FOURTH EDITION

Global Problems

The Search for Equity, Peace, and Sustainability

Scott Sernau
Indiana University South Bend

Long Grove, Illinois

For information about this book, contact:
Waveland Press, Inc.
4180 IL Route 83, Suite 101
Long Grove, IL 60047-9580
(847) 634-0081
info@waveland.com
www.waveland.com

Copyright ©2022 by Scott Sernau

10-digit ISBN 1-4786-4722-1
13-digit ISBN 978-1-4786-4722-5

Previous editions of this book were published by Pearson Education, Inc.

All rights reserved. No part of this book may be reproduced, stored in a retrieval system, or transmitted in any form or by any means without permission in writing from the publisher.

Printed in the United States of America

7 6 5 4 3 2 1

*To those who wish to understand the problem
so that they can be part of the solution.*

Contents

Preface   xv

Introduction:
The Global Century — 1

    The Call of the World   3
    Making a World System   6
    Empires in Collision   8
    Toward a Global Century   12
    Plan of the Book   14

PART ONE — Seeking an Equitable World: Issues of Inequality — 17

1 Class:
A World of Rich and Poor — 19

    The Global Divide   22
    Inequalities between and among Nations   22
    Realities of Global Poverty   28
    Theories of Class and Economy   30
    The Wealth of Nations: Adam Smith   30
    The Misery of Nations: Karl Marx   31
    Assessing the Views   33
    Economic Development: Modernization and Dependency Theories   38
    Modernization Theory:
      Time to Clean House   38
    Dependency Theory:
      Get Out of My House   40
    When Prehistory Repeats Itself   43
    Ending Extreme Poverty:
      Markets and Beyond   46

KEY IDEAS   49
FOR REVIEW AND DISCUSSION   50
MAKING CONNECTIONS   50
MAKING A DIFFERENCE   51

2 Work and Trade: The Global Assembly Line 53

The Division of Labor 55
Adam Smith: Efficiency   55
Émile Durkheim: Solidarity   56
Max Weber: Work Ethic   56
Karl Marx: Alienation   58
The New International Division of Labor   58

The Boundless Frontier: From East India to Amazon 61
Occasional Help Wanted   62
Working the Line: Life on la Frontera   65
Pushed to the Wall: Walmart and the "Big Boxes"   66

Made by Small Hands 68
Mills and Mines   70
Hooked by the World Economy   71

A Trade Free-for-All 73
David Ricardo: Comparative Advantage   73
Chain of Production around the World   73

Ordering the World Market 76
The International Monetary Fund (IMF)   76
The World Bank   77
From GATT to the WTO   77
FTAA: A Common Market in the Americas?   79
Other International Trade Groups   79

Trade That Is Fair for All 80

KEY IDEAS   82
FOR REVIEW AND DISCUSSION   82
MAKING CONNECTIONS   83
MAKING A DIFFERENCE   83

3 Gender and Family:
Overburdened Women and Displaced Men 85

Nietzsche Undone:
  From Superman to Supermom 89
Masculinity as Vulnerability:
  The Harder They Fall 93
Tired, Stressed Women and
  Angry, Alienated Men 94
Locked In and Shut Out 98
The Feminization of Migration 100

Global Family Changes 102
Marriage and Divorce 102
Parenting 107

Half the Sky 109
The Continued Perils of Being Female 109
Feminist Theory and
  World Feminist Movements 112

KEY IDEAS 114
FOR REVIEW AND DISCUSSION 114
MAKING CONNECTIONS 115
MAKING A DIFFERENCE 115

4 Education:
Access and Success 117

The Foundations of Education 121
And Who Will Care for the Children? 123
Education around the World 126
Great Britain 126
Japan 128
China 130
India 131
Mexico 133
Russia 134
Germany and Northern Europe 135

Opening Doors, Opening Minds — 136
Human Capital Theory 136
The School-to-Work Transition 138
Elite and Popular Education 139
Savage Inequalities at Home and Abroad 140
Pedagogy of the Oppressed 143

KEY IDEAS 145
FOR REVIEW AND DISCUSSION 146
MAKING CONNECTIONS 146
MAKING A DIFFERENCE 147

PART TWO Seeking a Peaceful World: Issues of Conflict 149

5 Crime: Fear in the Streets — 151

Seeking Security — 154
Street Crime and Youth Violence — 156
International Drug Trade — 160
Opium 160
Cocaine 163
Cannabis 165
Tobacco 166
Alcohol 167
New Recipes: Chemical Agents 168

Incarceration around the World — 170
International Crime Cartels — 171
Trading in Guns, Drugs, and People 171
Mexico's Drug Wars 172

In Search of Opportunity and Order — 175

KEY IDEAS 176
FOR REVIEW AND DISCUSSION 177
MAKING CONNECTIONS 177
MAKING A DIFFERENCE 178

6 War:
States of Terror — 179

- How States Made War and War Made States — 183
- From Limited War to Total War to Cold War — 186
  - Limited War 186
  - Total War 187
  - Cold War 189
- From World War to Regional Conflict — 194
  - War by Proxy 196
- The Global Arms Trade — 200
- Weapons of Mass Destruction — 205
  - Chemical Weapons 205
  - Biological Weapons 206
  - Nuclear Weapons 208
- Military Expenditures — 211
- The Last Great War? — 211
  - KEY IDEAS 214
  - FOR REVIEW AND DISCUSSION 215
  - MAKING CONNECTIONS 215
  - MAKING A DIFFERENCE 216

7 Democracy and Human Rights:
Having Our Say — 217

- Nationalism and the Nation-State — 221
- From Bands to States — 222
- Nationalism and Independence — 228
- Democracy and Its Alternatives — 230
  - The Age of Democracy 230
  - Authoritarianism versus Democracy 236
  - The Rise of Twenty-First Century Authoritarianism 239

"Dirty Wars":
   When Democracy Degenerates   240
   The Price of Democracy 242
   After the Repression 243
The Right to Be Fully Human   244

   KEY IDEAS 248
   FOR REVIEW AND DISCUSSION 249
   MAKING CONNECTIONS 249
   MAKING A DIFFERENCE 250

8 Ethnicity and Religion: Deep Roots and Unholy Hate   251

Ethnicity: Ties that Bind and Divide   255
Faith and Fervor: Religious Diversity   258
   Local Religions 258
   Christianity 260
   Islam 262
   Asian Religions 264
Ethnicity, Religion, and Power   264
   Resurgent Fundamentalism 267
   The God of the Poor:
      Liberation Theology 270
Identity and International Terrorism   271
   Revolutionary and State Terror 271
   The Power and Weakness of Terror 273
Alternatives to Terror   277
   Religion as Resilience 277
   Ethnicity as Resilience 278
   Moral Leadership as Resilience 278

   KEY IDEAS 280
   FOR REVIEW AND DISCUSSION 281
   MAKING CONNECTIONS 281
   MAKING A DIFFERENCE 282

PART THREE — Seeking a Sustainable World: Environmental Issues — 285

9 Urbanization: Cities without Limits — 288

The Urban Millennium: Worldwide Urbanization — 293
Dawn of the City 293
Triumph of the City 294

World Cities — 296
Megacities 299
Sprawling and Brawling Contenders 304

Cities as Dynamos: Central Places and Hyperurbanization — 306

The Shape of Urban Life — 308
Theories of Urban Culture 308
Theories of Urban Structure 308
Fantasy City: Postmodern Theory 310

The Shape of the City — 311
Global Ghettos: The Spread of Shantytowns 312
A Slum with a View 315
Autosprawl 317

Seeking Livable Cities — 319
Cities that Work 319
New Urbanism 320
Sustainable Cities 321

KEY IDEAS 322
FOR REVIEW AND DISCUSSION 322
MAKING CONNECTIONS 323
MAKING A DIFFERENCE 323

10 Population and Health: Only the Poor Die Young — 325

Counting Heads: World Population Estimates — 330
Marx and Malthus: The Population Bomb Debate — 330
Demographic Transition Theory — 333
Death Rate and Birth Rate 333
Life Expectancy 335
Fertility Rate 339
Changing Demographics 341

Population Control — 344
Migration — 346
Disease — 349
Infectious Disease: The Kiss of Death 349
HIV/AIDS 353
Pandemic 355
Chronic Disease: Dying by Degrees 357

Health Care — 361
United States 361
Canada 362
Sweden 363
Great Britain 363
Japan 363
Russia 364
China 364
Other Asian Countries 365

Living Well, Staying Well — 366

KEY IDEAS 367
FOR REVIEW AND DISCUSSION 367
MAKING CONNECTIONS 368
MAKING A DIFFERENCE 368

11 Technology and Energy: Prometheus's Fire or Pandora's Box? 371

Power Surge: The Advance of Technology 374
The Fires of Industry 375
Booting Up the Electronic Age 376
Global Cybercafé: The Social Network 381
Planet Hollywood: When Reality Is Virtual and Virtual Is Reality 383
Stalked by the White Ghost: Electronic Globalization 384
The Information (and Misinformation) Age 385

Energy: Fire from Above and Below 387
Wood 388
Coal 389
Oil 393
Natural Gas 396
Nuclear Fission: The Power of Ancient Suns 397
Nuclear Fusion: The Fire of the Cosmos 399
Alternative Energy: Sun, Wind, Earth, and Water 400

Chariots of Fire: Automobiles and Transport 404

Turning Down the Heat: Climate Change and Appropriate Technology 407

KEY IDEAS 412
FOR REVIEW AND DISCUSSION 412
MAKING CONNECTIONS 412
MAKING A DIFFERENCE 413

12 Ecology: How Much Can One Planet Take? — 415

- Planetary Boundaries — 419
- Food: We Are What We Eat — 420
  - Sowing the Seeds of Civilization — 423
  - Growing Business: Industrial Agriculture — 425
  - "We Are What We Eat" — 429
- Pollution — 432
  - Water: From Open Sewers to Toxic Canals — 432
  - Solid Waste: A Planet in Plastic Wrap — 434
- Deforestation and Desertification — 438
- Who Invited You? Invasive Species — 447
- Ecology and Economy: The Search for Sustainable Futures — 451

  - KEY IDEAS — 453
  - FOR REVIEW AND DISCUSSION — 454
  - MAKING CONNECTIONS — 454
  - MAKING A DIFFERENCE — 455

Conclusion: Making a World of Difference — 457

References 463

Index 477

Preface

This is an exciting time to be teaching about global issues and social problems. But it can be a daunting task. There is far more material than can ever be covered in a semester, and the issues of our time change with each day's headlines. I hope this book, *Global Problems: The Search for Equity, Peace, and Sustainability*, Fourth Edition, will make the task of engaging global problems a more manageable one.

We must go beyond the "toe in the water" syndrome. This is seen when a student of a foreign language learns just enough to say, "No, I don't speak . . ." in the target language, never learning enough to use the language and so forgetting it. A similar process can happen when we learn just enough to feel overwhelmed but never expand our skills and awareness enough to feel conversant in the ways of the world and at home anywhere on the planet.

We must also get beyond the "blue box" syndrome. This is seen in textbooks, where a newly realized issue or group is confined to discussion in boxes (often pale blue, but this depends on the taste of the publisher). For example, the history of the nation is told largely from the perspective of white men (often politicians and generals), but then there is a box for "Women in History" or "Great African Americans in History," as though this perspective was an afterthought rather than a central part of the story. Global issues are still often confined to the blue boxes of many texts. The story told is of events and issues within a single country, and an occasional box is included with information on "Marriage in India" or "Education in Japan." One gets the impression that these boxes provide interesting sidelines and tangents but something apart from the real story. Given its size and current world dominance, no place has been a greater offender in this area than the United States. But this denies the reality of our interconnected, interwoven world. A terrorist cell in Frankfurt today is in Boston tomorrow; a virus in Hong Kong yesterday is in Toronto today.

The book is divided into three parts, representing what I see as three key dimensions to the current global situation. The first part begins with the challenges of global inequalities: in life chances, wages and work, and gender and education. The choice to begin with inequality is not accidental but rather reflects my conviction that inequality lies at the heart of many global problems. The second section focuses on conflict and violence at all levels: from crime to politics, terrorism to war. Violence is closely linked to issues of social justice and human rights, and this connection is made throughout. The final section looks at the issue of sustainability and the problems of urbanization, crowding, and environmental destruction. These problems are immediate but also call on us to look ahead toward the kind of world that we are building.

Each chapter of *Global Problems* begins with a "Global Encounters" vignette. I have worked for years with overseas study and international education programs and have taught on Semester at Sea voyages. The opening vignette gives an example of college students encountering a striking situation and being asked to think about the broader implications of what they are seeing. The questions raised are central to the topic of that chapter.

I want students to be able to see the interconnectedness of our world and of people leading seemingly very different lives. Each chapter strengthens this local–global connection. The chapters explore social problems by focusing on key theories and providing enough history to understand the background of contemporary issues. The approach is both multinational and multidisciplinary. I have avoided burdening the text with a bewildering array of citations and have instead focused on the key insights and studies that most clearly inform the topic across disciplines. Both classical and contemporary theorists and writers are noted. Often I identify both the nationality and the discipline or background of the person cited, so students can get a better sense of the many areas of study that contribute to the whole.

So much has changed in our world since the Third Edition! A pandemic has gripped the globe. Authoritarian and nationalistic leaders, on both left and right, have strengthened their grip on power. The so-called Islamic State has risen and fallen, while other conflicts seem to go on endlessly. A changing global climate has moved from disputed analyses to daily accounts of record heatwaves, droughts, wildfires, monster storms, and melting arctic ice. All of these are discussed with the latest data and examples. And most important, students are encouraged to make connections between the headline issues and underlying causes. To assist with this, photos, graphs, and charts provide an accessible, up-to-date, and easy-to-understand visual format. For those who want to probe deeper and to learn more, links to more detailed data are provided.

I hope that students will think deeply and care deeply about global problems. At the same time, I do not want to indulge in gloom and doom to the point that the situation seems hopeless, for that can breed apathy and inaction. Each chapter includes and concludes with positive possibilities for global change. The "Making Connections" section at the end of each chapter offers reliable websites for more information. "Making a Difference" sections offer options for broader and often local involvement. They are also reminders that while the problems are substantial, there are many people, including students, who are committed to making a difference. These sections can form the basis for assignments, for further study, or for a class or group project.

This combination of elements allows *Global Problems* to serve social problems courses that seek a truly global perspective and context for analysis as well as courses in global issues, global studies, Third World studies, and international development.

Introduction

The Global Century

When Bob Dylan sang in the 1960s that the times were "a-changin'," he was quite right. The times are still changing; only now, they seem to change every year or every few months, and they encompass change that Dylan likely didn't consider. The term **globalization** was popularized in the mid-1990s, and it soon became the favorite label for our age. Our world has been coming together in dramatic new ways.

Globalization is sometimes used to describe only the increasing economic linkages between countries. Yet it is more than that. **Economic globalization** is reshaping our world marketplace. At the same time, **political globalization** is binding the world together in new forms of power and authority relations. **Cultural globalization** means that music, fashion, media, and lifestyles are transported around the world, reshaping how people live and even how they think. Economic, political, and cultural globalization are clearly intertwined, but they are also as distinct as their respective U.S. centers: New York, (economic), Washington, DC (political), and Los Angeles (cultural). By the end of the twentieth century few doubted that globalization, in some form, was here to stay.

Then came September 11, 2001. The world's most devastating terrorist attacks, directed against seats of global economic power (the World Trade Center) and political power (the Pentagon), raised new questions. What would the impact of global terrorism be on our shrinking world? Would fear of terrorism restrict the movement of people and products? Even that classic symbol of the shrinking world, the jet airliner, seemed somehow menacing. The 9/11 terrorist attacks were followed in short order by two wars, toppling the governments of Afghanistan and Iraq, launched by a U.S. government that seemed increasingly eager to use unilateral power and to avoid international agreements and power sharing.

Some have argued that the first great move toward globalization that began the twentieth century was stopped, even reversed, by the cataclysm of World War I. The great symbol of globalization of that era, ocean liners such as the *Titanic* and the *Lusitania*, became objects of suspicion, vulnerable to both natural disaster (icebergs) and terror (unannounced torpedo attacks). Is the world of the twenty-first century still coming together, or is it coming apart amid the flames of nationalism, terrorism, and war?

I firmly believe that globalization will not be reversed in the long term. Economic globalization has been shaken by tariffs and pandemics. Yet in the midst of threats of economic tariffs and sanctions, countries are still eagerly negotiating new free-trade zones and international accords. The very threat of economic sanctions shows how important trade is to every country on earth. Political nationalism is on the rise, but emerging powers need international alliances, global bases, and "blue water" navies. Even while shut in by a pandemic, global consumers ordered products online, drawn from around the world and delivered to their doorstep. Countries are racing to vaccinate their populations—for their own safety and often to assure the world they are again safe for tourists and business travelers.

While political turmoil and disease may interfere with the movement of people and products, nothing short of the complete collapse of the power grid seems to slow electronic globalization. In an age of cables and satellites, messages and information can circle the globe almost cost free. Business that cannot be conducted in person can take place globally and instantly on Zoom, on Microsoft Teams, or in Google Rooms. Governments around the world are seeking to build walls and fences to guard borders, yet I can watch protests against these actions occurring in real time on the other side of the globe—as well as occurring in my own downtown. Even as I lament pandemic limitations on travel, I can share my woes instantaneously on social media with friends and colleagues on five continents—mostly in English—and listen to the latest world beat music—in five languages—assembled for me. Cultural and social globalization continues undiminished. The United States may be in retreat from some aspects of global power, yet it remains a cultural superpower in music, film, and media. That power, however, is increasingly multicultural—a commercial re-export of ideas and art forms from around the world.

The Call of the World

One reason globalization will not be reversed is that it is ancient. Globalization began with the first humans to stride out of Africa. The world was first conquered by canoe and moccasin. Human hunter-gatherers placed strains on their local environments and moved on in search of new unexploited land. And humans were endlessly adaptable: Furs and fire could help conquer the cold, new materials could be employed for shelter, and simple vessels could follow coastlines and cross narrow straits. The first human explorers may have reached Australia, across a strait of open water, by 40,000 years ago. They were in Japan, the Philippines, and the many islands near the Asian coast by 30,000 years ago. People were in the Americas by 12,000 years ago—by some accounts, as much as 20,000 years ago. Those who came 12,000 years ago could have walked across what is now the Bering Strait that divides Alaska from Siberia, following routes opened by the low ocean levels of the last ice age and corridors between great walls of ice. If people came earlier, they must have worked simple but effective boats, perhaps a covered canoe or kayak of some sort, along the edges of the ice through frigid waters. In time, so-called prehistoric and uncivilized humans—that is, people who lived before the advent of writing and urban life—extended their reach to almost every point on the globe that wasn't buried under a mile of ice.

As the climate changed and populations increased, people began to settle in small farming villages. Some of these places occupied key trade routes and developed into substantial communities. By 10,000 years ago, the great trade centers of the Middle East were growing into major population centers. As farmers intensified their production, the first real cities arose around 5,000 years ago. For better or worse, globalization had begun as cities became linked to one another, first through trade routes and soon through conquest as the ambitious and the brazen seized land and created the first empires.

People set out in search of something beyond the horizon, driven by the desire for commerce (economic globalization), control (political globalization), and sheer curiosity (cultural globalization). Early civilizations were far more interconnected than we first supposed. We have learned to think in terms of Western civilization (Europe) and Eastern civilization (China). In fact, the ancient world had multiple interconnected and overlapping centers of civilization.

Mediterranean society included both the northern (European) shore and the southern (African) shore of the Great Sea. The idea that Europe and Africa were different continents would have seemed strange to ancient inhabitants of the Mediterranean region. Rather, they struggled for control, sought commerce, and explored out of curiosity from a circle of competing and cooperating power centers: Athens, Tyre, Alexandria, Cairo, Carthage, Rome, Venice, and many others at various times. Because later Europeans would become enamored of them as cradles of "classical civilization," Athens and Rome have occupied center stage in our understanding of the region. But the city on the Bosporus, straddling what we now consider to be Europe and Asia and variously known as Byzantium, Constantinople, and Istanbul, stood at the center of Eurasian commerce for a thousand years after the city of Rome fell into decline.

Another cultural hub centered on what Europeans later called the Middle East—the area bounded by the Tigris and Euphrates Rivers, the Persian Gulf, and the Iranian plateau. This area included some of the earliest kingdoms on earth: Sumer, Babylonia, and Assyria. Later empires wedded this land more firmly with Mediterranean regions: The great Persian Empire encompassed Egypt and threatened Greece; Alexander's short-lived realm spanned from Greece to India; and the Parthian Empire rivaled Rome. Starting in the 700s, this land became the center of Arab realms, based first in Mecca and then Damascus and Baghdad, which stretched across North Africa and northward to include all of Spain and traded with ports on both the Mediterranean Sea and the Indian Ocean. Parts of this area were later subsumed by several Turkish Empires that turned back the Crusades in the 1200s, conquered Constantinople in 1453, reached all the way to Vienna by the 1600s, and struggled on until World War I.

The northern rim of Africa from Morocco to Egypt has long been bound up with Mediterranean and Middle Eastern civilizations with which it shared sealanes and caravan routes. As the great Sahara Desert grew over several thousand years due to climate change and human impact, ties to the rest of Africa became more difficult. Lakes dried up, and the great granaries that fed much of the Roman Empire were buried under sand dunes. Travelers with those most durable of beasts of burden, camels, continued to make long and dangerous treks south, trading in places that became symbols of the remote and exotic to the outside world, such as Timbuktu. But Sub-Saharan African civilization continued to expand as well. Around the end of the first millennium of our age, West African farmers and traders, workers of iron who spoke a common family of languages known as Bantu, began one of the world's great expansions. In the succeeding centuries, they moved across Central Africa well into the eastern and southern parts of the continent. They often displaced other ancient African groups to remote deserts or rain forests as Bantu farming and trading communities filled much of the continent. But Africa, with its difficult soil and tropical diseases that plague both people and livestock, is not an easy place to farm. The Bantu farmers adapted to life in the tropics with dispersed interconnected communities, a vast network that later European explorers would fail to comprehend, just as they failed to understand the complexity of the dispersed village-based networks of North America.

In India, civilization began early along the Indus River. About the same time as ancient Egypt's civilization took root, more than 4,000 years ago,

Harappa civilization built great planned cities with streets laid out in grids and the world's first sanitary system for water and sewage. Subsequent power changes, often at the hands of a series of invaders from the north, first brought Hinduism and later mixed it with Buddhism, Islam, and several other faiths but always retained a particularly Indian flavor.

Finally, for much of the ancient and medieval period, the greatest center of power and culture was China. Originally this region comprised two centers: one in the north along the Hwang Ho or Yellow River and one in the south along the Yangtze River. In time, these centers merged and drew many of their neighbors into their sphere. Some remained politically and culturally distinct—Japan, Vietnam, Mongolia, Tibet—while exchanging ideas and influence with the Chinese. Traders came to China via great caravan routes across central Asia and by way of the sealane around Southeast Asia. Sometimes the Chinese welcomed the trade; at other times they built great walls, literal and figurative, to protect their empire from outsiders. In time, the core of East Asia, once no doubt as diverse in language and ethnicity as India, Africa, or Indonesia, melded into a vast land with a common sense of ethnicity, Han Chinese, and eventually a single dominant language, Mandarin.

Each of these centers of power and culture, at one time or another, saw itself as the center of the world, an oasis of culture surrounded by barbarians, infidels and heathens, and hostile hordes. Yet while the centers maintained their own cultural identities, they were always interacting with one another: trading; fighting; and exchanging ideas and innovations, merchants, and spies. The boundaries of cultures, like those of empires, were fluid and often overlapping. The Great Silk Road connected the Roman Empire and the Han Chinese Empire; it was a trade route that persisted for centuries. Sometimes merchants carried on a vigorous traffic in products and ideas with the very nomads beyond their borders that they most despised (Weatherford 1994). Once they became seafaring, traders and merchants, from the Phoenicians to the Arabs to the Portuguese, exchanged their products and ideas with traders along the coast of Sub-Saharan Africa and on the islands of what is now Indonesia.

The greatest seafarers of all may have been the Polynesian ("many islands") cultural groups that spread into the Pacific. Their ancestors had reached Fiji in the South Pacific almost 3,000 years ago (see Smith 2008). By the end of the first millennium, they had navigated sailing canoes across thousands of miles of open ocean to reach Tahiti, Hawaii, and the remote Easter Island. By the 1300s, they were settled in the islands of what is now New Zealand, perhaps the largest landmass outside of Antarctica still to be inhabited.

About the same time that Polynesians were landing in Hawaii, Norse sailors, or "Vikings," from Norway and Denmark were making the first connections across the Atlantic in single-sail oar boats. They settled first in Iceland, then Greenland, and finally found a tenuous foothold on the North American mainland in what is now the Labrador coast of Canada. In Iceland and Greenland, the Norse sailors encountered other intrepid sailors in much smaller boats, oceangoing kayaks that could weave in and out of narrow inlets and through the ice-strewn waters. The Norse called these people "Skraelings," meaning "babblers," since they couldn't understand their language. These people were part of a hunter-gatherer culture that had adapted to life on the edges of the Arctic Ocean in a series of communities that circled the North Pole. Known as "Inuit" in their language family, and later dubbed "Eskimos," this group provided trading partners for the Norse, until they eventually fell into hostilities. The Norse who landed in North America soon found greater hostilities from groups already there. These weren't Inuit, however, but Amerindians, descendants of the first ice age hikers, who now spanned North and South America. The Norsemen (they had yet to bring families) had iron axes and swords but no firearms around the turn of the second millennium. Outnumbered by hunter-gatherers proficient in the use of the bow and arrow, the Norse retreated from their first cross-Atlantic encounter (Diamond 1997).

After tenuous connections along icy northern routes, open-water seafaring allowed Europeans to extend their commerce, control, and curiosity to the Americas. Though they were slow to realize it, what they encountered in the Americas was also a network of empires and cultures with trade routes that spanned North, Central, and South America and the Caribbean. Intensive maize (corn) farming in Mesoamerica—what is now Mexico and Central America—allowed for great cities and realms that would finally end with the Aztec and Maya Empires. In South America, a trade network up and down the Andes Mountains permitted the rise and fall of great civilizations and finally merged into a single empire of the Quechua-speakers we have learned to call the Inca. In both North and South America, the desert, plains, and forestlands provided for myriad villages and the occasional city, such as Cahokia near present-day St. Louis.

Making a World System

The world of 1450 was one of scattered empires interconnected by a vast web of trade routes. For most people, however, life was local; they lived in towns and villages where farming could be sustained or in great nomadic groups of hunters and herders across dry and mountainous country on each continent. Then everything changed. According to some scholars, such as Immanuel Wallerstein, a whole new system of society and economics, a world system, was born (Wallerstein 2011 [1974]). According to others, such as Andre Gunder Frank, this was more likely an intensification of the empires that had been expanding for thousands of years (Frank and Gills 1993). In 1453 the great city on the straits connecting the Black Sea and the Mediterranean, and the passage between Europe and Asia, fell to the Turkish Empire. Europe was a varied collection of relatively small states whose nobility had developed a taste for Eastern commodities. With the overland routes closed by what they saw as a hostile force, where would they go?

In a small country on a sliver of land facing the Atlantic, a prince dabbled in improving trade and navigation by sea, earning himself the title of Prince Henry the Navigator. The prince encouraged ocean exploration, the only way that the tiny country of Portugal could ever be a wealthy power. His sailors braved open ocean waters to settle in the Azores, and then turned south toward Africa. They began by stopping at a series of trading ports along the African coast. Eventually they rounded the Cape of Good Hope, the southernmost part of Africa, with great new hope as they entered the Indian Ocean. The coast of East Africa was already dominated by Swahili traders of Arab and East African descent. With slower but more powerful ships and newly cast cannon, the Portuguese muscled in and dominated the Indian Ocean trade from Africa to India to the East Indies (now Indonesia) and eventually all the way around to China and Japan. Wealth flowed in. China and Ottoman Turkey remained powerful, but in terms of control of the world system, the 1400s became the Portuguese Century.

By the end of the 1400s, Isabel the Catholic of Castile and Ferdinand of Aragon were uniting Spain and driving out the last of its Islamic rulers. After years of war, they needed money. But the Portuguese controlled the African trade and the sea routes to Asia. When an Italian-born sailor, whom the English would call Christopher Columbus, showed up with great bravado and maps that horribly underestimated the size of the planet, he convinced them he could find a route to Asia by sailing west. What he found were two vast connected continents, one likely visited by Vikings and the other by Polynesians, largely cut off from his world for at least 10,000 years. The Spanish began by establishing colonies in the Caribbean, dominating, largely enslaving, and ultimately nearly exterminating the native population. Then two men from the poorest, meanest, toughest part of Spain decided to make good on the mainland. They discovered and dismantled the two extensive American empires that commanded great troves of gold and silver. The Spanish needed gold and used the cold steel of swords and armor and the hot lead of newly developed firearms to take it. Cortés plundered and dismantled the Aztec Empire of Mexico and Pizarro did the same to the Inca Empire of Peru. They were not professional soldiers bent on conquest but adventurers who formed "trading companies" for profit and plunder. Kim MacQuarrie (2007) calls Pizarro's group "a few hundred of well-armed entrepreneurs." As American gold and silver traveled in European ships to purchase goods in Chinese ports, the great American regional network was fully incorporated into a global world system, now dominated by Spain. The 1500s were Spain's *Siglo de Oro*, or Golden Century—the Spanish Century.

When Spaniard Ferdinand Magellan sailed to the Philippines and his ships continued around the world, Spain's trade routes became the first to completely circle the globe. While Spanish forces and entrepreneurs came to control great trade routes, they were losing control of another group of independent-minded entrepreneurs: the Dutch. The Netherlands gained independence from Spain but could never hold back enough of the sea to make Holland great on its own reclaimed land, so the Dutch took to the sea. They built better ships and formed bigger and better trading companies. Eventually Dutch burghers, or businesspeople, wrested control of global trade from the Spanish and the Portuguese. They established themselves in the Americas, Africa, and Asia, often replacing their rivals. The Dutch faced new rivals in the growing British navy as well as others, but in large measure, the 1600s were the Dutch Century.

France lagged as a naval power but developed powerful armies and then clamored to claim its share of the Americas, North and West Africa, and India. Paris flourished as a cultural and economic center. French became the lingua franca, or common language, of trade. With his armies victorious and wealth pouring in from around the world, Louis XIV reigned in Versailles for 72 years as the "Sun King." His power established French supremacy at the beginning of the 1700s, just as Napoleon's victories would reestablish it at the end of the 1700s. This was the French Century.

England had been rising in power since much of the Spanish Armada sank off its shores in 1588. United as Great Britain in the early 1700s, England first challenged the Dutch and then the French for global supremacy. The English gained ever-greater control in Canada and in India from their French rivals, only to lose the American colonies to a French-backed revolution. But with Napoleon defeated at Waterloo in 1815, the British Empire was unhindered and able to encircle the globe. British traders replaced the Spanish as the dominant force in much of Latin America and the Caribbean; they claimed ever-greater portions of coastal Africa and gradually gained control of all of South Asia, what is now India, Pakistan, Bangladesh, and Burma (Myanmar). Queen Victoria became Empress of India and reigned for 60 years over an empire on which "the sun never set." The 1800s were the British Century.

British dominance was challenged in the late 1800s by various European powers, most notably a newly united Germany. As the world industrialized, it was no longer sufficient to control trade routes; a great power also had to control raw materials to compete in growing industries

Empires in Collision

The 1800s were dominated by the struggle to maintain and extend these great empires. European nations vied with one another for dominance around the globe. Spain lost much of its great empire early in century to Napoleonic invasions at home and uprisings in Mexico and South America. It managed to retain Cuba and the Philippines until late in the century. Portugal held on to Brazil until 1822 and struggled to keep its hold in Africa. France gave up its last great stake in North America by selling the Louisiana Territory to Thomas Jefferson and the new United States of America, but it turned to creations such as its famous Foreign Legion (essentially a band of mercenaries) to extend its holdings in West Africa and Southeast Asia.

Africa became the center of a great land grab beginning in the 1880s. Until that time, most foreign possessions were small ports and territories on the coast. The interior of Africa remained, to the Europeans at least, unknown: the "dark continent." Increasingly, however, European states wanted the prestige and access to resources that came with owning a piece of the African continent. Britain dominated in the east and France in the west. Germany claimed the remaining portions. These three nations vied for control of weak states in the north, such as Morocco. Belgium claimed a piece out of the middle. The Belgian Congo, operated as the private domain of King Leopold, was many times over the size of its home country, with vast mineral and timber resources. By the end of the century, all of Africa was European controlled or dominated.

Meanwhile, the Russian Empire grew, as the great Eurasian land empire of the czars pushed its control south and ever eastward to capture small states and tribally held territory in the Caucasus Mountains and on to the Pacific. The result was a single land empire greater than any other since Genghis Khan (much the same territory, in fact) ruled. The expense of seizing and controlling this empire was enormous, however, and some portions were too far away to control effectively. Alaska was sold to the United States to help pay the bills.

The United States built a large land empire by extending control ever westward, adding Texas and then seizing the northern half of Mexico in the war of 1846. During the 1880s and 1890s, the United States completed its own push to the Pacific, capturing vast amounts of tribally held territories in the process. The so-called Indian Wars, made famous by dozens of western movies, were part of a worldwide movement of powerful industrial states against the remaining tribally held territories in North America, Africa, Central Asia, and Australia and New Zealand.

The nineteenth century ended with one final colonial war in which the United States seized the Philippines, Guam, and Puerto Rico from Spain and created a partially independent Cuba in the Spanish–American War of 1898. After the terrible bloodshed of the Napoleonic wars of the early 1800s, however, the Europeans avoided fighting great colonial wars with each other for much of the rest of the century.

This relative truce among empires was shattered by the cataclysm of the two great world wars of the 1900s. World War I erupted in 1914 amid jealousies, suspicions, and alliances among rival empires. The Russian Empire was huge and menacing but also impoverished and corrupt and showing signs of crumbling. The Turkish Ottoman Empire had ruled the Middle East since the Middle Ages but it was also in decay, "the sick man of Europe." The German Empire was strong in Europe but felt surrounded by enemies and the great reach of the French and British Empires. The final spark was the assassination of the ruler of the increasingly insecure Austro–Hungarian Empire by a Serbian seeking national independence.

By the time World War I ended in 1918, the Russian Empire had been destroyed. It was recast as the Union of Soviet Socialist Republics (USSR), or Soviet Union, following the Bolshevik Revolution. The Austro–Hungarian Empire was split into newly independent states. The Ottoman Empire was also broken up and given to the victorious British and French, who began to carve the area into states and emirates: Iraq, Kuwait, Jordan, Lebanon, and the protectorate of British Palestine. The German Empire was greatly reduced, with Germany being forced to give up its African possessions as well land in Europe to France and to the newly recreated country of Poland, which had previously been swallowed by Russian and German expansion.

In many ways, World War II (1939–1945) was round two in this great battle of empires. Adolf Hitler and his Nazi Party dreamed of reestablishing a third great German empire, or **Third Reich.** They dreamed of dominating Europe and controlling valuable resources in North Africa and the Middle East, especially petroleum. While Hitler is often accused of wanting to achieve world domination, it appears that the Nazis would have been content to allow the British to maintain a remnant empire, the Japanese to control Asia, and the United States to dominate the Americas. The world would have been divided into a few great empires, with the German as the most important. In Italy, Benito Mussolini dreamed of the glories of the Roman Empire and sought conquests in North Africa. In Asia, Japan sought an "Asian co-prosperity sphere," in which the European powers—Britain, France, and the Netherlands—and the United States would be replaced by Japanese dominance under the rule of Emperor Hirohito, who would control an even greater Japanese Empire. In Great Britain, Winston Churchill promised to prevent the "liquidation" of the British Empire. In the United States, Franklin D. Roosevelt envisioned a world of free trade without empires or spheres of control, one in which U.S. commercial interests would likely dominate.

Germany moved to seize the territory it had lost in World War I, and World War II began as Germany invaded Poland. Shortly thereafter, it invaded France and demanded the return of lost border territory. Joseph Stalin's Soviet Union joined in the invasion of Poland, as it tried to reclaim all the territory of the Russian Empire, which also included Finland. The need for resources, especially grain and petroleum, led the German Nazis to battle Britain for North Africa and to invade the Soviet Union.

To expand its own empire, Japan seized Korea and gradually extended its control over China, replacing the dominance of the European powers. Needing additional resources, especially petroleum, Japan attempted to disable the U.S. Navy, seize the Philippines, and then drive the European powers, all facing defeat at German hands, from Southeast Asia. The resulting war bled and bankrupted Europe and crushed Japan, and imperial ambitions crumbled. The Philippines became independent. The Dutch East Indies became the country of Indonesia. British holdings became Malaysia and Singapore. In India, Mohandas Gandhi, the Mahatma or "great soul," had been leading a nonviolent struggle for independence. After World War II, he achieved his goal of independence but not of unity: British India split along religious lines into Hindu-dominated India and Muslim-dominated Pakistan in 1947, with East Pakistan later achieving independence as Bangladesh. France fought in the early 1950s to retain French Indochina, but after a defeat at the hands of the revolutionary leader Ho Chi Minh, it withdrew too and the independent states of Vietnam, Cambodia, and Laos remained.

Independence came last to Africa. South Africa became independent as white Afrikaners gained power and sought to maintain white rule. Franz Fanon (2004), from the French Caribbean, closely watched the struggles of Africa. Seeing the poverty and oppression of those he called "the wretched of the earth," he called on Africans to purge the violence of colonialism with the violence of liberation struggle. Algeria, whose struggle inspired Fanon, fought the French army and European settlers throughout the 1950s and gained independence. Starting with the British Gold Coast, which reclaimed the ancient title of Ghana in 1957, Sub-Saharan Africa began to claim independence as a collage of countries whose borders often followed old colonial lines. The Belgian Congo became independent in 1964 and was renamed Zaire, only to have its name changed back to "the Congo" decades later. Whites in Rhodesia, named for British colonial administrator Cecil Rhodes, claimed independence to try to maintain white rule. This hope was defeated in a bloody civil war that gave power to the black majority; the country claimed the name of an ancient African civilization, Zimbabwe. Late to gain independence were the Portuguese colonies of Mozambique and Angola. After achieving independence in 1975, they almost immediately fell into civil war. One of the very last colonies, what had been German Southwest Africa and held by South Africa, finally became independent as Namibia in 1990.

The 1989 escape of Eastern Europe from Soviet control and the breakup of the Soviet Union in 1991 could be seen as signaling the end of the Russian Empire, although fighting in the Caucasus Mountains and in Ukraine, as well as unrest elsewhere, still continue. The end of the era of colonial empires in Asia came peacefully as Britain returned Hong Kong to China in 1997, and Portugal returned its old colonial port of Macau in 2000.

Throughout this time, nationalism remained a powerful motivator. For many, independence brought neither peace nor prosperity. The great irony in Africa is that independence came suddenly and relatively peacefully, as Europeans abandoned the old colonial idea, but in many cases, bloodshed followed independence.

Toward a Global Century

The 1900s might have belonged to Germany or to Germany and Japan but for the efforts of old rivals—Britain, France, Russia—who united to contain German and Japanese expansion. Decisive in the great global wars of the 1900s, however, was the nation whose access to both vast raw materials and vast wells of immigrant labor have made it the most productive and powerful industrial economy—the United States. The 1900s emerged as the American Century.

What, then, of the third millennium of our time, this century? Some see continued American dominance, or hegemony, in the world system. Others have looked first to the power of Japan and more recently to the sensational economic growth of China and declared this as a Pacific Century. We may be on the verge of something new: a truly intertwined global system without a single core. We may be at the beginning of a Global Century.

Debates about the nature of the modern world center around three powerful forces:

1. **Capitalism** is the profit-driven system of private accumulation and reinvestment that drives the world economy. In this scenario, the fundamental shift is new ways of doing business centered around the acceptance of money and private profit. The stagnant monopolies of the national monarchies are broken, and a new burst of productive energy is unleashed. Capitalism eventually penetrates all world markets and societies, transforming them and bringing them, for better or worse, into the world economy. We will explore the dimensions of global capitalism in the first part of this book on issues of inequality and the search for an equitable world.

2. **Imperialism** is the process of international domination and empire building. In this scenario, the key event is the rise of global imperialism based on military conquest and European firepower. Old trade systems are disrupted and replaced by one controlled by the great European powers, who become great because the very nature of this system allows for appropriation and control of the world's wealth. Imperialism proceeds in two great waves, the first beginning in the sixteenth century with the formation of the Spanish, Portuguese, British, French, Dutch, and Russian empires. This is an older form of mercantile ("get the gold") imperialism. It is replaced in the nineteenth century by a new wave of industrial ("get the materials and markets") imperialism. To the list of old imperialists are added other

newly industrial nations: Germany, Italy, Belgium, the United States, and Japan. The competition among these industrial powers eventually sparks the great world wars of the twentieth century. We will look at issues of conflict and the search for a more peaceful and democratic world in the second part of this book.

3. **Industrialism** is the fundamental shift in the basis of society, founded on harnessing nonanimal energy sources to drive productive machinery. In this scenario, the fundamental shift in thinking begins in a scientific revolution in the 1600s and quickly leads to the Industrial Revolution, beginning in Britain in the early 1700s. The subsequent diffusion of industrial production leads to the rise of industrial society with rapid population growth, urbanization, a growing industrial proletariat, and industrialized agriculture. Eventually the entire world enters the era of mass production and mass consumption. We will return to issues of developing technology, harnessing energy, and growing cities in the third part of this book, as we look at issues of sustainable change.

The continued global extension of commerce, control, and curiosity poses new and changing challenges. Economic globalization challenges us to be able to operate both effectively and ethically in the global marketplace. It has been said that one can buy in any language, but if one hopes to sell, he or she better know the language of the customer. This is also true of culture and society. To market global wares, one needs to understand the culture of the customer. To market wares ethically in a world filled with graft and exploitation, one needs to understand a great deal about world politics, society, and economic systems.

Political globalization challenges us to understand the nature of power and the meaning of **global citizenship.** Some have contended that many places have lost their sense of **national citizenship:** the rights and responsibilities that are conferred on those who are part of the nation. Yet we need somehow to claim a new sense of global citizenship: the rights and responsibilities conferred on all who are part of humanity.

Cultural globalization challenges us to understand and appreciate different ways of seeing the world, expressing ourselves, and building a satisfying life. **Culture shock** is the term applied to those who travel to new locations without adequate preparation and are overwhelmed by the differences. In a globalized world, it is possible to experience culture shock without ever leaving home. New people, new ideas, new ways of life converge on our communities and challenge our set ideas of how life should be lived. Cultural awareness and appreciation allow us to feel at home in a world of diverse ideas and ways of life.

There are no sidelines anymore. The entire globe occupies center stage, and the drama is enfolding our lives.

Plan of the Book

Globalization today is fraught with possibilities and dangers, as it has always been. A global reach brings new opportunities for prosperity and progress. It also brings new concentrations of power that monopolize opportunity and deny it to others. Globalization brings the promise of the empowerment of individuals and communities and the integration of these communities into a new world community of exchange and respect. It also brings the harsh possibilities of even greater exploitation of the poor and powerless and exclusion of the mass of humanity from the promised prosperity. Around the world, we see the irony of workers clamoring for jobs in the global economy and leaders begging for global investment while protests grow against international labor exploitation, mounting and unsupportable international debt, and the unchecked power of new and expanding global trade and finance organizations. The world cannot seem to agree whether this powerful genie of globalization is good or evil, but one thing is certain: The genie will not be stuffed back into the bottle. We must make it work for us.

In the chapters that follow, I offer brief overviews of some of the many issues that have emerged in our rapidly changing world. On one level, this book is a story of global problems: poverty, violence, and environmental destruction. On another, it is a story of persistent hope: the continuing search for equity, peace, and sustainability. I wish I could take you on a global tour to explore our changing world firsthand. In place of that, I have tried to illustrate big ideas with the real lives and situations around the planet. I have taught students as we traveled the world in various ways, including sailing around the world with Semester at Sea. Each chapter begins with an account from that voyage as students encountered a world that shocked, intrigued, delighted, dismayed, and angered them. They were warned they were not on a "cruise," but rather a voyage of discovery. I invite you to embark on your own voyage of discovery in the pages that follow—a global encounter with the people and ideas that are remaking our world. In these "Global Encounters" we will truly circle the globe, but I have also focused on three countries to examine in more depth: Brazil, South Africa, and India. Each is the largest established democracy on its continent, and each represents a country undergoing dramatic changes and becoming a major economic power. I hope that getting to know these three places better will also give you a window into the changes sweeping Latin America, Africa, and Asia.

Part One (chapters 1–4) focuses on a world in the grip of economic globalization and what it means to build an equitable world amid vast inequalities. We will look at how the world came to be so divided between rich and poor, and what this means for work, family, and education.

Part Two (chapters 5–8) looks at issues of power and conflict: the prospects for a more peaceful world emerging out of the cauldron of war, civil strife, and terrorism. We will start with conflict at the local level and with strong ties to inequality: the problem of crime. Then we will explore how warfare has created the world we know and the prospects for peace. We will also examine repression and human rights and finally the ways that key areas of identity, such as religion and ethnicity, have proved to be a source of both strength and turmoil.

Part Three (chapters 9–12) looks at issues of culture and the environment: what it will take to build a sustainable society that can nourish the needs of our grandparents and those of our great-great-grandchildren. We will start with a look at the great global cities that are dominating the planet, and then consider how population change is taxing the global system and ways to create healthier societies and healthier lives. The great mover in our world continues to be rapid technological change, and we'll examine the impact of technology, particularly in an age of growing energy scarcity. Finally, we will look at the ways we have remade the ecology of our planet, and the prospects for a world that sustains both livelihoods and life itself.

Clearly, there are no simple answers. But we must never assume that there are no answers. If we must abandon easy answers, we should not abandon hope but go on to tougher questions and seek better, even if more complex, answers. Our search for ideas, explanations, and answers will take us across the social sciences: anthropology, human geography and social history, economics, political science, and sociology. We will also need to draw insight from the natural sciences, especially for understanding the environment within which we must make our decisions. Finally, we will need to reference the humanities and humanistic pursuits: to learn from one another's stories and ideals, as captured in literature, ethics, worldviews, and the arts.

The goal is not to try to learn everything about everywhere but to weave together the strands we have gathered from many pursuits, and speak to the issues raised by a world in search of equity, peace, and sustainability. It is the fundamental challenge of our time.

PART ONE

Seeking an Equitable World

Issues of Inequality

1 Class: A World of Rich and Poor
2 Work and Trade: The Global Assembly Line
3 Gender and Family: Overburdened Women and Displaced Men
4 Education: Access and Success

An examination of global inequality is a logical place to begin any examination of global problems, since inequality is a part of them all. Even if inequality is not the cause of the problems, it is always an important part of how people experience global problems. Inequality and the struggle over resources and access to power and opportunity are at the heart of much of the world's conflict. Inequality is also a key issue in global sustainability. Both the very poor and the very rich can be hard on the planet. The poor may destroy land, wildlife, forest cover, and soil and water resources in a desperate struggle to survive. At the same time, rising levels of affluence in parts of the world have increased the energy appetite of many places, contributing to global climate change as well as the consumption of nonrenewable resources.

Inequality between people can operate along many dimensions: class, race, ethnicity, gender, religion, caste, region, nationality, language, and age, among others. The first chapter in part one is an introduction to an unequal world, with an emphasis on ideas about social class. Class analysis has typically focused on inequalities within a single national society. But for many in North America and Europe, the working classes, who make our industrial products and harvest our food, live in Latin America and, especially, in Asia. The excluded poor are particularly concentrated on the continent of Africa.

These groups are intertwined in a division of labor connected by global trade. Chapter 2 will examine the world of work and the ways that workers are interconnected in a web of trade relations. Of particular interest are the people who do the work and those who set the rules of the game and determine who gets ahead and who stays behind.

One cannot go far into the world of work without confronting issues of gender and family, examined in chapter 3. Many societies have had a sexual division of labor, with women responsible for some tasks and men for others. Even as this division breaks down, deep gender inequalities remain in the expectations of who will do what work and how they will be compensated. The balance between work and family, and all the unpaid work that may come with providing for the needs of children and other family members, challenges people around the world and is a key factor in gender inequality.

Finally, people everywhere look to education, discussed in chapter 4, as a means to mobility, to moving up into better work and better rewards. Yet education itself, in quality and availability, can be a key element of inequality. Without a good chance at a complete education, many other life chances will be severely limited.

These dimensions become more controversial when we look at how lives are interrelated around the world. If I happen to be rich and you happen to be poor, that is an issue of inequality. If I am rich exactly because you are poor, that is a problem of ethics and equity. Life is unfair, we are told, and with good reason. But must human society be built on inequitable relationships? The quest for social justice, a sense of basic fairness for all, is the common theme throughout the next four chapters.

1

Class

A World of Rich and Poor

GLOBAL ENCOUNTERS

Bahamas

The road to paradise can be bumpy. Braving late August in the Caribbean, we flew through the eye of a building hurricane. Eventually, we spun out of the clouds, to land in the Bahamas outside of Nassau.

Perhaps paradise doesn't present itself as well in the rain. Dropping through the clouds, we can see that the waterfront of New Providence Island is lined with homes and hotels all dressed in Bahamian pastels on palm-fringed properties. Just out of sight of the water, the landscape changes. Tired clapboard houses list in the wind, cattle wander around muddy clearings in the trees, and roads and fields are covered by brackish standing water.

On the ground, the highway follows the coastline past row upon row of expensive houses in Pastel Stucco and a bit of wrought iron. These are second homes for snowbirds from the United States, Canada, and Europe, and most sit empty during the rainy summer. The only competition for space comes from the gated grounds of large resort complexes. Club Med was here early on and newcomers abound—Sandals offers a paradise retreat to couples; others target other tourist niches. In Nassau, the old British colonial hotel is now a Hilton, its stately grounds largely filled with those waiting to board their cruise ships.

Nassau has beautiful old churches and stately historic houses on its hillsides, but the dominant skyline is offshore: towering ships and the castle. The castle looms over the city in unnatural shades of pink, topped with Las Vegas–like interpretations of gothic turrets, leaping dolphins, and a somewhat sinister-looking King Neptune. The scale is enormous, with huge towers connected by vaulted bridges. It dwarfs the British colonial hotel; it dwarfs Nassau itself. This is Atlantis. Once the object of high-stakes deal making between Merv Griffin and Donald Trump, it is now the property of "King Sol," a South African billionaire. The hotel is the centerpiece of a vast property that includes a water park and shark aquarium, all centered on the sunken city theme. The core of this operation, however, is the casino; all visitors are routed through it wherever they may be headed. A brilliant combination of Orlando, Las Vegas, and Hilton Head, the Atlantis is now the area's largest employer and dominates the economy as well as the skyline. Our cab driver, a large Bahamian woman, who is amazingly adept at hefting and tossing massive suitcases, nods and smiles when we mention Atlantis. "Yah, that King Sol, he employ a lot of people. And that good, we jobs here now. But he also run the town. He get what he asks for." Indeed, the small parliament house we pass in town seems slight compared to the great castle.

Atlantis is not in Nassau proper but sits off on Paradise Island, now connected to Nassau by a tall arching bridge. Paradise Island is a narrow slip of land that an earlier generation of sailors knew as Hog Island. Somehow, that name would not do for travel brochures and it became Paradise Island. Truckloads of sand and a fringe of planted palms completed the transformation. Its big-spending gamblers don't travel by cab but are shuttled by limo right from the airport to the casino. Our seatmate on the plane had tapped his Rolex and noted that the limo could have him in the casino, with a drink in his hand, in under a half hour. "But lock your doors as you go through Nassau, it's a sad sight. I don't ever leave Paradise." Who would?

The channel between Nassau and Paradise Island contains the cruise ship dock. The great orange boats of Carnival Cruise Lines bob in and out of the harbor like great orange life vests. The boats have jogging tracks, four pools, and a climbing wall for passengers to exercise off the copious meals. They stay for a single afternoon. All day the dock has two lines of the tanned and the sunburned coming and going from the ships, looking a bit like red ants streaming in and out. Unless they take taxis to the Atlantis, the passengers have a little time to walk around. They walk through the line of shops along Bay Street, mostly offering jewelry and Asian-made clothes. When we, too, walk from this circuit toward the east end of town, we are warned by a local woman to go no further. "Not good. There are bad boys up there robbing people. Better go back."

With friends who know the city well, I do get to travel inland to other neighborhoods and local restaurants. In the sunshine, Nassau can be a lovely and welcoming city with a rich history. I left with many questions, however, about this type of tourist-driven development. At its best, travel is about meetings, encounters, and exchanges. Yet we also know the dehumanizing side of tourism. The tourist becomes faceless, a disembodied wallet on a short timetable. The residents of tourist destinations are reduced to hawkers and haulers or a snapshot novelty. Perhaps humanizing these encounters would be the first step in humanizing development.

The Global Divide

Inequalities between and among Nations

The most glaring fact that strikes a world traveler (at least one who ventures beyond airports and look-alike resorts) is that the world is full of inequality. We live on a planet of rich nations and poor nations: glaringly, often grotesquely, unequal. Upon closer inspection, the inequalities do not fade but rather become more complex. Gross domestic product (GDP) is a measure of the total value of the goods and services produced within a country. It is one of several measures of the size of an economy, similar to the measure of gross national product (GNP) or gross national income (GNI). Dividing this by the population gives an estimate of average per capita income, while realizing of course that true incomes will vary widely around the average (see figure 1.1).

Even as the aircraft circles over the capital of some poor nation, the tall, gleaming buildings sparkle, the auto traffic forms long lines, and the tiny blue pools of elite hotels and secluded residences shine. Clearly, poor countries have many signs of wealth. The opposite happens in a wealthy country, sometimes even in the trek between the airport and a downtown hotel. The poor and the homeless shuffle along the streets: sometimes selling, sometimes begging, and sometimes waiting. Clearly, rich countries have many signs of poverty.

And, while the old adage about the rich getting richer and the poor getting poorer is often repeated, there is always a mix of people and places in between, everywhere. "These poor countries have no middle class, just rich and poor" is something I often hear repeated. Yet travel through the downtown of that capital or major city, anywhere, and you will see people, often in Western-style business clothes, hurrying to work, reading newspapers, riding trains. They buy hot dogs from street vendors in New York, tacos from sidewalk stands in Mexico City, and curried rice from vendors in New Delhi, and then they hurry into one of those look-alike office buildings. These are neither the idle rich nor the idle poor, but some version of a global middle class. Better-off in some places, more at risk of economic disaster in others, they nonetheless share many of the same worries.

This is the double divide: a big gap between rich and poor nations and a big gap between rich and poor within nations. Working in that latter gap are many in the middle, hoping and planning, wondering if they will ever climb to the top, and worrying that they might someday fall to the bottom. Income inequality can be measured by comparing how much goes to the top versus the rest (or the bottom) or by measuring the curve of inequality with a Gini index that ranges mathematically from zero (perfect equality) to one (absolute inequality) (see figure 1.2).

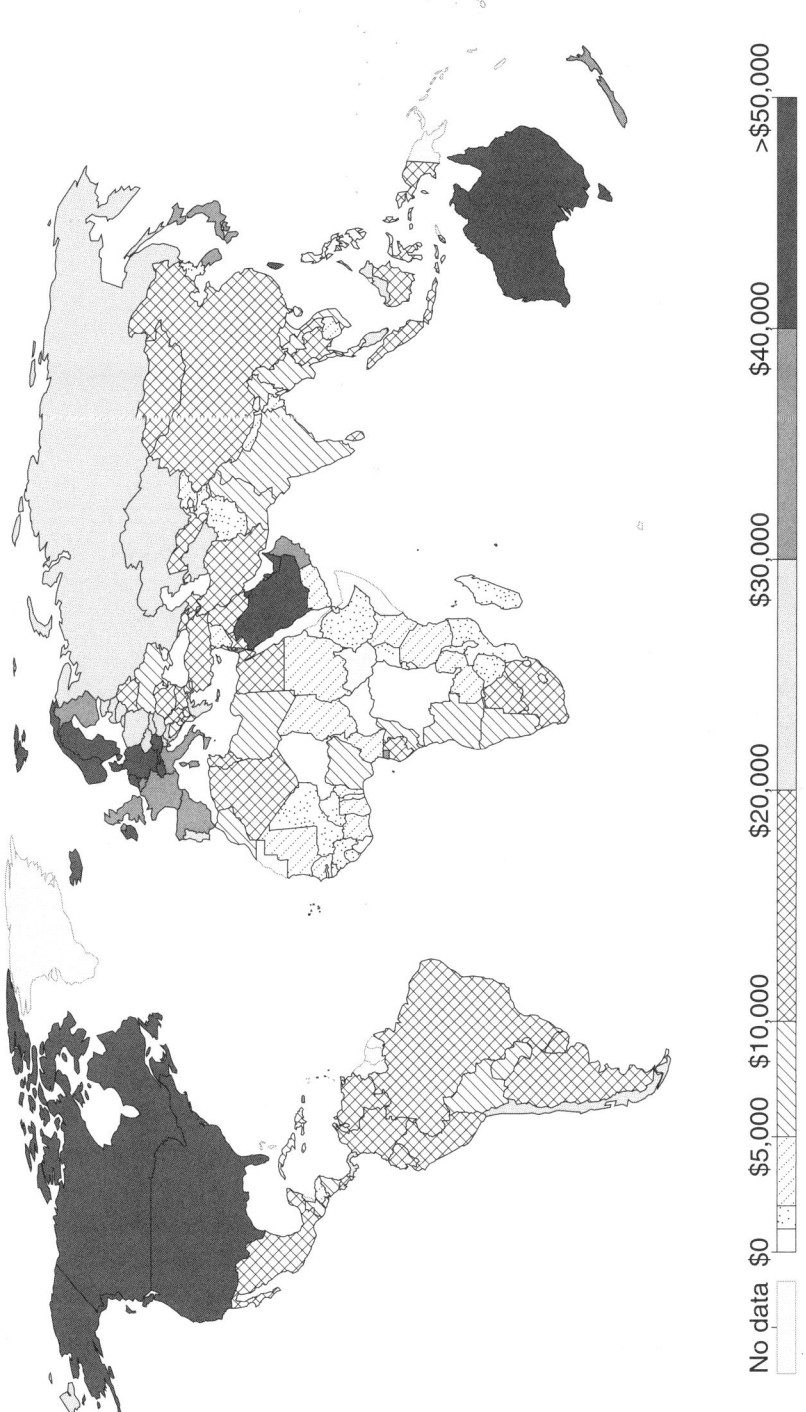

Figure 1.1 Map of global incomes, GDP per capita. (Source: Our World in Data.) For more detailed information, see https://ourworldindata.org/economic-growth.

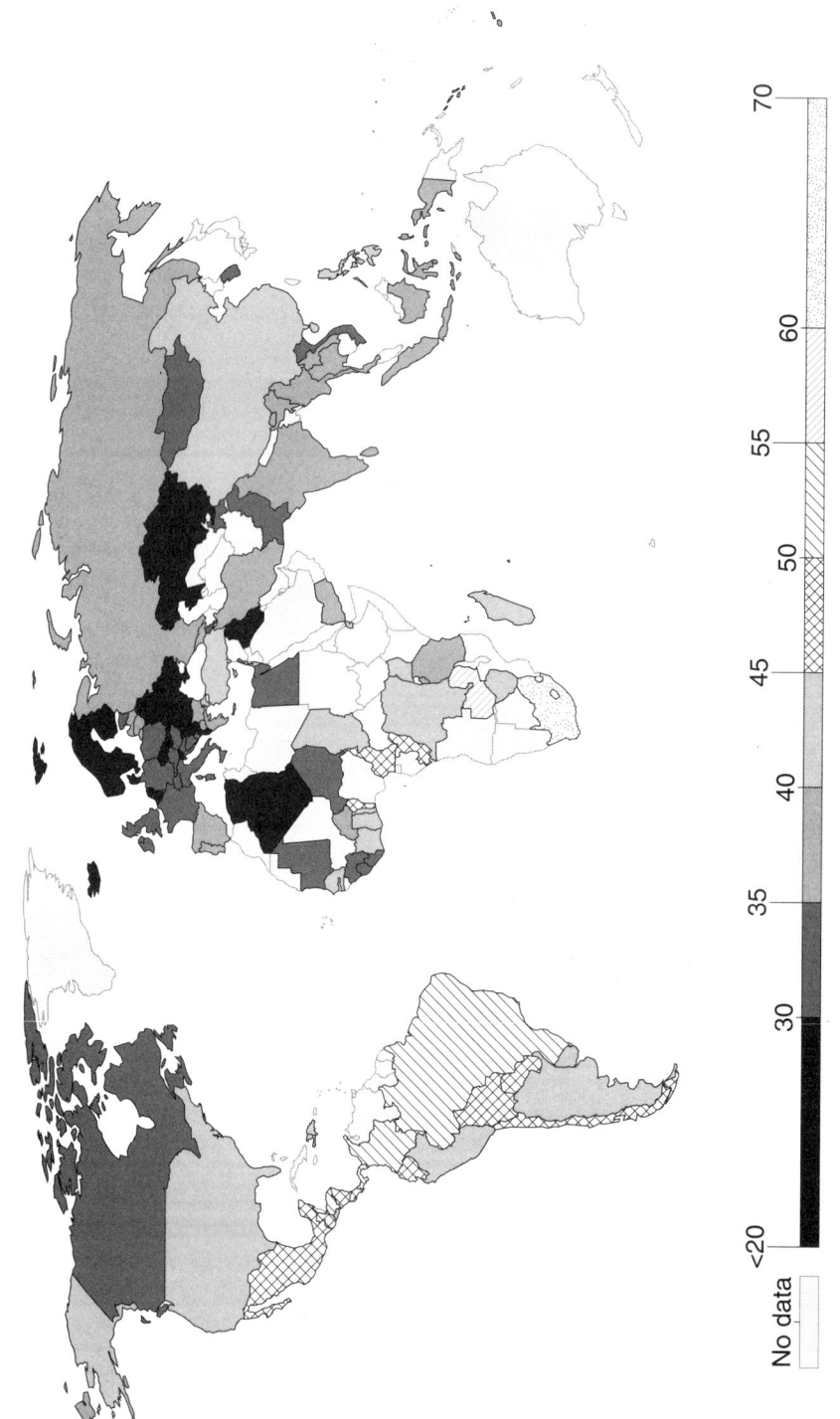

Figure 1.2 Inequality within countries, Gini index. (Source: Our World in Data.) For more detailed information, see https://ourworldindata.org/income-inequality.

São Paulo, Brazil, luxury high rises where the wealthy can literally look down on the poor.

The gap between nations is greater than the gap within any single country (United Nations 2003). There is some evidence that income inequality between countries is declining (Firebaugh 2003). This is not true uniformly around the world, however. Incomes in Sub-Saharan Africa have fallen absolutely, leaving much of Africa even further behind the rest of the world than in 1990. In 1820, Western Europe's per capita income was only about three times that of Africa's; by 1992 it was over 13 times that of Africa; and the gap continues to grow.

The closing of the worldwide gap is due entirely to gains in Asia and in two countries in particular. Both China and India have seen dramatic growth in overall income, with the rate of growth greatest in China. Since these two countries alone account for one-third of the planet's population, this has a big impact on the overall figures. Incredible gains have also been seen in the city-state of Singapore—now richer than its former colonial master with much faster growth than the UK—in South Korea and Taiwan, and in urban Thailand and urban Malaysia. The rural–urban gap remains large, however. Most of the gains have been in large commercial cities, while rural areas, especially in India, have lagged far behind.

This points to a common problem: Comparisons between countries may mean less than comparisons between groups and regions within the countries. Cosmopolitan and high-tech Mumbai (Bombay), India, may flourish along with Seattle, Washington, while the hill country of the northern part of the Indian state of Uttar Pradesh may languish along with the hill country of eastern Kentucky. In all this, however, one striking pattern emerges: The more-equal societies fare better on a host of social measures than the more-unequal societies. Comparing both the world's wealthiest nations and the 50 U.S. states, Wilkinson and Picket (2010) find that the more equal have a stronger community life, better social relations, better mental health with lower levels of stress, less drug use, better physical health and longer life expectancy, better educational performance, less violence, and lower rates of incarceration. Regardless of their overall standard of living, it would appear that deeply unequal places are often deeply divided and at risk for many social ills.

At the same time, the combined forces of globalization, technology expansion, and limited global regulation may have increased the profitability of capital and the power of the very wealthy, even as wages stagnate. The COVID-19 pandemic accentuated this as workers around the world faced layoffs and work restrictions with the greatest perils facing the most vulnerable—a pandemic is no time to be a street vendor in a crowded city as millions of Indians soon realized (Gettleman 2020). The pandemic, however, added to the wealth of those who could expand and even monopolize online vending: Amazon stock soared, and Jeff Bezos added close to 100 billion dollars to his wealth. It was also a good time for Facebook and Google, and for their emerging Chinese competitors. One estimate is that the world's workers lost four trillion dollars in wages even as the world's billionaires added four trillion dollars to their wealth (Oxfam 2021; ILO 2021; as compared at https://inequality.org/facts/global-inequality/). The Forbes list of world billionaires is a mind-boggling compendium of concentrated wealth, vast sums in the hands of a few, and not always the rich and famous but a mix of industrialists, retailers, tech industry tycoons, and global investors—most whose names you would not know (See https://www.forbes.com/billionaires/). The largest group resides in the United States, followed by Japan and Germany and the UK, but with growing global power in China and India.

The top of the Forbes list is still dominated by U.S. technology tycoons (see Table 1.1). They share the top with a few European fashion and retail fortunes, including the only woman (Françoise Bettencourt Meyers) at the top. New and growing fortunes from China and India, ranging from technology to heavy industry to food and pharmaceuticals, now make a bid for the very top.

The Forbes list used to be annual, now it is updated daily—and needs to be. Forbes can estimate gains and losses in this list based on daily stock market performance. The volatility is stunning; any list I put in this book will be obsolete by the time you read it. Consider the incredible "wins and losses" on ONE volatile day in February 2021: In the great horse race, Jeff Bezos (Amazon) was back at #1 with $192 billion—he made almost 2 billion dollars in one day. It

TABLE 1.1 The World's Billionaires

Rank	Name	Net Worth	Age	Country	Source	Industry
1	Jeff Bezos	$177 B	57	United States	Amazon	Technology
2	Elon Musk	$151 B	49	United States	Tesla, SpaceX	Automotive
3	Bernard Arnault & family	$150 B	72	France	LVMH	Fashion & Retail
4	Bill Gates	$124 B	65	United States	Microsoft	Technology
5	Mark Zuckerberg	$97 B	36	United States	Facebook	Technology
6	Warren Buffett	$96 B	90	United States	Berkshire Hathaway	Finance & Investments
7	Larry Ellison	$93 B	76	United States	software	Technology
8	Larry Page	$91.5 B	48	United States	Google	Technology
9	Sergey Brin	$89 B	47	United States	Google	Technology
10	Mukesh Ambani	$84.5 B	63	India	diversified	Diversified
11	Amancio Ortega	$77 B	85	Spain	Zara	Fashion & Retail
12	Francoise Bettencourt Meyers & family	$73.6 B	67	France	L'Oréal	Fashion & Retail
13	Zhang Shanshan	$68.9 B	66	China	beverages, pharmaceuticals	Food & Beverage
14	Steve Ballmer	$68.7 B	65	United States	Microsoft	Technology

Source: Forbes magazine. Retrieved June 15, 2021 from https://www.forbes.com/billionaires.

was a bad day for Elon Musk (Tesla Motors, SpaceX), who had surged to #1, but losing $347 million today put him at #2 with a paltry $173 billion. Also a bad day for Bill Gates (Microsoft) and Mark Zuckerberg (Facebook), each losing around $450 million. But it was a good day in China for Zhong Shanshan (Nongfu Spring); he made $1.3 billion—in one day—in beverages. Four people, all named Walton, each made $350 million, pushing their wealth close to $50 billion as Walmart sales remained strong during the pandemic.

In 2020, a year of struggle for many but huge profits for others, Bezos and Musk and 25 other super-billionaires paid little to no federal income tax thanks to tax loopholes and a focus on taxing income over wealth (Rappeport 2021). Bezos celebrated a good year by buying a 417-foot long "superyacht" for $500 million plus a smaller "support yacht" with a helicopter pad to sail alongside. While this price tag can be hard to fathom, it represents less than some at the top can gain or lose in a week, and building superyachts is a booming business (Matza 2021). Meanwhile the U.S. national minimum wage has stayed at $7.25 an hour for the last 12 years, and this is a weekly wage for the world's poorest workers.

Realities of Global Poverty

Of the world's 7.7 billion people, about 1.5 billion are well-off, living middle-class lives or above, mostly in Western Europe, North America, and parts of the Western Pacific (such as Japan and Australia). Increasingly, they share their level of affluence with rising middle classes in Latin America and Asia, and a small but growing African middle class and elite. Ten percent of the world's population lives on less than $2 per day, the World Bank's benchmark for extreme poverty (World Bank 2018a) (see figure 1.3). This leaves about 3.4 billion, almost half the world's population, somewhere in between. They live in very modest homes, heated by wood or coal if it is cold, cooled if possible by the open air when it is hot. They probably commute on foot, by bike, or by inexpensive public transit. Hovering in the middle, they are often trying to escape sliding into abject poverty, and trying to claim the air-conditioned affluence of the top segment.

Global poverty is declining, at least as measured by the UN and the World Bank. Some of this is the result of concentrated campaigns to alleviate extreme poverty. Much of the gains are also in just two countries, India and China, as well as a few smaller Asian nations. Rapid economic growth in these two countries has lifted millions out of poverty, particularly out of extreme poverty. In both countries, however, a huge divide remains between a relatively privileged and growing urban middle class and millions left behind in poor rural villages with limited access to education, technology, and secure employment. Around the world, almost 80 percent of the world's poor live in rural areas (World Bank 2021).

Numbers can also be controversial, especially with regard to poverty. A rural villager, who leaves behind the self-sufficiency of home and garden and close-knit community for an urban shantytown, where backbreaking construction work or selling vegetables in a market provides an insecure $2 per day, has "escaped" poverty statistically. Whether this person's life has improved dramatically may be harder to determine.

What is it like to live on less than $2 per day, or even how is that possible? In the eastern Congo, Umberta works as a porter in rural village. The only other work is breaking rocks to sell as gravel, and her arms are not strong enough. But she has the considerable strength and stamina to haul luggage, furniture, bags of grain—whatever is needed—for people in a community where there are no roads, only deeply rutted paths marginally passable on foot. In the morning, she hauls beds for a family moving to higher ground. They promise to pay her the equivalent of 50 cents, but only come up with 35. After hawking her services all afternoon, late in the day she is commissioned to haul heavy

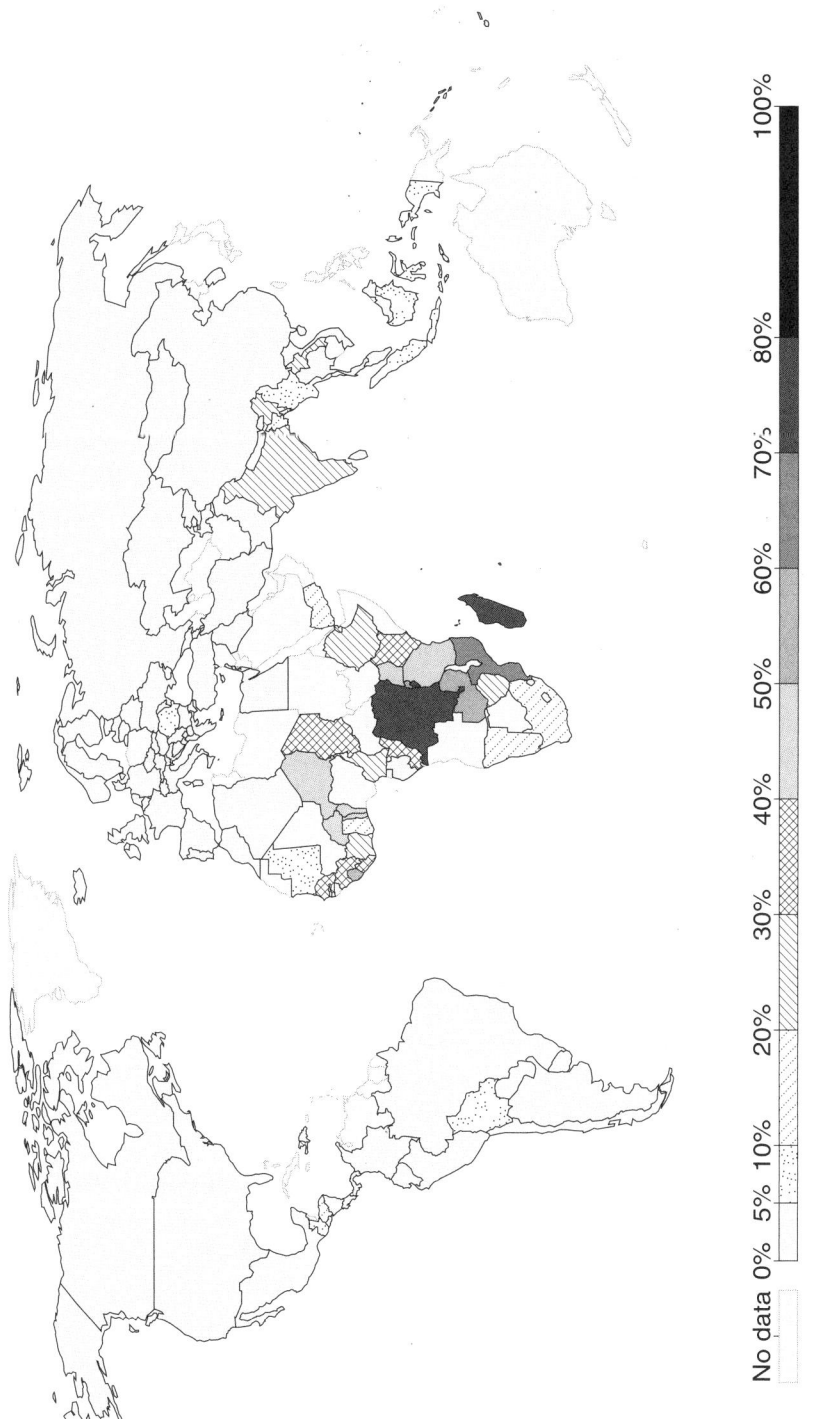

Figure 1.3 Regions of extreme poverty. (Source: Our World in Data.)

sacks up the same steep path. This time she gets her 50 cents. She takes the 85 cents to the local market where it is enough to buy some starchy cassava paste and a few very small fish, caught in the contaminated waters of a local lake. She takes this home to make a meal, their only meal for the day, for her five children. So goes another day in truly world-class extreme poverty. Bill Gates, one the world's richest men, shares some of their stories on his blog: https://www.gatesnotes.com/Development/Life-on-less-than-2-dollars-a-day.

Theories of Class and Economy

The Wealth of Nations: Adam Smith

Why are some nations rich and some poor? This question has puzzled social observers for centuries. One of the earliest attempts to answer this question came from a British analyst, Adam Smith. In 1776, the same year that America declared its independence, he wrote *An Inquiry into the Nature and Causes of the Wealth of Nations* (1937 [1776]). By this time, a century or more of political philosophers in Europe had debated the nature of the state. Now at the dawn of the Industrial Revolution, Smith pioneered a field that came to be known as political economy, which examines the relationship of the political state and the economy, both national and international.

Smith came out of a group of philosophers who became known as the **utilitarians,** very practical-minded people who saw the essence of morality as gaining the greatest good for the greatest number. They believed the way to do this was to allow people to freely pursue their own personal gains, some might even say selfish gains, with as little restraint as possible. Utilitarians believed in individual rights and freedoms, as Thomas Jefferson wrote in the Declaration of Independence that same year, "the right to life, liberty and the pursuit of happiness." (He originally had the word *property* in this sentence.)

Adam Smith believed that these freedoms would also lead to greater wealth. People needed to be free from greedy monarchs who might try to overtax and control commerce (although Smith, unlike Jefferson, remained a loyal subject of the British monarch). He believed in what the French called **laissez-faire,** or that the best government would let capitalists, merchants, and workers pursue their own goals without interference. In a famous phrase, he stated that the "invisible hand" of the market would ultimately turn this selfish ambition into the greatest good for the greatest number. Nations that followed this advice would grow wealthier, such as Britain and the Netherlands perhaps. Those that ignored this advice were doomed to fall into decline, no matter how rich their holdings in land and gold; Spain and Portugal were a case in point. Those who distrusted commerce and believed that society needed the heavy hand of the king and the church to function became known as **conservatives,** and people who followed Smith's ideas about free markets became known as **liberals.** They were indeed the liberal reformers of their days.

This philosophy has seen an enormous revival all around the world, as countries have turned to free trade and free markets in search of wealth. Its proponents are sometimes called **neoliberals** and their views **neoliberalism.** This has caused no end of confusion in the United States, where free trade and laissez-faire capitalism often underlie the philosophy of political conservatives. (The idea has been around long enough that now it is the **conservative** position.) Unlike Adam Smith, however, U.S. conservatives often want the government to be involved in issues of personal morality, so those who believe in a true hands-off approach to governance are sometimes called **libertarians.**

The Libertarian Party in the United States echoes Adam Smith's belief that giving individuals great liberties to pursue their own ends will ultimately result in greater wealth and greater good. While many are suspicious of the extremes of this position, dissatisfaction with government interference has led many around the world to endorse the free-market, free-trade principles of Smith. This approach is also known as **neoclassical economics,** the economic vision of the early utilitarians.

To be fair, Smith was not as blind to the dangers of laissez-faire capitalism as is sometimes supposed. He recognized that free trade was in danger not just from greedy, manipulative monarchs but sometimes also from greedy, manipulative corporations that might seek great monopolies. Smith, of course, was not thinking of Microsoft but of similar entities of his day, like the Hudson's Bay Company (Korten 2015).

The Misery of Nations: Karl Marx

Three-quarters of a century after Smith, Karl Marx looked at his ideas about the productive power of global capitalism and couldn't have agreed more. Capitalism, Marx agreed, was the most productive engine of economic growth ever conceived. But rather than an "invisible hand" that benefited all, Marx believed that behind global capitalism loomed four deep contradictions that would eventually cause the entire system to unravel:

1. **A growing divide between owners and workers.** Marx contended that every age was divided between those who owned or controlled the productive power of the state and those who depended on it for the actual work of production. In the slave societies of the ancient world, such as Greece and Rome, wealthy citizen-landowners depended on the work of slaves as well as foreign subjects to produce the wealth that made their cities and rural estates so fabulous. In medieval Europe, the nobility controlled society through an elaborate hierarchy of power known as feudalism. But the

wealth of kings and noblemen was dependent on the work of poor peasants. Sometimes the peasants had a measure of independence, but many of them were serfs—virtual slaves tied to the land and who owed everything to the landowner. Marx focused his attention on Europe in particular, but much the same arrangements existed in China at the same time, as well as in feudal Japan.

Capitalism and the capitalists eventually overturned the feudal nobility, as wealthy merchants and bankers became richer and more powerful than the old nobles. Industrial capitalism, with its demands for large investments in factory production, further gave power to the new capitalist class. They, in turn, depended on industrial workers, the proletariat, to do the hard and dirty work of industrial production. But capitalism took an ancient story to new heights: The new capitalists were far richer and commanded more resources than the ancients could ever have dreamed of. At the same time, Marx believed that industrial workers were being driven to a uniform level of misery.

2. **A continual crisis of profit for owners.** Despite their wealth, the capitalist owners could not sit back and relax, because capitalism proved intensely competitive. The capitalists always had to worry about being driven out of business by new competition. This competitive struggle forced them to try to increase production by getting more work out of their workers while also cutting costs by cutting wages to a bare subsistence level. The owners would only pay the workers the minimum needed to survive and keep working.

3. **Workers driven to the level of subsistence.** This is one of the contradictions of capitalism that Marx liked to note. As the system became more productive, the workers did not benefit but became more desperate. Greater productive power stemming from new machinery did not result in rising wages but in more displaced workers. These workers formed a "reserve army" of unemployed who would be eager for any work at any wage. Workers, who demanded better conditions, were therefore easily threatened with firing and replacement by these desperate displaced workers.

4. **Greater solidarity and class consciousness among workers.** The capitalists might try to hide the true nature of the system from the larger society by controlling the government and the ruling ideology. The workers could be divided from one another by race/ethnicity and position and told to fear competition from the unemployed "scoundrels" eager to take their jobs. Nonetheless, the result of working side by side with others in similar situations (unlike peasants, who might be widely separated from one another) would eventually cause workers to see their common condition. They

developed a sense of class consciousness and ultimately banded together to challenge the system.

Marx believed that ultimately the only effective challenge would be a revolution that overturned the capitalist system in favor of a system of common ownership for the common good, a system of pure **communism.** In the meantime, however, he encouraged workers and his fellow communists to work with progressive reformers to establish a minimum wage, reduce working hours, ban child labor, and improve the conditions and protections of workers everywhere. These efforts would not solve the problems of a system that he believed was ultimately rotten to the core, but they would raise awareness of the workers' plight and eventually lead to a groundswell of support for a new and better system.

Assessing the Views

So, who is right, or are we all just grasping at theoretical straws in trying to understand a changing world? One view is that Adam Smith was right all along but that his ideas have never been fully applied. Free markets and free trade work, this view contends, at least as long as there are certain modern institutions, such as the World Trade Organization (WTO), to make sure that everyone plays fair. For promoters of free-market capitalism, Adam Smith was basically right about how economies work; it is just that for over 200 years governments have been reluctant to step back and allow free markets to do their magic. Global trade will eventually benefit everyone, as it has already benefited some export-oriented countries in East Asia. Promoting business is good business for all, because wealth will eventually trickle down from rich nations to poor and from rich investors to poor workers. A key step is to limit the power of government and encourage **privatization,** which involves replacing government programs or functions with private enterprise. This view was embraced and exported in the 1980s by Prime Minister Margaret Thatcher in Great Britain and President Ronald Reagan in the United States, where it was dubbed "Reaganomics." It was sometimes seen as an Anglo-American idea in parts of Europe and viewed with some suspicion, but the idea proved popular around the world in the 1990s. Then the new century began with a prolonged global recession that deepened into a world financial crisis in 2008.

Faced with global economic crises and stagnation, the appeal of privatization and market deregulation has been tempered, in accord with Smith himself, who saw dangers in completely unregulated trade. The so-called **third-way economics** of Great Britain's Labour Party, an approach championed by former Prime Minister Tony Blair when he took office in 1997, has been heavily influenced by social theorist Anthony Giddens (1999, 2000). This approach has called for a smaller but still active government that promotes trade, even as it works to protect the rights of workers and assist those who have not benefited from globalization. In the United States, President Bill Clinton supported free-trade initiatives—such as the North American Free Trade Agreement (NAFTA), which went into effect in 1994—but sought to include labor and environmental protections. Advised by economist David Ellwood (1988), sociologist Mary Jo Bane, and other social scientists, Clinton proposed reforms to help those for whom globalization was not providing opportunities. In his 2000 campaign, President George W. Bush championed the benefits of small government and free trade around the country and around the world but also endorsed a "compassionate conservatism" that offered some help to those hurt by global neoliberal economics. As the Bush emphasis on free trade and unregulated financial markets seemed to bring the United States, and then world, to the point of economic catastrophe, there was again great interest in Barack Obama's message of charting a new course domestically and internationally that was more cooperative and inclusive.

In the 1990s and early 2000s Brazil managed to combat poverty and bring up the standard of living of the poorest Brazilians, while maintaining a high rate of economic growth and technological development. Brazilian sociologist Fernando Henrique Cardoso studied both Marx and Smith and wrote thoughtful accounts of dependency and development in Latin America as an academic (Cardoso 1977; Cardoso and Falletto 1979). He became a senator, then finance minister, and then president of Brazil. As president from 1995 to 2002, this dependency scholar seemed to embrace the neoliberalism of privatization and free trade. Cardoso contended that his policies were in fact **neosocial,** embracing smaller government and freer markets but, like Clinton's and Blair's policies, trying to use the power of government to assist those hurt by these policies while supporting investments in education. Cardoso won great praise for stabilizing Brazil's uncontrolled economy and at the same time preserving democracy. His successor was Luiz Lula Ignácio de Silva, a former laborer known for his fiery anticapitalist rhetoric. As president, Lula tempered that rhetoric and tried to maintain good relations with the United States while also keeping commitments to workers and Brazil's many poor. Policies to promote growth and a strong export economy were paired with programs like the Bolsa Família that offered subsidies to poor families who kept their children in school. The combination fueled growth and gave Brazil new global economic clout (Barrionuevo 2008). Lula left office as one the most popular national leaders in the world and was replaced by Brazil's first female president, Dilma Rousseff, a former Marxist guerilla who was imprisoned and tortured in the 1960s for opposing Brazil's right-wing military dictatorship and promised a more centrist "growth with equity" model of development. She was impeached by a right-leaning senate on charges of corruption. In the election that followed, amidst anger over corrupt politicians and high crime rates, Brazil elected a former military captain, and proponent of the far right, Jair Bolsonaro. An admirer of the U.S. Trump administration, Bolsonaro promised a law-and-order crackdown on crime and a fast-forward focus on economic development from the cities to the Amazon, with far fewer protections for workers, indigenous peoples, or the Amazonian environment.

Another view is that Karl Marx was right all along but that his ideas haven't been fully applied. A popular joke in Russia as it struggled with the economic transition toward capitalist markets was, "Everything the communists told us about communism was a lie. Unfortunately, everything they told us about capitalism is true." The Soviet government had told the Russian people that communism would bring them prosperity, modernity, and economic equality. It did not. The government had warned that capitalism would only bring poverty, inequality, unemployment, corruption, and crime. It did. What went wrong?

Some argue that communism is inherently flawed—that is, it doesn't take into account the realities of economics or human nature (although Marx was an astute observer of both). Others contend that it has yet to be fully tried. Still others believe communism began in the wrong places: Marx looked for revolutions in Germany, Great Britain, and maybe the United States, the advanced industrial nations of his time. Instead, communist systems emerged in Russia, China, Vietnam, and Cuba. Marx did not consider these places ready for true communism. What occurred in these countries was less an uprising of the urban industrial proletariat and more a peasant revolt. Marx himself noted that peasant revolts, though very common throughout history, invariably failed as the peasantry could not find an effective way to govern themselves without turning to tyrants. (The Greek word *tyrannos* originally referred to just this sort of a people's leader.) Marx believed that capitalism must emerge first, so that communism could harness its productive might. He also believed that a revolutionary consciousness, one committed to the rights and dignity of all workers, had to be cultivated before a true revolution could occur.

As a result, some are reluctant to call what emerged in Russia and China and several smaller nations *communism*. Marx's communist ideal saw the state, or centralized government, withering away as it was no longer necessary, now freed from its old role of protecting the dominant class. But Russia and China maintained strong centralized and bureaucratic states that only grew. As a result, they are sometimes referred to as **state socialist systems.**

State socialist systems have not fared very well. In 1991, economic and political problems splintered the Soviet system into Russia and many new republics, most of which are gradually moving toward private enterprise systems, even when led by autocratic former communists. The former Soviet bloc of Eastern Europe is also embracing free markets and privatized economies, some with more success than others. China has retained its communist-era bureaucracy but is wide open to foreign capitalist investment and trade. Vietnam and Cuba have retained a few communist slogans but are also courting foreign capitalist investment. To the neoliberal economists, this shows the ultimate weakness of communism. To the pure Marxists, it shows that these countries were not ready for true communism and that the capitalist world system wasn't ready to allow them to develop it.

Further, many find that what the communists told them about the evils of capitalism seems to be all too real. Eastern European economies are growing but also growing more unequal with high unemployment. The Russian economy is stagnant, with all the supposed evils of capitalism—poverty, unemployment, and corporate crime—but few of the benefits. Capitalist institutions have brought great economic growth to China, but human rights concerns remain. Moreover, some communist institutions, such as basic health care for all, are now threatened by new divides between rich and poor.

Marxists look at this and say Marx was right all along. Reforms, while important, never fully fix the system. Divisions between countries may be important for a time, but the real, ultimate division is between the rich capitalist owners, whose ranks get smaller and grow richer all the time, and the poor proletarian workers, who become more numerous and more impoverished with each decade. To these Marxists, the world is simply not yet ready to embrace a real alternative. World-systems Marxists believe that only a worldwide revolution can work; otherwise, communist states in a capitalist world will be pressured to play by capitalist rules. Other Marxists still look ahead to future crises of capitalism that will cause the workers in the advanced industrial states to demand a fundamental change in the system. They are at their strongest in highlighting the glaring problems in our current global economy. The challenge remains to devise and demonstrate a fully workable alternative.

Some prefer to call themselves "neo-Marxists" in that they propose new versions of Marx's thought. Others simply back what they call *political economy,* a term that would have been familiar to both Adam Smith and Karl Marx. Today political economy often refers to liberal or progressive approaches that contend that the power of government must be used to regulate the economy and to address problems of concentrated power and wealth.

Even when ruled by a single party, the pendulum of Mexican politics has swung between the politics of the left, with its ideology of a political economy of redistribution of wealth to the poor, and the politics of the right, with its ideology of what Latin Americans call *neoliberalismo,* seeking progress in free trade and free-market economics. The same pendulum has swung across Latin America. The 1980s and 1990s saw many Latin American countries rejecting leftist leaders in favor of the Washington Consensus of free markets, free trade, and privatization. Some countries did well; many did not. Some people within those countries did very well; many did not. Venezuela continues the leftist policies of Hugo Chávez, sometimes socialist but more often just populist, and his successor, Nicolás Maduro, often seems more authoritarian than the proponent of any coherent economic plan. Evo Morales of Bolivia was seen with deep suspicion by some and as a great leader of Bolivia's overlooked indigenous population by others, but after holding power for almost two decades, he was turned out by military action supported by the political right.

Unfortunately for Latin America, most countries have not been well served by either the left or the right. Left-wing populists have had a nasty habit of abandoning democratic principles in favor of continued power. Sometimes the leftists are thrown out, either by election or more often by force, with an uprising from the right. Whether civilian or military, the right-wing reformers have often proved ruthless in their pursuit of economic growth. Reform seems to mean union-busting, land grabs, and privatizing by selling assets to political cronies. Nevertheless, parts of Latin America have emerged from economic crisis with new vigor (Romero 2010) and the optimistic hope to dare that a new generation of leaders has found the right mix.

Many European states, particularly the Nordic countries, see a significantly larger role for government. While their political parties sometimes have the word *socialist* in their names, these are primarily welfare-state systems in which the economy is largely capitalist but the government is actively involved in promoting the welfare of its people, and some measure of equality, through government programs and income transfers.

The most common hybrid around the world looks to markets as economic engines of growth and development (that is, most production is private) and to the government as the guarantor of certain basic rights and opportunities through the redistribution of wealth, such as by taxing the wealthy more heavily and offering credits and subsidies to the poor. The scope of government involvement varies greatly: In parts of Europe, these programs are quite extensive; in North America, they are often quite limited. In his book *The European Dream*, Jeremy Rifkin (2005) contends that Europe's vision of the future is eclipsing the American dream. He argues that while the American dream was based on *belongings* and getting ahead for oneself and one's family, the European dream is based on *belonging* and a shared sense of common well-being. Rifkin believes that this alternate vision of what a society should offer makes Europeans more willing to accept widespread government involvement in promoting equity and the welfare of its citizens. He sees something to be learned in both the American and European approaches:

> At the risk of ruffling feathers on both sides of the Atlantic, perhaps there are lessons to share. We Americans might be more willing to assume a collective sense of responsibility for our fellow human beings and the earth we live on. Our European friends might be more willing to assume a sense of personal accountability in their individual dealings in the world. (p. 385)

The European model has produced some of the world's highest standards of living as well as some of the highest levels of human development. But as a number of European countries—Greece, Ireland, and Portugal in particular—face fiscal crises over their inability to pay for domestic programs, and as economically stronger European partners, such as Germany, are less willing to come to their financial aid, the European model may face new challenges.

Economic Development: Modernization and Dependency Theories

What made poor nations poor? Why do they so often stay poor, in spite of what seem to be great efforts to advance? For over half a century the debate on these points has been dominated by two broad lines of thought: modernization theory and dependency theory. Modernization theory combines a neoclassical understanding of the global economy with a theory of social change. Dependency theory extends the political economy of Karl Marx to an understanding of the workings of a world system dominated by colonial and postcolonial powers.

Modernization Theory: Time to Clean House

The underlying premise of **modernization theory** is that poverty is the basic condition of humanity. People have always been poor. An old adage says that we're born hungry, naked, and crying, and it goes downhill from there. Perhaps the same could be said about humanity in general. We entered the world with great needs, and until we acquired the huge productive capacity of modern society, we lived in poverty.

Modernization thinkers built their ideas on a basic dichotomy between traditional and modern societies that was popular in European social thought in the 1800s, as Europeans and their American counterparts tried to understand the changes brought by urbanization and industrialization. These two forces generated not only great social dislocations but also incredible productivity; on this point, both Adam Smith and Karl Marx agreed. But what of those societies that did not make the great, often painful, leap from traditional society to modern society? With low productivity, they were doomed to stay poor until they changed their ways. To prosper, they needed modernity.

Nations Today Need Modern Technology. Peasants working the land—maybe with the help of a draft animal, if they were lucky—would scarcely be able to feed themselves and would have little left over to better their lives; they would remain poor. Artisans and craftspersons using traditional methods might make beautiful things, but they could never make enough of them to raise themselves and their communities out of poverty. They needed industry: tractors, factories, assembly lines, and the energy to drive this production.

This was enough for the industrial age of the mid-twentieth century, but now with the electronic age, nations also need the computing power and endless electrical grids necessary to organize all this production.

Developing Nations Need Modern Ideas. It's not enough to have the goods without the knowledge and the will to use them. Traditional ideas must go. Traditional values—such as fatalism, patience, humility, communal cooperation, respect for the wisdom of elders and the old order, ties to the land—must be replaced by new modern values—ambition, entrepreneurship, advancement, achievement, and hard-fought competition. The modern ideal (even if rarely achieved) is an opportunity for all, regardless of one's inherited status, birthright, ethnicity, or place of origin, but assurances for none. Only hard work and productivity can bring success.

Developing Nations Need Modern Institutions. It is of no help to believe in education if all the schools are bad. It doesn't help to believe in entrepreneurship if there is no way to begin a business. To prosper, countries need modern governments. Electoral democracy should replace theocracy or monarchy; that is, parliaments or presidents should be put in place of religious leaders and kings. But this is the democracy of Thomas Jefferson and Adam Smith, a limited government that promotes individual freedoms. This government should be free of graft and also of paternalism; it will not promise to repay loyalty with patronage but rather to maintain an open playing field for all. It will be kept in place by a modern electoral process as well as by a free and unbiased press. Business needs to have a secure and stable environment in which to prosper; this requires reliable modern banks and financial institutions, modern insurance companies, and free-market institutions such as stock and commodity markets. Modern schools enroll all children and forego most religious instruction and memorization of ancient texts in favor of learning the skills of the modern technological world.

Achieving the Ideals of Modernization. Together, these views of modernity have provided a powerful vision of progress and prosperity. In the years following World War II, this was the dogma of the United States, Great Britain, Canada, and Australia and, to varying degrees, Western Europe and Japan. It was encouraged for the newly independent countries of Asia and Africa as well as U.S. allies in Latin America. Mixed with a healthy dose of neoliberal trust in free markets and free trade, this view came to define the **free world.** Modern technology would be exported by multinational corporations, building new facilities in the developing world as well as through the foreign technical and financial assistance and development loans from new post–World War II institutions, such as the World Bank. Modern ideas would come through a Western-model of education and Western-dominated global media. Modern institutions would be built with the help of Western managerial assistance as well as through international programs such as the International Monetary Fund (IMF), created at the same time as the World Bank and intended to stabilize national currencies and global economic trade.

Oddly enough, perhaps, modernization thinking also came to define the Soviet model of development, although in this case, it was mixed with the ideas of Karl Marx. Led by the Soviet Union, the communist world was also eager to modernize. Modern technology meant large-scale, state-owned heavy industry. Modern ideas meant the new socialist worker, striving for progress and rejecting traditional religious ideas for a new secular dream of work and opportunity for all, with the rewards of this productivity divided equally. Modern institutions included the complex bureaucratic framework of state socialism, with careful, rational planning ensuring continued gains in efficiency and productivity. These achievements would be exported around the world by Soviet technical advisors and investments and would become vanguards of enlightened revolutionaries across the globe.

One does not have to spend much time in Latin America, Africa, or South Asia to see that both the capitalist and the socialist visions of modernization have fallen far short of their ideals. To be fair, most in the modernization school of thought always believed that modernization would be slow and painful. But they also believed that progress was inevitable. In much of the world, people are still waiting.

Dependency Theory: Get Out of My House

Since the time of Joseph Stalin, national modernization had been a hallmark of the policy of the Soviet Union, but the founder of Soviet communism, Vladimir Lenin, had a slightly different conception of the world. Lenin loved Marxist ideas and preached them with fervor. But influenced by intellectuals among the Russian radicals (Bukharin 1925, 1973 [1917]), Lenin came to see Marx's picture of capitalist misery not as a state problem, operating within one nation, but as a global problem.

Lenin wrote *Imperialism, the Highest Stage of Capitalism* (1948), arguing that European imperialism—the wild expansion of European empires that was carving up Africa and would eventually help lead to World War I—was driven by the forces of capitalism. Capitalist industry needed new raw materials, more labor, and new markets. Its insatiable thirst for profit drove it on a mad, worldwide chase. But as the industrial empires imported materials, they exported misery. British industry grew while industry in India, a British colony, was crushed. British workers could live better than Marx had predicted only because Indian workers lived so poorly. The squalor, desperation, and misery that Marx had predicted were evident but only in limited fashion in

London, because they had been exported to Calcutta. This became the kernel of the idea of **dependency theory.**

Dependency theorists acknowledged that the Western world, or the First World, did bring many things to the poor nations, the Third World, but that most of them were negative and destructive. The destruction came with the European colonial empires but did not leave with them, because new institutions—including multinational corporations, foreign aid agencies, and the World Bank and the IMF—continued to practice neocolonialism. Even after achieving independence, poor countries were hopelessly dependent on the rich nations. And dependency brought evil in several respects.

Dependency Brought Exploitation. Poor countries were being ripped off. The terms of trade were rigged against the poor: The rich countries paid them poorly for their raw materials and then sold finished goods to them at high prices. The poor countries were not naturally poor; they had many resources. But the rich countries, not the poor, profited from that natural wealth and left behind little but despoiled, stripped, polluted land when the resources ran out. In the decades following World War II, the rich multinationals came less often in search of raw materials and more often in search of cheap labor, exploiting the people rather than the land. At one time, Europe, Japan, and North America sought out the country that is now Indonesia and once was the Dutch East Indies for its natural rubber. Now, companies such as Nike come to Indonesia to seek reliable, inexpensive labor to stitch athletic shoes made of nylon and synthetic rubber. To dependency thinkers, this shift only perpetuates the gross exploitation.

Dependency Brought Domination. If the terms of trade are so bad and the exploitation so obvious, why don't the poor countries object and throw the multinational companies out? They can't because they are at the mercy of the vast wealth of these companies and the countries that sponsor them. The newly independent states around the world are not truly independent. They depend on the rich nations for their livelihood (since their independent economies were destroyed long ago by imperial expansion) and so must play by rules set by the rich. National leaders are bribed or coerced into doing the bidding of rich countries and rich companies, even at the expense of their own people. Those who refuse face sanctions, embargoes, and even outright military intervention.

Dependency Brought Distortion. The economies of the poor countries no longer function as an integrated whole; they are entirely structured to serve the needs of wealthy foreigners and maybe a small internal elite. They got help (or borrowed money) to build roads and rails, but the roads and rails mostly lead to port cities to facilitate exports. The goods produced in these countries don't serve local needs, and the local people can't afford them; they are made for foreign markets. The people no longer are self-sufficient but depend on imports from the rich; thus they remain vulnerable to exploitation and domination. And so, the cycle continues.

The key to dependency thinking is that the poor were not always poor. They were made poor. And this is fundamentally different than the experience of the industrialized wealthy nations. Those countries may also have been undeveloped at one time, with little industry, but they were never underdeveloped. The rich countries developed by stripping wealth from the rest, underdeveloping them in the process (Frank 1967). The poor countries, at least not many of them, cannot do the same, because they are left at the bottom of the heap with no one else to exploit, except maybe their own rural, tribal, or minority populations.

Rooted in Lenin's ideas, dependency thinking gained ground in Latin America, also following World War II. Largely ignored by the industrial West, Latin America had done well in the 1940s, but then new investment and cold war politics seemed to make Latin America more miserable and poor. Dependency theory was clearly the minority viewpoint in industrial North America in the 1950s and 1960s. But as the poor countries remained poor and got even poorer in the 1970s and 1980s, its ideas gained currency. Even the success stories seemed to show failures. Some countries, such as Brazil, saw their economies grow, but inequality also grew and the lives of the poor did not improve. This was the problem of "dependent development" (Evans 1979) or "growth without development."

The most complete extension of dependency thinking came in the 1970s from Immanuel Wallerstein (2011 [1974]), who in a series of books laid out **world systems theory.** European capitalist expansion began in the 1500s. You will remember that "in 1492, Columbus sailed the ocean blue," and he was soon followed by every European adventurer who could borrow or steal a boat. Colonial powers created a world economic system that enriched the core nations at the expense of the periphery, their colonies. The world system continues to have a wealthy core supported by a poor periphery. The core of the core has shifted a bit—Amsterdam and the Dutch United Provinces in the 1600s, London and the British United Kingdom in the 1700s and 1800s, New York and the American United States in the 1900s. But the rich have only grown richer while the poor have grown poorer. Sometimes a small semiperipheral nation, such as Taiwan or Israel, serves in an intermediary role in advancing the interests of the rich nations.

This was a forceful diagnosis of the world situation, but it proved much harder to find a cure. If modernizationists are still waiting for the promised progress, dependency thinkers are still waiting for the promised alternatives. Communist China seemed to be charting an independent course but then came to embrace modernization and an export economy after the death of Chairman Mao Zedong. In Cuba in the 1960s, Fidel Castro promised a change but seemed to only move Cuba from dependency on the United States to dependency on the Soviet Union. In the 1980s in Nicaragua, the Sandinista government promised an alternative but became bogged down in corruption and an endless U.S.-sponsored civil war. Nicaragua and Cuba now compete with one another to get more foreign investment. In Africa, the best of theories all seemed to fall under the weight of factional fighting, internal and external corruption, and famine and diseases. The search for new ideas continues, and the poor are still waiting.

When Prehistory Repeats Itself

Each of the contending theoretical approaches offers its set of clashing explanations for why the poor are poor. To the first camp, China was poor because traditional, inward looking rulers failed to adopt new technologies and ways of doing business, holding all these ideas suspect and keeping their nation in a state of suspended development while European innovation sped ahead. To the second camp, China was held hostage not so much by its own government as by a wolf pack of militaristic nations—those of Europe as well Japan and the United States—that demanded economic concessions and political acquiescence to gross exploitation.

Similarly, one finds both theories at play as to why Latin America has been poor. In scenario one, Latin America had the misfortune of belonging to the wrong empire. Unlike Canada and the United States, its culture and society were Spanish rather than British, dominated by agrarian rather than industrial organization and values, by a crown monopoly rather than capitalist commercial interests. In scenario two, Latin America had the misfortune of being "ripped off" twice: first by Spanish and Portuguese mercantilists, then by British and North American industrialists.

Why is Africa poor? One scenario points to drought conditions, soil that lacks nutrients for growing crops, and an abundance of disease, coupled with a traditional village-based society that does not lend itself to national development. The second view points to the recent orgy of industrial imperialism that divided the continent and only began to relinquish its hold in the last few decades.

Have people indeed always been poor? The answer to this simple question hinges on what we mean by *poor*. There is an issue of definition and one of judgment. If we mean absolute poverty, or lack of basic needs, then we must note that most of humanity has lived very simply for most of human history with few material goods. Yet it is not clear that life was always miserable. Many tribal people, that is, those living in prestate societies, seemed to have lived quite well. A few still do.

Hunter-gatherers, our earliest ancestors, faced many dangers and challenges. Yet they also seemed to have relished roaming in the openness of the natural world, had healthy and varied diets of natural plants supplemented with bits of meat, and maybe enjoyed more leisure time to relax, tell stories, and build relationships than most of us will ever know (Sahlins 2018 [1972]. Simple hunter-farmers and fisherfolk in North and South America, in the Caribbean, and in the South Pacific often lived quite well before the Europeans showed up uninvited. Some of those European sailors, in fact, thought they had found paradise. Life for these tribal peoples probably was never pure paradise, but they managed to have a good diet from gardening (horticulture), supplemented by catching fish, seafood, and wild game. They seemed to have had a rich village life as well, even if almost none were rich by our standards.

The few autonomous tribal peoples that remain in the world may be eager to acquire a shotgun or are intrigued by an outboard motor, but they are often also eager to retain their independence and some semblance of their way of life. Certainly, if by *poor* we mean relative poverty, then these people have enjoyed a much smaller gap between the richest and the poorest than in more complex societies.

Did poverty arrive for these societies with European colonization, as the dependency and world systems approaches often contend? For many in the Americas and across the Pacific, as well as in Sub-Saharan Africa and parts of Southeast Asia, perhaps it did. They certainly already knew hunger and disease, and all but the simplest and most remote knew warfare. The terrible scourges of famine, plague, and genocidal war were rare, however, and the idea of desperate poverty—going hungry while others ate, going without while others prospered, begging with no accepted social role or vocation—was almost unheard of (McNeill 1991 [1963]).

But these things did not first appear in 1500. Europe and Asia, and maybe to a lesser extent Mesoamerica from Mexico to Peru, knew these things far earlier. They seem to have come not with the European empires (although the Europeans took them to new extremes) but with the first empires themselves. They came with civilization itself, if by *civilization* we mean state societies, with cities and rulers supported by large-scale agriculture. They came not at the time of the Industrial Revolution (although it brought a brutal new form of urban poverty) but toward the end of what anthropologists call the **Neolithic revolution,** the transition to farming.

Large-scale grain agriculture provided a food surplus that could be stored and shipped and could support mighty empires, from Egypt and Mesopotamia to the great river valleys of India and China. The granaries could support the pharaoh, the king, or the emperor and his armies. The ruler could, in turn, use armed military force to extend territory and bring more people under his (or very rarely her) control. Peasants worked the land. They answered to rulers who controlled the land, and their surpluses went to support cities, temples, and armies. Their own diet became dominated by one or two basic foods—often, a grain such as rice, wheat, or maize (American corn). Once drought came, they didn't have a variety of natural foods to which to turn, and they died in mass famines. When war came, large professional armies destroyed the crops. And relative poverty reached extremes. The great rulers lived a fabulously wealthy lifestyle and lacked for nothing, while the peasants had far less and may have been reduced to an existence of bare subsistence or starvation when hard times came.

This was the picture of poverty in the civilized world from about 3000 BCE in the Middle East and China and somewhat later in Mexico and Europe. It is still the picture of rural poverty in much of the developing world. Poor peasants have probably never chosen their fate but had it imposed on them from without. And while few want to remain poor and landless, they may have good reason to fear life in the city. As the cities grew in number and size, rural poverty found a counterpart in urban poverty: begging and work at poorly paid crafts, domestic service, odd jobs, and informal employment. This, too, is as old as the first cities, but it is now the way of life for many of the world's poor. Poor urbanites are almost never content to stay as they are, for they can clearly see what they are missing. They often bear the worst of the modern world's crime and pollution, yet they see few of its benefits.

Realizing the antiquity of poverty, along with its global spread through colonization, we can see that modernization and dependency have often been processes that occurred side by side. This understanding is important if we are to work for economic development that truly addresses human needs.

Modern technology, for better or worse, is essential to our world, and people need access to it. A few tribes may want to be left alone (although even the Kayapo of the Brazilian Amazon and the Inupiat of the Arctic have invested in satellite dishes). Poor farmers and poor urbanites need access to technology, only it must be the appropriate technology.

Modern ideas are also growing in importance, even if many of them prove to be more ancient than we originally thought. Once again, these must be appropriate. On the one hand, much of the world is suspicious of what they are sold as Western popular culture: images of instant gratification without responsibility, about "having it all" at the expense of family, faith, and community. On the other hand, they must realize that many in the West, young and old, have the same suspicions. Presumably modern ideas have roots that go back to our earliest tribal ancestors and strike a chord with people around the world, even if they are often ignored in practice: the dignity and worth of individuals, the rights of women and children, and the importance of opportunities for creative expression for all.

Modern institutions are also needed, even as they often fall short of their ideals. The World Bank, a long-time supporter of free markets, devoted its

2002 *World Development Report* to "building institutions for markets." Poor farmers and urbanites alike need reliable and accessible financial institutions and affordable credit. Rich and poor alike benefit from a stable currency, a graft-free government, a free and independent press, and a clear and equitable system of laws.

This is the *internal* side of reform and development (Bradshaw and Wallace 1996). Anthropologist Oscar Lewis (2011 [1961], 1968) contended that a **culture of poverty** emerged in poor communities in capitalist societies. This culture stressed **fatalism,** living for the day rather than planning for the future, and a distrust of outside institutions. Ultimately, Lewis believed, that view was passed on to the children and helped keep them in poverty. Many found Lewis's description compelling, but others saw it as "blaming the victim" (Ryan 1976). They believed that it was not the subculture of poor people that kept them poor but the external structures of a larger society that oppressed and exploited them. Modernization theory is much like the idea of a culture of poverty—in this case, applied to whole societies within a capitalist world. Certainly we can find many ways in which poor societies need reform, but this can become victim blaming unless we also look at the larger structures, as dependency theory reminds us.

The exploitation of workers around the world can only be changed by new global structures. People and their representatives must also be able to make decisions about their own needs and priorities without facing undue external pressure. Export economies are likely here to stay, but they can be balanced by efforts to meet local needs. A new generation of social scientists has called for development that is both broad-based and sustainable (Weaver et al. 1997).

Ending Extreme Poverty: Markets and Beyond

At the beginning of the twenty-first century, few examples of viable socialism remain. Market economies dominate, even in "communist" China. Yet markets have been slow to deliver the promised benefits to many. As described by former Brazilian president Fernando Henrique Cardoso (1996):

> It's as if the demise of real socialism coincided with some kind of Marx's "revenge." The economy reigns supreme, determining political choices and the limits of social action. And the free market emerges as a leading ideology, fostering competition and an exaggerated, narcissistic individualism that equate the realm of values with the dictates of efficiency.... Inherent in the ideal of progress is equity, seen as the convergence of standards of equality of opportunities—or social justice. This idea of equality has nurtured all modern utopias—from the liberal, centered on political equity, to the socialist, concerned with socio-economic equality. Today's demand for equity—denser, more powerful—is searching for new institutional vehicles. It is no longer the monopoly of one group or class. It is now a collective task—to give a human sense to development. (p. 44)

Even as some societies have attempted socialist or alternative paths, the global economy is dominated by global corporate capitalism. The challenge then is to tame corporate economic power and harness market forces for human needs. The world now faces those same **market conundrums** that have long vexed national societies. Markets work best under conditions of relative equality, but over time, they tend to produce conditions of extreme inequality. Pay-as-you-go markets might be acceptable delivery vehicles for food, education, health, and housing if everyone involved has similar market power. Yet in the "one dollar, one vote" logic of the market, some have tremendous power to claim whatever they want while others have no voice at all. The game of Monopoly begins as a free-for-all market and ends with all of the wealth and control concentrated in one player's hands, as the others go bankrupt. Real-world markets, when unregulated, often behave in the same way.

The assumption of market efficiency may also be wrong. Competition can force greater efficiency, but it can also lead to market inefficiency. Imagine trying to get around town in a city of nothing but competing toll roads: The libertarian's dream would be most motorist's nightmare: most of your time would go to paying tolls, and most of what you paid would go to the cost of collecting them. Likewise, four competing toll roads between two cities would likely be disastrous both economically and ecologically. In some cases, people want choice above all, as perhaps in fashion. While we might settle for simple quality clothes, most of us want more choice than the single "Mao suit" of rural China in the 1950s and 1960s. But in many other cases, a single quality choice is better than a multitude of poor choices: for instance, one product that lasts in place of 10 that don't, one good school in place of six bad ones, or one health insurer that will pay instead of 12 that may not.

Beyond problems of equity and efficiency, there is the tragedy of the market: the opposite of Smith's "invisible hand," in which individual decisions do not add to the common good but create the worst for all. It may be in my best individual interest to let everyone else use public transit while I drive on open, uncluttered roads. But what happens if everyone decides to do this? Public transit will go bankrupt while traffic jams clog the roads. There is no way out of this by private action, although some have tried helicopters. The only solution is a public commitment. As a counter to the tragedy of the market is Garrett Hardin's (1968) "tragedy of the commons." He believed that a space that belonged to all would eventually be neglected or abused by all: the collective farm or the world's oceans, for that matter.

The ultimate failure of the market can be seen in a basic disjuncture between basic beliefs and everyday life. Despite stereotypes to the contrary, Americans claim overwhelmingly that what matters to them most is family, friends, and faith. Yet most of their time is spent accumulating and caring for material possessions. Somehow, Americans have become captive to the market, and more and more people around the world are experiencing the same fate.

Markets are powerful. But much of what the world is seeking, markets do not provide. The challenge of the twenty-first century will be to tame the markets—promoting equality, opportunity, and second chances, while limiting wasteful and destructive choices and agreeing on social solutions. In that regard, the United Nations created a series of development goals to focus the world's priorities as it entered the third millennium of the Western calendar.

The UN Millennium Development Goals (MDGs) were the world's agenda for the first part of this century. They outlined the priorities that people from around the world have identified as necessary for a more equitable, peaceful, and sustainable world. Yet they are largely unknown by many in wealthier nations; certainly, they have received little attention in the United States.

One of the most vocal champions of the MDGs has been economist Jeffrey Sachs (2006). Sachs is a free-market economist who spent much of his early career advising Russia, Eastern Europe, and Latin America to adopt market reforms in the spirit of neoliberalism. His description of Western nations emerging out of poverty accords well with modernization theory. But Sachs has also become a champion of philanthropy, environmental sustainability, and people-driven economic change. He insists that the end of poverty is within our reach, but only with concerted collective effort:

> When the conditions of basic infrastructure (roads, power, and ports) and human capital (health and education) are in place, markets are powerful engines of development. Without those preconditions, markets can cruelly bypass large parts of the world, leaving them impoverished and suffering without respite. (pp. 2–3).

The success of the MDGs was mixed. Extreme poverty was greatly reduced and access to primary education increased. Access to clean water and electricity continues to expand. But many goals were not met fully, particularly in sub-Saharan African and in rural South Asia. The global agenda for 2015–2030 are 17 Sustainable Development Goals (SDGs) (see figure 1.4). Excitement about a new millennium has given way to concerns about a sustainable future. Yet in many ways, the SDGs are an expansion and update of the MDGs agenda. Even Sachs admits that 17 is quite a lot—"Ten were good enough for Moses," he quips in his talks—but they are interconnected, like the doughnut economic model (discussed in chapter 12), recognizing that healthy, productive people and healthy, vibrant communities on a healthy, sustainable planet biosphere are entirely intertwined (Sachs 2015). At the end of each chapter, I will often refer to the relevant SDGs and the steps we can take to achieve those ends. Time is short and the stakes are enormous.

Figure 1.4 Sustainable Development Goals. (Source: Ritchie, Roser, Mispy, Oritz-Ospina. "Measuring Progress towards the Sustainable Development Goals." SDG-Tracker.org. website [2018]).

Key Ideas

- The world faces a double divide: Income inequalities are vast between nations and the gap between rich and poor is growing rapidly within most nations.
- The perspective that draws on the work of Adam Smith, variously known as neoliberalism, neoclassical economics, or free-market economics, stresses the importance of free trade among nations and of reducing government interference in domestic markets.
- Karl Marx developed an approach to understanding history that is based on conflict between social classes. Marx contended that capitalism takes this conflict to new intensity in the struggle between owners and workers and that workers' rights could only be fully secured if there was collective control of the means of production.
- Modernization theory contends that low-income countries need modern ideas, technology, and institutions. Dependency theory and its extension, world systems theory, contend that poor countries face exploitation, domination, and economic distortions resulting from their dependence on rich countries.
- Globalization is radically altering the world economic system. Global interconnections are affording new opportunities to some. Global markets can increase the revenues of large corporations while at the same time

forcing wages down due to increased labor competition, and can increase global inequalities.

▶ Researchers, policy analysts, and activists from many backgrounds are seeking new ways to harness the forces of globalization to achieve broad-based equitable economic development that addresses human needs.

For Review and Discussion

1. What are the major causes of the "double divide" between and among nations? What factors are emphasized by dependency and world systems theorists, by modernization theorists, and by neoclassical economists?
2. Should we be more concerned by the gap in wealth between nations or by the growing gap within many nations? Are the causes of these two types of inequalities the same?
3. Look closely at the UN Sustainable Development Goals: Do these make sense as the world's priorities; are there other things you would want to include? Do you believe these are attainable by 2030? What are the most urgent actions that need to be taken?

Making Connections

The United Nations

▶ Look at the homepage of the UN Development Programme (www.undp.org). This agency of the United Nations collects a wide range of data on global well-being and economic development and publishes the annual Human Development Report.

▶ The Human Development Goals Report shows global needs and the progress toward reaching the SDGs. What are the key indicators of well-being? Where is progress being made? Where are we losing ground?

World Bank

▶ The World Bank collects vast amounts of data on the state of international development, with an emphasis on key economic indicators. See data.worldbank.org for maps, projects, trends, and a link to the latest world development indicators tables.

▶ How does the World Bank data compare with that provided by the United Nations Development Programme? What are the bank's emphases in measuring successful development? Are these being achieved?

Making a Difference

ONE: The Campaign to Make Poverty History

➤ One of the new high-visibility groups that are trying to focus international attention on the problems of extreme poverty calls itself ONE. Go to one.org to see the current priorities of this campaign. ONE has involved many high-profile celebrities from Bono to Angelina Jolie in its campaigns to change national policies and priorities. ONE invites political candidates from all parties to post videos, answering questions on their approach to world poverty. If you find that this group represents your convictions, you can sign their declaration, receive their emails, join their Facebook page, and stay in touch with antipoverty activists around the country and across the world. You can join One Campus at https://www.one.org/us/take-action/campus/ to link up with students and campus groups across the country concerned with global extreme poverty.

UN Sustainable Development Goals

➤ Look at ways to monitor and act on the global agenda for 2030 at Take action on the UN Sustainable Development Goals at https://www.un.org/sustainabledevelopment/sustainable-development-goals/. Begin with Goal 1: End poverty in all its forms everywhere. What data do they highlight on global poverty? Look at the targets for 2030 and then explore the links for ways global organizations are trying to achieve this goal.

2

Work and Trade

The Global Assembly Line

Global Encounters

Mauritius (Isle Maurice), Indian Ocean

We are sailing a route that would have been very familiar to a British sea captain of the 1800s: Cape Town to Mauritius, then on to Madras (which the Indians now call Chennai).

And we arrive to find that in many ways the party has started without us. Mauritius became independent in 1968. It almost immediately went into global export manufacturing in a major way. The entire island became a massive export-processing zone. As sugar prices fell, workers again left the cane fields for work in the city, Port Louis, named for a French king. Incomes grew and the government put the new tax revenues into health and education, achieving "First World" levels of life expectancy and literacy. With a ready port and a peaceful populace who could speak a bit of both French and English and who had been working in textiles for over a century, Mauritius was far more attractive to textile manufacturing than anywhere on the African mainland. The economy grew at rates that mainland Africans dream of, with incomes surpassing South Africa and everywhere else on the continent and approaching Eastern European levels.

With China hot on its fashion heels in textiles and footwear, Mauritius has gone upscale. The major remaining textile plant is for Ralph Lauren. At the same time, Mauritius has moved into technology, offshore banking, and tourism. These prove quite complementary. Tourists like hidden tropical locations but prefer them to have good shopping, ready ATMs, and fast internet service. Americans still can't find the spot (one guest book of 400 names showed only three from the United States), but the island draws many Europeans. Flights are regular from South Africa, where the elites describe Mauritius as their Hawaii. It's harder to get a flight from India, but the connections with booming Mumbai (Bombay) are growing. Mauritius is eager to again be the star and the key to a new Indian Ocean trade.

Mauritius has a growing economy that many on the mainland of Africa would envy. Its resources and location have been exploited by the Portuguese, Dutch, French, and British, in that order, but there was no indigenous population. Is this a success story? What are the keys to its success: location, language, determination, or something else? Could the rest of Africa follow its example and become centers of thriving trade? Would that be a good thing for the continent? Mauritius has been a model of political stability, and the United Nations has cited it as model of social harmony, although there are definite distinctions between its East African, Indian, and European populations. Under what conditions does trade provide shared opportunity, and when does it lead to inequality and conflict?

The Division of Labor

In societies with simple economies, both past and present, it is common for many people to be involved in the same tasks. There may be a division between genders and maybe another between nobility and commoners, but economic life is based on only a few divisions. For instance, in hunting-and-gathering societies, all the able-bodied men hunt, all the able-bodied women gather, and at times, all may work together, as in flushing out game or netting fish. In simple horticultural societies, all the men work in clearing the ground and all the women in planting gardens. In larger-scale agricultural societies, this becomes more complex. Especially in the past, there were noble classes that specialized in warfare (European knights and Japanese samurai) and oversight but never worked the land themselves. There were skilled artisans who produced prized products, but their work was usually only for the nobility or elite and so they were few in number. Today, as in the past, the great majority of people in agrarian, agriculture-based societies work the land. Men and women may work together, as in gathering a harvest or in complementary tasks: plowing, weeding, tending flocks and gardens, and so forth.

Complex societies with more technological economies are based on a complex division of labor. Few of us could maintain anything like our current lifestyle if we personally had to build, maintain, fix, and operate all the material goods that fill our lives. We each specialize in a single pursuit for income, maybe supplemented by hobbies and occasional "moonlighting," and then look largely to markets to provide the diverse goods of our society. This has been true in the industrial world for several centuries, but the degree of specialization and the extent of the markets continue to increase.

Adam Smith: Efficiency

Adam Smith (1937 [1776]) believed that the great efficiency of modern capitalist economies (even as they existed in his day) lay in their complex **division of labor.** Workers could specialize and so be more efficient. In his famous example of a pin factory, Smith noted that even the production of a single industrial pin (which might hold two parts of a machine together) would take one person a very long time to complete if he or she had to do all the work, from ore to final product. But if each worker only works with a single part of the process, workers become quite expert and very efficient in their own part. By combining their labor, workers produce the pins in great numbers at low cost.

The same idea holds for all industrial production. No one at General Motors could produce an entire automobile if he or she had to work alone. Even if the task were given to the most senior engineers, they would take a long time and probably do poor work (as they might not be proficient welders or painters or the like).

Smith saw this ever-increasing division of labor as the key to prosperity. If this efficient production were coupled with efficient markets, so that everyone could have access to the final product, the greatest prosperity would result. But even Smith saw dangers in this. He worried about the collusion of capitalists. Because only the owners would be familiar with the process as a whole, their ability to manipulate production and prices would increase. Further, because workers would be so specialized that they could not move readily between positions and certainly could not be self-sufficient, he worried that capitalists might also manipulate the labor market—the price paid for labor in wages and benefits. It is sometimes forgotten that Smith, the great proponent of free labor and free trade, believed that some government oversight would be necessary to prevent the collusion of powerful interests.

Émile Durkheim: Solidarity

While Smith focused on the economy, a century later, French sociologist Émile Durkheim (1964 [1895]) focused on the effects of a division of labor on overall society. He believed that simpler agricultural societies had strong common bonds, what he called *solidarity*, because so many were engaged in the same tasks. They worked together sometimes, or at least they understood each other and their common concerns. Drought or another affliction for one was common to all.

This solidarity was natural, even mechanical, as people came together without thinking about it. Durkheim referred to it as **mechanical solidarity.** He wondered what would happen to solidarity in modern late nineteenth-century societies. He concluded that they, too, could have solidarity, but it would be of a different type. He called this new bond **organic solidarity,** because he believed it was based on a complex division of labor in which each person contributed his or her specialty to the whole, just as the specialized organs of a body contribute to its overall well-being. People would be bound together because they needed each other.

Max Weber: Work Ethic

Social and political scholar Max Weber also saw a new ethic or sentiment in the new economies; in fact, he believed that a new way of thinking was crucial to building modern capitalist economies. In his classic book, *The Protestant Ethic and the Spirit of Capitalism*, Weber (1997 [1905]) argued that in northern Europe, Protestantism brought a new way of thinking about economic life. Whereas medieval Catholicism was often suspicious of material gain (calling it *avarice* or *greed*) and the desire to advance (calling it *hubris* or *spiritual pride*), Europe's Protestants, beginning in the early 1500s, began to think differently. According to Martin Luther, one's secular vocation was a gift from God and was to be pursued with as much vigor as one's religious duties. According to some Calvinists, wealth was not the root of all evil but could be a sign of God's favor: Had not God blessed Abraham and Solomon with great abundance?

But (and this was crucial) *wealth* did not mean *extravagance*. The Dutch burghers and the English Puritans dressed in black wool, not the extravagant colors of silk, satin, and lace favored by the wealthy of the High Middle Ages. To win favor with God and country, they were hardworking and shrewd but also diligent and frugal. So what did they do with all that money? If they were true Protestant capitalists, Weber believed, they would reinvest all that money to enlarge the enterprise and make still more money. Weber saw this ethic of frugality and diligence coming to the American colonies, with thinkers like Benjamin Franklin and his famous *Poor Richard's Almanac* (which made Franklin rich, even as he preached frugality).

There are continuing debates about Weber's thesis: Did Protestantism lead directly to capitalism? Or did an emerging middle class, who were not from nobility but certainly didn't want to be part of the peasantry, break with medieval norms to embrace both Protestantism and capitalism? Still, this seemed a powerful combination, and it drove the new American captains of industry during the nineteenth century. John D. Rockefeller, for example, was a staunch and stern Protestant, frugal except in charitable giving, but also a shrewd (some would say ruthless) businessman, who became perhaps the richest man ever. (In today's dollars, he was richer than Bill Gates.)

Weber was most concerned about the behavior of the new capitalist *owners*, but his idea, popularized as the **Protestant work ethic,** has often been applied to their *workers*. The maxim for workers is similar, even if the results are often more modest: Work hard, live frugally, invest carefully, and you will advance. In the 1700s, John Wesley, founding thinker of the Methodist and Wesleyan denominations, preached in the slums and flophouses of London a message that seemed to powerfully echo this ethic: Get saved, get sober, and get to work. Some of Wesley's converts indeed learned an organized, methodical (from which we get *Methodist*) way to both worship and work. Some even prospered. Interestingly, Wesley lamented that some lost their religious fervor after they became prosperous.

The ideal of hard work and frugal investment had already been long practiced by Europe's urban Jews, who all through the Middle Ages were a people caught between the medieval estates (or classes of nobility), the clergy, and the peasantry. In time, the hard-work ideal was embraced by Roman Catholics and others, as well. In the United States, it became the ideal for people from all religious backgrounds, preached by populists such as President Theodore Roosevelt, a common man despite his family's great wealth. Some have contended (Bellah 1957) that the Shintoism of Japan and the Confucianism of East Asia espoused a similar ethic that continues to encourage hard work in those regions. Modernization theorists (Wiener 1966) have contended that this ethic of getting ahead through ambition, hard work, and frugality was essential to building a modern capitalist economy.

Karl Marx: Alienation

Karl Marx (see McLellan 1977, 1988) saw many of these same changes in the world of work but mused about the darker side of such changes. He agreed with Smith that the capitalist system of production, coupled with an ever more specialized division of labor, led to greater productivity. But he worried that part of this specialization was the deskilling of workers. Instead of a gunsmith knowing how to make an entire firearm, he now punched out a single firing pin to be assembled into a whole that he could not make himself and that he might never even see. Such an individual amplified Smith's concern that deskilled workers were vulnerable workers, who could be replaced just like the cogs in a great impersonal machine.

Marx also believed that the movement from an agrarian to an industrial society could lead to greater solidarity among workers. Unlike peasant farmers, who might work as family units separated, at least some of the time, from their fellow workers, industrial workers, the proletariat, stood shoulder to shoulder on the assembly line and could forge a common bond of solidarity. But Marx also believed that the work ethic could be manipulated by the capitalist owners to keep workers divided and complacent. Competition between and within plants could keep workers divided, while religious threats and promises could be used to keep them from challenging the system.

Above all, Marx believed that modern industrial workers in capitalist economies experienced profound **alienation.** Work, he believed, was meant to be ennobling and purposeful, a source of pride and accomplishment. But modern industrial workers labored at routine, deskilled, repetitive tasks on minute parts of products that meant nothing to them and that they themselves might never be able to afford. And the truth was that most would never advance, no matter how hard they worked. Work was not just harsh; it was meaningless.

The New International Division of Labor

Around the world, the division of labor continues to become more complex, and new specialists continually emerge. Not just industrial workers but service and professional workers continue to specialize in increasingly narrower fields. Even highly educated people often know a great deal about a very narrow field of specialty. More and more physicians, for example, specialize in narrow subfields of medicine, and more attorneys practice only one type of law.

This is one way to cope with an ever more complex world. Having specialists may well be more efficient, at least in some ways, than having many people trying to be generalists. Some find this degree of specialization quite alienating, however, both as workers and as consumers who are being juggled between specialists.

The division of labor not only has grown within countries, but it has also grown between countries, with different parts of the world specializing in different tasks. The old international division of labor was a divide between producing raw materials and producing finished goods. In European colonial systems, the home country's cities produced finished goods—textiles, machinery, and so forth—from the materials produced by the farms, forests, and mines of its colonies. Workers in the colonies were often farmers, miners, and the like, and they provided these raw materials. Finished goods, increasingly industrial products, in the colonies would come from the cities of the home country. In the late 1700s, King George III believed that prosperity for all would come from the great cities of England, such as London, Manchester, and Liverpool, as they produced the finished goods from the cotton, timber, tobacco, sugar, and other products produced by the British colonies.

In 1776, Adam Smith (1937 [1776]) wrote that this was bad economics: Economies ran best on free and mutual trade, not on royal decrees. The same year, of course, Thomas Jefferson, writing for the American colonies, noted that this was also bad government and should be dissolved. The colonies were declaring independence. It is not a great surprise that the staunchest proponents of American independence often came from New England, which was poised to produce its own finished goods.

The new United States opted out of the old international division of labor as a producer of raw materials, only to rejoin it as a producer of finished goods. Throughout much of the 1900s, raw materials flowed into U.S. cities from Latin America (in particular), as well as Africa, Asia, and the Pacific, while U.S. industry sought to export finished goods around the world. This process continued through World War II, both between Europe and its colonies and between the United States and its less-developed trading partners. This began to change after World War II, however—gradually at first and then rapidly in the 1970s and 1980s. Industry was no longer tied to major industrial centers in advanced industrial countries. Even poor countries could provide electricity for production.

New harbors and new container ships could move products easily around the world. New communication systems could keep far-flung factories in touch with distant management centers. Industry could move, and it did. It moved to where manufacturing labor was the cheapest: Latin America, Asia, certain countries in the Pacific, and, in a few cases, Africa. The old industrial centers of North America, Europe, and eventually Japan experienced **deindustrialization,** as their factories moved overseas to **export-processing zones** in developing counties.

The advanced industrial countries became **postindustrial.** As large numbers of workers in poor countries moved from the farm to the factory, many in the richer countries moved from the factory to the office. Professional workers in rich countries today manage, finance, design, plan, advise, regulate, and program production that's carried on elsewhere. Job growth lies in computers, law, banking, accounting, and related fields. Other professional workers serve the financial, health, legal, commercial, and personal needs of postindustrial economies. Job growth also lies in more menial service tasks: cleaning and maintaining offices, making beds in hospitals and hotels, serving fast food to busy workers, and the like.

The new international division of labor is very productive, and so the total productive capacity of the world's economy continues to grow markedly. In many ways, it is very efficient; more is produced at lower costs. It has also produced a new solidarity among groups of workers, including women workers, around the world. And it has produced a new ethic of ambition and achievement.

But many, including many who would never consider themselves Marxists, wonder if Marx may have been right about the alienation inherent in industrial corporate capitalism. Many of these "new economy" workers are profoundly alienated, working ever longer hours at menial and sometimes seemingly meaningless tasks. Old connections of family and village are disrupted in the industrializing world, while old ties between employee and employer are disrupted in the postindustrial world. Ties to the land and to local communities are undermined, and workers feel like they are cogs in a huge and often very impersonal machine.

And *efficiency* refers only to means, not ultimate ends. Cigarette factories can turn out cigarettes far more quickly and efficiently than people "rolling their own." Weapons factories can turn out ammunition far more quickly and efficiently than pioneers pouring their own bullets. Yet, whether production either enriches or impoverishes the world is not always clear. Nonetheless, the size and power of multinational corporations is staggering. Of the world's 100 largest economic entities in 2017, 69 were corporations and 31 were countries (Global Justice Now 2018).

The first wave in the new international division was **offshoring:** the movement of industry and, therefore, manufacturing jobs to export-processing zones overseas and to special economic zones in China, which began in the 1970s and gained ground during the 1980s and 1990s. China has become the world's manufacturer, accounting for 28.4 percent of global production in 2018, compared to the United States' 16.8 percent (World Economic Forum 2020). Offshoring requires cheap transportation in container ships to move goods around the world, and cheap communications to monitor that movement.

While the first wave of offshoring took the jobs of industrial workers in the former industrial powers, offshoring can threaten the jobs of middle-class service workers. Offshoring had U.S. engineers designing products to be built in China. Now the engineering can be sent to India as well. Only the marketing and sales of the product remain in the United States, along with some of the central management. These positions may be challenged next. China is facing new labor demands and rising labor costs and so is eager to move beyond low-wage factories into new areas. Instead of just doing cheap piecework for JC Penney, a Chinese supplier is shifting to doing offshore managing of inventory and sales (Barboza 2010).

The rapid expansion of global technology, however, spurred the growth of international **outsourcing,** moving specific tasks to other locations in the world. The first country to dominate in this area was Ireland, which used its abundance of English-speaking, lower-wage workers and an abundance of underused transatlantic cable to encourage many North American countries to outsource data storage, insurance, and a wide range of record keeping tasks. Wages are now too high in Ireland for many, and India has become the great center of outsourcing. India offers a huge, highly educated, English-speaking population with labor rates that are still very low.

New areas for outsourcing are created daily. I regularly receive invitations to replace student workers, whether graduate or undergraduate, with talented students in India who can assist with research (much is now available anywhere on the internet), create databases, analyze data, search for sources, and generate bibliographies and anything else I might need for research and writing. U.S. students worry that by the time they graduate their intended job will be outsourced. Truth is that they may not have to wait; it could be outsourced while they are still students. Thomas Friedman (2006) has described this new playing field in *The World Is Flat*. He argues that technology is leveling the global playing field, making highly educated people competitive regardless of where they live. He wonders if U.S. workers will keep up with the highly technically educated Asians competing for their jobs.

The Boundless Frontier: From East India to Amazon

The push for cheaper products and higher profits has long driven industry to try to combine First World technology with Third World labor. The frontiers of industry have been on the move for over 400 years, incorporating slaves, immigrants, migrants, and displaced farmers among others in the search for low-cost labor. When textile mills grew in England in the 1700s, small farmers were driven off their land to make room for more wool-bearing sheep. The farmers, men and women, were then unattached labor who could be employed at low wages in the mill production, either as suppliers of spun wool or as mill workers. The resulting products were shipped literally around the world, marketed by giant government-sponsored but ultimately private corporations, such as the Hudson's Bay Company and the British East India Company. This pattern continues. Customers who phone in clothing orders to the retailer Lands' End are likely to be helped by the wives, daughters, partners, and occasionally sons of farmers, would-be farmers, and once-were farmers in southern Wisconsin. The clothing itself is made in cities and export zones by the wives and daughters of once rural-farming families in Asia and Latin America.

Great multinational ventures have reshaped our world. The Dutch East India Company ("VOC" in Dutch) may have been the first publicly traded holding company, a conglomerate of rivals founded in 1602 with big ships and big financiers. They helped win independence from Spain and fought the Portuguese for ports. Ultimately, they established Dutch trading ports from India to Japan, gaining control of the great Indian Ocean trade. The most profitable proved to be ports in the East Indies. Soon they were the Dutch East Indies, a colony that reluctantly ceded independence to Indonesia in 1949. They were ultimately exceeded in sheer reach by the British East India Company, founded in 1600. The London-based company had even more ships—you may remember the fanciful armada in the *Pirates of the Caribbean* film series. In the 1700s they fought the French and any other rivals to wrest control of India well before it would be an official realm of the British Empire. They dominated trade in China in the 1800s, trading tea and textiles—and increasingly opium, leading to two wars.

The push to connect oceans of commerce reshaped the planet as French engineers struggled to carve a canal across the Suez in the 1860s, and for U.S. engineers to carve a much more challenging canal across Panama in the early 1900s. Ships also grew from fast clippers to large hulled steamers to the great container ships that now ply the oceans. Capable of being fully loaded and unloaded by crane, the great old dockyards of London, Amsterdam, Dublin, and New York are now tourist districts while great new ports in Shanghai, Singapore (a British colonial enclave on the edge of Dutch realms), Yokohama, Long Beach, and Tacoma define transocean trade. These great ships now challenge the limits of the old canals. When a container ship of 20,000 containers (each a truck trailer worth of products)—one of the world's largest super-ships—became jammed in the Suez Canal in 2021, a fifth of global shipping came to a halt while heavy equipment went to work to set it right.

Occasional Help Wanted

Industrial demands have kept the United States and Mexico bound in a turbulent marriage of convenience for decades. During World War II, when labor was scarce in the United States, the U.S. government began the **Bracero Program.** From the Spanish word for "arm," a *bracero* is a strong manual laborer. The program was so successful that it was extended until 1964. The

Global commerce is driven by rising middle-class consumer demand, global internet connections, and the massive capacity of huge container ships whose container boxes can be quickly loaded and unloaded by cranes to continue their journey by train or truck.

goal of the program, however, was not to open the United States to Mexican immigration but to maintain a revolving door of labor migrants. Almost a century earlier, the United States had sought a similar arrangement with China to provide temporary Chinese laborers.

When the U.S. economy struck a recession in the mid-1950s and concerns were raised that too many braceros were staying on, the government began Operation Wetback. It is not clear if these workers had "wet backs" from swimming across the Rio Grande River, or from hoeing vegetable crops in the hot sun, but this derogatory term for illegal laborers become the title of a massive program that existed between 1954 and 1958. Mexicans working illegally, and many legal workers as well, were rounded up and returned to Mexico. In a few instances, Mexican Americans whose families had been in the U.S. Southwest since the land belonged to Mexico were rounded up and "returned" across the border.

The complexities of recruiting labor migrants in one direction while returning unwelcome workers in the other eventually led to the program's abandonment. In 1964, it was replaced by the Border Industrialization Program (BIP). This program allowed materials to be shipped across the Mexican border to neighboring cities, assembled by low-wage labor there, and then returned to the United States without export duties or tariffs. And so, the *maquiladora* was born, a plant whose only purpose was as an assembly turnaround point for industrial goods, particularly textiles and electronics. Throughout the remainder of the 1960s, *la huelga*, "the strike," raged on in California's farm fields, as Mexican migrant laborers struck for higher wages. The industrial demand, however, was more simply met by keeping the workers in Mexico and moving the products to the United States. Eventually, much fruit and vegetable production also moved south of the border in imitation of the fleeing industries.

In 1993 the North American Free Trade Agreement (NAFTA) was ratified, extending the special trade privileges of the Mexican border cities to all parts of North America. Discussion was renewed in 2001 and again in 2003 over new types of temporary labor arrangements between the United States and Mexico. Most of the laborers in question, however, would be neither industrial nor agricultural but rather low-wage service workers. Cooks, clerks, cleaners, and nannies—these are the jobs that cannot be simply relocated. For production, it is still easier to keep the workers within their own country (though often nowhere near their hometown and family) and to move the products.

The 2020 United States, Mexico and Canada Agreement (USMCA, or CUSMA in Canada) was touted as a major fix to the problems of NAFTA, but only added a few new restrictions and updates, essentially becoming NAFTA 2.0. It continues to allow for additional temporary workers, or guest workers, between the three signatories. Guest workers in the United States arrive on an H-2A temporary visa for seasonal agricultural workers and on an H-2B visa for temporary nonagricultural workers. An H-1B program allows temporary employment in specialty occupations such as engineering and nursing. Guest workers typically send a large portion of their earnings home as remittances. These are a vital source of income for families living in poor home-country communities with high unemployment. Advocacy groups such as the Southern

Poverty Law Center (see https://www.splcenter.org/issues/immigrant-justice/guest-workers) and Farmworker Justice (https://www.farmworkerjustice.org/advocacy_program/guestworker-programs/), however, note that the guest workers themselves are extremely vulnerable to adverse working conditions and labor exploitation.

Other countries with strong economies whose labor demands exceed the local labor force often turn to guest workers. The workers may work directly in agriculture or industry, or serve in service and caregiver roles such as childcare to free up the local labor force. Taiwan and Singapore have sought workers from Indonesia and the Philippines. The Persian Gulf states use workers from Pakistan, India and Bangladesh. European countries have drawn temporary workers from Turkey, from struggling Eastern European countries such as Moldova, and from South Asia. Host countries gain a flexible workforce without having to commit to the politically sensitive policy of largescale permanent immigration. Temporary guest workers gain needed employment but confront isolation and many months away from home and family, long hours with few rights and benefits and little recourse to legal action, and an uncertain future.

Working the Line: Life on la Frontera

A thousand-mile chain of twin cities has been created along the U.S.–Mexican border, or la frontera, as the Mexicans know it. The cities face each other across this long, chain-link line, the "Great Wall of the Americas," in a relationship that is at times symbiotic and at times parasitic: San Diego–Tijuana, Calexico–Mexicali, Nogales–Nogales, Douglas–Agua Prieta, El Paso–Ciudad Juárez, Del Rio–Ciudad Acuña, Eagle Pass–Piedras Negras, Laredo–Nuevo Laredo, McAllen–Reynosa, and Brownsville–Matamoros. As the fastest-growing part of Mexico, this border area is at once the most prosperous and the least appealing.

The twin cities facilitate the movement of products in and out of what in the United States are known as "twin plants" and in Mexico as maquiladoras. Juana Ortega works at an RCA plant on the U.S.–Mexican border, one of the first of a series of electronics maquiladoras that now dominate the economic life of the city of Juárez. She gets up at 5:00 in the morning to make breakfast for her three children as well as her sister and her uncle. Then she crowds into a van for the ride to work. The plant, like many here, is new and expansive, with an American-style corporate campus. Yet Juana feels her life here is as cramped and stifling as the hot, crowded ride in the van. Says Juana:

> This job is a terror. The noise. The monotony. The constant danger of the machine.... In the factory the line is the worst, it crushes your fingers and in the end your mind as well.
>
> They stuff us into vans. They stuff us into factories. They stuff it to you at work. It's stuff! Stuff! Stuff! ... You work till your bones hurt. You work till your eyes

hurt. The engineers make you work till you think you will drop, . . . always watching and hovering, stopwatch and clipboard in hand. (Peña 1997, 6)

Juana goes on to describe acts of collective sabotage against the line, breaking parts and the belts themselves that workers use to slow its relentless speed-up. Workers play stupid and play sick and sometimes revolt in wildcat strikes against what they see as the inhumanity of their workplace. Juana sums up her view of the situation:

What I regret the most is not the pain of working at something so degrading, so meaningless. It is instead the pain of knowing that we, the laborers, are capable of so much more. (p. 6)

Given the sheer size and power of many of the corporate entities that work the border, they quickly obtain the power to determine the labor market and the futures of entire communities. Alcoa, the aluminum giant whose conglomeration of subsidiaries produces hundreds of products, moved its automotive wiring plant to Ciudad Acuña. In 1996 Alcoa CEO Paul O'Neill, who later became U.S. treasury secretary, boasted at a shareholders meeting of the clean, modern plant and the company's growing profits. He was challenged by a janitor from the plant, who told a different story: wages of six dollars a day, covered-up accidents such as a gas leak that sent 100 workers to the hospital, and workers so regimented they were each issued an allotment of three pieces of toilet paper. Moved by the charges, O'Neill worked to improve conditions at the eight plants the huge firm (now AFL) owns in the city. Alcoa's wages have risen to the highest in the city but are still too low to bring about change in the ramshackle community. The frontera cities continue to try to define themselves in a changing world. Some are losing production to even lower wages in Asia. The question then is how to find legitimate employment for all the newcomers in these deeply divided cities. Tijuana is trying to redefine itself as no longer a place to find illegal drugs and prostitution, but as a hip new spot for entertainment and nightlife. Meanwhile Juárez continues to face ever more brutal drug–gang violence with the highest murder rate of any city in the world.

Pushed to the Wall: Walmart and the "Big Boxes"

The Victorians of the late nineteenth century loved fashion and home accessories, and they could find these items in boutique stores in growing urban centers. There, delicate stitching and elaborate feather and floral arrangements were done by very young women: new immigrants in the United States, Welsh and Irish girls in England, and French Canadian girls in Canada.

The department store made its appearance in France in the 1800s and soon dominated marketing. By the 1950s, urban department stores in the United States were moving to suburban shopping centers, first in California. Soon building planners in cold climates began covering the shopping centers, and the *mall* was born. Around the world, wherever people depend on cars rather than public transit and walking, U.S.-style malls have been built. Yet in some cities, the malls are being torn down because they have become obsolete. Some wealthy and trendy shoppers are returning to downtown and uptown department stores, but the biggest push has been to "big box," or massive, retail stores.

The biggest "big box" of them all is Walmart. This chain grew rapidly in rural communities by drawing people from aging town centers. Walmart hires mostly part-timers, sometimes keeping people just below the number of hours needed to qualify for benefits. Many of the store's workers are former homemakers as well as retirees who need added income. Young people and others displaced from the labor force comprise the reminder. Union activity has always been bitterly opposed.

Walmart has moved from small towns to big cities and now around the world. It is the world's single largest marketer of consumer goods. It is the world's largest enterprise by revenue, employing 2.3 million people globally. Its profits have been enormous. If Sam Walton, the founder, were still alive, he would be one of the three wealthiest people in the world. As it is, Walton family members, Sam's heirs, comprise five of the richest multibillionaires in the world.

The economic power of Walmart is also huge. Building so many stores, it is the world's largest contractor for the construction and building trades. Its market power spans the globe. Walmart was not built on fashion or quality. Its foundation is price. Its market position allows it to continue to focus single-mindedly on price. This has benefits for the consumer, but it also comes at a price to the world of work. The company that in the late 1980s championed its "Buy American" philosophy now accounts for 10 percent of massive U.S. imports from China. To do business with Walmart, companies must leave home; to ignore Walmart is often to go out of business.

For years, the progressive corporate leadership of jean maker Levi Strauss in San Francisco resisted taking its production overseas, where wages were (and still are) considerably lower. As Gap jeans and others weathered negative publicity about their overseas suppliers' sweatshops, Levi's held to its all-American image. But Levi's were sold in malls, where sales were declining. Their one hope was to sell their jeans at Walmart. But that would mean cutting costs, and the way to do that would be to move operations overseas. In the early 1980s, Levi's had 60 clothing plants in the United States. By 2004, it had none. Like Nike, Levi Strauss no longer makes clothes; it merely imports and labels them.

Walmart tries to have everything—except maybe walls. The biggest competitor is ever-growing Amazon. Amazon still has fewer employees and profits but is valued at several times that of Walmart and is constantly extending its global reach. Amazon's rivals are the old big boxes, which are going online, just as bookseller Barnes and Noble did to compete in cyberspace. The most successful Amazon competitor is Alibaba, owned by Chinese entrepreneur Jack Ma. Ma, critical of the Chinese government and now out of its favor, just saw his company fined $2.8 billion by Chinese regulators for monopolistic practices. Meanwhile, governments in Europe—even the Dutch—try to find ways to control these great global monopolies.

Made by Small Hands

One of the most remarkable marches in U.S. labor history wound its way from Kensington, near Philadelphia, toward Long Island, just north of New York City, at the beginning of the twentieth century. Hundreds of children—many of them missing fingers and others hunched over from various disabilities and accidents as a result of their work in the Kensington textile mills—marched under the leadership of Mother Jones, a grandmother and organizer from West Virginia. The children focused on a single demand: They wanted their 60-hour work week shortened to 55 so they could attend five hours of school a week.

In trying to negotiate this with the mill owners, they had been rebuffed, and now they marched with banners that read, "We Want to Go to School" and "More Schools, Less Hospitals." The children planned to march to Long Island, where President Theodore Roosevelt was vacationing with his own children, who were enjoying pony rides by the beach. Although Roosevelt

Work and Trade CHAPTER 2 69

Industrialization has often been fueled by children working at jobs requiring difficult and hard labor, as seen here in a Georgia cotton mill in the early 1900s USA [facing page], a brickyard in contemporary Nepal [top], and dockyards in Bangladesh [bottom].

came from a wealthy family, he was often quite sympathetic to progressive labor causes. But he was also reluctant to condone federal government involvement in what he believed were state and local issues. He had signed labor laws as governor of New York, and so he believed the governor of Pennsylvania should champion the children's cause.

The children went back to their 60-hour week, climbing into and restocking machinery and, like children in Pakistan and India a century later, making carpets. Six years later, the Pennsylvania legislature passed child labor laws, including limits on the work week. And many others who took notice of the children's march—including Theodore Roosevelt's cousin and later First Lady Eleanor Roosevelt—became champions of child labor reform both in the United States and around the world.

Mills and Mines

Child labor and the struggle to eliminate it have a long history. In many agrarian societies, children are valued farmhands and go to work by middle childhood. In medieval Europe, by age eight to 10, peasant children were typically either working the fields or had been contracted out as apprentices, essentially unpaid labor, to various smiths and craftsmen.

As societies became industrialized, child labor became institutionalized. Throughout the 1800s, in Great Britain and New England, children were favored to supply looms and machines with thread and materials because they could crawl through cramped spaces, often at great personal risk. By the late 1800s, immigrant children and young women were the favored workforce for textiles and a host of other industries. A jingle of the time chided the leisure class, "The factory is next to the [golf] links so the children at work can watch the men at play."

In Scotland and Pennsylvania, having children work as coal miners meant that supply shafts could be smaller. At a time when earth removal was difficult and expensive, children could be lowered into the most difficult pits in buckets to bring up the ore. When Japan began catch-up industrialization at the end of the nineteenth century, it also found children to be a ready and pliable labor force, and many worked to their deaths in the coal mines of "Battleship Island."

Children were also useful in the service economy. Ironically, the Victorian ideal of hearth and home often meant that less privileged children had to leave both for the workforce:

> For every nineteenth-century middle-class family that protected its wife and child within the family circle, then, there was an Irish or a German girl scrubbing floors in that middle-class home, a Welsh boy mining coal to keep the home-baked goodies warm, a black girl doing the family laundry, a black mother and child picking cotton to be made into clothes for the family, and a Jewish or an Italian daughter in a sweatshop making "ladies" dresses or artificial flowers for the family to purchase. (Coontz 2016, 6)

Hooked by the World Economy

Reformers in advanced industrial societies began to denounce the practice of child labor. The ideals of universal education and school as the appropriate place for all children were promoted. Yet the old practices have persisted, and more children are now at work around the world than ever before (see figure 2.1)

According to the International Labour Organization (ILO), there are 152 million children working worldwide, including almost one child in five in Africa. A large majority of these children (71 percent) work in agriculture. Another 12 percent work in manufacturing and 17 percent in services. By far the worst forms of child labor range from forced and bonded labor to prostitution and pornography. Seventy-three million working children are in what the ILO considers "hazardous jobs" (ILO 2017).

The demands of changing economics and the perils of family poverty place many children at risk of cruel exploitation. Ten million children are in chronic labor bondage in India alone. More than one million children work squatting before dusty looms in Pakistani carpet factories. Pakistani children sew soccer balls for Nike, Adidas, and other foreign contractors for as little as six cents an hour. Working a 10-hour day to stitch one ball, each worker receives sixty cents for an item that wealthier parents will buy for thirty to fifty dollars. The balls enter the United States tariff free and proudly labeled "handmade." No mention is made of whose hands.

These situations are not limited to South Asia. Children also work in Honduran factories that make trendy garments, in Brazilian orange groves that supply American breakfast tables, in toy factories in China and Thailand, and on assembly lines in Indonesia. Yet it is in South Asia where the extremes of poverty combine with a history of child labor to produce some of the greatest abuses.

In Lahore, Pakistan, child labor is driven by both domestic and external pressures. Brick making is an ancient enterprise that employs hundreds of children. This is not making mud pies. Children mold and form a thousand bricks a day, set out to bake in the hot sun. A family of five working together can earn about one dollar per day. A major export of the region is handwoven rugs. The carpet makers start as early as age three. The biggest selling point abroad is the number of stitches per centimeter (hundreds), as this denotes a hand-stitched rug. The only hands small enough to work these tiny stitches belong to the very young. A small carpet that takes weeks to make may net a vendor thirty dollars, of which fifteen may go to the workers (Garrels 2002).

Reformers are trying to change these systems. New informal schools allow children to work a few hours less per day so as to attend a few hours of school. Some schools are no more than covered porches, but for many of the young children, this is their first chance to hold a crayon instead of a needle. Unlike the madrassa schools, which only teach memorization of the Qur'an, these

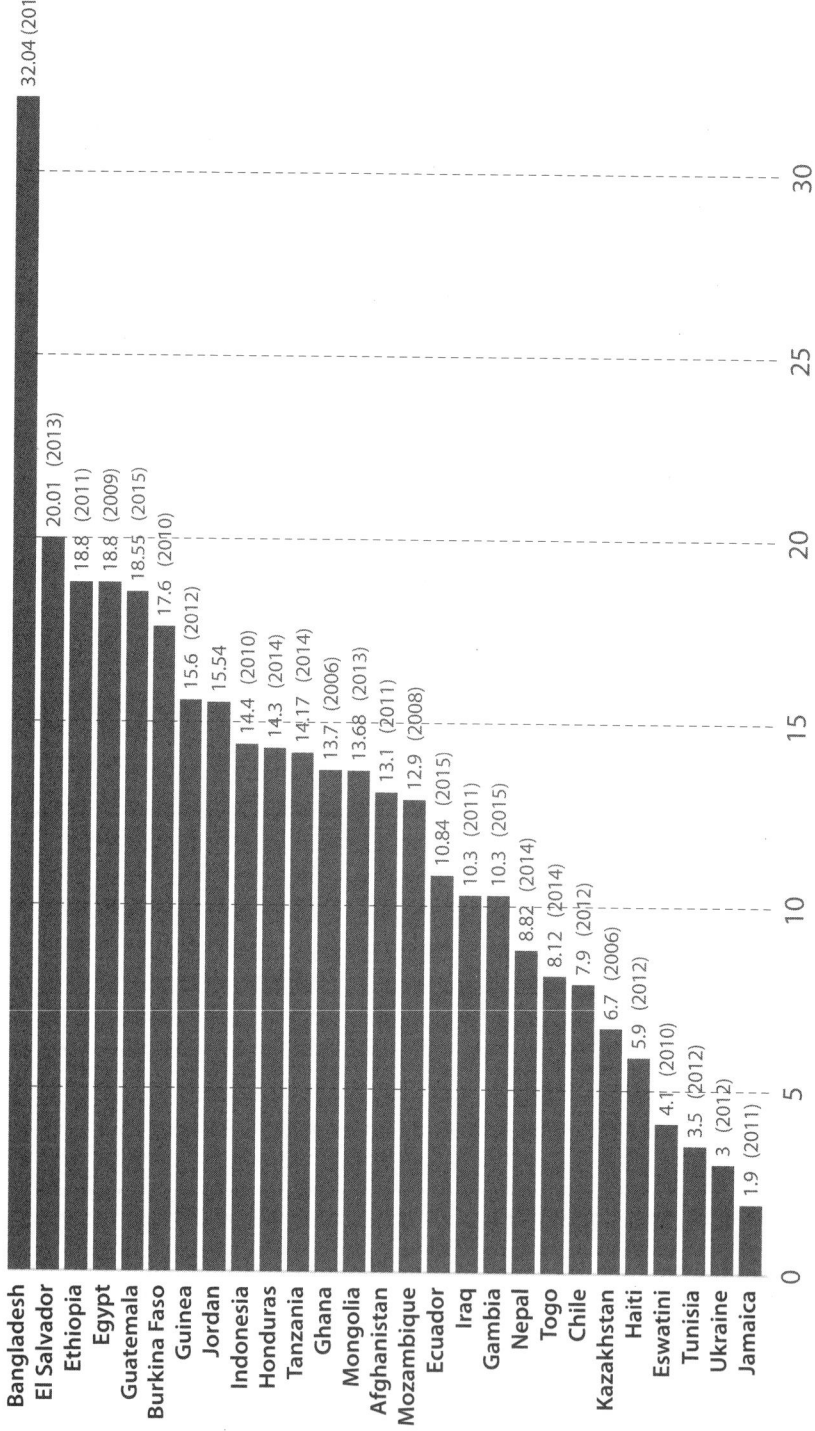

Figure 2.1 Child labor. (Source: Our World in Data.) For more detailed information, see https://ourworldindata.org/child-labor.

schools teach basic literacy and math, as well as practical skills, and, for a few, represent a chance to go on to regular education.

A Trade Free-for-All

David Ricardo: Comparative Advantage

The much-touted benefits of world trade are based on an idea that goes back to David Ricardo. Ricardo extended the idea of the division of labor to nations and regions (1996 [1817]). Just as Smith believed that national prosperity would come from each person working in his or her area of expertise and then exchanging goods in a free market, so Ricardo believed that national specialization, coupled with vigorous trade, was the recipe for world prosperity. Each area of the world should do what it does best, where it has a **comparative advantage** over others. For example, it makes no sense for Scottish farmers to grow bananas and coffee in a greenhouse when they can raise sheep for wool. With the money they get from the worldwide wool market, the Scots can purchase their morning coffee and bananas from Central America, or somewhere else where their production is cheaper.

If each place in the world does this and the wheels of trade keep turning, then the world will have the most efficient, most productive system possible. Free markets will foster this, since the place with the greatest comparative advantage in a product will be able to market the best quality at the lowest price. This seemed highly logical and formed the basis for many national economies. Of course, small countries often became highly dependent on one or two products in which they seemed to have a clear advantage, and this made them vulnerable to sudden shifts in the market (just like overspecialized workers).

This new international division of labor, however—with its emphasis not on finding cheap materials but on finding cheap labor for assembly—puts several new twists in the doctrine. What if the comparative advantage of a nation is in providing a cheap, docile labor force that won't demand higher wages or better conditions? What if the advantage lies in lax environmental laws, insufficient labor protections, and many desperate people looking for work? This is the darker side to comparative advantage.

Chain of Production around the World

Toys. The search for this elusive comparative advantage keeps many producers traveling the world, always trying to stay ahead of the competition (and often the regulators and union organizers). The manufacturers of toys, which are cheap and easy to ship but labor intensive to make, have often made the global trip.

Electronics. A microchip is a classic example of a high-value item that, by its very nature, is small, light, and easy to transport. In the 1980s many were assembled by young Asian American women, including immigrants and Southeast Asian refugees, staring into microscopes in the area near San Jose, California, that was dubbed "Silicon Valley." By the 1990s it was cheaper to have the work done on the other side of the Pacific, in places such as the Philippines and Malaysia. The plant arrangement, even the workforce, looked almost the same. Currently, global microchip maker Intel seems also to favor China as a location, with plants near Beijing, the global industry boomtown of Shenzhen near Hong Kong, and the free-trade zone near Shanghai.

Larger electronic consumer items rarely have a single manufacturing location. Whether the brand name is American (RCA) or Japanese (Sony) or European (Thompson), the parts come from all over the world. For television sets, "Made in the USA" became "Made in Mexico" by the 1980s, but this has since become the more mysterious "Assembled in Mexico from parts of various manufacture." The final assembly occurs in plants just over the Rio Grande River from the United States, but parts stream in from all over the world.

Textiles. Textile manufacturing has long depended on a steady supply of cheap labor, most often from young women. In the late 1700s farm girls came to the mills of Massachusetts. In the 1800s new mills emerged in Tennessee and Alabama and also drew young farm girls. By the 1900s the growing garment trade required waves of Southern and Eastern European immigrant workers to supply the sweatshops of New York. As the century spun on, new labor came from Asia and Latin America. Over time, it became easier to move the factories than the workers. Ironically, workers now sometimes lose their jobs to the very lands from which they came.

Textiles have joined the growing list of products that are assembled around the globe. In *Coat of Many Countries*, Josh Freed (2004) follows the manufacture of a sport coat across the planet. The Canadian manufacturer gets the wool from Merino sheep in Australia and ships it to India to be spun on the great high-speed, high-tech machines that have replaced the simple spinning wheel shown on the Indian flag. Ironically, that wheel was Mahatma Gandhi's famous symbol of self-sufficiency and independence. But now, the coat components keep moving: The shoulder pads arrive from China, the lining from Korea. They meet the cloth in Hamburg, Germany, only to be loaded on trucks and shipped deep into Russia, where border guards are bribed along the way. In central Russia, Soviet-era factories have been retooled to sew and stitch the sport coat by female workers so desperate for employment that they now work for lower wages than those in India. The coat makes another brief appearance in Canada to get the one accessory made there: buttons molded in a factory so automated that labor costs are not an issue. The coat then makes its final trek over the border to a store in New York.

Food. Not only what we wear and what we watch but increasingly what we eat is not so much grown as it is assembled:

> The catfish are trucked from the fish farms to the factory where they await the assembly line. The workers—also women, also black, also poor—are ready for them in their waders, looking like a female angler's society. But these women mean business. The fish come down the line, slippery and flopping. The sawyer grabs the fish and lops off their heads with a band saw, tossing the bodies back onto the line while the heads drop into a bucket. Down the line, women with razor-sharp filet knives make several deft cuts to eviscerate the fish and turn them into filets to be frozen. Many of the longer-term workers have lost fingers, especially to the saws. The company says they fail to follow directions and that they get careless. The women say they are overworked. They say they get tired. They say they slip in the fish guts that fill the floor. But through it all, the assembly line, like Paul Robeson's "Ol' Man River," "just keeps rolling along." The line that threads between these rows of black women is operated by a tall white man who supervises from a raised control booth, adjusting the speed of the line and noting the workers' efforts. One watches and wonders: is this the face of the new South or the old South? And what of what Marx called the "social relations of production"; is this the assembly line of the future or the plantation of the past under a metal roof? (Sernau 2001, 61)

The scene behind the counter at a fast-food restaurant also bears much more resemblance to an assembly line than to a kitchen. Ground-up beef parts from three continents become hamburgers and chemically altered oils from North and South America and Africa coat precut potato fragments and are whipped into shakes by workers following exact procedures as they stand in rows of standardized machines. This process was first refined by McDonald's, and has since been emulated by scores of competitors, as such fast-food procedures now permeate many parts of the service sector (Ritzer 2018; Schlosser 2012 [2001]). We have seen how fast-food processes could trim skilled culinary jobs to routines that can be done by anyone able to move quickly from machine to machine. But it didn't seem as though the actual fast-food jobs could be outsourced. Yet in Hawaii, where wage rates are high, if you drive into a McDonald's and talk into the annoying little microphone, the voice on the other end may be coming from rural California. The young person takes your order then flashes it back by internet to the one person actually in the store in Hawaii, who puts it all in the bag. Has McDonald's considered that it might be even cheaper if the person on the other side of the microphone were in India or the Philippines? They are apparently exploring the option.

Ordering the World Market

The International Monetary Fund (IMF)

At the end of World War II, the leaders of the capitalist world met at Bretton Woods, a resort in New Hampshire, to discuss the shape of the postwar global economy. It was becoming clear that no amount of sputtering determination on the part of Prime Minister Winston Churchill was going to hold together the British Empire in its current form. The Warsaw Pact provided for economic as well as military cooperation among Eastern Europe and the Soviet Union. But the Western allies were fearful of global economic chaos and of the formation of military–economic blocs, such as just-defeated Nazi Europe and Japan's Asian "co-prosperity" sphere. The alternative was to create international organizations to regulate world trade and the global economy. Several semi-independent organizations were formed, dominated by Great Britain and the United States. The **International Monetary Fund (IMF)** was created to regulate the world's currencies. Its original tasks were to avoid runaway inflation, prevent collapsing currencies, and facilitate trade by establishing exchange rates between currencies. One tool the IMF had at its disposal was lending money to prop up struggling economies.

Over time, the lending function became the dominant one. In order to get IMF loans, countries must agree to certain reforms, known as *structural adjustment*. Typically, they are called on to reduce government spending, including on social programs, and to privatize. Recall that privatization is the turning over of certain government-controlled functions to private enterprise, including banking, oil refining, and manufacturing. Often, governments are also encouraged to devalue their currencies to make their exports cheaper abroad.

The philosophy of the IMF from the beginning has been deeply rooted in neoclassical economics: Reduce government and encourage free markets and free trade as the route to economic stability and prosperity. The long-range consequences of this policy remain a source of intense controversy, and the short-range consequences are also mixed. Big, wasteful governments with inefficient programs, patronage jobs that build political support by hiring friends of the party in power, and reckless monetary policy such as paying debts by printing worthless currency have benefited from readjustment. At the same time, IMF demands have often included cutting food programs for the urban poor, cutting agricultural subsidies for poor farmers, and even cutting expensive health and education programs. Often the poorest citizens have borne the brunt of the pain resulting from fallout from these policies.

Opponents of free-trade doctrines often call for the abolition of the IMF. Others see the need for such an organization but question its absolute devotion to free-market, free-trade policies; to "shock therapy," which eliminates many government programs overnight; and to rapid transitions to market economies (Stiglitz 2002). Calls also have been made to expand the IMFs leadership to better include new economic powers. By agreement, the president of the IMF has always been European, while the head of the World Bank has always been an American appointed by the U.S. president.

The World Bank

The Bretton Woods framers of the new world order believed that newly independent and other developing countries would need outside capital to fund their development. They created the World Bank to provide loans for development projects that would speed the growth and modernization of supposedly backward economies.

In its early years, the World Bank seemed to favor large, showy development projects, such as huge dam and highway projects. Newly independent governments also favored these projects as symbols of national strength and pride. Unfortunately, many never delivered all the economic returns that had been envisioned. Governments were saddled with the massive debt incurred without the revenue to pay the debts. Often the governments needed to turn to the IMF to restructure their debts and their economies.

Over time, the World Bank learned from its early mistakes and sought more local participation, encouraged smaller projects, and insisted on stricter environmental standards and economic accountability. Big dam projects and expensive showpieces were increasingly rejected for funding. Despite these reforms, the World Bank still has many critics who argue that it lures poor countries into deep debt while ignoring more innovative micro projects that actually employ and empower local people.

From GATT to the WTO

Accompanying the effort to stabilize the world economy has been the effort to encourage and stabilize international trade. For centuries, this had been done through **tariffs.** The very first law passed by the new U.S. Congress, and signed by newly inaugurated President George Washington, was a tariff law that protected U.S. industries from cheap European imports.

Tariffs did two things: They allowed local industries to develop by making imported items more expensive, and they raised revenues for the new federal government. Early American manufacturers accused the huge British corporations of dumping products at less than cost in an attempt to put them out of business. It appears this is exactly what they were doing in the early 1800s, and tariffs compensated for the practice. In a time before the federal income tax, tariffs also provided the national government with much of its operating revenue.

Over the course of the nineteenth century, tariffs remained one of the most controversial aspects of political campaigns and national policy in the United

States. Exporters, such as Southern cotton growers, wanted low tariffs in both the United States and Europe so that they could export their own goods cheaply and in turn cheaply import what they needed to expand. Growing local industries and eventually labor called for higher tariffs to protect manufacturing jobs.

Around the world, tariffs became the way that young countries—such as the many Latin American countries that became independent in the 1820s—could raise revenues and control imports. When rebels or outside powers wanted to seize revenues, they attacked and seized the tariff collections in customs houses. When the British and U.S. governments were concerned about Latin American and Caribbean countries failing to pay their debts, they sent in the marines to seize tariff revenues. But few challenged the right of governments to collect these revenues or to protect fragile, local industries in their early stages.

In the decades following World War II, the controversy over tariffs was settled in favor of what become known as the **Washington Consensus:** the neoclassical view that trade was good and tariffs that limited trade were bad. **Free trade**—that is, trade free from regulations and tariffs—became the accepted doctrine. In 1947 this doctrine was institutionalized in the **General Agreement on Trade and Tariffs (GATT)** accords. GATT allowed some limited protections to be gradually phased out, but the overall goal was low or no tariffs and free trade.

In 1994 GATT was replaced by the **World Trade Organization (WTO),** which monitors trade practices around the world. Countries that place too many or unfair limits on imports can face punitive tariffs on their own exports. If countries can prove dumping in the WTO courts, they can place tariffs on these items or limit their export. Otherwise, the main rule of the game is free trade. Countries are also limited in their ability to keep out imports based on environmental or labor concerns or "unfounded" concerns over products' safety.

The tit for tat of world trade can be complex and far-reaching. Angered over France's protection of its own farmers and its tendency to favor agricultural imports, such as bananas, from its former African colonies rather than from Latin America, the United States put temporary punitive tariffs on French cheese and champagne. In 2002 President George W. Bush put protective tariffs on imported steel. The U.S. steel industry had been in decline for decades. Critics of the industry said the problem was out-of-date mills and techniques that couldn't compete with newer Japanese and European plants. American steelmakers and organized labor claimed the problem was the dumping of foreign steel at below cost to drive out U.S. suppliers. The domestic complexity of tariffs was evident in that the steel tariffs were popular with steelmakers and their workers, who said they were saving the industry, but unpopular with automakers and their workers, who claimed that higher steel prices raised the prices of their cars, both domestically and for export. The WTO accepted the tariffs as temporary measures but ruled against their extension. In response to these now-illegal tariffs, France temporarily put tariffs on U.S. farm products. Clearly, much more is at stake than the price of Brie in Los Angeles or the price of Wheaties in Paris. How far can governments go to protect their workers and their industries?

A common complaint is that the WTO still operates by the "golden rule": Those players who hold the most gold make the rules. The United States and European countries have found many arguments in support of exceptions for their own protected industries. Japan and China have used a long tradition of cooperation (some would say collusion) among government, banking, and industry to hide subsidies and anticompetitive actions. Small countries usually do not have these options and must dance to the tune of the more powerful players.

FTAA: A Common Market in the Americas?

The 2004 meetings of nations from across the Americas to discuss the Free Trade Agreement of the Americas (FTAA) caused quite a stir. The bold idea was to extend the North American Free Trade Agreement (NAFTA), which exists among Canada, the United States, and Mexico, all the way to the tip of South America.

Excitement ran high as proposals were put forward. Could the Americas become a common market as Europe had, moving for several decades toward an expanding European Union (EU)? Miami was pleased to play host. Maybe this would give it an advantage in the competition with Atlanta and Panama City to become the host city for FTAA institutions, much as Brussels has hosted many EU institutions.

The FTAA proposal was not without dissent, however. Cuba didn't show up. Costa Rica voiced concerns about market pressures from U.S. media conglomerates. And the streets were filled with protesters. Talks such as these often went unnoticed; the discussions around NAFTA had not raised a stir until much later. But ever since the World Trade Organization (WTO) meetings in Seattle in 1999, trade had become a media event. In Seattle, young environmental protesters (a few in whale suits) joined veteran union organizers and self-proclaimed "raging grannies" in chants against free trade and for greater social justice. The protesters dogged later trade talks in Washington, DC, and London, spilled out into mass protest in Rome, and then converged on Miami.

Other International Trade Groups

The pattern repeated itself, as President George W. Bush landed in Chile in November 2004 for the meetings of the Asian-Pacific Economic Cooperation (APEC) conference, a meeting of 21 world leaders to promote trade and economic growth. The Chilean government was proud to host the meeting of Pacific Rim countries that control half the world's economy. This event was evidence that Chile had joined the elite club of wealthy nations. But 30,000 antiwar and antiglobalization protesters were also there. Led by the Chilean Social Forum, 100 groups opposed to "corporate-led globalization" filled the streets. Topics that would have been confined to a macroeconomics classroom suddenly became the rage, quite literally, of the streets.

Every year powerful political and corporate leaders meet in Davos, Switzerland, for fabulous food, great scenery, and economic discussions as part of the World Economic Forum. It is quite difficult to organize mass protests in remote and expensive Davos. For years now, a counter meeting has been held in Porto Alegre, Brazil, long home to many of Brazil's labor activists. Those meetings in Porto Alegre have called for new models of trade that focus on workers and workers' rights rather than just corporate profits. In 2004 the group met in Mumbai, India, and in 2006 in Nairobi, Kenya; then in June 2007, the first U.S. Social Forum was held in Atlanta. These gatherings are often termed part of the antiglobalization movement, although many participants would argue they instead seek to reform the institutions of economic globalization to move from free trade to fair trade.

Other economic organizations have expanded to reflect the spread of global economic power. The Group of Seven (G7), consisting of the United States, Canada, Japan, the United Kingdom, France, Germany, and Italy, has often been superseded by a G20 that consists of other major powers and emerging markets, including Russia, China, India, Brazil, and South Africa.

Trade That Is Fair for All

Everyone loves a fair. Whether a small country affair or a great global exposition, a fair is a place of coming together, showcasing the new, and buying and selling. The entire global economy has become one great world's fair, with technology and new styles on display every month.

Trade is a force for change. Every country that has been drawn, willingly or unwillingly, into the world economy has changed rapidly. Japan was revolutionized from agrarian isolation to industrial might in a matter of decades following the visits of U.S. Commodore Matthew Perry in the 1850s. Perry had come demanding, with great courtesies and great guns, an opening of trade relations. Certainly China has been undergoing a commercial revolution as sweeping as any Mao-inspired revolution. India is racing to catch up. Latin America, from Mexico to Brazil to Chile, is also being completely rebuilt for participation in global trade. Africa alone has been largely passed over, except for raw materials, but this seems certain to change as the search for cheap labor pushes on.

The great world's fair of the twenty-first century has brought more products to more people than ever before. It has motivated economic, social, and sometimes political reform. The two great Asian powers, India and China, along with a half dozen or so small Asian nations have used the work and income provided by this fair to make significant reductions in poverty. Yet this fair, like the fairs of old, also has its downside. Global profits have created an international elite club of billionaires, while workers around the world continue to struggle under long hours and low pay. The burden of work falls unevenly, leaving some to toil far from their homes and families while others are idled in bypassed places. Can this fair be made fairer?

Trade could be used as a force for positive change. Countries wishing to participate in the WTO could be expected to sign labor and environmental accords. Instead of being required to weaken their protection of both workers and the environment, as the WTO has sometimes insisted in Europe, participants could be required to strengthen these protections. To join the great fair, countries could be required to agree to certain conditions for the global assembly line: no child labor; no banned chemicals; proper waste disposal; minimum wages; and inspection and enforcement of local ordinances, national laws, and global accords.

Before this can happen, however, the powerful players and wealthy nations will need to rethink the very foundations of the organizations that govern the world of work and trade. Is the goal to promote trade, at whatever cost? Or is the goal to promote development—economic, social, cultural, and human—and to use work and trade as tools in that process?

Global capitalism hasn't been pretty. But then neither were the attempts to build great spheres of influence that led to World War II nor the efforts to defend the aging empires that helped spark World War I. Economic globalization is likely, at least in part, to be here to stay. People have come to depend on the global supermarket to supply their needs.

Yet our greatest needs are still often best met locally: quality face-to-face education, quality personal health care, quality housing, livable communities with safe and pleasant spaces, and good infrastructure. Most of humanity's history is one of the largely self-reliant communities that traded mostly for novelties, adornments, and luxuries. This is a pattern to which we may need to return, at least in part. Of course, this shift in priorities would also mean that the more affluent consumers would need to do with fewer novelties, adornments, and luxuries and invest instead in the lives and development of communities both close to home and far away.

Economist Jeffrey Sachs (2006) embraces free market economics and is a champion of globalization, but he argues for a change in the rules of the game toward enlightened globalization:

> When all is said and done, however, the antiglobalization movement should mobilize its vast commitment and moral force into a proglobalization movement on behalf of the poorest of the poor, the global environment, and the spread of democracy. It is the kind of globalization championed by the Enlightenment—a globalization of democracies, multilateralism, science and technology, and a global economic system designed to meet human needs. We could call this an Enlightened Globalization. (p. 358)

Key Ideas

- Societies have been moving toward ever more specialization in their division of labor. This can provide for efficiency and technical expertise but can also leave workers feeling alienated from their work as they become small cogs in great production schemes.
- Some of the division of labor has been international since at least European colonial times, but since the 1970s, the world has seen an explosion of outsourcing of jobs and offshoring of production to other countries, creating a new international division of labor.
- Industrial production has shifted from advanced industrial nations, who are becoming postindustrial providers of services and technology, to newly industrializing countries such as India and China. The dominance of large retailers seeking to cut consumer prices has accelerated this trend.
- Sometimes the comparative advantage offered by a newly industrializing country is weaker labor and environmental laws. New opportunities are created, but so are opportunities for exploiting powerless workers, including children.
- International institutions have been created to attempt to regulate world trade and currency: the International Monetary Fund to regulate debt and currency, the World Bank to provide funding for development projects, and the World Trade Organization to monitor global trade and encourage open markets. These organizations have been given credit for spreading global prosperity, but also criticized for supporting powerful nations and interests at the expense of the poor and powerless.
- While economists debate the merits of free trade, new voices around the world are emerging to call for a fair trade system that respects the rights of workers.

For Review and Discussion

1. How has globalization changed economies and the lives of workers? Is it likely to lead to greater poverty or greater prosperity? What factors support your point of view?
2. What are the arguments for and against open markets and free-trade policies? Which ones do you find convincing?
3. Why do workers persist in jobs that are dangerous or underpaid? What are the most promising ways to promote the rights of workers?
4. Is "fair trade" possible in a world of great inequalities in wealth and power? What policies and actions can help promote fair trade?

Making Connections

World Mart

▶ Walk through your favorite shopping mall or big box retailer. Examine the "Made in" tags. What countries are represented? Are certain products centered in certain locations? What might these locations offer manufacturers? You may also be able to do this assignment in your own clothes closet.

UN Sustainable Development Goals

▶ Goal 8 of the UN Sustainable Development Goals is "Promote inclusive and sustainable economic growth, employment and decent work for all." See the challenges and action being taken on this at https://www.un.org/sustainabledevelopment/economic-growth/.

ILO

▶ Go to www.ilo.org for information on the UN-affiliated International Labour Organization (ILO). This site has information and articles on globalization, child labor, women's work, AIDS and work, global wages, and dozens of other topics. What are some of the new and continuing challenges that workers face across the continents?

Making A Difference

Fair Trade

▶ Explore *alternate traders* that may operate in your community or a neighboring city. Alternate traders (sometimes called *fair traders*) attempt to provide an alternative to exploitive international trade relations. They purchase products directly from local producers in low-income countries and communities, often giving special attention to local cooperatives, to women's and poor people's groups, and to products that are produced in socially and environmentally responsible ways. Products include clothing, coffee, and crafts. Often, these are sold with little or no payments to a person who acts as an intermediary, so that a large portion of the retail price returns to the producers.

Alternate traders with local outlets include Ten Thousand Villages (www.tenthousandvillages.com), SERRV (www.serrv.org), Equal Exchange (www.equalexchange.coop), and Marketplace: Handiwork of India (www.marketplaceindia.com). Others can be found at the websites of Fair Trade Federation (https://www.fairtradefederation.org/browse-ftf-members/) and Fair World Project (https://fairworldproject.org/choose-fair/mission-driven-brands/). Look at these sites for information on fair trade and then check for locations or outlets near you. If possible, visit a store, look at the items (bring your Christmas list if you like!), read the brochures, and talk with store personnel. How do alternate traders attempt to cope with the problems and inequalities of the global economy? Do they provide a viable alternative to the destructive and exploitive aspects of world trade? Why or why not?

Worker Rights Consortium

➤ In recent years, students on many campuses have become active in the anti-sweatshop movement. Go to www.workersrights.org formerly United Students Against Sweatshops). WRC campus affiliates are listed at https://www.workersrights.org/affiliates/affiliate-institutions/. Does your campus or community have a related chapter? If so, talk with the leadership about local issues. What current issues are featured on the national website? How do they propose taking action?

Fast Fashion

➤ Paris-based fashion reporter turned fashion investigator, Dana Thomas, writes in her 2020 book *Fashionopolis: The Price of Fast Fashion and the Future of Clothes* (Penguin Books) about the real costs in a world of cheap, fleetingly stylish clothes. Many of the world's top billionaires are in fashion (including three of the richest 12 on the Forbes list) yet the vast majority of textile workers – from Los Angeles to Jakarta – endure harsh, often brutal, conditions and some of the world's lowest wages. For one take on Nike, Victoria's Secret, Zara, Forever 21 and others, see https://theprettyplaneteer.com/fast-fashion-brands-to-avoid/. For suggestions on alternatives, see https://www.thegoodtrade.com/features/fair-trade-clothing. What makes an ethical company? Can it still be affordable? Do you consider social responsibility in your own clothing choices?

3
Gender and Family
Overburdened Women and Displaced Men

Global Encounters

India

India is a place of many divides: rich and poor, rural and urban, male and female, and north and south. In many ways it is a subcontinent of nations rather than a single country. India has long been ruled from the north: emperors in Delhi, Muslim moguls in Agra, and the British raj in Calcutta. New Delhi is the seat of modern political power. But these northern cities are also in the most troubled part of India. The region has the highest birthrates and the highest infant mortality, aging inefficient industry, and the most severe deprivation. Stories of abuse of women over dowry, caste divides, and child labor are often centered in the north. Calcutta, now called Kolkata, has seen deindustrialization with the speed of Detroit, Flint, and Gary. Students traveling to the north are amazed at the funeral pyres burning along the Ganges in Varanasi (Benares). They are also overwhelmed at the onslaught of beggars clinging to the vehicles and filling the sidewalks. In Agra they marvel at the elegance of the Taj Mahal, but only after struggling through the rings of homeless families that surround the train station. Delhi is the storied ancient heart of this country, but students can only catch glimmers of the city through a dense haze of auto exhaust and the fumes of wood and dung fires. On the train from Agra to Delhi, the shantytowns become denser as the sky turns from blue to tobacco-stain yellow to a thick brown-orange of moldering smog. Northern India has power and history but it is being left behind. Our guest lecturer, a proud resident of the southern state of Kerala, speaks of the north as the Cow Belt, the land of tradition and traditional poverty.

Cows do venture into the roads in southern India, but they better look both ways lest they be run over. Southern India is racing toward a high-tech future. India has more software engineers than anywhere in the world. They are not hard to spot: earnest young men in blue jeans and button-down white shirts. Their pocket protectors seem to hold the key to India's future. Our students traveling to Bangalore, the center of this IT boom, feel like they have entered the Silicon Valley of India. Bangalore, along with neighboring Hyderabad, is at the core of India's IT revolution. It struggles with limited infrastructure and huge numbers of immigrants to continue driving India's economic growth rate of around 6 percent per year. An economy growing that fast will double in every 12 years. Bombay (now renamed Mumbai), India's largest city, and Chennai (once known as Madras) also compete for this IT influx, moving beyond software into media. Mumbai and Chennai turn out more movies than Hollywood; here they speak of Bollywood. The films look like Rogers and Hammerstein high on hashish and the glories of Hinduism. Melodramatic plots always include lavish weddings; sinister, plotting mothers-in-law; and lavish dance numbers involving a cast of thousands, often joined by a few dancing Hindu deities. They also gross fabulous returns and now extend well beyond India's borders.

Chennai flourishes with "back office operations." The data processing for U.S., Japanese, and European firms can be done at a fraction of the cost here. Now even U.S. newspapers are looking at having their editing and layout work done here. Radiology clinics in U.S. hospitals can send digital files here in the middle of the night to be read and returned by a radiologist the patient will never see.

Our briefing from the U.S. consulate officer notes all the economic progress in southern India, much of it highly encouraged by the consulate, which often serves as booster and cheerleader for U.S. business interests. Then he notes the one exception: the southern state of Kerala. Kerala, he contends, lives largely on the remittances of its residents who have traveled abroad in search of work. Keralites can be found in U.S. hospitals and all across the Persian Gulf states. There is not enough work and little economic growth back home.

Too bad for Kerala, to miss out on such a boom of economic expansion. One must blame the women, the Christians, and the communists. Women have held prominent positions for a very long time in a state that has a matrilineal heritage, with inheritance following from not the man but the woman. Kerala is a religiously diverse place, with more Christians than any other group. The Christian families sought education for their girls as well as boys, and many have become teachers, nurses, professors, and physicians. Then there are the communists. Kerala likes to alternate who holds power, and about every other election, the control of the state goes to the local communist party, always popularly elected. The women, the Christians, and the communists: They have supported labor unions so that companies coming to Kerala must pay union wages and negotiate time off, and don't even think of using child labor in a state where virtually every child is in school. Poor Kerala: It has some of the highest unemployment rates and slowest growth rates in the county (see Biswas 2010).

The consulate officer also notes social indicators. Birthrates remain high in the northern Cow Belt but are falling in the south. They are lowest in Kerala, barely at replacement level, and just under that for the United States. India is also gaining in literacy, although rural dwellers and women lag far behind, and in some places, only a third can read and write. But not in Kerala. Literacy is 99 percent, higher than the United States, and women are more literate than men. Life expectancy is also rising in India, but health care can be hard to come by, especially in rural areas. Except in Kerala. Life expectancy and infant mortality statistics in Kerala match those of France, better than that in the United States, far better than for Americans of color. What is this with Kerala? How can a place that is so poor seem so rich? Blame the women, the

Christians, and the communists. They put all their money into health and education; they insist on schools and clinics for all and staff them with their own highly educated people. Our students who travel through Kerala are amazed at the complete lack of deprivation. There are no beggars, no homeless to be seen. The land is lush and green. It is a rural place of farms and fishing towns. It is beautiful. Of course, since international business is reluctant to locate in a place as strike-prone as France or Italy, the residents must often leave this land to work elsewhere. They lost their bid for the electronics industry, which needs low-cost assemblers as well as highly educated designers. So the people must go to California and Dubai, to Mumbai and Bangalore, and only return when they can to this lush and welcoming southern state.

Where is India's future? Certainly most seem to have their eyes on Bangalore. The government struggles to build the roads, the fiber-optic lines, and the electric power stations to keep the electronic fires of Bangalore burning. Mumbai and Chennai have their own plans to capture whatever IT industry won't fit in Bangalore. Even Calcutta, like Detroit and Cleveland, has plans for a comeback. Can a billion Indians all enjoy the consumer frenzy broadcast from Mumbai? Is that a picture of economic miracle or environmental disaster? Should we completely forget Kerala, moving forward on bicycles, living well on annual incomes that are below what many Americans spend in a week?

I wonder if somehow India in its great ingenuity could arrange a marriage between cosmopolitan Bangalore and rural Kerala—introduce those young men in jeans and white shirts to the proud and healthy women of Kerala in their beautiful and flowing flower-print saris. Can the global economic engine be harnessed to a commitment, to a sustainable quality of life? It won't be easy; cross-cultural marriages never are. But what is the cost of failure? To see the answer to that, one must only look out through the smog to the shacks along the tracks from Agra to Delhi.

Nietzsche Undone: From Superman to Supermom

Around the world massive changes are taking place in the relationship between work and family, and within that sphere, between men and women. It is not the change envisioned by feminists in the 1960s, nor is it merely a backlash against those changes. Rather, this odd mix of global economy, global culture, and global politics that we have come to call *globalization* is changing men's and women's roles across the continents. Unexpectedly (though it shouldn't be, given trends already afoot in the 1960s), women's roles are becoming ever broader and more encompassing and men's roles are becoming more limited and constricted, at least for certain men. This is not a story of female triumph, however, for only occasionally do women receive the full benefits of their new roles. Often they end up overburdened, just as men find themselves displaced.

The idea of women's liberation is much older than we usually imagine, but the idea of men's liberation may be older still. The ideal man of Athens was free from male drudgery, like plowing the rocky Greek soil, to discuss matters of importance in the city marketplace, to trade and converse, to worship on the hillside, and to vote in the assembly. The ideal man also tended a rural farmstead, so he could stay close to the land and know the joy of picking his own olives and stomping his own grapes. Meanwhile, the ideal Athenian woman, at least in the male mind, was largely cloistered at home, tending to a narrow range of domestic duties as befit her temperament. Likewise, the Renaissance man of fifteenth-century Italy knew the pleasures of both the city and the countryside and appreciated the best of each. He also knew the pleasures of both mind and body and indulged both, and he was equally adept in science, art, and politics. Of course, managing the affairs of such men about town was no small task, and so it took many a domestic woman.

When German philosopher Friedrich Nietzsche envisioned the emboldened Übermensch, it was clearly a super-*man* in most respects. All along, women have sought to challenge this, but only the rare woman has succeeded. Elizabeth I of sixteenth-century England danced, romanced, conspired, and maneuvered her way through the worlds of politics, art, theater, and global exploration, but she was always one mishap from losing the throne. She also chose to forgo matrimony as part of her having it all. Sor Juana Inés de la Cruz of seventeenth-century Mexico likewise probed the worlds of art, literature, and science, also by forgoing marriage in what appears to have been, at least initially, a marriage of convenience to the church. By the 1800s the number of women adventurers and explorers, philanthropists, and activists had increased, but we still remember them in part because they were so few: Sojourner Truth, Lucy Stone, Susan B. Anthony, Harriet Tubman, Jane Addams, Virginia Woolf, and Amelia Earhart.

The rising influence of well-educated and influential women in the 1800s was matched by the Victorian ideal of womanhood and emphasized that a woman's loftiest aspiration should be motherhood. Queen Victoria of England may have ruled an empire that stretched around the world, but she was often admired for her matronly ways and being the mother of many. The Victorian woman of Great Britain and the United States was expected to follow this queenly example. She should have many children and devote herself to their nurture. Her husband would dutifully devote his time to their economic comfort and sustenance. A man's home was his castle, and his wife's time went into maintaining that castle for her prince and his children, with ample help from servants and day laborers. Of course, only the upper classes and the small, well-off middle classes of the time could attain this cultural ideal. The reality for most women was more like the life of Cinderella before the fairy godmother showed up. Domestic tasks without the help of servants were long and arduous.

It is also misleading to simply note that many women did not work outside the home. In fact, businesses were often family businesses and farms were family farms, with women contributing a great deal of the labor and expertise needed for economic survival, even if they were not listed as landowners or business owners. Typically, women from all but the most elite classes were involved in economically productive activity, even if it was not wage labor. Only the wealthiest families could afford to have women in hoop skirts in grand Victorian homes or plantation houses supervising the work of others while doting on their children, even if this was the cultural ideal.

Women also began the movement into wage labor early in the U.S. and European industrial periods. Women—especially young, unmarried women from lower-income backgrounds—often went to work in the mills that were becoming common in the United States and Western Europe from about 1840. Textile mills, in particular, were major employers of women, almost as an industrial extension of the textile work that women had often done in their homes. By the turn of the twentieth century, a full one-fifth of U.S. women were in the paid labor force; many of these were immigrant women, trying to help their families survive and become established in growing U.S. cities. Women from middle-class backgrounds were expected to leave the labor force upon marriage. Often this was even required in certain professions, such as teaching. (Male teachers could continue teaching after marriage, as long as they could support their families on the meager wages.) If a middle-class woman lost her husband to death or desertion, she frequently found herself in dire circumstances and often turned to so-called quiet employment, such as using her Victorian home as a boardinghouse, to gain needed income.

In the 1920s, U.S. women worked sometimes as an expression of new-found independence (as they did again in the 1970s) and sometimes as a way of trying to share in the highly touted prosperity of the Roaring Twenties, which was not reaching everyone (as they did again in the 1980s and 1990s). Women in the 1930s often worked out of necessity, as the hard economic times of the Depression forced many women to postpone marriage or to replace or supplement the lost income of unemployed and underemployed husbands (a pattern that also returned in the 1970s).

World War II provided the global cataclysm that shattered entrenched powers, including male power, and opened new doors to women. American and European female labor-force participation reached its peak in the war years of the early 1940s. Now it was women's patriotic duty to go to work to keep the industrial "arsenal of democracy" churning while the men were at war. Women worked in heavy industry as Rosie the Riveters. They also worked in meatpacking and as bus drivers and "milkmen," fulfilling traditional male-dominated service roles.

When World War II ended, European countries that had lost huge portions of their manpower to war casualties—Germany and the Soviet Union, in particular—continued to need and encourage women to participate in industry. In the United States, however, women workers were told to go home. Millions of servicemen were returning home and looking for college educations and jobs. Women were encouraged to make room for them. Female university enrollments declined, and female labor-market participation plummeted.

Correspondingly, women married younger than ever before, and after years of declining fertility rates, they again started to have more children and at a younger age. The Victorian ideal of the domestic woman whose sole devotion was to home and family was revived, but now a growing middle class meant that more families could live this ideal. Women in the paid labor force were accepted, especially in female-dominated occupations, but mostly with the understanding that they were waiting to get married or wanted to buy a few extras. Their employment was acceptable as long as it did not involve taking "men's work."

Suspicion of career women was often fierce, as in Merle Miller's 1954 rebuke in *Esquire* magazine to "that increasing and strident minority of women who are doing their damnedest to wreck marriage and home life in America, those who insist on having both husband and career. They are a menace and they have to be stopped" (quoted in Miller and Nowak 1977, 164).

Much of the social life of the 1950s in the United States can be seen as a grand attempt to reverse the irreversible. Even in the 1950s, fully one-third of the U.S. labor force was female (and most were not working casually). Growing numbers of other women, many with significant education and work experience, found complete devotion to home less than satisfying (despite the "hosannas"). Yet this cultural vision of the domestic woman was so strong that many people were shocked when young women, as well as less-than-content older women, rejected the old-fashioned choice and followed in the footsteps of the emancipated girl (often their own grandmothers) of the 1920s and 1930s. They returned to higher education in large numbers in the 1960s and to the professional workforce, including the "big career," in the 1970s.

In one sense, the return of large numbers of women to the paid labor force was merely a continuation of earlier trends in the century, trends that had their roots in the expansion of industrialization. Yet there was something new: An increasing portion of these working women were seeking true careers, rather than temporary or low-wage employment. In 1900 wealthy women often received a good education, but it was intended to provide refinement—to make them more elegant, more cultured, and sometimes more pious domestic women. There were exceptions, including the women who left home to become missionaries and the extraordinary group of wealthy, highly educated women who advanced both social work and public health practices, as well as progressive social theory, at Jane Addams's Hull House in Chicago. These women were few, however. Poor women, on the other hand, often worked for wages but received little education.

The idea of large numbers of career women pursuing higher education and then using that education in professional employment was new and even shocking. But over time, this new idea transformed many occupations. Law was once a male-only domain, but law schools now enroll about as many women as men, and significant numbers of these women are older, returning students. Law school, with its emphasis on reading, writing, and communication skills, has been more permeable to women than engineering, where entrance often depends on early encouragement to pursue science and higher mathematics. Medical schools, with similar entry requirements, have been slower than law schools to enroll large numbers of women, but in 2019, over 50 percent of medical school students were female (AAMC 2019).

Instead of Superman, we found Supermom. But we also realized what classical Athenians, Renaissance Italians, and all the rest of the men's movements overlooked: You cannot fundamentally change the role of one gender without bringing about major changes in the role of the other. Liberation must go both ways. A second lesson is that liberation confined to a privileged class cannot triumph. This was understood by nineteenth-century feminists who worked for civil rights and progressive reforms. It was beautifully exemplified by the mid-twentieth century's greatest feminist, Eleanor Roosevelt (though she may have preferred a different label). Somehow this idea got lost in the individualism of the 1970s and the corporatism of the 1980s. Then, the liberation of privileged men often came at the expense of poor women, and the liberation of privileged women in the later portion of the twentieth century seemed to come at the same price. Supermom felt guilty, because deep down she knew she couldn't do it all without basic changes in society—essentially, in men's roles and expectations—and she could only do what she could because of the added burdens of her poor sisters.

Masculinity as Vulnerability: The Harder They Fall

Around the world, male privilege is persistent but precarious. Respect, prestige, privilege, and power go to successful men, not necessarily to all men. In an article called "The Good Provider Role: Its Rise and Fall," Jesse Bernard (1981), one of the first prominent female sociologists in the United States, noted that *successful* men were told to use their advantages to be good providers for their families. This was not just an ancient idea but actually gained acceptance in the 1800s, as the agrarian partnership of men and women gave way to a market economy dominated by business-*men*.

But not all businessmen proved to be successful. Some never reached their dreams; some succumbed to economic disaster. Whether for economic or personal reasons, many men found themselves unable to fulfill the good provider role and withdrew from the competition; frequently, in a time when divorce was rare, they simply abandoned their families. The good provider role seems to have had many deserters. Although these deserters were clearly vulnerable to economic downturns and wounded by social expectations, in one sense they were still privileged relative to their women. The men could move and start over, but the women they deserted were often left raising families with little means of support. In Latin America and to a certain extent in much of Africa and Central Asia, the idea of the man as provider and protector is culturally well established. But there, too, the number of deserters seems to be increasing.

Some men were always vulnerable because of their race, ethnicity, or class. African American sharecroppers and Irish American stockyard workers could never support their families in the proper style and either had to forgo family life or admit to being less than good providers (Bernard 1981). Currently within the African American community, men are more likely than women not to finish school and not to be employed. Men are far more likely to be incarcerated, as well. As black women struggle to maintain their families and communities without large numbers of contributing men, it is not clear that they are therefore privileged. It is clear, however, that poor black men are particularly vulnerable to loss and humiliation. In societies that accord other men respect, advantage, and power, they find only disrespect, disadvantage, and disempowerment.

This is increasingly true not only of U.S. black men but also of poor black men in Brazil, the Caribbean, Europe, and across Africa. The vulnerability of manhood is realized by Latino men in both North and Latin America, where changing economies limit their ability to be good providers. It is also increasingly realized by working-class white men, both in North America and now across Eastern Europe, who are far more aware of their vulnerability than their privilege.

In an era of heavy industry, men from low-income backgrounds often found their best opportunities in manufacturing. If these were unionized jobs with relatively high wages, they contributed to the male advantage. Men in these jobs earned considerably more than women in routinized clerical, service, and domestic positions. Yet as these unionized heavy industry positions become scarce, the men and their industrial skills are extremely vulnerable to termination, protracted unemployment, and new employment at far lower wages. Women in industry are also vulnerable, but those with skills applicable in the service economy may have more secure employment than the men of their families and communities. Men may still have certain privileges, more so than women, such as greater freedom from family responsibilities, but they are most acutely aware of their vulnerability. Their severe class disadvantage trumps their gender privileges.

This phenomenon is not purely new. In the 1800s the paneled offices and the boardrooms—as well as the decrepit boardinghouses, flophouses, and rescue missions—were all dominated by men: either men who had reached the top or men who had hit bottom. The place of women is also changing and in similarly complex ways. Women today are more likely to be seen in the boardrooms, but they are also more likely to be found in the rescue missions and the homeless shelters, not always as "sisters of mercy" but sometimes as guests.

Tired, Stressed Women and Angry, Alienated Men

Changing gender roles in the workplace are tied to changing gender roles in the home and family, with a change in one realm often forcing a change in the other. For example, women's growing economic independence has made it easier for them to leave abusive and unsatisfying marital relationships. This, along with other social and legal changes, is one factor in the rising world divorce rate. At the same time, the high divorce rate means that women are often left as sole custodians of children, often with limited child support and sometimes with limited income-earning potential of their own. The result is what has been termed the **feminization of poverty,** with the group most at risk of poverty being single mothers and their dependent children (Sidel 1998).

Women's expanded role in the workforce generally has not meant a relaxing of expectations for their family and domestic activities, such that many face the double burden of home and work responsibilities. Often, women still have primary responsibility for the care of children as well as the care of older adults in the family. Women also still shoulder the largest portion of the upkeep of the home, even when they are working full time (South and Spitze 1994; Stapinski 1998). Arlie Hochschild (2012) has termed this the "second shift" and noted the anger and frustration that women often feel when they find they are still doing the major portion of housework on top of their paid work.

This is a cross-cultural and almost worldwide phenomenon. Around the world, women spend more total hours in work than men, and mothers work the most of all (Scarr, Phillips, and McCartney 1989). In Japan, a majority of women are in the paid workforce, but they face wage discrimination that is the greatest in the industrial world, and barriers to upward mobility that are blatant by Western standards. Once married, they are still expected to be devoted wives and mothers who give all their effort to the home, even after a full day of work. Latin American women, now entering the paid labor force in ever greater numbers, likewise face what they call the *doble jornada*, or "double-day's journey." *Machismo*, that swashbuckling blend of male authority and male privilege in Latin America, appears to be breaking down, as more Latin American men regularly interact with their children and help around the home (Gutmann 2006). Even so, the main domestic responsibilities still fall to women, even those who are the primary wage earners. In Western Europe, where gender role changes have been most pronounced, the gaps in wages and workload are smaller but still present. Like North American and Latin American men, European men are more likely than ever to play and interact with their children but no more likely to participate fully in their daily care. Likewise, they are more likely than ever to help their wives and female partners at home but no more likely to shoulder all domestic tasks equally.

Sometimes this is a pretty clear story of continuing male privilege. Other times it is also a story of male alienation and vulnerability. The changing global economy is displacing many men, especially low-income and working-class men, from their traditional roles, even as it is overburdening women with new and double roles. Around the world, men who depended on strong backs and arms for their livelihood have been displaced by automation in industry and mechanization in agriculture, as well as by the constantly shifting nature of global production. Steelworkers in Gary, Indiana; Bethlehem, Pennsylvania; Manchester, England; and the former East Germany have all been idled by new more automated Japanese plants and by products that replace steel with molded plastic parts from Guangzhou, China. Dockworkers in Baltimore, Maryland; London, England; and Gdansk, Poland, have been idled by container ships that load and unload the world's wares with a single crane. Small farmers in Minnesota, Brazil, the Philippines, and South Africa have been idled as corporate-controlled heavy machines work the land in their place. Cattlemen in Montana watch their ranches turn into condo developments, while cattlemen in Sub-Saharan Africa watch their range land turn into desert.

Sometimes these men find alternative work. Security guards are in high demand in crime-plagued cities like Gary, Indiana; St. Petersburg, Russia; and Johannesburg, South Africa. Security seems to be manly work, although it is typically low paying in each location. Other men may try criminal activity or a variety of odd jobs—day labor, seasonal or informal construction work, small repairs, and sales. The alternative is often chronic unemployment: sitting around the tavern, the pub, the street corner, the village center, or the diner amid abandoned buildings, drinking coffee, beer, vodka, or homemade brew and talking about hard times with other men. These men don't feel privileged; they feel humiliated and disgraced or alienated and cheated. As one church conference in Washington, DC, noted, they're not deadbeats, just dead broke. Given the high rates of suicide, alcoholism, disease, and violent crime among these men, sometimes they are also soon dead.

Ironically, if there are women in the lives of these displaced men, they are often overburdened. They may have become the major wage earner for the family. Assembly plants in export-processing zones in Mexico, the Caribbean, and across East Asia are often reluctant to hire unemployed men, who may tolerate too little and demand too much. These plants prefer to hire young women. Strong backs aren't needed to assemble electronic components—just nimble fingers, keen eyesight, and endless patience. Young women bring these skills plus the willingness to work without complaint. Other plants draw on traditionally female skills, such as sewing seams in textile plants. Women in these plants often earn very little by Western standards, but they may become the major wage earners in their families, replacing the income lost by unemployed fathers and husbands.

Regardless, it is not easy for many men to step into what they have always thought of as female roles: taking over domestic tasks and childcare. So these remain primarily female activities. Left with nothing to do, the men seek alternate gratification or simply leave altogether. Faced with double and triple roles, women may feel crushed by the added burdens. Men may be as likely to feel resentful of the women as grateful. Somehow the world has changed, and it is hard to know whom to blame. Women may blame men for not "doing something for themselves." Men may blame other racial/ethnic groups: Displaced white men in both the United States and South Africa frequently blame black workers, and displaced black men in both the United States and East African cities frequently blame Asian entrepreneurs. Men also may turn to ultranationalist politicians and leaders, as they have in the United States, in Russia, and recently even in Austria, Fiji, and France. They may also blame women—the feminists, perhaps—for undermining the status they once knew.

Middle-class and upper-middle-class career men with children face stresses of their own. They often are expected to have the same single-minded devotion to their careers as the 1950s man, who was supported by his "domestic woman." But now the men are also expected to invest themselves more in the duties and demands of parenting. They face their own set of unrealistic demands and guilt as they confront what Hochschild (2001) calls "the time bind." The

Gender and Family   CHAPTER 3   97

Global economic changes have often displaced men from many of their traditional roles and jobs, sometimes only leaving seasonal and migrant work as with these strawberry pickers in Salinas, California [top]. At the same time, such changes frequently overburden women who often keep traditional roles and add new workplace demands, such as these Burmese (Myanmar) women working in a Thai shoe factory [bottom].

very expectation that child rearing is primarily a female endeavor can limit the options of men: Even when paternity leave is offered, the very few men who take it may be subject to suspicion or ridicule (Hochschild 2001). Swedish women are still more than four times as likely to take leave for childcare than men, but paternity leave has become part of the social fabric, not incongruent with ideas of manliness:

> Mikael Karlsson owns a snowmobile, two hunting dogs and five guns. In his spare time, this soldier-turned-game warden shoots moose and trades potty-training tips with other fathers. Cradling 2-month-old Siri in his arms, he can't imagine not taking baby leave. "Everyone does." (Bennhold 2010, p. A6)

Finding more equitable, more satisfying ways of combining work and family remains one of the challenges of this century for men and women, for their employers, and for their governments.

Women, especially rural women, are still the poorest of the world's poor, because they often bear heavy family responsibilities with only meager resources. In some urban areas, women are now more employable than men, but they see little of the benefits of this, for their incomes often go to supporting struggling families. Urban women have made substantial movement into middle-class employment but find it hard to continue to move up to top positions. Men still dominate in positions of power and privilege, although many poor rural and urban–industrial working-class men have lost ground. While they may be inclined to blame this loss on women's gains, most have lost out to global technology and global marketing, both still controlled largely by wealthy and powerful men.

Locked In and Shut Out

In ancient times, raiders sometimes killed men and captured women. Modern colonial and corporate raids often do the same, albeit figuratively. When local systems collapse under more powerful international forces, it is often the men's roles that are the most completely erased. This is because men tend to hold the positions of power, influence, and independence that are usurped by new forces and new masters. The men's roles of authority and autonomy are replaced by more distant authorities. The women's roles of caretaking and daily providing are still needed, however, and so are harnessed to the new system. Poor women become locked into the global economy, and poor men get shut out. Because the women are closer at hand than distant and abstract forces, they may become the objects of men's anger, frustration, and violence. While this violence is abhorrent and its consequences devastating, it must be recognized as a secondary reaction of the powerless to subtler but more powerful violence.

Examined side by side, common themes emerge from these repeated refrains. Women frequently bear the brunt of poverty. They continue to have primary responsibility for the care of children, as well as of sick and elderly family members. They continue to face discrimination and handicaps in the labor market, and attempts to gain greater education, independence, and upward mobility are frequently met with suspicion and outright hostility on the part of employers, fathers, husbands, and others. "When people who've had a little bit of education suddenly start acting uppity, they get slapped down," Jesús Sánchez told his daughter in the Mexico of two generations ago (quoted in Lewis 1961). "Take a look in the mirror and tell me what class you belong to, what your place is in society" (p. 482). Versions of these harsh words are still heard in many places and many families, especially in regard to ambitious daughters.

In increasing numbers of homes, the men are not there at all. Whether divorced, deserted, or just abandoned for long periods, the women carry on without male support. North Americans denounce "deadbeat dads" and "absentee fathers," Latin Americans murmur about the *machos* who prefer the streets to home, and Africans wonder why their traditionally strong families are now so often supported by networks of female kin with few men to be found. These female-headed families are sometimes called **matriarchal,** a term that is misleading because it implies that the women are powerful when in fact they are often overworked, overburdened, and victimized. A more accurate term is **matrifocal,** which means focused or centered on the mother and female kin. These families are increasing in number on every continent.

So, where are these men: the deadbeats, the dead broke, the machos, the bums, the deserters? The world has never lacked for individuals who have a difficult time enduring great responsibility, and cultural patterns around the world certainly contribute to this. But again, we would do well to look beyond personal and cultural peculiarities for structural causes. In their defense, many men have been displaced by forces they cannot control and may only partly understand. Traditional male roles—especially those that involved strength, independence, bravery, and self-reliant providing—have been severely undermined. Despite cultural variations, male roles in many societies have emphasized just these traits (Gilmore 1990). The man comes home from the hunt, the battlefield, the voyage, or the marketplace, tired and bruised, but loudly tosses down the goods and enjoys the acclaim of a waiting family and community. No more.

The unemployed steelworker in Gary and the laid-off autoworker in Flint, who once won approval for their ability to withstand the heat and grime and physical demands of their professions, now find themselves competing with teenagers for minimum-wage jobs that the teenagers do better. These men subsist on severance, on savings, and on women's employment. They drink beer, watch sports, and think about how they have become a liability rather than an asset to their families. The same story is repeated in East Africa, where proud herders who once withstood the heat and grime and physical demands of their profession, now are idled on government supported settlements, where they drink homemade beer and come to the same conclusion.

Women often find themselves locked in: locked in to a home full of never-ending demands or locked in (sometimes literally) to the demanding drudgery of an electronics or textile plant. Men often find themselves locked out: locked out of the labor market and eventually out of their families. Fatherhood around the world is shifting. While some men have the skills and background to become the nurturing, involved dad, many others find they are no longer needed or respected, no longer capable, of handling the demands of the new marketplace or the new home front (Furstenberg 1988). They become bitter, or despondent, drunk, or violent, or they just disappear. The women may at least have the support of matrifocal families, but unless the men join militias or gangs, they have only the camaraderie of the street corner.

The new global middle classes clearly have access to more opportunities, but these opportunities come with their own anxieties. The new middle classes—whether African American, Polish American, Mexican, South Korean, or Indian—are often painfully aware of the precariousness of their position. A sudden economic downturn can result in an equally sudden plummet from privilege (Newman 1999). Raising children, who were ultimately an economic asset in agrarian societies, is an expensive and demanding proposition for the urban middle class. Often, it requires two incomes from two separate professions. This creates demands that are very different from the side-by-side economic efforts of earlier families (Hochschild 2001).

It has been suggested that the very idea of a career was created for a man who was largely exempted from family responsibilities (Slater 1970). This is not likely an option for a career woman. She faces criticism and guilt over neglecting her work if she invests too much at home and over neglecting her family if she invests too much at work. The man feels that security in this precarious situation can only be won by making a heavy investment at work, yet he knows he is now also expected to be available at home. The challenge lies in how quickly we can open nongendered opportunities and how thoroughly we can make these opportunities family friendly.

The Feminization of Migration

A slave ship is seized off the West African coast before it can deliver its cargo of human beings. Many are shackled below decks, waiting to be sold. This is not the seventeenth century but the twenty-first century. Slavery has returned. By some estimates, the illegal trade in humans is exceeded only by the illegal trade in drugs and arms. West Africans, tricked or sold into bondage, are sold to sweatshops, docks, and insurgent armies. In the Brazilian Amazon, "debt peons" work for huge ranches, bound to the land, without contact with families or homes. Some started so young and so long ago that they have forgotten their names (Le Breton 2003). In Southern Europe, women from Albania and the newly independent Eastern European countries are promised high-wage jobs in Greece and Italy. The women then have their documents seized and are sold as domestics, laborers, and even prostitutes (Karakatsanis and Swarts 2003). Even when authorities deport them, they have often been pulled off trains by traffickers and sent to new locations to be sold again. The trafficking in people, often women and girls, is the darkest side of a recent pattern of the feminization of international migration.

In their book *Global Woman: Nannies, Maids, and Sex Workers in the New Economy*, U.S. social commentator Barbara Ehrenreich and U.S. sociologist Arlie Hochschild (2003) have compiled accounts of how wealthier countries in the last decades have been flooded with immigrant female domestic workers, creating what some are describing as the "feminization of migration." Labor migrants have traditionally been men. For instance, Chinese laborers in the United States in the 1800s were overwhelmingly unmarried men. In southern Africa, men have long left home to work in mines and industries. Men from South Asia and North Africa have traveled to the Persian Gulf to work in the oil industry. Traditionally, women were left at home to care for the children and elders and to wait for the return of their men. Increasingly, it is the women who are leaving.

The first large-scale migration of women independently was out of Ireland in the 1800s. Young Irish women traveled to England and France and then to the United States in large numbers. Some worked as shopgirls and millworkers, but the largest portion worked as domestics. The Irish maid became a common feature in large, posh Victorian homes. Ironically it was the movement of women into professional positions in Europe and North America that led to the recent surge in international domestic migrants. The Latina domestic in the United States and the Turkish domestic in Germany have become commonplace. This pattern is now expanding around the globe, as pockets of prosperity become magnets for domestic workers from less-thriving economies. Filipina maids have become common in Hong Kong (Constable 2007). Sometimes the mix is unusual, and increasingly, it is not the male overseas laborer who supports the household back home but the female.

Women have taken to the seas, the back roads, and the backwaters in new ways as well, turning traditionally female occupations into services in the new global economy. They cut hair on cruise ships and give massages at overseas resorts. They have also taken to informal and independent sales. The traveling salesman touted in the *Music Man* is often now a traveling saleswoman. Selling cosmetics is big business. In 2020 U.S. citizens alone spent $49.2 billion on cosmetics and beauty items, only $4.8 billion less than the Brookings Institution's estimated annual amount needed to provide basic education to all children in 46 low- and middle-income countries (Statistica 2020; Steer 2014).

Dugout canoes ply the waters of the upper reaches of the Amazon River and its tributaries. They carry a myriad of hues for painting faces and potions mixed from exotic herbs. These are neither for some sort of war party nor for a "medicine man" or tribal shaman. This is the Avon lady. Avon is big business in the Amazon. It's a huge industry all across Brazil, and the Amazonian Avon ladies are coordinated from high-rise offices in São Paulo. Brazil has more Avon beauty consultants (over 400,000) than it has soldiers.

What do Amazonian women buy from these Avon armies? Lipstick, of course, and a bit of eye shadow. Even in the rain forest, a Brazilian woman must look her best. They also buy skin creams that lighten the skin, essentially by burning off the outermost layer. Color is important in Brazil, and lighter skin tones are often the most prized. The Amazonian women might do better, it would seem, with the Skin So Soft creams that are reputed to repel mosquitoes. They pay with what cash they have on hand or perhaps offer a chicken in exchange. A successful Avon lady can earn far more than a rural teacher. She might even be able to hire a paddler so that she can hold an umbrella over her head for protection from the sun (one doesn't want to get too dark) and sort her wares for the next stop (Royle 1996).

Global Family Changes

Marriage and Divorce

Around the world, people are marrying later and divorcing more often. The changes in the last half of the twentieth century were most dramatic in the United States but mirrored changes that took place first in Europe and somewhat later in Latin America and Asia. Modernization theorists tried to divide the world into *traditional* and *modern* patterns of family life, describing a great transformation from the traditional family life of large **patriarchal** (male-dominated) extended families to the modern arrangements of smaller nuclear families, as described in the work of prominent U.S. social theorist Talcott Parsons (1964) and family sociologist William Goode (1963). This can be misleading, however.

The glimpses we get of family life in simpler societies suggest a more complex pattern. Hunter-gatherers seem to have married for love and lust, raised small nuclear families with the help of close community and perhaps grandparents, and occasionally divorced and remarried, all much the same as today (Fisher 2004; Nanda 2019). In family life, at least, it seems that prehistory repeats itself. The story of Nisa of the Kalahari Kung people (Shostak 2000) is full of falling in and out love, happy and unhappy marriages, domestic violence, and interpersonal struggles and intrigue. Her life could serve as the plot for any modern American soap opera, except the actors would need to wear even fewer clothes.

In simple horticultural societies, such as were common in Sub-Saharan Africa and across the Pacific as well as in the Americas before Columbus, people tended to marry early and they had to consider family obligations in their decisions of whom to marry. But they still exercised some choice, and wives often wielded considerable power and influence. In a significant number of these societies, the couple would live with the wife's family, a system anthropologists call *matrilocal.*

With the expansion of agriculture and its demands, agrarian societies developed, having characteristics that we have come to consider traditional: male-dominated, extended families with arranged marriages. Marriage was a union of families. It was about economic considerations, such as control of the land and inheritance, and as such needed to be strictly controlled. Romantic love was known and even celebrated in song and tale, but it was also dangerous. People who fell in love with the wrong people threatened the stability of the clan or kingdom. From Camelot's Guinevere and Lancelot to Shakespeare's Romeo and Juliet, romantic love led to war and disaster. Tales from Asia, such as the tragedy of the Jade goddess, suggest the same. People knew of love but feared it (Fisher 2004; Nanda 2019).

Men were traditionally concerned about legitimate heirs and property. Social position and land were matters of inheritance, and marriage was a way, often the only way, to secure one's future. Female virginity before marriage was essential. Women were often closely guarded, cloistered, or veiled, and after marriage, their role was focused around the home and farm. Women were often viewed as property, like land, with few rights of their own, and in some societies, such as in the Islamic world and parts of Africa, wealthy men could own more than one wife. This was forbidden to Christians but often occurred informally in Europe and Latin America, as wealthy and powerful men took mistresses. Children have traditionally been viewed as the most valuable property to come from marriage, and large families with many children to work the land and provide security in old age were prized.

Industrial changes shattered much of this pattern. Family patterns do not change overnight, however, and around the world, changes are still taking place. Families are smaller and more flexible. Arranged marriage is still practiced in Asia, particularly in India, but instead of children being betrothed at eight and nine, arrangements may be made between the families of two college graduates, each of whom can claim veto power over the match. For the 5,000 years that agrarian societies dominated much of the world, marriage was about property, work, and kinship obligations. Romance was a dangerous game for the wealthy. Companionship came from same-sex peers. Increasingly, or maybe once again, marriage is about romance and companionship for young people around the world. This makes marriage more optional. Many are waiting longer to marry and are thus more likely to engage in marriage-like behavior, such as living together (Nanda 2019).

The idea of marriage as primarily about companionship rather than just legitimizing procreation has also accompanied a decades-long struggle for marriage equality for same-sex couples. Rapidly changing cultural attitudes have resulted in the legalization and recognition of same-sex marriage in much of the Americas and Western Europe along with South Africa and the Pacific. Most of Eastern Europe, Asia, and Africa, however, remain deeply resistant to the idea (see figure 3.1).

Marriages based on romance and companionship may be more appealing, but they are also more fragile. World divorce rates continue to rise. In the United States, the divorce rate has been increasing since the late 1800s. It reached a peak in 1946, only to drop markedly during the 1950s. For a brief time, earlier ideals of motherhood and family again dominated, and divorce carried a great stigma. This changed during the 1960s, and divorce again peaked in the 1970s. Divorce rates in the United States have plateaued since that time. Divorce has likewise increased in much of Europe. However, U.S. divorce rates remain the highest in the industrial world (see figure 3.2), in part because marriage remains very popular in the United States. Northern Europeans are slower to marry in the first place and so less likely to have a formal divorce. The Roman Catholic Church has long held a strong stance against divorce, and rates are lower in staunchly Catholic countries, such as Ireland, Italy, and Poland. Yet numbers can be deceiving: In Italy, cohabitation outside marriage and church-sanctioned annulments of marriages mean that coupling and recoupling can occur without formal divorce.

For a long time, the lowest divorce rates in the industrial world were found in Japan. The reason for this, however, was not necessarily happier marriages but a strong stigma against divorce coupled with lower expectations for marriage. Consider the following:

> Yuri Uemura sat on the straw tatami mat of her living room and chatted cheerfully about her 40-year marriage to a man whom, she mused, she never particularly liked. "There was never any love between me and my husband," she said blithely, recalling how he used to beat her. "But, well, we survived." (Kristof 1996, 33)

Not all Japanese couples are this distant, of course, but it is a common pattern, particularly among an older generation:

> Osamu Torida furrowed his brow and looked perplexed when he was asked if he loved his wife of 33 years. "Yeah, so-so, I guess," said Mr. Torida, a cattle farmer. "She's like air or water. You couldn't live without it, but most of the time, you're not conscious of its existence." (Kristof 1996, p. 34)

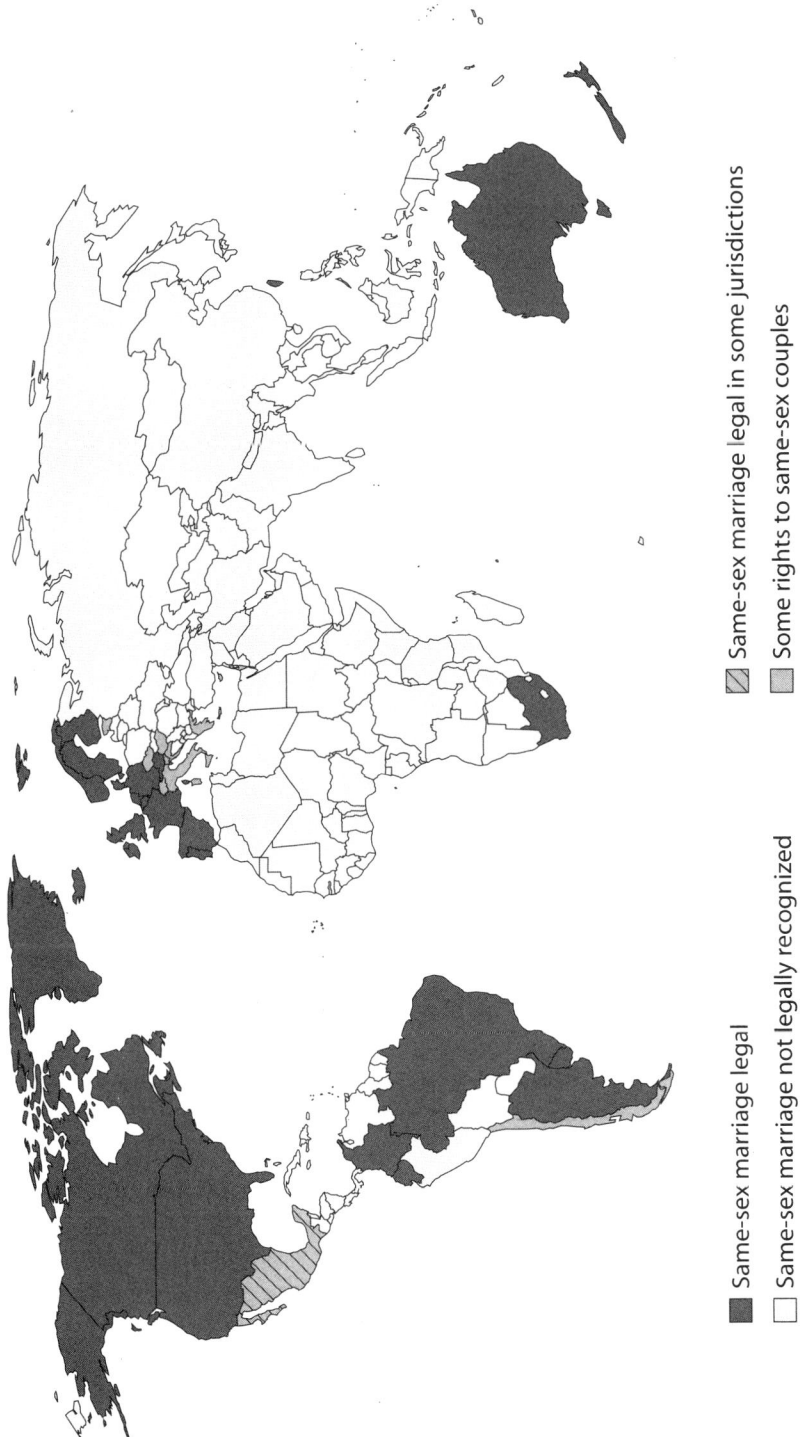

Figure 3.1 Same-sex marriage recognition, 2019. (Source: Our World in Data.)

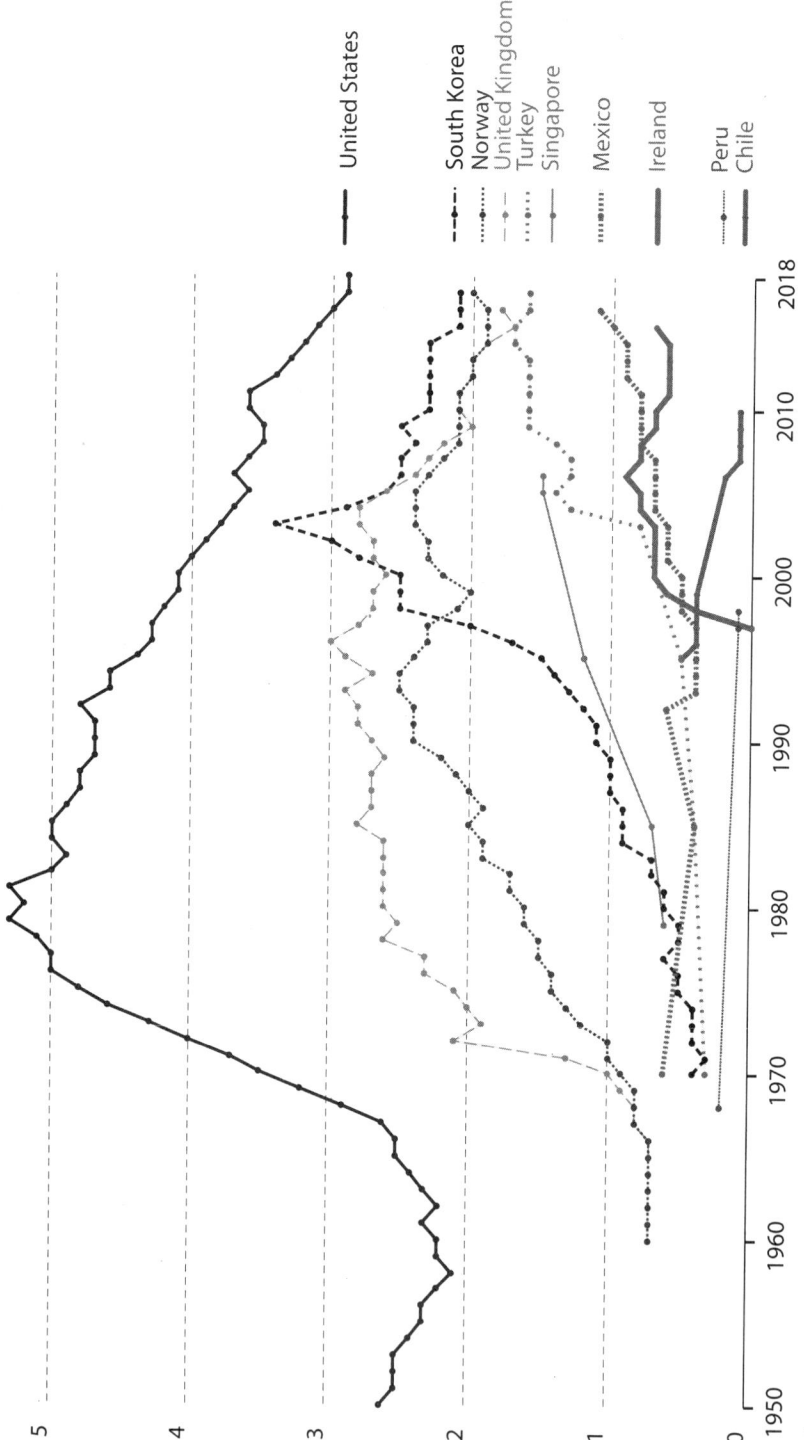

Figure 3.2 Divorce rates per 1,000 people, 2018. (Source: Our World in Data.) For all countries and trends over time, see https://ourworldindata.org/grapher/divorces-per-1000-people.

The demands of work and obligation are a common theme. But these hardworking marriages have also proved quite durable. This was once also common in the West, and it is now also changing in Japan. Most new divorces are now initiated by women who are tired of being afterthoughts in their husband's busy lives.

Divorce rates are also climbing all across Latin America, in spite of a strong Catholic and agrarian heritage. Only the semiarranged marriages of India seem to be particularly enduring. But the pattern seems inescapable: It is the people who marry out of obligation that seem to feel compelled to remain together. People who choose to marry and choose whom to marry sometimes choose to break up.

The emotional struggles of divorce may confront men and women equally, but the economic consequences do not. Since men more often command greater economic power and since women often have the primary responsibility for children, divorce places many women and their children at risk for poverty. This feminization of poverty is becoming a global phenomenon.

Parenting

Changes in work and marriage have also complicated the task of parenting. Mothers have long worked with their children close at hand, and many still do: with young children playing in the back of the vendor's booth, in the shade next to the farm field, and next to the loom and the cookware at home. At any Latin American, African, or South Asian market, there are a lot of children: the older ones sewing, painting, or stacking fruit and the younger ones watching the crowds slip by. Itinerant vendors have it harder, as they sling their small children on one side of their body and dangle their wares from the other.

This arrangement becomes more complicated as work pulls mothers into less family-friendly environments. In Europe, governments eager to get children on a strong start and to encourage births provide a generous maternity leave followed by heavily subsidized childcare. Mothers (and often fathers, if they wish) can spend the first year with their babies on full or near-full pay and then leave their growing infants in the hands of caregivers at a variety of day care settings, such as France's heavily subsidized *écoles maternelles*. In China and India, the caregiver is more likely a grandmother or other older family member. In the United States, the pattern is mixed. Low-income parents may find some help with subsidized day care, while others either use private day care, trade shifts between parents, or seek home-based jobs that can be done with children alongside.

The challenges grow for single parents who don't have a partner to help. In the United States, single parenting is the single greatest risk factor for poverty. A common cycle is evident: Women in communities in which few men have stable employment eventually begin their parenting alone or with an unreliable partner. The single parent, in turn, may find it even harder to escape the poverty of the community. The connection between single parenting and poverty is mediated by the surrounding society. Single fathers in the United States, a small but growing group, are less likely to be poor than single mothers (U.S. Bureau of the Census 2004), since men tend to earn more and can often only get custody if they can show economic stability.

Public policy also makes a huge difference. Sweden has one of the world's highest rates of single parenthood yet also one of the lowest rates of child poverty. How can this be? First, many single mothers in Sweden do have a partner present but have chosen not to marry. Second, even when the woman is truly on her own, the choice to have a child is often made later in life, when she is more financially stable. Finally, a strong system of government supports for children—health, education, and childcare—make it easier to raise a child without a partner. In Africa, Latin America, and low-income communities in North America, single mothers most often depend on a network of family and neighbors to informally provide support and childcare.

The greatest challenges are those that young single parents or teen mothers face. The patterns here are more complex than they may first appear. Despite the tremendous alarm of concern over teen mothers, the teenage pregnancy rate in the United States is at an all-time low. Why, then, the alarm? It is also true that teen marriage is at an all-time low, so that over 95 percent of births to teenagers occur to single mothers. In earlier times, including the 1950s, it was not uncommon for a woman to be married at 18 and to be pregnant at 19, or perhaps the other way around. So, there were lots of teen mothers, but they were older teens and they were married, even if many of those marriages were unstable. Births to teens are increasingly to unmarried teens and sometimes to younger teens, a pattern first seen in the United States but now becoming common elsewhere. A teen mother at 13 or 14 is much less likely to have completed secondary school and be ready to begin parenting than a teen mother at 18 or 19.

The main reason that younger girls are getting pregnant is they can now do so. In most societies of the past, a girl of 13 or 14 would not have yet menstruated. Some experimented sexually and others were sexually abused, but they didn't become pregnant because they weren't biologically able. A pattern not fully understood—a high-calorie, high-nutrient diet, coupled with a low level of exercise—has resulted not only in a higher proportion of body fat among young women but also in menstruation at a younger age and the possibility of pregnancy.

In simple horticultural societies, it was not uncommon for girls to first menstruate at 15 or 16 and to be married by 16 or 17. Premarital pregnancy wasn't a problem. Agrarian societies continued to marry off most young women at a young age and strictly chaperoned the rest to avoid pregnancy. In situations where chaperoning failed, marriage quickly followed an unexpected pregnancy. The so-called shotgun marriage was common in colonial America, where it seemed to carry little stigma (Coontz 2016), and again became common in the 1950s in the United States (Rubin 1992 [1976]). With the average age of menstruation at around 13 and the average age of first marriage creeping up to 26, U.S. women now have a 13-year window of possibility for premarital pregnancy.

After a brief rise in the teen pregnancy rate in the early 1980s, the rate is again falling in the United States, due to greater emphasis on sexual abstinence by some and to greater attention to contraception by others:

> Researchers often sum up the findings in one tidy phrase: "less sex, more contraception." But there is nothing simple about their puzzlement over the reasons. (Bernstein 2004)

This pattern has prevailed in much of Europe for some time, where beginning sexual activity is planned and preceded by a contraceptive decision. The United States has one of the highest rates of teenage pregnancy in the industrial world because it neither chaperones, as is common in Asia, nor has the broad and open availability of contraception common in Europe. Thus, U.S. teenagers are seemingly getting mixed messages about the onset of sexual activity. Just as this double message seems to be declining in the United States, it is increasing in Latin America. Traditional chaperoning and early marriage of girls is declining, but many families are reluctant to talk about contraception (*South Bend Tribune* 2005). As a result, unmarried teenage pregnancy rates are growing in many Latin American cities and among some U.S. Latinas. As education about AIDS (acquired immune deficiency syndrome) grows in Latin America, there is a gradual movement toward more open discussion of safe sex. AIDS is a huge concern in Africa, but poverty, limited choices, and limited information still lead to high rates of young pregnancy. At the same time, AIDS has brought to modern Africa what was the most common reason for single parenting in the United States and Europe a century ago: the death of a parent.

As rising divorce rates, falling marriage rates, and delayed marriages make single parenting more common around the world, governments and communities are confronted with the task of easing this burden for both single parents and their children. Rising unemployment and underemployment, coupled with disabling diseases, also mean that in many communities (and in poor communities, in particular), even extended and two-parent families may have only one wage earner, and this person is increasingly likely to be female and poorly paid.

Half the Sky

The Continued Perils of Being Female

The United Nations Population Fund 2000 report noted that conditions for women around the world had improved since 1994, when 179 countries pledged to do more for their women. Yet the report also noted that throughout the world, women continued to be victims of violence, sexual exploitation, and discrimination—at great cost both to their own well-being and to their countries' economies. The report cited links among abuse, illness, early death, dangerous abortions, and personal degradation. The UN Department of Economic and Social Affairs report, *The World's Women 2020: Trends and Statistics* (n.d.), notes 25 years of progress in education, legislation, and women in leadership. It also notes the setbacks of COVID-19 and the many tasks remaining: "Twenty-five years since the adoption of the Beijing Declaration and Platform for Action, progress towards equal power and equal rights for women remains elusive. No country has achieved gender equality, and the COVID-19 crisis threatens to erode the limited gains that have been made." UN Sustainable Development Goals (n.d.) highlight the challenges ahead:

- Globally, 750 million women and girls were married before the age of 18 and at least 200 million women and girls in 30 countries have undergone FGM (female genital mutilation).

- In 18 countries, husbands can legally prevent their wives from working; in 39 countries, daughters and sons do not have equal inheritance rights; and 49 countries lack laws protecting women from domestic violence.

- One in five women and girls, including 19 percent of women and girls aged 15 to 49, have experienced physical and/or sexual violence by an intimate partner within the last 12 months. Yet, 49 countries have no laws that specifically protect women from such violence.

Women have been gradually moving into prominent positions in governments around the world. Globally, the percentage of women in national legislatures has slowly risen from 12 percent in 1997 to almost 25 percent in 2020. During this time, several Latin American countries, including Brazil, Chile, and Costa Rica, elected their first female president. Cuba has a very high representation of women, and Mexico has almost doubled its female representation in just over a decade. Saudi Arabia has gone from zero representation in 2011 to almost 20 percent in 2020 (World Bank 2020a). Germany's Angela Merkel has been at the center of European politics for over 15 years, but new, younger leadership is also emerging—Jacinda Ardern became prime minister of New Zealand in 2017 at age 36 and Sanna Merin became prime minister of Finland in 2019 at age 34. Overall, Europe has seen a greater rise in female representation in government than have North Africa and Asia (see figure 3.3). Globally, most heads of state, judges, and legislators are still overwhelmingly male.

Women also still earn less than men, on average, around the world (see figure 3.4). This gap has been closing, in part due to the displacement of men from secure employment, as noted earlier in this chapter. In fact, most of the gains of U.S. women relative to men have been the result of men losing

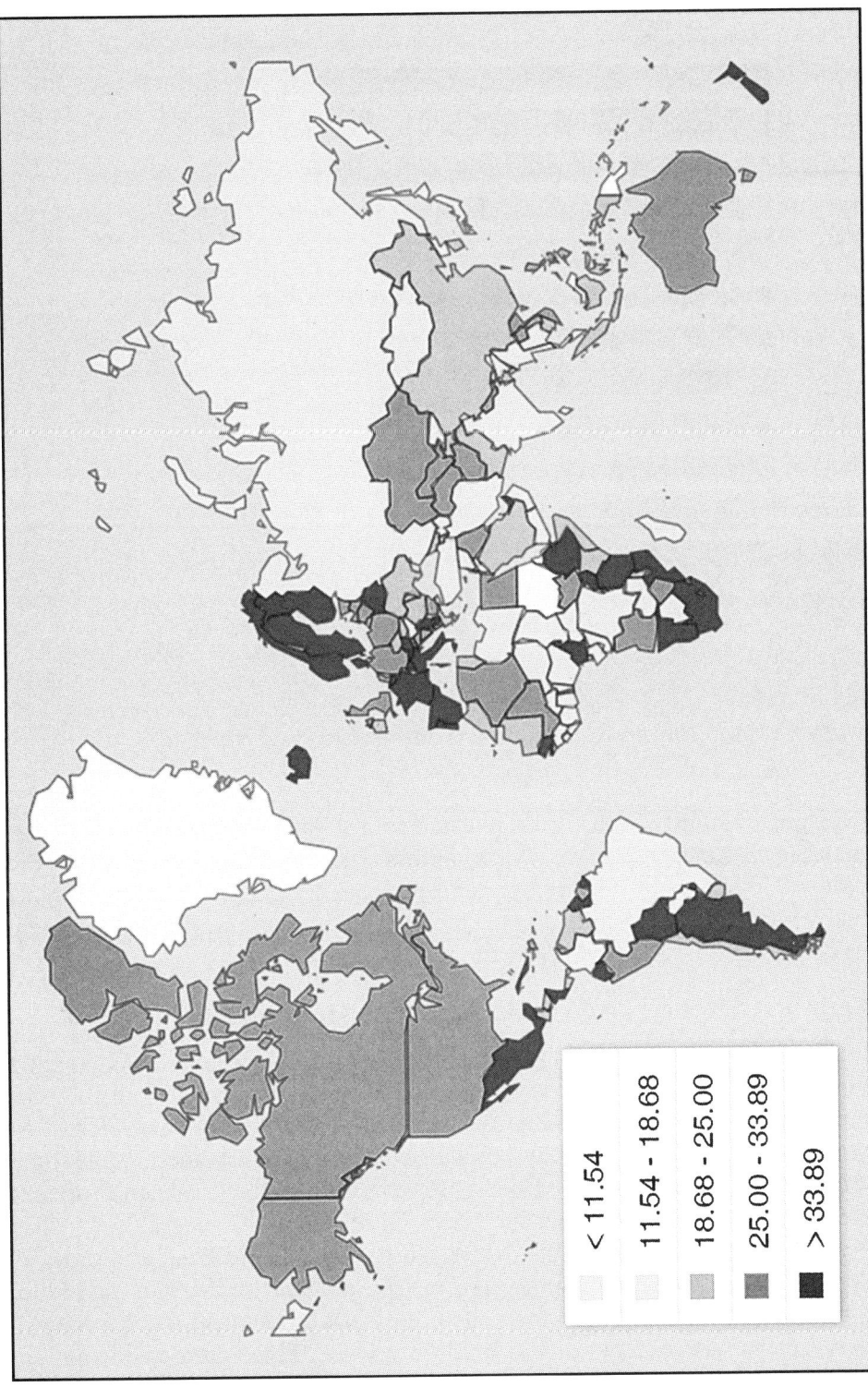

Figure 3.3 Proportion (%) of seats held by women in national parliaments, 1997–2020. (Source: World Bank.)

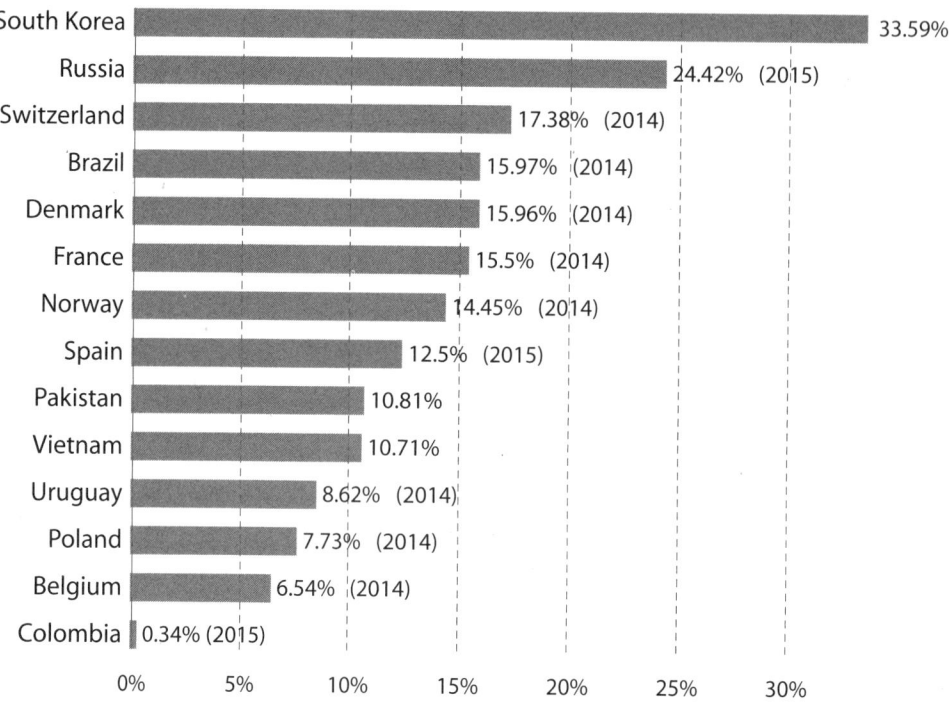

Figure 3.4 Gender pay gap in selected countries. (Source: Our World in Data.) For maps and further data see https://ourworldindata.org/economic-inequality-by-gender.

high-wage unionized jobs. Europe has a somewhat smaller gender-wage gap than North America. Japan, which has less class inequality than much of the industrialized world, has greater gender inequality. Japanese women report many hurdles to advancing to upper levels in the business world, and Japanese women's earnings are well below those of Japanese men.

Feminist Theory and World Feminist Movements

For at least the first 5,000 years of civilization, which were characterized by large-scale agrarian and pastoral societies, men dominated both the economic and political life in most societies. Feminist theorists have referred to this as our "legacy of patriarchy," or male control and dominance. While some feminist writers have ascribed this patriarchy to a particular history of religious and political thought in the West (Gimbutas and Dexter 2001), it has been the pattern as well across North Africa, the Middle East, and most of Asia (Ruether 2005). Patriarchy, like racism, is about more than individual attitudes. Rather, it refers to the structure of institutions and whole societies in ways that subordinate women, children, and anything considered feminine.

A worldwide feminist movement has grown to challenge these structures. The women's movement in the United States first emerged in the 1840s and was associated with movements for the abolishment of slavery, temperance (the banning of alcohol, consumed mostly by men and which led to abandoned families and domestic violence), and suffrage (the right to vote). The road was a slow one: Abolition came in 1865, but the right to vote for U.S. women was not national until 1920. Interest in the prohibition of alcohol came and went. Suffrage movements also grew in Great Britain, which did not grant women the right to vote until 1927.

The U.S. feminist movement again gained strength in the 1960s and 1970s, alongside other movements for greater equality and civil rights. Today women's movements have emerged in Latin America and in Asia. The UN Conference on Women stressed the link between women's rights in particular and human rights in general. Hillary Clinton spoke of this connection in her address to the group:

> It is a violation of human rights when a leading cause of death worldwide among women ages 14 to 44 is the violence they are subjected to in their own homes.... If there is one message that echoes forth from this conference, it is that human rights are women's rights—and women's rights are human rights. (Clinton 1995, 5–6)

Only recently has there been much talk of a men's movement, or a masculinist movement. In his book *Iron John*, U.S. poet Robert Bly (2004) called on men to get back in touch with their masculine side, not the "savage man" who is brutal and violent, but what he termed the "wild man," who enjoys his masculinity. A Maasai elder, in an ancient East African herding society known for the bravery and fierceness of its *maroni* (warriors), makes a similar distinction: A good maroni fearlessly takes up his spear and shield to face the enemy or the lion, a good maroni readily lays down his spear and shield when nurture rather than valor is called for, and a great maroni knows when to do what. The growth of the Promise Keepers organization for evangelical Christian men and the Million Man March for African American men showed renewed interest in male roles and men reclaiming their responsibilities. Both movements, however, seem to have stressed reclaiming earlier roles and responsibilities, which may not be available or even desirable for men in a changing world economy and culture.

Feminist movements continue to work for the rights of women. But feminist theory has also gone on to reconsider how societies construct their ideals of masculinity and femininity and often devalue the latter. Sometimes there may have been utility in assigning women the role of nurturer and tender of the home and community and having men specialize as warriors, physical laborers, and procreators. But the contemporary world has less need of all three men's roles. Societies, communities, and families are going to be forced to rethink and broaden the roles for both men and women and to welcome and assign equal value to the contributions of each.

In their book *Half the Sky: Turning Oppression into Opportunity for Women Worldwide,* Nicholas Kristof and Sheryl WuDunn (2009) quote the Chinese proverb that women hold up half the sky, but they then go on to document how women are often not allowed to share power and responsibility in equal measure, limiting not only their own lives and development but also the development possibilities for their communities and countries. Kristof and WuDunn argue that educating and empowering women is the single best way to fight poverty and extremism. Women aren't the problem, they are the solution—or at least half the solution, with men committed to creative change as the other half.

Key Ideas

- ➤ Gender relations and expectations are changing around the world. In many strained societies, the pattern has been for women to become overburdened with old and new tasks even as men are displaced from traditional roles and tasks.

- ➤ Gains have been made in gender equality in the last two decades. But nowhere in the world do women experience full parity in society, work, and government with men. In many of the poorest places in the world girls lag behind boys in access to schooling. Everywhere in the world women are underrepresented in top government and corporate positions and have average wages lower than their male counterparts.

- ➤ Changes in almost every society around the globe have made choices about whom and when to marry as well as the choice to divorce more common. Relations between spouses and between parents and children have often become more equal, but sometimes also more contentious.

- ➤ Women are particularly at risk for human trafficking, exploitation, and sexual violence. These risks are greatest in conflict zones but have also become part of a global pattern.

For Review and Discussion

1. Why is it that in some parts of the world, women are overburdened with many tasks, while men are displaced from many of their roles? Why can't the men just take on some of the tasks being done by women?

2. Are global changes making for stronger, happier, and more equal families and marriages, or are they undermining the traditional strength of marriages and families? What are the losses and gains?

3. What are particular challenges and dangers faced by women in the world? What must be done to make the world a safer, more equitable place for women and children?
4. Do you consider yourself a feminist? What do you see as the positives and negatives of that term? Do you see gains being made by global women's movements? Is there a need for a global men's movement?

Making Connections

UNFPA
> The United Nations Population Fund (which still uses an old acronym, UNFPA) is at www.unfpa.org. This UN agency works worldwide on issues of family planning, prenatal care and women's reproductive health, and related issues. It has at times been controversial amidst some groups for its promotion of contraception availability and education. The site has a wealth of information on maternal issues, as well as human rights issues for women and girls, such as ending sexual violence.

UNESCO
> Look at the United Nations Economic and Social Council (UNESCO) International Women's Day site at https://en.unesco.org/commemorations/womenday. Which aspects of gender are addressed? What are some of UNESCO's major initiatives? What does UNESCO do to address gender equality?

UN Sustainable Development Goals
> Goal #5 is Gender Equality: "to achieve gender equality and empower all women and girls." See the challenges and efforts on this vast project at https://www.un.org/sustainabledevelopment/gender-equality/. Look at the Facts and Figures for the challenges, and then follow the links to the literature prepared by the many organizations tasked with addressing different aspects of these challenges.

Making a Difference

Half the Sky
> A website to extend the challenge of the book by the same title can be found at www.halftheskymovement.org. The site contains stories of women from around the world who face challenges, and it provides the names of its partner organizations, located around the world, working for the

empowerment of women and girls. Included are organizations centered around education, maternal health, economic empowerment, combating sexual violence, and more. Decide which issues interest you and why.

Women's Shelters

➤ What services does your community offer abused, homeless, or troubled women? Check your local United Way or directory of social services to see what is offered in your area. Also ask about advocacy and information programs offered locally on domestic violence, sexual assault, and gender issues.

Women's Health Services

➤ What does your community offer in the way of women's health services? Check for a local chapter of Planned Parenthood (www.plannedparenthood.org) and find out what it is doing to deal with the problem of unplanned pregnancy. Look at the global site (https://www.plannedparenthood.org/about-us/planned-parenthood-global). What is being done globally by Planned Parenthood? Are there other organizations active in your community or schools, such as "abstinence-only" groups? How do the philosophies and approaches differ?

NOW

➤ Go to the website of the National Organization of Women (NOW) at www.now.org. Look at their initiatives in global feminism https://now.org/now-foundation/global-feminism/ and developing a Young Feminist Taskforce https://now.org/yftf/. Find a local chapter and visit it, if possible, to discuss issues. What topics/issues are you able to discover as you navigate the sites?

4

Education

Access and Success

Global Encounters

India

Southern Tamil Nadu state is a land of temples. Great towering temples to Shiva and Vishnu rise from the crowded streets of Kancheepuram, and huge sculpted elephants and bulls of granite from the eighth century loom over the beaches of Mamallapuram. But the greatest temples line the highways that connect these ancient cities to Chennai (formerly Madras). Gleaming new temples with towers and pointed domes whose antiquity is less than five years. They are not built in the southern style but look a bit more like exuberant losers in a design contest for a new Taj Mahal. They are temples to learning. Only a decade ago, learning in this area meant attending the stately buildings of Madras University, a bit of Cambridge on the edge of the Georgetown area of what was British Madras. The temples line the highways and sprawl along the rice fields. They have great entry arches and billboards. Some of these temples are Christian and others have the picture of a respected bearded and robed swami as their founder. They are all colleges. We pass a huge new medical school, a nursing school featuring both modern and alternative medicines, and many temples to engineering and the industrial arts. Their huge campuses will not fit in crowded Chennai and so they sprawl outward along the highways with students arriving in lines of buses. The narrow roads have wide shoulders bulldozed into the red mud and are lined with tiny stores, tin-roofed houses, and thatched huts. Some of the huts are so new, they are built right on the new road bed, occupying a bit of mud in the few months between the clearing and the paving of this land. Newcomers from the city and the country have come here to work.

They also share the road with other newcomers: Hyundai motors, a French glass factory, and the postmodern architecture of Pentasoft Technologies. The streets of Chennai are crowded with the old and not-so-old India, crammed with vehicles, and have no room for the new India. So, new is moving out in great swaths of sprawl. The land is cheaper, at least until a few years ago, and there is less congestion on the new highways, at least for the moment. As the road widens it also opens a new e-highway: high connectivity cable to support information technology.

We risk a highway crossing to move on to see the rice paddies, and behind them the ramshackle housing of the migrant construction workers. Just beyond, the great temple-like buildings of Jeppiaar Engineering College sprawl across the horizon. It is a cliché to say India is a mix of old and new. All the world is the new intruding on, layering over, and mixing among the old. But India is especially fervent, even reverent, about each. Only here is traditional clothing—the saris of the women, the longyi wraps of the men—worn every day, for work, not festivals. Here our host's parents tend the temple they built on their land for two and a half hours every day, while he grapples with lawyers and figures profit margins. We ride a bullock cart over the red earth and chat in English with our host and his photographer as I frame the view in my digital camera. From the ship's photographer, I have learned the rule of thirds: foreground, rice paddies; middle ground, thatched temporary shacks; background, the new temples of learning. Past, present, and future superimposed.

The signs amid the construction warn: "Drive slow, you are entering the new millennia." More than one? I wonder. All I see are lines of shacks lining the roadway to the horizon. What of this sign? Is that a typo or is there more than one new millennium, maybe depending on who you are? I have seen the new millennia as we traverse this stretch of highway, dubbed the "One in a Million Office Park." And I can report: The new millennia have a lot of highway overpasses. They have a lot of mud, embedded with broken brick and plastic refuse. And they have lots of squatter housing huddled between the road and the high rise—waiting and hoping.

Brazil

Brazil, for all its color and exuberance, for all its cultural blending and diversity, remains a divided land. Brazil is divided by social class and is one of the most unequal countries in the world. In Salvador da Bahia on Brazil's northeast coast, the contrasts are incredible. Great towers of condominiums overlook the bay with balconies of subtly varied colors. These towers would make a contemporary, sophisticated addition to Chicago's Gold Coast or Manhattan's East

Side. They have their private cable car access to the beach. Beaches in Brazil are supposed to be public, but that doesn't mean that the public needs to have access to all of them. Private beach parties bring together those who have truly arrived. The upper classes in Brazil live well. Middle-class apartments shoulder up next to theirs, a bit older and shabbier, not quite as tall, and in need of maintenance. The middle class in Brazil is large but precarious. They look up to the taller towers of their wealthier neighbors and aspire; they look down at the tumbledown shacks below and they wonder.

Everywhere in Salvador, often in pockets between nicer housing, one finds the layer upon layer of cramped, one- or two-room do-it-yourself housing that Brazilians call favelas. I'm leading a group of students to visit one of the most progressive of these favelas. We walk through eroded but safe streets and meet the community leaders. They have a small radio station that reaches the neighborhood for both entertainment and organizing. A minimally staffed clinic treats emergencies and does public health education. A few years ago, the main issue of concern was cholera, and the warning signage remains. Once the residents connected to the city water supply, and no longer had to depend on a muddy brown stream for their water, concern over cholera faded and was replaced by programs to educate on the dangers of AIDS.

The centerpiece of the work is the community school. Several dozen young children welcome us to their courtyard and the three stories of small classrooms. We play capoeira, Brazilian martial arts dancing, with them. We take paints out to the courtyard and join them in adding designs, names, and phrases in English and Portuguese to the walls. My students hand out crayons and markers and are soon surrounded by children begging for more, and for the paper to use these on. Begging aside, this school is fun and encouraging, at least until about age 12. There are no secondary school opportunities in the favela, and few children ever go on to higher education. Above us is more of the favela but there is no tour there, for the upper part is still ruled by drug "lords": lords of a small and poor realm, but possessive nonetheless.

These are the dilemmas of many countries around the world, including advanced industrial countries: How can we educate all children, rich and poor, male and female? And what should they learn? What should the standards be, and who should decide on the curriculum? And how do we keep them safe and engaged throughout the long process of getting a good education, especially when school is an enclave in an otherwise dangerous world?

The Foundations of Education

The idea that children belong in school is actually quite new. For most of human experience, formal education was for a select few. Most learning was practical and occurred between parents and children, masters and apprentices. Beyond this, value was given to the ancient stories, verses, and rules that defined a people and their culture. Even the simplest bands often have esteemed storytellers who guard the ancient wisdom. For instance, the oral stories of Dreamtime among Australian Aborigines are complex, vivid, and highly valued as a source of understanding. In larger groups, tribal elders, both male and female, have guarded the ancient stories and passed them on through the long practice of memorization.

At first, writing didn't help much. A written text could replace a human memory, but writing was a complex and hard-to-learn business. It was limited to a few dedicated scribes who worked their styluses over clay tablets first in Sumer, then wrote on papyrus in Egypt, and later wrote on paper in China and parchment in European monasteries. They kept accounts; they copied laws; and they began to write down the ancient tales of heroes, victories, and calamities, as well as the sacred verses and the honored proverbs. Mastery of this material, *education*, could be a means to advancement.

At several times in the history of China, the imperial bureaucracy was filled by merit; only those who passed the entrance exams were given positions. For centuries, however, the civil service exams consisted mostly of showing that one had memorized the writings of K'ung Fu-tzu (Confucius) and other important texts. In ancient Greece, knowledge was highly valued, but schooling was associated with leisure. As such, it was the pursuit of aristocrats and their children and a few esteemed philosophers, some who opened their own schools, many who tutored, and most who were quite poor. In 343 BCE, Philip II of Macedon could afford to hire Aristotle to tutor his son, Alexander, in social and natural philosophy. From Aristotle, Alexander learned political theory, biology, astronomy, and mathematics, but he also needed to study the arts of cavalry and infantry offense to lead the campaigns that would make him Alexander the Great.

One of the great things that Alexander did was to found a city on the Egyptian coast that, like many other founders, he named after himself. Alexandria became a center of learning. It was home to a great museum, not just a collection of objects but a research laboratory of sorts, where the muses inspired wise minds. It also had a great library, filled with great scrolls in many languages; written on some were new ideas in science and philosophy, and on others ancient sacred and honored texts. The librarians were no slouches, either. One, a fellow by the name of Eratosthenes, measured with incredible accuracy the circumference of the world based on measurements of the inclination of the sun's rays.

But libraries are expensive and difficult to maintain. The one at Alexandria fell into ruin and burned. The next great centers of learning were Islamic universities—in some ways, the world's first. These great centers of learning gathered what had not been lost from ancient Greece, including the wisdom of Aristotle that Alexander had carried across the Middle East. They had the mathematics of Pythagoras and added the "new math" disciplines like algebra.

European learning was centered in the great monasteries for close to 800 years, but gradually, in the newly powerful cities, new universities emerged: Bologna, Oxford, Cambridge, the Sorbonne, and so forth. Still, learning remained largely the domain of priests, monks, sometimes nuns (such as Sor Juana) and other religious specialists, a handful of scribes and philosophers (in Europe now called *Doctors of Philosophy*), and the children of aristocrats. The subjects also changed little. The first universities in the United States all had similar curricula: theology and sacred texts, mathematics, rhetoric, and the ancient languages of Latin and Greek, mostly useful for reading ancient texts and tales. However, most children learned as they had before: from their parents and elders and from master tradespeople.

By the 1700s the key to education for laborers in Great Britain did not lie in the great universities of Cambridge and Oxford but in **apprenticeships.** In these outgrowths of the medieval guilds, the skills associated with trades were learned from master tradespeople. In the colonial United States, apprenticeships also flourished but with the added expectation that basic literacy and math skills also be taught to help the apprentice become an effective tradesperson and citizen. In fact, across the southern U.S. colonies, where slavery flourished, slaves and apprentices often worked in similar trades, both bound to their masters. The apprentices were taught the skills, including literacy, that would be expected of a free citizen; the slaves were not.

Not everyone was satisfied with this system. A bright, young printer named Benjamin Franklin had gone as far as the apprenticeship system would allow, but all of his flair for science, math, and language would not be enough to get him into a university. He persuaded the prominent citizens of Philadelphia to sponsor an academy that would be open to all, regardless of family status or religion. (Gender and race remained contentious well into the late 1800s.) Franklin envisioned a more practical education, stressing English skills rather than Latin. The sciences would also be prominent, each with a practical application: biology for agriculture, astronomy for navigation, chemistry for pharmacology, and physics for engineering. Eventually his academy would provide the foundation for the University of Pennsylvania, although it would be decades before his more practical curriculum would dominate, even in public universities.

In a similar spirit, Thomas Jefferson claimed as his greatest accomplishment not writing the Declaration of Independence or serving as U.S. president but founding the University of Virginia. He built it in a classical style he had found in his own studies at Williamsburg. But he envisioned providing an education for all with the interest and ability, one rooted in the practical needs of a democracy. Education for democracy was also the driving vision of the great progressive reformer John Dewey, who was working at Columbia University in New York around the turn of the twentieth century. He argued for active learning, not rote memorization, as a route to active and informed citizenship.

These changes were slow to reach much of the rest of the world, which by Dewey's time, was dominated by European colonial powers. The epitome of cultured education, limited to a tiny elite, was education at one of the famous universities of Europe (a goal also sought by many in the United States). When schools were founded in Asia and Africa, they were typically based on the model of the colonial power. Thus, British education dominated in India and East Africa, while French education prevailed in French West Africa. The language, the history, even the uniforms were those of the colonial power. Many were mission schools, designed to teach religious values. In Latin America, religious orders also dominated the schooling, and both religious- and government-sponsored education followed European models: first Spanish and later British and French. In Central Africa, the Belgians maintained control of the vast Congo, in part by providing elementary education to all who could reach a school, but secondary education was available only to Europeans.

Everywhere in the colonized world, secondary education was for the few and higher education was the dream of only a small elite. Again, most people continued to learn as they had for centuries from family, elders, and master tradespeople. When Africa and Asia emerged from colonial control in the mid- to late twentieth century, one of the most pressing problems for the new governments was how to teach the masses, as well as what to teach them.

And Who Will Care for the Children?

Pakistan, a very poor nation of over 220 million people (one of the 10 most populous nations in the world), does not find it easy to educate all of its children. According to the United Nations, nearly 44 percent of the five-to-16-year-old age group is not in school (UNICEF n.d.). The madrassa schools often make up some of the difference and sometimes are the only places where girls learn literacy skills. The madrassas carry on a tradition of Islamic education, heavy on memorized texts that can inspire reverence or, as some worry, inspire radicalization (Bashir and Ul-Haq 2019). Moreover, Pakistan faces a big gender gap in education: Female illiteracy is twice that of males. Public schools are understaffed and ill equipped. Another problem Pakistan faces is that many poor rural and urban families depend on their children to contribute to the family income through work. Pakistan is often cited as one of the countries with the worst child labor abuses, but having children work is part of the social structure, as it is in many societies.

In the poorest and most rural parts of Latin America, South Asia, and Africa, the struggle has always been to get every child to school. Just like on the historic U.S. frontier, the local school in such an area may be small and poorly equipped—a one-room schoolhouse, if that—and larger schools offering higher levels of education may be too far away. For many rural U.S. children, the problem was also that they were needed on the farm, whether that farm was their family's homestead or whether their families were sharecroppers or migrant laborers working on the land of others. Providing consistent schooling for all remains a struggle in many places in the United States.

In poor, rural regions of the world, this struggle is greatly magnified. Children's labor is needed, especially as farm laborers. And when the farm economy breaks down, children are often needed as family wage earners. Even if Pakistan can provide schools for all, it will be a real struggle to get all children into those schools. It is not that parents don't care about their children's education but that every family member, including the very young, is needed to help, to provide income and food as well as look after siblings while parents are away seeking food and income.

Schools are more available to everyone in urban areas around the world, which is one of the attractions of city life for rural migrants. Yet even in the cities, schools in poor neighborhoods are often poorly maintained and poorly equipped. Absenteeism is high, as children are still needed as laborers, working as street vendors, sewing and helping run family businesses, and tending to younger siblings while parents are at work. This is common in the burgeoning cities of Latin America, as well as in parts of Africa and Asia, and even in Los Angeles and New York.

Education around the world is also very unequal by gender. When resources are scarce, families may have to decide which children will have the privilege of education and which will work to support that education. Often it is boys who are given the chance to pursue education. In many cultures, young men are more likely to stay close to home, to bring a wife into the family, and to support their parents in their later years. Girls may marry out to become part of another family, and so educating them is seen as a poor investment. Also, in cultures in which men interact in the marketplace and the community and women remain almost entirely at home, men are seen as needing at least basic math and literacy skills to buy and sell without being cheated, while women are believed to have less use for these skills. Interestingly, in cultures in which women remain to support their parents and men live with their in-laws, as well as in places in which women traditionally have had more prominence in the marketplace, the educational gap between boys and girls is the smallest.

While providing all children with a primary education is difficult, providing them with a secondary education has proved even harder. Around the world about two-thirds of all children never receive a high school education or its equivalent. Secondary schools are often far away for rural children. Poor urban children are needed for work and child care by the time they leave the primary grades. And in locations where good jobs are scarce, the practical benefits of a secondary education may not be obvious. Even in the United States, poor communities with few job opportunities and high unemployment among adults often have the greatest difficulty keeping their children in high school through graduation. It is too easy for children, and sometimes parents, to look around at the lack of economic opportunities and ask, What's the use?

Mauwa Funidi is a college graduate who works in a college library in Kisangani, Congo (Kristof 1996). She has a good education and what looked like a good job that would secure her place in the middle class of her country and provide for her extended family.

But the Congo is a troubled place. After its independence leader, Patrice Lumumba, was killed, the Congo was ruled by an absolute dictator, Mobuto Sese Seko (1967–1997). Mobuto ruled for most of the first three decades that the Congo was a nation, following its colonization as a vast private estate of the king of Belgium. Since Mobuto's death, the resource-rich country has been torn by civil war, refugee crises, and foreign intervention.

Mauwa's library has almost no books; none have been purchased since 1982. Books aren't much in demand, since university classes rarely meet. Even if the library had books, many of the people couldn't read them. Many places in the country are too dangerous for children to attend school, and so literacy rates are falling along with incomes. Mauwa's own salary has plummeted to $11 a month and often goes unpaid. Her extended family, once prominent and not stifled by unemployment, cannot count on her to provide for them. Instead, they must look to her sister, who has a more lucrative job at the Take-a-Peek bar.

Many in the Congo hope that education will be the answer to national development and personal success. But Mauwa already has a good education. There is simply not enough national stability and infrastructure for her to use it.

What constitutes the best route for completing a secondary education varies greatly around the world. In Europe, vocational programs and apprenticeships, both with traditions going back centuries, often begin in secondary school. Children who do not do well on tests or do not have an early desire for higher education are moved into vocational tracks and apprenticeships that will prepare them for trades. Japan and much of Latin America also use this model. In the United States, tracking is less formal and apprenticeships are often limited to a few trades. Yet in high school, children are often still divided into college-bound and vocational tracks, which may be very different from each other.

The United Nations collects data on current mean years of schooling around the world (see figure 4.1). It also estimates projected years of schooling for those just entering. The latter is increasing almost everywhere in the world. Ethiopia has a mean under three years of formal education, but newly entering students can expect an average of 8.5. Australia has the highest projected average of 22 years of school (UNHCR 2020).

The United States offers the opportunity to go to college to a larger portion of its students than most countries, ranging from community colleges to huge universities, although costs—and the nature of the experience—vary greatly. This is somewhat less common in Europe, where apprenticeships in trades have centuries-old roots but may still require rigorous preparation at the secondary school level, including in mathematics. In Japan the opportunity to get into a respected college is very limited and intensely competitive. In many poor countries, university education is limited to a very few.

The paths between these programs and between school and work are varied. There is worldwide agreement, at least at the national level, about the importance of education. There is much less agreement, however, about the related questions of how much? For whom? And of what type?

Education around the World

Great Britain

Well into the 1800s education was still primarily an avenue for the elite in Great Britain. Most factory workers and farm laborers had little formal education and were likely to be illiterate. Children of the elites went to private boarding schools, called *public schools*, such as Eton and Exeter. These schools prepared them for admission to an elite university, such as Oxford or Cambridge, and for a career. Such an education was especially important for the younger sons of landed gentry, who would not inherit their father's land and so needed a profession in law, medicine, government, the church, or the military. As fewer of the elites were large landowners, passing on privilege to their children increasingly meant giving them an elite education.

The boarding schools in Great Britain still flourish, though few are quite as exciting as the fictional Hogwarts known to Harry Potter fans. Britain's new rich see these schools as a way to give their children elite breeding, profitable acquaintances, and an entry into the upper level of British society. Just as many Americans seek an Ivy League education, British students covet admission

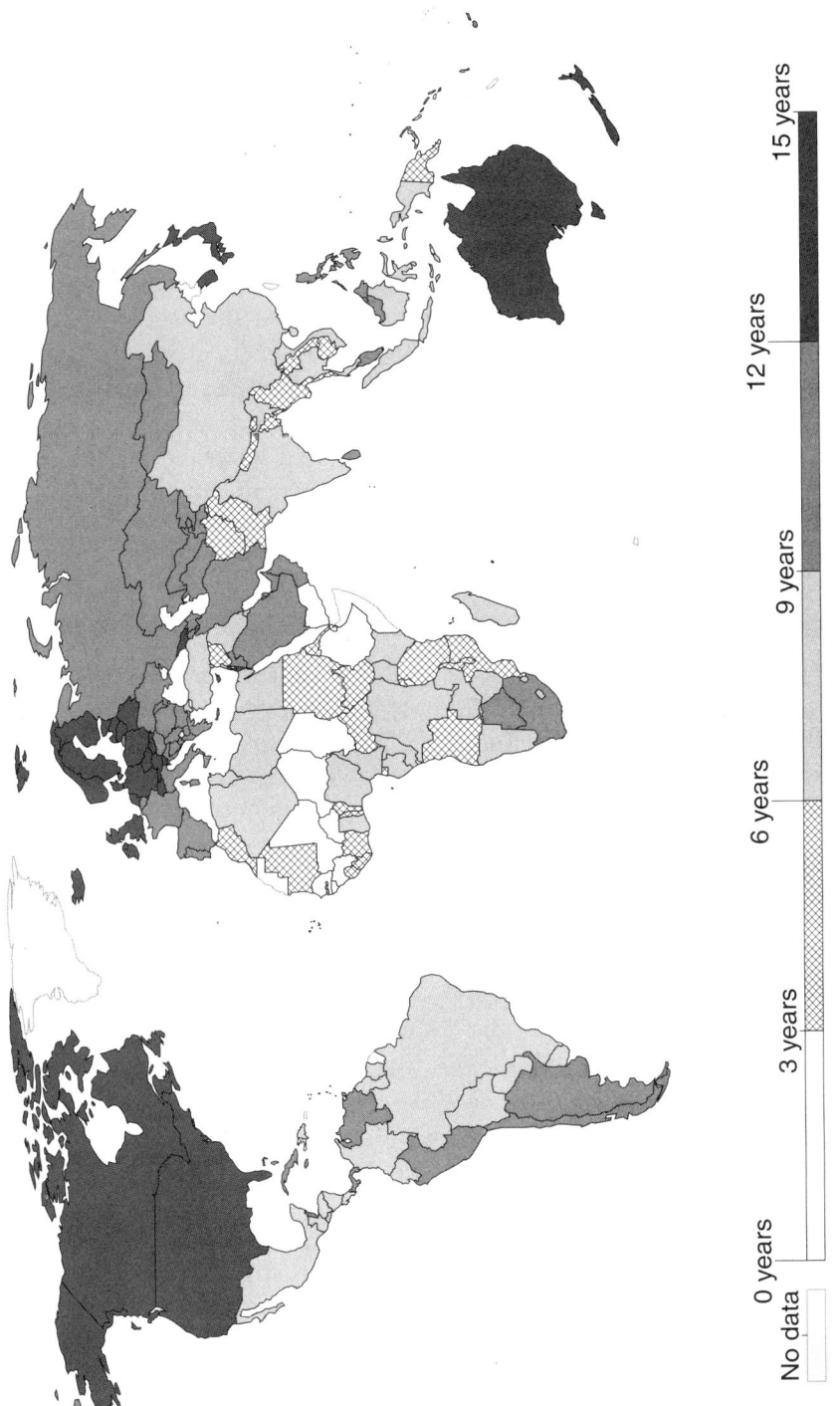

Figure 4.1 Mean years of schooling, 2017. (Source: Our World in Data.). To see how this has changed over time and for more detailed data on trends, see https://ourworldindata.org/global-education.

into Oxford and Cambridge. Most government officials, as well as business executives, can claim an "Oxbridge" degree from one of these two universities.

At the same time, there has been an effort in Great Britain to extend the reach of popular education. As early as the 1800s Robert Raikes began the Sunday school movement. This was not about religious education, although it had a strong moral component. Rather, Sunday was the only day that poor, young laborers were not working in the mills and factories; so it became their one day for school. Across Britain, historic efforts for universal primary education were often coupled with efforts to limit child labor: Children could only be in school if they weren't already in mines, mills, and sweatshops.

State-supported day schools now educate over 90 percent of British children, for whom an invitation to Eton may be as remote as an invitation to Hogwarts. College entrance is competitive, with the government paying most costs for those who do very well on the entrance exams. As occurred in the United States during the Reagan administration, government support for higher education began to decline in Great Britain in the 1980s, with a greater financial burden falling on the students themselves (Gutek 2022).

Japan

Education has long been valued in Japan, but it, too, was originally for only a small elite. In the early 1800s most Japanese children worked alongside their parents on peasant farms. Industrialization brought even harsher work, as children were used to dig coal in narrow mine shafts and to work in new industries, much as they did at this time and earlier in the United States and Great Britain. Industrialization also brought the need for a more educated population, and in 1872 the first laws were passed for mandatory basic education as part of Japan's governmental reforms.

With roots in earlier Shinto and Confucian models, Japanese education traditionally stressed discipline, order, and harmony (some would say conformity), as well as a great deal of study and memorization. Beginning in the late 1800s, however, Japan became much more enamored with Western science than with Chinese Confucian texts, and the focus of study shifted to math and science, where Japanese students continue to excel. Standardized tests, now popular in the United States, have also played a major role in Japanese education, especially in moving students on to higher levels.

Japanese high school graduation rates are high (over 95 percent, more than 10 percent higher than in the United States), but space in major universities is limited. While over 80 percent of Japanese students go on to postsecondary education, including vocational training, only just over half enter a major university (MEXT n.d.). A university education continues to carry significant prestige. This makes the university entrance process of supreme importance among the Japanese. It is not based heavily on family wealth or on a well-written essay or portfolio; rather, standardized test scores are the key criteria. Without high test scores, options for college are limited, even for the wealthy. But students who do not get into a major university are not abandoned, for Japan also has an extensive apprenticeship and worker training program.

Japanese high school students not only spend more time in school and study longer than their U.S. counterparts, they may also attend Saturday "cram schools" to give them an edge on the tests. Japanese schools also tend to have fewer electives and extracurricular activities, as they might distract students from the core subjects. Given the intense competition to get into key universities, U.S. observers are sometimes surprised to find how relaxed the atmosphere in Japanese colleges is, with students often studying less than their U.S. counterparts. Having been admitted, Japanese students often feel that they have arrived. They have honored their family and secured their future, so they can now relax a bit after the intense entrance competition. Traditionally major Japanese corporations recruited employees directly from the major universities and then offered their new hires essentially lifetime job security. Thus, while Japanese students felt much more stress than U.S. students as they prepared to enter college, they felt much less job and career stress as they left. However, this customary hiring process (*shūkatsu*) is changing, and now Japanese graduates face the same anxiety as their U.S. counterparts (Shabata 2019).

One reason for the traditionally high level of Japanese industrial productivity and quality appears to be that their workers are so well-educated, especially in math and science, compared to those in many other countries. For a while, many in the United States looked at Japanese successes on international test scores and in industrial productivity and innovation and wondered if Americans should adopt a more Japanese model. At the same time, educators in Japan visited the United States in hopes of adopting ideas for Japanese schools, making them more flexible and creative and offering more interaction and less rote memorization. Even though U.S. students lag behind their Japanese counterparts all through school, they seem to do very well in graduate school and in entrepreneurship, which require self-initiative and creative risk-taking.

In many ways, while they have been a study in contrasts, the U.S. and Japanese systems are starting to look more alike. Many U.S. proposals for school reforms are for measures already in place in Japan, such as greater use of rigorous standardized tests, longer school days, a "back to basics" curriculum with fewer electives and more emphasis on math and science, school uniforms, an emphasis on order and respect, and a greater emphasis on parent involvement in their children's education. At the same time, while proud Japanese parents still come to hear their uniformed children sing the school song in heartfelt unison, Japanese schools are becoming more flexible and have a new regard for hands-on learning.

China

Chinese education is both ancient and continually changing. Chinese Confucian society long honored the scholar as the most respected citizen below the emperor. At various times in China's long history, both the trusted advisors to the emperor and the administrators of regional provinces were scholars who had come up through the ranks of the civil service branch of government by passing examinations. These examinations tested knowledge of and ability to memorize ancient texts, including poetry, prose literature, and Confucian dissertations on the meaning and achievement of good government.

K'ung Fu-tzu, the man to whom the Westerners gave the Latin name of Confucius, lived from 551 to 478 BCE, a period known as "the time of warring states." He wrote about how to achieve good government and, with it, a harmonious society. These ideals were not easy to implement, and the rules of scholars were often interrupted by the rules of both foreign invaders and local warlords. Yet the ideal of dedication to scholarship and advancement through formal education remains rooted in the culture of China, and of much of East Asia to this day.

Another man had a different view of the making of a just and harmonious society. Mao Zedong, the Chinese Communist revolutionary who came to power in 1949, replaced conservative Confucian ideals with revolutionary communist ideals. But Mao also looked to education to advance the nation, in large measure by raising a new generation in the principles of Marxism, as interpreted by in his once-famous "little red book" of sayings. Westerners often made fun of "Confucius says" statements and either ridiculed Mao's little red book or saw it as dangerous propaganda. Yet the Chinese have long believed that education should shape the heart as well as the mind, perhaps a philosophical version of the basis of many religious schools around the world.

Contemporary Chinese education continues to emphasize moral education, rote learning, hard work, and mathematics. Now there is an increasing focus on technical training as well. The Chinese Communists placed great emphasis on expanding basic education to everyone, but like most of the developing world, educational quality and availability are much greater in urban than in rural areas. Many Chinese continue to look to formal education as their best means of advancement, even if it increasingly involves understanding the intricacies of an export economy, rather than the doctrines of either Mao or Confucius.

The surging interest in getting into top schools, and the limited number of spaces in those schools, has led to intense competition among students and their parents. An elite education can mean access to ever-expanding and lucrative professional and business opportunities. Not making the cut into a top school does not doom one to poverty but can mean being tied to industrial work with long hours and limited advancement. In the past, overseas education was crucial, and while it is still highly valued, top slots in Chinese universities are also coveted.

Even for young children, school days can be very long, as parents supplement public education with expensive tutors, often straining the family's finances. And the pressure on children and their "tiger mothers" can be intense (*Economist* 2018). While still promoting academic advancement, China has created a television program that encourages intense Chinese parents to relax a bit for the sake of their children (Pak 2021). The need to expend limited resources on a child's educational success also is keeping Chinese birthrates low, even as the government has lifted restrictions on the number of children a couple is allowed to have.

India

India is a huge country of more than one billion people, and so everything comes in large numbers. India may have more software engineers than any country in the world, including the United States. But, because of lack of jobs at home, India "exports" many of its highly trained technical and health professionals. Well-educated Indian physicians, businesspeople, and technical experts are found all across Europe and parts of Asia and Africa, and Indian Americans on the whole are the single most educated U.S. immigrant group. After years of effort, literacy in India is just over 74 percent, but this still leaves hundreds of millions, women in particular, without functional literacy (World Bank 2020b).

Most Indian children receive some primary education, but classes can be very large, with 50 students, and attendance—by both teachers and students—can be sporadic (UNESCO 2008). Expected education for school-aged children in India has climbed to over 12 years, a sharp rise from the current 6.5 mean years of schooling for all adults, and 5.4 years for women (United Nations 2020). These gains are well ahead of neighboring Pakistan and represent efforts by the nation and state governments, but they also mask continued deep regional and urban–rural divides.

Many rural children, especially girls, have to work to help support other family members. In some states of India, where male dominance has been the rule for centuries, the female illiteracy rate is very high. In others, such as Kerala in southern India, where women have traditionally held prominent positions, the educational levels of girls and boys are much more equal.

About 70 percent of Indian youths go on to secondary school, and a university education is a coveted opportunity (UNESCO 2008). Yet even for a university graduate, the job market may be tight, and having a career may mean leaving the country for another location, where technical skills and mastery of English are valuable commodities.

The contexts in which children learn vary greatly around the world, as seen in these classrooms in a government-run girls' school in India [top] and in a rural village school in Malawi, East Africa [bottom]. Overcrowding and limited facilities are common challenges.

Mexico

For more than 1,000 years preceding the arrival of the Spanish in the early 1500s, the pre-Hispanic Mexicans—the Amerindian peoples of Mesoamerica, such as Aztecs and Maya—valued education greatly. That education consisted largely of studying astronomy (with related mathematics) and memorizing ancient tales, just as with many other ancient peoples. Yet their accomplishments were substantial. Maya used place value and the zero perhaps before the people of India and certainly before Arabs and later Europeans adopted their use. They precisely calculated the orbit of Venus long before Copernicus ever ventured his theory about planets orbiting the sun.

Mesoamerican education was heavily class-based, training warriors, priests, administrators, and merchants for their roles. Yet it could also be a means of advancement for those who were especially promising. Following the Spanish conquest, education became the privilege of the Spanish elite, but not the peasants and certainly not the "Indians." The Catholic Church dominated Spanish education for the entire 300-year colonial period, from the 1520s to the 1820s.

Mexican independence fighters in the early 1800s, although they were Catholic and included prominent priests, were influenced by the European Enlightenment ideas of broad-based secular education for all. In the 1860s President Benito Juárez, of Zapotec Indian ancestry, sought reforms that would remove the church's influence in education and expand education to all, including the indigenous population. These ideas, among others, sparked a civil war with Mexican conservatives backed by the French Foreign Legion, about the same time as the U.S. Civil War. Juárez won and public education was expanded, but the struggle to provide public education for all continued through the Mexican Revolution, a decade of turmoil between 1910 and 1921.

Providing public education is a goal enshrined in the Mexican constitution, but the struggle to achieve this goal still continues (Gutek 2006). In Mexico school attendance is compulsory for students ages six to 18. Yet rural schools, especially those in remote and non-Spanish-speaking areas, often offer at most six years of public primary education. Continued education can mean traveling long and difficult distances. Quality secondary education is competitive, especially the later years leading to college.

Getting into college is not that difficult for urban residents. The Autonomous University of Mexico (UNAM) in Mexico City is one of the largest universities in the world, with over 300,000 full- and part-time students, thanks in part to largely free tuition. But students struggle to pay for living expenses while studying, key classes are often full or not offered, strikes by university workers are not uncommon, and many students never graduate. The title of *licenciado*, essentially "one who holds a bachelor's degree," is coveted in Mexico and is used as a personal title, much as *doctor* is used in the United States. A more secure education is offered, for those who can afford it, at private universities such as the Technológico de Monterrey, from which many of Mexico's business leaders, and increasingly now its political leaders, have come.

Mexico continues to expand higher education and to offer an increasing range of private business and technical schools, often with strong English components. But like many developing nations, it struggles to employ all of its graduates, especially in secure, well-paying professions.

Russia

Czarist Russia did not experience the profound industrial changes and reforms that altered Great Britain and the United States during the nineteenth century. While Russia had a long tradition of literature and arts (think of many great Russian authors and composers), the vast peasantry could never read or appreciate these works, and education for the masses was not encouraged.

One of the great changes promised by Vladimir Lenin and the Bolshevik communists, who took control during the Russian Revolution of 1917, was education for all. Education would not only be the basis for technical advancement, as Russia was eager to catch up to Western Europe, but it would also be a moral force as it created "the new socialist man" (although the communists also tended to be strong proponents of education for women). Study in the traditional subjects would be wedded to study of Marxist–Leninist doctrine, and instead of educating the elite, the schools would produce a new generation dedicated to the advances of the working class and international communism.

By the time Joseph Stalin took control in 1924, the international emphasis had declined and pride in Russia was a core tenet. The horrors of World War II only increased this nationalist emphasis. By the 1950s Americans saw Soviet education as filled with propaganda. Russian students not only learned the Marxist–Stalinist ideology in school, but after school, they donned uniforms as Young Pioneers and learned group work, leadership, and the glories of socialism. To be fair, U.S. education in the 1950s was also filled with nationalism and the glories of capitalism. George Washington and Abraham Lincoln looked down from classroom walls in place of Karl Marx and Vladimir Lenin, the textbooks often commented on U.S. successes and Soviet failures, and after-school activities involved flags and uniforms and pledges in the Boy and Girl Scouts in place of the Young Pioneers.

Soviet education was highly centralized and very inflexible, but it had some great technical successes. The launch of *Sputnik* and the Soviet lead in the space race were often seen as evidence of strong Soviet science education; in fact, these events sparked a new interest in science education in the United States, as it sought to catch up. In the 1980s Mikhail Gorbachev's glasnost, or "openness," meant new openness in the school curriculum, as well.

The breakup of the Soviet Union in 1991 meant further changes in education. New textbooks were much more muted about the glories of communism, but Russian achievements of the communist era—great authors, composers, scientists, World War II heroes, and cosmonauts—were, and are, still featured prominently. Today the Russian government must contend with other problems: how to encourage entrepreneurship in a system that has traditionally held this in suspicion, how to continue to provide virtually free higher education to highly qualified applicants amid declining government revenues, and how to provide jobs for a highly educated population that is living in a stalled and declining economy.

Germany and Northern Europe

Compared to the U.S. system of education, the German system can seem extremely regimented. Children do not begin school until about age seven but by age 10 are already taking examinations that will help determine their future careers. The main secondary school, *Hauptschule*, prepares them to pursue a technical and vocational education. A smaller, selective track, *Gymnasium*, is rooted in a classical education that serves as the basis of a future university career. The decision is not final at this early age, for there are a number of "bridges" from one track to another, but increasingly the paths diverge.

Those who do not get into the university track are hardly abandoned, for Germany has an extensive system of technical training and apprenticeship that goes back to the medieval guilds. Likewise, the classical university preparation is rooted in the great German universities of the Middle Ages, with a new emphasis on business and technology. Few students come to the end of their career path without a clear direction of where they are headed in the workforce, and Germany prides itself on having one of the world's most productive and capable workforces.

The school-to-work transition is even stronger in Sweden, where the government has tried to guarantee that every young person will be on a track that will lead to a productive working career (Nothdurft 1989). Higher education, though often of a technical nature, is seen as crucial, and few Swedes drop out of the system. For those who struggle in the rather regimented system, there are alternative schools and programs, each also tied to a particular niche in the economy.

Beginning in the Clinton administration, U.S. policy also started looking more closely at the school-to-work transition and the congruence between school training and the needs of the workforce. Most Americans, however, are uncomfortable with the amount of government involvement and the degree of early decision making that are part of the Northern European systems.

Opening Doors, Opening Minds

Human Capital Theory

Is education the key to national development? A strong affirmation that it is, is known as **human capital theory**. It has been advanced by economists such as Gary Becker (1964), who held joint positions in economics and sociology at the University of Chicago and won the Nobel Prize in Economics for his application of economic theory to social issues. Becker reasoned that just as investments in physical capital (say, a more technologically advanced factory) would increase productivity and efficiency, so, too, education could be seen as an investment in human capital, increasing the productivity and efficiency of humans. Highly educated people can do more and do it better and so contribute more to national development.

This idea has been very influential in national development policy. The World Bank, driven largely by economic theory, often discourages what it sees as wasteful government spending, but it does encourage governments to spend on education (World Bank 2018b). The logic is that this is an investment in the future productivity of the country and just as important as building a better power grid or a better road system. In general, few would argue with this logic, especially educators, who see this as a strong rationale for public support of education, including higher education. Students paying hefty tuition bills also want to believe this theory: that education is an investment in a more productive and so more lucrative future. And in most ways, it is.

Some countries have used this approach to considerable success. First Japan, then Singapore, and now places all across Asia, including India, have favored strong investment in education. Education has been key to rising standards of living of countries such as Japan and Singapore. Now, many countries in the world, especially in Latin America and the Caribbean, as well, tout their highly educated workforces. Spending on education also correlates strongly with overall well-being. Those that spend the most as a percentage of GDP are the Nordic countries, and others in Europe and the Pacific also score very well on overall well-being and happiness (see figure 4.2)

Yet for some, the returns on education have been slower. India, with its vast population, has had a difficult time finding productive employment for all its highly educated workers and now "exports" some of its most educated workers and professionals to other places in the world. As noted earlier, Indian Americans are the most educated immigrants in the United States, but many came because they could not use their education to full effect in their home country. The Philippines is another Asian country that tends to "export" educated workers in a "brain drain" to other parts of the world because the economy has not grown fast enough to employ them all.

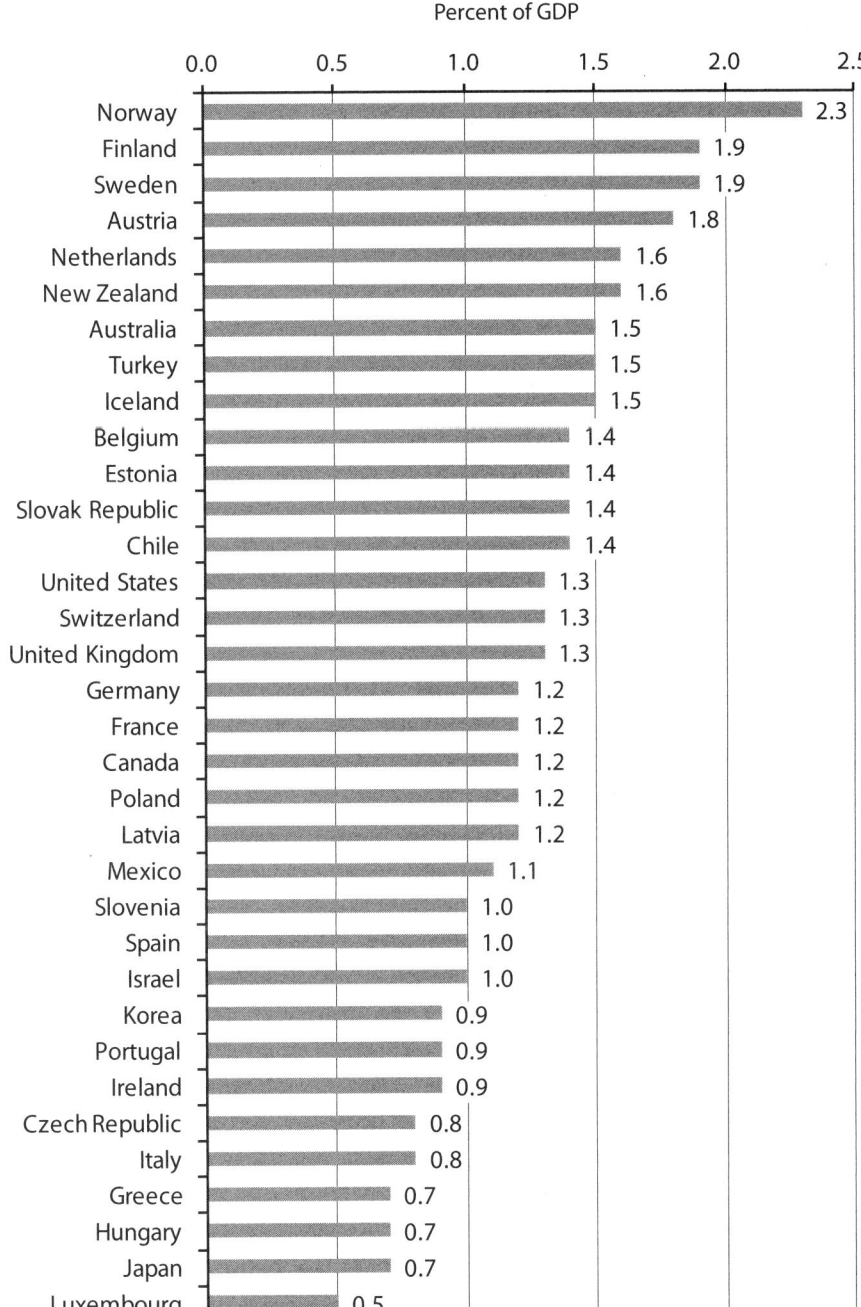

Figure 4.2 Spending on education: Selected countries, 2018. (Data from Organisation for Economic Cooperation and Development [OECD].)

Even in hard times, education can make people more resourceful and aware, and a good education can be a valued possession in its own right. Retirees traveling to Elderhostels and auditing college classes are not trying to increase their productivity but rather their awareness, intellect, and interest in life. Yet for education to become a true investment in human capital that will offer a return in productivity, it must be connected to a viable means of application. Any college student who has graduated during a recession or slow economy will likely agree that an education alone is not enough. It must be matched with opportunities for productive application.

The School-to-Work Transition

As mentioned earlier in this chapter, the United States started to focus more specifically on the school-to-work transition during the Clinton administration. Does what is learned in school clearly prepare students for the expectations of the workplace? Are students learning the skills that employers are seeking? Is there a clear path from education to employment?

Recently many more academic programs in the United States have begun to stress internships and ways to gain practical experience as part of the educational process. At the same time, constant shifts in the state of knowledge in any given field and the likelihood workers will go through many positions and maybe even many vocations and professions, each with different skills, mean learning that is too narrow may not be as useful as a broader education that stresses critical thinking and communication skills, which are useful in many contexts.

Generally the European and Japanese educational systems are much more closely tracked than those in the United States and Canada. In Europe and Japan students make decisions and take exams at earlier ages that will determine the directions of their future careers. Students in the United States are often allowed to remain undecided longer and to have more second chances in returning to school and in changing programs. At the same time, U.S. students often get less clear career direction and are less likely to be on a path that leads directly to employment; this means they run a greater risk of falling through the cracks in the system. Students in developing countries often face both perils: Programs may be highly selective with few second chances, yet they may also offer few assurances, unless the student is from a wealthy or well-connected family.

Around the world and especially in the United States, there has been intense debate over national standards and international competitiveness. Concern began to grow in the United States in the 1980s and 1990s that U.S. students know less, especially in the areas of math and science, than their counterparts elsewhere and that this hurts U.S. competitiveness. One reason given for the competitive success of European and Asian advanced industrial economies is the high level of technical and mathematical competence of even assembly line workers. The U.S. system, with its more flexible structure and emphasis on choice and creativity, has successfully promoted a culture of innovation and entrepreneurship, although some have argued it does less well in areas such as quality control. There has been a strong push to address this with a program of nationally mandated examinations and standards.

Elite and Popular Education

Arguments about human capital also hinge on what types of education constitute useful human capital. Human capital theorists are often proponents of **technical education,** the "how-to" of industrial production and commercial enterprise. Many of the world's educational systems have instead inherited patterns of **classical education,** rooted in the finest ideas and ideals of the past, and **elite education,** intended not to make one rich but to make the children of the rich more refined. From this view, education was not a necessary means to wealth, but wealth was often a necessary means to a quality education. Since the goal of elite education was refinement, rather than productivity, the course of study often focused on rhetoric and refined speaking, the study of ancient texts and languages, and other marks of distinction.

Elite and classical types of education were not limited to Europe but found expression in many of the world's civilizations. Yet once European colonial powers came to dominate the world, the elite education of the dominant powers, such as Great Britain and France, became the model for many educational systems around the world. In Africa elite students often learned more about the literature and history of the colonial "mother country" than of the cultures and problems of their own communities. In Mexico, in the seventeenth and eighteenth centuries, the elites studied the great writers of Spain and the great Latin classical and ecclesiastical texts; in the nineteenth century they studied the great thinkers of France and Enlightenment Europe. Rarely did the studies ever turn to the heritage and thought of Mexico itself.

Increasingly around the world, national texts—many of them approved, produced, and distributed by national governments—seek to promote national patriotism by emphasizing the story, or at least one version of the story, of nation building within that country. Schools of technology and industry have also become much more common. The debate remains, however, as to what constitutes a good education. Should it be classical or technical, narrow or broad? Or are these false dichotomies? And of course, whether a student learns to use the proper fork or to use a forklift depends a great deal on his or her social class origins.

Savage Inequalities at Home and Abroad

The type of education a student receives and the quality of that education vary greatly depending on that student's position in society. We have already noted the persistent gender gap in education. A persistent region gap is also found around the world. Namely, children in rural areas are less likely to attend school, less likely to graduate from higher education levels, and less likely to have access to buildings and supplies than their urban counterparts. Within urban areas, elite districts and wealthier neighborhoods have the finest facilities, while schools in poor urban areas reflect the distress of the surrounding neighborhood.

This regional difference is somewhat less pronounced in Europe and Japan, where strong national programs and national funding of education have reduced such differences. The regional gap is particularly marked in Latin America, however, with the exception of a few places with strong national education programs, such as Cuba, or places of a very small size, such as Barbados. In Africa the regional gap is so great that schools seem to exist in different worlds, with modern schools in the national capital and rural locations with few or no opportunities for formal education.

There are also persistent racial and ethnic gaps. Education can reflect a racial hierarchy. Before the dismantling of apartheid in South Africa, the type of school one attended depended on his or her racial classification. Schools for whites were well equipped with books and supplies and had a student–teacher ratio of 18:1. Schools for black South Africans were often in old, dilapidated buildings (or sometimes no buildings at all), lacked basic supplies, and had a student–teacher ratio of 42:1 (World Almanac 1991). A similar situation existed in parts of the United States before U.S. courts mandated desegregation. Schools for African Americans typically had limited facilities, little equipment, and high student–teacher ratios. In rural areas, it was not uncommon for schools for black children to have a shorter calendar, since many children worked in the fields well into the autumn.

Schools in the southern United States began to desegregate in the 1950s following the 1954 *Brown v. Board of Education* decision. By the 1970s school desegregation orders had reached many northern cities, and angry confrontations shifted from southern states, such as Arkansas and Alabama, to northern cities, such as Boston. South Africa began to dismantle its apartheid laws in the early 1990s and accelerated the process after the 1994 election of African National Congress leader Nelson Mandela to the presidency.

Still, in both the United States and the Union of South Africa, racial and ethnic differences persist. In the United States the test scores and graduation rates of Hispanic and black children continue to lag well behind those of white and Asian American children. A history of social disadvantage is coupled with continued residential segregation and differences in language and culture.

These differences are seen in varying forms around the world. In Latin America children with strong ties to an indigenous or Amerindian heritage often struggle in schools that were modeled on European norms and European languages, such as Spanish and Portuguese (just as American Indians in nontribal schools in the United States have often struggled). In Africa and Asia ethnic minorities often struggle in schools that do not reflect their language, religion, or heritage. These are particularly divisive issues in countries that are trying to forge a common identity out of many diverse groups. Nigeria, the largest country in Africa, has dozens of ethnic groups and languages, three major religious traditions (Christianity in the south, Islam in the north, and many traditional African religions in between), and a British colonial past. Indonesia, the fourth largest country in the world, has literally hundreds of languages and ethnic groups scattered across hundreds of islands, religious diversity (a Muslim majority with Christian, Hindu, and traditional tribal religions all represented), and a Dutch colonial heritage.

In countries such as these, what should be the language of instruction: a national language, such as Bahasa Indonesian in Indonesia; a colonial language, such as English in Nigeria; or each of the local languages? Which religious holidays should be observed, and which ethnic customs and learning styles should be represented? Sometimes, the answers to these questions vary by education level. It is not uncommon in parts of the world to find primary instruction in the local language, reflecting renewed local pride and determination; secondary education in the national language, reflecting an attempt at nation building and establishing a common culture; and higher education in a dominant European language, such as English or French, reflecting the realities of international power and resources. From all this diversity, however, a common pattern tends to emerge: Students who are the most different from the mainstream of the society—in language, religion, race/ethnicity, heritage, and so forth—tend to struggle in the school system and to complete less schooling than their majority-group peers.

All these attributes—race/ethnicity, region, neighborhood, and so forth—are typically intertwined with **social class.** Children of privilege have always received more attention to their education than children of poor and working-class families. For almost four decades, writer Jonathan Kozol documented the problems and inequalities in U.S. schools. Kozol graduated summa cum laude from Harvard in the 1960s, was a Rhodes Scholar, and went to work teaching in a low-income public school in Boston's then-primarily African American neighborhood of Roxbury. He was promptly fired for reading "unauthorized poetry" to his students and so began a long career in alternative education and critiquing the U.S. educational system. His first scathing critique, *Death at an Early Age: The Destruction of the Hearts and Minds of Negro Children in the Boston Public Schools* (1967), drew national attention to the problem of inner-city schools. Kozol documented not only the poor condition of the schools but also the message conveyed to children in this system—that somehow it was they, not society, who were failing and thus to blame.

Kozol's work also drew the attention of international community activist Ivan Illich. After having worked in many parts of the world, Illich founded a retreat center near Cuernavaca, Mexico, and was bringing progressive thinkers from around the world to discuss the many vexing social problems of the 1960s. Kozol went to this center, where he met another educator, Brazilian Paulo Freire. Freire's writings had earned him the anger of the generals who ruled his native country, and he was in exile in Mexico. Freire compiled the insights gained from his experiences in a widely read classic on educational reform, *Pedagogy of the Oppressed* (2018 [1968]). Freire argued that true education was more than either elite or technical education; it was a liberating experience. He believed that liberation came when oppressed peoples understood the true nature of the system that dehumanized them (and ultimately dehumanized their oppressors, who had to maintain the system). They regained and liberated their humanity through education that included *conscientização*, what became known in English as "consciousness raising."

Inspired by Freire's ideas, Kozol proposed to write a second book on education that went beyond calling for greater equality to calling for radical changes in the ideology of U.S. education—from teaching children to accept a fundamentally unjust system to teaching them to analyze and ultimately change that system. Freire warned Kozol that such a book might not be well received, and it wasn't. The book, *The Night Is Dark and I Am Far from Home* (1975), drew angry retorts and far less acclaim. Kozol stopped writing on public education for some time and turned his attention to related concerns, such as adult literacy and homelessness; he also continued to work on alternative education. For a time, Freire joined him in Boston.

Kozol returned to the public schools as a visitor in the late 1980s and was shocked by what he found, calling it, *Savage Inequalities* (1991). This was segregation not written into law but enforced by divided communities with little in common. It was inequality that was not based on a national formula but on the fact that school districts could only spend what local property taxes generated, and poor neighborhoods had little property of value. Kozol vividly recounted how poverty; substandard housing and medical care; and dangerous, segregated, and hopeless neighborhoods deplete the possibilities open to poor Latino and black children (1995), as well as how children are resistant to these blights and have an amazing ability to continue to look for hope and new possibilities (2000). He continued to denounce a system that he saw as separate and unequal and profoundly immoral in the way it fails poor children, in *Shame of the Nation: The Restoration of Apartheid Schooling in America* (2005).

The United States has taken up the task of seeking more effective and more equal education many times in the decades since the 1954 *Brown* decision overturned legal segregation by race. The most recent attempt has been No Child Left Behind legislation, which set national standards and rewards and penalties for schools based on test scores. In the spirit of Freire, Kozol denounces the emphasis on rote learning to prepare for a very limited test and the way schools in poor areas may be penalized for their poverty; instead he advocates for an education that encourages critical thinking and engagement. In struggling inner-city schools, he contends that liberal education has been replaced by prisonlike rule enforcement and rote instruction that is unimaginative, culturally barren, and almost robotic. The United States, like much of the world, is still seeking an effective pedagogy for all its children.

Pedagogy of the Oppressed

High in the Andes Mountains of Bolivia, Quechua-speaking women have long had little power and little voice. In one NGO-sponsored program, these women travel long distances to take part in a brief but intense educational experience based on Paulo Freire's models. Working in groups, they struggle to write answers on crinkled butcher paper to questions in Spanish. "Who are the illiterates?" The women think and write, "Those who cannot read and write." They talk some more and then add, "Those who do not understand their lives and their situations." The women talk some more. "The wealthy do not understand our lives and situations; to us, they are the illiterate ones." The women laugh and then go on with the questions.

In Kenya a school for girls struggles to keep the girls in and others out, including angry former employers, such as pimps and others in the sex trade. Many of the girls are homeless, some have children of their own, many have been exploited by various employers in the bustling capital of Nairobi, and few have any other resources. Rather than keeping the girls in school, family members may try to pull them out, especially if their incomes are needed by the family. Yet the Mukuru Promotion Centre operates coeducational schools in one of the poorest slums of Nairobi. Free primary education is guaranteed in the Kenyan constitution, but "free" does not include the cost of uniforms and school shoes, county fees, or fees charged to cover the cost of exam paper, or even firewood. The center partners with the government and UN agencies to make sure that schooling is truly available to all. Once students are there, the emphasis is on assuring that all have a sense of belonging and building a new national future. It is a precarious venture, but the staff draw encouragement from seeing teenage girls who enter looking old and sad and "used up" begin to regain their youthful enthusiasm and again laugh and sing and learn (Mukuru Promotion Centre 2021).

The schools operated by the center show some of the struggles of educational systems around the world. The world is still seeking pedagogy of the oppressed to reach the poor and the exploited and pedagogy of the dispossessed to reach those who have lost their homes, cultures, and livelihoods. The elements of that pedagogy are still developing, but the key issues have been well defined.

Inclusive Education. There must be a place for every child, regardless of gender, region, or race/ethnicity. The world is moving toward an international consensus, affirmed in documents such as the UN Rights of the Child, that all children should be in school and stay in school long enough to keep up with their peers and to progress to higher levels. It is true that, for millennia, many children were taught in informal contexts, and there is still a place for family-based learning, for learning from elders, and for learning from practical service in the community. These are all strengths of traditional societies, and rather than be abandoned, they could well be added to the educational systems of modern advanced industrial societies. Japan, perhaps more than any other country, has captured this aspect of both traditional and modern learning.

For almost every child in our interconnected world, however, a meaningful education will involve some formal education. Education must also include adult learners. **Functional illiteracy** in adults is a problem in the United States as well as in the world's poorest countries. Often the best way to ensure that children will learn to read is to make certain that their parents know how to read, maybe through multigenerational family literacy programs.

Equal Education. Societies have many inequalities in their institutions, but educational inequality underlies many of the other inequities. It cuts across many of the problems considered in this book. Quality education for girls, who go on to be workers, mothers, and community leaders, is one of the best predictors of population stability, family well-being, and hope for the next generation. Nations with little access to education for women also tend to have exploding populations, high infant and maternal mortality rates, low levels of family well-being, and high rates of worker exploitation. Societies with marked differences in educational access and quality, coupled with intense segregation between racial and ethnic groups, also tend to be marked by turmoil, unrest, ghettoization, and even civil war.

Again, there is broad international consensus on this idea. In the United States, President George W. Bush and Congress took up the slogan "no child left behind." Yet in countries rich and poor, certain groups and places remain neglected, with crumbling facilities and few resources.

Practical Education. If education has no apparent application and hard work in school brings no clear rewards, then it will be dismissed by the poor as a worthless investment and will be distrusted by all who don't already have their future secured. Education must include useful skills in communication, analysis and problem solving, and working with complex systems and technology. Some of these skills can be measured by standardized tests, but many can only be assessed by involved instructors working closely with their students, as has typified education from its beginning.

While the language of national competiveness is often used, in a globalized world of multinational entities it is misleading to assume that nations compete as single entities. Each student and each community must be able to compete and to cooperate to build a successful future. Learning needs to lead to internships, apprenticeships, entry-level positions, and other opportunities for its useful application. To be effective, education must open doors.

Liberal Education. This term, as captured in the phrase *liberal arts college*, does not refer to a political ideology but to broad exposure to the best of humanity's hopes and ideas. Good education doesn't just train; it liberates, as Freire hoped. Students are learning not just to be workers but also to be citizens.

Too often this realization has only meant political indoctrination. Students learn a glorified version of their own history—whether in Russia (or the former Soviet Union), China, Great Britain, or the United States—so as to become patriotic, nationalistic citizens who will support and advance their country. This aspect of education has been adopted, as well, by many developing countries seeking to establish and glorify a national heritage. But in a globalized world, students need the broad, inclusive learning that allows them to become global citizens. This means understanding both the rich heritage and the persistent problems of many places and having the critical-thinking skills to address these issues. Effective education should also open minds.

Key Ideas

> Education has ancient roots in human culture, and scholars have been revered in many societies. Yet formal education was often limited to tutoring for the children of the ruling class, while others received practical instruction from their elders.

> Many countries are still struggling to get all their children into school. Many who begin primary school do not make it to the secondary level. Challenges include the need for children to provide income and do chores for family members, as well as the fact that schools may be located in distant or dangerous areas. Many cannot afford school fees. In parts of Africa, the Middle East, and South and Central Asia, girls are still less likely to have access to education, especially secondary education.

- ▶ School systems around the world have been built on national traditions, and many have adopted systems from colonial powers. These systems vary in their emphasis on style of education—particularly creativity versus memorization—and on the subjects and the focus.

- ▶ Human capital refers to investments in knowledge that make workers more productive. Technical education is weak in many poorer countries and jobs may be scarce for graduates. Even advanced industrial countries often struggle with the school-to-work transition and how to best prepare graduates to contribute to the labor force.

- ▶ The quality of education often varies greatly between city and countryside and between rich and poor neighborhoods. This is a problem the United States shares with much of the developing world.

- ▶ Educational reformers such as Brazilian Paulo Freire have argued that education should liberate as well as inform and should raise the consciousness of the oppressed to challenge systems of exclusion and oppression.

For Review and Discussion

1. Should all countries insist that all children be in school? To what level? What is the answer for families who insist they need their children to help with the work?

2. What should a school curriculum emphasize: national traditions and culture, technical skills, literacy skills, or creativity? Who should decide this: national or local governments, individual schools, or teachers themselves?

3. How would you answer a child from a poor family and neighborhood who says that education is a waste of time since jobs are scarce and many educated people are unemployed?

4. What do you see as the educational strengths of school systems in the United States, Europe, Japan, China, and elsewhere? Are there particular strengths that you think might be adopted by other countries and systems?

Making Connections

Wide Angle "Time for School"

- ▶ PBS's *Wide Angle* series has been following children in countries around the world as they make their way through their national school systems. Subjects include Japan and Romania, rural West Africa and Nairobi in East Africa, as well a school in a Brazilian favela. The series and accompanying stories can be found at https://www.pbs.org/show/time-school/. You can follow the children's growth and experiences over the 14-year study in a 90-minute video at https://www.pbs.org/video/time-school-time-school-2003-2016/. What are the particular challenges of poverty, gender, conflict, and social attitudes seen in the lives of the children? In what ways do they struggle for an education? What seem to be the keys to success?

United Nations

➤ Go to the website of the United Nations Economic and Social Council and examine "Education Transforms Lives": https://en.unesco.org/themes/education. What are the particular gains and challenges around the world in education for all?

➤ Visit the site of the United Nations Children's Fund or UNICEF (www.unicef.org). It offers good information on the status of children, reports on the Year of the Child, and other material. What are the current key concerns of UNICEF concerning the well-being of children?

UN Sustainable Development Goals

➤ Goal #4 is Quality Education: "Ensure inclusive and equitable quality education and promote lifelong learning opportunities for all." Go to https://www.un.org/sustainabledevelopment/education/. What are the challenges ahead in achieving this goal? How has it been impacted by war and refugees and by COVID-19? What are some of the projects being undertaken to promote inclusive education—for ethnic minorities, for girls, for rural and isolated children? What are some of the efforts toward lifelong education, and what would that involve?

Making a Difference

Local Tutoring

➤ Opportunities abound in many communities for people to tutor both children and adults. This can be a great opportunity to learn firsthand about educational challenges and the possibilities and difficulties of upward mobility. Find out what programs are available in your community from a campus community relations office, local school district, or local public library. Also learn about national programs, such as America Reads and America Counts, that may provide training and stipends to tutors; your campus should have this information. Spend time tutoring a child needing extra help, tutoring an adult working toward a GED or improving academic skills, or with a family literacy program that is seeking to improve reading skills for both parents and children. Some programs require an ongoing commitment; others are drop-in or after-school programs that can be visited occasionally. What academic deficiencies is this program trying to address? What did you experience in the diversity of needs, backgrounds, and learning styles? What are the possibilities, as well as the limitations, of this program in promoting academic and career success?

▶ School districts and community agencies also often have tutoring programs targeted at immigrants, migrant laborers, and refugees. Many of these programs focus on ENL, or English as a new language. Others include a wide array of subjects and academic content support. Some of the English programs, especially those for Spanish speakers, are set up as *intercambios*, where the conversation is half in each language. Each participant in the pair gets the opportunity to teach the other a bit of his or her language while also practicing the other language. What opportunities are available locally? What challenges become apparent in such programs?

Part Two

Seeking a Peaceful World
Issues of Conflict

5 Crime: Fear in the Streets
6 War: States of Terror
7 Democracy and Human Rights: Having Our Say
8 Ethnicity and Religion: Deep Roots and Unholy Hate

Most of what fills our news is conflict. Take any news source, whether paper or electronic, and take out all the news about crime, war, terrorism, domestic disputes, civic disputes, and political disputes; what you have left is pretty slim. Even as we recognize conflict as a part of life, we must also confront the fact that in a world of ever deadlier weapons and means, human conflict could destroy life itself. Conflict may be inevitable, but is violence an inevitable part of human life?

Issues of conflict are placed here right in the center of our look at global problems, because that is exactly how it often works. Conflicts are often rooted in inequity and tensions between unequal groups. At the same time, conflicts are often what threaten to undermine our efforts for an enduring and sustainable society; it can destroy hope and opportunity. Conflict can abruptly destroy in a great nuclear mushroom cloud or it can slowly destroy as it degrades our environment and depletes our resources and ability to work together.

Chapter 5 begins this section where conflict hits the streets and local lives everywhere: crime. Often closely tied to poverty, and perhaps especially to the resentment and twisted ambition that comes from being poor amid the affluent, crime is a bridge from part I to this section.

But most violence in the world, and certainly violence on the grandest scale, is often state violence perpetrated by powerful interests. In chapter 6 we will examine ways in which war has shaped the world we know, and how it could also destroy that world.

Increasingly, however, struggles between groups do not take the form of large-scale formal warfare. State power, and violence, is more often used against its own citizens. So, in chapter 7, we will next look at the global struggle for democracy and human rights. Is democracy only about elections, or is there also a sense of the rights and responsibilities of active citizenship? Are human rights universal and can governments be held accountable for how they treat their own people?

Likewise, many of those striking back at powerful states and institutions are doing so in the name of causes that extend beyond national boundaries. People are divided by beliefs and heritage that may span many countries or may divide a single country. Humans have long been motivated and inspired by a myriad of spiritual and cultural traditions. These are a source of strength, and also of deep and intense conflict. Chapter 8 concludes this section with a look at religion and ethnicity, examining the beliefs people hold about their identity and place in the world, and what happens when these beliefs come into conflict. Why do some beliefs provoke such violence, while others compel people to overcome divisions and reach out to strangers? The search for peace in a divided and conflicted world is the common thread that runs throughout this section.

5
Crime

Fear in the Streets

Global Encounters

Brazil

Women on the ship can learn the art of personal self-defense from specially trained RAs: a bit of martial arts technique, but mostly how to avoid being a victim of assault, when to scream and struggle, how to attract help. These are good things to know, whether on a college campus or in a new city on a different continent.

After several days of open water, we awoke to the sight of a dramatic skyline of towering buildings that seem to leap suddenly from the sea. Up on the top deck, the full sweep of the bay comes into view. The city of Salvador, the capital of Bahia, sits to our east atop a 200-foot bluff. Church steeples and wrought iron balconies dominate the old city, and then give way to shoulder-to-shoulder high-rise apartments and offices just to the south. A huge elevator straddles the cliff, taking passengers from the port up to the old city. Once centered on a market square and a place known as the whipping post, it was the hub of the transatlantic slave trade. This area fell into decay until an independent group—Olodum—found exciting ways to combine music and learning and to engage the area's young people. As Olodum's renown spread, local officials recognized the potential of the area. It is now back in action, draped in bright colors, with shops, open air plazas and markets, and music.

There is always music in Brazil. African rhythms crossed the Atlantic with the human slave cargo and followed the routes of their diaspora. From here one set of rhythms, combined with dance and often social protest, moved north toward the Caribbean where it flourished as Reggae. A slightly different beat gave rise to Samba, which spread to the south, taking root in Rio de Janeiro and becoming the national dance. With the Spanish and Portuguese came the guitar and the harp, but the beat of Latin America is not Latin; it is African. The marketplace of the old city still hums, although tourists are few. Many are southern Brazilians who come north to enjoy the country's cultural roots. The transatlantic tourist trade now consists of Germans and French plus a few others who shop for colorful clothing and Brazilian gems. North Americans, at least when Semester at Sea is not in port, are fewer. Unlike Rio to the south, a poster of Salvador is not on every U.S. travel agents' wall. The revival of the old city remains tenuous. Some buildings seem no more than colorful Hollywood-style facades over decaying structures. A few wrong turns on the winding streets and the look of the neighborhood changes abruptly. Decay rather than décor becomes the dominant impression, and vendors are as likely to offer drugs as gems. There are no tourist police. Students learn that there are boundaries to this revival, boundaries that are crossed at considerable peril.

Having wandered just a little too far down one of these intriguing streets, one young woman steps from the zone of entertainment into a danger zone. She is grabbed by several men who try to drag her toward a vehicle. Well-trained in the self-defense course, she screams and kicks and waves, and others—alerted by the same course—run to her aid. Her attackers flee, taking only her camera, and she returns to the ship with a few bruises from being held so tightly. Surprisingly, before we leave port, the camera is returned. It had shown up in a secondhand store. Before hocking the item, apparently the thieves had taken pictures of themselves on the street in front of their homes and left the images on the memory card. They are promptly arrested. We laugh nervously about their folly, and she tries not to think about the police suggestion that she was almost part of a kidnapping that is used as a gang initiation. Interest in the self-defense course increases.

Are global fears about crime and security justified? What makes some places so fraught with criminal activity while others seem so much safer?

Seeking Security

The world is afraid. It is not clear that life is any more precarious than it has ever been, but stories of new dangers and terrors abound, and safe retreats no longer seem so safe. Sometimes, the responses of people are innovative.

Some shopkeepers in New York have given up on dogs and are trying tarantulas. They don't eat much and can crawl around jewelry cases and window displays, discouraging smashing and grabbing. Tarantulas are actually quite timid, but signs warning about large, hairy, poisonous spiders do get intruders' attention.

In Johannesburg, South Africa, the measures are more extreme. Once divided by apartheid, this city is now deeply divided by extremes of wealth and poverty. Coupled with high unemployment, this is a recipe for high crime rates. As criminals have become bolder or maybe more desperate, brazen crimes such as carjacking have become common. Cars stopped at lights or, for that matter, for any purpose risk being invaded and seized, the owners robbed, kidnapped, or assaulted. Heavy-duty locks don't seem to work well, so drivers now seek the ultimate customization: underbody flame throwers. A tank of flammable material is stored under the car door (one hates to think what happens in an accident), and an igniter and nozzle are pointed out in the direction of the door handle. If any unauthorized person reaches for the door, the driver hits a button that sends a fireball flaming out toward the attacker. As yet, there is no safety equivalent for those who must ride the bus.

Johannesburg is a bustling city of gold, located around huge gold mines. But not everyone has gold. And in a changing economy, many do not have jobs. The result of old injustices and new economic turmoil has been extraordinary crime rates. Parts of downtown Johannesburg have been all but abandoned; tall buildings deemed too dangerous sit empty. Taxi drivers in Soweto, the famous black township that has gained new vitality, often refuse to go downtown. Imagine catching a cab in Harlem or the South Bronx and the driver refusing to take you to midtown Manhattan. Homeowners have taken to installing what they refer to as "rape gates." A metal gate closes the upstairs from the downstairs. If intruders get onto the roof, the residents flee downstairs and close the gate. If the intruders break in at the first floor, they retreat upward, closing the gate below them like barring some medieval castle. Then the homeowners hit a button to summon the very common private security services. Within minutes, armed security men arrive with automatic weapons drawn, ready to retake the house. In slum communities, which are far more dangerous, no one can afford private security, so where police action is slow, mob rule and vigilante justice have become the norm (Bearak 2009).

While some of these attempts at security bring smiles, many are deadly serious. In the United States the purchase of handguns for home and personal defense is a growing multimillion-dollar business. Long marketed primarily to white men, women and people of color have become the largest target audiences. The weapons have also seen a continuing trend to greater lethality: firing more rounds, more quickly, with more penetrating power. The results have not been promising: A gun in the home is 22 times more likely to be used against a family member by accident (four times) or in a suicide (11 times) or in an act of domestic violence (seven times) than it is to be used against an intruder.

The United States has by far the highest rate of gun violence among major nations. In 2019 the figures for gun-violence deaths in the United States, Canada, and the UK were: 396,000 (U.S.), 47,000 (Canada), and 4,000 (UK). Thus, gun-violence deaths in the United States were more than eight times higher than in Canada and 100 times higher than in the UK (Aizenman 2021). The United States also has the highest rate of gun violence in comparison to major nations in Asia. The U.S. rate of 4.43 deaths per hundred thousand is over 100 times the rate in Japan, China, or Indonesia (Aizenman and Silver 2019). In general, stable Asian countries have very low rates of gun violence. The highest rates of gun deaths are in turbulent countries where a toxic mix of political turmoil and corruption, together with guns and drug trafficking, has taken hold. Compared to the United States, gun death rates in Venezuela and El Salvador are 10 times higher, five times in Brazil, and twice as high in the Philippines. By comparison, Middle East conflict zones seem "safer": rates of gun deaths in Afghanistan and Iraq are lower than in the United States.

The number of shooting rampages across the United States seems to have skyrocketed since the expiration of the 2004 act banning assault weapons. The 2011 Arizona shooting of Congresswoman Gabby Gifford and the death of six bystanders by a gunman with a history of mental health problems who was still able to buy a high-capacity handgun (which would have been banned under the expired assault weapons ban) led to calls for a more reasoned approach to weapons regulation (Kristof 2011). In 2021 President Joe Biden called for a ban on assault weapons after a shooting at a Boulder, Colorado, supermarket in which 10 people died. But a long U.S. history of associating guns with liberty, coupled with a powerful gun lobby, makes this unlikely (Connolly 2011).

The problem with using a gun for deterrence is that often it is only the criminal who has a weapon and is ready to use it when a crime occurs. Some places in the western United States have even tried to reverse a long-standing trend toward controlling the circulation of firearms (the first thing Wyatt Earp and his brothers did when they came to old Tombstone was to ban gun possession in the town), instead of encouraging citizens to carry firearms. This has been done in other locations as well. In urban Brazil, women have been known to pull handguns out of their purses in shopping markets to fire on would-be thieves. While this seemed to reduce supermarket theft, the crossfire could be deadly and of limited use against purse snatchers, who ended up not only with the money but also the gun.

Many stores, and now many neighborhoods, in Brazil have resorted to hiring heavily armed security guards. Likewise, where police protection has failed, neighborhoods in Latin America and Africa often hire private security forces. Traveling in groups in pickup trucks (as do the police in much of Latin America), the forces can quickly turn into vigilante groups that "prevent trouble" by targeting and sometimes killing anyone who is poor and suspicious, including street children.

One of the extreme examples of this growing dependence on vigilante groups, often operating with the support and even involvement of police and local authorities, is Nigeria. Nigeria is beset by deep divides of wealth, religion, and politics, and violence often results (Spencer 2017). Overwhelmed, authorities allow and encourage the Bakassi Boys (youth vigilantes) to patrol markets and have even made the Vigilante Group of Nigeria an official NGO. Some fight terrorism, some guard pipelines, some fight violent gangs, and some become violent gangs. Amid rising urban crime rates and with governments that often cannot afford to staff large and effective law enforcement agencies, urban dwellers are seeking creative and sometimes-violent alternatives. The results in Latin America, the United States, the Philippines, and turbulent regions of Africa are not encouraging as the death toll mounts (see figure 5.1)

Street Crime and Youth Violence

What spurs such waves of urban violence? Poverty is certainly a factor, but places of great poverty have not always been places of great violence. Inequality appears to be an added factor—poverty in the midst of wealth, especially sudden wealth. Equally important are issues of dislocation and unemployment (Wilson 1996).

In places where rich families have always been rich and poor families have always been poor, each may accept their place as inevitable. But when the rich have suddenly come into their wealth, the question for the others is, "And why not me?" Cities with high unemployment, especially youth unemployment, leave many seeking alternative ways to use their talents and ambitions. The same skills that might move someone up the corporate ladder—planning, ambition, networking, marketing, and a willingness to take risks—might also make one effective in a criminal enterprise. It is all a matter of where the opportunities lie.

In many urban areas, there are decreasing opportunities for newcomers to use their skills in legitimate ways. Economies based on white-collar services and management may offer little to those with a less polished demeanor and few formal academic skills. Cities such as New York, which have seen growth primarily in what has been termed the **FIRE economy** (finance, insurance, and real

Crime CHAPTER 5 157

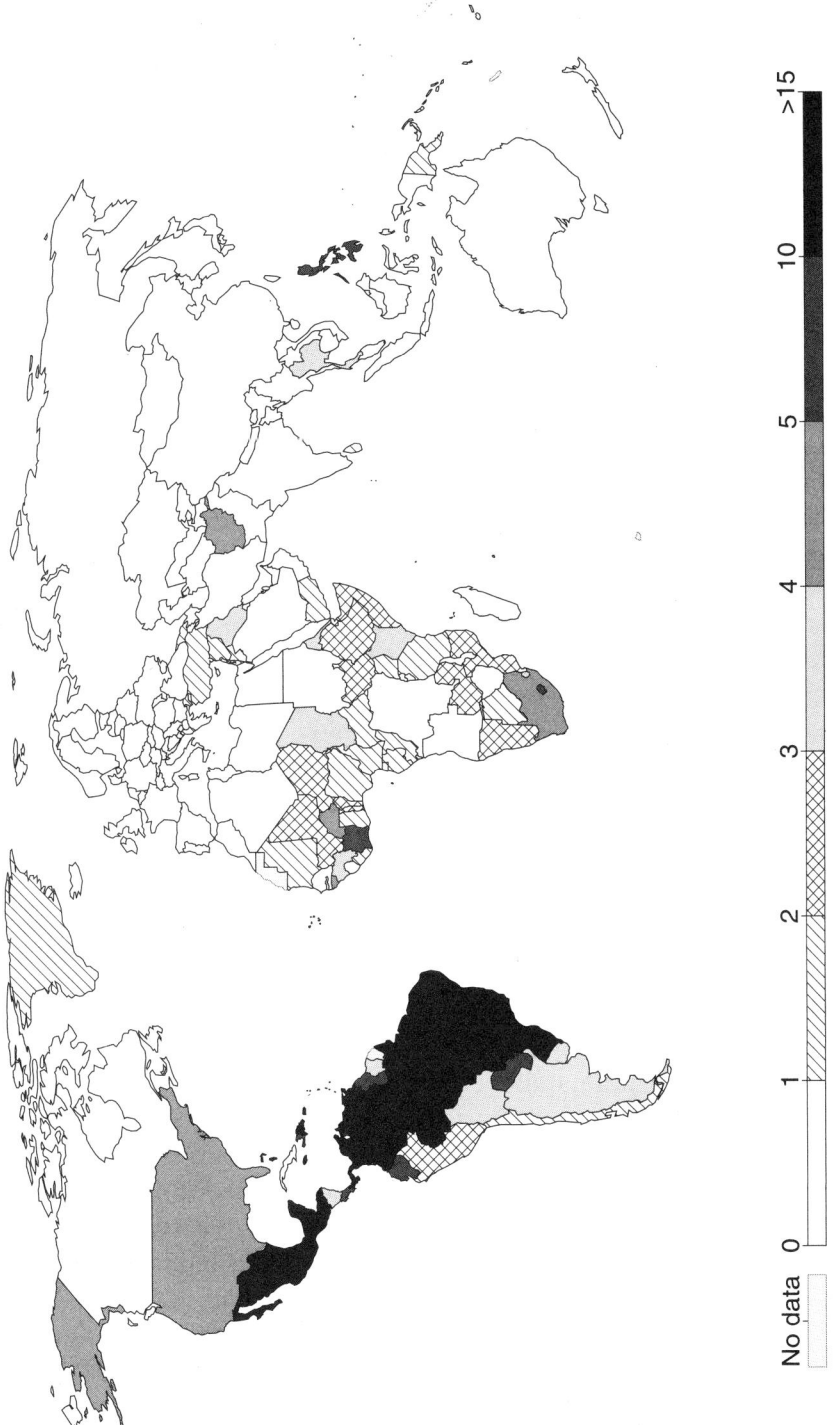

Figure 5.1 Murders by guns, selected countries, 2017. (Source: Our World in Data.) For more data on homicide around the world, see https://ourworldindata.org/homicides.

estate), leave many "burned" and excluded. According to Philippe Bourgois, "Obedience to the norms of high rise, office-corridor culture is in direct contradiction to street culture's definitions of personal dignity—especially for males who are socialized not to accept public subordination" (Bourgois 2003, 114).

For groups such as the young Puerto Rican men that Bourgois studied in New York, the changing economy has meant huge cultural and social dislocation. The residential dislocation of movement to and within a large city further interrupts old networks that might have led to the workaday world of the legitimate economy. Instead, the most immediate opportunities are in the crack cocaine trade. The work is dangerous and not as lucrative as the young men pretend it is (they're far from drug lords), but they can get some ready cash and dream of making it big. The real story is not so much about crack, Bourgois contends, as it is about social marginalization and alienation.

Such dislocation is common around the world. Tijuana is one of Mexico's fastest-growing cities, but many of its new industries prefer to hire young women. For young men, some of the most immediate opportunities are in the illegal trafficking of people, drugs, and other items across the border.

Rio de Janeiro and São Paulo, Brazil, are two of the world's fastest-growing cities; São Paulo is now perhaps one of the three largest cities in the world. New high-rise apartments continue to go up, and new office buildings are being built to serve the computer industry, the growing media, and the agricultural export economy. New cars fill the crowded streets. The middle and upper-middle classes, while always worried about economic crises, continue to grow. So do the ranks of the poor, both in and around the cities. Shantytowns fill the lush hills above Rio, looking down on the fabled beaches and bustling streets, but there are few points of access into the legitimate economy. As a result, crime in Rio and São Paulo also continues to soar. Middle-class women wonder whether they should include a handgun in their purse along with their makeup. Helicopter services for successful businesspeople have become increasingly common in São Paulo as a way to get to work that avoids both the traffic and the crime of the streets. The fear of crime was one of the factors that propelled far-right candidate Jair Bolsonaro to the presidency. The former army captain and one-time supporter of a military regime known for human rights abuses, Bolsonaro promised a crackdown on crime.

Brazil's problems are some of the most extreme but also echo the problems of other divided cities, such as Los Angeles, Miami, Detroit, and Washington, DC, in the United States. These problems are compounded when social and cultural dislocation are joined by political corruption and disruption. The deadliest city in the world is perhaps Bogotá, Colombia, with a murder rate more than three times that of New York (and more than 30 times that of Toronto or Tokyo). Bogotá is a city divided between rich and poor. It is also a transit point in the drug trade and the capital of a country rocked by political violence. Countries torn by war and violent revolt often find this violence taking root in their cities, even after the war has subsided.

Sometimes the relationships between political and urban violence are transnational. In the 1980s many young people from Nicaragua, Guatemala, and El Salvador fled the political violence in their home countries. Some went to Los Angeles, where their poverty, dislocation, and familiarity with danger made them prime recruits for urban street gangs. When some of them returned home, they brought with them new skills in urban gang activity, including experience in drugs and violence that spurred the growth of street gangs in their home countries.

French sociologist Émile Durkheim worried that growing urban areas would be prone to **anomie,** an internal sense of lawlessness and displacement that results as people leave the tight network of their home villages. Durkheim himself focused on suicide, a great concern of his day, rather than drugs or homicide. But his concern that cities would become places of turmoil, both internal and external, is echoed by observers of places like Bogotá and São Paulo, New York, and Miami.

Yet cities are not always high-crime zones; places such as Tokyo and Toronto are known for their orderliness and relative safety. In fact, some of the most dangerous places in the world, on a per capita basis, are not cities at all but rural areas and villages that have undergone great dislocation and upheaval—political, social, and cultural. Afghanistan remains one of the world's most violent countries, but far more dangerous than the capital of Kabul are those outlying areas, where civil authority is absent or corrupt, the opium drug trade is an enticement, and the line between political violence and criminal violence is often blurred.

Rural areas in the United States have had high rates of violent crime: the rural Dakotas, northeast Arizona, south Texas, and rural counties all along the southeastern United States (American Demographics 2000). In all these areas, crime rates corresponded with exceptionally low-income communities of color and with extremely high rates of unemployment: the Dakota Native Reservations, such as Pine Ridge and the Rosebud in the Dakotas; the Navaho–Hopi reservation system in Arizona and New Mexico; the Mexican American communities along the Rio Grande; and the African American communities of the southeastern states. Each of these areas has suffered extreme political, social, and cultural dislocation, and each provides few opportunities with accompanying high rates of alcoholism, domestic violence, and other turmoil. In 2018 violent crime in the rural United States exceeded the national average, driven by new drug problems such as opioids coupled with dislocation and job loss in rural white communities (Mahtani 2018).

U.S. sociologist Robert Merton (1938) drew on Durkheim's ideas and argued for a **strain theory** of criminal activity. Strain occurs when society does not provide the means to achieve the goals a culture considers desirable. This is occurring around the world as people, particularly young people, are bombarded with images of desirable consumer objects but have no means to obtain them. Merton argued that in such cases people may reject the socially approved means and either "retreat," perhaps into alcoholism or drug use, or "innovate." Innovation can take the form of an informal economy, in which people create their own employment on the margins of legal commerce, or it can include more overtly criminal activity. In places of great turmoil, the borders of the legal economy, the informal economy, and the criminal economy may be blurred. Merton noted that there was also the option of rejecting both the cultural goals and the means, and seeking a new form of society—some who we might label criminals see themselves as revolutionaries and freedom fighters.

Richard Cloward and Lloyd Ohlin (1966) argued that these responses are much more likely in settings in which the relative opportunity structure favors criminal activity. Ambitious young people at an elite college may be surrounded by friends and associates with risky schemes to get ahead: hedge funds, start-up companies, venture capital, new internet ventures, and so forth. Ambitious young people in a depressed neighborhood nearby may also be surrounded by friends and associates with risky schemes: profitable drug deals, illegal gambling ventures, smuggling, fencing goods, and so forth. In fact, both groups may face situations that are ethically dubious and potentially illegal, but the dangers of violence and incarceration are far greater on desperate city streets than in comfortable corporate suites.

International Drug Trade

Opium

Drugs have been bound up with power, violence, and crime for a long time, in relationships that often transcend borders. Some of the first international drug lords were none other than the lords of the British East India Company, ultimately making Queen Victoria the top drug kingpin (or queenpin) of her day. In the early 1800s the British emerged as the top mercantile power in South and East Asia. They were becoming the masters of India (which at the time included what are now Pakistan and Bangladesh) and were eager to build a vigorous trade with the great power on the Asian continent, China. China was rich in porcelain, silk, and many other luxury items that could turn a fine profit for the East India Company.

While the Europeans were fascinated with Chinese luxury goods, the Chinese tended to disdain European imports, and so the British could not find a strong market in which to sell as well as buy. After many tries, they finally found their commodity: **opium.** Opium and related narcotics, such as heroin and morphine, are made from the seeds of a poppy that grows across southern

Crime

Rocinha Favela, Rio de Janeiro, the largest favela in Brazil [top] can be marked by violence, drugs, and tense relations with the police but mostly by a vibrant street life of getting by amidst poverty and limited employment, and finding good times with friends and extended family.

Asia. In any of its forms, the refined extract of this poppy is powerfully addictive. Opium was being used in medicines in Europe and North America, where it was touted as a cure for many ailments and a good way to soothe the nerves of wealthy ladies (many of whom became addicted).

The addictive power of opium made it a powerful commodity in China. Smoked in special rooms set aside for this purpose, so-called opium dens, it attracted many Chinese customers, especially men, seeking to escape for a moment the turmoil and dislocation of China's crumbling empire. British traders could transport the opium from poppy fields across South Asia and sell it in China's crowded urban centers. Even as the Chinese government tried to stop the trade, local officials could always be bribed to permit this extremely profitable traffic. They pleaded with the British to end this unconscionable trade, but the lords refused.

Finally the Chinese found an incorruptible official to travel across China and destroy shipments and block further traffic. The British lords responded with war. The British justified the Opium War of 1839–1842 on the grounds that China was interfering with British trade, but the trade involved was simply the drug trade. Even though Great Britain did not have vast numbers of troops, it did have a powerful navy, and British steam-powered gunboats could control the coasts and move up and down the great rivers, such as the Yangtze, at will. Chinese resistance collapsed, and the opium trade, along with other trade concessions, continued. China was finally able to ban the opium trade in 1917, only to have it reimposed by the Japanese occupiers in the 1930s. Addictive drugs thus proved not only profitable, and a good way to support a war effort, but also an effective means of social control.

Profitable drug traffic, once established, is hard to end. In time, opium addiction in many forms found its way around the planet. (The great fictional British detective Sherlock Holmes was portrayed as an addict.) In the twentieth century, heroin, a highly refined extract that can be easily injected, became the narcotic of choice. It was associated with the youth culture in the 1950s and 1960s, claiming high-profile music stars such as John Lennon and Janis Joplin among its addicts. Heroin also became the drug of choice for the dislocated urban poor of Europe and the United States, just as its chemical cousin opium had been for the dislocated urban poor of China.

While opium poppies can be grown in many places, the center of cultivation remains South and Southeast Asia. Poppy cultivation supported the Mujahedeen rebels in Afghanistan, who fought Soviet troops; it briefly supported the Taliban, who for a while tried to stop the cultivation as un-Islamic; and it now supports regional commanders and warlords in remote parts of that country. Warlords found it profitable to be drug lords, as well, and drug trafficking and weapons trafficking often are interrelated. For many years, the center of poppy cultivation was the so-called Golden Triangle, which includes parts of Laos, Thailand, and Myanmar (Burma). The extent of this cultivation has declined, as governments have found that it interferes with other profitable ventures in the area. Myanmar and Afghanistan, both with struggling national governments and long-standing regional conflicts, remain the world's two major supplies of opium.

Morphine continues to be used for pain relief from the battlefield to the hospice center, where in the latter case addiction may not be a major concern in comforting the terminally ill. Heroin addiction remains a major problem and difficult to safely treat. For years, policy makers insisted on banning substances such as marijuana, claiming that lesser drugs were **gateway drugs** leading users to stronger substances, including heroin. For many, however, the gateway drug is often a prescribed painkiller, particularly any of a number of opioids. From the once widely prescribed Oxycodone to powerful fentanyl, these were widely prescribed for decades as pain relievers. When they failed to control the pain, the prescription ran out, or the user simply became dependent on their effects, the next step was often illegally obtained opioids and heroin. In 2020 Purdue Pharma was convicted of three criminal charges of paying doctors and medical record suppliers to promote, prescribe, and expand the use of their brand opioid, OxyContin, while suppressing known risks. Opioid addiction has become a global problem, yet 80 percent of the global opioid production goes to the United States.

Cocaine

Perhaps as ancient as the cultivation of poppies in Asia is the cultivation of coca in South America. The leaves of the coca plant can be brewed into a tea or chewed to serve as a hunger suppressant and a mild stimulant, roughly equivalent to smoking a cigarette or having a cup of coffee. When the extract of the coca leaf is refined into a powder, it becomes a much more powerful drug: **cocaine.**

Cocaine has a long history and was a common ingredient in many patent medicines. Coca-Cola, first put out as a medicine rather than a beverage, got its name from two of its original ingredients in 1885; the cola nut and cocaine from the coca leaf. As concern about the dangers of cocaine grew, it was gradually taken out of products. In Coca-Cola, it was replaced with another, less potent, stimulant: caffeine.

Powdered cocaine became a popular drug of choice in the 1960s, fashionable enough to have songs written about it. Powdered cocaine was seen as less dangerous than heroin and could be inhaled rather than injected. Always quite expensive, it became the drug of choice for the young and well-off. A modified method of preparing the drug, essentially a cooking process, resulted in crack cocaine, or **crack,** which could be smoked. This new form was cheaper and more available and so quickly made inroads into low-income communities.

The rise of the cocaine trade transformed entire regions in the Andes highlands of South America. Poor farmers in Bolivia found in the coca plant the only crop with a guaranteed world market. Yet farmers rarely saw much of the profit. Rather, they often saw their communities devastated by violence, as drug traffickers fought one another and their governments. Backed by the U.S. military, regional governments made forays into the countryside to destroy crops and refining stations (Weatherford 2012). The center of the cocaine trade fell in Colombia, and entire cities were transformed.

The largest **drug cartel** came to dominate the city of Medellín, Colombia, in the 1980s. Before his death in 1993 Pablo Escobar organized the Medellín traffickers into a cartel that dominated the world market and even Colombian politics through bribery, intimidation, and assassination. No judge, municipal official, or legislator who refused the cartel's money and influence was safe, and many were killed. At the height of its power and wealth, the Medellín cartel became so bold that their schemes were mind-boggling. At one point, U.S. and Colombian agents discovered a submarine under construction in the Andes Mountains. The traffickers planned to somehow move it down into the ocean and use it to slip under U.S. Coast Guard supervision. The Medellín cartel was intensely anticommunist; some dubbed them "cocaine capitalists," for they certainly believed in free trade, and they used their profits to support right-wing paramilitary groups. At the same time, leftist rebels realized the profit potential in the coca plant and also began to use cocaine money to finance their need for weapons and supplies.

Cocaine turned parts of Colombia into war zones, and in the form of "crack," it seemed to do the same thing to many American cities. New York, Los Angeles, Detroit, and Washington, DC, were particularly hard hit. The shock of the crack epidemic filled newspapers with accounts of this powerful new drug, which would drive its addicts to do anything. Also common were stories of "crack babies" born to addicted mothers. The babies were so physiologically and psychologically scarred that they were presumed to be the next generation of killers.

In truth, crack cocaine, while addictive and dangerous, is probably no worse for an individual than anything smoked in Shanghai, China, in 1850. But it became an epidemic in vulnerable communities, which collapsed under the added weight of addiction. Rival street gangs fought over local control. Money, much of it coming from outside these exceedingly poor communities, poured into the illegal economy, just as legitimate sources of income were disappearing. The effects on many low-income, often African American, communities were so devastating that some claimed crack was an intentional plan to destroy black America. The desperation and violence of the crack economy took hold across many U.S. cities, deepening already existing problems of deindustrialization and urban dislocation.

The U.S. government's response of declaring a "war on drugs" truly looked like a military operation in parts of Latin America and the Caribbean. Efforts focused on destroying the supply lines coming into the United States. Drug interdiction became a primary task of the U.S. Coast Guard. Since drugs were intertwined with politics in Latin America, antidrug activity often involved action against rebels and even governments. The United States accused President Manuel Noriega of Panama of being involved in drug trafficking and used this as part of the rationale for invading the country in 1989 and deposing him.

The United States has also supplied helicopters, night-vision goggles, and Special Forces to Colombia and Bolivia to fight drug suppliers and, by extension, rebel groups who have reputed drug ties. These countries, along with Peru, continue to be the center of cocaine manufacturing. Highland peasant farmers are often caught in the crossfire, unfortunately, and complain of the destruction of their farms, whether or not they contain coca plants. Many in Latin America have argued that these dramatic military sweeps distract from the real problem, which is not the growing supply in Latin America but the growing demand in the United States.

Cannabis

The **cannabis** plant produces a useful fiber, **hemp;** a quite powerful drug, **hashish;** and a somewhat milder drug, **marijuana.** These drugs also have a long history. They became popular in the United States with the so-called beat generation of the 1950s, and their rates of use soared in the 1960s, such that "hash" and "pot" became common terms. Hashish had long been used in South Asia, however, and had a certain appeal for those interested in Indian mysticism, including high-profile international figures.

Much more common was the inexpensive and easily attainable marijuana. Less potent and less addictive (though its dangers and addictive qualities have often been debated), marijuana became a common social drug. Even today in the United States, about one-third of the adult population admits to having tried a form of cannabis, usually smoking marijuana. In fact, politicians who came of age in the 1960s often have had to dodge probing questions about their use of this illegal drug.

Cannabis is grown and trafficked widely around the world. But its ability to grow in any mild climate (or on a windowsill, for that matter) has made it less profitable to traffickers. Mexican marijuana coming into the United States must compete with many homegrown varieties.

The legalization of marijuana has long been controversial. Early films such as *Reefer Madness* (1936) portrayed it as a powerfully dangerous drug. The most extreme of the purported dangers have not been verified, though medical professionals note that frequently inhaling *any* kind of smoke is not a healthful practice. In the 1970s 11 states started to **decriminalize** possession of small amounts of marijuana. In the 1990s five states—California, Oregon, Washington, Alaska, and Maine—approved marijuana's use for medical purposes, such as controlling the nausea that comes with chemotherapy and the anxiety of PTSD (posttraumatic stress disorder). Colorado largely ignored small-scale use of marijuana and then in 2012, along with Washington State, allowed its so-called recreational use, which did not require a prescription or approved-use card. By 2020 a majority of states allowed some medical use of marijuana, but its use was still opposed in many Southern, Midwestern, and Plains states. Ten states allowed recreational marijuana in 2020, although federal laws against its use, sale, and transport remain. Proposed legislation such as the MORE Act would remove marijuana from the federal list of scheduled substances, expunge the record of those convicted of minor marijuana charges, and tax its legal sale.

The most successful experiment in decriminalization has been in the Netherlands, where so-called coffee shops (some of which sell no coffee at all) are allowed to sell small quantities of marijuana and hashish. The product cannot be resold, it must be consumed on the premises, and no disorderly conduct is allowed. Since customers typically walk to these establishments or use public transport, there is also no danger of impaired driving. In the Dutch social context, this has worked very well, and drug-use rates for Dutch youths are no higher than those in the United States. The idea that cannabis will be a "gateway" drug, leading to other drug use, has probably been diminished, in that the purchase and use of this substance are completely separate from other more potent drugs, which are still illegal. Most significantly, incarceration rates for drug offenses in the Netherlands are a fraction of what they are in the United States.

Tobacco

The most widely trafficked drug in the world is not illegal (except in the tiny state of Bhutan): It is **tobacco,** with its addictive stimulant, **nicotine.** Tobacco was first grown by American Indians in the southeastern area of North America. Like **peyote** in the western part of the continent, tobacco was generally not used as a daily leisure activity but rather for ceremonial use. In the 1600s the newly formed European colonies needed a cash crop to support them, having failed to find gold and other precious items. As tobacco pipe smoking became fashionable in Europe, tobacco became that cash crop for the British American colonies. In the Caribbean, it was second only to sugar production.

Tobacco can be grown almost anywhere the soil will support its nutrient demands, but much of the production remains in the United States, Canada, and Cuba. Cuba's niche is hand-rolled cigars, while the United States has dominated in mass-produced cigarettes. With smoking rates falling in North America, each of these locations is heavily dependent on tobacco exports. Smoking rates are very high in parts of Asia and Eastern Europe: Three-quarters of the men in Vietnam and two-thirds of the men in Russia and China smoke, although the rates are much lower for the women in Asia. In comparison, less than one-quarter of the U.S. population, both men and women, smoke.

As a result, large U.S. tobacco companies have aggressively marketed their product overseas, particularly in the growing markets in Asia. The Marlboro man, originally created to get men to smoke what was seen as a women's brand, has been one of the world's most successful advertising images. He still rides the range, but increasingly on billboards across East Asia. Exports have been the key to survival for U.S. and Canadian tobacco-farming communities and have helped the North American balance of trade with Asia. Yet as smoking-related illness continues to climb in Asia, one wonders if this is not continuing a pattern of trade in addictive substances that dates back to the Opium War.

Alcohol

Despite high-profile challengers, the world's preferred drug of choice for the last 7,000 years has been **alcohol.** The brewing of beer goes back to prehistoric times, probably to the very beginning of the cultivation of grains. Wine production is also ancient. While wine-tippling Romans became part of our lore about wealthy excess, alcohol has also been the drug of choice of the poor.

During the European Middle Ages, grain was hard to store and distribute in a manner that was safe from mold and rats, unless it was brewed into beer. At certain times, European peasants may have gotten large portions of their calories from beer and basically been tipsy for a good share of their working lives (Braudel 1979). Maybe it relieved the drudgery and deprivation that accompanied their lot.

Distilled spirits became common only in the early industrial period, when simple metal machinery for distilleries became common and inexpensive. Distilled spirits required much less space for the transport of the same amount of alcohol and so lent themselves to wider distribution. Brandy may have begun as a more compact alternative to wine.

The common drink of choice in the seventeenth to nineteenth centuries, however, was rum distilled from sugarcane. Rum figured prominently in a triangular trade that existed among Europe, Africa, and the Americas. Slaves were brought from Africa to work on the sugar plantations of Brazil and northern South America and the Caribbean. Sugar from the plantations was brought into New England by traders and distilled into rum. The rum was consumed locally, exported back to Europe, and used in part to pay off crews on the slave and trade ships and to buy more slaves in West Africa.

Today any visitor to a duty-free shop in an airport knows there remains a brisk international business in spirits. Wine exports are vital to the economies of France, Italy, Spain, and Portugal and increasingly so to places as diverse as Chile and Australia. Beer exports have long been important to Germany and the Netherlands. Beer was also one of the foundations of economic growth in Monterrey,

Mexico, and fueled the development of truck transport and related industries, such as glassmaking, in the area. Mexican beer exports continue to climb.

Attitudes toward alcohol, and thus its impact, vary greatly around the world. Alcoholic beverages are not allowed to be sold in strict Islamic states in the Middle East, except sometimes in stores catering to non-Muslim foreigners. Alcohol is forbidden to Muslims, but adherence to this practice has varied widely around the world. Many Christian groups— including Mormons (Latter Day Saints), Seventh-Day Adventists, and some Baptists and Pentecostals forbid or strongly discourage the consumption of alcohol.

The temperance movement against the consumption of alcohol in the United States and Great Britain was strong for nearly a century, from the 1830s to the 1930s, and was closely tied to Christian religious convictions as well as the feminist and abolitionist movements. Revival preachers spoke against the evils of alcohol, but some of the most determined protestors were women, who saw temperance as part of overall social reform. Men wasted family resources on alcohol and then became abusive, and alcohol and tobacco had long been intertwined with slavery and other social ills. By 1900 the emphasis had shifted to alcohol and urban poverty and urban decay, as growing immigrant and industrial cities faced mounting problems. Alcohol consumption was banned in the United States in 1920, with the passage of the Eighteenth Amendment, only to be restored 13 years later with the passage of the Twenty-First Amendment, in part, as an effort to revive the Depression-stricken economy.

Alcoholism continues to be associated with a wide array of social problems, from domestic violence to impaired driving. Alcohol is implicated in 56.6 percent of incarcerations in the United States, which includes 57.7 percent of inmates who committed a violent crime (NCADD 2016). National rates of alcoholism are highest in Russia and parts of Eastern Europe, where a tradition of heavy alcohol consumption, especially among men, has been coupled with political and economic dislocation that has resulted in, among other things, very high unemployment rates, also especially among men. Extremely high rates of alcoholism have also plagued the American Indian communities in the United States and Canada, similarly coupled with social and cultural dislocation and soaring rates of unemployment. Alcoholism in both Russia and among Native North Americans is also associated with high rates of aggravated assault, domestic violence, divorce, and, striking in both contexts, suicide.

New Recipes: Chemical Agents

Mind-altering substances can also be produced from common substances in the laboratory or someone's modified kitchen. Lysergic acid diethylamide or **LSD,** a hallucinogen that can occur in nature due to the action of certain molds and also can be synthesized, was the preferred mind-altering substance of the 1960s. It was often used to attempt to expand consciousness and perception, in ways similar to the use of peyote in the Southwest United States and the use of various hallucinogens by shamans and tribal religious specialists in South America and elsewhere (although with far fewer social controls over its use and the results). The use of LSD was popularized and even glamorized by high-profile proponents, such as Timothy Leary, and rock songs such as "Lucy in the Sky with Diamonds." But when LSD use became associated with vivid and at times agonizing adverse effects, known as "bad trips," it fell out of favor.

In the 1990s new **designer drugs,** such as MDMA ("ecstasy") and PCP ("angel dust"), gained popularity, sometimes in concert with the rise of a version of international electronic music that became known as *techno*. Powerfully addictive **methamphetamine,** or "meth," which can be "cooked" in small labs and even home kitchens, has provided a new alternative for homemade production to the drug trade. Meth use became the epidemic of the early twenty-first century, striking hard in rural U.S. communities in the Midwest and South that were often not considered "drug hot spots." Meth use now rivals that of powered cocaine (NIDA 2020). It is both powerfully addictive and incredibly damaging to the body. While meth can be "cooked" anywhere with the right supply of ingredients, such as common decongestants, it has also become a lucrative product for the Mexico–U.S. drug trade. Meth can be made in large batches by drug cartels with ready supplies and relative immunity from authorities and then moved across international borders.

Simpler homemade substances are often the preference of the world's urban poor, especially the youth. In an alcove next to a street theater in Guatemala City, a group of 10 or 12 boys cluster, many holding plastic bags containing a thick, yellow liquid (Konner 1991). The children are homeless except for this alcove, many fleeing families who were abusive or simply too poor to keep them. "The glue makes you loco, crazy," they admit. "It hurts your brain." But it also quells their hunger pangs and boredom, and so its use persists. Glue is cheap and available, sold in plastic bags by adults who clearly know these street kids are not assembling airplane models. Some Latin American street youth have turned from glue to aerosol inhalants, which provide a quicker high and less of a headache. They are, however, equally dangerous, especially in causing long-term brain damage.

Elsewhere in Central America the drug of choice is **bazooka** (a twist on its Spanish name, *pasuco*). Bazooka is generally an ill-defined mix of homegrown marijuana spiked with crack cocaine and sometimes other chemicals, rolled into a fat "joint" to be smoked. Frequent border crossers think it could be the next profitable drug recipe in urban California, Texas, or Florida.

Incarceration around the World

Societies are burdened not only by the effects of crime itself but also by the difficulty and high cost of incarcerating convicts. Nowhere in the world is this a bigger problem than in the United States, where incarceration rates have soared five times as fast as the population. With over two million incarcerated individuals, the United States now holds 25 percent of the world's prison population, and a greater proportion of its population is behind bars than in any other country. The United States has more total prisoners than even more populous China and India (see figure 5.2).

In the 1980s the U.S. rate of incarceration was third in the world, behind the Soviet Union and South Africa. Rates in those countries dropped with the breakup of the Soviet Union and the end of apartheid in South Africa; in both cases, there was a release of many political prisoners. Even though crime rates in both Russia and South Africa have grown dramatically since then, the prison populations have not climbed as rapidly. In contrast, in the United States the prison population grew in the 1980s and 1990s, even as the crime rate fell.

The single biggest factor behind this increase was drug sentencing. Tougher drug laws and mandatory sentencing meant more prison time for more people. In the 1980s the Reagan administration's "get tough" approach to drugs and crime meant longer sentences. This trend toward greater punishment for drug offenses slowed down at the beginning of the Clinton administration. But when Clinton was accused of being "soft on drugs" and references to his own college-age marijuana use became common, policy again shifted toward tougher enforcement, including the "three-strikes rule" for those convicted of three felonies. Many drug-related offenses in the United States are felonies. Over 1.3 million of the two million Americans behind bars are serving time for nonviolent offenses, usually drug-related crimes.

Incarceration rates in the United States have been declining since 2006, due in part to changes in sentencing for drug violations in poor communities; specifically, the black imprisonment rate has fallen by 33 percent. Despite this decline, a vast racial gap in incarceration exists in the United States, with black Americans five times more likely to serve prison sentences than white Americans (Nellis 2016; Gramlich 2020).

The approach to drug use varies greatly around the world. Some countries, particularly in the Middle East and Asia, have very strict drug laws. In many of these societies, drug laws are coupled with strict social controls and expectations that make illegal drug use uncommon. Other countries, such as Thailand and Mexico, which have been transit points for the drug trade, have turned to stricter enforcement, although it has been undermined by corruption (always a problem where drugs can generate large amounts of money) and the underfunding of law enforcement efforts (Elsner 2005). Many European countries,

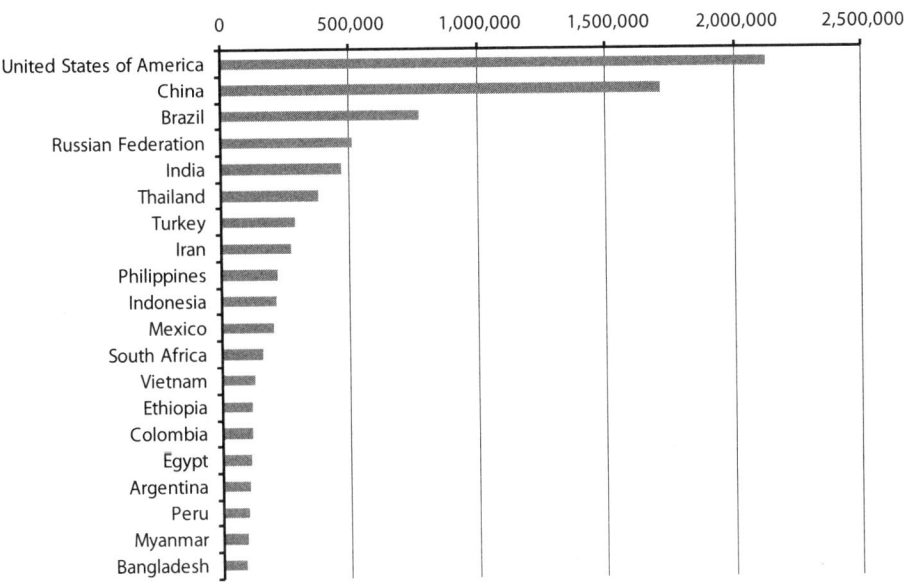

Figure 5.2 Countries with the most prisoners, 2020. (Source: World Prison Brief, Institute for Crime & Justice Policy Research.)

particularly the Netherlands and the Scandinavian countries, have treated drug use less as a criminal problem and more as a public health problem. As a result, they have invested less in incarceration and more in drug treatment for chronic offenders (Karberg & Beck 2004).

International Crime Cartels

Trading in Guns, Drugs, and People

Crime trends around the world are difficult to gauge. Some locations, such as southern and western Africa and parts of Latin America and Eastern Europe, have clearly seen rising crime rates, often as part of political and social disruption and growing inequality. The United States saw a long downward trend in crime throughout the 1990s, but that trend started to reverse for property crime at the beginning of the twenty-first century, accompanying a general economic downturn with rising unemployment (FBI 2004). Fear of crime also seems to have increased in cities around the world, partly as urban dwellers have become less sure they are safe by living in presumably good neighborhoods. The world may not have more criminals than ever before, but it certainly has more weapons, and the criminal element is better armed and hence deadlier than ever.

The United States has a long history of urban gangs: Irish, Italian, even Jewish and Polish (Steinberg 2001). What has changed is that urban gangs now often have ready access to high-capacity firearms: automatic pistols, rapid-fire shotguns (such as the infamous "street sweeper"), and automatic and semiautomatic versions of military assault rifles. During the 1980s the hallmark of gang violence shifted from the switchblade stabbing to the drive-by shooting. Both are dangerous to rival gang members, but the latter also brings far greater dangers to passers-by, such as children and neighborhood residents. This pattern has been echoed in Latin America, Africa, and Central Asia, where weapons sometimes originally obtained for civil war and unrest have made their way into the hands of now heavily armed criminal gangs. At times it is difficult to determine whether a group is a revolutionary army or just a criminal gang, as drug trafficking, weapons, and violence against civilians often characterize both.

One ironic twist to the growth of free markets with less government regulation has been greater opportunities for national and international crime cartels. States emerging from the former Soviet Union—Russia, Ukraine, and Belarus, in particular—saw a surge in organized criminal activity, or "Mafia capitalism." Crimean resorts once favored by communist officials suddenly became the haunts of crime figures in Armani suits, brokering illegal trade and extortion on their ever-present cell phones. China has worried about organized criminal activity in Hong Kong and the former Portuguese-controlled port of Macau. Italy has seen a decline in blatant Mafia activity in the south, but there are new rumors of graft and corruption and possible ties to organized crime at the highest levels of government.

Though the weapons and methods have become more sophisticated and the scope of activity has gone global, the favored criminal activities all have a long history: drug trafficking, prostitution (now often including the global trafficking in women), extortion and kickbacks, and weapons trafficking. New concern has arisen about trafficking in so-called weapons of mass destruction, although most of the trade involves small arms, such as automatic weapons and grenade launchers.

Concern about international crime and international terrorism has also led to a rise in international cooperation among law enforcement agencies. Organizations such as INTERPOL (International Criminal Police Organization) attempt to coordinate police efforts across international boundaries, although different procedures and political agendas often complicate international anti-crime cooperation.

Mexico's Drug Wars

"Drug wars" has been a popular phrase since the U.S. Reagan administration declared war on drugs. In Mexico, however, the violence that has exploded since Mexican president Felipe Calderón moved against the drug

Military-style police arrest in Santa Lucia, El Salvador. Gangs have moved into transnational spaces such as the feared Mara Salvatrucha-18 (MS-18), born in the movement of poor young men between Los Angeles, California, and El Salvador. Drugs and violence are part of this world, as are gang-identifying tattoos and the fears and ambitions of displaced young Salvadorans.

gangs in 2006 can only be compared to war. According to the Council on Foreign Relations (2021), Mexico has seen over 300,000 drug-related homicides since 2006. The dead include students, journalists, and politicians. Ciudad Juárez, across the border from El Paso, Texas, had long been a violent community, with women working in the maquiladora factories particularly vulnerable to violence over years of unsolved murders. But as rival gangs battled for control of the city, while also battling local, state, and federal police and then the Mexican army and marines, Juárez has become the most violent city in the world. Most casualties are among gang members or the police and military, but hundreds of others have also been killed in attacks on drug clinics, businesses, and even on a children's birthday party.

While Mexicans debate causes and responses to the extraordinary violence, a familiar pattern is in place: Though always called Mexico's drug war, it involves a familiar international movement of drugs, guns, and people. Illegal drugs flow north from Mexico into profitable markets in the United States. Money and U.S. weapons, particularly high-capacity assault-style weapons, flow back into Mexico. U.S. guns are readily available, and powerful semi-automatic assault weapons can often be converted back to fully automatic military-style weapons, giving the gangs more firepower than local police. The smuggling of people is often involved, not just to carry guns and drugs, but also to transport undocumented workers who are hoping to reach the United States. In several dramatic cases, large numbers who had paid gangs for safe transport were murdered in remote areas. Police corruption has been a constant problem, as well as police forces too intimidated by assassinations to be very effective. The Mexican government has come to depend more and more on the military for antigang assaults, but the military has also been charged with rights violations, corruption, and abuses. One of the deadliest of the gangs, the Zetas, consisted originally of former military members who left, often taking weapons with them, to become enforcers for drug cartels. They have now set off on their own and, as they expand south into Mexico, have also recruited former counterinsurgency fighters from Guatemala, many U.S. trained, to join their ranks. The strong push by the Calderón administration has led to a strong pushback by the gangs in targeted killings of police, mayors, and military personnel and families, and also to greater turf wars among the gangs. As one leader is killed or captured, others fight to take over the drug and human trafficking routes and distribution points.

Some also point to broader connections between the United States and Mexico in these wars. While the North American Free Trade Agreement (NAFTA), and now the United States–Mexico–Canada Agreement (USMCA), have brought some economic benefit to parts of Mexico, these agreements have also displaced thousands of farmers who can no longer compete with cheap farm imports. Those who have been displaced seek work and survival in the United States and in Mexico's major urban centers, particularly in the north of the country. The factories that remain often prefer to employ young women, leaving young, poorly educated men with few options. The lure of money and excitement offered by the gangs can be particularly powerful to those with no other prospects, even as they know that their lives will likely be fast, brutal, and short. The United States worries about spillover violence in its own cities, particularly near the border. Meanwhile, Mexico's Central American neighbors, and countries further south, watch with concern that they could be the next to fall into this deadly vortex of drugs, guns, and corruption. As it stands, two of Mexico's principal drug cartels moved 90 percent of their U.S.-bound cocaine trafficking operations to Central America (UNODC 2012).

In Search of Opportunity and Order

What can be done to address the worldwide problem of crime? Political conservatives often emphasize the need to restore order. Police forces must be strict but also efficient and effective, with high professional standards. In parts of Latin America the police now dress in combat attire and ride around in the backs of pickup trucks, often carrying automatic weapons. They are an intimidating force but are also often suspect. They look more like an occupying army than an agent of law enforcement, only a bit more sophisticated than the Nigerian Lord's Resistance Army vigilantes.

Mexico had long favored this style of policing, but in major urban areas, at least in the more prosperous areas, the U.S. model of single or paired police officers riding in a patrol car (or in some cases, even on a bicycle), well-dressed and sporting only a small automatic pistol and handcuffs, has replaced this older model. Efforts to eliminate police corruption are difficult, especially when salaries are very low compared to the profits possible through graft, extortion, and bribes. In Brazil police in prosperous urban areas have also shifted to a friendlier, more professional look. Those who patrol the poor urban and periphery slums, however, still often look more like a patrol in 1960s Vietnam than a modern police force, as they move through in combat boots and helmets, carrying automatic rifles that are continually pointed into the shifting shadows. A recent move against drug lords and gang members in Rio de Janeiro's largest slum included the usual helicopters and armored personnel carriers of military-style assault. But it has also been combined with community-based policing Brazilian-style, with police teaching capoeira and partaking of other activities in the slums to get know and build the trust of residents, particularly the young men.

Criminologist James Q. Wilson has written about the need to restore order to urban spaces as part of restoring urban vitality. In an influential essay called "Broken Windows" (1982), Wilson and George L. Kelling note that signs of urban decay and disorder—broken windows, gang graffiti, and the presence of loiterers—give an impression of abandoned spaces, which terrify law-abiding citizens and welcome further crime. Wilson's ideas were influential in the anti-crime administration of former New York mayor Rudolph Giuliani. Fixing up abandoned buildings was not controversial, but heavy-handed police action against the indigent and homeless (who may not have been criminal but gave areas a disorderly appearance) clearly was. Still, many credited the ideas with a reduction in New York's crime problem and an improved image for the city.

While political conservatives have stressed order, political progressives have often championed opportunity—legitimate, hopeful opportunity—as the solution to crime. Sociologist William J. Wilson (1996) has argued that the answer to urban crime and disorder is to open the opportunity structure by supporting educational improvement and full employment policies. He contends that many poor urban residents endorse mainstream values but find no way to live out those law-abiding, family-oriented values in neighborhoods that have been abandoned by legitimate businesses and institutions.

Urban and rural residents who are fearful of crime often speak of their desires for both greater order and greater opportunity. Crime prevention seems to hinge on elements of both. Careful, professional policing coupled with neighborhood involvement not only builds trust but also reduces the local power of criminals and the attractiveness of crime. Policing efforts that focus on building a sense of trust and security have been effective in communities in both the United States and Europe and might offer hope for Latin America and Africa. At the same, their effectiveness also seems to depend on the availability of legitimate alternatives to criminal activity that offer opportunities for advancement and hope for the future.

Key Ideas

> - Although crime has a long history, fear about growing, violent crime is a feature of many places, both urban and rural, around the world.
>
> - Social and economic dislocation has left many, especially many young people, on the margins of the economy and can drive those with few other opportunities into criminal activity.
>
> - Much crime has taken on global dimensions, particularly in the trafficking of people, weapons, and drugs. Traditional drugs such as opium and cocaine remain highly profitable, while powerful new drugs have entered the international market.
>
> - One result of drug activity and the violent conflict it has produced is growing levels of incarceration, and the accompanying overcrowded prisons in many countries, particularly in the United States and Latin America.
>
> - In addressing crime, political conservatives often stress restoring a sense of order, whereas progressives argue for more open opportunities for marginalized groups. Amid rapid economic and social change, many societies are struggling to strike a balance between order and opportunity.

For Review and Discussion

1. What factors have been cited as causes of crime and violence? Which do you believe are the most important causes?
2. Why are some societies, and some cities, so much more violent than others?
3. How have countries responded to the problem of illegal drugs and drug trafficking? Which solutions do you see as the most effective? Would you support decriminalization of some or all drugs or would you support tougher penalties and enforcement?
4. What has driven the rising rates of incarceration? Are there alternatives to prison that seem promising?
5. Is crime inevitable? Are there measures that can be taken to reduce the level or the danger of crime?

Making Connections

United Nations Office on Drugs and Crime

➤ The interconnection of drugs and crime with other social ills and struggles can be overlooked in a strict law enforcement perspective. The UN Office on Drugs and Crime (UNODC) includes a page where they link efforts to combat destructive drugs and crime to the UN Sustainable Development Goals, including challenges of poverty, education, and employment. See their links at https://www.unodc.org/unodc/en/sustainable-development-goals/index.html.

Bureau of Justice Statistics

➤ Current statistics and trends on crime in the United States can be found at www.bjs.gov. What current trends in crime and incarceration do you note? On what types of criminal activity does the U.S. government focus its activities?

Drug Enforcement Administration

➤ Go to the site of the DEA, the main U.S. drug enforcement agency (www.dea.gov). What are the prime concerns of the DEA and how does it approach issues of drugs and addiction?

INTERPOL

➤ The International Criminal Police Organization, INTERPOL, has a site at www.interpol.int. It has a huge amount of information on international crime, including drugs and drug trafficking, money laundering, and trafficking in children, as well as international crime statistics. Further information on U.S. and international crime can be found at www.fbi.gov the site of the Federal Bureau of Investigation (FBI).

El Jefe

➤ In summer of 2021, the Mexican government filed suit against U.S. gun manufacturers, claiming they were abetting violence in the country's gang conflicts. One of the most popular status symbols for Mexican gang leaders and drug lords is to own a Colt *El Jefe* ("The Boss"). It can come gold-plated with engravings drawing on Mexican heritage – including Day of the Dead. Look up images of the 38 caliber *El Jefe*, or its more powerful cousin, the 45 caliber *Jefe of Jefes*, online. Why do these weapons, and others, have the look that they do? Do gun manufacturers have a responsibility – or even a legal liability – for how their products are marketed and used?

Making a Difference

Gun Controversies

➤ Efforts to reduce the prevalence of weapons and gun-related violence in the United States are described at www.bradyunited.org. The site is named for the efforts conducted in the name of James Brady, who was shot in the attempt to assassinate U.S. President Ronald Reagan. The site strives to remain nonpartisan and data-centered, but gun control is a very controversial topic in the United States. The most complete counterpoint can be found at the site of the National Rifle Association (www.nra.org), a huge site with many articles on crime and violence from a progun position. How do the two sites differ in their assessments of the nature, causes, and solutions to crime and violence?

Amnesty International

➤ This international human rights organization collects data on incarceration around the world and champions the rights of detainees to legal counsel and fair trials. Visit the group's website at www.amnesty.org. What are some of the current issues in crime and incarceration?

6

War

States of Terror

Global Encounters

Vietnam

Ho Chi Minh City, still often called Saigon by its residents, reflects the mid-morning sun back at us in the multiple hues of postmodern glass towers. The tallest buildings all seem to have cranes still perched on them, finishing their construction. The tops tout their sponsors: Citibank, Prudential, Sheraton, and Sofitel. Modern Saigon's skyline has its eyes fixed on the future. This city and the country are also deeply rooted in the past. We tour the history museum and find amid the usual artifacts a repeated theme. Room after room features a martial diorama: one Vietnamese hero after another leading the people in a heroic defense against invading Chinese, Mongols, Khmer, Thais, Manchus, and others. It is always a national struggle against a foreign power. The French and the Americans get their own museum. It was once known as the War Atrocities Museum, now softened to War Remnants. Our students who visit this cataloguing of U.S. atrocities feel discomfort that goes beyond just the gruesome depictions of war. Many of the supposed perpetrators were young Americans of just their age. Here they are now wandering with Vietnamese guides. Would there be animosity or resentment? They find neither from their gracious hosts who may have had relatives on both sides of the conflict. Of course the museum does not catalog atrocities committed by the Vietcong or their northern supporters, but even in these halls an understanding seems to emerge between the hosts and guests: This is not about the brutality of one side but the realization that war is organized brutality, only glorious from a distance, always ugly up close.

I skip the atrocities for another memento of the conflict that the Vietnamese know as the American War. The Reunification Palace is a museum housed in what had been the presidential palace and war headquarters of South Vietnam. The tanks that crashed the gates still stand outside and a helicopter waits quietly on the roof. Inside are the mementos of a strange regime that the United States tried futilely to prop up: one floor of maps and old radios to monitor the war, one of great meeting rooms in a strange blend of old Chinese and 1960s California styles, and one floor of gambling rooms and theaters for leaders who couldn't travel within their own country.

The next day students venture north out of the city to climb through the Cu Chi tunnels. Vietcong lived in these tunnels for years at the height of the war, hiding from U.S. bombings and using them as staging grounds for sudden attacks on Saigon. The students are awed at the life and determination these tunnels represent, even if it now feels more like man-made spelunking than the terror-filled battles these dark chambers must have witnessed. Following the tour, visitors can now, for an extra fee, fire off rounds from various war-era weapons. Several students take to this activity with glee, while others are mortified at the commercialization of a national tragedy. Do the trigger-happy students know what the clatter of these weapons meant to young Americans and to thousands of Vietnamese of all ages during the war years? The trip leader is a senior passenger on our voyage, a retired infantry colonel who served two terms of duty in Vietnam. A quiet man with an easy smile, he just shakes his head: "I don't blame the young people, I don't think they can understand what those weapons represent, but I'm disappointed that the Vietnamese seem to be making an amusement center of this place."

In place of the trek north, I make the short journey south into the Mekong Delta. We venture out by ferry into the wide Mekong, then by small boat, and eventually by rowboat to navigate through the narrow channels and canals that separate islands with mythical and garden names: Dragon Island, Unicorn Island, and Coconut Island. These places still support crops that feed the hotels of Saigon but are also eager for their share of the direct tourist revenue. We pass other boats filled with Japanese and German tourists, all smiling as we navigate these lush jungle channels. The students I'm with have only a vague notion of the history of this area, one of the war's great early battlefields: "Hadn't Dad talked about 'the delta'?" "He was some sort of SEAL or something, I think in boats, maybe?" A few remember the controversies surrounding Senator John Kerry and his swift boat adventures, and I try to fill in some of the history that our guide is less than eager to discuss in detail. It isn't clear if he is just too polite to discuss such things with Americans or, like much of our party, too young to know much of the events that troubled these lush lanes.

Most sobered are those students who travel to Cambodia, some with visiting parents. The killing fields of Pol Pot's Khmer Rouge remain, with bones and teeth still littering the land they are walking across. Here amid the remains of two million murdered Cambodians, no one asks to fire off a few rounds. Yet Cambodia is also looking ahead. After being nearly abandoned, Phnom Penh is slowly rebuilding, although the pavement often ends with the tourist district. Even remote Angkor Wat, home of the great Khmer temples, is seeing a new building boom. Glitzy hotels, most only a few years old, line the way in and out of the temple grounds. At night, the students find the strip oddly reminiscent of Las Vegas. They must remind themselves that unlike at Caesars and the Luxor, the ancient temples next to the hotel strip here are real.

What are the lessons of this complex and changing place? Two simple understandings might have spared the United States a decade and a half of misery: One, the regions of Vietnam are many and varied and not easily united, and north–south divisions run deep. And two, in spite of this, the sense of nationalism is strong, and while foreign involvement is welcomed, foreign domination has been hated for two millennia. What the United States saw as a battle over global communism, the Vietnamese saw as one more chapter in an ongoing struggle for national independence. A more recent lesson is the near impossibility of successfully imposing a centrally planned economy on the people here. If U.S. military ambitions failed miserably, so too did the economic ambitions of the Leninists of Vietnam and the Maoists of Cambodia. This land also speaks of the limitations of war as foreign policy. Decades of peaceful relations have brought more to the people and done more to make Vietnam a stable, pro-American place of opportunity than was ever accomplished by all the military hardware the "free world" could muster.

Less clear are the lessons for the future. The city that most still call Saigon is a comfortable place: modern and familiar enough to make one feel at home, exotic enough to be interesting. But what is its future? Should it aspire to be the Singapore of Vietnam? And the contradictions remain. How long can a government embrace all that global capitalism can offer and still claim to be communist? And how long can a government claim revolutionary legitimacy without holding free elections? For now, most people seem content with the heady combination of united independence and steady economic growth, elusive ideals for Vietnam for centuries. In a land too long torn by war, no one wants to disturb the peace. At least not yet.

How States Made War and War Made States

Why something like war—so costly in lives, investment, and destruction—has been so persistent and so prominent as a part of the human experience is a perplexing question. Longtime war correspondent Christopher Hedges (2003) offers a psychological answer: "War is a force that gives us meaning," turning ordinary lives into extraordinary moments in history and heightening our sense of purpose, honor, heroism, and even passion. American sociologist and social historian of conflict, Charles Tilly (1975) contends that the modern world is addicted to war, in part because the modern world is the product of a millennium of wars.

Has warfare always been part of human existence? It is hard to know. While there are some human cultures that seem almost exclusively peaceful, they are rare and usually isolated. (There might have been many more that were not so isolated and so were overrun.) Some ancient cultures, such as the Maya culture of Mexico, once thought to be very peaceful, have turned out to have been highly involved in warfare.

Even the animal kingdom doesn't offer much hope. Chimpanzees, once thought to be peaceful animals, have been observed attacking other bands and ganging up on individuals, engaging in primal (or at least primate) warfare. There may be a gender issue here: Young male chimps like to shake sticks and intimidate rivals, behavior rarely seen among females. But observers have also noted mother–daughter attack teams. Sometimes, the fight is over territory, but most often it is over dominance.

Human tribal warfare seems to have been much the same—sporadic skirmishes over territory and dominance, a chance to prove one's courage and, occasionally, a very human addition: revenge for past grievances. Yet with rare exceptions, tribal warfare did not take many lives. Sometimes the tactics—ritual announcements and expressions of bravado—even seemed designed to offer maximum opportunities for courage and minimal opportunities for carnage. This changed as large agrarian empires became the norm in the Middle East, India, and China around 5,000 years ago and to a lesser extent in Mesoamerica and the Andes somewhat later. Perhaps warfare is not so much built into our genes as it is built into our societies.

Empires are the result of conquest. In short, they are about war. Kings and emperors are primarily war leaders who derive their power and prestige from conquest. In such a situation, war becomes chronic. Logistics and weather often prevented year-round conflict, so there were seasons of war. The Bible speaks of spring as "the time when kings go forth to war" (2 Kings 11:1). The peasants must have often hoped for a long winter. The great problems for the conquerors were often ones of logistics, such as feeding and moving large armies (and later their horses). The maximum size of an empire was determined by how long it took the king's armies to reach the furthest corner. Paying for a large army depended on success. Tribute and loot from conquered states would pay for an army to march on to new conquests.

As a result, empires fed on invasion. The mighty got mightier, and small tribal entities were engulfed. The reverse was also true, however. Any setback in military fortunes would make it hard to reward one's soldiers and would embolden one's enemies. Empires lived by expanding, but larger areas were harder to administer and left ever-growing borders to defend. As such, all the great empires eventually collapsed, often by some combination of turmoil from within and a new invasion by an enemy from without.

During the Low Middle Ages in Europe, about 500 to 1000 CE (sometimes dubbed the Dark Ages for the collapse of central power and the chronic fighting between rival groups); the problem of raising armies was handled through feudalism. China and Japan also used a similar system at times when there was not a single strong central ruler. Under feudalism, a king depended on his lords, who may in turn have depended on knights or samurai underneath them, to provide his army. The lords and their knights provided protection to peasants under their domain, although that protection may have been little better at times than a violent crime syndicate offering protection to a businessperson. In return, the peasants and artisans provided the lords and knights with the food and supplies needed to live well and to wage war. Sometimes the peasants also fought, but the key force was composed of mounted knights with expensive armor and weapons.

Kings relied on staying in the good graces of their lords to stay in power. As a few kings again grew in power, beginning around 1000 CE and continuing for the next four centuries or so, they were again gradually able to field paid armies answerable only to themselves. As weapons and tactics changed, kings came to prefer armies of professional soldiers hired from within their realm or paid foreign mercenaries. Hired Swiss "mountaineers" with some very nasty pikes and hired Turkish "horse archers" proved very effective against feudal knights, while British yeoman archers, essentially small farmers in service to the king, decimated French knights in famous battles of the thirteenth and fourteenth centuries. Eventually the rise of guns and artillery permanently wedded a ruler's fortunes to his ability to mass and arm large armies.

Chronic warfare forced the consolidation of diverse regions into national identities that could muster large, unified armed forces. Those who failed to do so were overtaken by those who succeeded. The modern nation-state was formed. Tilly (1975) contends that "the state made war and war made the state" (p. 42) and that this combination of warfare and state formation reshaped, and in fact created, the continent. He writes, "A thousand years ago, Europe did not exist" (1990, 38).

A Europe of competing nation-states was forged in 500 years of war between 1000 and 1500 CE. Then the idea was promptly exported. In 1500 Europe was a continent of small nation-states that looked weak and fractious compared to the great empires in what are now China, India, Mexico, and Peru. But their intense competition gave Europeans a great desire to expand abroad, and their frequent fighting pushed them to develop the means to do so. For the first time, European ships were capable of sailing the open ocean. Ships also always had an important drawback: It was difficult to fight from aboard a ship, as various rams, boarding planks, and catapults all had their limitations. Europe also had another innovation, as artillery had become cheap and effective enough to be a major factor in warfare. Cannons had limitations, too, however; they were heavy and hard to haul over distances—except aboard a ship.

The Chinese had invented gunpowder and the navigation compass and had built some of the first great trading ships, but it was Europeans in small, relatively new countries, such as Portugal, Holland, and England, that turned the combination into world empires. The combination of ships and guns gave the Europeans a portable force that soon spanned the globe. Spanish galleons reached and conquered the Americas south of Florida at the turn of the sixteenth century. Portuguese men of war rounded Africa at about the same time (establishing outposts along the way), drove the Arab traders from the Indian Ocean, and forced their way into Asia. By the mid-1600s, bigger and better Dutch ships fought the Portuguese out of South Africa and the West Indies (Indonesia). They also sailed across the Atlantic to seize islands in the Caribbean and neighboring shorelines (Aruba, Surinam, St. Martaan, and others) and an island and shoreline further north on the Atlantic (New Amsterdam, later recast as New York City).

The most powerful navy of all was created by the British, who used it to build the world's largest empire: North America, north of Mexico along with points in the Caribbean such as Jamaica; much of eastern and southern Africa, the latter seized from the Dutch; parts of western Africa, Nigeria and Ghana; all of India, including what are now Pakistan and Bangladesh; and trading interests in China, Southeast Asia, and across the Pacific. The process was gradual. Britain spent much of the 1700s in constant war with its great rival, France, eventually winning complete control of Canada and India. The British Empire faced only one great setback: the loss of the American colonies to determined irregular armies with the final decisive help of the French fleet. France retained control in much of western Africa, many points in the Caribbean (losing Haiti in the second great new world revolt in 1811), in Southeast Asia (including Vietnam), and in the Pacific (including Tahiti).

From Limited War to Total War to Cold War

The nature of warfare also continued to change. Military historians speak of the shift from **limited war** to **total war.** Rival monarchs often fought limited wars with small professional armies augmented by hired mercenaries. Total war came to involve the mobilization, and risk the destruction, of an entire society's population and economy.

Limited War

Until the late 1700s most armies were quite small. Europeans in the 1200s dreaded the great Mongol hordes, ravaging their eastern lands, but in fact, Genghis Khan used relatively small groups of highly mobile cavalry. Limited war often had strict rules of conduct and ideals of honor and glory. Wars began with formal declarations such as the U.S. Declaration of Independence. In grand fashion, the Duke of Wellington preceded the battle of Waterloo with an officer's dress ball. The preferred tactic of this era was a tight formation on an open battlefield attended by much pageantry. At the least, this tended to keep noncombatants out of the fray, much more so than the siege tactics of the Late Middle Ages. European ideals of chivalry, or the ideal knight, were promoted by both church and state as a way to limit the plunder and pillage of a violent age. Likewise, in Japan, Samurai knights fought with a strict code of honor, the Bushido Code, the way of the warrior. The Mongol armies struck terror by violating some of the European rules, but they, too, had their ideals of what made a brave and honorable warrior.

Warfare, even if limited, always ran the risk of degenerating into wholesale slaughter and plunder. The European Thirty Years' War (1618–1648) between Catholic and Protestant factions devastated Central Europe, destroyed thousands of towns and villages, created huge refugee crises, plundered fields and led to famine, and resulted in massive civilian deaths far beyond the number of combatants killed. Yet the ideal of the time and the centuries to follow replaced medieval chivalry with the so-called gentleman at arms, popularized in books such as *The Three Musketeers*, who was loyal to king and honor and country.

War was still ultimately about brute force, but codes of conduct were often taken very seriously. At the battle of Yorktown, the final engagement of the American Revolution in 1781, one of the final issues of debate among the victorious French and American commanders was whether the British defenders, outnumbered and hopelessly surrounded, had put up a spirited enough defense before surrendering to be accorded the full honors of dignified defeat, with their own bands playing mournful tunes as they laid down their firearms while their gentleman officers kept their own swords.

Total War

Warfare became increasingly less limited in the 1800s. Napoleon violated contemporary rules of engagement by attacking without warning. Commanders of the armies he defeated complained that this was because he was a Corsican peasant, not a true gentleman. Napoleon used the populist ideals of the French Revolution to advance a new idea: mass mobilization, an entire nation at war. All of France's resources were poured into his war efforts. Armies also grew dramatically in size. Napoleon's Grand Army of the Republic numbered over 600,000 as it marched toward Russia in 1812. This vast force moving east onto the Russian steppes was many times larger than any Mongol horde that had ever invaded from the opposite direction.

Rapid industrialization was also changing the face of war. In many respects, the American Civil War (1861–1865) was a turning point from agrarian limited war to modern, industrial, total war. The weapons were changing: the first battle of iron-clad ships, the first sinking of a ship by a submarine (hand-operated), the first use of aerial reconnaissance (hot air balloons), the first use of a machine gun (the Gatling gun), the early use of repeating firearms in place of single-shot weapons, and the use of much larger artillery pieces. Europeans watched Americans slaughter one another on the battlefield in unprecedented numbers and claimed Americans just didn't know how to fight a proper war. The truth was that the American commanders on both sides were well-trained in the tactics of the Napoleonic era, but the weapons had become far deadlier in the intervening 50 years.

From the day the first war was fought until the Civil War, the primary weapon had been the spear. The hunter's spear was no doubt the first weapon, and in various forms—short javelins, long pikes, and horse-borne lances—it remained the weapon of choice. Archers launching arrows (modified spears) could be deadly, especially in rough terrain, but battles were usually decided by groups of charging spear men, either on foot or on horseback. Even in the era of firearms, the deciding moment of battle was often the bayonet charge, essentially a long gun turned into a spear. But now the commanders learned, from Gettysburg to Fredericksburg, that charging shoulder to shoulder was certain suicide.

As the war dragged on, the tactics shifted. The Southern states of the Confederacy had the most experienced and capable commanders, with a long history of military service, but the Northern states of the Union had greater industrial might and sought to exhaust and strangle the South. Union ships, increasingly steamers, blockaded the South. Rail links and trains became vital nerve systems. The final and ultimately successful Union commander, General Ulysses S. Grant, had no better success with the frontal infantry assault than his predecessors had had. Rather, he won the Civil War with slow, bloody campaigns that attacked shipping and supply centers, and he increasingly levied massive artillery bombardments against urban centers, as his opponents took refuge in trench warfare. He sent his subordinate, General William Sherman, on a march through the South that ripped up railroad tracks, burned down major cities, and sought to terrorize and demoralize the population. The ideal commander at the beginning of the war had perhaps been General Robert E. Lee, the South's gentleman warrior. But the grim face of war that emerged was that of Sherman, who destroyed infrastructure and displaced civilians, contending simply that "War is hell."

The hellishness of modern war fully dawned on Europe and the world with World War I. This conflict began high hopes for a quick victory, and the first battles included drums and bagpipes and bayonet charges. The conflict quickly moved into a long war of attrition, with soldiers digging ever-larger networks of trenches to hide from ever-deadlier artillery. Coils of barbed wire and newer machine guns made infantry charges hopeless. The first large-scale use of poison gas added to the horror and the misery. Population centers could be bombarded with huge guns or bombed from the air, and each side tried to starve the other with blockades: the British using surface ships and the Germans using submarines. Industrial centers worked around the clock to turn out more and deadlier weapons. The bloodiest battles ever fought were the ultimate result. Some 600,000 died in a matter of days at the Somme offensive, the size of Napoleon's entire Grand Army and more than 10 times the dead at Gettysburg. By the time the war ended, nearly an entire generation of Europe's young men had been wiped out.

World War II raised the stakes to new heights. Nazi Germany claimed it could make war more humane by using brief *blitzkriegs* that would "shock and awe" the enemy into quick surrender. At first successful, their destructive might was soon matched by that of the other large industrial powers: Great Britain, Russia, and eventually the world's largest industrial economy, the United States. To finally win the war, U.S. industry was turning out a major ship every day, along with hundreds of aircraft. As each side tried to destroy the industrial capacity of the other, civilian centers became the primary targets. German aircraft flew daily raids in the "blitz" of London and devastated whole cities, such as Canterbury. German ground forces besieged and starved entire Russian cities, such as St. Petersburg. The Allied powers returned the devastation, bombing German industry and ultimately turning to firebombing, which created huge firestorms that consumed entire city centers and their populations in Dresden and throughout the country. The Nazis retaliated with missile attacks on London.

The same pattern was repeated in the Pacific. Japanese troops displaced, enslaved, massacred, and terrorized civilian populations as a weapon of war, seeking to force surrender through terror. Later in the Pacific War, the U.S.

Army and Navy tried the same strategy from the air, seeking to bomb Japan into surrendering. Targeted industrial bombings gave way to massive firebombings, which had an even deadlier effect, for Japanese homes were built of wood rather than the brick, stone, and stucco of old Europe. A single firebombing of Tokyo created a vast firestorm that may have killed over 100,000 people. No poison gas was used in this war, but phosphorus and napalm (a jellied petroleum product) were clearly weapons of mass destruction. The annihilation of cities culminated with two atomic bombings that largely destroyed the entire cities of Hiroshima and Nagasaki, killing well over 100,000 in the short term and far more in the long term from the effects of burns and radiation poisoning. Total war had reached its apex.

Cold War

The realization that weapons technology had reached the point at which warring nations could entirely consume one another changed the nature of war. People spoke of the next great conflict, World War III, as a cataclysm that might destroy the planet, and indeed, it could have. But facing this prospect, the next great war was not a total war but rather a **cold war,** a new form of limited conflict.

The United States and the Soviet Union were allied in World War II by virtue of having the same enemies. Once those enemies were defeated, however, relations between the two countries quickly became strained. The first half of the twentieth century had been a struggle among multiple powers, but in the wake of the Second World War, two nations emerged as superpowers and vied for vast spheres of influence, offering different visions of the postwar world. Yet the specter of that war, which took the lives of 20 million Russians, coupled with the threat of growing nuclear arsenals, kept the two superpowers from direct open warfare. Instead, the cold war was marked by a battle over influence, by an arms race, and by regional conflicts, or "proxy wars," in which what would have been civil wars became part of the struggle for dominance between the two superpowers.

The first and bloodiest of these conflicts was in Korea. Following World War II, the Korean peninsula was divided into a Soviet-occupied North and a U.S.-occupied South, just as Germany was divided into zones of occupation that became East and West. In 1950, as the Korean zones were looking to become permanent, the North launched a massive invasion of the South, quickly capturing Seoul, the southern capital, and almost overrunning the rest of the peninsula and reuniting Korea by force. The United Nations Security Council, with the Soviet Union absent as part of a boycott over contested procedures, voted to condemn the invasion and help the South. United Nations forces, under the command of U.S. General Douglas MacArthur and made up largely of U.S. and South Korean forces, broke out of their small holdout perimeter and drove the North Korean army all the way to the Chinese border.

The situation grew more complex, however, as the Chinese Communists under Mao Zedong had just completed their takeover of China. They announced that if the UN forces pushed to their border, they would consider it a grave threat and intervene. This they did, and large numbers of Chinese forces drove the UN forces back south, retaking Seoul. A UN counteroffensive pushed the Chinese and North Koreans back to the original 38th parallel. MacArthur wanted to push on, bombing and even invading China, if necessary, to win a decisive victory, such as the one that had ended World War II. The use of nuclear weapons to speed this victory, as had been done at the end of World War II, was also discussed.

But this was a new age. This seesaw conflict was referred to as a United Nations **police action,** not a war. China was huge and could fight on for a very long time, even in a losing conflict. The Soviet Union had not directly intervened but had recently tested its own nuclear weapons. If it responded to a nuclear attack with a similar counterattack, the world could fall into nuclear war. American president Harry Truman fired MacArthur and returned to the bargaining table. The United States' cold war policy became not the destruction of communism but rather its **containment.** A stalemate ensued and an accord, never signed by South Korea, was drafted in 1953 to accept, for the time being, the current status. This civil conflict and police action cost South Korea perhaps three million civilian casualties and devastated both North and South Korea.

In time, South Korea was rebuilt with extensive foreign investment. North Korea remained in the hands of its Soviet-installed leader, Kim Il-Sung. On his death in 1994, he passed leadership on to his son, Kim Jong-il. He in turn selected his son, Kim Jong-un, who became Supreme Leader in 2011, more in the manner of an imperial succession than a communist ideal. Kim Jong-un has continued a repressive regime that has become ever more bankrupt. But this poor country maintains a million-man army and the legacy of years of war preparation: massive artillery pointed at Seoul, missiles that can reach Japan as well as South Korea (and maybe even the United States), and a nuclear program geared to producing nuclear weapons. The specter of an unpredictable leader in a reclusive state with little to lose, heavily armed with the world's deadliest weapons, is one of the cold war's great legacies.

When communist forces took control of China in 1949, the Nationalist government fled to the island of Formosa, which had been a Japanese possession for much of the century. The Chinese Communists lacked the naval power to invade, especially with a U.S. fleet blocking the strait. The Formosa-based government became Taiwan, the Republic of China, and long claimed to be the rightful government of the entire country. For two decades, it was treated by the United States as the legitimate government of China in exile, and it held China's UN seat. Thawing relations with mainland China in the 1970s led to a "two China policy" and then full recognition of the Communist government in Beijing. The Chinese government considers Taiwan to be a renegade province of China and demands its reunion with the mainland. Many Taiwanese would like to see Taiwan formally independent, but it remains as it has for over 50 years as a small, prosperous entity left in political limbo.

The other great Asian cold war battleground was Indochina, particularly Vietnam. France had administered Vietnam as three colonial departments, but the independence plans of the late 1940s sought to form a unified country. The dilemma for Western Europe and the United States was that the hero of independence and likely winner of any election would be Ho Chi Minh, who was considered a communist. In fact, while Ho was heavily influenced by Marxist theory, he was also a Vietnamese nationalist, who sought to chart a course that was independent of both China and the Soviet Union. The compromise plan of 1954 represented a by now familiar pattern: Vietnam would be temporarily divided into a northern sector under Soviet influence and a southern sector under the influence of the United States and its allies. However, when this division appeared to be gaining permanence as it had in Korea, Ho's followers formed the Vietcong, supported by the north, and Vietnam plunged into civil war.

What would have been an isolated civil conflict in a poor, remote region took on global dimensions as the United States came to view this fight, like the one in Korea, as a struggle to contain communist expansion. This required trying to support a series of increasingly corrupt South Vietnamese governments and the ever-increasing presence of U.S. forces. After over a decade of war and losing more than 50,000 soldiers, the United States agreed to a peace treaty in 1973 and withdrew its forces. When the peace collapsed in 1975, so did the South Vietnamese government, but the United States did not reintervene.

All Vietnam became communist, and spillover wars toppled the governments of Laos and Cambodia, which had also become the site of a proxy war, with the Soviets supplying arms to forces battling an opposition backed by the Central Intelligence Agency (CIA) and supported by U.S. bombing. Cambodia fell under the control of a particularly brutal revolutionary group, the Khmer Rouge, which followed a twisted version of Maoist peasant communism. Namely, it depopulated the cities to return the country to its agrarian roots, killing anyone considered an enemy of the revolution. As many as two million people died in the "killing fields" of a Cambodian holocaust. This bloodshed was finally stopped by a Vietnamese invasion. China, which had supported the Khmer Rouge, responded with a brief invasion of Vietnam, which was heavily supported by the Soviets. Meanwhile, border conflicts developed along the Soviet–Chinese border.

While the Western alliance of Europe and the United States still spoke of the Communist Bloc as a single entity, it was clear by the 1970s that old animosities and new rivalries divided the communist states. Vietnam, like China, has since pursued economic reforms that have moved it closer to the capitalist world economy, while Cambodia struggled to rid itself of the dark legacy of the Khmer Rouge and develop a growing export-oriented economy. In the 1990s U.S. President Bill Clinton visited Vietnam, a sign of warming relations. All the countries of Indochina remain among the poorest in Asia and the world.

The cold war legacy in the Middle East and South Asia is less obvious but equally enduring. India and Pakistan remained rivals, with border disputes that were not resolved at the time of their partition in 1947. This was a legacy of colonialism but took on a cold war character, with the Soviet Union generally backing India, resulting in U.S. support for Pakistan. India and Pakistan have fought four regional wars and now face each other with their respective arsenals of nuclear weapons.

In the Middle East, the Israeli–Palestinian conflict also emerged from the ashes of colonialism. Once part of the Ottoman Empire, this area fell under British control. Great Britain essentially promised the same land to both its Arab allies in the world wars and to European Jews escaping the ravages of the holocaust and European anti-Semitism. The United Nations tried to divide this relatively small disputed area between the two groups. But given the fervor of Zionist Jews to quickly create a homeland and the anger of the Palestinian Arabs who were displaced, war quickly broke out. The Soviet Union backed the Arab cause, especially when it was led by Arab socialists such as Prime Minister Nasser of Egypt, and the United States strongly backed and armed the Israeli effort. Again, a regional dispute over the spoils of former empires turned into a cold war battleground.

In Iraq, the United States first supported the anticommunist Baath Party. Yet strong U.S. support for the Shah of Iran led the Baath leadership, including Saddam Hussein, to turn to the Soviets. When the Iranian Revolution toppled the Shah and brought the anti-American Ayatollah Khomeini to power, the United States again shifted its support and began to arm Saddam Hussein as a bulwark against radical Muslims. In Afghanistan the Soviet Union resorted to invasion to support an unpopular client government. The United States, in turn, supported the collection of Islamic resistance groups known as the *mujahedeen*. With U.S. assistance, they ultimately forced a Soviet withdrawal but then fell into fighting among themselves. Control finally went to Pakistani-borne fundamentalist movement, the **Taliban.** In both Iraq and Afghanistan, the United States ultimately invaded to topple governments that were in many ways relics of cold war politics.

In Latin America struggles between elite land-owning families and displaced individuals, between military and civilian governments, and between different philosophies of development, some of which were a century-and-a-half old, took on new importance as cold war battles. The United States helped topple left-leaning elected governments in Guatemala in 1954 and in Chile in

1973, which were replaced by procapitalist military dictatorships as a way to prevent communist (and hence Soviet) influence in the Americas. The Soviets backed successful revolutions in Cuba and Nicaragua and an unsuccessful one in El Salvador. The United States backed opposing forces and counterrevolutions. In Cuba in 1961 the CIA supported a failed invasion of Cuban exiles at the Bay of Pigs, seeking to topple Fidel Castro. In Nicaragua the United States overtly and covertly aided the Contras, who sought to topple the Sandinistas, the leftist government that had taken its name from an anticolonial nationalist.

While all these global regional struggles could be termed a "true" world war, like the first two world wars, the cold war's primary focus remained Europe. At the end of World War II, U.S. and British troops had moved into Germany from the west while Soviet troops had advanced across Eastern Europe. Both sides were determined to have friendly governments with kindred systems of government in their zones of control. Germany was divided into two occupation zones: The Soviet zone became East Germany, and the U.S.–European zone became West Germany. Berlin was also divided, and West Berlin became an island of Western and U.S. control in the midst of East Germany. The Soviet Union promoted communist governments in the Eastern European countries under its control, many of which had some socialist sympathies. Together with the Soviet Union, Poland, Hungary, Czechoslovakia, Romania, Bulgaria, and East Germany formed an alliance known as the **Warsaw Pact.** To counter this alliance, the Western European countries allied with the United States to form the **North Atlantic Treaty Organization (NATO).**

Just as at the beginning of World War I, Europe was divided into hostile alliances, but now with the realization that a full-scale war could destroy the continent. Prime Minister Winston Churchill of Great Britain warned of an "iron curtain" descending on the continent, and this became the metaphor for the time. The iron curtain became an actual wall separating the two Berlins in the early 1960s, as the Soviets attempted to prevent East Berliners from fleeing into the more prosperous West. Vast armed forces faced each other on either side of the iron curtain. NATO, fearing the larger size of the Warsaw Pact forces, refused to rule out nuclear retaliation for a Warsaw Pact invasion.

The 1960s saw tense standoffs, especially over the status of Berlin. NATO airlifted supplies to its isolated half of the city to get around an embargo. Tensions eased a bit during the late 1960s and early 1970s, as President Richard Nixon, famous as a staunch anticommunist, decided on a policy of **détente,** or limited cooperation, to ease tensions. Tensions reignited in the late 1970s over Afghanistan.

In the 1980s President Ronald Reagan dubbed the Soviet Union an "evil empire" and accelerated the arms race. Yet the Soviet Union was changing. After a series of turnovers in leadership, Mikhail Gorbachev came to power and declared new policies of *glasnost* (openness) and *perestroika* (economic reform and restructuring). The Soviet Union started to make moves toward reducing its military arsenal and challenged the United States to follow suit. At the same time, glasnost and perestroika set in motion a series of events that few could have predicted. Hungary tested the new openness by allowing people to move freely into neighboring Austria, a seemingly small shift. But as with a hole in a dike, this small movement soon became a flood of people from all over Eastern Europe, and the Soviet Union did not move to plug the breach. Soon it was pointless to try to blockade other borders; the iron curtain was being shredded. The Berlin Wall was deemed to serve no purpose and was no longer defended, and mobs started to tear it down. The decade that began with talk of an "evil empire" ended with the Warsaw Pact dissolving, borders opening up across Europe, and Germany ready to forge ahead toward reunification.

Two years later, in 1991, the Soviet Union unraveled after a failed coup attempt against Gorbachev. The republics that made up the Union of Soviet Socialist Republics began to declare independence. The first to go were the small Baltic republics of Latvia, Lithuania, and Estonia, which had been forcibly pressed into the Russian Empire, after which they became briefly independent and then were reconquered by Stalin. When the republic of Russia itself, led by Boris Yeltsin, a Communist Party member known for divergent ideas, declared itself independent, the Soviet Union was over.

Some declared that the United States, NATO, and the Western alliance had triumphed. However, looking upon the tremendous cost of the conflict—the hugely expensive arms race and the cost of proxy wars in places such as Afghanistan and Vietnam, which had bankrupted the Soviet Union and left the United States with a trillion-dollar deficit—it seemed that perhaps both sides had lost a great deal. As south Asia and the Middle East remain in turmoil, as Africa struggles to get rid of the legacy of cold war–supported dictatorships, and as Latin American commissions find new evidence of proxy "dirty wars" from this period, the shadows of this world war, like the two before, still cast a pall over the planet.

From World War to Regional Conflict

World War I ended with the creation of the League of Nations in 1919 and the hope that this new international alliance would keep the peace. World War II ended with the creation of the United Nations, as well as the International Monetary Fund (IMF) and the World Bank, and the hope that development, trade, and arbitration would replace global conflict. The cold war ended with the hope for a "new world order" and a "peace dividend" and saw the creation of organizations such as the World Trade Organization (WTO) to orchestrate this new world of prosperity and freedom.

In fact, the hope that World War I would be "the war to end all wars" was shattered by the rise of fascism and militaristic states. The hope of stemming global conflict at the end of the World War II was dimmed by the emergence of superpower rivalries. The optimism at the end of the cold war was soon beaten down by a world of regional conflicts and the rise of international terrorism.

Yugoslavia, a post–World War I creation, came apart in the early 1990s—not peacefully, but amid a vicious civil war characterized by numerous atrocities, including **ethnic cleansing.** African conflicts were no longer strategic and were largely ignored until the Rwandan holocaust of 1994 claimed the lives of half a million people. New states often fell into the hands of authoritarian leaders who could not hope for world domination but frequently had old scores to settle with rivals and sought national glory and regional power through war and repression. While peace studies programs continued to emphasize U.S. and Russian relations and cold war ideas such as deterrence, it was becoming increasingly clear that a new world disorder of regional and civil conflicts was becoming the norm.

Regional conflicts and civil and ethnic strife have a long history, but they were often overshadowed by the rules of empires and superpowers. Rome tried to enforce a rule of order within its sphere of influence, the *Pax Romana*. Likewise, Genghis Khan and his grandson Kublai Khan enforced peace and order within their vast domain even as they pursued conquests beyond it. The British saw their empire as extending order, decorum, and peace to a world of small rivalries. The United States and the Soviet Union both tried to bring a semblance of order and control to their spheres of influence. With these powers removed, old rivalries reemerged and new ones were created and manipulated by the ambitious.

Regional conflicts have always had a way of involving the prevailing power. In the middle of the first century BCE, the Roman general Pompey marched to put down unrest in the east (what we now call the Middle East), and his rival, General Caesar, marched to put down unrest in the west. Both ended up as conquerors who extended the empire to enforce the peace. During the height of their imperial era in the 1800s, the British often moved in to protect their commercial interests, stayed on to arbitrate regional conflicts, and remained as conquerors and administrators. This is essentially the story of the British takeover of India. During the 1900s the United States often intervened in Latin America to protect its commercial interests and became heavily involved in regional conflicts as a result.

The specter of **international terrorism** has now added a new dimension to regional conflicts: the threat that they might spawn terrorist actions that will be felt far away, most particularly in the great power centers. The United States has found it very difficult to quickly restore order and then withdraw from places such as Afghanistan and Iraq. One of the great questions for the United States in the twenty-first century is whether it will try to impose order, a *Pax Americana*, as the world's great power (a few have used the now unpopular term of *empire*), or whether it will try again for multinational solutions and organizations.

Small-scale conflicts pose new problems for the global order (see figure 6.1). Most are civil wars, fought by factions within a particular country, but they typically spill over to destabilize entire regions. Fighting in Liberia spilled into Sierra Leone, which in turn led to conflict in the previously stable Ivory Coast. Wars in Central Africa have bled into one another, with factions in one country supporting and occasionally taking refuge with factions in another. Internal and regional conflicts are particularly prone to the use of terrorism as a weapon. Long before al-Qaeda, Tamils fighting for independence in Sri Lanka "invented" the suicide bomber. In Colombia, long-standing battles among government forces, paramilitary forces supporting wealthy landowners, and two rival guerilla groups have turned the country into a bloodbath of war, terror, assassination, and drug trafficking.

Often, it is difficult to tell where war, terrorism, and crime begin and end, as each overlaps the other. One side's martyrs are another's terrorists; one side's freedom fighters are another's criminal gang. Civilians are often caught in both the acts of terror and the antiterror crackdowns in seemingly endless cycles, as has been seen in Northern Ireland and Sri Lanka and most recently in Israel–Palestine and Iraq. British actor and writer Peter Ustinov contended that "terrorism is the war of the poor and war is the terrorism of the rich" (Veterans for Peace 2003).

Often the preferred weapon for local warlords is not weapons of mass destruction but children with automatic weapons. Watching rival bands of teenagers in West Africa, who wear oversized T-shirts and high-top athletic shoes and fire off irregular but lethal arrays of automatic small-arms fire, it can be hard to tell if one is looking at a street gang or an army. In parts of northern Uganda, children spend the night huddled in bus stations and other public places in small cities, not because they are homeless but because their rural families send them into town for the night. In the rural areas, they are vulnerable to kidnapping by the Lord's Resistance Army. Once taken, the children are often tortured and forced to participate in killings and atrocities until they become calloused killers themselves, with nowhere to go but into the "army." Female soldiers face the added risk of sexual slavery in the armed camps.

War by Proxy

One way to keep the peace in the absence of effective multinational cooperation and international peacekeeping is to strive for a balance of power, or of terror, among "great powers." As European nation-states gained strength but not complete continental dominance, they competed for spheres of influence, each hoping it could muster a series of checks and balances on its rivals. This

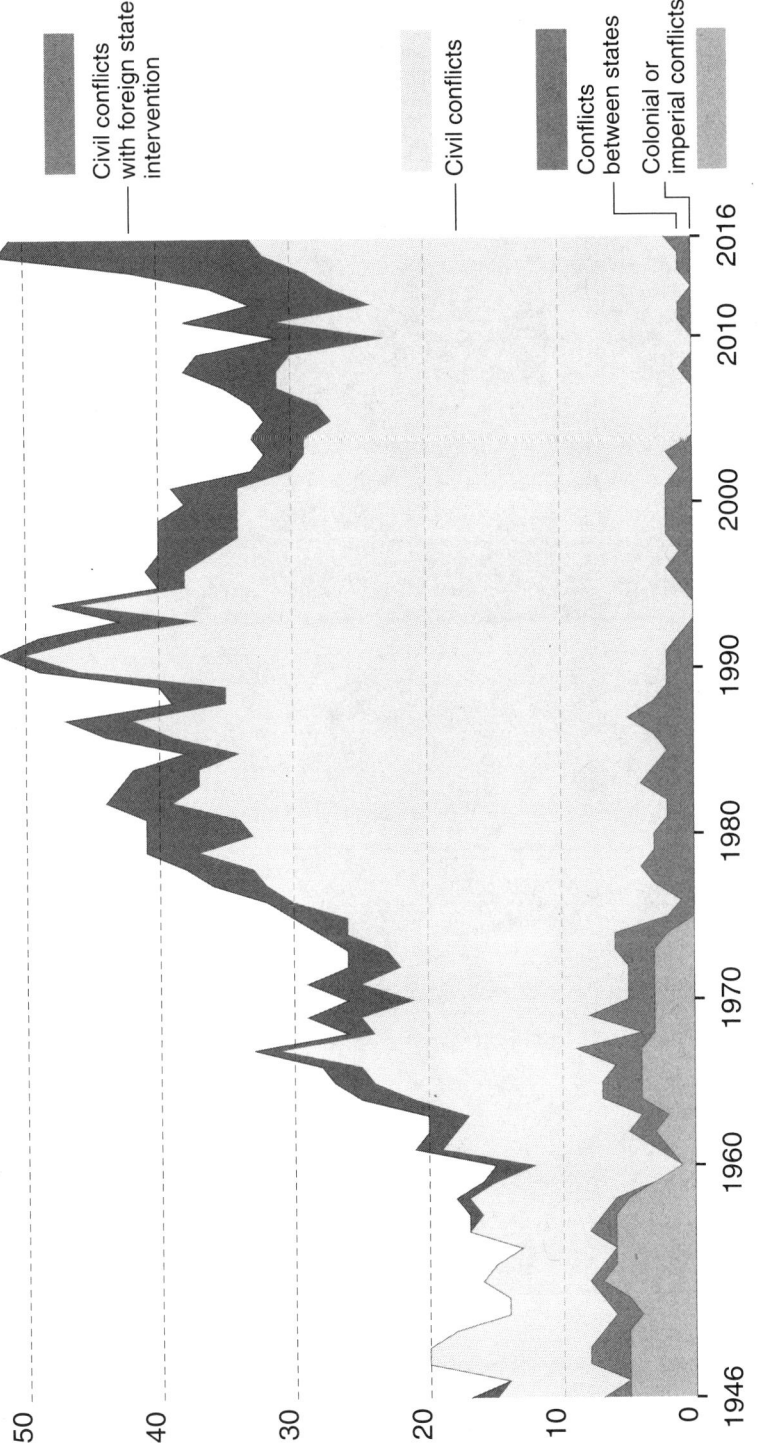

Figure 6.1 State-based conflicts, 1946–2016. (Source: Our World in Data.) For more information, see https://ourworldindata.org/war-and-peace...

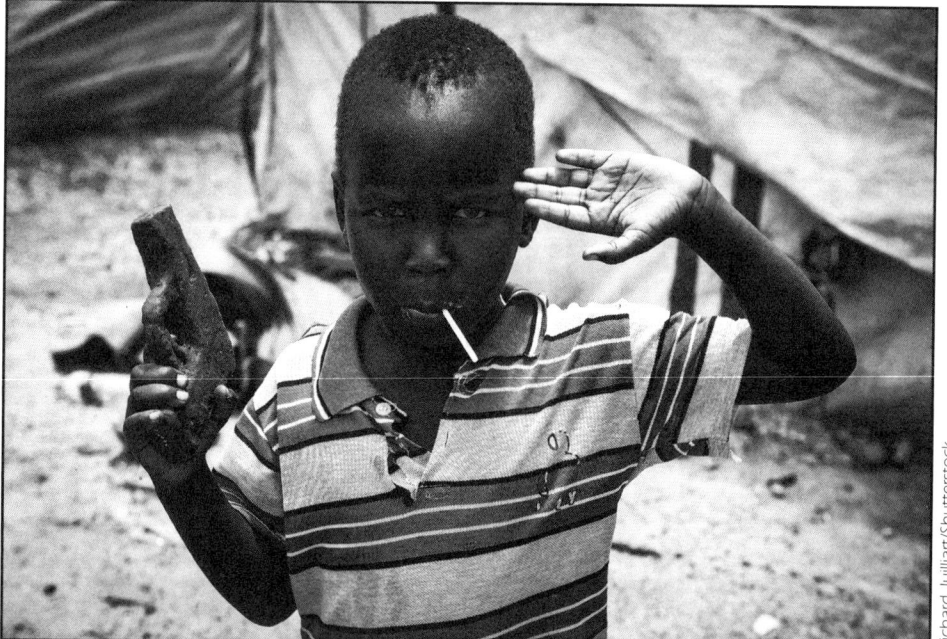

The face of war is ancient, but the warriors are often very young. Two boys of the country of South Sudan, newly independent and wracked by civil war. One seems hardly bigger than his gun [top], the other is clearly learning from what he sees [bottom].

approach dominated Europe for the century between the end of the Napoleonic Wars in 1815 and the start of World War I in 1914. Great Britain, France, Austria, Prussia (and later Germany), Russia, the remnants of the Ottoman Empire, and eventually a united Italy, faced each other with large armies and modernizing navies, staring across a chain of smaller buffer states. Sometimes powers would clash, as when Britain and France joined to keep Russia from seizing too much power from Ottoman realms in the Crimean War. Sometimes they clashed head to head as with Prussia and France in 1870. But they also met to confirm the borders and monarchs of Europe and well beyond, even as they divided Africa between them in the 1880s. It was an uneasy peace but largely free of the huge and long wars of the past. This tense balance finally imploded in the chaos of World War I as shifting alliances and restless proxy states plunged the continent, and to a lesser extent the world, into war.

The world's answer to this cataclysm was the creation of the League of Nations, an international body to settle disputes and maintain order. Despite the early enthusiasm of U.S. President Woodrow Wilson, the United States never joined, and the powers of league were very limited. A new set of great powers plunged into World War II. With even more desperation in a nuclear age, this was followed by a second attempt at a global body of cooperation, the United Nations. This time the United States joined, and the international body resides in New York City. Five of the large victors formed a UN Security Council: the United States, the Soviet Union, China, France, and the United Kingdom. The UN depends on the financial support of member states and on participation by their armed forces in peacekeeping missions. Despite its weakness it has been the world stage for conflict dispute and has engaged in a myriad of peacekeeping interventions.

The beginning decades of the twenty-first century have seen the rise of nationalism in many of the old powers—Russia, the United Kingdom, and the United States—and in powers of the past seeking to reassert themselves: China most particularly, but also Turkey, Iran, and Saudi Arabia. New alliances have emerged, and with them new proxy wars. Conflict between Saudi Arabia and Iran has stretched across the Mideast, but really centered on the civil war in Yemen, with each supporting one side. Syria exploded into civil war after the repression of democracy movements that emerged with the Arab Spring of 2011. The conflict created a space for the so-called Islamic State to take territory and terrorize local populations. In time, it also saw the hesitant intervention of the United States, the forceful intervention of Russia, and the limited intervention of Turkey, Saudi Arabia, and the Iranian-backed militia. With the most limited resources, Iran seems to have come to an early understanding with religious and revolutionary militia, such as Hezbollah, who often fight with greater determination than weak national armies. The United States found its greatest success working with the Kurdish militia group, the Peshmerga.

The wars of our time are almost all civil wars, fought between factions within a nation. This hardly means, however, that these are purely internal affairs. Major and minor powers provide increasingly sophisticated weaponry—rockets, missiles, and drones can provide terror from the air for those without a sophisticated air force—training, reconnaissance from spies and aerial surveillance, well-armed mercenaries and militias, and bribes to local warlords. The level of human suffering in Syria and Yemen—from direct attacks and the destruction of infrastructure to the consequence of these attacks, which lead to famine and disease—is incalculable. The next grab for Africa may not be in a grand conference as in the 1880s but in backroom deals supporting factions and proxies to gain power, influence, and prized resources.

The Global Arms Trade

An added legacy of the cold war is a world awash in weapons. Not only did the United States and the Soviet Union arm themselves to extraordinary heights, but since they found it best not to confront one another directly, their preferred strategy was to arm client states in proxy wars. Soviet arms poured into the hands of leftist governments and rebel movements, while the United States armed right-wing governments as bastions against communism. Many of these weapons remain in circulation.

The deadliest weapon the world has ever known in terms of the sheer numbers of people killed is probably neither high-tech nor a weapon of mass destruction but the lowly AK-47 Kalashnikov automatic rifle (see Chivers 2010). It was designed by Mikhail Kalashnikov in 1947 (hence AK-47 for automatic Kalashnikov of 1947) for the Soviet army, which continued its production until 1960; after that, the other Warsaw Pact countries continued production. Bulgaria still makes and sells the Kalashnikov. There may be 50 million of these weapons in the world.

Cheap, with an extraordinary rate of fire that makes them deadly at close range, they are the favorite of the world's small-arms dealers and their many clients. The Vietcong used the AK-47 against the United States, and the Khmer Rouge used it to slaughter their own population. For a while, every leftist guerilla in Latin America carried an AK-47, and now every well-armed drug trafficker, whether rightist or leftist, carries the same weapon. Afghan warlords and their followers sleep with their Kalashnikovs, and these weapons fill the black markets of Karachi, Pakistan. Somalis fighting for warlord Mohamed Adid used AK-47s against the U.S. Army Rangers in Mogadishu, and the insurgents in Iraq attacked U.S. forces with Kalashnikovs. They brought absolute terror to Sierra Leone and Liberia. AK-47s are flooding the multiple war zones of the Congo, many now made in China rather than the former Soviet

Taiz City, Yemen [top] and Homs, Syria. Civil wars are not small-scale to the civilians trapped in their midst. Urban warfare combined with massive airstrikes by "supportive" powerful allies create scenes of mass destruction.

nations. In war-torn regions, a locally produced AK-47 can be purchased for as little as $20, less than a bag of rice. Even the poorest warlord can steal enough to arm a cadre of teenagers with enough AK-47s to terrorize a city.

From Baghdad to Bogotá to Brazzaville, the term **small arms** refers to the ever-present combination of automatic assault weapons and rocket-propelled grenade launchers. While they are not much use against a tank, a lucky shot will bring down a helicopter. They are deadly weapons of terror against lightly armed opponents and civilians and bystanders of all types.

Some of the world's handheld weapons are more sophisticated. Any minor arms dealer in Afghanistan can get you a Kalashnikov or a grenade launcher, but talk longer and bring out more foreign currency and you may be able to secure a Stinger: a shoulder-fired, heat-seeking missile designed to bring down high-altitude aircraft. During the Soviet war in Afghanistan, the CIA found that one of the most effective ways to bleed the Soviet army and to support the mujahedeen was to supply them with Stingers, since the Soviets depended on airpower and air supply to fight across the vast, rugged terrain. It proved a remarkably effective tool of guerilla warfare. The only problem was that there was no way to collect all the Stingers at the conflict's end and bring them home. The high-tech Stinger is not much good in urban combat, unless one's opponent has helicopters, but it would make a lethal weapon for terrorists to use on a civilian aircraft. No one knows how many Stingers are still in circulation.

Small arms are sold by any number of international arms traffickers. Larger weapons are sold by governments to allies and increasingly to the highest bidder. Eastern Europe inherited a Soviet arms industry that remains in demand around the world and provides an important source of income. Old-style Soviet and Eastern European automobiles are not exactly popular collectors' items around the world, but many governments are glad to get a good buy on a Russian-style tank. Cheap and durable, old Soviet Bloc arms continue to travel the globe.

By far, however, the world's foremost arms supplier is the United States (Wezeman et al. 2021, see figure 6.2). While many U.S.-manufactured goods have lost ground to foreign competition, U.S.-made arms are still the gold standard (Lipton 2008). Some of these weapons are provided as part of aid packages to allied governments. Many, however, are sold to bring earnings as exported goods. The most favored customers are friendly governments that can pay in cash. Many of the biggest buyers are in the Middle East (see figure 6.3).

The most coveted imported weapon, and one with strong U.S. dominance (although there is competition from France, Russia, and even Israel), is the jet fighter, a high-speed strike aircraft that can quickly reach targets in a neighboring country or in a remote or rebellious part of a leader's own country. The tremendous might of airpower was demonstrated in the wars in the Persian Gulf, Afghanistan, and Iraq. Before that, Israel used U.S.-made strike aircraft to lethal effect against its many Arab enemies.

For many years, the most highly demanded aircraft has been the Lockheed Martin F-16. There are over 2,000 in the U.S. Air Force and another 2,000 in the air forces of 24 other countries, and additional demand could push the total past 5,000 (Tirpak 2020), but new competitors continue to enter this profitable

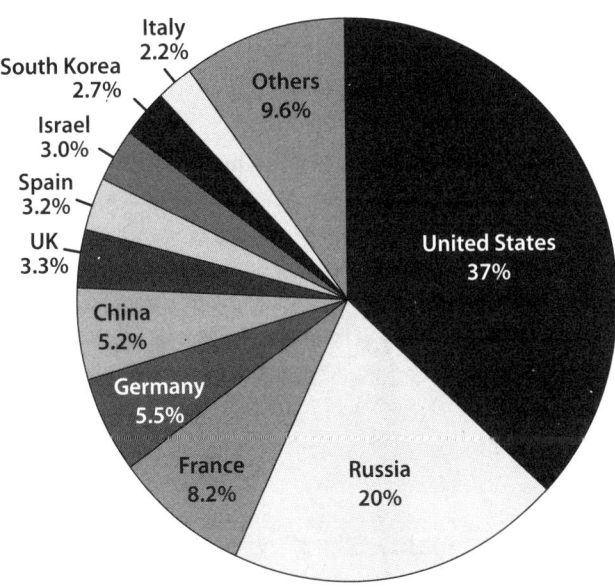

Figure 6.2 World's largest arms exporters, 2016-2020. (Data from SIPRI.org.)

market. Like a classic car, this 1979 fighter keeps buyers coming back for new models that offer a wide-ranging package of options: air-conditioned cockpits, HARM antiradar missiles, standoff air-to-air missiles, Harpoon antiship missiles, global positioning systems, JDAM satellite-guided bombs, and laser-targeting pods, as well as more powerful engines and larger payload capacities.

Israel flies more F-16s than any other country besides the United States; in the mid-2000s alone it possessed over 300 (Larson 2020). One reason this small country needs so many F-16s is that its Arab neighbors continue to order more. Eighty F-16s, complete with the latest and most powerful General Electric–built engines, went to the tiny United Arab Emirates in 2004. Some U.S. allies receive these as part of military aid packages, while others, including petroleum-producing states, can pay as they go.

The U.S. military is eager to replace its aging fleet of F-15 aerial combat planes with state-of-the-art F-22 Raptors and to replace the F-16 with the F-35 Lightening, radar-evading "stealth" planes of enormous capability and cost. The F-35, plagued by delays and cost overruns is the centerpiece of the Joint Strike Fighter program. It is used by the U.S. Air Force and by the Marine Corps, and by many NATO countries and U.S. allies. So far only Israel has used it in combat. Russia and China are challenging its dominance with sophisticated, and expensive, stealth fighters of their own. The aerial arms race poses many practical and ethical dilemmas. Turkey was to purchase F-35s as part of

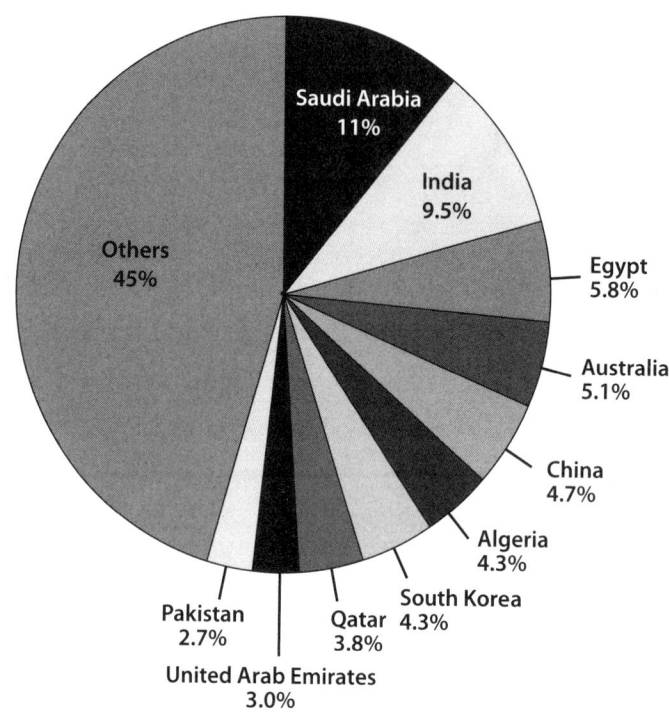

Figure 6.3 World's largest arms importers, 2016-2020. (Data from SIPRI.org.) For more data, see https://www.sipri.org/research/armament-and-disarmament/arms-and-military-expenditure/international-arms-transfers.

a NATO agreement, an agreement placed on hold after they also bought highly sophisticated Russian missiles. The Trump administration had planned to sell F-35s to the United Arab Emirates, drawing concern about introducing a new generation of expensive and deadly weaponry into the tumultuous Middle East. In Yemen, Saudi use of American-built aircraft in raids that resulted in massive civilian causalities raised the question of who shares responsibility for such actions.

Cheaper alternatives are also emerging. The United States first used attack drones in the Gulf War and has continued to use the missile-launching Predator drone against high-level targets accused of being part of terrorist organizations. More recently, Iran and Iranian-backed groups such as the Houthi rebels of Yemen have used drones in attacks against Saudi Arabia and other targets. In the brief 2020 conflict between Armenia and Azerbaijan over disputed territory—an enclave of Azerbaijan with an Armenian majority—Azerbaijan was able to quickly win the upper hand before turning the situation over to Russian peacekeepers. The key was missile-firing drones and small "kamikaze" drones that crash into targets, such as tanks purchased from Israel and Turkey with oil revenues. The Armenian army, motivated but with an older generation of weapons, simply had no effective response. The power to strike from the air with small, nimble craft that do not require a pilot is not lost on various national leaders seeking to yet again modernize their arsenals.

Weapons of Mass Destruction

While conventional arms continue to cause most of the carnage in war zones, much attention has been paid to what have become known as **weapons of mass destruction (WMD),** the term identified with nuclear, radiological, chemical, and biological weapons. This term is something of a misnomer. Conventional weapons—such as those dropped from the bombers of World War II, the huge payloads that can be dropped from large bombers such as the B-52 in carpet-bombing campaigns, and the Pentagon's 22,000-pound MOAB (nicknamed "mother of all bombs")—are clearly weapons of mass destruction, but they are not placed in this category. At the same time, chemical and biological weapons are really weapons of mass casualty, but they cause little physical destruction. For a while, these were included as "nonconventional" weapons or ABC (atomic, biological, and chemical) weapons. But the WMD designation has captured the popular imagination, and so the name has remained.

Chemical Weapons

Chemicals have a long history in warfare. The Byzantine Empire defended its shores for centuries with a secret substance known as "Greek fire," probably a modified petroleum product a bit like napalm that burst into flame when it hit water. Regardless of whether it actually sank ships, it certainly terrified enemy sailors.

Incendiaries, chemicals that burst into intense flames that are difficult to extinguish, were used with devastating effect against German and Japanese cities in World War II. Capable of consuming whole cities, they were certainly weapons of mass destruction but were not considered chemical weapons in the same category as poison gas (though huge fires kill many with toxic smoke and fumes). Incendiaries were also used in Vietnam; one of the most famous photos of the time shows a young female burn victim, fleeing naked from a burning village. Vietnam also saw the use of **defoliants,** chemical agents such as Agent Orange that cause the leaves to fall from the trees and so make hidden troops more visible from the air. Agent Orange has been shown to have many enduring toxic effects, but again, it was not considered poison gas.

The first large-scale use of poison gas was during World War I. The German army began an attack on French trenches with the release of green chlorine gas.

The lung-searing effects of this strange new weapon sent the defenders fleeing in panic and sent both sides in the war scrambling for more chemicals. One of the favored chemicals was **mustard gas,** a heavier-than-air yellow vapor that sank into enemy trenches. After both sides equipped their forces with gas masks, the gas proved less effective but added one more dimension of horror and misery to trench warfare. Recognition of this led to agreements to ban the use of poison gas after the war, a ban that was observed throughout World War II, perhaps in part because these weapons are not well-suited to highly mobile warfare, in which attackers find themselves driving right into their own poison clouds. Following the Second World War, the United States and the Soviet Union both developed far more deadly chemical weapons, especially new types of nerve agents that can kill on contact and be loaded into bombs, artillery shells, and missiles.

While the world has lived with the threat of such incredibly lethal chemicals ever since, their use has been quite limited. Communist forces may have used poisons late in the war in Laos. There is good evidence that in Afghanistan the Soviet Union used **mycotoxins,** mold-based poisons that caused what Afghans called "the bloody diarrhea." When the Iran–Iraq War of the late 1970s and early 1980s fell into trench warfare, Saddam Hussein turned to World War I–vintage mustard gas. When the Kurds in the north of Iraq rebelled following the 1991 Gulf War, he attacked their villages with poison gas from the air in strikes more aimed at spreading terror than defeating armed forces.

Many small countries have been interested in chemical weapons, "the poor man's nuclear bomb," because they are cheap to produce yet can terrify potential enemies. One of the greatest fears is that these weapons will be secured by a terrorist group for use in a major urban area.

Biological Weapons

A top-secret aircraft carrier submarine slips close to the California coast. When it surfaces, small bombers with collapsible wings are lifted to its deck. The planes take off and fly over San Diego, where they release their payloads of clay-shelled bombs. The bombs burst open at low altitude, showering the ground with fleas—fleas contaminated with the deadly bubonic plague, the "Black Death." The fleas bite inhabitants, and soon a terrible scourge of plague is devastating the city.

This is not the plot of the latest James Bond movie or *Matrix* remake. It was an actual attack plan of the Japanese army in 1945, never carried out because the Japanese navy wanted to save its secret submarines for launching *kamikaze* attacks in defense of the home islands. Japan had already secretly used these biological weapons with terrible effect in China, killing unknown thousands. At the time, it was claimed as a naturally occurring disease. At the same time, of course, the United States was working on its own top-secret program of mass destruction, the **Manhattan Project,** which developed the nuclear bombs that drove Japan to surrender before the decision to attack with infected fleas and a variety of other deadly biological weapons could be reconsidered.

As biotechnology expands, new concern grows about **biological weapons:** deadly strains of viruses and bacteria that could be spread over a large area or set in motion to spread themselves. Disease has always been a deadly enemy. Attila the Hun had to abandon his invasion of Italy and planned capture of Rome in part because his army was ravaged by the plague in 452. Rome's defenders actually believed it to be a divine reprieve.

Disease can also work against defenders. In the Peloponnesian War, Athens's defense against Sparta collapsed in the 420s BCE when a plague (perhaps typhus), arriving on supply ships, ravaged the crowded masses within the walls, killing civilians, soldiers, and even their leader Pericles. Socrates saw in this horror more of human folly than divine justice. Cortés was able to seize the Aztec capital of Tenochtitlan (now Mexico City) in 1540 in part because the Aztec defenders were ravaged by a smallpox epidemic that killed their emperor and decimated the crowded and besieged city. When the Spanish were largely spared the ravages of this European disease, to which they had partial immunity, it seemed as though their god must be mightier than the patron god of the Aztecs. Likewise, Francisco Pizarro and a handful of Spanish adventurers were able to conquer the Incan Empire in part because the Inca were also being decimated by smallpox, which had likewise killed their emperor.

Although in each of these cases microbes decided the war, none of them were intended actions. Rumors of intended biological warfare have persisted. In 1347 Mongol invaders reportedly shot the corpses of plague victims over the walls of a Crimean fort to spread the disease to the defenders (Weatherford 1994). Whether the plague arrived by catapult or had previously entered through traders, this terrible disease swept into Europe from Central Asia and killed over one-third of the population of the continent before it subsided.

There are multiple accounts of Europeans and Americans attempting to spread smallpox to Indigenous Americans through gifts and trades of infected blankets. Whether such an act of germ warfare ever occurred and whether it was effective (since smallpox travels best person to person) is questionable. What is clear is that smallpox and related infections decimated the indigenous peoples of the Americas and later the Pacific, killing perhaps 90 percent of the original population (Diamond 1997).

The very idea of using biological weapons made sense formerly in the context of total war and now in the context of terrorism. Pathogens and germs are not easy to control and don't act quickly enough to be useful on the battlefield (even though in both the American Civil War and World War I, the greatest killer was infection stemming from conventional wounds). These organisms do, however, have tremendous potential for terror and disruption. A minute quantity, easily concealed, could have tremendous impact, especially if it began a chain reaction of contagion.

Key problems have been the issues of storage and dispersal. This is what the Imperial Japanese Army hoped to do with clay bombs and small explosive charges—to spread but not kill the infected fleas. **Anthrax**—a disease caused by a bacterium that can remain dormant for a long period in spore form and then become active once inhaled into warm, wet lungs—has long been favored as a potential weapon and was studied and stockpiled by both the United States and the Soviet Union. Its distribution through the U.S. mail in 2002 showed both the power and the limits of biological weapons. Anthrax is not highly contagious between people and does respond to certain antibiotics, if treated quickly. Deaths were limited to a handful of early victims who came in contact with contaminated mail. The act completely disrupted the U.S. Postal Service, however, and had the attacks continued, they could have disrupted all mail service and the U.S. economy for a very long time. The fact that the agent was a minute powder, easily concealed in envelopes, added to the fear factor and the difficulty of tracing its source.

Other pathogens are harder to control but could be deadlier. By the 1980s, the UN World Health Organization had eradicated smallpox, the scourge of the planet for centuries. Since the virus can only live in humans, it became extinct "in the wild" once a worldwide vaccination campaign reached the last villages. It still lived in laboratories in the Soviet Union and the United States, however. Both claimed research purposes but also seemed to worry that the other might try to reintroduce it as a weapon of war. Now, over 40 years later, most of the world is no longer being vaccinated against smallpox and a release of the virus, if it still exists somewhere, could be catastrophic. (Remember the 90 percent fatality estimate among Indigenous Americans.) A 1980s triumph, the first complete eradication of a disease by human effort, is now a twenty-first century mystery: Does it remain somewhere, and could someone try to reintroduce it? The prospect is unlikely, but as with the anthrax scare, the power of an unknown, unseen killer has an ample chilling effect.

Nuclear Weapons

The weapon that completely changed the face of war—the ultimate weapon of mass destruction, capable of destroying whole cities, whole nations, and maybe life itself—is the power of a tiny atom's nucleus, first harnessed and used during World War II. The United States held a brief nuclear monopoly from 1945 to 1949, and then the Soviet Union surprised the world by testing its first nuclear device. The **nuclear arms race** had begun. The United States then raised the stakes by testing a thermonuclear weapon, a **hydrogen bomb.**

The first weapons worked through **nuclear fission,** in which a heavy, unstable nucleus of uranium or plutonium was split, releasing the energy of thousands of tons of conventional explosives. Thermonuclear weapons began with a fission bomb to generate the huge amount of heat needed to fuse hydrogen into helium. This is the process that drives the sun. Such a weapon could release enormous amounts of destructive energy. Again, the Soviet Union raced to catch up with the United States and tested its own hydrogen bomb. Then the bombs became bigger. One Soviet bomb tested was the equivalent of 50 million tons of conventional explosives, or 4,000 times the power of the bomb that destroyed Hiroshima.

The delivery method for these weapons was the intercontinental bomber and carrier-based aircraft, but developing technology in the 1950s produced the **intercontinental ballistic missile (ICBM),** which could be launched from one continent to devastate another. By the early 1960s, the United States had thousands of these weapons, while the Soviet Union only had a handful. There was also a reversal in geographic advantage: The position of the Soviet Union on the edge of Europe meant that most of its armed conventional forces could quickly rush into a European war, which meant the United States had to base forces in Europe or move them across the Atlantic. But it also meant that U.S.-based mid-range missiles in Europe could easily strike Soviet territory. The Soviets attempted to gain a similar advantage by placing missiles in Cuba, within close range of the United States.

The resulting crisis produced a classic cold war stalemate. The United States spotted the missile emplacements (it regularly spied on Cuba with U-2 aircraft) and demanded their removal. Cuba was blockaded, and U.S. military leaders wanted to bomb the installations before they could become operational. Publicly, President John F. Kennedy and Soviet leader Nikita Khrushchev sounded stern and uncompromising. But we now know from their private statements that they secretly wondered if they were blundering into a war that would massacre millions in its first hours. Khrushchev pulled the Soviet missiles from Cuba, and Kennedy secretly agreed to remove the U.S. missiles from Turkey, a NATO ally on the Soviet border.

The conflict showed the madness that had entered the world. Both powers had tremendous weapons potential and were spending huge sums building ever more massive weapons and more far-reaching delivery systems. Yet neither side dared to use its weapons. Which side had more and better weapons, a crucial question in all prior conflicts, mattered little when each side had the capability of utterly destroying the other. The policy that resulted was **deterrence,** having the weapons to make sure the other side did not use theirs in a stalemate of mutually assured destruction. This was always an uneasy stalemate, for each side also worried that its massive weapons would be vulnerable to a first strike. Hiding missiles underwater in moving submarines was one answer to this problem, but it only added to the nightmarish quality of the situation: boats like the U.S. Trident submarine, a true doomsday machine, lurking underwater and carrying enough firepower to destroy every major city on the planet. Tension mounted in the early 1980s as the United States accelerated its arms spending, and some members of the Reagan administration spoke of the possibility of a winnable nuclear war. The demise of the Soviet Union brought a moment's respite, as tension eased between the two powers and both relaxed their nuclear readiness.

The problem was that the nuclear "club" was expanding. Both France and Great Britain conducted nuclear tests in the 1950s. China was added in the 1960s. Israel and South Africa secretly developed nuclear weapons in the 1970s and 1980s. The 1990s saw some hopeful signs. One was that Brazil, Argentina, and Algeria all abandoned their nuclear programs. In addition, the new republics that inherited the Soviet nuclear weapons chose to give them up. South Africa dismantled its nuclear arsenal and signed the Nuclear Nonproliferation Treaty.

But new dangers also emerged. India and Pakistan abandoned their pledge not to develop nuclear weapons, and each tested weapons designed to intimidate or at least warn the other of their nuclear capabilities. Most troubling was that nations with reckless prior records and with possible ties to terrorism became interested in nuclear weapons. Iraq's nuclear program was halted first by an Israeli bombing raid in 1981 and then again by the first Gulf War and weapons inspections in 1991. A UN program similarly thwarted Libya's interest in nuclear weapons. Iran continued development of a nuclear program, claiming they only sought peaceful uses in electrical power generation. Their increasingly sophisticated equipment was producing weapons-grade uranium—a higher level of enrichment than needed for power plants—and it was becoming quite clear that Iran had an interest in nuclear weapons capability. The Iran nuclear accord, signed in 2015 with the five permanent members of the UN Security Council as well as the European Union, created a monitoring and inspection system to assure that weapons and weapons-grade material were not being produced in return for a relaxing of international sanctions against Iran. In 2019 this agreement was scrapped by the Trump administration and has proven difficult to revive with deep suspicions on all sides.

At the same time, North Korea has conducted a variety of nuclear tests, including one very large test that they claimed was a hydrogen bomb. And they continue to test larger and longer-range missiles with the potential to threaten Japan and even the United States. Seoul, South Korea, a more likely adversary, is within easy artillery range of the North. Their tests and boasts have shown how nuclear weapons can alter the global balance of power, giving new power to smaller nations, as well as to the aggressive and the reckless. Much attention has focused on the actions and intensions of regimes in Iran and North Korea, which highlight the dilemma of nuclear proliferation. Other countries may decide to follow this nuclear path, and the availability of lost or poorly protected nuclear materials worries those who believe they could be acquired by terrorists.

Military Expenditures

> Every gun that is made, every warship launched, every rocket fired signifies, in the final sense, a theft from those who hunger and are not fed, those who are cold and are not clothed.
> —President Dwight D. Eisenhower, April 16, 1953

Interestingly, one of the first U.S. leaders to raise concern over the cost of military spending was President Dwight Eisenhower, a former World War II general, as he looked at the rising costs of the cold war. In his farewell speech as president on January 17, 1961, Eisenhower both defended the need to contain the Soviet Union and expressed open worry over the consequences of that effort:

> In the councils of government, we must guard against the acquisition of unwarranted influence, whether sought or unsought, by the military–industrial complex. The potential for the disastrous rise of misplaced power exists and will persist. (Dwight D. Eisenhower, *Public Papers of the Presidents*, [1960–61], 1035–1040)

American sociologist C. Wright Mills (1956) wrote about this concentration of power that was dominating U.S. society. He saw military leaders, corporate leaders who often depended on military contracts, and political leaders who depended on cold war fears for their positions as forming a **power elite** that controlled the U.S. economic agenda. Spending by the U.S. military continued to grow and reached a peak during the Vietnam War. It declined, especially in real-dollar amounts, somewhat during the late 1970s. New concerns about the Soviet Union and an attempt to deal with perceived threats through new military superiority during the Reagan administration again led to a rise in military spending. Military spending in the United States declined following the breakup of the Soviet Union and the end of the cold war. The rise of global terrorism brought a huge increase in U.S. military spending following the attacks of September 11, 2001. The United States was already spending more on arms than all of its adversaries combined. By 2005 the United States was spending as much on its military as the rest of the world's major powers combined, and continues to far exceed any rivals (see figure 6.4). China has greatly increased its military spending to expand its air and naval power, and now holds second place in spending.

The Last Great War?

German novelist Hermann Hesse, who often wrote of war, speculated that perhaps war, like slavery, would someday be gone from human history. Historian John Mueller (1993) contends that war is a "thoroughly bad and repulsive idea, like dueling or slavery, subrationally unthinkable and therefore obsolescent" (p. 214). Already, formal war, like formal slavery, is disappearing. Yet

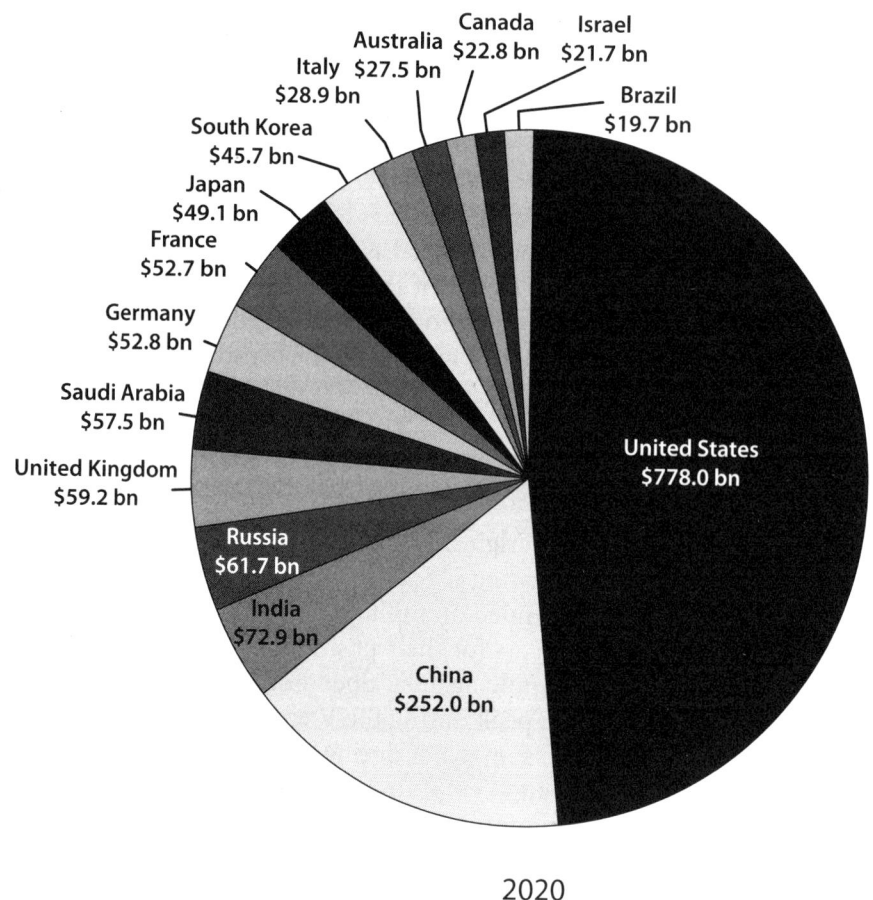

Figure 6.4 World military expenditures. (Source: "Military Spending," by Max Roser and Mohamed Nagdy. Our World in Data.) For detailed data, see https://www.sipri.org/databases/milex.

the end of formal war has not brought world peace, any more than the end of formal slavery has brought global economic justice.

Can we build a more peaceful world? The issue is practical as well as philosophical: It is not that violence is nasty and nonviolence is nice. Rather, it is simply that reliance on violence is no longer practical. Some see hope in the emergence of so-called people-power movements, which are not easily stopped by force. Examples of this are inspiring but uncertain. People power succeeded in toppling the corrupt Marcos regime in the Philippines in the 1980s (where the term was coined) and reversed a corrupt election in the Ukraine in 2004–2005. The crucial moment in both, however, came with the defection to the opposition of key military and security leaders, something that was rumored but never occurred in China's Tiananmen Square uprising.

Others, such as Samuel Huntington (1996), see hope in the triumph of democracy. Allied leaders in both world wars saw themselves as advancing a struggle for democracy that would eventually lead to a more peaceful world, since democracies, where people have some say in their fate, seem less prone to plunging into war than do dictatorships. The second Bush administration's doctrine justifying the war in Iraq is based in part on the idea that spreading democracy, even by force, ultimately will bring a more peaceful world. Others worry that part of the Bush doctrine established a new emphasis on **preemptive strikes,** attacking a foe in expectation of what might be done in the future, such as the development and use of weapons of mass destruction. The early days of World War I, and in some sense even the Pearl Harbor attack of World War II, have often been justified by their proponents as preemptive strikes to weaken future foes. Neither of these actions, of course, prevented war but led to a chain reaction of expanding warfare.

Others see hope in globalization and the increasing economic interconnection of countries that would make war too risky and too expensive to consider. *New York Times* commentator Thomas Friedman (1999) describes an only partly tongue-in-cheek "golden arches theory of conflict prevention," noting that no two countries with McDonald's restaurants have gone to war against each other. Can it be that simple? Did Baghdad only need a Happy Meal to turn things around? Friedman may have a point in the broadest sense that while globalization can stir hatred that breeds instability and civil conflict (Chua 2003), it may make large nations eager to maintain peace and stability, if only to protect world's stock markets.

In his book, *The Pentagon's New Map*, Thomas Barnett (2004), of the U.S. Naval War College, contends that the world is divided into a **functioning core** linked by globalization and a **nonintegrating gap,** a large swath around the equator that includes most of Africa as well as the Middle East and parts of Southeast Asia that incubate terrorism and conflict. This is where the world's wars and military interventions continue. The goal of war and interventions, as well as economic policy, he contends, is to shrink this gap. Yet Yale law professor Amy Chua (2003) contends that it is the very attempt to export free-market democracy that is breeding ethnic hatred and global instability. Both may be right, such that the result will not be a great global war but instead a "world on fire" with many smaller conflicts.

During the 1990s the military task of the United States and its NATO allies (Canada and much of Western Europe, at the time) shifted from containing the Soviet Union and winning any sort of conventional battle to peacekeeping assignments and interventions in regional conflicts and human rights crises, such as occurred with the breakup of Yugoslavia. Africa continues to provide situations in which Western powers are called on to intervene, sometimes in their own former colonies: Somalia, Rwanda, Liberia, Sierra Leone, and Sudan. The tasks associated with peacekeeping can be very different from the challenges of fighting and winning a war, as the United States has found in its occupation of Iraq.

Sometimes the call for assistance is for natural, rather than man-made, disasters. Following the terrible destruction in Southeast Asia caused by the tsunami in late 2004, many nations not only pledged financial help but also used their naval and military air transport capabilities to rush in relief supplies. The U.S. military, with an extensive network of air transport, was particularly valuable. Some see this type of effort as a great distraction from the military's main duties. Yet the logistical challenges of natural disasters—rushing in supplies, maintaining communications, moving personnel, keeping the peace, and restoring order—are very similar to the logistical challenges of war. The U.S. National Guard has been used in cases of natural disaster, civil disturbance, and international conflict. Humanitarian relief is still a small task, however, compared to the global investment in military preparedness. The United States pledged $383 million for tsunami relief in 2005, or just over one million a day, at a time when it was spending over one billion a day—a thousand times the tsunami effort—on general defense spending and close to another one billion per day on the Iraq conflict.

Less than one-quarter of the world's military spending would be enough to meet the total UN estimate for international development, well-being, and poverty elimination: health, housing, education, and environmental protection. One wonders if such a shift in priorities would not also lead to a much more stable and less conflict-prone planet.

Key Ideas

> - The modern nation-state grew out of centuries of war in Europe and then around the world. Preparing for war has become such a large part of national identity that in many places it is difficult to undo the institutions of weapons and warfare.

> - European powers fought great colonial wars and negotiated peace treaties that redrew the map of the world. World Wars I and II represent the climax of several centuries of such conflict.

> - Warfare became increasingly "total" up through World War II, which saw the wholesale destruction of whole cities.

- Knowing the destructive power of a third total war, the United States and the Soviet Union engaged in four decades of "cold war," often using small proxy conflicts as struggles for power.
- While major powers retreat from large-scale formal confrontation, many regional and local conflicts, informal wars and civil wars, continue to rage.
- New fears have emerged that regional conflicts and terrorist activity may resort to the use of nonconventional arms—weapons of mass destruction—which include chemical, biological, and nuclear weapons.
- The global arms trade remains a huge source of revenue for some, and a huge expense for many countries. Devoting needed resources to human development will require countries large and small to shift priorities from weapons to economic and social development.

For Review and Discussion

1. If war is so terrible, why do so many appear ready to fight over international and internal disagreements? What is the appeal of war to governments? To individuals?
2. How has warfare changed over the centuries? Has human conflict become more or less humane?
3. What drives the current regional conflicts in the world? Can alternatives to war be found and accepted?
4. Who are the major players in the global arms trade? What would be needed to turn this expenditure from weapons of destruction to tools of human progress?

Making Connections

Center for Defense Information (CDI)

- The CDI at https://www.pogo.org/center-for-defense-information/ collects and presents vast amounts of issues on defense spending and weapons proliferation. Information is here on everything from small arms to nuclear weapons, with an emphasis on U.S. controversies and priorities in spending. A watchdog group, they tend to be critical of overspending.

Project Ploughshares

- A Canadian peace organization under the auspices of the Canadian Council of Churches at https://ploughshares.ca/ provides information on weapons and conflicts worldwide, with an emphasis on peacemaking.

Stockholm International Peace Research Institute

➤ A global think tank at www.sipri.org, this group collects data on conflict zones, arms control, and international security; it is consistently rated one of the top global think tanks on armaments and security issues.

Making A Difference

Peace Groups

➤ Student interest in war and peace peaked in the 1960s, when many college students faced the possibility of military draft and serving in the Vietnam War. The conflicts in Iraq and the Middle East have renewed interest in peace movements. Are there peace groups on your campus? If so, what forms do they take? Do they have religious or spiritual themes? Are they politically active? Do they include social justice themes or domestic issues in violence?

United for Peace and Justice

➤ This group serves as a clearinghouse for hundreds of peace groups around the country. See their site at www.unitedforpeace.org. Their issues of concern include military spending, nuclear disarmament, global justice, and immigrant rights. Look at "Issues" and "Campaigns." See if there are activities near you. What are their current campaigns and activities?

7

Democracy and Human Rights

Having Our Say

Global Encounters

Myanmar (Burma)

Our ocean voyage has just become a river cruise. Off both sides are intensely green rice fields waving in the morning breeze. Water buffalo wander through the fields and down to the river for a drink. The fields are interrupted only by clusters of ancient trees and sudden and unexpected flashes of gold. It seems every low hilltop, every grove of trees, and every small tributary is marked by the gleaming gold bell of a Buddhist stupa. Some are no larger than a big potbelly stove, and others are surrounded by ornately carved pagodas. Where the small tributaries reach the river the juncture is almost always marked by a village of maybe 20 to 50 houses. They have thatched roofs, and many have bundled thatch walls. The more substantial have weather planks under the thatch, and all those near the water rise up on stilts. There are no roads, just clusters of the hollowed-out boats we had encountered at sea.

All that's missing from this river scene is Katharine Hepburn and Humphrey Bogart. Or maybe it should be Bing Crosby and Bob Hope, bumbling along on the road to Rangoon. We have entered the Yangon River, one of the major channels in the lowlands of the Irrawaddy Delta. This is the watery highway that Rudyard Kipling lauded as the fabled "road" to Mandalay. Kipling wrote the poem but he never came to Burma. George Orwell did, and spent five years here. His Burmese Days (2008 [1934]) is not his best-known work but is an interesting glimpse into this quixotic land. The Burmese call Orwell "the prophet" and claim that Animal Farm and 1984 were inspired not by Russia or events in Europe but by his days in Burma. Independent from British India since the end of World War II, the country whose leaders call it Myanmar has been ruled by an unpredictable military dictatorship since 1962.

Visiting the land that calls itself Myanmar is to live in a world of ambiguity and paradox. I'm sure that training in Zen would be useful to cope mentally with this postmodern police state. While U.S. officials are in the ship's union denouncing the national government, polite and courteous officials of that government are in a conference room stamping our visas. Then there is the matter of what currency to use. It is illegal to have U.S. dollars without a permit, but almost everyone, down to rural market vendors, will gladly accept them—often only singles, however. That's useful because it is hard to know what to do about the currency. There are several. The official kyat is listed at 6.3 to the dollar. At that rate, you'd need to be a millionaire to buy a Tiger beer. The government trades at 400 to the dollar, but you can't find anywhere to exchange the money legally. The real rate is about 1,200 to the dollar, which makes the largest domination printed, 1,000 kyat, worth about 80 cents. The government occasionally announces that other denominations are suddenly worthless, which is too bad, especially since most people can't get access to the banks and have to hold cash. You can only get the higher rate through the black market, though it's not really a black market since trading is done openly on the streets and the traders seem to have no trouble turning in their dollars—permit or not. But one never knows. A child approaches us on the street in the downtown and asks for a dollar for a chain of ten postcards. This is common everywhere in Southeast Asia. But then she mumbles something about being quick before the police come. When we hesitate, she runs off. Many things are illegal here, including riding a motorcycle in parts of the city and honking your horn, but are quite openly tolerated (as we note while dodging honking motorcycles). But it is also means that if anyone runs afoul of the government there are plenty of grounds for making a minor arrest.

The government of Myanmar is actively promoting tourism. So far, business has been slow. The country gets less than 1 percent of the millions who trek through neighboring Thailand every year. Still there are Japanese and Australians and a scattering of Europeans, particularly Germans, who go everywhere. Travel snobs who find Vietnam too touristy head for Cambodia and Laos. Those who are fed up with the touristy welcome of Thailand try Myanmar. Still, just by docking at this port, we have multiplied the number of Americans in the country several times over and become the largest invasion of Americans in Myanmar since World War II. We can't get all the way up the river to the city, so shuttle buses take us on a 40-minute drive between our berth amidst the teak logs and the city that was formerly known as Rangoon, now Yangon. Waiting there is the Trader's Hotel, which offers a wonderful high tea. The neighboring national history museum displays the great Lion Throne, the symbol of Burmese authority, once carried off to London and now returned. A sprawling market sells an amazing array of products that one is not supposed to buy. With a quick flick of his pliers, a crouching man replaces my dead watch battery (for one dollar, of course) while two of his companions keep watch, blocking the view of his actions from the street.

Over all this activity towers the great golden bell of the Shwedagon Pagoda, topped, we are told, by a 760-carat diamond. From up here, we can look down on the two tall buildings—the Traders Hotel and a Japanese office building—in this sprawling city whose only dominating feature is that gleaming diamond in the sky. The platform of the pagoda is filled with statues of the serene and contemplative sage of the Theravada Buddhism that dominates in Southeast Asia. The great Buddha statues often have a hand raised in a gesture of reassurance: Life is suffering, but there is a way beyond suffering. The largest Buddha in this complex is not ancient but quite new. It was donated by the government. "To give a great Buddha is to gain forgiveness and to gain merit," our guide explains. The guide then looks at the giant statue with a Buddha-like smile, "Those who have many bad deeds that need to be forgiven, they must give the greatest Buddha." He walks on without further comment.

Everywhere we go, guides, hoteliers, and shopkeepers are more eager to talk than one might expect. No one mentions opposition leader Aung San Suu Kyi by name; she is just "the lady." No one ever speaks of the junta by name either. In good colloquial English, they are often just "those guys." Many express *admiration for the United States and, sometimes, worry about the growing power and influence of China. To most Burmese, that nearby great power is much more threatening than the distant United States.*

Unable to develop commercially and facing international sanctions, the government seems bent on plundering the country's available resources. Our dock is piled high with huge logs culled from the rain forest, some being loaded onto the deck of an old freighter with South Korean flags. Rubies, almost a Burmese monopoly, continue to find their way onto the world market. So does opium. When the Taliban briefly cracked down on Afghan opium, Myanmar became the world's largest supplier. Now that Afghanistan is back in the drug trade, Myanmar is only number two, but still a major player. Sanctions mean that even U.S. and international drug enforcement agents cannot make official contacts in the country. Sanctions have led to a great informal economy, and to the darkest side of illegal trade, such as trade in women and girls for prostitution. AIDS is spreading faster here than anywhere outside of Central Asia.

What I remember most, however, are those friendly Burmese people with the Buddha smiles. Will they continue to endure? Will the situation blow up with antigovernment and anti-Chinese sentiment, as in the closing days of Indonesian crony capitalism Suharto-style? Or will they become a pawn in struggles between great powers, as has so often happened here in Southeast Asia?

I have no answers to these questions. For now, I'm satisfied that our students can now find Myanmar on the map. They have asked some good questions and grappled with those infamously contradictory answers. Somewhere between the golden pagodas and the barbed-wire checkpoints, they have seen both the beauty and the beast in this land, enough to be sobered by both.

Within days of our departure, the government suddenly announced it was moving the capital from Yangon to a remote interior location. In fall of 2007 the country was rocked by protests over high prices and continued repression. The protests were led by the Buddhist monks, some of whom were beaten and others confined to monasteries. In spring of 2008 a terrible cyclone ravaged the Irrawaddy Delta all the way to Yangon. The villages we had visited were utterly destroyed. Fearful of outside intervention, the government refused to allow American or European aircraft to provide relief supplies and left tens of thousands of villagers on the flooded delta to fend for themselves without food or clean water. The United Nations was able to broker the delivery of some relief supplies, and groups such as UNICEF remained active in the area. The tragedy and continued repression raised many unsettled questions (see Reynolds 2009): How does the international community sanction a repressive government without hurting the people? To provide relief, should the international community negotiate with repressive regimes, enter disaster areas without government approval, or seek other means to reach desperate people?

Nationalism and the Nation-State

The road to democracy is long and uncertain. The ever-unpredictable Myanmar military surprised the world in 2010 by releasing Aung San Suu Kyi from house arrest and allowing her to head the dominant political party. She is barred from serving as president but has held several official positions, and was clearly the face, and voice, of civil authority. In 2012 President Obama and Secretary of State Clinton visited the country and met with her. It seemed that the needle was nudging to the democracy that Myanmar has never really known. Then tensions exploded with the military crackdown on another of Myanmar's many minorities, the Muslim Rohingya. The military had long fought other groups, such as the largely Christian Karen, but this time the crackdown was especially brutal. The military said that the Rohingya were not citizens but aliens who snuck in from Bangladesh (many have been in Burmese territory for centuries). They said they were Islamic terrorists. Villages were burned, residents were massacred, and a mass migration toward refugee camps in Bangladesh began (BBC News 2020).

Human rights advocates waited for Nobel Laureate Suu Kyi to speak out against these actions. She defended them. The military still had a monopoly on coercive power, and their actions were often popular in the Buddhist majority population. By siding with the military's action, Suu Kyi gained strength and won big in the 2020 election. Nevertheless, the military declared the election fraudulent, rearrested Suu Kyi, and resumed direct rule. This time the general population rose up in dismay and took to the streets—workers, students, women's groups, and others. Then the shooting began. After heavy-handed tactics to disperse groups failed, the military returned to what it knows best—direct assault with live ammunition. At least 500 were killed. And the future? The world has responded with sanctions (Thrush 2021), but it can be hard to sanction a junta that does not answer to popular opinion and already is adept in black market trade: timber, gems, opium, and more. The greater the atrocities the harder it becomes to relinquish power for fear of being called to account and prosecuted (Fisher 2021).

As we see by the events in Myanmar, war is only one form of state violence. Often, the worst forms of violence are perpetrated by a nation against its own citizens and residents. It may be the bloody violence of a massacre or execution or the more subtle violence of exclusion and repression. Military governments were common between the 1960s and the 1990s. Direct military rule is now rare. Authoritarian governments remain, but more often they hold some form of election and leverage their control of the economy and the media, as well as armed support from their military, from militias, or from some form of national security apparatus including "secret police." Repressive as they may be, such governments need to maintain a coalition of control and a veneer of legitimacy, and so are less likely to use direct force than military governments.

Imperialism drove the nineteenth century; nationalism drove the twentieth. **Nationalism** is the intense belief in the worth, rightness, and glory of one's own nation. **Nation** is itself a slippery term. Used in the context of the League of Nations or the United Nations, *nation* simply means an independent entity with full sovereignty; it answers to no higher power, except as it may freely enter into treaties. **Sovereignty,** as we will see, is also a slippery concept. Does it mean a nation can do whatever it wants, or are we all answerable to a higher moral or social order?

There is an older root of the word *nation* captured in the word *nationality:* people who share customs and culture, maybe language, and certainly identity—an ethnic group. The Latin root of the word (*natio*) refers to "birth," as one is born into the nation, and implies this older meaning of ethnic identity. Political scientists often prefer to refer to a sovereign government entity as a **state.** For an anthropologist, a *state* is an entity with centralized power and the ability to exercise coercive force, something more than a tribe.

I have used the term *state* in these latter two meanings in the previous chapter. This can be confusing, though, since people in the United States of America and in Mexico use *state* to refer to a subnational entity, such as a province (and it certainly wouldn't help matters if the United Nations started calling itself the United States!). The two terms can be combined as **nation-state,** which is, strictly speaking, a sovereign entity that represents the interests of people who share a common culture, presumably a common language, as well as a common territory. Burmese kingdoms had long and proud histories before being subjugated by the British Raj that ruled India and the entire subcontinent. Fiercely independent, the Burmese rejected British rule and Imperial Japanese dominance in World War II and established the independent country that now calls itself Myanmar. But the majority Bamar population share this land with over 100 culturally distinct ethnic groups.

The trouble for our taxonomy is that this term no longer fits many places, most of which have multiple cultures sharing one land. A single land with a single culture and ethnicity perhaps describes tiny nation-states, such as Slovenia, but not even Belgium and certainly not Switzerland. Japan comes close, but certainly not the United States. The nation-state is a fairly recent invention, and it may already be fracturing.

From Bands to States

The simplest way people have organized themselves is what anthropologists call a **band.** It's a small group of people working and traveling together.

Hunter-gathers (what's left of them) often live in seminomadic bands. They don't and can't control all the territory they use. Their decisions are collective, or made by the group: adults, young and old, men and women. From what we can still see of bands in equatorial Africa and a few remote places, some members are obviously more articulate and persuasive than others. Decision by consensus doesn't mean perfect harmony; sometimes it might look more like a contentious family gathering, with sarcasm, insults, and old grievances. All are involved, however. It is a participatory democracy.

Once a human group settles down to tend gardens, practice horticulture, or raise animals (which is called **pastoralism**) and the population of the group grows, band leadership becomes more difficult. Not everyone can be heard in one meeting. There are new responsibilities: Horticulturalists have land, often communally owned, to defend, and pastoralists have herds to defend. These groups are often governed as **tribes.** Tribes have recognized leaders who speak for them to other groups and who come together to judge disputes, mark off land, punish offenders, and defend territory. They typically have little permanent power beyond their ability to gather followers and the prestige they have gained over the years.

The tribes most familiar to North Americans are the American Indian groups that originally occupied the continent. Some have called these people "the First Nations," but they were not nation-states; they were sovereign tribes. Europeans liked to call the native leaders "chiefs," using an old French term (and we're stuck with it), but this can be misleading. To speak of "Indian princesses" is even more misleading, unless one is speaking of South Asia. A better term might be **elders.** Often there were multiple roles: talking chiefs, the wise ones; war chiefs, the brave ones; and others. Certainly, one person could command great respect. The settlers at Jamestown met the commanding Chief Powhatan, a person of such charisma and political influence that they called the loose alliance of tribes under his control by his name and decided that his daughter, Pocahontas, was a "princess." But even mighty Powhatan did not declare war or make peace; he *advised* war or peace.

When Europeans and North Americans think of tribes, they may also think of Africa, which at the time of the European conquests was, in fact, a huge collage of many forms of government that included bands and tribes. But all our origins are tribal. Europe was also once a land of tribes, and we still call modern nations by their names: the Belgae, the Germani, the Scots, the Britons. Readers of the Jewish Torah and the Christian Bible also know the 12 tribes of Israel, each led by its elders; politically, Moses was much like Powhatan. The "judges" of the book of Judges were elders, or "chiefs," gifted in dispute settlement (wise ones) and in defending territory (brave ones). Occasionally the related tribes acted in concert under a charismatic leader.

A bit more centralized is the **chiefdom,** in which a single leader starts to exercise more central control, commanding armies and perhaps controlling economic life by redistributing goods to those in need. At the time of the Roman Empire, what had been tribes beyond the borders were becoming more organized (perhaps in self-defense) as chiefdoms: The Franks, the Goths, and the various Germanic tribes were, strictly speaking, chiefdoms. This also became true among the Polynesians in the Pacific, again often under the stress of war. Every now and then, a great chief would organize the chiefdoms and looser collections of tribes into a single entity, usually for military purposes. Attila the Hun was a great chief. He brought together a diverse collection of groups and put them on the move, changing the faces of both China and Rome. The man who fought Caesar in Gaul (modern France, named for the Franks), a fellow who would be more famous if he had won (and if modern tongues could pronounce his name), Vercingetorix, was also a great chief. The man who united Hawaii, and whom Europeans called "King" Kamehameha, was a great chief. When he first united the nomadic tribes of Mongolia, Genghis Khan was a chieftain, and he went on to become a great chief.

When the chief became a permanent fixture and passed rule on to his descendants and when he (unlike tribal leaders, these were almost always men) organized a professional fighting force, perhaps a standing army, and had other officials under his command so that he could truly *rule* with the power of coercive force, the state was born. A state usually came with agriculture and intense cultivation of the land, as well as a larger population. Typically, it was ruled by a king.

When my children were smaller, they sometimes liked to play king and queen, with the requisite princes and princesses and maybe the dog standing in as a dragon. In the midst of one of these games, there was typically a pause and this question: "OK, I'm the king, but just what does a king do?" This is not easy to answer. Kings rule, clearly. But what constitutes rule? They were the final arbitrators of disputes. King Solomon deciding which woman should get a disputed baby is a famous example, but this would only be likely in a very small realm; otherwise, the king would need to appoint administrators. Kings sometimes embarked on great building projects: the pyramids, the Hanging Gardens of Babylon, the Great Wall of China. But mostly, kings went to war. Kingdoms were built by conquest. To again use a biblical example from the Old Testament, the elder Samuel is recorded as having warned the people that if they demanded a king, he would seize their finest fields and produce and even their daughters for his own use, and he would take their sons for his armies. But he would, they hoped, defeat their enemies.

Kings were in an almost common state of war, and so it is not surprising that some were far more successful in this enterprise than others. These kings established empires by conquering other kingdoms. The empires they created, however, were not nation-states but multiethnic, multilingual conglomerations of the tribes and kingdoms that they had overrun. Multiple religions and practices were often allowed, as long as the superiority of the ruling city and its ways was acknowledged. The emperor ruled, sometimes with the lesser rulers still in place, as the king of kings or appointed his own staff. Alexander the Great, for example, left local rulers in place throughout the fringes of his empire and appointed his own people to rule Persia in the empire's center.

The Romans worked through local kings or their own governors as convenience allowed. From about 2300 BCE—when a tough village kid who took the name of Sargon I conquered a large swath of the Middle East and created the Akkadian, or first Babylonian Empire—until almost 1500 CE, the multicultural empire was the world's usual complex form of social organization. The Mediterranean world saw the Egyptian, Greek, Roman, and Holy Roman Empires. The Iranian plateau and Mesopotamia saw the Babylonian, Assyrian, Persian, Alexandrian, and Parthian Empires. India was consolidated by the Mauryan Empire. Its great emperor, Asoka, converted from Hinduism to Buddhism, renouncing war in the process, but also tolerated as many as 600 different religious practices and languages. The later Mughal Empire included both very tolerant Muslim rulers and at least one "fundamentalist" and also allowed the cultural, linguistic, and religious complexity of India to remain.

China began to unite under the Shang Empire (about the same time as Sargon I in the Middle East), later fell into a series of warring states, and was then reunited by the powerful leader, Qin Shi Huang, who created the Qin (or Chin) Empire in 230 BCE, about the time that Rome was coming to prominence; it is from Chin that the name *China* derives. His Han successors started to build a more cohesive culture with a greater merging of people and traditions than those in the West, and we still refer to the dominant ethnic group in China as the *Han Chinese*. China remained diverse, however, with multiple religions, languages, and ways of life.

The nation-state, the modern country, emerged from this pattern slowly. Charles Tilly (1990) writes, "A thousand years ago, Europe did not exist" (p. 230). That is, no one had a sense of being part of a common entity, any particular group of countries, nor had they any reason to. According to Tilly, "In 990, nothing about the world of manors, local lords, military raiders, fortified villages, trading towns, city-states, and monasteries foretold a consolidation into national-states" (p. 230). Rulers dominated but rarely governed. "The emperors, kings, princes, dukes, caliphs, sultans, and other potentates of 990 prevailed as conquerors, tribute-takers, and rentiers, not as heads of state that durably and densely regulated life within their realms" (p. 229). For example, Richard I, the Lionheart, a much admired and famous king of England and leader of the Third Crusade, only spent a few months of his time as king residing in England.

Gradually, over the next 500 years of almost continual war, those rulers who were unable to conquer vast lands found that the best way to consolidate their power was to forge a national identity within their boundaries. This created at least three recognizable nation-states: England, France, and Spain. Each united around a common religion—Catholicism for France and Spain and the Anglican Church for England—and even more slowly around a common language—Parisian French for France, the King's English for England, and Castilian Spanish (the language of Madrid) for Spain. As described by Weatherford (1994):

> Unlike rulers before them, who had been willing to rule over many different nationalities speaking different languages, wearing different clothes, and practicing different cultures, Ferdinand and Isabella installed a new homogeneity that was very much a precursor of the totalitarian movements of the twentieth century. They equated nation, language, race, and religion. To be one of their subjects, one had to speak Spanish and be of European ancestry and Roman Catholic faith. (p. 151)

This, however, was a slow process. Napoleon tried to inspire French national pride and to impose control with a standardized language, laws, and school system. It wasn't easy. He seized Nice from the Italian dukes of Savoy, but to this day, the street names are also given in the local language, Niçois, something of a French–Italian hybrid. Down the coast, Prince Rainier of Monaco held an independent principality for more than 50 years, and the dialect of the entire region remains distinct. In Spain, as late as the middle of the twentieth century, General Francisco Franco tried to strengthen the role of Catholicism as the national church, wipe out regional languages such as the Catalan of Barcelona and the Mediterranean coast, and centralize control in Madrid. To this day, the Basques of northwestern Spain use their own language and agitate for independence. England is still a land of dialects and regional distinctions, and the idea of the United Kingdom of Great Britain and Northern Ireland (the official national title) is even more tenuous as the Scottish seek more legal autonomy, the Welsh work to keep alive their language and culture, and Northern Ireland moves to reach accords with the Republic of Ireland.

Italy and Germany did not unite into single nations until the 1870s. Both countries retain strong regional identities and north–south distinctions, with differences in dialect and culture. The 1990s saw the dismantling of big multiethnic states into smaller versions of nation-states. The Soviet Union broke up into nationally defined states with nationalist ideologies: Georgia for Georgians, Armenia for Armenians, Estonia for Estonians. The trouble (and it can be real trouble) is that all of these entities still contain ethnic and religious minorities. Yugoslavia, a multiethnic state, broke into small nation-states starting in 1991: Slovenia, Croatia, Serbia, and Macedonia. The struggles again mounted over minorities: What about the Serbs in Croatia and the Croatians in Serbia? And Bosnia, with a mix of three nationalities, fell into a terrible civil war. Czechoslovakia managed a rare "velvet divorce" in 1993 when its president, Vaclav Havel, refused to try to hold the country together by force. The result was a

Czech Republic in the west (which still contains the formerly divided territories of Bohemia and Moravia) and Slovakia for the Slovaks in the east.

While the power of nationalism in Europe has remained strong, it has always had its nobler and baser sides. The twentieth century saw particularly brutal forms of European nationalism. It was a favorite tool of dictators and demagogues, who used national images to win elections, rally masses, and ultimately turn those masses to violence against their neighbors, both internal and external. In the 1930s, Benito Mussolini's Fascists carried ancient Roman symbols and preached the glories of the Italian people and their destiny.

The ugliest, yet perhaps most masterful, use of nationalism was that by Adolf Hitler and the Nazis. They spoke to German anger after the nation's humiliation after World War I and promised a new era of glory for the German people, German culture, and the German nation. The call for all the Germans together, in one greater Germany, provided the excuse for the takeovers of Austria and Czechoslovakia, the invasions of Poland and France (each with German minorities within territory that had been part of Germany), and the expulsion of and eventual effort at exterminating Jews, Gypsies (Roma), and others who did not fit the national ideal.

When Hitler invaded the Soviet Union in 1941, Joseph Stalin was not able to rally defenders to the cause of international socialism, especially since much of what the people had seen of Stalinist socialism was brutality and misery. Yet he found he could rally at least the Russian people to a defense of the homeland, Mother Russia. Nazi invaders treated them as inferior people, and the Russians fought back with the same tenacity that had exhausted Napoléon in his Russian invasion. Those who did not rally to the cry of Russian nationalism—conquered Chechens, for instance—were deported to the icy east by Stalin.

More recently, in the 1990s Slobodan Milošević rallied the Serbian people around the idea of a greater Serbia. Serbia, now poor and disorganized, was once an important kingdom in the Balkans and had made a heroic defense against Turkish invaders. Milošević's idea of a resurgent Serbia struck a chord of national pride. Gradually, it became apparent that Milošević's nationalism included brutal attacks on Muslims and all non-Serbs in Bosnia and the province of Kosovo. The dark side of nationalism had surfaced once again.

Having faced centuries of bloody conflict fueled by nationalism, many Europeans are turning to a new vision: **Europeanism** and **transnational union.** In one sense, this is not new. For centuries after the fall of the Roman Empire, European states tried to recreate a new Christian empire that would reunite the core of Europe. Despite its power, the attempted Holy Roman Empire never really succeeded, as it was observed by the French writer Voltaire to be "neither holy, nor Roman, nor an empire." Napoleon once envisioned a United States of Europe (of course, with a French core). Hitler envisioned a fascist Europe with a German core.

The new idea of a united Europe is one that intentionally disperses power without a single core. The European Union (EU) has its headquarters in Brussels, Belgium. The European Parliament meets in Strasbourg, France, and its court system is headquartered in Luxembourg. The EU began as a unit of economic cooperation, the Common Market. Economic cooperation has extended now to a common currency, the **euro.** Political cooperation has included the coordination of common laws and policies, although each member state still retains its own lawmaking function. There is great ease in traveling across large areas of Europe without customs stops, currency exchanges, and other interruptions. It's similar to moving from state to state in the United States or across the Canadian provinces. (As in Canada, though, the prevailing language may change.)

In some ways, transnational unionism and national splintering complement one another. One reason that tiny European states can thrive is that they are part of a larger economic and political entity. How much this should be a larger cultural entity is more controversial. Usually open Denmark has shown considerable resistance to union, in that the Danes want to retain their Danishness. So, too, for the Finns, who have long been dominated by larger powers and are not eager to lose Finland's hard-fought independence. Great Britain, who withdrew from the European Union in 2020, has all along kept a certain distance from the united continent, just as the island does geographically, wanting to maintain strong ties with the United States and other English-speaking countries around the world and not eager to give up time-honored traditions such as the British pound.

How much can one unite economically and politically and still remain unique culturally? Can one be a nation without a state? These are questions that go beyond Europe to a world that is often both coming together and coming apart.

Nationalism and Independence

Twentieth-century nationalism not only fired Europe but increasingly fired the world, often in struggles against Europe. Japanese nationalism glorified the country's emperor as the embodiment of all that was unique and glorious about the Japanese people. Emboldened by a new sense of national pride, Japanese leaders challenged first Russia in the Russo-Japanese War of 1905 and then the powers of Western Europe and the United States in World War II.

In Vietnam, Ho Chi Minh explored socialist ideas but used the power of nationalism to inspire the Vietnamese people throughout the middle of the twentieth century. He called on them to restore their ancient honor and power by evicting the French, the Japanese, the French again, and finally the Americans.

One of the great tragic misunderstandings of the Vietnam War was that the United States persisted in seeing it as a struggle of international communism, while for most Vietnamese, it was a struggle for national independence. Commonalities of language, religion, and culture fired broad national aspirations.

One of the most powerful was the idea of Arab nationalism, evicting the Turks, Germans, Italians, British, and French (at varying times) and creating a common Arab nation under Islam. The most eloquent voice for Arab nationalism was Egypt's President Gamal Abdel Nasser, whose popularity and power in the region was founded on this idea. Egypt even went as far as to merge with Syria to form the United Arab Republic (UAR) in 1958, with the hope that others would join. In fact, the union split apart within three years, although Egypt continued to call itself the UAR until 1970. Instead of a single Arab state that spanned North Africa and the Middle East, what resulted from squabbles among the colonial powers, as well as squabbles among the Arab leaders, was a mélange of over a dozen small states, emirates, and sultanates, each with limited power.

Nasser's disappointment was not new. One-hundred fifty years earlier, Simón Bolívar had envisioned Latin American nationalism, a great United States of South America, free from Spain but united with a common language and heritage. What emerged instead in the early 1800s were many small states, often fighting border disputes with one another. Pan-African nationalism fared little better. In 1957 Kwame Nkrumah, a powerful orator and the first president of independent Ghana, preached Pan-Africanism that would span all of black Africa, with common goals and cooperation. Africa was instead divided into a myriad of small states, filled with internal conflicts and often at odds with one another. The vision of black nationalism remained and inspired African American leaders in the United States, but its goals remained elusive.

Where a national identity didn't exist, many leaders of newly independent states decided that it had to be created. The country of Indonesia was forged from what had been the Dutch East Indies, a land fought over by colonial powers for centuries. The world's fourth-largest country, it contains hundreds of islands; hundreds of languages and ethnic groups; a Muslim majority with significant Christian, Hindu, and animist minorities; and incredible cultural diversity. In the 1930s Indonesian nationalist Achmed Sukarno came to the forefront of groups demanding independence, democracy, and national unity. The Indonesians fashioned a new flag and even a new language. Indonesia needed a language, and it wasn't going to be Dutch. Imposing the main language of Javanese, which was spoken in the capital and by the largest population, wouldn't work either, as it would likely be just as resented. So a minor language related to Malay was chosen to be Bahasa Indonesian, the language of the country.

When Raden Suharto came to power in 1967 in a bloody coup that took the lives of as many as 700,000 people, he began an enterprise of nation building. Centralization of the economy proceeded, and the schools were mandated to teach a common Indonesian identity. Other entities, such as the former Portuguese colony of East Timor, were added to the nation. Javanese people were transplanted to remote and sparsely populated islands to spread the population as well as to homogenize the culture. Suharto envisioned a united world power. Instead, when he was driven from power in 1998 amid charges of incredible corruption and an economic collapse, the country itself started to fray. Fighting between Christians and Muslims became frequent. Certain ethnic groups, such as Chinese merchants, were targeted for attacks. Catholic, Portuguese-speaking East Timor fought for and finally gained independence in 2001. One reason this was so strongly resisted by the national government was the realization that a chain reaction of independence movements could occur that could unravel the entire country.

The creation of national identity where none has previously existed can be amusing at times, brutal at others. Iraq exists as it does because British colonial administrators drew lines on a map as they divided the former Ottoman Empire. Yet Saddam Hussein sought to create a strong Iraqi nationalism that was distinct from Arab nationalism. In his version, he, as the great father of Iraq, was successor to the mighty Nebuchadnezzar of Babylon (whose palace ruins lie within the country) and the great Muslim leader Saladin (who ironically was a Kurd, the group Saddam Hussein attacked with poison gas). The character of the leader aside, it seems quite artificial.

Perhaps nationalism is always based a bit on legend and glorifying a confused past. When U.S. schoolchildren stand and pledge allegiance to the flag under the watchful portraits of George Washington and Abraham Lincoln, this, too, is nationalism. In most classrooms, the children represent dozens of different nationalities from across the globe, standing on land taken from over 500 different tribal entities. What they have in common are certain symbols and a tradition that is about 225 years old. Many might prefer to term their feelings for the flag *patriotism*, rather than *nationalism*. The distinction is subtle: Is it that one's own feelings are patriotic and those of his or her enemies are nationalistic? Patriotism, which means devotion to the *patri*, or fatherland, perhaps denotes less of a single ethnic heritage.

Democracy and Its Alternatives

The Age of Democracy

Democracy, or rule by the people, is both an ancient idea and an elusive one. The 1990s saw a great increase in the number of electoral democracies around the world, as authoritarian governments, ruled by unelected powerful leaders, fell in Eastern Europe and Latin America, while democratic gains were made in parts of East Asia and Africa. Yet democracy has not always fulfilled its promises. Moreover, many modern democratic systems are plagued by corruption, human rights abuses, misinformation and public manipulation, poor leadership, and suppression of minority rights.

A world of electoral democracies—national governments chosen by popular vote—is new, but the idea of popular participation is not. One could argue that it is not only ancient but also even prehistoric. Human bands and tribes often had a process of collective decision making that involved a large portion of the group. This system was often quite informal but not always. The Iroquois of what is now the northeastern United States were led by a variety of male elders, or chiefs who were ultimately answerable to women *electors* in a system that involved all adult members and included representation at multiple levels: village, clan, tribe, and ultimately the Iroquois confederacy of tribes itself. Some claim that this arrangement (without the female electors) served as a model for the new United States of America; we know at least that Benjamin Franklin admired the Iroquois system.

Tribal democracy gradually gave way in many places to **monarchy,** or rule by a hereditary leader, as kingdoms and empires spread across the planet. The power of these kings nonetheless varied greatly. Kings in the Middle East and the Mediterranean at times ruled as absolute monarchs, having complete authority over the lives of their subjects. The Egyptian pharaohs at the height of their power were considered divine beings who essentially owned all of Egypt, its land and its people—a true and absolute monarch. In other times and places, however, the king was more like the great elder above tribal elders, the most revered chief. African kings often held such a position, and as far as they hold their offices, present-day African leaders continue to do so. Limited monarchs—ancient kings who were answerable to elders or medieval kings who were answerable to nobles—became the basis of later constitutional monarchies, in which a parliament enacts a code of laws and a king or queen presides over and enforces them, if even in a largely ceremonial function.

In the ancient Middle East, kings often had great authority, but a tradition of laws also emerged. The great Babylonian King Hammurabi set down a code of laws in the 1700s BCE that gave privileges to the wealthy and those of noble birth but recognized certain rights of the poor, as well. Attacks on the person, property, or family of even a poor man would be punished, at least with a fine. Hebrew prophets, who served as royal advisors, reminded kings that even if they ruled by decree, they were still bound to a moral law to protect the poor and powerless and to respect the families and properties of their subjects. This advice was sometimes ignored, but kings who abused their power faced rebellion by religious and military leaders as well as by tribal elders.

About the same time as the Persian kings and the Hebrew prophets, Chinese scholars also pondered the essence of good government. The shadowy figure of Laozi (Lao Tzu)—a teacher and maybe a librarian, maybe a retired government official, and certainly a respected elder—is reputed to have fled a China torn by warring states and ruthless kings sometime in the sixth century BCE. Laozi believed in limited government, with local autonomy and personal freedom. He denounced the corruption of his day and sought a better way, the *Tao*, or way of heaven.

We know more about Laozi's somewhat younger contemporary, a scholar and minor government official, K'ung Fu-tzu (551–479 BCE), whom Westerners know under the Latinized name of Confucius. Confucius believed in strong but just government, based on loyalty and responsibility. Children should show respect and loyalty to their parents, women to their husbands, people to their leaders, and all to their king. But in return, each holder of a respected position was bound by obligation to lead firmly but kindly, with moderation and good judgment. Confucius's ideals were not immediately embraced, but his writing was preserved. China's mighty emperor of the Qin Dynasty, hardly a man of moderation and kindness, was not impressed with these ideals and sought to burn everything that Confucius wrote. Later Han rulers saved the remnants of his writing, however, and government officials had to pass tests based on memorizing the words of Confucius, which have influenced centuries of families and governments in East Asia.

The ancient Mediterranean world knew of democracy, though it didn't always approve of it. The most famous ancient democracy was practiced in some Greek city-states, most notably Athens. A **city-state** is a city that functions as an autonomous unit under its own leadership. In the Greek case, the state was small, a city and the land it controlled, and the nation, all Greek-speaking people, was large but mostly defined by a sense of common heritage rather than a cohesive political entity. The smaller size of the city-state allowed for participatory democracy; everyone could have a say. Well, not really everyone. Women and slaves had limited political rights and no political voice. Free male citizens could serve on juries, vote in assemblies, and help decide the direction of government. By the time of its golden age under Pericles (c. 450 BCE), the Athenian experiment with this limited participatory democracy had reached its peak.

Other systems were also in competition. Sometimes Greek city-states were ruled by kings, and sometimes they were ruled by a group of oligarchs, or wealthy powerful men. (**Oligarchy** is rule by a powerful elite.) Sometimes the king or the oligarch would oppress the common people so badly they would rise up under the leadership of a **tyrant,** who would lead them in rebellion. The tyrant would then rule as a revolutionary dictator. Some were just, impartial, and effective, but many were not (as you can probably guess from the meaning the word *tyrant* has taken on in English). Sparta was largely in the hands of a military dictatorship, ruled by those who had come up through the ranks in Sparta's many wars. The need to hold both conquered slaves and conquered lands under close control meant that the military dominated all aspects of Spartan life.

Greek political philosophers debated which form of rule was best: monarchy, oligarchy, military dictatorship, dictatorship of the masses, or democracy. One of the most famous answers to this question came in Plato's *Republic*, written in 360 BCE. Plato wasn't much of a democrat; he worried that the masses would always fall behind a **demagogue,** someone full of empty but appealing slogans who would appeal to their basest desires—a Milošević or a Hitler perhaps. Plato believed a ruler should be chosen from among those known for their wisdom and who cared nothing for luxury. Plato's rulers would have great power but no real wealth; they would be too noble to want any. We call Plato's ideal ruler the **philosopher-king,** but this was not a hereditary monarch. The ruler's own children would get no special privileges, nor would any other individual, for the ruler would preside over a **meritocracy** (rule by the most meritorious) and distribute goods according to need without regard for rank. Plato's ideal rulers were essentially philosopher-communists, an ideal that would have modern appeal but be hard to realize in practice.

Plato had an especially bright "graduate student" by the name of Aristotle. Aristotle believed in more limited government and respect for the rights of free men. His most enduring political idea is that of **natural law:** the idea that ethical principles are apparent in nature to all well-educated, reasonable men and so form the basis of human rights and good government. Recall from chapter 4 that Aristotle took a job in 343 BCE as tutor for the son of King Philip II of Macedon, a bright lad by the name of Alexander. He went on to conquer most of the Middle East and became known as Alexander the Great. Alexander had great admiration for the culture and learning of Athens; perhaps Aristotle had advised him to be a philosopher-king. But in governance, he seemed to prefer the Persian model of an absolute monarch, who appointed administrators to serve at his whim. His generals continued this pattern after his death. Athenian democracy would later be rediscovered and idealized by Enlightenment Europeans, but as a practical matter of governance, Greek democracy died with Alexander.

Rome began under the rule of kings, but for several hundred years it was governed as an imperfect republic. Republican Rome was in many ways an oligarchy, with the Roman senate controlled by wealthy men. Yet the Romans loved laws. They wrote a lot of them and created courts to rule on them. Rule by law was important, in that senators were bound by precedent and agreement and could not rule by whim. The laws favored the wealthy but in time gave increasing protection to the poor, or the **plebeians,** and even accorded certain rights to slaves and to women.

The Romans never perfected their republic; in particular, in times of war and crisis they often turned to dictators. Their most famous dictator, Julius Caesar, was made ruler for life. His life didn't last when it was rumored that he also wanted to be crowned king; he was stabbed in the senate in 44 BCE. His adopted son, Octavian, won in a rivalry with one of Caesar's favorite generals, Marc Antony, and ruled as Emperor Augustus. Although the senate continued with power firmly in the hands of the emperor, Rome went from a republic to a pure empire. The Roman emperors were supposed to handpick their successors (rather like Mexican presidents for much of the twentieth century). Sometimes this was hereditary, as when a son inherited the throne. Sometimes it went to a great general, and sometimes the army imposed its person in a classic military dictatorship. Some emperors aspired to be philosopher-kings (Marcus Aurelius), some rose through the ranks and were surprisingly adept (Hadrian), and some came to power through intrigue and ruled as madmen (Nero and Caligula). In time, the Roman Empire grew so large that the emperors tried dividing its rule in half, forming one eastern and one western empire. The western empire collapsed around the time of Attila, while the eastern half survived another thousand years as the Byzantine Empire, with eastern-style absolute rulers.

The legacy of Roman law continued to influence Europe, especially through the Roman Catholic Church, and it was exported around the world under European colonialism. The key problems of government—how to select capable rulers and how to balance power and competing factions—were never fully solved by the Romans. This turmoil accelerated their downfall, and the same unanswered questions continue to beset a world in turmoil.

Medieval European kings were feudal rulers whose rule depended on the loyalty of a hierarchy of nobles underneath them. From dukes to marquises, counts, earls, barons, and on to knights in various times and places, titles still held, though without much authority. This system could lead to ineffective government but provided a check on the power of kings. When English nobles forced King John to sign the **Magna Carta** in 1215, they were protecting their own rights and lands. Yet in time, that document came to stand for the rights of all Englishmen and is now held as one of the bases of British democracy. In contrast, in France the king continued to centralize power. Louis XIV was the "sun king" because every matter of state revolved around him personally. Popular discontent meant his successors were deposed in revolutions. In 1776 the American colonies became a republic, as did France in 1789, by throwing off the rule of a king. Both countries today have presidential systems, with the executive power held by an elected president. In Great Britain the king gradually ceded power to a parliament composed of both lords and elected representatives in a pattern of parliamentary democracy.

During this time, political theorists again debated the nature of government and human rights. British philosopher Thomas Hobbes (1588–1679) wrote his classic book *Leviathan* at the time of the English civil war, a struggle between the king and the parliament. Hobbes believed people needed a strong government, and this was best seen in a strong and mighty king, or a *leviathan*. (Since this refers to a sea monster, one wonders about his choice of imagery.) For Hobbes, government was not divinely imposed; there were neither divine kings nor kings who ruled by divine right, but a social contract entered into by people to protect themselves. In a famous statement, Hobbes contended that the natural state of humans without government was "war of all against all," in which life was "solitary, poor, nasty, brutish and short." Even a strong government that limited individual freedoms was better than this. Although Hobbes argued for a very old form of government, authoritarian monarchy, his language shifted to arguments about social contracts and protecting rights, issues that would be debated for the centuries that followed. Of course he also wrote at a time when his knowledge of actual human society before the time of European kings was less than the glimpse contained in this chapter.

John Locke (1632–1704), Hobbes's predecessor and fellow English political philosopher, like him saw government as a social contract between individuals. He wrote, however, not to champion a king but to denounce an abusive monarch. As such, his treatises on government were filled with warnings against the excesses of government. According to Locke, the only right to rule came from the consent of the governed. People formed governments to protect their God-given rights: life, liberty, and property. To do this, they sought to create a just system of laws. Kings who did not respect these laws and basic rights had no right to rule.

These arguments will sound familiar to many in the United States because they form the basis of the U.S. Declaration of Independence. In 1776 Thomas Jefferson adopted Locke's ideas to frame his accusations against King George III. Jefferson argued that people formed governments to protect the rights given to them by their creator: life, liberty, and the pursuit of happiness (a more lyrical way of denoting property and livelihood). When a government infringed on those, it was the right, even the duty, of the people to throw off that government.

Like Locke, French philosopher Jean Jacques Rousseau (1712–1778) wanted to limit government. Unlike Hobbes, Rousseau believed that people in their state of nature were basically noble and good. Society and power corrupted them. If power corrupts, it is best limited, and the greatest possible freedoms should be given to the people. Rousseau also influenced the American revolutionaries, whose success in turn inspired France's own revolution a few years later in 1789.

Debate continued over Rousseau's idea of decentralized power. Jefferson and his "democratic republicans" argued for a decentralized system in the new United States, with power retained by the states and localities. Federalists, such as Alexander Hamilton and James Madison, argued the need for more centralized control as a way to maintain order. Rousseau's ideas seemed to be more influential in the United States than in France, where even with the king gone, control was still highly centralized in the committees in Paris and soon in the hands of one revolutionary leader, Napoleon Bonaparte.

Authoritarianism versus Democracy

These debates continued into the twentieth century. In Russia a monarch, Czar (from the Russian form of *Caesar*) Nicholas II, was deposed and executed at the end of World War I. A republican government took power briefly, only to fall to Vladimir Lenin's Bolsheviks, a group of revolutionary Marxists. Karl Marx had believed that socialist reforms, and even eventually communism, might possibly come through democratic means, especially in places such as Great Britain and the United States, where democratic institutions were well established. Lenin disagreed. As he looked over the ashes of the World War I, he believed that the state of the world had deteriorated so badly that only a revolutionary vanguard, a dedicated few who were truly committed to Marxist ideals, could lead the people to communism. A revolution of the **proletariat** (working class) would be followed by a dictatorship of the proletariat. The government would remain forceful and centralized, but it would use its power to advance, rather than repress, the workers. The Soviet dictatorship was born.

On Lenin's death in 1924, Leon Trotsky discussed a return to earlier Marxist ideals, but Joseph Stalin, who ultimately triumphed, sought to strengthen the centralized dictatorship and his own rule, while supporting like-minded governments abroad. On Stalin's death, Nikita Khrushchev returned to the idea that maybe in small countries around the world, electoral processes could bring socialist reforms. Finally, Mikhail Gorbachev argued in the 1980s that Marxist principles and democratic ideals were not incompatible and sought semidemocratic reforms.

Whereas in the United States socialist or communist economics was typically associated with dictatorship and undemocratic government, in Europe a variety of democratic socialist parties sought to combine public ownership with democratic government. Some touted the ideals of the young Marx and of Trotsky; others sought to create a new hybrid economy with a democratic base.

In Germany a monarch, Kaiser (from the German form of *Caesar*) Wilhelm, was toppled at the end of the First World War, and his government was also replaced with a republic. As Germany continued to struggle with the aftermath of the war and a deep depression, however, the party that gradually drew more and more votes was the Nazi Party of Adolf Hitler, which would ultimately dismantle the electoral process for a return to dictatorship under a *führer*. The Nazi platform and National Socialism combined state involvement in the economy with a powerful, centralized, and militarized nationalistic dictatorship in a system known as **fascism.**

This system also prevailed in Mussolini's Italy and Franco's Spain. Germany, Italy, and Spain all had ultraconservative right-wing dictatorships, while the Soviet Union had a radical left-wing dictatorship. They were rivals, even before the Second World War. The Soviet Union fought a proxy war with Italy and Germany in Spain, with the Soviets supporting leftist republicans and Hitler and Mussolini backing Franco. But they also had similarities; they were essentially **totalitarian;** they engaged in extreme authoritarian rule that tries to control all aspects of national life.

Both forms of dictatorship continue to influence the world. Even after the Soviet Union began its reforms, countries such as Albania and North Korea continued Stalinist-style dictatorships. Latin American military governments in the 1950s (Guatemala), the 1960s to the 1970s (Brazil and Argentina), and the 1970s into the 1980s (Chile) often had many of the characteristics of fascist dictatorships. Left-wing dictatorships claimed to rule for the people and often jailed the middle and upper classes; right-wing dictatorships claimed to protect property and champion the needs of business and often jailed labor leaders and labor union members. Both, however, sought to maintain strict control of both the economy and the society.

Democracy continues to gain ground, as more governments are based on elections. Fareed Zakaria (2007) notes that this is not always "liberal democracy" with a strong respect for human rights and individual liberties. Some of the world's most brutal leaders, such as Hitler and Milošević, came to power in a democratic process (and some highly respected leaders, such as Pope John Paul II and the Fourteenth Dalai Lama of Tibet, did not). Elected leaders in East Asian countries—South Korea, Taiwan, and Singapore, in particular—have ruled with strict laws and limits on freedom of expression, although each country has seen liberal democratic reforms. Sometimes their leaders have contended that they are not undemocratic, only Confucian: seeking order and demanding loyalty but also feeling the responsibility of a "parent" to dutifully guide and protect the citizens.

Democratic governments have also been plagued by charges of corruption. Scandals and investigations of government corruption have echoed across Europe, the United States, and Mexico. Charges of corruption have often brought down elected governments. In 1999 one of a series of military coups in Pakistan replaced the elected government, which was charged with corrupt dealings with General Pervez Musharraf, who himself stepped down in 2008 to avoid impeachment proceedings. In Algeria and Turkey, military-backed governments have intervened in the electoral process to prevent the election of people from Islamic militant groups, who are charged with being undemocratic in character, even though they command a large enough following to win an election. What should be done when a group whose ideology indicates it may not retain democratic institutions is poised to win an election? The appropriate role of government, an issue that long ago absorbed Hobbes and Rousseau, has resurfaced: In an age of terrorism, how much government control is needed to maintain order?

British Prime Minister Winston Churchill is said to have remarked that democracy is the worst system of government in the world—except for all the others. Democracy is fraught with practical problems, to be sure. How do you create effective government without having autocratic government? Locke was a proponent of checks and balances between powers. This became one of the hallmarks of the U.S. Constitution, a balance among a lawmaking body (Congress), a law-executing executive body (the president), and a law-interpreting judiciary (headed by the Supreme Court). Ancient Rome had likewise tried to balance different spheres of power, especially the Senate and the consuls and later emperors. Locke favored a strong emphasis on the lawmaking bodies.

Interestingly, European countries that kept monarchs in power sought a strong balance in their parliaments, and now that monarchs are largely figureheads, actual governing power is largely in the legislative branch, the parliaments. The prime minister is first and foremost a representative of the party that holds a legislative majority. In contrast, countries that abandoned monarchy, such as the United States, created a strong presidency in its place.

Even though the U.S. Constitution devotes most of its space to Congress as the prime organ of government, U.S. presidents have used their position over time to gain greater power. For example, while the U.S. Congress has the power to declare war, the U.S. president is commander in chief of the armed forces. No war has been formally declared by Congress since World War II, yet the president has great discretion in the use of U.S. military force. The War Powers Act of 1973 was an attempt by Congress to reclaim some of this authority. The act requires presidents to notify Congress within 48 hours of military action and to seek congressional approval for any combat operation over 60 days. Yet presidents have claimed that extended peacekeeping, antiterrorism, and anti-insurgency actions are not covered by this act.

Parliamentary systems can lead to deadlocks among multiple competing groups or unchecked power when one group holds clear control of the legislature. Power, however, remains in the hands of a group or party. Presidential systems give more direct power to an individual. Most of Asia, including the major powers of Japan and India, use a parliamentary system. Much of Latin America uses a U.S.-style presidential system, and most of the African countries employ modified presidential systems. The danger in these is that the president personally holds great power, which may be used to create a dictatorship under an electoral guise.

A related problem is the issue of control by political parties. While parties are sometimes not even acknowledged in constitutions, such as the U.S. Constitution, they are major players in most governmental systems. A **one-party system** gives complete control to a single party, even if others are allowed. China continues to be dominated by the Chinese Communist Party, which controls the governing process. For 75 years, Mexico was dominated by a single party, which always selected the president. Even Japan's openly contested parliamentary system was dominated for years by a single party.

The United States, Great Britain, and Canada are examples of government systems (presidential in the U.S. and parliamentary in Great Britain and Canada) that have been dominated by two-parties, although the nature and even names of the parties have shifted. An active two-party system can prevent entrenched control by a single faction but may become entrenched itself and eliminate other voices. France and Italy have long had multiple parties competing for control. This can be highly democratic, giving voice to many ideas and groups, but the government can be weak and based on shifting coalitions and complex electoral alliances.

The Rise of Twenty-First Century Authoritarianism

Each year the British publication, *The Economist*, issues a world democracy report and an index based on free and fair elections, press freedom, and other measures of working democracy. In 2020 the top five democracies were all parliamentary systems in countries with modest populations: Norway, Iceland, Sweden, New Zealand, and Canada. The bottom five were corrupt and embattled presidential systems, or outright dictatorships: Chad, Syria, Central African Republic (CAR), Democratic Republic of the Congo (DRC), and dead last, North Korea. However, parliamentary India, "the world's largest" democracy, has slipped from 27 to 52 since Prime Minister Modi, a Hindu nationalist with authoritarian tendencies, came to power in 2014. *The Economist* places India among 52 "flawed Democracies" (*Economist* 2020). Freedom House moved India from "free" to "partly free" in their 2021 report, noting intimidation of journalists, suppression of human rights organizations, and attacks on Muslims (Thakur 2021). In the former Soviet sphere the heavy-handed "presidential" autocrats of Belarus and Turkmenistan have ruled since independence. Now, Eastern European counties, like Poland under President Andrzej Duda and Hungary under Prime Minister Viktor Orbán, in office since 2010, appear increasingly authoritarian.

Few these days speak of "the triumph of democracy." India is not alone, the largest world powers have moved toward one-man authoritarian rule under a banner of nationalism. Vladimir Putin claims to be restoring Russia's rights and "respect" among world powers, even as political opponents are poisoned and the constitution changed to keep Putin in power. China's Xi Jinping holds more absolute and indefinite power than his recent predecessors, with re-education camps for religious and ethnic minorities, limits on democracy in Hong Kong, threats to Taiwan, and a campaign to assert China's global economic and military reach. China has asserted territorial claims in the South China Sea by creating new artificial islands that sprout airstrips and are populated by a vast navy. China's Belt and Road Initiative, an investment in development and infrastructure abroad, expands China's influence across Asia and into Africa, recalling the lore of the ancient Silk Road. When U.S. President Donald Trump talked about jailing opponents, called the U.S. press "the enemy of the people," and refused to accept election results, many wondered if even the world's longest established modern democracy might be taking an authoritarian turn under the nationalism of "America First."

Fear of crime led to the election of authoritarian leaders in Brazil and the Philippines. Seeking regional preeminence, leaders in Turkey and Saudi Arabia draw on Islamic nationalism and ancient glories to assert the power of their regimes. In Venezuela, the government claims it is anti-imperialist, and Bolivarian, evoking the name of the revered liberator of South America, Venezuelan born Simón Bolívar. Yet the patterns of changing the constitution, seeking to control the congress and the courts, and restricting the free press are familiar and predictable, regardless of proclaimed ideology.

"Dirty Wars": When Democracy Degenerates

With the exception of a handful of Islamic monarchies and emirates, all the countries in the world have constitutions based on democratic principles. Yet democracy in practice is fragile. Often democratic documents comprise a thin veneer covering a government run by a "president for life."

Africa, in particular, has been burdened with presidents who never quit. Mobutu Sese Seko ruled the country he called Zaire (Congo) for 35 years with complete control of the government and the economy. Daniel Moi ruled Kenya for 24 years from 1978 to 2002; Muammar Gadaffi ruled Libya for 42 years from 1969 to 2011; Robert Mugabe ruled Zimbabwe for 37 years from 1980 to 2017; and Hosni Mubarak ruled Egypt for 30 years from 1981 to 2011. Typically, these rulers win an election in which the opposition has little opportunity to organize or challenge the system. Saddam Hussein won reelection in Iraq, first winning 97 percent of the vote and then topping that by winning 100 percent in the next "election." While few believe these results, the winner is allowed to claim the title of "president" in international circles.

Often long-standing rulers claim only they can keep their countries together. As the ruler consolidates both economic and political power, this becomes a self-fulfilling prophecy. Somalia fell into chaos after the departure of its longtime ruler, Said Barre, whereas Indonesia struggled through political and economic turmoil to restore democratic institutions after 35 years of Suharto.

The other way to power in many countries across South Asia, Africa, and especially Latin America has been through military takeover—what the French have termed the **coup d'état,** or seizing of the state. During the cold war, seizing power was often done under an ideological guise: either to advance or to prevent communism. In 1954 the CIA assisted in deposing a leftist-elected government in Guatemala, which led to a series of military rulers that continued into the 1980s. In the 1960s and 1970s Brazilian generals dominated the political process in that country with the brutal suppression of human and political rights.

In 1976 the Argentine military seized power from chaotic political factions. It began what became known as the **dirty war,** in which thousands of political opponents, labor leaders, and others considered dangerous were detained, often tortured, and killed. To "be disappeared" became a chilling reality for many Argentineans, and bodies are still being found in the ocean and in mass graves. A quiet but persistent protest movement grew, with groups such as the Mothers of the Plaza de Mayo standing in silent protest with large pictures of the "disappeared."

In 1970 Chile elected a socialist president, Salvador Allende. After three years of controversial policies, the military, under General Augusto Pinochet, seized power and ruled for the next 15 years in a regime that likewise targeted labor and opposition leaders. Silent protests took such creative forms as "dancing with the dead," in which wives, perhaps widows, of the "disappeared" danced in the main square with invisible (missing) partners. Pinochet finally agreed to a referendum on his rule in 1988, claiming to be the only one who could retain order in the economy, the military, and the bureaucracy. He lost overwhelmingly, and the democratic process was restored.

Sometimes dictators are elected in an open process. Hitler and the Nazis won a series of elections in the 1930s, using nationalistic rhetoric to draw support and increasingly blatant acts of terror to disrupt the opposition. Slobodan Milošević came to power in a similar fashion in Serbia following the breakup of the Yugoslav republics.

One of the most grotesque distortions of the electoral process occurred in the small West African nation of Liberia. The regime of the country's longtime dictator Samuel Doe was coming to a close, and guerilla forces sprang up to fill the power vacuum. A tough street kid named Charles Taylor, who had fled to the United States, participated in various petty crimes, and then slipped out of a Massachusetts jail on a rope of sheets, returned to Liberia to lead one such group. Taylor proved as resourceful and ruthless as any of the local warlords and guerilla leaders. He assembled an irregular force, consisting largely of boys in or near their teens, who were recruited or kidnapped into his army. Armed with smuggled AK-47s and rocket-propelled grenade (RPG) launchers, as well as machetes, his "army" moved throughout the country, killing opponents and sometimes whole villages and pursuing a policy of terror that included public executions and tortures, organized rapes, and the mutilation of suspected opponents and their family members. Taylor's army had no uniforms, unless Nike sneakers count, and few supplies, but a mixture of fear, guilt, anger, and drugs drove them on.

As the fighting persisted, international intervention took the form of a West African peacekeeping force in 1995 and a mandate to hold an election in 1997. Charles Taylor ran in the election. His campaign slogan was direct, "I killed your pa, and I killed your ma." The implication was that if he was not elected, he would go on killing. Taylor won. Once in office, he proceeded to organize and support insurrections in neighboring countries: Guinea, Sierra Leone, and the Ivory Coast. The bloody involvement in Sierra Leone, in which cutting off the limbs of children was a favorite terror tactic, finally resulted in Taylor's indictment on war crimes charges. As new rebel groups fought him for the capital of Liberia, West African countries again sent in peacekeepers in 2003, and in 2005 Liberians voted in free and competitive elections to select the first female elected head of state on the African continent, Ellen Johnson Sirleaf.

The Price of Democracy

Is democracy always the best answer to a nation's troubles? In practice, it certainly has been imperfect and even dangerous. Zakaria (2007) claims that if the task of the twentieth century was, in the words of U.S. President Woodrow Wilson, "to make the world safe for democracy," then the task for the twenty-first century is to make democracy safe for the world.

During the turmoil of post–World War II independence, some contended that poor countries needed a strong hand, a development-oriented dictator, and could not yet afford the luxury of democracy. Yet the world's experience has been that dictators often plunder and distort economies and rarely provide a sure route to progress. Argentine political scientist Guillermo O'Donnell (1979) sees democracy as a key element in social development yet also notes that institutions must be built to support the process, and that takes time. A free and independent press that strives for objectivity is one of those institutions that have been fragile everywhere in the world.

What is the price of democracy? In 1959 U.S. social scientist Seymour Martin Lipset noted that as national wealth increased, so did the likelihood of democracy. Political scientists Adam Przeworski and Fernando Limongi (1997, as cited in Zakaria 2007) put an exact figure on it: $9,000. With a per capita income of less than $9,000, a majority of democratic regimes collapse. With an income over this amount, none have.

Yet if democracy is also a major determinate of social progress, as well as its outcome, even poor nations must struggle to gradually build democratic institutions. Countries as diverse as India and Costa Rica have shown that it can be done. With a long history of statehood that included a number of remarkably enlightened leaders, followed by a period of British colonialism that, while very imperfect, included many of the trappings of formal democracy, India has remained democratic since its independence in 1947, despite being one of the world's poorest major countries for much of that time and having had several major leaders assassinated.

Likewise, Costa Rica, a country of European immigrants who found few native peoples to enslave and imported few slaves, also began early to lay the groundwork for democratic institutions. While other Central American countries were embroiled in revolutions, Costa Rica abolished its army. This was an important signal of its internal as well as its external intentions, for Latin American armies are much more likely to see action against their own people than against foreign armies. While Costa Rica is not much wealthier than its neighbors, it, like India, has maintained very high levels of health care and education and enjoys a life expectancy on par with those of the world's wealthy nations. Democracy does not guarantee economic progress, but it does afford the people a say in how limited resources will be used.

After the Repression

Another question for precarious young democracies is what to do after the repression. Should the emphasis be on bringing the guilty to justice, compensating the victims, or bringing about reconciliation between embittered enemies?

Following World War II, the trials in Nuremberg convicted many Nazi leaders of war crimes. Following this model, after losing power in Yugoslavia, Slobodan Milošević was tried for war crimes by the World Court in The Hague, Netherlands. In both cases the accused claimed they were being made scapegoats by the victors. After losing his grip on power in Chile, Augusto Pinochet remained a senator, and military leaders were shielded from prosecution as a way of avoiding new trouble. The elderly Pinochet was finally charged with crimes in Spain, since some of his victims had been Spanish nationals.

Following the collapse of apartheid in South Africa, the government created a Truth and Reconciliation Commission. After a period of repression, secrecy, and misinformation, both truth and reconciliation can be elusive. But South Africa was determined to have neither "don't ask, don't tell" silence after repression nor "Nuremburg justice" handed out by the victors. In *No Future Without Forgiveness*, Desmond Tutu (2000) describes the work of the commission, hearing stories not only of torture and repression but also of small acts of kindness, and witnessing people stepping forward to both seek and offer forgiveness. He concludes:

> At the end of their conflicts, the warring groups in Northern Ireland, the Balkans, the Middle East, Sri Lanka, Burma, Afghanistan, Angola, the Sudan, the two Congos, and elsewhere are going to have to sit down together to determine just how they will be able to live together amicably, how they might have a shared future devoid of strife, given the bloody past that they have recently lived through. They see more than just a glimmer of hope in what we attempted in South Africa. (p. 282)

Robbin Island, where Nelson Mandela spent his prison years, has become a popular destination, though many South Africans make the short trip out to the island as more of a pilgrimage than a tour. We stand in Mandela's cell and visit the quarry where he labored. We also hear the tales of the grim existence on this island for other past prisoners. One of them is now our tour guide. This has become part of the South African experiment: to expose, to forgive (former wardens as well as prisoners are invited to become guides), to vow never again, and to go forward.

The emphasis is still on truth and reconciliation. It is an impressive effort. At the Irish mission church, the guide notes he was recently pleased to host Gerry Adams, who was visiting to learn the lessons of South African reconciliation that might be applied to Northern Ireland. We are continually amazed here by the human capacity to forgive. There are exceptions. Some black South Africans remain deeply angry, but more common are those who are deeply hurt, in many ways, yet are convinced that reconciliation provides the only hope for even deeper healing.

The Right to Be Fully Human

John Locke and Thomas Jefferson began their statements on government with a proclamation of human rights. The language of **human rights** has continued to gain currency in the world, but it is not without controversy.

Nations have long recognized, at least in theory, the idea of **civil rights,** or the rights of citizens. When African Americans sought the right to vote without hindrance and to attend integrated schools and use public facilities, they used the language of civil rights. Their rights of citizenship, guaranteed by the U.S. Constitution and intentionally extended to them by the post–Civil War amendments to that constitution, were being violated. Many around the world still seek full protection of their civil rights, but are there also basic human rights, which need to be respected by all governments, regardless of national laws and customs?

Jimmy Carter was the first U.S. president to specifically make protecting international human rights a major foreign policy goal. The Reagan administration retreated from this stance initially to return to a cold war–based foreign policy, but the demands of addressing humanitarian needs and protecting human rights has continued. During the Clinton administration, NATO, under

U.S. leadership, intervened in the fracturing Yugoslavia, claiming to protect the human rights of Bosnians and of Muslims in Kosovo. A remarkable shift occurred in 1994, when U.S. forces were poised to intervene in Haiti to remove a military dictatorship and restore to power to an elected socialist president, Jean-Bertrand Aristide. The United States would intervene again 10 years later in 2004—to help remove him from power and the country.

As the political globalization of the world proceeds, more questions about human rights are being decided at the international level. In 1948 the United Nations drafted its Universal Declaration of Human Rights, which was followed by statements on the rights of children, women, refugees, and other groups (see figure 7.1).

This trend toward the globalization of human rights has not gone unopposed. One major power that has resisted this movement has been China. While China has opened its economy tremendously in recent years, it has proceeded slowly toward making democratic reforms. Students demanding greater democratic freedoms were brutally repressed in Tiananmen Square in 1989. China has adamantly contended that pressure based on international human rights is politically motivated, violates its sovereignty, and does not take into account

---

Article 1. All human beings are born free and equal in dignity and rights. They are endowed with reason and conscience and should act towards one another in a spirit of brotherhood.

Article 2. Everyone is entitled to all the rights and freedoms set forth in this Declaration, without distinction of any kind, such as race, color, sex, language, religion, political or other opinion, national or social origin, property, birth or other status. Furthermore, no distinction shall be made on the basis of the political, jurisdictional or international status of the country or territory to which a person belongs, whether it be independent, trust, non-self-governing or under any other limitation of sovereignty.

Article 3. Everyone has the right to life, liberty and security of person.

Article 4. No one shall be held in slavery or servitude; slavery and the slave trade shall be prohibited in all their forms.

Article 5. No one shall be subjected to torture or to cruel, inhuman or degrading treatment or punishment.

Article 6. Everyone has the right to recognition everywhere as a person before the law.

Article 7. All are equal before the law and are entitled without any discrimination to equal protection of the law. All are entitled to equal protection against any discrimination in violation of this Declaration and against any incitement to such discrimination.

Figure 7.1 UN Universal Declaration of Human Rights, First Seven Articles. (Source: United Nations.)

When democracy seems to fail, massive street protests have mobilized thousands—even amidst COVID-19. Crackdowns on democracy have led to huge and persistent street protest in Hong Kong in spite of harsh police actions [top]. The death of George Floyd in Minneapolis, under the knee of an arresting police officer, led to some of the largest collective action ever seen—protests in many U.S. cities, large and small, and parallel actions in cities around the world as this in London [bottom].

> - Freedom from discrimination—by gender, race, ethnicity, national origin or religion.
> - Freedom from want—to enjoy a decent standard of living.
> - Freedom to develop and realize one's human potential.
> - Freedom from fear—of threats to personal security, from torture, arbitrary arrest and other violent acts.
> - Freedom from injustice and violations of the rule of law.
> - Freedom of thought and speech and to participate in decision-making and form associations.
> - Freedom for decent work—without exploitation.

Figure 7.2 *The Seven Freedoms. (Source: United Nations.)*

its unique culture and history. China contends that its policies in Tibet, its limitations on democracy in Hong Kong and harsh actions against protestors, its "re-education camps" and forced labor for Turkic speaking Muslim Uighurs in western Xinjiang Province, and even its actions toward Taiwan are all "internal matters" that should not be placed on international scrutiny.

The other major power resisting the move to a more encompassing international law on human rights has been the United States. Only the United States and Iraq refused to sign the UN Declaration on the Rights of the Child. The United States has also refused to allow the world court jurisdiction over its citizens. Again, the argument has been national sovereignty and the concern that politically motivated actions would be taken against the United States.

Following the September 11, 2001, terrorist attacks and the war in Afghanistan, the United States has been keeping prisoners at Guantanamo Naval Base, a part of the island of Cuba to which the United states holds a long-term lease (over Cuban objections). Unlike typical prisoners, many of the detained do not know all the charges against them, most have no legal counsel, and the few lawyers involved do not know the charges against the detained. In fact, these people are not considered prisoners of war and thus are not subject to rules regulating such prisoners. The U.S. government claims they are "enemy combatants," a unique status that provides neither the usual protections of civil detainees nor those accorded to prisoners of war.

To try to extract information from the prisoners in their wire "cages" at Guantanamo, they were interrogated. The Bush administration said that it did not allow torture but that prisoners might be placed in "stressful" conditions.

This included temperature manipulation, sleep deprivation, and sexual ridicule. Do such actions constitute torture? In the 2006 case of *Hamdan v. Rumsfeld* the Supreme Court concluded that military commissions set up by the Bush administration to try detainees at Guantanamo Bay lack "the power to proceed because its structures and procedures violate both the Uniform Code of Military Justice and the four Geneva Conventions signed in 1949." As a presidential candidate, Barack Obama (as well as his opponent, John McCain), spoke out against ill treatment of prisoners, and Obama vowed to close the Guantanamo prison camp. This has proven difficult, particularly in finding places to receive the inmates. Both Canada and Great Britain have used similar patterns of indefinite detention in other locations, and both have also been challenged in the courts as violating basic human rights.

The challenge before the world is that if international institutions and declarations are to be meaningful, there can be no exemptions for powerful nations. Human rights must apply to all of humanity, regardless of national interest and perhaps despite the claims of long-defended national sovereignty (see figure 7.2). German writer Johann Goethe, a contemporary of Jefferson, put it succinctly: "Above the nations stands humanity."

Key Ideas

- For millennia people lived in small bands and tribes that often allowed a great deal of participation in governance by many or all members. With large agricultural empires, power becomes concentrated in a ruling elite, and often a single hereditary monarch.

- Democracy has been tried since ancient times but has often seemed unwieldy and fractious compared to its alternatives. In recent decades, the number of democratically governed countries has grown dramatically, but true functioning multiparty electoral democracy is still elusive in many parts of Africa and Asia. Even in countries with an established democratic government, citizen participation in public affairs is often low.

- Human rights abuses and repression of democratic processes are common in elected regimes who refuse to leave power, as well as in military regimes who have seized power.

- Following World War II, the United Nations drafted a comprehensive Declaration of Human Rights and has followed this with statements on the rights of refugees, children, women, and others. How much the international community should intervene in independent countries over questions of human rights remains controversial.

For Review and Discussion

1. Do you consider yourself patriotic? Do you consider yourself nationalistic? What is implied by these terms? Are they hopeful, or dangerous, or both?
2. What are the advantages of European-style parliamentary democracies, and of U.S.-style presidential democracies? Which model would seem preferable for new nations?
3. What are the strengths of one-party, two-party, and multiparty systems of government?
4. Should countries with weak human rights records be placed under economic embargoes, or some type of political or economic sanction? Can the world community both respect national sovereignty and press countries for greater human rights? How is this best done, and what are the roles of governments, of the UN, and of nongovernmental human rights organizations?

Making Connections

UN Office of the High Commissioner for Human Rights

➤ Go to www.ohchr.org for information on many aspects of international human rights, including for women, children, and indigenous peoples. This site also offers information on international agreements and human rights training and education. Update on human rights issues can be found at https://www.un.org/press/en/human-rights. On what issues of human rights is the United Nations currently focusing its attention?

UN Sustainable Development Goals

➤ Goal 16 is Promote just, peaceful and inclusive societies. See the overview at https://www.un.org/sustainabledevelopment/peace-justice/

UN Declaration of Human Rights

➤ Go to https://www.un.org/en/universal-declaration-human-rights/index.html to view the UN's Universal Declaration of Human Rights. Which of these declarations of rights are most at risk in the world today?

Making a Difference

Amnesty International

➤ This international human rights organization was introduced in chapter 5. Amnesty campaigns around the world seek to end torture and human rights abuses while championing the causes of political prisoners and other so-called prisoners of conscience. Go to the group's website (www.amnesty.org) to find out about their current causes, letter-writing campaigns, and other activities. There may also be a chapter on your campus or in your community. What are their current concerns with regard to democracy and human rights?

Human Rights Watch

➤ At www.hrw.org, you will find large amounts of information on human rights, including prisons, women's rights, rights and HIV, refugees' rights, children's rights, and so forth, as well as region-by-region coverage of key human rights crises. See the information in the "Topics" section that addresses the trafficking of women and children, abuses of refugees and detainees, and other issues. How are they trying to address these problems?

8

Ethnicity and Religion

Deep Roots and Unholy Hate

Global Encounters

Brazil

Brazil is divided by race. Yet the country has been proud of racial mixing and integration: Interracial marriage is not uncommon and cities are much less racially segregated than in the United States. Racial categories are more subtle and complex. Brazilians don't think in terms of black and white, even with regard to race. In Brazil one can be coffee colored, or maybe coffee with a bit of cream, or coffee with lots of milk. A North American can change race simply by getting on an airplane going from New York to Rio. But race is also very much institutionalized into the divides of Brazil, and always intertwined with class. In colonial days, a well-off person of mixed parentage was pardo, "blended," whereas a person whose parents were poor white and poor black was mulatto, "a mule." Even today a Brazilian might change racial identity by gaining education and income.

While race relations tend to be cordial, the association between color and class remains. Our guest lecturer termed it "cordial racism." In Salvador a full 80 percent, probably more, of the population has a large amount of African heritage, yet color still divides. The Barra shopping mall has three levels. The bottom is discount stores, and most of the shoppers are working-class people of color. One floor up, the quality of the store merchandise improves, and both the clerks and the shoppers seem to have more "milk" in their coffee-colored complexions. The third floor has elegant boutiques and is connected to a special floor of the parking garage so that its shoppers can step directly into the courtyards of their favorite stores. Suddenly, it seems, the clerks have all become blondes and light brunettes, matching the prevailing tone of the clientele. There are a few clerks who North Americans might consider black, but these are all young, fine-looking individuals, stylish in the latest clothes and jewelry, and very hip. "Oh yes," Brazilian friends tell me, "if you are black you must be very cool—then you are accepted, at least casually." I am left wondering whether race relations in Brazil are not really so different from those in the United States.

Brazil is divided by religion. This country was once almost all Roman Catholic. But that was only because African spirituality was suppressed by convention and by law. Now Condomblé (cone-dome-BLAY) is legal and its temples and styles of dance and music are everywhere in Salvador. This was the religion of the African slaves, rooted in West African Voudon, and a bit like Haitian Voodoo. The orixá (or-eesh-a) are West African deities or powers who were long honored under saints' names to keep out of trouble with Catholic authorities in a manner similar to Amerindian deities elsewhere in Latin America. Now they have their names back and many devotees, most of whom also consider themselves Catholic. Services are open to all and advertised rather than kept secret; they are a potential tourist draw, and several of our students attend.

At the same time, evangelical and Pentecostal Protestantism is on the rise. On any given Sunday, there may be more Protestants at services in Brazil than Catholics. The Protestants are still far fewer, maybe 20 percent of the population, but while Brazilian Catholics may rarely attend Mass except on special *occasions, the Protestants know how to "do church," often several times a week. Some of the Protestant churches are small storefront Baptist churches with schools and soup kitchens for the urban poor. Some are exuberantly Pentecostal, with exorcisms, healing chants, and swooning worshipers in a fervent worship style that looks more like Condomblé than a Catholic Mass.*

I am most intrigued, however, by the largest church in the city, seating far more than the Catholic cathedral. It is the Universal Church of Jesus Christ, the Brazilian form of the modern megachurch. Its founder is a very wealthy man who owns businesses throughout the city and sells franchises to would-be pastors who want to use the name and open their own Universal Church. Universal Church leaders also have a vision for Brazil: All the poor countries of the world are either Roman Catholic or non-Christian, they claim; to be a modern, prosperous country, Brazil needs to be an evangelical country. The Roman Catholic response is a modern "counterreformation" led by a singing and dancing priest who has his own television show. His praise songs have pop tunes and upbeat lyrics and his events look more like a variety show than a traditional Mass. Like many things in Brazil, religion can be a political statement, but it seems to thrive best as a media spectacle.

South Africa

One can learn a lot from cab drivers. They are often wonderful guides to both the seen and unseen sides of a city. Sometimes they also provide a window into attitudes that are only visible in the relative privacy of one's own cab. Students ride with a cab driver who gives them his view of the safe and unsafe parts of the city. They are warned away from the black neighborhoods, since for all the changes, he claims, blacks are still dangerous, unruly, and immature. In quieter tones he raises the old fears of black-on-white rape, but mostly he dismisses the blacks as incorrigible children. The students look at the dark curly hair of his head and the deep mahogany brown of his driving arm. Does this "colored" man realize that if he decided to drive a cab in New York or Chicago he would immediately be considered black?

Sometimes attitudes are more subtle. Our own driver for an outing likes to contrast "Western" ways and attitudes that are forward looking and energetic with "native" ways that are backward and smack of tribalism. It takes a while before it becomes clear that there is a skin color associated with these "attitudes." At other times, nothing is subtle. One older white man tells a group of students that he is sure that AIDS is God's answer to the "overbreeding" in the townships. They can only respond with stunned silence.

Social relations in South Africa are complex and continue to change. We visit Desmond Tutu's church, St. George's Cathedral, from whose pulpit he fought apartheid with his own mixture of anger, humor, and spiritual conviction. Amid the liturgy of this beautiful old church, I am struck by the fact that sitting here in South Africa, I am in one of the most multiracial congregations I have ever visited. Tutu would have his parishioners clasp hands and raise them in the air—"You are the rainbow people of God," he would remind them. I like the metaphor but as we clasp hands to pass the peace, I am reminded that there is really no rainbow of clear differences. There are just finely graded transitions in the shades of brown—more alike than different—subtleties that could be easily overlooked, but have at times divided continents.

I realize that we have barely ventured beyond the tip of this vast continent—the tip of the iceberg, we would say, or as Africans put it, the ears of the hippo. You can't know the massiveness of the hippo from its exposed ears, but I suspect you can get a hint of its disposition. In the evening light, this really may be the fairest cape in the world. It also remains a cape of storms, some of which are poised to blow across the continent.

Ethnicity: Ties that Bind and Divide

Theorists such as Karl Marx and Max Weber thought that ethnicity might play a reduced role in the commercial capitalist world of the future, in which trade, not blood, would be the primary tie. In some aspects they were right, but the twentieth century also witnessed a resurgence of ethnic identity and pride.

Ethnicity is based on a sense of common heritage, common culture, and what U.S. social theorist Donald Horowitz (2001, p. 3) calls "the language of a family tie." But ethnicity is also more than this. It not only tells who is "in," or one of *us*, but also who is "out," or one of *them*. Norwegian sociologist Frederick Barth (1998 [1969]) focused attention on ethnicity as a boundary, a divider between us and them, based on some presumed common ancestry. The common bond may be based in language, cultural practices, and stories or legends of heroic ancestors who did great deeds, were blessed by the gods, sprang from the soil, and so forth. The historical basis of the accounts does not matter as much as the boundary, the sense that others of this group are "our people."

The prehistoric and ancient worlds were mosaics of different ethnic groups. We see glimpses of this prehistoric diversity in places such as Irian Jaya and Papua New Guinea, north of Australia, where there are hundreds of different groups, all with their own languages, variations of rituals and religious practices, and tales of their origins. In many places, this persisted well into the ancient world. The complexity of Indian society that often awes visitors is rooted in its history as a subcontinent that has had hundreds of languages, hundreds of variants in religious practice, and both subtle and glaring differences in dress, food, and daily life. As late as the arrival of Europeans around 1500, the land that would become the United States had at least 500 different ethnic groups, with many more in what would become known as Latin America.

The process of nation building, described in chapter 7, has gradually reduced this ethnic diversity. Languages are disappearing at the rate of dozens per year, as elder members die off and younger members of tribal and ethnic groups only know the national language or a regional dialect. Yet there has also been a resurgence of ethnic pride and interest in ethnic identity. In the United States, the Cherokee, Mohawk, Chippewa, and Salish struggle to keep their native languages from dying. In Great Britain, groups likewise struggle to keep the Celtic languages (Welsh, Irish, and Scottish) alive amid the universal use of English. Catalans in eastern Spain, Provençal in southern France, and many other languages are being kept alive, not because they are needed for communication, but because they carry a group's sense of ethnic identity and heritage, things they are loathe to lose.

About the same time that ethnic diversity was being submerged into the broader ideal of nationhood—essentially, the high tide of European colonialism—another potentially dangerous concept was created: the idea of race. **Race** originally referred to nothing more than a collection of tribes or ethnic groups, as in the *German races*. Gradually, from the 1600s through the 1800s, the term took on a new meaning: a group of people with common physical and sometimes psychological characteristics, due to their common origins. Biologists occasionally refer to races of birds or bears, populations of animals that while they are still part of a single species, have come to have easily distinguishable physical characteristics. Most social scientists as well as medical scientists now agree that dividing humans into separate "races" just can't be done with any sense of precision, given the full range of human diversity. Yet people have tried for centuries, often with strong political and economic motivations.

The Romans would never have thought of themselves as *Europeans* and their southern neighbors as *Africans*. *African*, in fact, referred only to a single province in about what is now Tunisia. They were all *Mediterranean* peoples. They were quite aware of their *ethnic* differences and held many ethnic stereotypes about Greeks, Jews, Egyptians, Gauls, and so forth. They were often certain that they themselves, as Romans, were superior; that is, they were **ethnocentric,** placing their own ethnicity and its ways at the center of the world and judging all others accordingly. Ethnocentrism is not a uniquely European concept, however; it appears everywhere. The Chinese believed they were the Middle Kingdom, and all around them were inferior habitations of barbarians.

One aspect of the ethnic resurgence that we have recently seen is groups reclaiming their original names. They want to be known not by the names given them by outsiders (Sioux, Winnebago, Auca) but rather what they called themselves in their own language (Lakota, Ho-Chunk, and Hauorani, respectively). There's another reason for this shift. The names given to groups by outsiders often translate to something like "savages," "brutes," or "dog-eaters." The names they have for themselves typically translate as "the people," "the real people," or "the first ones." Every group seems to favor itself and be suspicious of others; people are ethnocentric. The ancient Romans were ethnocentric but not racist; in fact, they did not have a concept of racism.

After years of contact and the slave trade, the many diverse peoples of Africa became "black" and were envisioned as a single race. This was remarkable, given that Africa was a huge continent with the world's tallest (Tutsi) and shortest (Mbuti) people and that their skin color ranged from light brown to deep ebony. At the same time, the tremendous diversity of Europe—from pale blond and red-haired Scandinavians to black-haired and olive-skinned Sicilians—all became "white," another race.

In the United States this was a convenient shorthand. Most Europeans in the American colonies had come from Northern Europe and were quite light-skinned, while most Africans had come from the Bantu peoples of West

Africa and were quite dark-skinned. Seeing the world in black and white came to make sense. Essentially, however, it was a categorization of privilege, not color. The black race could be enslaved for perpetuity, while the white race could only be held as indentured servants for seven years (Takaki 2008). In time, notions of black and white would divide schools and communities.

New groups were not always welcomed into the white race: Jews and Italians, among others, brought darker complexions and new religious and cultural diversity. In time they "became white"; they didn't grow pale but were gradually accepted into the world of the more privileged (Brodkin 1998). A more elite designation, **White Anglo-Saxon Protestant,** or **WASP,** still kept them out of the most selective groups. Color was a convenient but elusive marker. Some light-complected blacks could "pass" for white, while some Southern European and multiethnic whites were suspected of "being black."

In the apartheid system of South Africa, roughly from 1948 to 1990, racial classifications took on extreme importance as categories of privilege: white, Asian, colored (mix race), and black. Yet even the apartheid-era South African authorities had difficulties, and every year the courts declared some blacks to be colored, some coloreds to be Asian, and so forth. Human ancestry is always complex and often ambiguous. Most of us just take our grandmother's word on who our real ancestors are! Yet around the world, 500 years of European dominance—coupled with earlier events, such as the invasions of Africa by lighter-skinned Arabs and the invasions of India by light-skinned Aryans—means that light is often favored over dark.

Light remains the color of privilege. In India today, 70 years after Gandhi declared all colors and creeds equal "children of God," mothers still purchase creams to lighten their daughters' skin color. Brazil has claimed to be free of the racial segregation and turmoil of the United States. In many ways it is, yet a clear distinction remains. Brazilians don't speak of black and white; they have dozens of color terms, so that a black woman from the United States may find that in Brazil she is no longer black but "coffee without milk." Even the quickest observation, however, shows that the wealthy and privileged of Brazil are overwhelmingly light complected—if not white, at least "coffee with lots of milk"—while the poorest groups have darker skin colors and African or Amerindian features.

One's color designation can even change along with social status: Having a college degree can lighten someone a few shades, at least in how he or she is described. As noted in chapter 3, Brazilians love cosmetics: lipstick, hair color, and especially skin cream. The most popular skin cream doesn't block the sun or repel mosquitoes; rather it burns off the outermost layer of skin to lighten its color. Brazilian skin color comes in many rich hues, but dark-complected women know from the ever-present Brazilian television and magazines that light is the color of beauty and wealth, and they don't want to be left out.

Faith and Fervor: Religious Diversity

Local Religions

The world of prehistoric humanity must have been one of incredible religious diversity. Just as each ethnic group had its own language or dialect—probably related to that of its neighbors but still distinct—so, too, each group would have had its own variant of religious practice, which is still evident today among many tribal groups. This diversity of religious practice, as it survives today, is often simply labeled **tribal religions,** although not solely the domain of true tribes—these reflect the spirituality of regions and peoples before the dominance of the world's global religions.

Anthropologists sometimes group many of these religions as **shamanism** for the informal spiritual specialists, the *shamans*, who exercise spiritual powers. These are often men, sometimes women, and sometimes a "third gender," such as the *berdache*, men who rejected the traditional male roles, in American Indian societies. These tribal religions are also often labeled **animist,** for a belief in spirits and spiritual forces that animate the natural and human world. Among hunter-gatherers whose lives are closely tied to nature, these spirits are typically nature spirits. Among more settled tribal peoples, such as horticulturalists, the important spirits are often spirits of their ancestors, such as the cloud-dwelling *kachinas* of the Hopi.

Often, in both shamanism and animism, there is a strong sense of the natural world. Land is holy, either because it is the place of nature spirits or because it is the dwelling place of the ancestral spirits. This reverence is seen in American Indian and African tribal religions and seems to have been part of European and Asian religions as well. The ancient Shinto religion of Japan retains some of this reverence for nature and the ancestors. Such religious practice often involves an altered state of consciousness, perhaps with the help of mind-altering herbs (mushrooms and so forth) or the mind-altering effects of extreme physical exertion (such as marathon dancing, fasting, body piercing, or enduring the heat of a sweat lodge).

Tribal religions are in slow retreat around the world, as they have been for the last 2,500 years. Nonetheless, tribal practitioners remain in isolated areas. Tribal religion colors the practice of many major religions, such as Latin American Catholicism, and shamanistic practice has again come into vogue. Sometimes this is part of an ethnic resurgence, as people try to reclaim their heritage by reviving ethnic religious practices as well as language.

Tribal religion is also doing well in some very cosmopolitan places, where it influences New Age religious practice and people seeking new forms of spirituality. The books of Carlos Castaneda reportedly reveal secrets of a South American shaman. There is also the more anthropological work of Bradford

Keeney (1994, 2004), a psychologist who travels the world studying tribal religious rituals and healing. He can also pack a stadium in Miami with people swaying and rocking to shamanistic rhythms.

Animistic religions often, though not always, also espouse the concept of a supreme spirit or creator. Sometimes the creator-spirit is remote and can only be accessed through lesser spirits, as was common in West African religion (often known to Westerners only through popularized versions of "voodoo"). Herding peoples in Africa, the Middle East, and Central Asia all seemed to have had a stronger sense of the closeness of one Great Spirit, who was their own shepherd.

Around 600 to 500 BCE, the world's religious landscape began to change markedly. Scholars and philosophers were asking deep questions about the one behind the many, and about whether religion was about tradition and ritual or about morality and ethics, or both. And they were writing their ideas down. Agrarian empires moved beyond ancestral spirits to worship a pantheon or collection of named gods, often with a ruling god who reigned among the gods, just as the emperor reigned among dignitaries. The lasting effect of this was minimal, however, for when an empire fell, so did its gods, often to be replaced by the apparently more powerful gods of the new conquerors.

During this time period (600–500 BCE and perhaps earlier) Hebrew prophets, seeing portions of the nation fall to Assyria and then to Babylon, wrote about a god who was not defeated even when his people were. This god was also more interested in personal and social conduct, "doing justice and loving mercy" in the words of Micah, than in the specifics of religious ritual. During this time and continuing through the great age of Athens, the Greek philosophers distanced themselves from the ancient pantheon of gods. (Socrates was called an atheist for doing this too much.) Greek Stoics wrote about "the great spiritual fire" that burned above and beyond the lesser gods and about personal and civic duty as the basis of a religious life. Similarly, K'ung Fu-tsu and Lao Tzu in China wrote about the "way of heaven" and the duties and ethical living that were to be the hallmark of a religious person. In India Hindu philosophers organized the diverse collection of practices and beliefs that were coming together into Hinduism. They wrote about Brahma, the eternal one, who was the center and unifier of all things, and how a faithful person should live to attain spiritual advancement. One Hindu prince went further than others in his search for right living and right thinking. Prince Siddhartha Gautama (ca. 563–483 BCE) left his throne to fast and meditate on the human suffering he saw. Enlightened as the Buddha, he taught his followers about noble truths and an eightfold path of right living.

As these ideas spread, they became the basis of the world's first great religions, those that transcended tribal and ethnic boundaries and won converts from many backgrounds. Over the centuries several more great religions developed. The most significant of all, in terms of eventual numbers of converts, began when a Jewish teacher reclaimed and extended the ideas of the prophets. Jesus of Nazareth (ca. 4 BCE–30 CE) claimed that the entire complexity of Hebrew religion was captured in the call to love God with one's entire being and to love one's neighbor as oneself. Jesus's followers—including his most prolific interpreter, Paul of the Roman city of Tarsus—put his life and teachings into the Greek language and in a form that built on Greek philosophy. In three centuries, the way of Jesus the Christ (or deliverer), **Christianity,** became the religion of the Roman Empire.

Between 570 and 632 CE, another teacher challenged a pantheon of gods to call his followers back to the ancient pastoral or herding idea of one god, the great shepherd. Muhammad put these ideas into his book, the Qur'an (or Koran), which had many similarities to Jewish and Christian thought. He drew a small but fervent following, and the religion of **Islam** was born, soon spreading throughout the Middle East.

Later prophets and teachers extended, reformed, and combined elements of these faiths into Sikhism, Baha'i, and other religions, each with a smaller but dedicated following. The main story since about 600 CE, however, has been the spread of the great religions to all parts of the globe (see figure 8.1).

Christianity

A full one-third of the world claims some type of Christian affiliation. When the Roman Empire split into a western Latin half, centered on Rome, and an eastern Greek half, centered on Constantinople, the Christian church also began to divide into a Latin-based Roman Catholic Church with the pope, the Bishop of Rome, as its head, and a Greek-based Eastern Orthodox Church, with the eastern (Byzantine) emperor in Constantinople and the patriarch of Constantinople at its head. By 1000 CE, the cultural, political, and linguistic

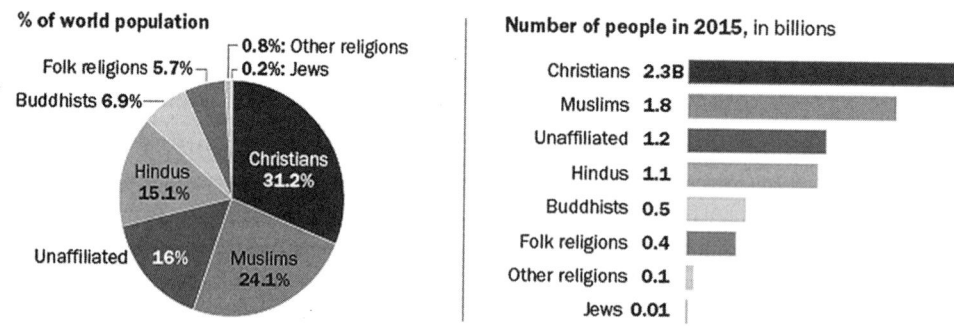

Figure 8.1 *Largest religious groups, 2015. (Source: Pew Research Center. April 5, 2017.)*

divisions became an official split, or schism, that still divides Europe into East and West. Just over 500 years later, the Protestant Reformation began in force in Switzerland, Germany, the Netherlands, and eventually England. After a series of struggles, including the bloody Thirty Years' War of the 1600s, Christian Europe was again divided, this time with Western Europe splitting into a Catholic south and a Protestant north.

The original division survives to this day, with Eastern Orthodoxy in its various national forms (Greek Orthodox, Russian Orthodox, Serbian Orthodox, and so forth) dominating in Russia and Southeastern Europe. Roman Catholicism remains the dominant religion in Italy, France, Spain, Portugal, Austria, Hungary, and southern Germany (up to a line that roughly marks the farthest extent of the Roman Empire). Among Protestants, the Lutheran Church dominates in northern Germany and the Scandinavian countries, the Dutch Reformed Church dominates in the Netherlands, the Anglican Church dominates in England, and the Presbyterian Church dominates in Scotland. Two outposts of Roman Catholicism in Northern Europe—Ireland and Poland—remain the most staunchly Catholic countries.

European Christianity is dominated by state churches that claim huge memberships but are marked by little active involvement by members. In many countries, affiliation in the dominant or state church is over 90 percent, but weekly church attendance is below 10 percent (Jenkins 2011). A typical Sunday morning may find a Danish Lutheran pastor standing in a huge, ornate church preaching (or more likely lecturing about helping the poor around the world) to 15 or 30 people. The pastor's salary is paid by the state, so there is no financial worry, and if the pastor is sincere about helping the poor, he or she may garner community respect but little religious fervor. All Danes are enrolled at birth in the Lutheran Church, unless their parents insist otherwise, but few see the need to regularly participate. A similar pattern is seen in much of Catholic Europe, where Catholicism is an important part of national heritage and identity but attendance at Mass and adherence to the dictates of the Vatican are very limited. Even previously devout Ireland and Poland have seen Mass attendance drop markedly, especially among the young.

Some have spoken of a post-Christian Europe, but what has mainly declined is the power of the state church. Many Europeans have spiritual interests and convictions, in spite of mistrust or apathy toward the dominant church hierarchy, and there has been some growth in the number of smaller, more evangelical, gospel-based religious groups. Immigration from North Africa, as well as South and Southeast Asia, has also meant a significant increase in the number of Muslims living in Europe.

In North America the United States and Canada have historically had Protestant majorities, with strong pockets of Catholicism in French-speaking Canada and in Irish, Polish, Italian, Mexican, Puerto Rican, and Cuban areas in the United States. Latin America has always been overwhelmingly Roman Catholic, given its primarily Spanish and Portuguese heritage. There has been rapid growth of Protestant faiths in many parts of Latin America, however, especially conservative evangelical and Pentecostal groups (emphasizing lively worship and the signs of the Holy Spirit, noted among early Christians at the celebration of the holiday of Pentecost). Places such as Guatemala are now as much as 20 percent Protestant. Because participation in Catholic Mass has been declining, on any given Sunday in Mexico there are more Protestants than Catholics at worship, by some estimates.

Christianity has also seen explosive growth in Sub-Saharan Africa, where many tribal religionists have become Christians, often of the evangelical or Pentecostal forms. The Presbyterian faith and evangelical Christianity have also exploded in South Korea, one of the few Asian nations where this has occurred so widely. Christians are scattered across all of the Asian countries, but South Korea now claims some of the world's largest churches, a few with congregations over 10,000.

Islam

Islam burst out of Arabia shortly after Muhammad's death. Arab conquerors carried the religion across North Africa to Morocco and across the Strait of Gibraltar to all of Spain and even into southern France, where they collided with the knights of the Frankish kingdom. The Moors, a mix of Arabs and North African Berbers, ruled Spain for centuries, until they were gradually driven back and finally expelled by the Catholic monarchs Ferdinand and Isabella in 1491, the year before they sent Christopher Columbus on his famous voyage.

The center of Arab power shifted from Arabia to Baghdad, in what is now Iraq. Persia became Muslim, and Arab traders carried the Islamic faith to their outposts in what is now Indonesia and Malaysia. Many Central Asians converted to Islam. One such group invaded and ruled most of India, where they were called *moguls* (from which we get our word for powerful leaders). One Central Asian group, the Turks, eventually conquered the Arab lands, first as the Seljuk Empire, which battled the European Crusaders, and later as the Ottoman Empire, which ultimately invaded Europe, capturing Constantinople (now modern Istanbul) in 1453 and reaching as far as the outskirts of Vienna in 1688. This was the high tide of the Islamic Empire.

The Ottomans were driven from Vienna by the Catholic Polish cavalry. (It is claimed the bagel owes its origin to pastries shaped like stirrups and baked by grateful Viennese.) Islamic lands fell to European Christians from the time the Portuguese drove the Arabs from the Indian Ocean and the Dutch seized the islands that now comprise Indonesia. The pattern increased when Napoleon seized Egypt from the Turks in 1798, to be followed by the British until Europeans controlled all of North Africa. Following World War I, the entire

Middle East was dominated by European powers. They were "infidels," or unbelievers, to many of the inhabitants but new "crusaders" in the rhetoric of Osama bin Laden and Islamic nationalists.

Evidence of the reach of Islamic civilization can be seen in magnificent structures from the Alhambra Palace in Granada, Spain, to the Taj Mahal in India. Having seized the domain of Alexander the Great and the Byzantine Greek Empire and thrived while Europeans were experiencing what would be their Dark Ages, Islamic scientists and philosophers formed an important bridge between the learning of the classical Mediterranean and Middle Eastern world and that of modern Europe (Berkey 2002).

Islamic political power has been in sharp decline for centuries, yet the religion continues to expand. About one-fifth of the world adheres to the Muslim faith. The largest Muslim nation is neither Arab nor Middle Eastern but the country of Indonesia. The second largest Muslim population is in India, where they are a minority in a Hindu country, but such a vast country that even its minorities are huge. Pakistan and Bangladesh, carved as Islamic states from Hindu-majority India, are the next most populous. The Arab nations, with the exception of Egypt, tend to be small in population but are historically important to Islam and now have oil wealth that gives them power beyond their size.

The Islamic belt slices across portions of Southeast, South, and Central Asia; across Iran and the Arabian Peninsula; and all the way across North Africa. A rough line across the Sahel, the dry region that separates the Sahara in the north from the wetter country to the south, divides Africa into a Muslim-dominated north and a Christian-dominated south. Sometimes, the line divides countries in two. Nigeria, Africa's most populous country, is roughly divided into a Muslim north, which dominates the national politics, and a Christian south, which dominates the national economy. Rivalries between the two resulted in the Nigerian Civil War (1968–1970) and continued tension. As the north of the country faces drought while the southern part of the country faces floods, both possibly the result of global climate change, more Nigerians are moving to the "middle belt," and conflicts, including those between Muslim cattle herdsmen and Christian farmers, became a frequent occurrence (Campbell 2018). The volatile situation is now often sparked by actions of the terrorist insurgency Boko Haram and the subsequent military crackdowns in the north of the country (John, Abubakr, and Mullen 2015).

The line of division also slices into two halves what until 2011 had been the vast country of Sudan. The government in Khartoum has been in the hands of Islamic nationalists, mostly Arabs, who have been accused of having ties with extremist groups. Southerners include the Dinka, the Nuer, and many ethnic groups, who adhere to tribal and Christian religions. They had fought for independence, or at least autonomy, for years. In a 2011 referendum, southerners voted overwhelmingly for independence, with 99 percent voting to break ties with the north to form the new nation of South Sudan. Many hoped independence would bring peace, but conflicts have sometimes pitted one southern group against another, with traditional cattle raids no longer consisting of a few men with spears, but at times up to one thousand men with AK-47 automatic weapons.

Asian Religions

India remains home to most of the world's **Hindus.** Despite being concentrated in a single country, this is still one of the world's largest religions, with 800 million adherents. The large number of Indians living and working overseas has spread the influence of Hinduism well beyond India's borders. Interest has also grown in the ancient practices and ideas of Hinduism. When the Beatles left England to study with the Maharishi Mahesh Yogi and his adapted form of meditation—transcendental meditation—came in vogue, and the Western world reawakened to Hindu ideas. Other Hindu-based disciplines, such as the practice of yoga, also continue to gain in worldwide popularity.

Buddhism began in India but never completely took hold. It quickly spread to other countries, however, and Sri Lanka, Thailand, Myanmar, and Cambodia are now all predominantly Buddhist. Buddhism has had great influence in China, although Buddhism's most prominent spokesperson is in exile from Chinese authorities, the 14th Dalai Lama of Tibet. A contemplative form with fewer rituals, Zen Buddhism, has had great influence on Japan; although given the open-ended nature of Japanese Zen, it is hard to say just how many would consider themselves practicing Buddhists.

The most difficult place to do an accounting of believers of any kind is China, the world's most populous country. Mao's Communists were officially atheist, and many Chinese claim no religion. There has been a revival of interest in the three "great ways" of China—Taoism, Confucianism, and Buddhism—and there has also been a renewed growth in Christianity. A few Chinese minority groups, primarily along the Mongolian border, are Muslim.

Any accounting of the world's major religions must consider the tremendous intermingling of faiths that has taken place (Eck 2002). There are today more Muslims in London, Detroit, and Chicago than in most Arab capitals. There are more Jews in New York than in Jerusalem, as well as more Hindus than Episcopalians.

Ethnicity, Religion, and Power

Religious and ethnic diversity have had tremendous power to fuel violence. History is full of accounts of one ethnic group's attempt to subjugate or exterminate another that was seen as threatening or inferior. Ideologies of race and religion have often been used to provide added justification for these acts.

Both Christians and Muslims (and no doubt, many others, such as the Mesoamerican Aztecs) have used religion to justify their conquests. They have also fought among themselves: Protestant versus Catholic Christians, Sunni versus Shi'ite Muslims, and so forth. These conflicts persist in many places in the world: between Catholics and Protestants in Northern Ireland; between Jews and Arabs in Israel and Palestine; among Muslims, Sikhs, and Hindus in India; between Muslims and Christians in Indonesia; and between Hasidic Jews and African Americans (many of Caribbean origin) in the Crown Heights neighborhood of Brooklyn, New York.

One way to view these conflicts is to believe they are rooted in human nature and due to the expanse of human history or ancient hatreds. Harvard historian Samuel Huntington (2011) believes that the post–cold war world will see a "clash of civilizations," in which the great civilizations that have emerged based on religion and ethnicity and that still hold conflicting values will continue to clash in conflict: Western Christian, Islamic, Chinese, Indian Hindu, and so forth.

The history of hate is long, yet so is the history of accommodation. Many religions and ethnicities intermingled in many of the great empires: the Persian, the Alexandrian, even the great Mongol Empire of Genghis Khan and his grandson, Kublai. Amy Chua (2007) argues that what allowed the greatest empires to flourish was in fact their broad tolerance (not necessarily equal respect) for many religious and ethnic backgrounds. Even that great modern imperialist, Queen Victoria, spoke of the British Empire as a place of brotherhood between people of many creeds and colors, once petty rivalries were subdued by careful British paternalism (or in her case, maternalism).

Many places known for violence have also had periods of cooperation. When Lebanon burst into violence among Muslims, Christians, and Jews in the 1970s and 1980s, the battles repeated the same bloodshed that had occurred in this land during the Crusades. Yet for decades Beirut was known not for hostages and terror but for cooperation and accommodation among all of its religious and ethnic groups, the cosmopolitan "Paris of the Mideast." Yugoslavia fell into war in the 1990s among Orthodox Serbs, Catholic Croats, and Muslim Bosnians. These rivalries went back to the earliest days of the Ottoman and Austro-Hungarian Empires, but Yugoslavia had also known 45 years of relatively peaceful cooperation prior to this.

Much hate seems distinctly modern. Donald Horowitz (2001) rooted his theories of ethnic conflict in the idea of competition. Struggles for dominance once an empire or ruler falls, as well as struggles between people who are fearful that loss in this competition will forever submerge their hopes and their way of life, are what fuel ethnic strife. Economic competition has played a major role in many such struggles. So has political manipulation. Dictators from Hitler to Milošević to Saddam Hussein have known how to play on ethnic and religious divisions, fears, and rivalries. Promising a better future has long been the rallying cry of politicians, but promising a better future by quashing someone who is profiting at your expense has been a great rallying cry to violence. Merchant minorities, sometimes called *middleman minorities*, who operate businesses amid other groups, have been especially vulnerable. Hitler moved against the Jews in Europe, Idi Amin moved against the Indians in Uganda, and anti-Chinese violence shook Indonesia with the fall of Suharto in 1998. Loss of historical territory, inevitable in a world of shifting boundaries, can also be a powerful rallying cry. In each of these cases, the immediate motivation may have been economic or political, but religion and ethnicity, sometimes combined in a hypernationalism, have proven far more powerful in inciting war—from ancient Sparta, to the Crusades of the 1100s, to modern calls for *jihad* (or holy struggle).

The tragic convergence of these factors was seen in 1994 in Rwanda. Two ethnic groups, the Hutus and the Tutsis, had shared the land for centuries. Under European colonial administration—in this case, Belgian in the early 1900s, which favored the Tutsis at the expense of the Hutus—the divisions and resentments deepened. Upon Rwanda's gaining independence in 1962, the groups had fought, and both sides feared the other. The stage was set. All it took was a group of particularly fiery Hutu leaders, both religious and political, to call their people to arms, to crush their opponents "like insects that infest the land." As the story unfolded, a shocked world saw the scope of the brutality: 1.5 million killed, many hacked to death with machetes as they huddled in churches for protection, while leaders, including a prominent priest, chided the attackers that "the graves are not yet full." The international community was slow to respond and quick to move on to other problems, dismissing this as "ancient hatred" (BBC News 2004).

One of the questions raised by this tragedy was how to best respond. The Belgians and French and a handful of UN observers were late coming to Rwanda in force, too late to stop the bloodshed. Remembering this, the French were quick to step into the Côte D'Ivoire (Ivory Coast), their former colony, when the fighting in Liberia threatened to destabilize that country. Similarly, the British intervened to restore order in their former territory of Sierra Leone. Small African nations have come to look to "big brothers" in times of crisis, but is this a new form of colonialism? The United States, distracted by Iraq and remembering its losses when it got involved in interclan fighting in Somalia, resisted sending troops to Liberia, where it had historic ties. Instead, a West African force led by Nigerians intervened. The Nigerians were welcomed but also sometimes mistrusted, as some had ethnic ties to certain factions fighting in Liberia.

Resurgent Fundamentalism

Just as many believed that the power of ethnicity would decline in the modern world, some also believed that the influence of religion would decline. Writing in the 1960s, British sociologist Peter Berger (1967) believed that amid growing modernization and diversity, people would have to hold their beliefs more tentatively and tolerantly; they would become more secular, or at least more liberal, as the "sacred canopy" of religion was pulled back. Similarly, U.S. theologian Harvey Cox (2013 [1965]) believed that the diverse cities of the world, with their international, cosmopolitan nature, would necessarily become examples of "the secular city."

Berger may have been correct about London and Cox about Boston in the 1960s, but elsewhere, sentiments were changing. The end of the twentieth century saw a sharp rise in highly conservative, traditional, and literal expressions of religious faith. At times, they have also been militant expressions.

Perhaps it was the pressures of a cosmopolitan, globalizing world that drove the movement. In his book *Jihad vs. McWorld*, Benjamin Barber (1995) sees two opposing forces acting in the world. One, he termed *McWorld:* the capitalist, corporate-controlled, economic uniformity typified by McDonald's and huge corporations. The other, he termed *jihad*, borrowing the Islamic word for "holy struggle," in his usage, referring to all reactionary struggles against modernity and globalization, the fierce call back to tribe and tradition, to religion and noncommercial absolutes.

In the 1980s the most prominent face of jihad, in this sense, was the Ayatollah Khomeini, religious and political revolutionary and leader of Iran, denouncing the United States as the "Great Satan" that dominated and tempted the faithful. In the beginning of the twenty-first century, the most recognizable face of this type of jihad is probably that of Osama bin Laden. To him, perhaps the power of McWorld was best seen in the twin towers of the World Trade Center. Barber fears that both McWorld and jihad may be fundamentally undemocratic—one represents rule by money, the other rule by fear.

The collision between these two forces is not always violent. It may take the form of a cultural clash. Pakistani rock star Salman Ahmed, lead singer of the band Junoon, fills auditoriums in his home country with people who want to hear his version of international rock and roll, while ultraconservative religious leaders denounce this worldly display, in some cases calling for a ban not only on rock but on all music as "un-Islamic."

What can be misleading in these current examples and in Barber's choice of terms is that this reaction is not unique to Islam. What has been labeled "religious fundamentalism" has taken root around the world.

Fundamentalism originally referred to a type of very conservative, Bible-oriented, and largely rural American Christianity. Around the beginning of the twentieth century U.S. Christians who rejected so-called liberal tendencies in many churches called for a return to the fundamentals of the Bible. These included not only fundamentals of belief but also often of lifestyle, such as prohibitions against dancing, drinking alcohol, watching movies, and playing cards. These "worldly" pursuits were believed to tempt and distract the true believer. For the most part, American Christian fundamentalism initially rejected political involvement as being worldly, although some southern politicians adopted its themes (and fervent style of preaching). Involvement in politics was largely limited to issues such as opposition to the teaching of evolution and to the selling of liquor on Sundays.

This changed in the 1980s with the rise to prominence of Jerry Falwell and his Moral Majority. The early fundamentalists who had found a political platform were likely to be populist Democrats, but in the 1980s fundamentalist support went to the Reagan administration and conservative Republicans. Falwell's followers still avoided direct political campaigns and instead called Americans back to a more "moral" time, as characterized by traditional gender roles and family structure, traditional (i.e., nineteenth-century) attitudes toward sexuality, and opposition to other trends it considered unbiblical. More direct political involvement came with the creation of the Christian Coalition under Pat Robertson in 1984 and its expansion under Ralph Reed and during the presidential campaigns of Pat Robertson, Gary Becker, and others. What became known as the **religious right** became a major force in the Republican Party and the country as a whole.

Islamic fundamentalism may be an awkward hybrid term, but it captures the notion that many of these same ideas, backed by the Qur'an rather than the Bible, have gained prominence in parts of the Islamic world. This fundamentalism is seen in a form of Islam known as Wahhabism, which gained influence in Saudi Arabia and has been exported to other countries through Saudi-supported madrassas and religious organizations. This form of fundamentalism also looks to a literal interpretation of the scripture and its direct application to modern life. Like Christian fundamentalism, Islamic fundamentalism is also opposed to alcohol and smoking, to "lewd" publications and movies (and maybe to all movies and theater), to immodest dress, and to many forms of entertainment—in particular, dancing and popular music (in some cases, to all music). It also favors traditional gender roles and provides strict punishment for offenses. In its more extreme forms, this includes cloistering women in their homes, unless they must be out (and then a traditional veiled covering is worn), and forbidding them to drive and in some cases to work. Criminal punishments are based on the Qur'an and include executions, stonings, and cutting off the hands of thieves and other offenders. Homosexuality and any form of extramarital sex are severely punished.

Many of these fundamentalist practices are seen in Saudi Arabia, although often moderated by local custom. They reached an extreme in Afghanistan under the Taliban, which means "student," or one who strictly studies the Qur'an. Many of these practices are ancient, although over the centuries a number of Islamic rulers have been extremely tolerant of religious and social diversity. Of note, however, is the fact that Islamic fundamentalism, like its Christian counterpart in the United States, has grown more political. The Iranian Revolution installed a government based on strict Islamic fundamentalist principles. Many Muslim countries now have Islamic political parties that call for a strict Islamic state, based on fundamentalist interpretations.

Other religions also have their fundamentalist forms. Ultraorthodox Jewish factions call for a particular type of modesty in dress, traditional gender divisions and family forms, a rejection of certain aspects of the modern world, and a strict and literal reading of the Torah, or Jewish law. In Israel, political parties that wed these beliefs to the conviction that God has promised them all the land of David and Solomon have gained influence in the government.

Hindu fundamentalism would seem to be an oxymoron, given that Hinduism is known as an incredibly diverse and highly tolerant religion. Yet within India a movement is gaining political and social power that likewise stresses traditional Indian lifestyles, family forms, and gender patterns; rejects certain aspects of the modern, commercial world; and is suspicious of secularists and non-Hindus in positions of power.

It is easy (perhaps especially easy in a cosmopolitan university) to condemn fundamentalist movements as shortsighted, anti-intellectual, antimodern, or just out of touch with a changing world. Yet these movements are clearly speaking to the personal and spiritual needs of many people and seem to represent a global hunger for a more stable and more moral social order.

Global fundamentalism also poses some major problems. Barber (1995) suggests they are fundamentally undemocratic. This perhaps remains to be seen. In the United States, Christian fundamentalists certainly endorse the democratic ideals of the U.S. Constitution and often speak of the "Founding Fathers" (even though most historians do not envision George Washington, let alone Thomas Jefferson or Benjamin Franklin, as much of a fundamentalist). Their mix of religion and politics sometimes clashes with the constitutional ideals of the separation of church and state. In addition, they have often objected to the American Civil Liberties Union's idea of free speech and have been vigorous opponents of campaign finance reform.

Islamic parties have been big vote getters in many Muslim nations that hold elections, but the commitment of these parties to continuing a liberal democratic tradition, as opposed to a theocracy of religious leaders and laws, has been questioned. In Iran a reformist elected government has seen many of its proposals vetoed by religious leaders, who still hold the final authority. African democracies have been more plagued by paternalism and tribalism (i.e., favoring one's own ethnic group), but now they are seeing new challenges from a fervent and possibly radical Islamic resurgence in Pakistan, Egypt, Lebanon, Algeria, Nigeria, and Somalia, among others. Often these groups draw support from a populace tired of corrupt or ineffective, and often Western-backed, governments, who see the Islamic groups as more dedicated and sincere, in spite of often violent tactics. Whether the repression and outlawing of these groups is protecting democracy or subverting it depends on one's view of the intentions of these political entities. Often what results are cycles of revolutionary terrorism and state repression that serve no one but the combatants.

Israel has functioned as a democracy since its founding in 1948. Still the country's so-called religious parties have often sought to conform Israeli law to their version of Jewish religious law and worry about the growing number of Israeli Arabs who can vote. Some wonder if Israel can really be both a Jewish state, defined in religious and ethnic terms, and a modern liberal democracy, with the expectations of pluralism. Likewise, India has been a democracy since its founding in 1947, but the demands of Hindu fundamentalists may run counter to the ideals of a pluralist democracy, which seeks to protect and include people from many cultural and religious backgrounds.

This may be a problem of mindset rather than religion in itself. In *American Fascists: The Christian Right and the War on America* journalist Chris Hedges (2007) looked at one set of dangers. In a follow-up work, *I Don't Believe in Atheists*, Hedges (2008), contends that some of the new advocates of atheism share the same intolerance of other traditions and heritage, as well as other ways of thinking, as religious fundamentalists. Amartya Sen (2007) contends that to end terror we must rethink our basis of identity from a narrow single dimension used by ideologies of hate to a broader sense of identity that can encompass the many things we have in common with others around the world.

The God of the Poor: Liberation Theology

Not all the mingling of religion and politics has occurred on the religious and political right. There is also a history of blending religious convictions and progressive politics.

Upon his conversion to Buddhism, the Indian leader Asoka (300 BCE) renounced warfare, embraced religious and ethnic tolerance, and sought to alleviate the suffering of the poor. Christian influence in the late Roman Empire restrained the excesses of the emperors and led to the abolition of the gladiatorial games. In the United States during the civil rights movement of the 1960s, many of the challenges to segregation, the demand for voting rights, and the Poor People's Campaign were led by African American religious leaders. Latin American politics have likewise been influenced by liberation theology, a set of ideas coming out of the Catholic Church that, at the core of the gospel, is a message of liberation for the poor and oppressed. Pope John Paul II tried to restrain what he saw as too much political involvement by Catholic clergy, but progressive priests in many countries formed base communities of poor *campesinos* (peasant farmers and country people) and workers and led campaigns for the poor.

The political landscape of the twenty-first century, however, has been most affected by religious fundamentalists, especially by what some prefer to call **religious extremists,** who hold very strict interpretations of their faith traditions and sometimes appear willing to use force to enforce these ideas. Religion, in this case, is closely allied with nationalism, as in calls by fundamentalists to preserve the United States as a Christian nation, India as a Hindu nation, Israel as an orthodox Jewish state, and Muslim countries as Islamic states under Islamic law. "Hard-liners," who combine religion, ethnicity, and nationalism, have been a force in the creation of repressive states, while "extremists" have combined the same elements into national and international terrorism in efforts to topple and remake some of these same states.

Identity and International Terrorism

Revolutionary and State Terror

Terror has a long history. It has been most often used to build states and empires. Cities that resisted Genghis Khan's invading armies in the thirteenth century were often massacred en masse, while those who surrendered were shown leniency, creating a powerful incentive to join rather than oppose the empire. In the twentieth century, state-sponsored terror conducted against enemies of various regimes claimed more lives and inflicted more suffering than ever before imagined, even if the exact numbers are hard to tally. An estimated six million people were killed in the Nazi Holocaust, many millions in the Stalinist purges, several million in China's Cultural Revolution, two million in Cambodia's "killing fields," and 1.5 million in Rwanda, and these numbers do not include terror in the pursuit of international war. Terror has also been used to oppose rulers. The Assassins, a sect of Shi'a Islam who inhabited the mountains of Persia and Syria in 1090–1275, used carefully planned murders to intimidate and oppose Christian and Ottoman rule. Their leader, an extremist Muslim, used both mind-altering drugs and promises of eternal paradise to motivate the killers.

Many troubled locations are trapped in cycles of revolutionary terrorism, combative rulers and states, and state repression, including what some would call **state terror.** The classic case has been Israel and Palestine during the *intifada*. Palestinians fighting for groups such as Hamas, Hezbollah, and the al-Aksa Martyrs Brigades all seek an independent Palestinian state and many also seek the destruction of the state of Israel. They gain support from other Palestinians who may not share their complete political and religious agenda but who have a long history of grievances against Israel and its allies and who respect the utter dedication of these groups, as well as the charitable work they often do in Palestinian communities and refugee camps. Bombings and ambushes have been the favorite tools of their terror.

The ability of zealots backed by experts in the dark arts of terror to dominate the news is clearly seen in the **suicide bomber,** detonating explosives, which have been packed into a car or strapped to the bomber's body, in crowded places. Suicide bombings were a regular part of sectarian violence in Iraq, often used by radical Sunnis against majority Shi'a, who have at times responded with militia attacks of their own. They were a major tool of the Taliban resistance and shadow groups in Afghanistan. An increasingly common response has been to attack these groups from the air with unmanned drones, a response that is both feared and deeply resented by communities on the ground. Drone attacks have spread around the world and are typically responded to by calls for greater security and with more repressive measures to attain that security.

This cycle of attacks and response has a long history in Israel. Since suicide is forbidden by Islamic law but martyrdom, dying for the faith, is glorified, supporters call these "martyrdom acts" rather than "suicide bombings." To Jewish Israelis these acts that randomly kill innocent people are the height of reckless, ruthless terror. While their perpetrators agree that terror is the intent, they argue that the victims are not innocent, as they are in collusion with a repressive Israeli state, and that the martyrs are soldiers of faith.

Israel has responded to these attacks with assassinations and targeted killings of suspected leaders and activists in these Palestinian cells, often killing them from the air in attacks that also take the lives of bystanders. Another common retaliation has been the bulldozing of the houses, orchards, and the fields of families of suspected terrorists and sometimes whole communities. To the Israelis, these are acts of self-defense; to the Palestinians, they are acts of repression and state terror. In fact, when taken along with the searches, beatings, and humiliation they experience at the hands of Israeli troops, these acts justify further acts of martyrdom. Both sides are armed and aided by outside supporters, and the cycle continues, despite attempts to negotiate a settlement.

This same cycle ripped apart Sri Lanka, the island nation just south of India, for several decades beginning in the 1980s. Once considered a place of peace and tranquility that, while poor, excelled in health and education, Sri Lanka was shattered by fighting between the revolutionary Tamil Tigers—Liberation Tigers of Tamil Eelam (LTTE), representing a Hindu Tamil minority with ties to India, and government troops representing the Buddhist Singhalese majority. The Tamils claimed they were an oppressed minority and sought their own independent state. While some groups worked nonviolently, the Tigers increasingly resorted to horrific bombings that made nowhere on the island safe; they claim to have invented the suicide bomber. Fighting and the state's response sent many Tamils into refugee camps, where they were displaced and without work and without much hope. The camps, in turn, became prime recruiting ground for new Tigers, just like the Palestinian refugee camps.

The bloodshed in Sri Lanka never captured the world's press in the same way as the Israeli–Palestinian conflict. The government finally trapped the rebels on the north of an island and crushed the LTTE in 2009. Still this battle between the Tamils and the Singhalese, between Hindus and Buddhists, provides a powerful reminder that religious and ethnic tensions spilling into terrorism are not limited to conflicts among Muslims, Jews, and Christians.

The Power and Weakness of Terror

Terrorist attacks in the Middle East reached their pinnacle with the savagery of the group that calls itself the Islamic State of Iraq and Syria (ISIS). Emerging out of the chaos in Syria to claim swaths of territory and then gaining a foothold in Iraq, they had grown tired of the older al Qaeda leadership

Towering security wall dividing the West Bank town of Bethlehem. Fears of terrorism have led to attempts to contain threats, although this can lead to isolation, division, and repression that spur new cycles of terror.

and offered a new apocalyptic vision to fight. Many saw themselves as not just restoring an ancient caliphate but also ushering in "the end of days." It didn't matter how vast the forces arrayed against them were, they believed their faith and fervor would unleash divine retribution on an evil world and they would triumph. Non-Sunni Muslims who opposed them were infidels who could be enslaved and Sunni Muslims who opposed them were heretics who could be killed. Within this framework, any action could justified. Despite spectacular early success, they made enemies of everyone who was not a part of their inner circle and were exhausted and defeated by forces—Russian and American along with Kurdish, Turkish, and Iranian-backed Shiite militia who could never have seen themselves as likely allies. ISIS left behind scarred communities and scarred landscapes whose ancient heritage was destroyed. They also left behind the reminder that groups, whether defined by religion, ethnicity, or just an apocalyptic fear of a world order that is ultimately evil and corrupt, can mobilize followers to commit outrageous acts.

Violent terror in the United States has come less from radical Islamic groups than from far-right hate groups. These groups can readily mobilize fears aimed at democratic institutions and multiculturalism and promote an apocalyptic vision of the righteous struggle against "dark powers" controlling the world order.

While al Qaeda and ISIS have receded from the headlines, a variety of groups across a huge swatch of northern and eastern Africa pledge "alliance" to them. This appears to be a way to give legitimacy and cohesion to splinter groups fighting ethnic, territorial, and economic battles across troubled and often impoverished regions. Nigeria has Boko Haram (Boko is a nickname for Western education, haram the term for a religious prohibition). Attacks have terrorized northern Nigeria with mass kidnappings of school children, with hundreds taken in 2014—some never to return—and again in 2018, and then hundreds of boys in 2020 and 300 schoolgirls in 2021, all from northern regions of the country. In their ideology anything that might be considered "Western," from voting in an election, to wearing shirt and pants, to attending a public school, is a sign of corruption and banned. They have spilled into neighboring nations. French forces have been called in to maintain order in Mali and former French West Africa, and U.S. forces have been engaged in actions in Chad and elsewhere (many of these strictly covert until an ambush or attack makes its way into the news). Boko Haram claimed allegiance to ISIS until they were repudiated.

In Somalia al Shabab (the youth) controls large areas beyond those controlled by the very limited government; their tactics, such as the beheading of children, are clearly designed to instill terror and submission. Their reach, or at least that of affiliate groups with similar allegiances, has now stretched as far south as Mozambique. Since 2017 the insurgency has claimed 2,500 lives and left 700,000 homeless (BBC News 2021b). Their recruits are mostly the young and unemployed from communities that seem to have no future despite rich ruby mines and gas fields nearby. Their victims are most often other villagers but may also be government officials or gas field workers. Al Shabab of Somalia has claimed allegiance to al Qaeda, and in Mozambique to ISIS in a pattern more like that of transnational drug cartels than a coherent movement. These local splinter groups all find support in desperate regions that have often experienced cycles of exploitation of people and resources, intertwined with long periods of abandonment and neglect. Yet they also seem to obstruct hope of escape from such cycles. AK-47s fill the region instead of vaccines, clean wells, and clinics.

The power of terror lies in its ability to grab headlines and command attention. It is not easy to become a famous humanitarian, but it's not all that hard to become a famous (momentarily at least) assassin. There are not many ways that 19 men from the Middle East could suddenly change the politics and policies of the world's powers and command the attention of the entire world, but the terrorists who hijacked planes and caused them to crash on September 11, 2001, did just that.

The weakness of terror lies in its inability to effect the lasting changes the terrorists and their supporters so desire. The event that has become known just by its date, 9/11, was first and foremost a terrible human tragedy that took the lives of people from around the world—from European financiers to Central American custodians, all working in the World Trade Center. From the perspective of the al-Qaeda leadership, it seemed to be a great success: the biggest act of revolutionary terrorism ever (it still pales before examples of state terror unleashed during wartime) struck at the heart of the world's superpower and riveted world attention. Yet in terms of achieving the goals of this Islamic extremist collection of terror cells, it was a complete failure.

Intended to divide and undermine the United States, it brought about tremendous national unity and a resurgence of patriotism. Inspired in part by anger over the U.S. military presence in the Middle East, it resulted in the next few years in huge U.S. military deployments in Afghanistan and Iraq. Motivated in part by U.S. support for Israel, it led to greater support for Israel as a fellow country fighting terrorism. Al-Qaeda was angered by U.S. and British embargoes and no-fly zones over Iraq, which they saw as an attack on Arab peoples, but their own attack provided grounds for a new, more aggressive doctrine that resulted in the full-scale invasion of Iraq. When the United States invaded Afghanistan after the 9/11 terrorist attacks, it toppled the one truly friendly regime to al-Qaeda, the Taliban, with many al-Qaeda loyalists killed and its leadership sent into hiding. In terms of commanding attention, the 9/11 hijackings and attacks were spectacularly successful; in terms of fulfilling long-term goals, they were a complete failure.

Opposition to terrorism takes many forms. Syrian opposition fighters celebrate a victory over the Islamic State (ISIS) in 2016 [top]. Iraqis in Washington make known their sentiments in 2014 [bottom].

Terrorism has been called "the weapon of the weak," for it has typically been favored by those who cannot field large, victorious armies. As the weapons available to terrorists increase, the world can only hope that both the proponents of revolutionary terror and those of state terror will realize that terrorism is also a weak weapon, one that almost never produces the desired outcome.

Alternatives to Terror

Religion as Resilience

Religious conviction and cultural heritage have also been used to effect nonviolent change and reconciliation. The towering figure of nonviolence in the twentieth century was a small, personally unimposing man, Mohandas Gandhi, whom Indians called the *Mahatma*, or "great soul." Gandhi believed that social change began with an inner spiritual change. "You must be the change you seek" was his famous motto. He also believed that as vital as deep spiritual conviction was, if it was not tied to tolerance and nonviolence, it would become a weapon of destruction.

Gandhi was deeply inspired by his own Hindu roots, especially the ideals of the Bhagavad Gita, and also by insights of others practicing different faiths, notably Christian pacifist and Russian writer Leo Tolstoy and the ethic of Jesus in the Sermon on the Mount. Gandhi called his program *satyagraha*, meaning the energy and power of the soul, driven by truth and love. His campaign of nonviolent resistance to injustice, tolerance for all faiths, respect for all castes and ethnicities, and respect for the cultural heritage of India won worldwide recognition in the early twentieth century and paved the way for India's post–World War II independence.

Gandhi's ideals were not accepted by all, however. Even though he favored a tolerant, multireligious India, he could not prevent the 1947 partition into a Hindu-dominated India and an Islamic state in East and West Pakistan. He was murdered by a Hindu hard-liner who resented his accommodation of Muslims. Yet his ideas lived on to inspire the Reverend Dr. Martin Luther King, Jr., in his commitment to nonviolence as well as that of many lesser-known leaders in the American civil rights movement, such as Ella Baker, and many other leaders across Asia and Africa.

In the antiapartheid struggle in South Africa, where Gandhi first started to form his ideas, a nonviolent campaign of resistance was led by Bishop Desmond Tutu of the Anglican Church and Allan Boesak of the Dutch Reformed Church. Throughout the 1970s and 1980s they held rallies, staged boycotts, lobbied for international sanctions and pressure, and pleaded to the moral conscience of their church members. The apartheid system eventually collapsed in the early 1990s without a violent revolution.

In the late 1960s the 14th Dalai Lama of Tibet fled the country, as China pressed harder to incorporate the once-independent country culturally and politically into China. Some of his followers proposed a guerilla war in the rugged Tibetan plateau to try to keep the Chinese out. The Dalai Lama instead chose a pattern of nonviolent resistance and continued dialogue with Chinese leaders. In over 60 years, he has not won independence for Tibet and now often speaks only of earning autonomy. He has, however, become a widely recognized spokesperson for Tibetan Buddhism and its ethic of compassion and is a symbol of enduring Tibetan culture. The respect he has garnered in the international community, as well as among his own people, has kept Tibet, once remote and largely unknown, in the forefront of the media throughout the world, forcing Chinese authorities to carefully consider their policies and image in Tibet.

Ethnicity as Resilience

Some movements draw strength from ethnic heritage, often with strong ethical, social, and spiritual values but not always rooted in the language of a major religion. The **Zapatista** movement in Chiapas, Mexico, drew heavily on Maya traditions and culture in its campaign against what it sees as Mexican government repression and economic exploitation in the extremely poor state of Chiapas. The movement's charismatic spokesperson, "Subcomandante" Marcos, insisted that the real *comandantes* are the indigenous village elders.

The Zapatista national liberation army (EZLN) looks like a typical armed Latin American rebel group, wearing ski masks and carrying rifles. Yet the rifles are not AK-47s, but antiquated hunting guns and sometimes no more than wooden cutouts. Members claim that the masks are to protect them from reprisals and that the guns are mere symbols of their determination to fight for their rights in the spirit of other indigenous and populist revolutionaries, such as Emiliano Zapata of the Mexican Revolution. Interestingly, EZLN's main weapon seems to be the internet. Their international friends maintain their website (www.ezln.org) and publish resolutions from the elders and scathing critiques of Mexican society and international capitalism. It has shifted its demands over time but has maintained its indigenous and local character, with many of the new leaders being Maya-heritage women (Hackbarth and Mooers 2019; Klein 2019).

Moral Leadership as Resilience

Nonviolent groups are often not as good at grabbing the headlines as their violent counterparts, who get immediate attention with spectacular terrorist attacks and other acts of violence. Even in this, however, some nonviolent leaders, Dr. King and the Dalai Lama among them, have been particularly effective in getting media attention.

Nonviolent groups are also not as easy for governing authorities to disparage and dismiss. State and federal governments, as well as popular opinion, often dismissed groups such as the Black Panthers as dangerous criminals. Yet this was hard to do with other groups, such as King's Southern Christian Leadership Conference and the hundreds of college students who formed the Student Nonviolent Coordinating Committee. These young people endured attacks and insults to nonviolently insist on desegregation, and their moral power was hard to dismiss.

Gandhi believed that once he had wrested the moral high ground from the British Empire, his struggle would be ultimately won. In South Africa, the apartheid government portrayed Nelson Mandela as a dangerous communist and terrorist, but this was not an easy charge to make against Desmond Tutu, a dignified bishop who spoke eloquently about brotherhood and reconciliation. Similarly, long after many revolutionaries have been forgotten, El Salvador's Catholic archbishop Oscar Romero, killed for his nonviolent defense of the rights of poor campesinos, is still remembered and his ideals pursued.

There is always the danger that nonviolent actions will be overtaken by more spectacular violence. In Kosovo a nonviolent Muslim movement in the 1980s and early 1990s founded Albanian-language schools and community services in opposition to the government of Slobodan Milošević. It was their armed resistance, however, that got the attention and support of Western Europe and the United States and then drew horrible reprisals and repression from the Milošević government in 1998. In the occupied territories of Gaza and Palestine, Palestinian groups, many with strong Muslim convictions, have organized schools and relief programs, used boycotts and strikes as major means of protest, and generally drawn on the arsenal of nonviolence. Some of their fellow Palestinians see these methods as too slow and ineffective, yet it may be the one way forward as more and more Arab leaders see advantages in peace with Israel over absolute support for the Palestinian cause.

Even as many in the world have come to view the Middle East, and the Arab world in particular, as hopelessly filled with violence and terrorism, the Arab Spring of 2011 showed the willingness of many, and many young people, in Arab countries to take to the streets in nonviolent demonstrations for democracy, reform, and human rights. Starting in Tunisia and quickly spreading to Egypt, Bahrain, Morocco, Syria, and Libya, these movements challenged entrenched governments. Libyans and Syrians faced violent repression from the government, and Syria and Libya broke into civil war, but in Tunisia, Egypt, and Morocco reforms were enacted without massive violence and cycles of terror.

In his book, *The Unconquerable World: Power, Nonviolence, and the Will of the People*, Jonathan Schell (2003), peace fellow at the National Institute in New York, describes what he sees as a progression from (1) traditional war, now obsolete in a nuclear age, to (2) "people's war," guerilla fights that depend on popular support but often lead to growing cycles of violence, with many civilian casualties, to (3) nonviolent revolution and nonviolent rule. While Schell respects the power of Gandhi's spiritual calling, Schell's call for nonviolent revolution and rule is more practical than theological: Traditional war and people's war lead to mounds of corpses. Only patient, persistent, nonviolent action can preserve both freedoms and traditions and provide what uprisings—popular, religious, and ethnic—hope to attain.

As people look for alternatives to terror in struggles around the world, several repeated lessons emerge:

1. Religious fervor and ethnic identity can be dangerous when manipulated by demagogues and be used to justify attacks on "the enemies of God" or "those who would destroy our people." But these same traditions and convictions can motivate people to make tremendous personal sacrifices, to stand in solidarity with one another, and to seek creative cultural, social, and political alternatives to violence.

2. While nonviolent change may be slow, it is often more enduring than the change brought about by force. Often it is the only way out of a cycle of terror and repression. It is not just about being "holier" or kinder, it is about playing for the long game.

3. The ethic that is rooted in many spiritual traditions and that may be most needed is that of compassion and forgiveness. History can be a great source of wisdom and understanding, but people and places can also be "sick with history" as the story of myriad grievances. Letting go of these grievances is hard for the aggrieved and resisted by leaders who know that playing on grievances will build a quick following. Yet as Gandhi, Tutu, and the 14th Dalai Lama learned, tremendous power results when truth is coupled with compassion and forgiveness.

Key Ideas

> Ethnicity, ties based on a sense of common heritage, has seen a resurgence of importance in many places around the world. Ethnic pride can renew interest in a people's cultural heritage but can also lead to divisions and tensions within multiethnic states.

> Ethnocentrism is seeing one's own ethnic heritage as superior and judging other cultures based on one's own cultural standards. Racism as an ideology extends these supposed differences based on skin color or other physical markers. Even societies that have relatively low levels of racial

and ethnic tension often have positions of privilege dominated by certain racial or ethnic groups.
- Tribal and local religions have been a part of humanity for millennia but in many places are giving way to faiths with adherents around the globe. Significant growth has been evident in Christianity and Islam.
- Religious belief has been used to divide and attack groups, and also to encourage forgiveness and understanding. Recent decades have seen a revival of religious fundamentalism in evangelical Christianity, conservative Islam, Orthodox Judaism, and nationalistic Hinduism. In some places this has led to growing tensions between groups.
- Religious and ethnic groups who feel threatened by national or international powers have at times turned to extremism and terrorism to advance their cause. Trouble spots in the world often become caught in cycles of revenge, or spirals of terrorism and repression.
- Some leaders have used spiritual and moral convictions, along with traditions and ethnic heritage, as ways of promoting nonviolent cultural revival and humanitarian service.

For Review and Discussion

1. Why have religion and ethnicity so often been rallying points for conflict? What is needed to promote understanding between racial, ethnic, and religious groups?
2. Terrorism has been described as "the weapon of the weak." In what ways is terrorism powerful? In what ways is it weak or ineffectual?
3. One danger of harsh crackdowns on groups associated with terrorism is that repression may lead to new resentments and further violence. Is there a way out of this cycle? Can societies keep people safe and still promote reconciliation between groups?

Making Connections

International Day for Tolerance
- In 1996, the UN General Assembly declared November 16 as the International Day for Tolerance. Each year activities are planned around this commemoration. For recent activities and priorities, see https://en.unesco.org/commemorations/toleranceday. What are the current priorities?

Pew Research Center

▶ The Pew Research Center presents a wide range of data on the world's religious landscape, including fastest growing religions and shifts in religious affiliation. See https://www.pewforum.org/2017/04/05/the-changing-global-religious-landscape/. Are there trends in world religious affiliation that you find striking or surprising? Pew also lists information on religious affiliation in the United States, see https://www.pewforum.org/religious-landscape-study/. On the national map, could can select any state and look at affiliations in the state. What groups are well represented in your area? Which are a small minority?

Religious Tolerance

▶ A Canadian site at www.religioustolerance.org offers a wealth of information on world religions, with good treatment of Islam and Asian religions as well as atheism, agnosticism, and new religions. Posted by a religiously diverse group, it provides balanced coverage that does not promote any one perspective, except for the importance of tolerance.

Making A Difference

World Council of Churches

▶ The World Council of Churches, an international affiliation of Christian groups, at https://www.oikoumene.org/ seeks to "inspire the worldwide fellowship of churches to work together for unity, justice, and peace." Themes include the disarmament, economic justice, gender justice, and health, but their focus changes with time and relevance. The site also contains links to information about churches around the world. How do various traditions approach the theme of nonviolence? Are there ways that local groups and places of worship are becoming involved?

Plum Village

▶ Vietnamese Zen Buddhist monk Thich Nhat Hanh (1926–) has worked for peace and reconciliation based on the principles of Buddhism for half a century. He first worked for peace during the Vietnam War and since that time has continued his efforts in exile in France at a site called Plum Village. Dr. Martin Luther King, Jr., nominated him for the Nobel Peace Prize. Information about his work, about the Unified Buddhist Church, and ongoing efforts for interpersonal and global peace can be found at www.plumvillage.org. What are some of the current emphases at his center? How does it draw on both Buddhist and Christian traditions?

Tibet

► The world's most prominent Buddhist leader is the 14th Dalai Lama of Tibet, who received the Nobel Peace Prize for his work for nonviolent solutions in Chinese-occupied Tibet. His ideas and work are featured at www.dalailama.com. More information on peaceful attempts to preserve the cultural and religious heritage of Tibet can be found at www.tibet.com, the official site of the Tibetan government in exile.

PART THREE

Seeking a Sustainable World
Environmental Issues

9   Urbanization: Cities without Limits

10 Population and Health: Only the Poor Die Young

11 Technology and Energy: Prometheus's Fire or Pandora's Box?

12 Ecology: How Much Can One Planet Take?

Sustainable development is development that meets the needs of the present without compromising the ability of future generations to meet their own needs.

—Brundtland Commission of the United Nations, 1987

It seems that in a matter of a few years, sustainability has moved from academic concept to buzzword of our age. Conferences, meetings, even fairs and festivals now tout "going green," being sustainable, and caring for the environment. The truth is we have become alarmed. Most of the ideas, and truly most of the warnings, go back decades. But for the first time, we are actually seeing the very fabric of our global home being altered by global climate change. With every new natural disaster, one is inclined to wonder: Is this just a freak occurrence or one more bit of nature's revenge?

Sustainability is about meeting our current needs and, more than that, living a good life. And it is about leaving our planetary home in good enough condition that future generations will also be able to meet their needs, and hopefully also live good and rewarding lives.

For too long, issues of human need and issues of the environment have been kept separate. This is a false division. People who are affluent enough not to have to worry about their next meal can worry about polar bears and redwoods. The poor just worry about their families. Yet no one suffers more from global environmental degradation than do the poor. And we are realizing that our fate is bound up not only with one other but also with the fate of life itself. If global climate change accelerates, both the polar bears of the arctic and the 150 million people of Bangladesh will be swimming for their lives. In this section, we will look at both the human-built environment and the natural environment, and the close relation between the two.

Chapter 9 begins this section with a look at the great human migration to cities. For the first time in human history or prehistory, cities will be where most of us live our lives, and they offer both great opportunities and great peril to our well-being.

The push into cities is driven by global population growth and the attempt to live a good and healthy life. Chapter 10 explores what is happening with global population shifts, which are intimately bound up with the factors of our births, health, and eventual, or untimely, deaths. Health and health care are very much problems of inequality. But increasingly they are also interwoven with the state of our environment: what we eat, drink, and breathe.

There is no way to examine our changing world and our prospects for the future without considering technology. People have always been toolmakers, but many of their inventions served for centuries or more. Now, it seems, last year's hottest inventions are obsolete by this year. The pace of change is staggering. My favorite corollary to Murphy's Law is, "if you understand it, it's obsolete." This has tremendous social as well as economic and environmental impacts. Since the beginnings of the industrial age, however, our inventions have tended to have one thing in common: They use stored energy, often lots of it. In chapter 11 we discuss that energy is not inexhaustible and we are now facing the resulting costs: new competition for scarce resources and new environmental dangers as we search ever harder to feed our energy appetite. The twenty-first century will no doubt be a century of great inventions, but unlike the last several, it may have to be a century of inventions that use less, not more, energy.

Cities, technology, and human society itself are still part of the ecology of life on the earth. The final chapter looks at food, water, land, and the earth's ecosystems. Will they sustain a good life for all, or collapse under mounting pressures? Sustainability is about the global present, the state of the world, and also about our global future: The kind of world that the youth will inherit and what they will pass on to generations to come.

9

Urbanization

Cities without Limits

Global Encounters

China

A handful of harbors in the world have a special power to stir the imagination. New York has spires and that statue, San Francisco has the hills and that bridge, Sidney has a signature opera house, all reflected in blue deepwater ports. In many ways, Hong Kong can match all these. We emerge out of morning mists and haze to towering hills and to ever-taller buildings that seem to challenge the mountains for dominance. One hillside is covered in ancestral tombs; this is a gateway to a land with a long ancestry. But everywhere in Hong Kong, what is in your face is the new. Great suspension bridges connect the islands. Towers boast postmodern curves and spires. A convention center with a Sydney

Opera House–like roof juts into the harbor on reclaimed land. Other reclaimed land is being prepared for what will purportedly be the next claimant to the title of the world's tallest building. Escalators lift people to higher neighborhoods while a great cable tram pulls them to the top of Victoria Peak. At night, the great towers put on a light show of changing colors and dancing lasers that glow over the port waters in a setting that seems poised for a science fiction movie. Hong Kong has come a long way in the less than the 200 years it has served as the meeting point of what we have learned to call East and West.

In the midst of all these structures is a great press of humanity, a higher population density than anywhere else on earth. People working, going to work, coming from work. And there is always shopping. Our ship's ramp drops at a berth that directly connects us to the Ocean Terminal Mall. Beyond this are high-rise malls and specialty malls. It is hard to get from one mall to another only because the streets are filled with myriad markets. If the name brands are too pricey in the malls—and Hong Kong is no bargain—one can select from a half-dozen knockoffs in the street stalls. Riding up the cable car lifts one from the street frenzy into a world of green. But it is no escape from shopping. At the top of Victoria Peak is another great mall, towering over the city, and offering "retail therapy." There is no escape. We are immersed in the Great Mall of China.

Since 1997 Hong Kong has placed SAR after its name. This stands for Special Administrative Region. After more than 150 years as a British colony, it reverted back to China. China, for its part, agreed to a plan of "one country, two systems" for at least 50 years. Hong Kong will be part of China, but a unique part, with its own economic and political systems. Right before the transition, elections were held for the regional government to ensure a precedent of democracy. Not everyone believed the assurances, and many left for Canada, Australia, and California. Some are still leaving Hong Kong, replaced by mainland Chinese eager to enter. But most are watching and waiting. Opinions still differ. Our one Chinese international student speaks of how happy everyone is over the "glorious" reunification after so many years. Our Hong Kong interport students are not so sure. Certainly in walking the fashion-conscious streets or in reading the local English-language papers, there is no absence of capitalism and a fair measure of openness. The university students who guide my field practica repeat a local quip: Here we have freedom without democracy. At least without national-level democracy, and it is, however, not clear just how much regional autonomy Hong Kong will be allowed to keep.

For now, Hong Kong has more immediate problems with which to concern itself, such as housing. Almost half the city lives in public housing. Much of the new private housing would look fine along Chicago's Gold Coast, but Hong Kong is also a place of back streets crammed with deteriorating apartments. The city's residents are also worried about competition. Not exactly foreign competition, since their main competitor is China. People in Hong Kong are making less all the time, as the city depends on managing the enormous production of the Pearl River Delta. All those "Made in China" tags on our clothes and toys rarely say where in China. Some are made in Shanghai in booming special economic zones, some in newer industrial parks around Beijing, but a huge amount is made in the special economic zones just over the border from Hong Kong.

And it is still a border. As I travel to the mainland, the train stops at the border of Hong Kong's New Territories. I fill out immigration forms and make my way through customs. Residents from both sides of this divide do the same. I can then board another train to travel upriver. The city outside is Shenzhen. Until recently, just a small border village, it is now a city of several million. This is not charming China, but a city of bland apartments to hold the workers who pour in from all over the country to work in the export processing plants. Fittingly, a huge lighted "Walmart" sign glows from the top of the tallest. The train rumbles through a bit of remaining countryside with ponds and ducks and older housing, but all are shadowed by new buildings. Industrial cities line the Pearl River just as they lined the St. Joseph a century ago, but magnified a hundredfold.

I get off in Guangzhou, the place Westerners knew for many years as Canton. In the midst of the Pearl River is an island filled with European colonial architecture. In the 1800s everyone had a piece of this place: the French, the British, the Germans, the Swedes, and the Americans were all here, each claiming a trading "concession." The hated concessions are long gone and the buildings are museums, but the French, British, Germans, Swedes, and Americans are back, along with the Japanese, Australians, Canadians, and anyone else looking for inexpensive manufacturing. They all seem to gather in the opulence of the White Swan Hotel, congregating and greeting their far better-dressed Chinese hosts.

Once off the island, one sees few Westerners at all. Accompanied by a Chinese friend, I move through the back streets of Guangzhou, towering over the traditionally small-statured southern Chinese like the jolly gringo giant. But the place is changing. Migrants are moving in from all over the country into this city of eight million and counting. I am repeatedly warned to guard my handful of belongings because petty crime has skyrocketed. Apparently not everyone finds the work they originally seek. Tensions are strongest with the Muslim ethnic minorities coming in from the remotest corners of western China. The food is still gloriously Cantonese, as is much of the language, but more Mandarin is now heard everywhere among newcomers.

My host is a lover of old towns, and she takes me to back alleys where the elderly still battle one another over fast-paced games of mah-jongg and Chinese chess. These neighborhoods seem safer than the main streets, not nearly so much to steal. But they are disappearing fast amid a building boom to accommodate more newcomers in tall towers. Some have described the rural-to-urban rush in China as the largest mass migration in human history.

India

I plunge into the heart of the city of Chennai (formerly Madras) to take a group of students on a field practicum on gender and poverty. We board a great magenta Volvo bus to bully our way through the chaotic and choked streets of Chennai. For the speed of our progress we could have walked, had there been anywhere to walk, but we finally reach a conference center. After thoughtful but somewhat predictable lectures by two prominent women, a local government official and a lawyer, we continue on to what everyone just calls the "slums area," the Nampet Choolaimedu, an old brick-making pocket in the city. Our guide gets on the bus; Mrs. Kumari is a cheerful woman who I later learn is the housekeeper of the entrepreneurial older woman, a local university professor, who organized the trip. We step off the magenta bus and fall off the map, at least off the city map. In this labyrinth of ancient brick and thatch live 10,000 families.

How does one approach a place like this on a "tour"? And we did have to have the reddish-purple bus? I'm glad to see students hesitating with their cameras as I do with mine. Crime is not the issue here, but cross-cultural conflict is. A busload of camera-toting foreigners on a brief "slum tour" can seem more like a mass drive-by shooting than any real academic or interpersonal engagement. These cameras are expensive. Some look ready to fix their bayonet-mount lenses and charge. We hesitate, put the cameras into totes, and hear the warning to stay close to Mrs. Kumari.

The dirt paths with broken bits of block that separate the buildings—one can't call them streets—are so narrow that we have to move single file. On both sides are buildings of red brick and thick pasty mortar, with roofs of matted thatch or occasional corrugated fiberglass. Windows are metal screens covered in cloth, or simply openings cut into block and brick. Residents greet us from mats on door fronts, and children start to gather and run ahead. We are invited to duck, and ducking is necessary, into some of the homes, feeling the embarrassment of intrusion. But at Mrs. Kumari's insistence, we duck into dark one-room dwellings, with a few mats on the floor. A few rough-cut boards serve as shelves for a few clothes and a pot or two. Such a place will house a family of four, five, or more, with attached dwellings holding the extended family. We are far enough along in our travels that students don't react with shock. We have been through the favelas of Brazil and the townships of South Africa, and there is a certain sameness to urban poverty. The décor only changes a bit: in Brazil, photos of Jesus shared the wall with West African deities; here Jesus and Shiva, St. Thomas and Vishnu often share the wall. Even the good-luck charms of sticks and shells that hang over the doorways are similar.

This is a place of hope and change as well as despair. South Africa is making a national effort to replace the worst of the shanties. Here in India, the efforts are often done state by state. In the north of the country, places like Calcutta may have as much as 75 percent of the population in slums, what northerners call bustees. Another 10 percent may be less fortunate, living life on the streets in what has been dubbed the City of Pavement Dwellers. Here in southern India the prospects are better. New capitalist fervor is bringing technology and jobs, while an old socialist heritage compels each local and state government to renew the commitment to housing. A government program is replacing the thatched roofs with corrugated fiberglass. There is electricity, although provided on such thin wires they don't seem like they could support much demand. Water is provided daily by truck to fill a large black cistern from which residents draw their household needs. And gradually the old one-room houses themselves are being replaced by two- and three-story apartment buildings, and residents can purchase an apartment on a 20-year mortgage with no down payment.

We cram shoulder to shoulder between the rows of houses and lines of laundry, talking about the improvements. I move the student next to me off a large flat stone. It is not a doormat but a place to grind flour. Gradually the cameras come out. As soon as they do, the children gather. There seems to be a transnational affinity between children and cameras. Just as in Latin America and South Africa, they queue up in formation and insist on having their pictures taken. Then they eagerly look at the result in the digital screen. I oblige, thinking what a strange global family photo album I am creating place by place. It might make an interesting oversize book, the kind that Barnes & Noble sells on discount at the front door: Children of the World's Slums. Smiling kids in old T-shirts, almost always with dark complexions, some holding dogs, others with chickens in their hands, most with arms around friends and siblings. Note the backdrop of tin, plastic, thatch, concrete, and handmade brick, and try to guess the location.

Maybe location doesn't matter, for these places line the back alleys of each of our global villages. One student, himself from a poor background, replied that rather than feeling guilty for not doing more here, we should be shamed by how many similar places there are back home, where we can do a great deal. Time to put away the cameras and return to our shipboard home. Perhaps future groups will be armed with miniature printers to leave copies of the pictures behind with the children. If only we could promise to return with the tools to help them build a secure and hopeful future.

The Urban Millennium: Worldwide Urbanization

Somewhere around the beginning of this, the third millennium (for those who follow the Western calendar), something momentous happened that will continue to reshape our times, regardless of the calendar we use. Unlike the new millennium itself, the event wasn't celebrated with fireworks. It was noted mostly by demographers, who are not known to be an overly boisterous bunch.

What happened? We became an urban world. Just over half of the world's population now lives in cities and urban areas.

Dawn of the City

In one sense, this was a long time coming. The first cities emerged around the dawn of agriculture, sometime well before the dawn of the third millennium BCE. We have many accounts of the founding of the early cities, but they are all shrouded in legend: Romulus and Remus being raised by wolves before founding Rome, Gilgamesh descending from the gods to rule Uruk, and so forth.

Probably the first cities were at key points on trade routes, maybe walled and fortified to protect the traders and their goods. The walls of Jericho, one of the world's first cities between 8000 and 5000 BCE, are most famous for falling down, but they must have been an imposing feature on the desert crossroads. Villages had already been around for several thousand years and were growing larger, but the first cities offered a social complexity that was new to the world. Cities were not only centers of trade. Some also became centers of religious observance, and some served as the homes of rulers who could commandeer the surpluses of surrounding fields of grain to support themselves and ruling elites along with religious leaders, craftspersons, and eventually soldiers to secure it all.

The early cities emerged by 3500 BCE throughout the Middle East: in Asia Minor (modern Turkey), all throughout Mesopotamia, and at several points along the Nile River. Somewhat later, great cities emerged along the Indus River, and along the great rivers of China by 2500 BCE. In time, well-watered valleys and lush lowlands in what are now Mexico and Peru would also see the building of great, complex, fortified cities between 500 BCE and 1500 CE.

With cities came civilization. The earliest cities of the Sumerians in southern Mesopotamia, with strange names such as Ur and Uruk, are still being excavated from the sands and the swamps to reveal complex urban networks. It is always dangerous to accord "firsts" to anyone, for history has had many cradles of civilization in many places, but between 4000 and 2000 BCE, this was the land of firsts. The Sumerians were some of the first people to use the wheel, to bake bread, and to keep track of it all in writing. The oldest writing samples we have are not great religious texts but something like accounting ledgers stamped on clay. Cities collect an abundance of goods, and someone has to keep track of it all.

Cities have also always provoked considerable ambivalence in people. The book of Genesis in the Bible gives credit for the first city to the murderous Cain and notes how Abraham, the father of Western religion, left the city of Ur and lived in the desert, where he could see the stars and be close to God. His nephew made the bad choice of going to the city, none other than Sodom, whose name has become synonymous with depravity and evil.

Even older than the account of Abraham is the ancient Sumerian (and later Babylonian) story of King Gilgamesh, who ruled Uruk. He was a mighty ruler, descended from the gods, but he also grew to be a tyrant and a slave driver. The people were crushed under his demands for higher walls and bigger monuments. Finally, the gods sent someone to be his friend, one equally strong but wild man who talked to the animals and understood the forest and the desert. To his shame, Enkidu was won over to the attractions of the city (in most accounts, women and baking have something to do with it), but he remained in touch with the wild. Only when Gilgamesh had his friend Enkidu, the wild man, was he whole and humane. It seems that the inhabitants of the earliest cities, telling and later writing one of the world's first epic stories, already sensed that life in a mighty city came at a great price.

Triumph of the City

Ambivalent or not, great civilizations were dominated by great cities. In the Indus Valley of India, by 2500 BCE, cities were laid out on careful grid patterns, much like Midwestern U.S. cities today. And they included an important innovation that would not appear in many European cities until industrial times: indoor toilets that fed into covered sewage systems. In China, for thousands of years following about 2000 BCE, powerful emperors built ever-grander cities around the area of the current city of Beijing, protected by ever-longer networks of walls and dominated by ever-grander imperial palaces. In Mesoamerica, near present-day Mexico City, the great city of Teotihuacán grew up around the obsidian trade and dominated a vast region about the same time as the rise of Rome, before likewise collapsing and falling to northern "barbarian invaders" around 750 CE, several centuries after the fall of Rome.

Rome stands as the ultimate city of the ancient world, with a population of between one and 1.5 million people at its height. It was the city of great public works, a huge aqueduct bringing fresh water, "circuses" ranging from gladiatorial games to chariot races to great mock sea battles fought in the flooded colosseum, a center of a trade network that stretched all the way to China along the Silk Road, and the power center of a mighty empire. Rome was the queen city of the Mediterranean world. It was also a city of beggars and thieves, a city dependent on slaves and on regular shipments of grain from abroad to feed its masses, a city prone to unrest and civil strife, and a place whose crowded neighborhoods were rank with filth. These themes continue to be present in ambivalent and contrasting views of the modern city: as the "pearl" of the region or the exploiter of the region, as the place of noble pursuits or the place of depraved pursuits. Cities have been the centers of great flourishes of thought and culture.

The Golden Age of Athens lasted less than 50 years in the middle of the fifth century BCE between two devastating wars, but for several centuries, the city was the home of great art, science, and philosophy. Aristotle, one of the most famous of the hometown philosophers and scholars, claimed in the *Politics* that one comes to the city to live and stays to live well. Living well may have been more difficult for the Athenian women cloistered in their homes, for the slaves laboring long hours to support a leisure class, and for the inhabitants of lesser cities forced to pay tribute to Athens at the height of its power. Regardless, this one city produced incredible insights into everything from democracy to astronomy to natural history to health care.

In terms of learning, the only rival to Athens was Alexandria, founded by Alexander the Great, on the Egyptian coast. A vast library held books (in scroll form) in many languages from around the world. Moreover, scholars from many places and ethnicities who worked in the library and museum measured the circumference of the earth (Eratosthenes, 276–194 BCE), conducted advanced mathematics (Hypatia, ca. 370–415 CE), and both collected and advanced learning from around the Mediterranean and across the Middle East.

While the European cities fell into decline, cities such as Baghdad flourished with the wealth of the empire and carried on the studies of astronomy, mathematics, and philosophy that had begun in the Greek-speaking cities. The European Renaissance was also centered in great (though by our standards, small) cities. Renaissance Florence may have had no more than 70,000 people, but among them were Michelangelo, da Vinci, Giberti, and scores of artists, writers, and scholars.

One of the most striking features of medieval cities was their compact size. Houses were crowded along tangled, narrow streets. If an original wall still stands, it often encloses a city not much larger than a modest modern neighborhood. For centuries the only city of any significant size in Europe was Constantinople, the capital of the Eastern Roman and Byzantine Empires, on Europe's eastern edge. Gradually, beginning in the 1500s, growing empires brought growing cities: Seville in Spain, Lisbon in Portugal, Amsterdam in the Netherlands, and eventually London in England. As the British Empire grew, so did the importance and size of London. The matriarch of a global empire, London, stood as perhaps the first truly global world city.

In the preindustrial world, often only the center of a great empire would grow to substantial size as a center of trade and government power. Cities rose and fell with the fortunes of their empires—or collapsed under the whims of changing climates, shifting water courses, and shifting political winds. Only three cities stood as the world's largest for a full three centuries each. All roads, and shipping routes, led to Rome at the height of the Roman Empire; Bagdad at the height of the Abbasid caliphate was a crossroads of learning and culture that brought together the learning, and mathematics, of ancient Greece with that of India; and Beijing, envisioned by Kublai Khan, flourished during the heart of the Ming dynasty as center to a vast Chinese realm of influence.

Industrialization changed the face of the cities. The first factories were clustered along scattered sites of waterpower, but eventually, cities built on coal power clustered around rail and shipyards. In the eighteenth century, London, as well as Liverpool and Manchester, became a city of industrial might and also of soot and ever-present smoke billowing from "dark satanic mills." In the United States, cities of mills such as Brooklyn, Yonkers, Hoboken, and Newark grew up around the port of Manhattan. Other major cities also took root around industrial might: Baltimore, Pittsburgh, and Chicago. It was the incredible influx of people from Europe (many of whom were displaced farmers whose own countries could not supply enough jobs) in the late nineteenth and early twentieth centuries, however, that eventually made New York the world's largest city.

In the later years of the twentieth century, New York was overtaken by another great industrial city—Tokyo, Japan—and soon by many others. The rush to the cities had begun. Great world cities of over five million people now dominate every continent, some having doubled in the course of a decade.

World Cities

The pace of global urbanization is staggering. In 1950 the world had one city with over 10 million people: New York. In 1995 it had 14. By 2021, 32 cities surpassed 10 million people. The largest are concentrated in Asia and Latin America (see table 9.1). Almost all of the on-going urbanization boom is in the developing world with major African capitals now joining the list.

In 1950 New York's competition was largely limited to the great capitals of Europe: London, Paris, Moscow, and the industrial heartland of Germany. By the turn of the twenty-first century, none of the five largest cities in the world were European: Tokyo, Mexico City, São Paulo, New York, and Mumbai (Bombay). The great Asian centers are slowly being displaced from the top 10 by burgeoning African cities: Cairo, Egypt; Lagos, Nigeria; Kinshasa, Congo (DRC); and Addis Ababa, Ethiopia. Such megacities will face enormous challenges to provide housing, education, transportation, water, and, in particular, stable jobs.

Table 9.1 Ten Most Populated Cities in the World, 2021

Rank	Name	Country	2021 Population
1	Tokyo	Japan	37,339,804
2	Delhi	India	31,181,376
3	Shanghai	China	27,795,702
4	Sao Paulo	Brazil	22,237,472
5	Mexico City	Mexico	21,918,936
6	Dhaka	Bangladesh	21,741,090
7	Cairo	Egypt	21,322,750
8	Beijing	China	20,896,820
9	Mumbai	India	20,667,656
10	Osaka	Japan	19,110,616

Source: Data from World Population Review

The cities in Europe and North America continue to grow by means of international **immigration.** A few U.S. cities are now growing explosively due to **internal migration,** such as the Phoenix area and Las Vegas, Nevada, which grew 83 percent in the 1990s, springing from the desert thanks to the "circuses" of the gaming and entertainment industry and air conditioning. The real growth, however, will be in the "sun belt" of the developing world—the Global South. Europe, North America, and Latin America are all already at least two-thirds urban, with many countries, including places such as Chile and Argentina, having urbanization levels above 75 percent. Two-thirds rural just a decade or two ago, many African and Asian nations are now majority urban (see Figure 9.1).

Who is urban and who is rural hinges on debatable criteria, such as the number of communities over 20,000. Many rural people are already dependent on neighboring cities, and in India and China, villages can run together in great agglomerations of population. But a city is distinct from a mere agglomeration of people. It has a complexity and interconnectedness of its own. The exact size of a city depends on who gets counted and who does not (such as people who are displaced or homeless or illegal "squatters"). It also depends on how one figures the extent of a metropolitan region. For example, based on the incorporated city itself, Houston is by far the largest city in Texas, but Dallas–Fort Worth is the largest combined metropolitan area.

The next generation of world cities will be a dizzying array of newborn giants. What do you know about Chongqing and Jinan? Unless you are from China or you study or do business in East Asia, these could be kinds of soup,

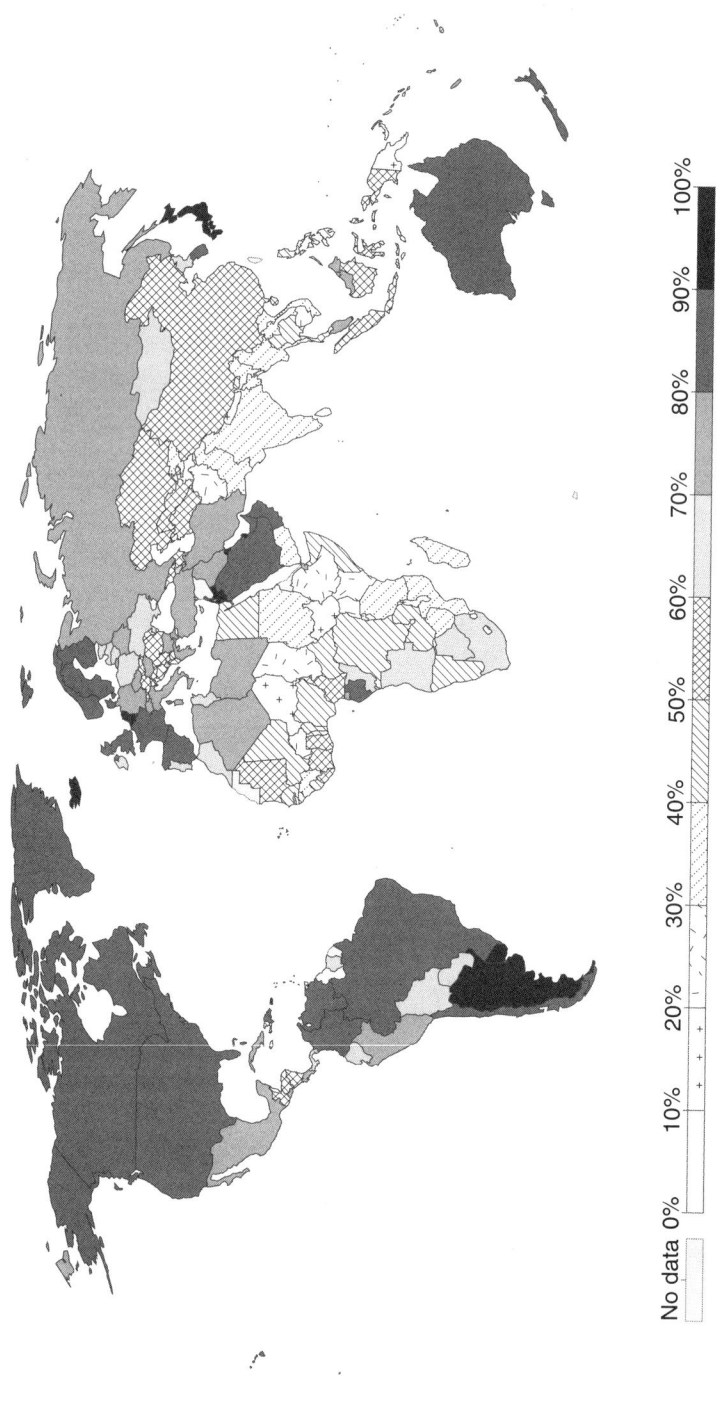

Figure 9.1 Share of people living in urban areas, 2017. (Source: Our World in Data.) To see this movement over time, see https://ourworldindata.org/urbanization.

for all you know. They are, in fact, Chinese cities of growing industrial might, each with over seven million people. They are each the size of greater London or Chicago.

Megacities

Who are the actors in this global drama of urban life? Read on for a brief tour of a few of the world's current **megacities.**

Tokyo. Following World War II, Tokyo, the ancient Japanese city of Edo, was a charred husk. It did, however, command a magnificent natural bay on a crowded, mountainous island. As Japan rapidly urbanized, Tokyo grew to become the world's most populous city and is likely to remain so well into this century. It is also one of the most crowded and one of the most expensive cities. The land around the imperial palace in Tokyo is worth more than that of all real estate of some entire countries. Rents are exorbitant, and buying a house is often an unattainable goal.

Yet for decades jobs were plentiful, wages rose to some of the highest in the world, and Tokyo grew to be one of the world's premier commercial and financial centers. Only New York has more major banks and corporate headquarters. The price of this success has been intense air and water pollution and constant crowds. Tokyo's clean, efficient, and profitable subway system is so popular that the operators have had to hire "pushers" to pack everyone (politely, of course) onto the trains before they continue on a rush-hour commute that seems to have no end. Almost anything from anywhere can be purchased in Tokyo, even air to breathe. Commuters who are feeling faint amid the fumes and crowds of the city can stop and buy a few breaths of pure oxygen to revive their energies and carry them home.

Tokyo can intimidate someone who is unprepared, yet it is also a vibrant, bustling, and hugely productive city. Whether it can maintain its premier role, as Japan suffers a recession and confronts new competitors, remains to be seen. In the meantime, people cram onto the trains to work 12-hour days and dream about visiting a Zen garden in Kyoto to meditate and restore their calm.

New York. For several decades the world's largest city, New York is the only U.S. city likely to remain among the world's "big ten." It is really a vast urban agglomeration that spans several states. Where the New York metropolitan area ends is hard to say, but the core has always been the island of Manhattan. The city grew as a port, with rail lines from Hoboken, New Jersey, and before that the Erie Canal upstate, carrying people and goods inland. The city awed the world from the 1880s on with ever-taller buildings, new and amazing bridges, and growing financial might.

Between 1880 and 1920, 20 million people came through New York's gate of entry at Ellis Island, past the Statue of Liberty (a gift from France in 1884) with its promises to the poor of the world and into a city of incredible diversity, boasting hundreds of languages. Some went on, but many stayed. Two-fifths of the U.S. population has ancestors who came through this one portal.

Industry spilled over to the manufacturing and shipbuilding of Brooklyn, one of several cities later incorporated into New York, while chemicals and railways went to neighboring New Jersey. Manhattan itself flourished in finance, commerce, and culture, from the theater dominance of Broadway to the Harlem Renaissance of African Americans in the 1920s. Manhattan's financial power became concentrated on Wall Street and began at the same time as did urban decay in Harlem. The skyscrapers still soar on Manhattan's south end and in Midtown, where high property values and solid bedrock allow them. The spaces in between still fill with newcomers in Chinatown and in Harlem, which is experiencing something of a renewed renaissance. Vitality has returned to Times Square, shoppers still crowd Fifth Avenue, and art and culture still flourish on Broadway and throughout Greenwich Village and SoHo.

Many newcomers, however, now prefer to bypass this crowded core and find their dreams somewhere farther out in the metropolitan sprawl. The Flushing area of Queens, home to the 1965 World's Fair, is still a world's fair of newcomers and people from dozens of nationalities and ethnicities. Indian temples crowd near Ethiopian cafes and Chinese markets. New York remains a slice of the world.

It is also a city that intimidates and frightens. The city of dreams is also known as a city of crime and despair, of endless hurry, and of a certain harsh, even ruthless character. As far back as 1916, an anonymous poem, "While the City Sleeps," captured these images:

> Stand in your window and scan the sights,
> On Broadway with its bright white lights.
> Its dashing cabs and cabarets,
> Its painted women and fast cafes.
> That's when you really see New York.
> Vulgar of manner, overfed,
> Overdressed and underbred.
> Heartless and Godless, Hell's delight,
> Rude by day and lewd by night.

Of course, this image may have attracted the curious even as it repelled the cautious. Yet even the more contemporary Pico Iyer (1997), the British Indian globe-trotting writer who lives in Tokyo, wonders about New York:

> The lighting is harsh, the contrasts are stark, and the effects are as loud as the tabloid headline in your face. When I think of New York, I think of people with an unearthly pallor, dressed all in black; of black jackets and white ties; black limos and white lies. (p. 80)

In spite of this, New York remains a magnet for capital and for people from around the world who are sure, to paraphrase the words of the song "New York, New York," that success in New York can translate into success anywhere.

Mexico City. The middle of Mexico is no place to put a city. The Aztecs were said to have been led here by an ancient prophecy, but they may have been driven here by hostile neighbors. They ended up on a snake-infested island in a large, shallow lake. The lake has all but dried up, leaving Mexico City as one of the few great cities that is nowhere near a major body of water, unless one counts the water below the surface. It is essentially a city on a high-altitude swamp. Yet here the Aztecs expanded the work of their predecessors to create a city that awed the Spanish conquistadors in 1519, who followed Cortés over the pass between the two volcanoes that pierce the skyline. As reported by Bernal Díaz del Castillo (1963 [1568]):

> And when we saw all those cities and villages built in the water, and other great towns on dry land, and that straight and level causeway leading to Mexico, we were astounded. . . . It was all so wonderful that I do not know how to describe this first glimpse of things never heard of, seen or dreamed of before.

Over time, the lake was filled in, paved over, and pumped dry. But the city continued to flourish. In the early 1800s, Robert Southey could still write, "Queen of the Valley! Thou art beautiful! Thy walls, like silver, sparkle in the sun" (2004 [1805]). For generations, canals sliced through this city (a few remain in the heavily touristed gardens of Xochimilco), giving Mexico City the name of Venice of the New World. The title is as appropriate as ever but not in the original sense. Venice, that medieval city of great canals, is sinking into the ocean. Mexico City is also sinking—a full two stories in the last century—because water is pumped out of the underground aquifer upon which the city was built in an attempt to satiate the thirst of a city of 20 million people.

Mexico City is not a city of skyscrapers. They would sink into the ancient lake and crumble under earthquakes. Mexico City has reason to fear earthquakes, as an unstable lake bed is about the worst place to be in a quake. A 1985 temblor brought terrible devastation. A couple of tall buildings in the city have been built on giant rollers that will rock and roll through an earthquake, a technique now being tried in Japan. With so many people and so much danger in building up, the city sprawls in a great concrete sea that seems to go on for as far as the eye can see. The city now fills the ancient valley and spills over into neighboring plateaus; it climbs up steep mountainsides in communities that cannot be reached by urban services. One of its neighboring cities (one cannot really call this a suburb) is one of the largest cities in Mexico. Built on the flats of the dry lake bed, Netzahaucoyotl (named for an Amerindian poet, diplomat, and king) claims three million people in a vast holding tank of the working poor.

This huge expanse of city has one of the most extensive and least expensive subway systems in the world. But even this system cannot effectively span the sprawl, so urban fringe dwellers ride minibuses that connect to bigger buses or eventually to the subway in multihour commutes over huge distances. The more prosperous people drive along avenues packed in daylong gridlock and contribute to the area's terrible smog. This high-altitude, mountain-ringed environment has some of the worst air in the world. A brown haze with the taste of old tobacco hangs over the city much of the winter, obscuring the view of the great volcanoes. One of those volcanoes continues to smoke itself, maybe in solidarity with the city, and adds to the natural threat.

Market reforms and globalization have brought new industry and commercial activity to the corridors that spill out of this city into the neighboring states. These forces have also widened the gap between rich and poor urban dwellers, and the crime rate continues to rise. The city's streets are threaded by old Volkswagen taxis with the front seats removed to allow passengers to squeeze into the back. Although this seems ingenious, visitors are warned against entering unknown taxis, some of which trap them for a robbery, rather than whisking them to their destination.

A city of poverty, crime, smog, natural hazards, and unsightly sprawl would seem to be a place to flee from, rather than a magnet for much of the country. It is true that Mexico City is also a fabulous collage of varied neighborhoods, great restaurants, and world-class museums and cultural events. But what draws residents is the promise of work. Increasingly, that promise is going unfulfilled, which is why Mexico City will probably never be the world's largest city, as once predicted. The displaced continue further on, to the exploding cities on Mexico's northern border and to bigger promises in the country that lies just beyond.

São Paulo. The quintessential Brazilian city may be Rio de Janeiro, where the mountains meet the beach and the rich and the poor live crammed between them. The capital of Brazil now lies in the interior in the planned city of Brasilia, neatly carved from the forest. But the economic dynamo of Brazil, well on its way to being one of the world's largest cities, is São Paulo. The industry and business in this hardworking city, from computers to automobiles to entertainment, generate much of Brazil's wealth and employ its most prosperous citizens. But the seemingly endless forest of high-rises gives way to equally endless slums. The city that is the biggest producer and consumer in all of Latin America is also a city in which two-thirds of the residents are poor.

The poor and the middle class have one thing in common, however: Neither can get anywhere fast in this traffic-choked city. Only the rich, who can afford one of the many helicopter shuttle services, can whisk over the gridlock and the carjackers to get to their board meetings. São Paulo is New York with the heat turned up—a city whose power is obvious but whose charm resides in patient and determined, hopeful and creative residents.

Shanghai. Long China's most outward-looking city, Shanghai is now also China's largest, a vast commercial center whose ties often seem closer to Taipei, Hamburg, and New York than Beijing. The northern Chinese may look on Shanghai with suspicion: too greedy, too capitalist, and too foreign. Yet the residents of Shanghai are proud of their city's place as a center of Asian commerce, a hip yet hardworking cosmopolitan dynamo. Every day, the city pulses with the pedals of millions of bicycles as its residents commute to work. On weekends, the parks are filled with one-child families, enjoying a brief time off.

The future of Shanghai remains uncertain, however. How large can it grow? What will happen to this city of bicycles, as ever more of its citizens can now own automobiles? Will they speed its growth or choke it?

Mumbai (Bombay). When Westerners picture a large Indian city, they often imagine the nuns of Mother Teresa's order, pulling the diseased and the derelict from the gutters to die in peace. That is one face of India, but Indian cities are not dying in peace. India is huge, more populous than all countries of Africa combined. It has been a largely rural, village-based society, but the rush to the city is on. Calcutta, also largely a British colonial creation, continues to grow. Delhi—the old Delhi that long ruled India and the New Delhi that is now its capital—dominates the north and will soon be one of the biggest metropolises in the world.

But India's most dynamic city may be Mumbai, on the coast that faces the Arabian Sea. It is an economic giant with a global reach. Call a "help" line about your computer, and you may get a young man in Mumbai who speaks crisp English and has a complete command of Microsoft Windows and the problems of gigabyte hard drives. Everything in India comes in numbers that boggle the mind. There are more poor people in this one city than in most countries. There are also more software engineers in this city than in any city in the United States.

Lagos. This is another site that wasn't meant to be a city. The name Lagos means "lagoon," and the city is built on three low-lying islands, coupled with a sprawl to the interior, and only a handful of bridges to connect the tangled masses of millions of people. This congested bit of coast, chosen by the British navy, is at least as unpromising a place for a great city as, well, the island of Manhattan.

Lagos is now the biggest city in Africa. It is the commercial core of Africa's largest country and will soon be one of the largest cities in the world. It's a city of maddening snarls and tangles and crammed neighborhoods that look and sound like the transported ethnic villages that they are. Even the Nigerian government gave up and moved the capital out of this city. Yet the city adds a million residents each year, all seeking opportunity.

Nigeria has oil, but that industry provides few jobs. Most of the work in Lagos is what residents create for themselves, as they have for over 40 years. Baker (1974) described the early stages of this population surge in 1970s:

> Lagos was unlike anything I had seen before in Africa; it was more like an overcrowded city in India. . . . People are jammed into this area, almost all of them selling something to someone. . . . Whole sections of the town are devoted to headscarves, and women walk nonchalantly down the street with two- or even three-foot piles of these scarves on their heads. . . . All night the city is alluring: candle flames flickering in the small shops or on stalls by the roadside, green or pink electric light bulbs casting eerie shadows in beer parlors. (p. 16)

Sprawling and Brawling Contenders

Industrial Giants. Carl Sandburg (1992 [1916]), a Chicago-based reporter and writer, described his hometown in these classic lines that celebrate the industrial city:

> Hog butcher for the world,
> Tool maker, stacker of wheat,
> Player with railroads and the nation's freight handler;
> Stormy, husky, brawling,
> City of the big shoulders.

There is no longer as much bellowing and commotion in the stockyards, as occurred in Sandburg's day. Instead, the bellowing and commotion continue in the Chicago Board of Trade building, as traders wrestle over the prices and delivery of products. Likewise in Cleveland and Pittsburgh, where smokestacks on the horizon are often dormant but tall office buildings now punctuate the skyline, managing the products that are manufactured elsewhere.

This is no longer just a North American and European phenomenon. Taipei, Taiwan, the city-state of Singapore, and the special port of Hong Kong all grew as industrial giants but have now become largely trade giants, filled with managers debating deals on products made elsewhere. The new industrial giants are often near the old centers: Juárez, Mexico, on the U.S. border, and Guangzhou, China, a short drive from Hong Kong.

Culture Capitals. Other cities, while active in global trade, draw their prominence from cultural enterprises. Paris, France, and Milan, Italy, are filled with savvy businesspeople, but their draw is as leaders of fashion and style. A new sport coat may be spun in Delhi, India, lined in Seoul, Korea, padded in one of the megacities of China, and then stitched in Novgorod, Russia. But the corporate owners—Canadians, Americans, and Germans—still come to Paris to study next year's styles.

Of course, styles and centers of style may change quickly. Several top corporations are interested in what their French fashion spies can find—in Tokyo:

Loic Bizel leads visitors through alleys packed with wild-haired youngsters, makes his way into tiny boutiques tucked beneath stairwells and points out fatigue-inspired jackets, hand-painted sneakers and plaid miniskirts. . . . Fake fur trims, oversized sunglasses, dogs dressed to the T, chains and gemstones embedded in shirts and hats of all shapes are "in."

(Kageyama 2004, B-1)

If they can't afford a French spy in Tokyo, trend-conscious businesspeople can at least log on to www.japanesestreets.com. Trend watchers contend that Japan is shifting from being a manufacturing powerhouse to an exporter of culture, tapping into the creativity of the streets in the world's largest city. The trend-setting competition is not far away—Seoul, South Korea, spreads its Gangnam style around the world through the power of K-pop. And next? Shanghai is already shifting from imitation to innovation. Or perhaps, watch the *sapeurs* strolling the streets of Kinshasa, DRC, in their finest *haute couture* evoking the nonchalance of the *flâners* strolling the streets of nineteenth-century Belle Époch Paris (Draper 2013).

Nonetheless, through its power in film and international media (and though the French may cringe), the world's cultural capital has been Los Angeles. California styles are sent around the world on film and video. Of course, the styles are not always created in the studios; often, they emerge on the streets of a city where hundreds of cultures and styles mingle. And since this is Southern California, the mix may occur in any of the myriad small cities that link together in the urban jigsaw puzzle. Keeping up with the Kardashians, the Jenners, and the Wests may result in the mix of luxury accessories and high-end athletic wear that is "Calabasas style."

Cities of Desperation. No tour of the world's important cities would be complete without visiting those that are truly places of desperation and destruction. Mogadishu, Somalia, remains torn apart by the chaotic violence and unending poverty of that struggling almost-nation. Kinshasa, in the Democratic Republic of the Congo, has millions of people and almost no jobs, except those that can be invented informally. The hospitals there have no doctors, no medicines, and often no lights. Civil war, government corruption, and economic collapse have all but destroyed the urban infrastructure and social structure. In the past, people abandoned collapsing cities to return to the countryside, leaving only the ruins of Teotihuacán or Babylon. Yet in Somalia and the DRC, the countryside may be even more dangerous. There is simply no place to run.

Other cities are not collapsing but struggling desperately. Karachi, Pakistan, is on its way to being one of the world's largest cities. It hasn't yet staked a major claim on Asian trade, however, and the national capital is far to the north. The streets of Karachi are filled with millions who live in poverty and face very uncertain futures. These streets have also become one of the great recruiting grounds for extremist and terrorist organizations.

There may be hope, however, in the incredible resilience of both the cities and their people. Beirut, Lebanon, once the "poster child" for the desolation brought by civil war, is slowly healing and regaining its international prominence. Calcutta, India, still has millions of poor but also millions of middle- and working-class Indians, who are cautiously optimistic about the future.

Cities as Dynamos: Central Places and Hyperurbanization

Whether global urbanization is a cause for hope or alarm or both remains controversial. Can the planet support all these megacities? Can these cities support all their people? "Cities are the fundamental building blocks of prosperity," claims Marc Weiss of the Prague Institute for Global Urban Development (quoted in Zwingle 2002). The industrial and commercial activities of cities account for over 80 percent of the global gross domestic product (GDP) (World Bank 2020c). American-Canadian urbanist Jane Jacobs (1970, 1984) saw cities as the necessary engines of productivity, creativity, and prosperity for their countries. She contended that places with great cities such as her home of Toronto in Ontario, Canada, flourish, while those without great, complex cities fall into decline.

Jacobs's ideas represent a line of thinking in geography known as **central place theory.** It suggests that regions need central places where key functions converge, and these central places, in turn, tend to prosper and grow. It is true that for all the squalor and misery in the cities in poor countries (and in parts of many of the cities in rich countries), urban dwellers are better off on many measures than their rural counterparts. They earn more money, they are closer to schools and health clinics and other social services, and they tend to have a better education and longer life expectancy. Even though cities grow little food, the people who live there tend to gather it from many places, and urban dwellers are sometimes less prone to hunger and famine than rural dwellers. For all these reasons, people continue to come to the cities, even when jobs are scarce and life is hard.

Whether the cities will fulfill their promises is less clear. The migrant who leaves southern or north-central Mexico to come to a border town like Tijuana or Ciudad Juárez will likely earn more money and have more possessions and opportunities than someone who stays behind. At the same time, the migrant will face industrial pollution and urban filth, high crime rates, ugly transient housing conditions, and social dislocation due to living far from his or her family, traditions, and roots. Are the economic gains worth the price? For many, they must be, for people continue to come. And while many return home for visits and pilgrimages and many hope to retire to their home region or village, most continue to work in the growing cities.

A related question is whether the advantages of life in the big cities are due to advantages inherent in city life or the fact that governments tend to neglect rural areas in favor of urban showplaces, especially when those places are also national capitals. From Mexico City to Nairobi, urban capitals often gleam with new high-rise offices and hotels and impressive government buildings, while rural areas are left to deteriorate. British social scientist Michael Lipton (1977) called this **urban bias.** City life, especially in a state or national capital, is better because governments drain resources from rural areas to invest in cities, where their prestige and power are more likely to lie.

One area in which both Lipton and Jacobs agree is that many developing countries are dominated by a single, overlarge metropolis. They have experienced **hyperurbanization** (Timberlake and Kentor 1983), in which the city's size is far out of proportion to the level of industrial and commercial development of the country. Further, this growth is often concentrated in a single **primate city** that dominates the economic, political, and social life of the country and often accounts for a large share of the country's total population. Buenos Aires, Argentina; Quito, Ecuador; Nairobi, Kenya; Abidjan, Ivory Coast; and Bangkok, Thailand all are primate cities in that they are the primary centers of national life. But they are also the "800-pound gorillas" of the developing world. Their demands determine national policy. Also, when they decline, the country declines, and when they are in crisis, the whole nation is in crisis.

Cities in the United States have always had a dispersed urban pattern: commerce in New York; government in Washington, DC; rail and foodstuffs in Chicago (as well as Omaha and Minneapolis); film and television in Los Angeles; industry in shifting corridors from Buffalo to Pittsburgh to Birmingham. This is partly a function of size. New York's shipping industry had to compete with other contenders on a long coastline, from Charleston to New Orleans and later San Francisco and Seattle–Tacoma. The cities tended to grow up around resource bases and commercial nodes, with jobs coming first and people following the labor demand.

Many European countries have had much more single-city dominance: Paris, Copenhagen, and Brussels. Historically these cities were supported by extensive empires or trade networks, however. In many poorer countries, there is little to support the dominant city but uncertain government investment. Likewise, there is little to support the residents other than what they can create for themselves in the informal economy.

The Shape of Urban Life

People have been pondering the advantages and perils of urban life since the time of Gilgamesh. The urban explosion that Europe and North America experienced with the beginnings of nineteenth-century industrialization (and is now rippling around the rest of the world) led to a new analysis of urban life.

Theories of Urban Culture

German social analyst Ferdinand Toennies (1988 [1887]) wrote about the shift in social relations from **gemeinschaft,** the face-to-face world of community, to **gesellschaft,** the more impersonal and institution-mediated world of society. French sociologist Émile Durkheim (1951 [1897]) wrote about the *anomie*, or an internal sense of displacement and rootlessness that urban dwellers would experience when cut off from village community and tradition. German social theorist Georg Simmel (1964 [1905]) believed that urban dwellers cope with the onslaught of too many people, sounds, sensations, and demands by becoming more withdrawn and indifferent to external stimuli, including people.

These images of the harried and withdrawn urban dweller still capture many of our negative views of the city. This is how rural Midwesterners may think of New Yorkers, how rural Mexicans often think of *chilangos* (Mexico City dwellers), how exuberant Brazilians think of *paulistanos* (people of São Paulo), and how rural villagers in Kenya think of the residents of Nairobi. In fact, these stereotypes may have some truth to them. Greeting a New Yorker with a smiling "Howdy, y'all" may not get the desired warm response. Yet we must be careful about too quickly dismissing the vitality, creativity, and distinct variations of urban life.

Upon studying Italian Americans in Boston's West End, U.S. sociologist Herbert Gans (1982 [1962]) contended that urbanites don't really leave the social life of the village at all; they recreate it, becoming "urban villagers." In big cities around the world one can enter an "urban enclave" (Abrahamson 1996) and immediately be struck by the sights, sounds, and smells of an ethnic community. The urban villagers may gather on the corners, in the pubs or coffee shops, in the bakeries or delicatessens, or on the steps of places of worship to chat and gossip, maybe in their home language, just as they or their parents or their grandparents once did in a rural village.

Theories of Urban Structure

This alternative perspective points to the importance of the social structure of the city and of people's participation in shaping that structure. Simmel and Durkheim may have been right in suggesting that cities bombard people with strange stimuli and ideas, but Gans and Abrahamson may also be correct in noting that people contend with this bombardment by creating safe and comfortable enclaves, where the traditions and connectedness of community persist.

One of the first systematic studies of urban life and the structure of the city came out of the new department of sociology at the University of Chicago at the beginning of the twentieth century. Robert Park (1967 [1916]) did not let his students sit back behind the gothic walls of this great university but instead plunged them into the heart of the city to drink in the pubs, hang with the gangs, investigate the institutions, and explore the ethnic neighborhoods to understand the life and structure of the city. He drew his ideas from **human ecology,** the study of people and their environment, and often borrowed concepts from the new field of **environmental biology.** Park (1914) believed that urban neighborhoods go through patterns of succession similar to the stages of a forest:

1. **Invasion:** A distinct new group begins to move in.
2. **Resistance:** The established group attempts to defend its territory and institutions.
3. **Competition:** The two groups compete for space and control of social institutions such as churches and schools.
4. **Accommodation and cooperation:** Eventually the two groups settle into a stable pattern of interaction.
5. **Assimilation:** As cooperation increases, the two groups begin to merge, eventually intermarrying.

Park believed that while conflict was inevitable, it would lead to eventual accommodation and assimilation. Not everyone examining modern cities is so sure, however. Some groups seem to have been excluded and segregated for a very long time, such as the Jews of pre–World War II Europe and the African Americans of the post–World War II United States. Yet assimilationists who follow Park believe that a new blending of traditions will indeed come in time. In particular, the demands of an interconnected marketplace and the expanse of urban opportunities may overcome people's initial desires to remain in more isolated enclaves (Sanders et al. 2002).

Park's University of Chicago colleague Ernest Burgess (1967 [1916]) attempted to describe the sectors of the city, which he believed fall into recognizable zones that form concentric circles: the commercial core, the industrial belt, the zone of working-class housing, the zone of middle-class and upper-middle-class residences, and so forth. This pattern fits older cities built on open terrain (like Chicago) fairly well. Newer urban agglomerations, built around highways and forced into canyons and irregularities (like Los Angeles), fit the pattern less well. One might also need to update Burgess's zones and add a few more: the zone of look-alike condominiums, the zone of endless strip malls, and so forth.

Beginning in the 1960s and 1970s, as cities around the world, and particularly in North America and Europe, went through increasing turmoil, new ideas of the forces that shape cities came to the forefront. These views were shaped more by the political economy and looked at how power and wealth determine urban structure and life. Neighborhoods are shaped not just by natural selection but by policies of segregation and integration, by which groups hold political clout, by the willingness or unwillingness of banks to offer mortgages, by absentee landlords, and by real estate speculators. This line of inquiry continues to be examined by U.S. urban sociologists, British urban geographers, and others who have new concerns about how global power and wealth continue to reshape world cities (Sassen 2000). In the twenty-first century, the banks and absentee landlords and real estate speculators may be halfway around the world, yet their impact is felt in the local neighborhood.

Fantasy City: Postmodern Theory

If you would like to see the world's tallest skyscraper, take a yacht between huge manmade islands, shop the world's fanciest indoor malls, or maybe ski in the world's largest indoor ski slope, there is only one destination for your vacation: Dubai. The city is the urban core of one of the seven emirates of the United Arab Emirates currently undergoing a frenzy of new construction. Strict Islamic laws are set aside for beverages, apparel, and almost anything else for vacationers in this slice of escapism on the otherwise troubled Persian Gulf. To some this looks like Las Vegas on growth hormones, to others petrodollars run wildly amok, but to increasing numbers of Europeans, Middle Easterners, and Americans, this is a sunny postmodern paradise, a fantasy city where, yes, you can snow ski in air-conditioned comfort while the desert sun sizzles outside.

New urban thinking has been influenced by **postmodernism,** that eclectic set of views that challenge modernist assumptions and seek to give voice to other marginalized perspectives. *Postmodernism* has come to mean many things, but it was first used as a description of architectural styles. In the 1950s and 1960s, modern architecture was dominated by what was known as the **international style,** largely because it looked the same everywhere in the world. Buildings were big rectangles, set on their sides in suburban areas and on their ends in the urban core, with rows of look-alike windows and little adornment. The idea was that buildings were great machines and should be built for efficiency with clean lines. The trouble was that many people did not want to work in a machine or live in a city dominated by sameness and uniformity.

Beginning in force in the 1980s and continuing through the 1990s, new buildings again borrowed themes from the past. Skyscrapers were topped with gothic arches and spires, which had not been seen since the Chrysler Building went up in New York in 1931. Courtyards with fountains and pools made a comeback, and echoes of Tudor England, provincial France, and the Alhambra in Spain graced both commercial and residential buildings. Some believe that this postmodern trend has accelerated to the point where we now live in "fantasy cities" (Hannigan 1998), where the lines between reality and imagination are blurred.

One of the fastest-growing and most-visited U.S. cities is Las Vegas, a hugely popular and populated collage of Egyptian pyramids, Roman palaces, fake volcanoes, leaping fountains, and green suburban lawns that sprout from the desert like some drug-induced mirage. In Orlando, Florida, the theme parks seem to blend with the city, so much so that it is hard to tell which is which. The most popular destination in the United States has been the Mall of America in Bloomington, Minnesota, near Minneapolis.

In one sense, the mall is the recreational center of the great marketplaces of the world's great cities, complete with diverse wares and vast entertainment options. Yet most malls are also entirely climate controlled and corporate controlled, managed by strict regulations set not by a government but by private mall management. This is becoming an international phenomenon. Families play under the Eiffel Tower and the onion domes of St. Basil's (in miniature) in Guangzhou, China, while Tokyo is so full of ornate wedding palaces, fantasy hotels, themed bars, and other buildings evoking every culture that ever was (and a few that never were) that it is often hard to know where the real ends and the facade begins.

Some have suggested that these places are popular because they help people to escape their fears of crime and disorder in real cities and allow them to mingle in spaces that pretend to be cities. Few people walk in the heart of downtown Los Angeles, but "Downtown Disney" in suburban Anaheim is crowded every day of the week. Shut out, as well, are people from the poor and working classes, who cannot afford to access these spaces. It may also prove harder to shut out urban problems than we may think. Prostitutes, many of them from middle-class backgrounds, now work the "avenues" of the Mall of America, just as they do the streets of Amsterdam and Bangkok. Drugs, homelessness, and crime are invading these safe spaces, as well.

The Shape of the City

There are many things you can't get in Addis Ababa, an ancient capital high in the mountains of Ethiopia. But you can have great-looking shoes. Shoeshine boys are everywhere, hauling their equipment and hawking their services. All across Africa prosperous young people seek American-style sneakers, such as Nike high-tops. But older, prosperous Africans like nice shoes, and here in this place of dust and rock, where everyone walks everywhere, shoes need frequent shining—hence, the ever-present, hardworking shoeshine boys.

If you have your shoes shined in Ethiopia, please tip well. This is not because the shoeshine boys are homeless and starving, although many of them live in tight communal quarters and eat very simple local dishes. It is because they have a family to support, often a big family. Most of the shoeshine boys have come from the Ethiopian countryside, where food is scarce and jobs are often nonexistent. They save as much of their earnings as they can and send the money back to their villages. In some cases, they are the major supporters of their families. How poor does one have to be to depend on a shoeshine boy as your family's major wage earner? Ethiopian annual incomes hover at about $350 a year.

Around the world, people are flocking to the cities to seek opportunities. The opportunities they find are modest, however. Some find work with large multinational corporations. More often, they find work in the so-called informal economy, working semi-independently at menial and occasional service jobs, such as shining shoes. For these refugees from rural poverty, the city rarely fulfills its promise of the good life, but they will remain so long as it offers a chance at survival.

Once a month, the Ethiopian shoeshine boys get to go home. They see their families and turn over their savings. Maybe they will play a bit. They might even walk to the top of one of the ridges in this rugged land to see the sunset. They won't need to wear shoes.

Global Ghettos: The Spread of Shantytowns

Towers in the sky and periurban sprawl have been competing abodes of not only the captains of commerce and industry but also the world's urban poor. In most cities in poor countries, the poor have crowded into shantytowns on the city's edge.

As New York grew in the 1890s, poor Irish immigrants, "the shanty Irish," crowded into shantytown shacks of broken boards and cast-offs along such outlying derelict areas as New York's Fifth Avenue (near 101st Street). The Irish slums were ruled by "plug ugly" gangsters in hobnail boots with pulled-down caps and blackjack clubs or pistols in their pockets. Respectable New Yorkers avoided the place. Modern New Yorkers know this same area as a fashionable part of Manhattan, giving a glimpse of how far and how fast this city has grown.

This pattern was repeated across the United States and then across Latin America as American cities boomed. In the rugged, often mountain-ringed cities of Latin America, the shantytowns climb the surrounding mountains.

Settlers (**squatters** is a more common term) invade the land, desperate for a toehold on urban opportunity. The shantytowns ring the city and climb higher and higher into the hills, carving out steep dirt roads that often erode. Water and electricity rarely reach these places, and residents must climb down the steep ruts to get to work, to collect water from delivery trucks, and to dispose of any trash they don't want next to or can't use in their "handcrafted" homes of cardboard, scavenged tires and tin, and occasional bits of wood and concrete.

This is the life above Mexico City, Lima, Quito, La Paz, and many Latin American capitals. The names given them by their residents are evocative: Lucha de los Pobres (struggle of the poor) and Ciudad de Esperanza (city of hope). Brazil's lofty slums, known as favelas, are infamous for their size, poverty, and crime. Latin American governments have debated how to deal with this urban influx: expel the invaders and bulldoze their homes, give them title to the land and try to incorporate them into the urban political process, or just ignore them and let them try to eke out a living on their own resources. Often, promises are made and not kept.

One of the few creative and successful efforts has been made by Jaime Lerner, an architect who became mayor of Curitiba, Brazil. Like many Brazilian cities, Curitiba has seen explosive growth—an elevenfold increase in 50 years to over two million—and grinding poverty, with the average family income below $100 per week. Rather than following the typical Latin American development plan of more highways and car-oriented shopping centers, Lerner stressed repurposed buildings, affordable express buses, and safe pedestrian paths. The result has been a cleaner, greener, and safer city (2018).

In the lowlands of Southeast Asia, the poor cannot gather on the mountainsides; instead, they live on stilts over wetlands and waterways in urban fringe *kampongs*, an Indonesian word. The Latin American poor get slums with a view, and the Southeast Asian poor get waterfront property. The trouble is that the water is often filthy and disease ridden, with floating garbage and dead animals amid the warm currents perfect for cultivating cholera. Here, the poor do laundry, bathe, and travel in search of urban opportunity. Kampong-like slums also crowd the Amazonian and coastal cities of the Brazilian northeast and the low-lying ports of West Africa.

Perhaps the closest the United States gets to a kampong is in parts of East St. Louis that lie low along the Mississippi River. Writer Jonathan Kozol (1991) describes neighborhoods where the urban poor swelter in a chemical stew dumped on them from above by industries that probably will not hire them and face authorities that are more likely to close bridges to contain them than to build bridges to integrate them. Children try to play, caught between the asthmatic haze that hangs in the air and the sewage-filled chemical soup that leeches up from the ground. Other low-lying and low-income communities are slung along to the south through the region known as the Mississippi Delta.

In crowded urban spaces shantytowns are often pressed against the high-rises of new urban development as seen here in the poor favela and impressive skyline of São Paulo, Brazil, [top] and Dobi Ghat below the rising skyline of Mumbai, India [bottom]. São Paulo and Mumbai are two of the world's 10 largest cities.

A Slum with a View

The Spanish, the Portuguese, and the people in their Latin American colonies believed in the city as a center of power and influence. The central square was the gathering point, and the twin symbols of power—the cathedral and the government palace—often faced one another across this square. The wealthy and powerful lived nearby. Wealthy Latin Americans have therefore been slow to abandon the central city to the poor.

The British and the citizens of their American colonies, however, have always idealized the green countryside and been somewhat ambivalent about the city. So while great mansions were built near the city center, where some still stand as museums, restaurants, and bed and breakfasts, there was an earlier movement outward. Many of the greatest mansions of New York were built far north (at the time) along the Hudson River in the late nineteenth century.

In the United States, where the flight from the central city began early, central cities began to become synonymous with poverty, or the inner city. Urban tenement houses filled with poor immigrants from the 1880s to the 1920s. In the decades that followed, as rural African American farmworkers, sharecroppers, and others moved north, they often found places to stay on the edges of the downtowns of major cities: New York's Harlem, Chicago's Bronzeville, Detroit's Near Eastside, South Central Los Angeles, and the hearts of Baltimore and Washington, DC. In the eastern United States, they filled old neighborhoods that had been vacated by earlier immigrants, cramming into the tenements and kitchenette apartments divided out of larger houses.

As the number of low-income newcomers grew, the question of where to house them also grew. In the late 1950s Chicago's Mayor Richard J. Daley proposed scattering them in public housing throughout the city. Opposition to this was so intense that he chose instead to build upward, creating the Robert Taylor Homes and Cabrini Green between 1958 and 1962. High-rise poverty was born. Initially the buildings provided an attractive alternative to tenements and kitchenettes. Yet having so many poor people in one place also proved attractive to the criminal element, rather than to legitimate employers, and the buildings often fell into decay. The Robert Taylor Homes and Cabrini Green have been torn down, to be replaced by planned communities of multifamily, multi-income housing. Whether replacement efforts become gentrification (the sites are prime city locations) or recapture the original vision of mixing low-income families with diverse institutions and opportunities remains to be seen.

Other towers have changed residents as the cycle has continued. The great multicolored towers of Cedar-Riverside in Minneapolis were once filled with low-income residents, many of them African Americans. The towers are again filling, this time with Somali refugees who have come from the East African deserts to the northern U.S. plains, often with help of Catholic Charities and Lutheran Social Services, both active in this traditionally Northern European community. Saturday night finds the towers full of strange new sounds and aromas. Sunday morning finds Somali Christians wrapped in white, lightly woven blankets, which they wear over their Western attire, riding the buses to local churches. Many still hope to return to their troubled country. If earlier patterns hold, many will stay. The question remains, though, what they can make of this "ghetto in the sky" and whether they can find success in this distant city.

For decades, the fortunes of African Americans in U.S. cities have been constrained by intense **segregation.** Cities in the Northeast and Midwest of the United States are often two to three times more racially segregated along black–white lines than their Canadian counterparts; in the 1990s some were as segregated as South African cities at the height of apartheid (Massey and Denton 1993). This intense segregation is lessening, not so much due to policies of integration as to new immigrant influxes that continue to restir the U.S. urban "mixing bowl." Cities from New York to Los Angeles and now even Minneapolis are immigrant metropolises, with an ever-changing mix of nationalities and ethnicities. Some immigrants find their foothold in enclave economies among their coethnics, but the continued changing patterns of international migration continue to stir the pot. Korean, Chinese, and Lebanese Americans often find their niche as intermediary minorities, serving a largely black or Latino clientele. Others move quickly from enclaves into new and diverse neighborhoods (Nee et al. 1994; Sanders et al. 2002). Shifts vary by city and the nature of the changing economy: Houston is rapidly integrating, Washington DC suburbs are becoming more diverse, but Chicago retains many of the marks of "legacy segregation" (Williams and Emamdjomeh 2018).

Just west of Cedar-Riverside in Minneapolis, the Phillips neighborhood and Lake Street business district bustle with scores of differing ethnic groups from Asia, Latin America, and Africa in a city that was once more known for blonds and Swedish meatballs. In Chicago the Near West Side was the traditional home to immigrants. There, pioneering sociologist and social worker Jane Addams operated Hull House from the 1890s into the 1930s, celebrating the many cultures while providing basic health, education, and social services to help newcomers cope with daily life and advance their version of the American dream. Today this area still bustles with Chicago's Chinatown, Little Italy, Little Mexico, and more. Meanwhile, Chicago's northeast draws new immigrants from India, Armenia, Georgia (in the Caucasus), and elsewhere. Manhattan's Harlem and Chinatown still receive newcomers, but many now find their first homes in the Flushing section of Queens, where dozens of groups intermingle. Each of these has brought new vitality as well as new challenges to their cities.

The difference between a ghetto and an enclave is that the first is forced and often long term and the second is chosen and typically short term. The difference between a slum and a first start is hope. Ensuring that hope is well founded makes all the difference.

Autosprawl

Mesa, Arizona, is big. Just how big, I can't say, because given the rate of growth, my estimate would be obsolete by the time this book reached print, but Mesa is heading toward half a million people. Mesa is also one of the fastest-growing places in the United States. It is already bigger than Minneapolis, and it is bigger than St. Louis. But Mesa is not a *city*, at least not in the way we have thought of cities. It is a suburb of Phoenix. It may be the biggest suburb in the world.

Phoenix sits at the center of one of the fastest-growing metropolitan regions in the United States. Like most U.S. cities in the West that boomed after the dominance of the automobile, it is built around great highways and expansive spaces. People moving here don't want to be confined to high-rise apartments in the manner of Manhattan or Hong Kong; they came for sun and for space. As a result, as the Phoenix metro area continues to sprawl, much of the growth is in neighboring communities, such as Tempe and Mesa. Mesa is no place to walk, even in the winter when temperatures are pleasant. Rather, it is a place to drive: past sprawling malls and huge, one-story, big box megastores, past new subdivisions, out to your place in the sun.

Is this the good life or the end of community? Will it thrive and bloom in the desert, or will it bake to death in its own greenhouse gases? This remains to be seen. In the meantime, residents can pick up a chilled latte, turn on the air conditioning in the car, and drive out to see the sunset.

Urban sprawl is not just urban growth; it is the spreading of the urban population over an ever-greater expanse. Some U.S. cities, such as Detroit, reached their maximum population in the 1950s and have been losing population ever since. The greater metropolitan area, however, continues to grow in number and certainly in extent. Growth also occurs in suburban locations, as more distant exurban locations gradually become suburban. As the city itself becomes an ever-smaller and sometimes ever-poorer part of the metropolitan region, it loses power and influence. Meanwhile, farmland and open spaces are lost to suburban housing and shopping.

Early cities had to be compact, since the residents needed to get everywhere by walking. The development of the streetcar in the late nineteenth century allowed the expansion of cities, as residents could live farther out and commute to work and shopping by rail. Still, the most coveted place was the city center, where the rails converged; it held the most important buildings and the most extensive shopping. This was changed by the dominance of the automobile, however. Gradually, the streetcar rails disappeared between the 1920s and the 1950s, perhaps with the prodding of automobile manufacturers, who were eager to make their product indispensable.

Cars change the basic urban equation. Central city areas quickly become congested with traffic and can rarely provide enough parking for all the cars. Gradually stores begin to abandon these areas, and the central cities of big urban areas begin to cater mostly to outsiders who arrive by air; witness the growth of convention centers in many central cities. The centers of smaller cities often just fall into decline. At the same time, cars allow people to move their homes (and their garages) ever farther out into new "green fields" and then to travel to suburban shopping surrounded by "miles of free parking." The movement is complete as businesses move out to suburban commercial parks and light industry finds new suburban industrial parks. For many suburban dwellers, there is no need to enter the heart of the city.

This pattern was completed as the U.S. federal government built beltways around large cities in the 1960s and 1970s. These were intended to move cross-country traffic around urban centers on the national interstate, but they quickly became attractions themselves. New **edge cities** (Garreau 1991) sprang up along these beltways, often at the junction of two or more large freeways. These are not suburbs but sprawling, car-dependent conglomerations of office space, shopping, and truck shipping, which together often generate far more income than the urban center.

For a century cities were defined by their tall buildings. Louis Sullivan built the first skyscraper in Chicago in the 1880s. New York dominated in this area for decades, with each new building taller than the last: the Chrysler Building, the Empire State Building, the World Trade Center towers. Chicago reclaimed the title of having the world's tallest building in 1973 with the great black spire of the Sears Tower (now called the Willis Tower).

Sears built the 108-story skyscraper, virtually a huge vertical city. It is a complete entity where thousands can work and live without stepping outside and where one could and still can find anything—anything, that is, except Sears. To find a Sears store, one had to go out to the many suburban shopping malls. To find the Sears corporate headquarters, one had to head out via Chicago's beltway to a vast corporate office park of postmodern, low buildings, ponds, and open space. In the late 1990s the Sears Tower lost its standing as the world tallest building by a few meters to the twin Petronas Towers of Kuala Lumpur, Malaysia. These were all dwarfed in 2010 by the incredible 154-floor Burj Khalifa in Dubai, over a half-mile tall. But even as oil money built the Petronas and Burj Khalifa towers, cheap oil—which enables low-cost commutes between suburbs and cities—was already making towers obsolete in much of the world. The al-Qaeda attacks on the World Trade Center in 2001 and the COVID-19 pandemic of 2020–2021 have each called into question the wisdom and safety of many people packed together in a great tower.

As automobiles come to dominate more places around the world and as urban dwellers continue to fear crime and congestion, more and more of the world's great cities are continuing to sprawl. Some, like Singapore and Hong Kong, don't have much room to grow and so continue to push upward. In many others, rich and poor alike play a game of leapfrog, each trying to claim its space on the city's edge to find affordable housing or to have "the best of both worlds."

The trouble with life on the edge is that the edge keeps moving. Cities, unlike some physicists' models of the universe, cannot expand indefinitely, and some are showing signs of collapse. In some cases, the privileged are returning to selected urban neighborhoods in a process of **gentrification.** This can bring new resources to old communities; it can also displace the poor who are already there.

How much cities will expand is a matter of political economy as well as human ecology. The future of sprawl will depend in part on the willingness of governments to invest in public transportation, to protect green space, and to limit exurban development. It will also depend greatly on the price and availability of oil to fuel long commutes in air-conditioned automobiles, or perhaps on the ability to find alternatives in electric vehicles.

Seeking Livable Cities

Cities that Work

Where are the cities that are thriving, livable, and working? Many examples could be touted. One commonly cited is Copenhagen, Denmark:

> Copenhagen is wonderful—a bustling, cosmopolitan city of 1.5 million full of scenic canals, tidy parks, lively squares, relaxed taverns and coffeehouses, well-preserved old buildings, safe streets, cheerful people, and the enchanting 150-year old Tivoli Gardens amusement park.
>
> Yet it is no fairy-tale land: Copenhagen faces many of the same problems that bedevil North American cities. Its richness and vitality stem not from any happily-ever-after magic but from creative responses to difficult urban situations. (Walljasper 1994, p. 158)

Solutions to the problems in Copenhagen have included tax sharing between the city and suburban and rural areas; a view of low-income areas of the city as incubators for people on their way up rather than dead ends; a ban on cars in a network of downtown streets that goes back to 1962; and a view of urban renewal that relies on refurbishing older neighborhoods to maintain their community fabric and architectural integrity, rather than relying on bulldozing the old.

While Europe has had a head start in reclaiming cities as livable, exciting, yet pleasant spaces, the ideas are taking hold around the world. This focus has been dubbed the **new urbanism,** and it has several basic features. Somehow, traffic must be tamed to allow pleasant walking spaces. As much as people love their cars, few want to live in a drive-by city. Rather, pedestrians can meet and mingle, and they can stop and shop.

New Urbanism

New urbanists welcome urban diversity; the eclectic mix of people is one of the attractions of urban life (Duany et al. 2010). Enough order must be maintained so that all people, including young families and the elderly, feel safe. Once basic order and safety have been ensured, the more variety the better. (Everyone likes to people watch.) Urban spaces must allow places to pause, rest, and enjoy the scenery, whether in a park or a sidewalk cafe. This can be achieved in the narrowest spaces, a single table on a medieval street, as long as lingering is welcomed. The urban space may shimmer in tinted glass, polished metal, and glistening lights, or it may brood in stone and stucco and half-timbered lodges. Either way, it must be attractive. People do not want to linger and mingle in a sterile, machinelike setting.

New urbanist ideas have taken hold in many cities that are eager to reclaim old industrial districts, renew neglected waterfronts, and bring back a mix of people (and their money) to urban districts. Some of the most dramatic renovations have been in old industrial and shipping sectors: London's dockyards, San Francisco's embarcadero, Baltimore's inner harbor, Montreal's Old Quarter, Cleveland's lakefront, and so forth. In many places, these developments represent a long-awaited rebirth of the city.

Critics contend that the new urbanists are too concerned with appearances and have not dealt with the deeper political economy of the city (Marshall 2001). For instance, poor and working-class neighborhoods are displaced to create new playgrounds for the middle classes. Jobs in heavy industry are lost and are replaced, if at all, only by low-wage service jobs that maintain, clean, and service the new urban spaces.

The challenge remains to create cities that work and that work for all sectors. New urbanist designs have restored vitality to old and decayed urban cores. They now need to reclaim vital neighborhoods throughout the city, not posh but pleasant places for people of all ages, incomes, and backgrounds. As we look to the developing world, can we even begin to talk about bringing the finer aspects of culture, social events, higher education, and cross-cultural experiences to the poor, transient, and displaced? Jane Addams's century-old experience at Hull House suggests that this is exactly where to begin—with people who appreciate the finer parts of urban life but have not yet been fully included in the life of the city.

Sustainable Cities

By the very nature of concentrating so many people in a small space, cities place great strains on their surrounding environment. Yet city dwellers, who live in compact cities and use public transportation, may actually use fewer of the world's limited resources than someone "living large" out in suburban or open rural places. Cities around the world are trying to become more livable, likable spaces and to do so in ways that are sustainable and that will allow them to thrive in a future of possibly scarce energy and water resources. Many European cities have benefitted from compact designs that new urbanists favor to also save energy on heating and cooling and transportation. In the United States, Portland, Oregon, has combined a greenbelt around the city to contain sprawl with a light-rail system to move people efficiently to a revitalized, walkable downtown. Now large U.S. cities, even those not always associated with ecofriendly practices, are following suit. Even the "hog-butcher for the world" has gone green. Chicago continues to develop its rail and bus system as an integrated transportation system that covers the city. Bikers can store their bicycles at Millennium Park in a bicycle parking garage and even take a shower before walking to their downtown high-rise office. The city is even experimenting with "green roofs" that grow native plants and keep their buildings cool while trapping rainwater to avoid runoff and helping to freshen the urban air. Urbanist Ebenezer Howard (1850–1928) wanted "garden cities"; the new push is "green cities." The Sierra Club has launched a nationwide effort across the United States for cities themselves to sign on to ways to reduce their carbon emissions without waiting for federal government action.

Many cities across Europe are already well ahead in this effort. And cities in developing countries are realizing they, too, must find new models as alternatives to car-driven and petroleum-fueled development. There is no shortage of auto showrooms in Shanghai, but the city also has been developing fast light-rail while trying to maintain broad bicycle lanes. Unable to afford rail, Curitiba, Brazil, became a leader in "rapid bus transit," using conventional buses in special lanes with prepaid low-cost tickets that move commuters with little expense. Innovations to make cities livable for all residents may also be a great first step in making them more sustainable for future generations.

Key Ideas

- Trade centers developed earlier than cities, but cities emerged as a major form of human organization around 5,000 years ago with beginnings of large-scale agriculture. Cities grew in size and importance with the great agrarian empires.
- Industrialization changed the look and purpose of cities as they became centers for the manufacture and distribution of industrial goods.
- Cities continue to grow around the world as now over half of the world's population live in urban places, making this the first urban millennium. The greatest growth is in the developing world, with the world's largest cities soon to be all in Latin America, Asia, and Africa.
- Africa and South Asia remain more rural than the rest of the world, but are urbanizing at some of the fastest rates.
- Urbanization in China and India is creating huge cities in a matter of years, and increasing the divide in technology and life chances between city and countryside.
- Many cities in poor countries are ringed by shantytowns and squatter settlements. Almost all of the world's great cities have areas of concentrated poverty.
- Transportation often gives shape to a city: Older cities were often clustered on waterways and rail lines. U.S. cities, especially newer cities in the Sun Belt, have sprawled over vast areas with huge highways to accommodate the needs of cars.
- Under such labels as "new urbanism" and "sustainable cities," architects, planners, and citizen groups are working to create more livable cities that provide both a good life and good livelihoods for their residents.

For Review and Discussion

1. What has given rise to the great migration to cities currently taking place? If cities are sometimes difficult and dangerous places in which to live, why do they continue to attract so many newcomers?
2. What large cities have you visited? Did you find them appealing or intimidating, exciting or overwhelming? What aspects of geography, architecture, transportation, and culture give these cities their particular character?
3. What are the key elements of a healthy and livable city? How are these achieved?

Making Connections

New Urbanism

▶ Visit the site of the Congress for New Urbanism at www.cnu.org. Here, you will find the principles of this influential school of thought and its current activities. Click on Charter Awards to see scenes from across the United States and other countries, which places this movement in its historical context and argues that cities can be reclaimed from decline and auto-sprawl. The site also lists resources, upcoming conferences, local chapters, and ways to get involved. What aspects of urban redesign do they advocate? Do you find their ideas and models appealing?

Livable Cities

▶ You can learn more about community spaces, transportation, architecture and sustainability from International Making Cities Livable at http://www.livablecities.org/. Note the articles and conference reports with designs for alternative urban development. How do they propose to halt and reverse trends toward ever-greater urban sprawl and make cities healthier and more livable?

Sustainable Cities and Communities

▶ UN Sustainable Development Goal 11 is "Make cities inclusive, safe, resilient and sustainable." See more on global urbanism and efforts for change at https://www.un.org/sustainabledevelopment/cities/. What aspects of an urbanizing world are noted? What are the UN goal's targets to make this a more equitable and sustainable process? Follow the link to UN Habitat at https://unhabitat.org/ .Look at campaigns for climate-smart cities, the campaign for housing, and their urban policy. Why is a national urban policy needed?

Making a Difference

Neighborhood Organizations

▶ Check with your municipality or campus-community office to find out what neighborhood groups and associations are active in your area. Try to attend one of their meetings or visit their offices. Are they city sponsored or independent? What are their key issues: crime, planning, property values, traffic, or others? Are there ways for citizens and student groups to become involved? Note in particular, groups in troubled or transitional neighborhoods and those in neighborhoods bordering the college campus.

Community Revitalization

➤ Many low-income individuals and families live in areas of concentrated poverty and limited opportunity. Where are these locations in your community, and what efforts are being made toward bringing positive change? Visit a community center, neighborhood association, nonprofit community development corporation (CDC), or other community-based organization working in a low-income community. Learn about the community demographics: Who lives here (income, race and ethnicity, family composition, many youth or many elderly, etc.)? Has this changed over time? Is the area undergoing a transition? What is the housing situation? Are there many absentee property owners, subdivided large homes, apartments, public housing, and so on? What, if any, are the area's employers and retailers? What are the most pressing problems, and what is being done to address them? Are local residents actively involved in these efforts? You may find activities in which you can assist, whether on your own or with a group.

10
Population and Health

Only the Poor Die Young

Global Encounters

South Africa

We board the large tourist bus to travel to the township of Spandau to work with Operation Hunger. "Township" is used in a unique way in South Africa to refer to those very poor communities created by apartheid to house black African workers. Fifteen years after the crumbling of apartheid and over 25 years after the first free election in which all could participate, the townships remain. In many ways, they are the South African incarnation of the shantytowns that ring and sometimes penetrate the sprawling megacities of the world. We saw Venezuelan ranchitos and Brazilian favelas, but these South African shantytowns have a unique place in the national life. Fans of Paul Simon and Ladysmith Black Mombasa know a bit of township music, and aficionados of the full range of township jazz know far more. On the waterfront, one can book a safari, a whale-watching tour, a winery tour, or a township tour. This strikes me as bizarre. Imagine long lines of Japanese tourists in Los Angeles boarding a tour bus in Santa Monica to cruise the scarred streets of South Central, take pictures of public housing and storefront churches, and listen to hip-hop.

I hope we will do better today. We are working with Operation Hunger, a service organization that has been in the townships since the 1970s, at a time when one had to be very careful to work for change while not appearing to threaten the system that created these communities in the first place. We have a large group, 40 students, and a very big bus that can barely fit down a township street. Meaningful encounters across cultures, and particularly across social class, can be extraordinarily difficult. Good preparation helps, as does an extended stay that allows for gradual introductions. We have had the preparation of experiencing other communities but only a bit over a week to learn specifically about South Africa. And then, there is that bus. On other trips, we have tried to travel in smaller VW minibuses, preferably older and less overwhelming, but today our large numbers require the full tourist cruiser.

As we drive out of town and past the airport, the country within a country continues. The highways are the best we have been on since leaving the United States. They aren't lined up with the scruffy auto repair and used parts shops, which seem to be so much of life on the road in Latin America. Here we get strip malls and minimarts. The BP station where we pause is new: the bakery goods are fresh and the coffee is good. At the same time, the view on each side of the road changes with every turn. Closer in are beautiful houses: the colors and frilled peaks of British colonial Victorians and the rounded curved fronts of the Dutch Cape style. On the other side are the newest and most ramshackle shanties. Nothing we saw in Latin America looked this unsubstantial. Ragged pieces of corrugated metal perch precariously on frames of scrap wood, cardboard, and scavenged car parts. A line of communal outhouses stand shoulder to shoulder along the road with their back sides toward us in a communal mass mooning of the highway, effluent running out and into a drainage ditch.

There is no room for a bus in this dense tangle of metal and boards woven together, so it is a relief to learn that our intended community has been renovated. The government is in the midst of the long slow process of turning informal shantytowns into formal settlements. Up to half the residents often need to be relocated to make room for small two- or three-room concrete-block homes surrounded by a bit of ground. We wind our way through such houses, built just four years ago, as our bus turns, backs up, and maneuvers through the streets. We are directed to a large tent next to a cluster of roofless homes. A tornado had come through Spandau and taken off the metal roofs and several layers of block from some of the houses. The exposed walls show concrete blocks less than six inches thick and assembled without reinforcing metal bars. These buildings were certainly a considerable improvement over the shacks but did not stand up well to the storms. Several men wave through the roofs of their houses, hoping we are connected somehow with a government project to repair them. We are not. We are here to weigh children, assess their nutritional state, and encourage the start of "door front" gardens.

As we pull in, children emerge from everywhere, waving, smiling, mugging for photos. We try to wave them away from the tent and unload. Our guide and leader is Clement, a quietly enthusiastic man who has worked with Operation Hunger for years. He gives us our tasks and then goes out to address the gathering children and parents in Afrikaans, their only common language. Meanwhile, we try an exercise in rapid mobilization. Weighing teams are created for the lines of children. Cards are distributed to get ages and addresses. Birth dates must be converted to months, and weights recorded and charted in kilograms. Two teams on the bus work on converting the data into graphs showing the range of weights for boys and girls by age and location. Clement mentions that children are sometimes slightly shy (we see very little evidence of this), associating white people holding clipboards with the medical teams that give them shots. He suggests a small prize for each who agrees to be weighed. We have brought some crayons and pencils and tear pages out of the few thick coloring books that a few students have brought. He also notes that rather than wasting any unwanted food from our box lunches, leftovers could also be given out. The students quickly decide to give out most of the lunches (while scheming about a fast-food stop later). Lunches are divided into a mix of treats and proteins. As the children are weighed, they get a mark on their hand, and then go to the side door of the bus where a shuttle line delivers toys and treats. The work goes quickly, but there is no shortage of confusion with more than 100 children, most of whom know only a few words of English. As we work, we are serenaded by strains of "Amazing Grace," in English, coming from a tent meeting.

Once everyone is weighed and fed, we leave briefly to find our own lunch and finish the charting. Our long-suffering bus driver manages to get us back to the tent site, and Clement goes over the results with the students. He then talks with several local community leaders about the families with the children most at risk. For some reason in this community those most underweight are boys. The parents claim they are out playing all day while school is not in session and often miss meals. On school days, they must walk a long way from home. The community reps attempt to persuade several families to begin gardens. These will initially be "door front" gardens, for there is little other land. Maybe when the tent comes down its site can be a community garden. We set off around the little grid of streets armed with rakes and hoes to plant a few seeds in the sand. Here no one seems to ever use the metal end of the tools; rather the handles are used to poke holes for a few seeds. The gesture seems almost futile as I watch the rake handles sink into the soft sand.

With the gardens in place, we have a little time to chat with the townspeople who have watched our day's efforts. Young children are everywhere, wanting to teach and learn songs and clapping games, and mugging for our ever-present digital cameras. We are invited by some of the teenagers to a house that has a courtyard of sorts made of scavenged boards and camper tops. A stereo is cranked up and we learn some line dancing while a couple of students teach them their best hip-hop moves. It takes a while to get our students to put down the beaming little kids and wave good-bye to our hosts.

As we drive away with exuberantly waving children behind us, I wonder about my initial hesitations. Maybe we had overcome the barriers of class, culture, and race to truly connect with a community for at least a day. Our students are exhilarated by what they could accomplish and deeply moved by the hospitality shown in return. Maybe this was more than a cultural safari; maybe it was truly amazing grace.

China

Shanghai, at one time China's fast-growing commercial hub, has many things to offer. For instance, there's cable access television. Tune in to hear the singing bachelors. This is not some bizarre new blending of U.S. reality television shows: American Idol meets The Bachelor. This is the new reality of modern China.

The Chinese bachelors are indeed singing for both notoriety and love. The problem is that there are too many of them. For years, China's birth rate has been skewed toward boys. In some rural areas, there are as many as 134 boys born for every 100 girls; the national average is somewhere around 119 for *every 100. Chinese parents want a boy who will marry and bring a wife home to them, not a daughter who will eventually leave them to join her husband's family. In the distant past, all they could do to achieve this goal was to beseech their ancestors to give them a boy. Rumors of female infanticide abounded. Now they can turn to ultrasound and other medical procedures to determine the sex of the fetus and then decide whether to abort it or not.*

The result is that more boys are born than girls are. But these boys are supposed to honor their parents by gaining success in the workplace, getting married, and having children. These singing bachelors have found economic success in Shanghai. But they haven't found wives. After two decades of skewed birth rates, there are not enough women to go around. So, the bachelors do what everyone does in Shanghai: They advertise. On cable access, they talk about their successes, their promotions, their wealth, maybe even their new car. And they sing. Interested women can call in. The competition is fierce.

If a singing bachelor is successful and does get a wife and they have a child, one wonders, will he wish for a boy or a girl? And what will the parents tell the next generation about the worth and value of each?

Counting Heads: World Population Estimates

How many people are there in the world? The last time I checked, there were 7,871.053,815. Obviously, I didn't count them. You can get the current figure from the U.S. Census Bureau and its world population counter, at www.census.gov/popclock/ or at https://www.worldometers.info/world-population/. The Census Bureau doesn't count either, but instead prints UN estimates based on census figures, reporting, and estimates from the world's countries, which they update continually based on projected birth rates.

Attempting precision at keeping this head count is silly in one sense, as we can only estimate and the figure is obsolete as soon as it is posted. Yet it is a reminder of how carefully we have tried to chart and tabulate the world's growing population. What is harder to estimate are the effects this growth and change will have on our planet.

The world's population, like the world's wealth, is very unevenly distributed. Of the close to eight billion people on the planet, just over 1.4 billion are in China. Almost another 1.4 billion live in India, soon to be the world's most populous nation. Overall, about three-fifths of the world's population lives in Asia. The remaining population is roughly evenly divided among Europe, Africa, North America, and South America.

A similar ratio holds when comparing the largest countries: Of the current 10 most populous countries, one is European, one North American, two are Latin American, one is African, and the other five are Asian (see table 10.1). Of these 10 countries, one is high income (United States), four are middle income (China, Mexico, Brazil, and Russia), and the remainder are lower income. Two are losing population (Russia and China), and the rest are growing. Mexico recently replaced Japan, which is losing population, in the number 10 spot. Nigeria is the fastest growing of the big 10; along with its West African neighbors, it has one of the highest population growth rates in the world. As shown in table 10.1, its population is expected to double by the year 2050, replacing the United States as the third most populous country in the world. Ethiopia and DRC Congo will join the top 10. Perhaps this will prove to be the African century!

How many people can this planet hold? No one knows for sure, and that has caused concern for some time.

Marx and Malthus: The Population Bomb Debate

For centuries, leaders saw a growing population as key to their power. The Spartan Greek leaders bribed their handful of citizen-warriors to spend enough time with their wives to procreate a steady supply of new boys to grow into

Table 10.1 World's 10 Largest Countries in Population: 2020 and 2050

	2020			2050	
Rank	Country	Population (millions)	Rank	Country	Population (millions)
1	China	1,439	1	India	1,639
2	India	1,380	2	China	1,370
3	United States	331	3	Nigeria	403
4	Indonesia	273	4	United States	379
5	Brazil	212	5	Pakistan	338
6	Pakistan	221	6	Indonesia	320
7	Bangladesh	165	7	Brazil	232
8	Nigeria	206	8	Ethiopia	205
9	Russia	146	9	Bangladesh	201
10	Mexico	129	10	Dem. Rep. of Congo	193

Source: UN, 2019. World Population Prospects 2019. United Nations Population Division.

citizens. They were needed to defend the city and to keep the large population of slaves in line. Too many of the "wrong sort" could be a problem. The biblical book of Exodus has the Egyptian pharaoh worrying about the rapid growth of the enslaved Hebrew population. Sufficient slaves were needed to do the work, but too many could be dangerous.

For millennia the world's population grew slowly. Disease and disaster, often human made, kept the death rate high. And while the beginning of agriculture meant a larger food supply, it also meant a more concentrated population, sharing their grain supplies with rats and insects, and consequently more diseases. The world had about 300 million people by 1000 CE and maybe 500 million by 1500 CE. The planet was well into the 1800s before it passed the one billion mark.

At least one person worried about this growth. British economist Thomas Malthus (1766–1834) noted a trend in human population growth: It was not linear but rather exponential, an upward rising curve that seemed to grow ever steeper. Malthus's mathematical reasoning went this way: The food supply was also growing, but it tended to grow in linear fashion, a straight upward line. Population had the power to grow exponentially: It doubled every so many decades (1926 [1798]).

The power of this doubling is dramatic. The Indians tell a tale of the man who invented chess. For compensation from a grateful king, he asked only for one grain of wheat on the first chess square, two grains on the second, four grains on the third, and so forth. This didn't seem like much to ask, except that the amount of grain needed for the 64th square would be more than all the grain the world has ever produced. The food supply would never be able to keep pace with this exponential growth.

In the 1800s crowded London and Paris were already showing the strains of a large population. Malthus (1926 [1798]) warned that this was only the beginning. The French have a simple riddle: Suppose you have a pond with a growing water lily patch that doubles in size every day. It will cover the pond in 30 days. On what day will it cover only half the pond? The answer, of course, is the 29th day. Again, dramatic changes come with exponential doubling.

Malthus believed that since "passion between the sexes" was inevitable—and he wrote before contraception was common—this growth was also inevitable. It would continue until it outstripped the food supply. Then the population would collapse through catastrophe: wars over food along with outbreaks of disease and famine. In time, even if things stabilized, the cycle would only begin again. Some say it was Malthus who gave economics its nickname as "the dismal science."

Yet most nineteenth-century leaders were not worried. Napoleon encouraged all French women to do their patriotic duty and bear more French citizens. Only in this way could France match the size of Russia and the German states and send out vast armies. Those vast armies would conquer enough land and seize enough food to fuel this growth, and so Napoleon marched disastrously into the vastness of Russia. The British also looked to their empire to help with growth: Excess population could be transferred overseas. Britain was small and getting crowded, but who could imagine an end to the vast open spaces of Canada, the U.S. colonies, Australia, and southern Africa? These lands seemed empty by comparison to Europe, and where they were not, they could be emptied through war, removal, and disease.

Another European economic thinker, Karl Marx (1818–1883), also disputed Malthus. People were a land's greatest strength, Marx contended. If they were miserable, it was because they were not able to enjoy the fruits of their labor. Once land and wealth were redistributed to the poor workers, there would be enough for all. Many leaders of poor countries in the twentieth century (and especially those influenced by Marx) continued this line of thought. In China, Mao Zedong claimed that the people, in all their many millions, were the country's glory and power and that the Westerners who sought to limit China's growth were only fearful of this growing power. A similar line came from the other end of the political spectrum. Fascist leaders, such as Francisco Franco in Spain, banned contraception, claiming it was anti-Catholic but also seeing power in numbers. In Italy, Benito Mussolini, like the ancient Spartans, told Italians it was their patriotic duty to increase their numbers.

By the 1970s the population growth curve had reached its steepest incline. Doubling was taking place within a single decade. Observers wondered how long it would be before "the pond" was full and choked with growth and at what point no increase in the food supply would be enough to feed the world. The Club of Rome, a group of concerned observers, issued a report on "the limits to growth." The most famous statement on the problem came from Paul Ehrlich in his 1968 book *The Population Bomb*. Ehrlich used the logic of exponential numbers to show the ultimate absurdity of unchecked growth. He pointed out that, eventually, each person would have about two square meters in which to stand and nowhere to move, grow food, or otherwise use for his or her survival. Ehrlich looked at a world of three billion and said it simply could not grow to six. He was, at least in the absolute sense, quite wrong.

The world has passed the seven billion mark and not yet collapsed. There is enough food for all—at least, if we could get it to them. Yet growth always comes at a price. This planet of almost eight billion has overcrowded megacities, eroded farmland and diminishing water supplies, disappearing forests, and many species that have become extinct or are on the verge of extinction, driven off by the pressure from a single species. What will the price of growth be in the future?

The simple answer is a world of more poverty. The UN projects the world's population will grow to almost 10 billion by the middle of this century (UN Department of Economic and Social Affairs 2017a). A lot depends on the policies of the next few years. But there is agreement on one factor: Almost all of that growth will take place in poor regions of the world (see figure 10.1). The rich have growing economies, while the poor have growing populations. The rich get richer, it seems, while the poor get pregnant. A simple theory proposes to explain this pattern.

Demographic Transition Theory

Demography is the study of human populations: their numbers, movements and migrations, and characteristics, such as age and race/ethnicity. Demographers are particularly interested in the vital statistics of human life: births, deaths, and migrations. A **demographic transition** is a change in the pattern of population growth and distribution. **Demographic transition theory** proposes that there is a predictable pattern to population growth as a country develops.

Death Rate and Birth Rate

In many preindustrial agrarian societies, the **death rate,** or the proportion of the population that died in a given year, and the **birth rate,** the proportion of the population that was born in a given year, were both quite high.

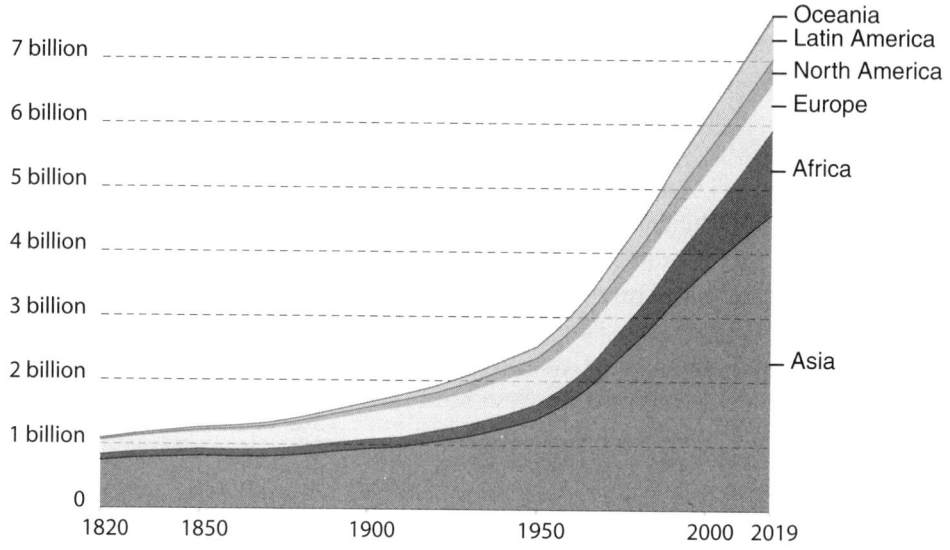

Figure 10.1 Population growth by region. (Source: Our World in Data.)

As long as they were in balance, with similar numbers of birth and deaths, the population remained stable. At some point—perhaps due to better nutrition and sanitation for a larger number of people and the control of certain highly infectious diseases—the death rate began to fall. But people in these changing agrarian societies continued to have large families due to cultural expectations, the hope that children would provide economic security in old age, the need for farm labor, and the uncertainty that their children would survive to adulthood.

During times of demographic transition, with a falling death rate but a very high birth rate, the population soars. This occurred in Europe and the United States in the 1800s and into the early 1900s. European and North American cities grew rapidly, and much of the explosive population growth was channeled into growing industries. The excess population of Europe, those who neither could find land to farm nor industrial work, were "exported" in great out-migrations. They moved to the great open spaces of Canada, the United States, Argentina, South Africa, and Australia, where frontier land—opened in part by the decimation of native populations through European-introduced disease, war, and removal—beckoned to newcomers.

The United States, in particular, took in huge numbers of immigrants for the time: 30 million between 1880 and 1920. These immigrants filled the coastal cities and pushed relentlessly into the interior. The tide of immigrants slowed as the birth rate began to fall in Europe and European-heritage communities in the United States.

For farmers, children have traditionally been a source of pride as well as labor and security. For urban industrial workers in crowded housing, raising children proved more difficult. Children could still be a source of labor, however, if they were put to work in the factories. Yet all across Western Europe and North America in the late 1800s and especially by the early 1900s, the idea was taking hold that children should be in school, not in factories. Putting children through school was expensive. As women's workplace moved from the home farm or family business out into the city, caring for children also became more difficult. Cultural expectations about large families began to shift, interest in contraception (often illegal at the beginning of the twentieth century) grew, and family size began to fall.

Life Expectancy

Despite ongoing disease and war, death rates have fallen everywhere in the world over the last 50 years. There have been temporary reversals in this pattern in certain locations, including in areas experiencing intense civil war and the height of the AIDS crisis in some African nations. Yet even these occurrences haven't changed the overall trend.

An easier figure to imagine and comprehend than the death rate of so many per 100,000 is **life expectancy,** and this is often used in international comparisons. Life expectancy is an estimate based on projections of death rates, and so it is less precise than counting the actual numbers of deaths. Even so, it allows us to compare numbers that make sense at the individual level: how long one can expect to live.

Remember that life expectancy is an average. A country in which the life expectancy is 45 probably does not have large numbers of 45-year-olds passing on. More likely, it has a very high rate of **infant mortality,** or the proportion of children who die before reaching their first birthday. Since life expectancy is an average, having a large number of deaths among people of very young ages brings down the average dramatically, even if the country has some people who reach very old ages.

Life expectancy has extended almost everywhere—at least until 2020 when COVID-19 and related disruptions in the economy and health care delivery system lowered global life expectancy. In the United States life expectancy retreated by almost a full year. Japan leads the world in life expectancy, followed closely by the northern European countries (see figure 10.2). The difference is not necessarily attributable to lifestyle, although it can have some effect. The United States has a higher rate of obesity than most of Europe and certainly Japan and has had a high-fat diet for a longer time (although others are catching up on this). But Americans are also now less likely to smoke cigarettes

336 Part Three　　　　Seeking a Sustainable World

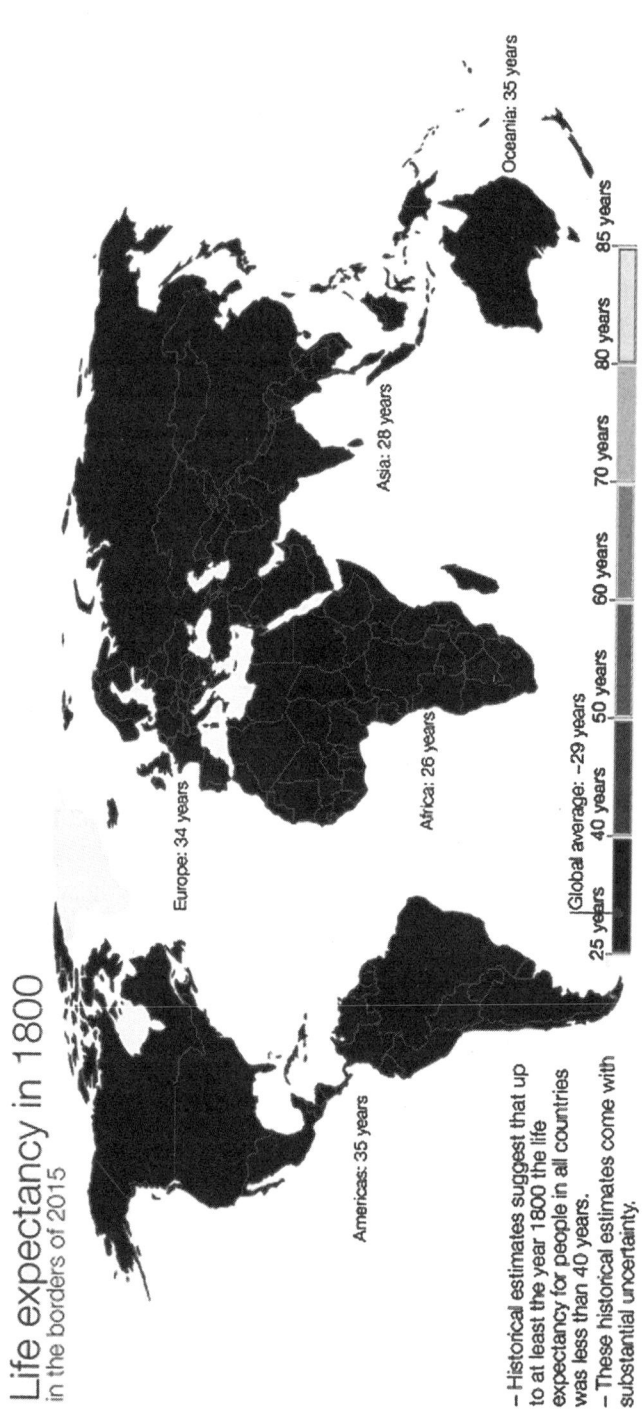

Figure 10.2 (continued on pages 337 and 338)　Maps of life expectancy in 1800, 1950, and 2015. (Source: "Life Expectancy," by Max Roser, Esteban Ortiz-Ospina, and Hannah Ritchie. Our World in Data.) For more information and charts showing changes in life expectancy over time see https://ourworldindata.org/life-expectancy#:~:text=The%20United%20Nations%20estimate%20a,life%20 expectancy%20of%2072.3%20years.

Population and Health CHAPTER 10 337

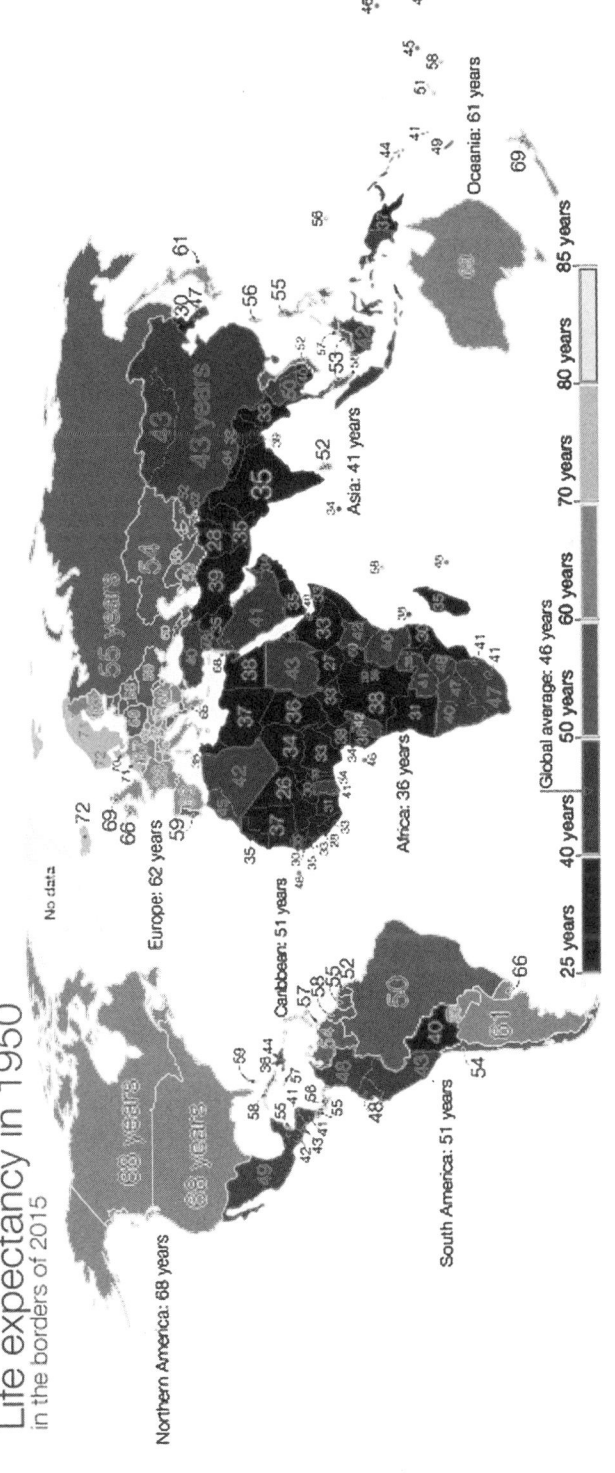

Figure 10.2 (continued) Maps of life expectancy in 1800, 1950, and 2015.

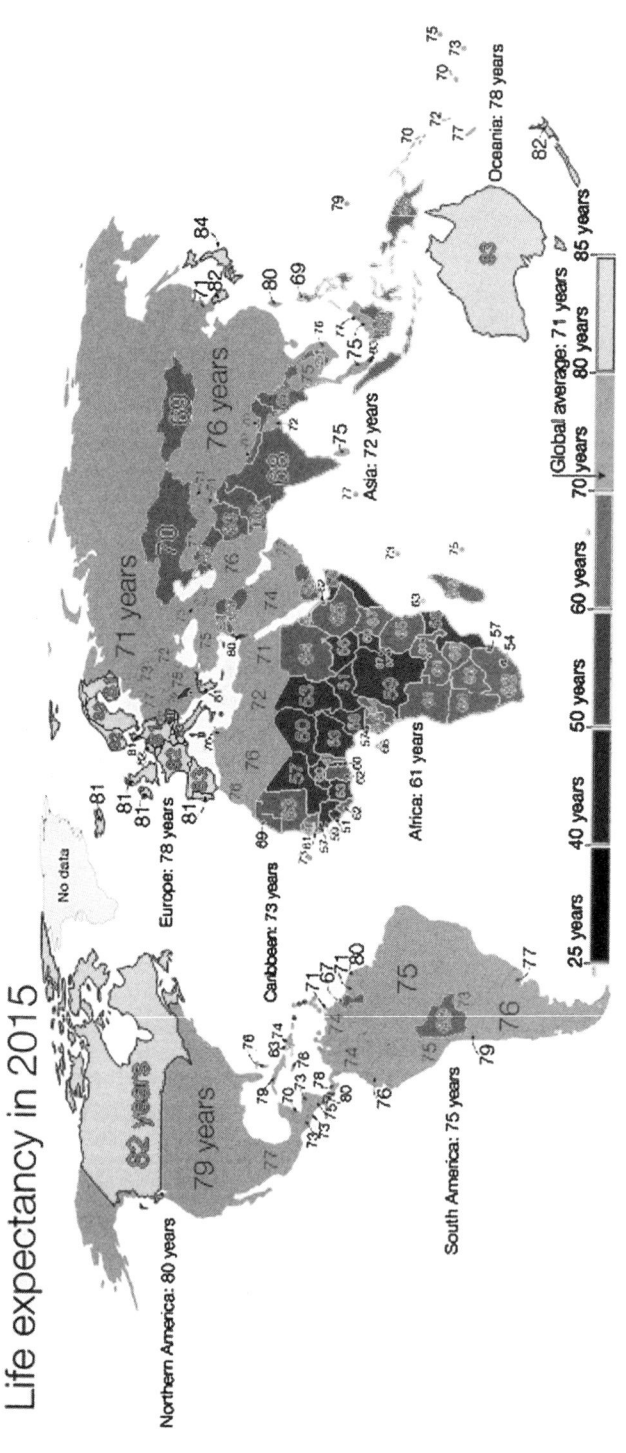

Figure 10.2 (continued) Maps of life expectancy in 1800, 1950, and 2015.

than Europeans or Japanese, and smoking is one of the greatest health risks of all. Both Americans and Japanese suffer from work-related stress. The biggest difference is that many more in the United States, especially in poor and nonwhite communities, lack good access to quality health care, especially prenatal and early childhood care. This raises the U.S. infant mortality rate and lowers the life expectancy.

Infant mortality rates have declined dramatically since 1950, particularly in areas of the world such as Africa, where improved health care has been provided to mothers and children. Regardless, there is a huge gap in infant mortality around the world, ranging from an average of 52 infant deaths per 1,000 births in the African region to an average of just seven deaths per 1,000 births in the European region (World Health Organization 2021).

Fertility Rate

Life expectancy provides a more intuitive way to think about the death rate, and the **fertility rate** provides a more intuitive way to think about the birth rate. Like life expectancy, the fertility rate is an average projection based on current rates—in this case, the birth rate. The fertility rate is the number of children the average woman will have in a particular country.

The fertility rate in the United States around the turn of the twentieth century was close to six; that is, the average woman bore six children in her lifetime. This would also have been a measure of family size, except that not all of the children survived. Moreover, some may have been "apprenticed out" as young as 10, and the older children may have already been married and having children of their own when their youngest siblings were born to the family (Hareven 1982).

In recent decades, the fertility rate has dropped markedly around the world, from also around six to now closer to three. And as demographic transition theory would predict, this rate is not evenly distributed (see figure 10.3). Fertility rates in parts of Africa, parts of the Islamic world, and a few locations in South Asia still range between four and six. Meanwhile, fertility rates in parts of Europe and Japan have fallen below two. The fertility rate makes an enormous difference in a country's future. A fertility rate of four, with most of the children surviving, will double a country's population every generation; if the mothers begin young, this could be every 15 to 20 years. If the fertility rate falls below two and the country does not experience net in-migration (people coming into the country from elsewhere), then the population will begin to age and decline in number.

Fertility rates are highest in rural areas, in the least industrialized regions, in places with traditional gender roles, and in locations with a strong religious and cultural ethic of the value of large families. The very highest fertility rates are in Islamic regions of Africa, such as northern Nigeria. Until recently in the United

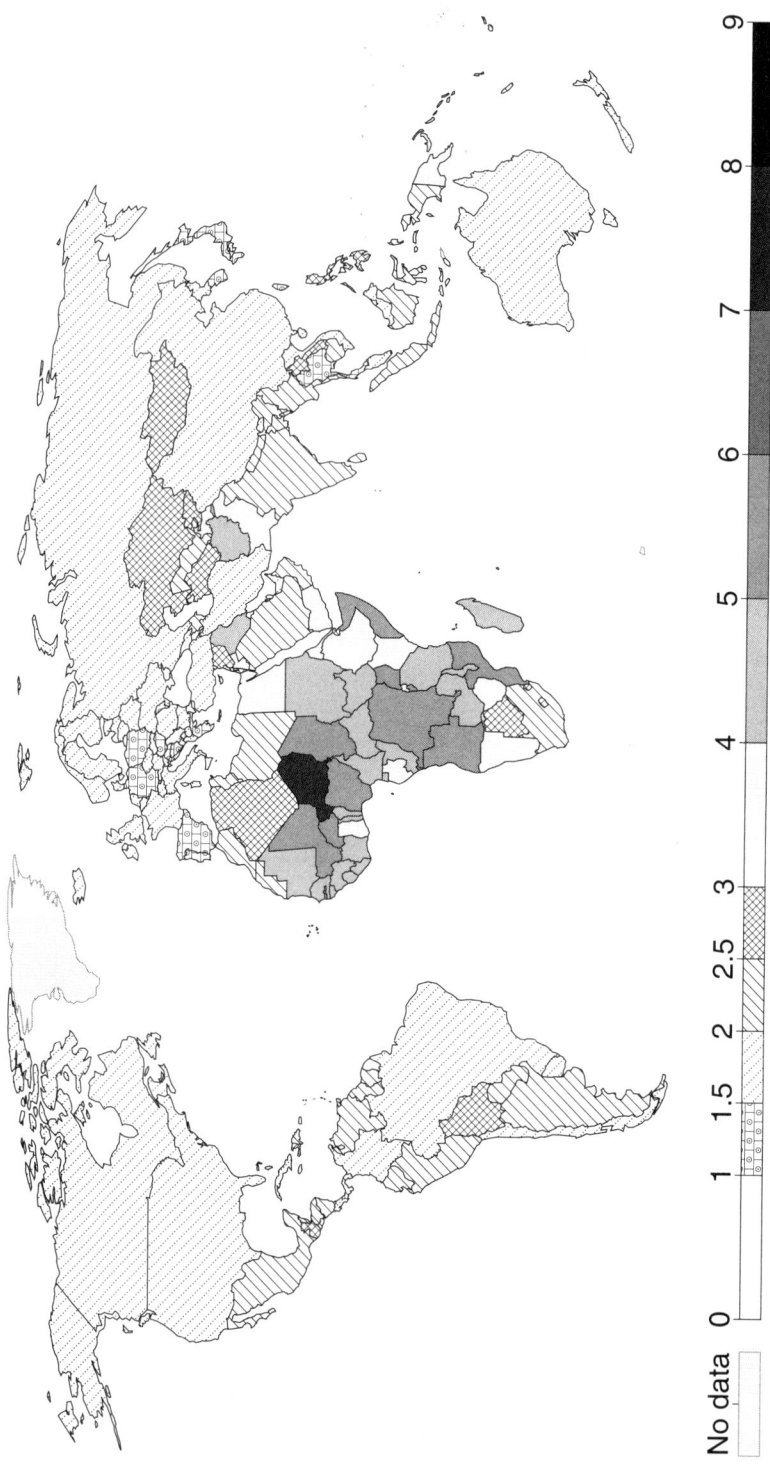

Figure 10.3 Fertility rates around the world. (Source: Our World in Data.) For more information: see https://ourworldindata.org/grapher/children-born-per-woman?time=2019&region=World for an interactive map to see global changes since 1500.

States, the fertility rate was substantially higher in Utah, with its strong Mormon heritage, than in other portions of the country, averaging 4.3 in the 1960s.

Yet fertility rates have fallen markedly even in parts of the world that have, until recently, stressed the value of large families. The fertility rate for Mexico is now barely at replacement level. The United States has dropped below replacement level, with average fertility per woman of around 1.7. It grows only due to immigration and the composition of its population changing accordingly. Groups with higher immigration rates—Hispanics as well as some Asians—grow rapidly mostly due to immigration.

Changing Demographics

In Western Europe, fertility rates are consistently below replacement level. These countries will therefore see aging populations and shrinking populations unless immigration from elsewhere in the world fills this void, a process that would change the religious and cultural complexion of Europe as well as its physical complexion.

Japan has been particularly struck by the "birth dearth." While the Japanese value children, theirs is an extremely urbanized country, with crowded living conditions and many women in the paid labor force. Japanese parents invest heavily in their children, seeking to get them the best education and preparation for it, and this makes children expensive. Most Japanese couples only have one or two children, and some forgo having children all together, devoting themselves to professional pursuits. With a fertility rate around 1.4, the Japanese population is aging quickly, and the government has tried incentives to encourage more births. Japan is an ethnically homogenous society that has not attracted or sought large numbers of immigrants.

Heading the list of shrinking countries is the one with the world's largest land area: Russia. The nation, as a single entity, lost just over half its population when the Soviet Union broke up into small republics in 1991. Russia now combines a very low birth rate with net out-migration, as many seek to leave but few seek to come to Russia, with its troubled economy.

As mentioned previously, the direst predictions about global overpopulation came in the 1970s as the planet added people at a faster rate than ever before. That growth rate, about 1.7 percent a year, has since fallen to about 1 percent a year. To understand what these rates mean, try the economists' so-called *law of 72*. (This works for compounding interest as well compounding population growth.) Divide 72 by the rate of growth to get the time to the next doubling. A population growing at 1 percent will double in about 72 years, at 2 percent in 36 years, and at 4 percent in 18 years.

Growth is based not only on the fertility rate but also on the age of the population—a kind of shadow effect of previous growth. Countries with rapidly growing populations have very young populations—lots of children and young people. Even if these young people start to have only a few children themselves, the population will continue to grow for some time, just because there are so many people in their prime childbearing years. This effect keeps Mexico's population growing slowly but steadily, even as fertility rates drop. Until recently, it kept China's population growing in spite of attempts (more effective in urban than in rural areas) to enforce a one child per family policy in 1980. Even with a declining overall fertility rate, the world population will continue to grow until a larger portion of the population ages past their prime childbearing years. The most significant effect, however, will not only be in the rate of growth but also in the place where it will occur.

By the middle of this century, the world's population will grow from almost eight billion to somewhere between nine and 10 billion, depending on how one does the predictions of how fast fertility rates will fall. But virtually all of this growth will be in poor countries. As noted earlier, in today's world, the rich grow their economies and the poor grow their populations. A similar pattern occurs within countries, where urban, two-income, upper-middle-class families tend to have fewer children than rural, low-income and working-class families.

This demographic pattern has important implications for individual countries. Western Europe, Japan, Canada, and the United States all have aging populations and wonder how they will provide for them as retirees, as they continue to comprise an ever-larger portion of the population (Fishman 2010). These countries also often debate how much they should open their borders to immigration to bring in younger workers and how doing so would affect their societies and economies. Russia, Ukraine, and other parts of the European portion of the former Soviet Union face the prospect of outright population decline—as much as 28 percent for Russia and a huge 40 percent for Ukraine by midcentury, according to UN population estimates. Poor countries, in contrast, worry about how to cope with the demands of a young and growing population. A population with many children needs a large number of schools. Children, like older adults, also require more health care. And as they graduate from school, they need jobs, requiring an ever-expanding economy and labor market.

Changing demographics are also changing the world as a whole. An increasingly larger portion of the world's population will be in Latin America, Africa, and Asia, giving greater numerical clout to these regions. All the world's explosively growing megacities will be in these places. If a large number of people try to move from fast-growing poor areas into slow-growing richer areas, the movement of peoples and cultures will be enormous—a countertide to the large number of Europeans who moved out into the world in the 400 years between 1520 and 1920. Should this occur, it would also mean that despite economic gains in some regions, most of the world's children would be born into poverty. Tremendous economic growth and expansion of social services would be needed just to keep pace.

"Around here," the queen in *Alice in Wonderland* explains, "one must run as fast as one can just to stay in one place." This seems to be the situation for the world and especially for the world's poorest regions. Humanity has experienced 10,000 years of economic growth and incredible invention since the first humans began tending crops. After all that, is the average peasant or slum dweller in one of the world's poor regions any better off—in terms of nutrition, health, livelihood, and well-being—than the hunter-gatherer who watched the glaciers melt? It is hard to say.

What happened to all that growth and inventiveness? Inequality took some of it. The wealthy of the world are certainly better off in material terms, even if other measures of well-being are less clear. But population growth also used up the benefits of these efforts. We grow more food but have more mouths to feed. We build bigger dwellings but have more people to house. We have faster-paced economies but more people to support. This sense of running just to keep up is most evident in the world's poorest places. Jobs are created but not enough for many new job seekers. Schools are built but not enough for ever more children. New food and water supplies are tapped but not enough for exploding urban populations.

Prosperous places on the planet face their own version of this treadmill, as population and prosperity combine to increase the demands on their environment and infrastructure. New highways are built but can't keep pace with the numbers of new cars and added miles driven. Efforts are made to improve efficiency and lower emissions from those cars, but if a country doubles its fuel economy as it doubles the number of vehicles on the road, it sees no net gain in lowering emissions. And so it goes, running hard to stay in one place.

It is not clear that crowding is always bad. Some of the most crowded places on the earth—Hong Kong, Singapore, Manhattan—are also some of the most prosperous and economically productive. Congested regions, such as the Ruhr Valley of Germany and Tokyo Bay, have pollution problems but also offer good health care and nutrition and have healthy populations with long lives. On the other hand, some of the world's most sparsely populated countries—Niger, Burkina Faso, Mongolia—are also some of its poorest. Yet we know that a dense population places great demands on resources and infrastructure. Tokyo and New York thrive by trading their commercial wealth for resources from all over the world, something that is not an option for very poor communities. Rapid population growth, even in a sparsely populated region, can undermine even the most careful of economic plans.

No one knows for sure how many people this planet can support. Previous estimates have tended to greatly underestimate levels of natural resources and human resourcefulness. In the 1800s some thought the United States could never reach 100 million, since there would not be enough pasture land for all those people's horses. Recall that Ehrlich (1968) did not believe the earth could support its present eight billion. It is in fact, supporting that population, though not always very well, and it can no doubt accommodate more. This growth has come, however, at a great price to the natural world—to species that have been driven to extinction, to fossil fuels that cannot be renewed, and so forth.

A crucial corollary to the question of how many is the question of how much. Americans consume energy and resources at a rate between 10 and 20 times that of Mexicans and 30 to 50 times that of South Asians. If everyone wants to live at the level of consumption enjoyed in the United States, then the planet may not be able to support the current eight billion, let alone more.

Population Control

Controversy continues to rage over how to best limit the world's population growth and whether this is even desirable or necessary. One view, common in many parts of the developing world, contends that the problem is poverty and economic injustice, rather than population. People are miserable, the argument goes, not because there are too many of them but because they are getting too little of the earth's abundant resources. This idea echoes Marx's

Cape Flats, township near Cape Town, South Africa. Population growth by itself does not always create poverty, but dense, poor, young, segregated populations create huge challenges in providing housing, education, health care and employment.

contention but is also popular with those who oppose **contraception,** or birth control, for religious and cultural reasons. At the World Population Conference in crowded Cairo, Egypt, the Vatican, drawing on Roman Catholic tradition, found itself in agreement with representatives from many Islamic states (Tagliabue 1994). People are not the problem; the inequitable distribution of wealth and resources is.

The counterargument has been around since Malthus: No matter how much we increase production or better distribute resources, our efforts will always be outstripped by the exponential curve of population growth. Population is the primary problem.

These two arguments need not be mutually exclusive. If it is indeed true that humanity's inventiveness over the past millennium has been used up by both inequality and population growth so that many people are no better off, then both a more equitable distribution of resources and a slower rate of population growth will be needed to provide a better life for those many people.

Debate also rages on how to best achieve population control. For a time, China used strict sanctions, primarily economic, coupled with a strong push for contraception, including sterilization, to enforce its one-child policy. While this policy never emphasized abortion, it tended to tolerate the use of abortion to achieve its target. In contrast, the United States, first under the Reagan administration and then again under the George W. Bush administration, moved to withhold funding for population programs that included access to abortion.

Contraception has been controversial for a very long time. Tribal peoples have used contraceptive herbs, as did women in ancient Greece and Rome. Contraception was controversial for more than 100 years in the United States. Feminist leaders in the late 1800s and early 1900s went to jail for promoting and distributing contraceptives. If motherhood was a woman's highest calling and civic duty, then contraception was a crime against both nature and the state. Yet even pioneer families in the American West circulated information on how to make homemade condoms.

Contraception became far more accessible with the approval of oral contraceptive pills in Europe in the 1950s and the United States in the 1960s. The media touted this as a "sexual revolution," but what really happened was a "fertility revolution." Fertility rates for U.S. and European women plummeted from the 1950s to the 1970s. Access to readily available and inexpensive contraception, along with the education and social acceptability to use them effectively, has been the key to declining fertility rates.

Attitudes change more slowly than technology, and often men seem more reluctant to accept contraception than women do. But even in traditionally "pronatal" countries, where a strong value is placed on large families, attitudes are beginning to change.

Fertility rates in the United States and Europe did not decline simply because new drugs became available. There were also new attitudes about the role of women and about their place in higher education and careers. This was crucial to the change: *careers*. Around the world, women work in fields and markets with small children tagging along or slung over their backs. Women pursuing higher education and professional employment, however, often choose a smaller family size. The state of women's education in a country is often a very good predictor of its fertility rate. More-educated women are more likely to wish to space out their children, to invest heavily in only a few children, to use contraception effectively, and to have the social power to convince others—both the men in their lives and an earlier generation of women—that this is a good approach for them and their families.

Population conferences, such as the one in Cairo, have also often featured controversies over the best route to lowered fertility: improved contraception, improved education, or an improved standard of living. Interestingly, these tend to be inseparable. The most successful approaches have often included all of them.

Women with broader life options choose to limit and space childbearing. They also tend to be healthier and to have healthier children. With more children surviving and more options for the future, the pressure to have many children as a form of "social security" also declines. Even when abortion is legal, in such situations, its rate may actually decline, as women make choices about family size in advance of pregnancy, rather than being pressured to seek abortion after conceiving. Combinations of urbanization, education, changing cultural attitudes, and access to family planning all point to population growth leveling off by the end of the century (see figure 10.4).

Migration

Demographers are interested in not only how many people there are but also where they are going. People have been on the move since the first ancestral human strode out of Africa to explore points unknown. Within remarkably few generations, humans were in South Asia and then Southeast Asia. By 40,000 years ago they seem to have been lashing together rafts and crossing to Australia with their newly domesticated dogs. By 12,000 to 20,000 years ago they were crossing the Bering Strait, either on foot or by boat, making their way between the walls of ice and then turning south to seek the bounty of warmer climates.

In the middle of all this movement, two great waves of **migration** stand out. The first came with European colonization of Africa, the Americas, and parts of Asia. Millions of Europeans eventually relocated to these "new worlds."

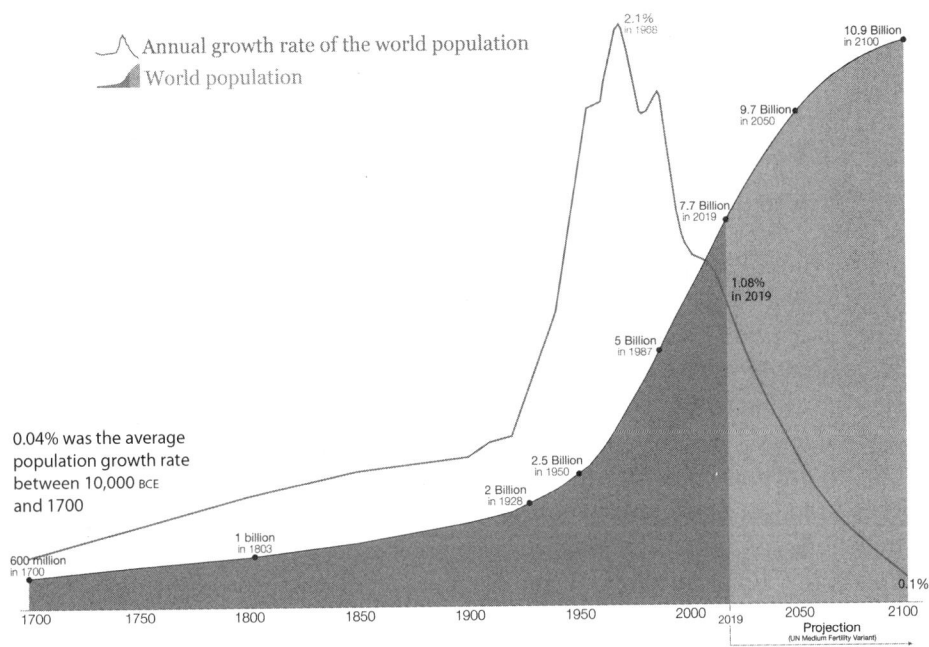

Figure 10.4 World population growth, 1700 to 2100. (Source: "Future Population Growth," by Max Roser. Our World in Data.)

This movement also accompanied the greatest population collapse in history: the decimation of the original peoples of the Americas, particularly through the introduction of Eurasian infectious diseases. The labor shortage that came with this population collapse was filled by exporting poor Europeans and then by moving millions of Africans as slaves across the Atlantic.

The second great wave of movement, larger in sheer number than the first, is occurring right now, as people from Africa, Latin America, and parts of Asia are leaving the troubled economies and dangerous political turmoil of the postcolonial world for safer and more prosperous regions. **Immigrants** leave their home countries to permanently settle elsewhere. **Labor migrants** travel abroad to seek work with the hope of someday returning home. **Refugees** are defined by the United Nations as those who have "a well-founded fear of being persecuted for reasons of race, religion, nationality, membership of a particular social group or political opinion" (UNHCR 2014, p. 2). If immigrants and labor migrants seek opportunity, then refugees above all seek safety. Those who flee their homes but remain within their countries of origin are labeled as **internally displaced.**

These labels and definitions are sometimes ambiguous: Is someone who is fleeing utter economic collapse and turmoil an immigrant or a refugee? Whether he or she will be granted entry and asylum, or the right to remain in a new country, may depend on how this question is answered by the authorities and the courts. The United Nations estimates there are 80 million forcibly displaced people globally, including 26 million refugees, and close to 46 million internally displaced people in the world (UNHCR 2020).

Each of these groups changes their host country or region in profound ways. Having a large number of internally displaced people can destabilize both a government and an environment, as can having a large number of refugees in a poor neighboring country. In Lebanon, Palestine, and Sri Lanka, refugee settlement areas have been places of extreme poverty and great unrest, serving as recruiting grounds for militants. Refugee camps in Africa have devastated fragile environments and placed huge strains on fragile governments.

When jobs and resources are available, however, immigrants and refugees can also be sources of innovation and prosperity. Immigrants often have high rates of entrepreneurship; they start new businesses in new locations, and many work very long hours. The immigrant boom fueled U.S. economic growth and industrial might at the beginning of the twentieth century, and immigrants have also brought growth and prosperity to places such as Canada, Australia, and Israel. But immigrants can also significantly strain schools and social services, especially if they are concentrated in few locations. Immigration has remade the faces of cities such as Los Angeles and Miami, as well as Sydney, Australia, and Toronto and Vancouver, Canada.

The greatest challenge can come in hosting refugees who have often had to leave with little time for preparation and maybe only the possessions they can grab and carry. The world's top receivers of refugees are Turkey, Colombia, Pakistan, Uganda, and Germany. The top suppliers of refugees include Syria by far, then Venezuela, Afghanistan, South Sudan, and Myanmar (UNHCR 2020). These are often linked: Syrians in Turkey and to a much lesser extent Germany, Venezuelans in Colombia, Afghans in Pakistan, and South Sudanese in Uganda. These are all fleeing political unrest and conflict ranging from oppression to civil war. Violent organized crime, often centered on drug trafficking, has now also entered the mix, sending many Guatemalans and Hondurans to seek safety in Mexico and the United States.

Honduras is a classic example of the dilemma of migrants. Much of Central America struggled with political violence in the latter part of the twentieth century, often in the grips of a U.S.-Soviet tug of war. Then in the twenty-first century, violence shifted from insurgencies and death squads to drug cartels and gang violence. Cities like San Pedro de Sula, Honduras, became murder capitals as rival gangs fought for territory amidst an otherwise collapsing economy. A government with a president who himself has been accused of involvement in trafficking was no help. Then came the hurricanes. In 2020, unprecedented back-to-back hurricanes slammed the city, burying people's homes and livelihoods under layers of packed mud. "We are doomed here," said Magdalena Flores, a mother of seven, standing on a mattress that peeked out from the dirt where her house used to be. "The desperation, the sadness, that's what makes you migrate." (Kitroeff 2021).

Those fleeing Honduras and other Central American countries represent the new face of refugees. Environmentalist Lester Brown has warned for years that climate change and degraded land would lead to failed states unable to maintain effective control of their territory and of resulting "climate refugees" (Brown 2011). The United States was first surprised by the size and determination of this out-migration, with many unaccompanied minors, during the Obama administration. The Trump administration responded with harsh detentions, higher barriers as part of a promised "wall," and a "remain in Mexico" policy for asylum seekers—using the coronavirus pandemic as justification for practices that violated international agreements. When word was out that the Biden administration was softening this policy, the northward flow resumed—sometimes parents walking and carrying children, but often teenage boys sent north by their parents on a desperate mission of escape. To remain is to be recruited into a gang or risk death at the hands of the gangs, or to just watch family members dig through the mud in search of any bit of their former lives that might remain.

Disease

Infectious Disease: The Kiss of Death

When people travel the world, they take many things with them. The most dangerous things are their breath and their blood. When humans travel and mingle, they often inadvertently transport dangerous microbes: viruses, bacteria, and parasites. Most are annoying, but some are deadly. A disease that spreads rapidly through a population in a particular location is an **epidemic** (they suffer at the epicenter of the infection). Once the epidemic spreads across continents and even around the globe, it is **pandemic.**

Through their activities, humans have often made their communities wonderful breeding grounds for microbes. Hunter-gatherers, however, seem to have been healthier than we first supposed. They ate a diverse, all-organic diet; exercised a great deal; and lived in small, isolated bands that were not the best breeding ground for dangerous microbes. The greatest danger they probably faced was parasitic worms and microscopic organisms that lay in wait in the natural world. Any backpacker who has stopped for a cool drink from what appeared to be a clean stream or lake, only to contract a persistent stomach ailment related to the parasite *Giardia*, can understand the danger.

Healthy individuals probably developed some resistance to these dangers, but things got worse when people started rearranging their environments. Domesticated animals became a valuable food source, but living in close proximity to these animals posed a real danger (Diamond 1997). Many of the "poxes" that have plagued herding societies and then traveled to their farming neighbors probably moved to humans from their livestock. Their names still reflect some idea of their origins: *chicken pox* or *cow pox*, which is closely related to one of history's greatest killers, *smallpox*.

Agricultural people, or grain farmers, didn't fare much better. Storing grain was a great way to provide for winter or drought, but it was also a bonanza for rodents. Mice and rat populations soared as these opportunists moved in to gobble stored grain, a year-round food supply. They brought with them a whole new array of microbes, as well as fleas to help transport the infection. People—who were now living in close quarters in villages and, worst of all, in cities—helped by transporting diseases through breath, water droplets in coughs and sneezes, dirty hands, and just plain pus. People were most at risk in poor and crowded urban spaces, where they were literally breathing down one another's necks. Crowded cities also faced a perennial problem that persists to this day: sewage. Human waste often ran in the streets and seeped into the waterways that provided water for cooking and drinking. The combination was deadly.

Great plagues devastated all the ancient cities with regularity. Famous plagues killed major portions of the urban populations of Athens, Alexandria, Carthage, Rome, and London. The most intense killer in Europe and Asia was **bubonic plague,** the so-called Black Death. Probably originally a disease of rodents, fleas carried the infection from rats to humans, who then shared it with each other. Several ancient "plagues" may have been caused by other diseases such as typhus. The first cases carefully enough documented to diagnose were during the Plague of Justinian in the sixth century (*Washington Post* 2021). Killing upward of 50 million, it was a major factor that prevented the Byzantine rulers of Constantinople from reassembling the full Roman Empire. Urban life was dangerous, and armies camped together were highly vulnerable.

Whole cities were decimated by plague with regularity in the fourteenth century. Refugees fleeing the cities would carry the infection into the countryside. Then the disease would subside, seemingly in a great divine reprieve. But it would live on somewhere, probably in wild rodents, waiting for the right time to return.

In 1333 the plague took hold of famine-stricken China, whose already weakened population was highly susceptible to infection. The plague moved westward with the caravans of traders and raiders. In what may be the first act of biological warfare, Tartar raiders are reported to have catapulted their plague-ridden corpses over the walls of the trading city of Calla in the Russian Crimean. Traders became infected and brought the plague to Constantinople and Venice. By 1347 the plague had found a home in famine-stricken northern Italy. Its source was still mysterious, and Jews were blamed for poisoning the wells. In England one-third to one-half of the population died, forcing a truce in the Hundred Years' War with plague-stricken France. Malnourished peasants in Russia and Poland succumbed quickly, and the Black Death began an eastward return march.

Before it left Europe, the Black Death had killed perhaps one-third of the entire population in a great demographic reversal. Rising populations suddenly fell. The survivors moved through a world in which labor was scarce, and so wages rose. Whole areas of the countryside were so depopulated that feudal agriculture collapsed. Some think the Black Death may have permanently changed European society. The last major outbreak of plague killed 50,000 in Marseilles, France, in 1720. Bubonic plague is not gone, however. Carefully monitored cases show up every year; today it is kept in check by human immunities, vigilance, and drugs.

Smallpox is a virus that travels from person to person. Closely related to animal diseases, it came to specialize in human hosts. The Antonine Plague that shook the Roman Empire to its core in the second century, killing perhaps five million, was likely smallpox, perhaps mixed with measles. The "plague" subsided but the infections continued to scar Europe for centuries. Waves of smallpox swept over Europe, Asia, and parts of Africa until many people developed a partial immunity to the disease. No such disease and no such immunity ever took hold in the Americas until Christopher Columbus showed up with a few sick sailors. The disease swept the Americas with an intensity only possible for a new invader. When the first lost Spaniards traveled across what is now the southern United States in the last years of the fifteenth century, they found a powerful civilization. Within a couple decades, later explorers found nothing but empty ruins and abandoned pyramids. Groups such as the Natchez had disappeared without a trace.

When Hernán Cortés attacked the great Aztec capital in Mexico in 1521 he had a secret weapon: smallpox. The disease killed an Aztec emperor and demoralized the defenders. The Spanish seemed largely immune, as if the gods had abandoned the continent's first inhabitants to favor the invaders. A few years later, in 1533, Francisco Pizarro attacked the vast Incan Empire with a handful of soldiers. He triumphed through treachery and disease. Smallpox killed many of the Inca, including their emperor, and left the empire in confusion and civil war.

A century later English colonists aboard the *Mayflower* had drifted hundreds of miles off course and were facing starvation in the chill of Cape Cod,

Massachusetts. When they disembarked, they noted the emptiness of the Americas, which was partly due to its inhabitants' less-dense settlement patterns than those of the Europeans. But the main reason for this "emptiness" was most likely due to the impact of disease. The new arrivals were saved by finding the food stock of an entire native village that had abandoned the site in the wake of disease, probably smallpox. The colonists took the food, gave thanks for God's provision, and went on to explore a continent that seemed to have been emptied to make room for them. Thus, European colonists didn't find an untamed wilderness, they found a continent devastated and depopulated by disease, microbes released when the first sick sailor breathed a sigh of relief at reaching landfall.

Smallpox continued to attack Europe, especially whenever populations were weakened. It became the first disease to be inoculated against, as it was noted that milkmaids who contracted a mild form of cow pox seemed immune to smallpox. When London was hit by smallpox in 1720, the same year of the last outbreak of bubonic plague, inoculations began and eventually reached even the royal family. That same year, smallpox struck in Boston, and a Boston clergyman and scientist began giving inoculations, despite intense suspicion. Gradually the idea gained acceptance. George Washington may have saved the Continental Army from destruction by inoculating his weakened, malnourished troops at Valley Forge. The methods were crude—exposing a cut to infected cells to stir a mild infection that would offer protection against the inhaled disease.

Perhaps you've seen references to Native peoples attacked in early germ warfare with smallpox laden blankets. One British commander may have tried, and others considered this approach, but it never proved feasible. Smallpox doesn't live long on surfaces. It is most quickly spread like COVID-19: person to person, breathing respiratory droplets. The U.S. army didn't intentionally unleash the great killers of the First Nations of the continent, smallpox and measles, any more than Rome's enemies intended to unleash the same killers on the legions, but in so many cases the germs proved to be the decisive killers.

Smallpox continued to take lives around the world well into the twentieth century. The UN World Health Organization (WHO) eventually launched a massive global campaign to eradicate the killer. Aided by better vaccines and by a virus that only infected humans and so could not hide in animals, the campaign succeeded in 1977, when the last smallpox case was reported in Africa. This campaign represents one of the world's greatest successes in fighting global disease.

Ironically, however, the fear of smallpox has returned. After the last naturally occurring case had ended, both the United States and the Soviet Union continued to keep vials of smallpox virus, each fearful that the other might try to use this killer as a weapon. Some of these vials are today unaccounted for, especially those that were part of Soviet bioweapons programs. The fear that terrorists might get hold of the smallpox virus and use it with terrible effect against populations that are no longer vaccinated and do not have a natural immunity to the disease has led some to call for renewed vaccination programs.

Cholera is a bacterial killer. It infects the digestive tract and kills through the dehydration that results from uncontrolled diarrhea. Not only is this an undignified way to go, it is also especially dangerous for young children. Cholera epidemics strike with ferocity and then disappear for a while. It appears the bacteria can live in warm water, waiting to be transported and to contaminate a drinking water supply. Once the disease has hit, poor sewage facilities move the bacteria quickly from a diarrhea-stricken victim to the next new host.

A cholera epidemic killed thousands in China in 1830 and then began a spread around the world that would claim the lives of millions over the next 20 years. It had reached London in 1832, had died down, but resurfaced in 1849–1849. Toward the end of that outbreak, John Snow, an insightful physician, recorded the location and deaths related to cholera, discovering they occurred near a particular public well. Snow convinced local officials to remove a water pump handle from the well, so it could no longer be used. Immediately, new cholera cases subsided and the connection between contaminated water and disease was established, along with the usefulness of careful demographic research!

Yet cholera epidemics continue to kill millions around the world, recurring every decade or so. The bacterium that causes cholera was identified in the late 1800s, and it was discovered that this disease responds to antibiotics. Death can often be averted with simple rehydration therapies. Cholera continues to kill, however, now mostly as a disease of the poor.

The fight against cholera also demonstrates the importance of improved sanitation. Death rates in European and North American cities began to fall long before the advent of antibiotics in the 1940s and later medical advances. The key disease fighter in the early 1900s was the sewer. But around the world, dysentery, cholera, and other diarrhea-causing intestinal diseases remain major killers, particularly of children. Providing a clean, covered water supply is the essential element in preventing these killers.

The other great weapon against disease has been improved nutrition. Major epidemics and plagues often followed famines and wars, times when populations were greatly weakened.

HIV/AIDS

In the 1980s the world's attention became riveted on a new killer, **AIDS, or acquired immune deficiency syndrome.** The disease is caused by **HIV,** the **human immunodeficiency virus,** which can remain dormant in the host for a period of months or years before attacking the body's immune system with enough force to cause AIDS. People with AIDS typically die of pneumonia or another infectious disease that takes over once their immune system has been disabled. HIV is spread by exposure to contaminated body fluids, particularly blood. It has most often been spread by sexual contact, the sharing of needles among intravenous drug users, and exposure to unsafe blood supplies.

AIDS appears to be another zoogenetic or animal-to-human crossover virus. It is related to diseases that infect felines and primates. It may not be so new; perhaps as early as the 1930s the virus made the leap from animal hosts to humans in West Central Africa. The ability of this virus to quickly mutate, or change its form, has been one of the difficulties in creating a vaccine. By the early 1980s the virus had left Africa and traveled with its human hosts around the world. Over 33 million people have died of AIDS (UNAIDS 2020), and over 38 million are living with HIV. No place on the planet escaped this pandemic, but over three-quarters of the cases have occurred in Africa.

The southern African countries—South Africa, Botswana, Zimbabwe, Zambia—all experienced HIV infection rates of 20 percent to 40 percent. For some communities, an entire generation and much hope for the future was lost. Government agencies and medical services lack a sufficient number of healthy people to staff them. With over 40 million orphans in Sub-Saharan Africa alone, social services were overwhelmed to the point of collapse. Since the virus can pass from an infected mother to her child, some of these children were born infected, compounding their needs.

In Africa HIV/AIDS has spread by various means. Prostitution is common in areas where work keeps men away from their families for months or years at a time. When the men do return home, they may return infected and spread the virus to their wives. The medical system has at times been as much a problem as a help. African hospitals depend more on blood transfusions than their European and North American counterparts, which have access to other treatments and drugs, and African hospitals have found it harder to secure and monitor their blood supply. Risky behaviors—some ancient, such as polygamous marriage, and some more recent, such as roadside and township prostitution—will need to change to control the spread of the disease in Africa. Sometimes the choices are difficult. Journalist Marc Lacey (2003) tells the story of girls whose only way to remain in school is to find a "sugar daddy" who will pay the school fees in return for sex.

Africa is not alone in terms of the complicated set of risk factors that people face. Thailand, a home to an international drug trade and sex trade, was particularly hard-hit and has launched a major campaign against HIV risk factors. Other countries, such as China, were slower to address the problems. In still others, such as India, the government has made major efforts but the message has been slow to reach the countryside. In some of India's poorest roadside villages, prostitution is almost the only source of income, and girls as young as 12 are quickly maneuvered into becoming prostitutes for those traveling the roads. Similarly, young Thai girls are often sold or tricked into the service of pimps, who confine them in the Bangkok sex trade. In both cases, these girls become new links in the chain of HIV transmission. The highest rates of new infection are now in Eastern Europe and Central Asia, where countries spun off from the Soviet bloc have been facing disrupted economies and societies.

The fight against HIV/AIDS must be based on preventing infection, but new drugs also give hope to those already infected. When first released, these drug combinations were so expensive that they were beyond the means of poor people in poor countries. Now treatment can cost as little as $1 a day, although this still constitutes much of the daily income of the world's poorest people.

Pandemic

New dangers for other infectious diseases also continue to surface. A world of people in motion is also a great worldwide web of potential infection transmission. A "mad cow" in England can spark a global panic in the world livestock industry within 24 hours, and a sick chicken in China can start an epidemic in Toronto within a month.

The world's deadliest year of disease was not during the height of the Black Death but the influenza epidemic of 1918. Spread globally by soldiers returning from World War I, it killed more people around the world than the war had. The United States lost 115,000 people to combat in World War I and 500,000 to the flu epidemic that followed. No one knows what made this particular flu so deadly. It killed over 21 million people, or 1 percent of the world's population (World Health Organization 2007).

Every year new influenza strains emerge, many of them in China and East Asia, where close proximity between farmers and livestock, especially chickens and pigs, seems to allow enterprising viruses to adapt to a change of host. Soon they go on a global tour. In 2010 global alarm was raised as the swine flu virus shifted from likely infection of hogs to humans, with Mexico at the epicenter. Fortunately this flu infected children and young people at higher rates, while older adults had some immunity from prior exposure to similar viruses. The result was a lot of misery but fewer fatalities, with most young people recovering fairly quickly. Although no flu-like virus has ever struck again with the virulence of the 1918 strain, world health officials continue to wonder and watch for mad cows and suspicious chickens.

The world has been on the edge of pandemics not just with the influenza virus but with the spiky protein covered pathogens known as coronaviruses. Like influenza viruses, the coronaviruses can infect a variety of animals and can cross over to human infection. In 2003 one such virus moved beyond a simple head cold to a serious respiratory infection known as SARS (severe acute respiratory syndrome). SARS shut down global trade in major cities from Guangzhou, China, to Toronto, Canada, before being contained by especially vigilant international action. Middle East Respiratory Syndrome (MERS) emerged in Saudi Arabia in 2012 but quickly died out. The WHO was still trying to understand the risks posed by animal coronaviruses shifting hosts to humans when people started to fall ill in Wuhan, China, in 2019. The culprit was a new or "novel" coronavirus, sars-cov-2, which was causing a new disease they dubbed COVID-19 (the coronavirus disease of 2019, not very creative naming). This variant was so dangerous because it was not always obviously dangerous. In some people, the disease felt like a mild cold. In others, it felt like a terrible case of influenza. And in others, particularly the elderly and those with "comorbidities" or other health risk factors, it struck with deadly force. In some victims it attacked the lungs, destroying tissue and dropping oxygen levels suddenly and precipitously. In others it triggered out-of-control immune responses, including inflammation of the heart, kidneys, and other vital organs. Risk factors rose with age, but this virus hit with unpredictable consequences. And it was highly contagious. Those with mild or even no symptoms could carry the disease to others. And they did—around the world. The disease was showing up in San Francisco and Seattle even as it was being identified and verified in China. Others brought it back to Italy where young people unwittingly infected elders in their household and extended family. From Italy and European hotspots it quickly traveled to the crowded spaces of New York City. Some parts of the world were quite effective at containing the spread with very few fatalities, such as Vietnam, Taiwan, and New Zealand. Others, including much of Europe, did reasonably well at first and then struggled with a second wave in the winter of 2020–2021. And some places with large urban conglomerations and leaders who were slow to respond to the crisis faced massive mortality: Brazil with almost half a million deaths, Mexico with a quarter million, and the United States with over 600,000 (Johns Hopkins 2021). India fared better at first, then amidst crowded conditions and a premature relaxing of restrictions, surged to over a third of a million deaths and massive social disruption.

Mask wearing, common for infection protection in parts of East Asia but rare elsewhere, became the norm before a massive global vaccine effort began to turn the tide of infection. Over a year of global contagion had taken 3.5 million lives. Like pandemics before, it is also altered economies and threatened to change the global balance of power.

It proved far faster to develop vaccines than to test and deliver them. Within weeks of the novel coronavirus being identified as the cause of the new illness, vaccines were developed in biotech labs around the world. Two used a method that had been tested on other viral illness but never developed into a vaccine. The Pfizer/BioNTech vaccine and the Moderna vaccine used a strand of messenger RNA, carrying the genetic fingerprint of the virus to teach the human body to mount an immune response. No virus was present, in fact, the labs needed no virus samples—they only needed the sequenced genome of the virus sent to them in an email attachment from colleagues in China to begin development. When the genetic code arrived by email, Moderna had a vaccine prototype ready in two days in January 2020, before many had even heard of the disease, and before most realized the world was facing a pandemic (Neilson et al. 2020; Wallace-Wells 2020). It took months to test each of the vaccines in traditional human trials, proving some of the newest technology to be incredibly effective, and then a huge effort to distribute the vaccines.

Wealthier countries secured supplies of vaccines—their own in some cases—or rights to purchase one of the major vaccines. Poorer countries were often left out. Delivery was a huge challenge for all but particularly in places with overstretched health care systems and little capability to maintain the very cold temperatures that the innovative messenger RNA vaccines required. Meanwhile some countries hedged by overbuying; in the fall of 2020 Canada secured 300 million doses for 30 million people, five times what it would need even with double doses. The United States went from suffering the most number of cases and fatalities to having by far the largest number of vaccines—if it could only convince everyone to receive it. The WHO organized COVAX to deliver vaccines to Africa and Latin America. The first vaccine, the British AstraZeneca, manufactured in India, arrived in Ghana and Ivory Coast in late February 2021, beginning the huge challenge of global vaccination (BBC News 2021a). The lessons learned in vaccine development and distribution could prove vital in conquering other diseases. But as countries in Africa entered the middle of 2021 with almost no one vaccinated, the realities of global inequality outweighed the miracles of new biotechnology. Meanwhile, other vaccine campaigns to eradicate long-standing killers were interrupted and suspended, threatening to further postpone a healthy and vibrant future in much of the world.

Chronic Disease: Dying by Degrees

Some infectious diseases are not acute killers, like smallpox and the Black Death, but slowly incapacitate their victims over time. With new drugs that contain but do not cure the disease, HIV/AIDS may be shifting from an acute to a chronic infection. TB, or tuberculosis, can be deadly but often has a slow disabling progress. Many of the parasitic infections that have long plagued humans follow this pattern.

The WHO office at the UN has targeted a number of these diseases for eradication (World Health Organization 2007). Long underfunded, the efforts have gained a major benefactor from the multibillion-dollar Gates Foundation. Other groups have targeted specific diseases. The Carter Center has focused on Guinea worm, which has disabled millions in West Africa. The Carter Center has also focused on river blindness, transmitted by a biting fly, which gradually takes the sight of thousands in West Africa. Young children, some only as old as three or four, become "seeing-eye children," whose full-time occupation is to lead blind elders around. The disease thus not only disables its victim but takes the childhoods of these children, who have no time for play or study.

In warm, wet locations, schistosomiasis, borne by snails that thrive in perpetually wet irrigated fields, slowly saps the energy of its victims and is particularly devastating to children. Haitian villages have long known the horror of "monster men," afflicted with a mosquito-borne worm that causes elephantiasis. The lymph nodes in the limbs and groin swell, giving the disease its name. The swelling and secondary infection can be so severe as to cause second-degree burns. The victims not only suffer intense pain but also the social isolation that comes with the disfigurement and horrible odor caused by the disease. Medical workers, backed by foundation money, are trying to get everyone in infected areas to take a harsh pill that kills the young worms and prevents the disease and to eliminate the sewage collection ponds that breed it. Like smallpox, these diseases have no nonhuman hosts to complete their life cycle and can be completely eradicated.

One disease not responding well to global efforts is **malaria,** which is caused by a parasite that is transmitted by mosquitoes. It can be deadly, and even the less-acute forms are often thoroughly disabling. Although it is now concentrated in certain regions (see figure 10.5), malaria once circled the warm areas of the globe. It was the "fever and ague" that afflicted U.S. pioneers and settlers along river bottoms and wetlands in the southern part of the United States. Even before the doctors of the day understood the disease (they believed a lethal "miasma" arose from stagnant waters and poisoned the air), they had a powerful weapon to combat it. The Amerindians of South America had discovered that a bitter tree bark could cure the disease, and this became the basis of the one of the world's first truly effective medicines: quinine. The well-off took quinine pills, while the poor brewed the coarse bark into a bitter tea. But in any form, quinine was effective—for a while.

Over time the malaria parasite has grown resistant to quinine, which is no longer recommended for many cases. Malaria was in retreat for a long time, given the spread of effective medicines coupled with the draining of wetlands in many locations. It persisted in the tropics, until a new weapon was deployed in the 1950s: DDT. This pesticide was used widely around the world. In prosperous temperate cities, it was a way to control the annoyance of mosquitoes; in poor tropical areas, it became the first line of defense against mosquito-borne malaria. DDT was found to have disastrous environmental and public health side effects, however, and its use has been discontinued in wealthier countries; it was banned in the United States in 1972. It has sometimes been replaced by newer and more expensive alternatives. A new line of defense against malaria was found in newer drugs, first chloroquine in the 1940s, and

Population and Health CHAPTER 10 359

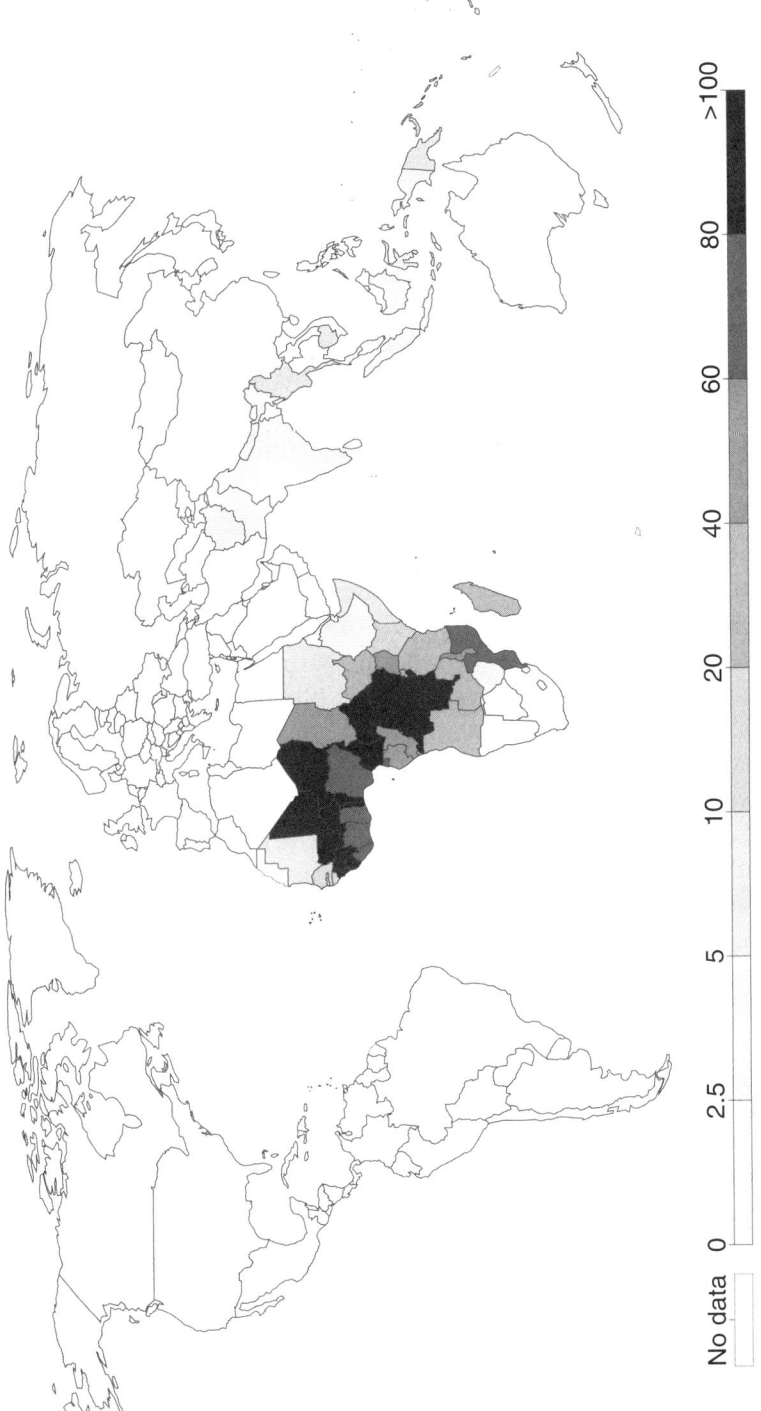

Figure 10.5 Worldwide distribution of malaria (number of deaths per 100,000 people). (Source: Our World in Data.)

then a third generation of more expensive drugs emerged as new strains again proved resistant to existing treatment. Poor countries can afford neither the more expensive mosquito-control programs nor the more expensive drugs, and so malaria is making a comeback in these regions. Some want to expand the spraying of DDT, even though it has many known dangers to both wildlife and humans.

Malaria can be a killer, particularly of children. In 2019, 229 million cases resulted in just over 400,000 deaths, mostly of children in Africa (CDC 2021). But malaria can also become part of chronic reinfection, with adults having many bouts of malaria over a lifetime, losing productive time to chronic fatigue and suffering a wide range of long-term organ damage. New hope has been raised by experimental vaccines, although this parasite has proven elusive and not an easy vaccine target. Until there is a breakthrough, malaria remains one of the world's greatest challenges for eradication through careful public health screening, isolation, treatment, and removal of risk factors. Meanwhile, climate change could also alter risk patterns as slightly higher elevations favored for settlement will no longer be above the malaria zone.

Many of the world's chronic diseases are not infectious (caused by microbes or germs) but are the result of work and community and lifestyle. These diseases are often very modern. During the height of deep shaft coal mining in the United States, coal miners often were disabled and sometimes dead by their 40s, what we would now consider midcareer, due to chronic diseases such as "black lung," caused by breathing coal dust. Careers and lifetimes were even shorter in the coal mines of Japan's Battleship Island at the beginning of the twentieth century. Miners in the great, deep mines of South Africa have long suffered both accidents and chronic infirmities. While conditions have improved in some mines, the occupation remains one of the most dangerous in the world. Occupational hazards are the source of many chronic diseases: Textile workers inhale lint dust, and industrial workers inhale fumes from toxic metals. Some workers are permanently bent, stooped, or partially blinded by working under intense and uncomfortable conditions for long hours.

Communities filled with pollutants are also disabling. In the inner cities of the United States, poor children have extremely high and rising rates of asthma and lung disease. Toxic waste sites are often located near low-income communities.

Much chronic illness is also related to lifestyle. The worldwide spread of tobacco use—particularly in the form of packaged cigarettes that encourage chain smoking—is one of the leading disablers and killers. A high-fat diet, often a Western "export," kills and disables through heart disease and stroke. High-sugar and high-calorie diets also contribute to diabetes, a major disabler of African American, American Indian, Native Hawaiian, and Polynesian peoples and a growing threat to children and young people.

The WHO (2005) notes obesity as a growing threat to people in the more prosperous nations of the world. The United States is a leader in this problem, and many European countries are not far behind. Obesity is also increasing in Latin America and Asia. The combination of fast-food—high-fat products that are consumed quickly—and the sedentary lifestyle of the video age has spread this chronic ailment around the world.

Health Care

Every society in the world has given a prominent place to the healing arts. Yet even now that science-based modern medicine has become the norm, countries vary greatly in how they deliver care and attempt to address health issues.

United States

The United States spends a great deal of money on health care—more in fact, than any other country in the world. It spends half again as much as Canada and more than twice as much as Sweden, both countries that have longer life expectancies, lower infant mortality rates, and overall better health.

Several factors go into making U.S. health care the world's most expensive. For example, U.S. physicians are among the best paid in the world, and hospital and insurance administration in the United States is costly. Technology is also expensive, and the United States is a world leader in advanced medical technology.

With such well-paid doctors and advanced medical equipment, why don't Americans fare better on overall outcomes? Over half of the U.S. expenditures on health go toward the last six months of life. Of course, it is hard to know in advance just when those last six months will be, but exceptional efforts to prolong the life of someone who is terminally ill can be very expensive.

Another factor is that the United States does not do as well as other countries in spending on preventive health care. It has by far the largest portion of its population uninsured or inadequately insured of any nation in the advanced industrial world. While some Americans receive outstanding care, those without private insurance often receive only emergency care, with little opportunity for regular checkups or prevention. This is especially true of uninsured pregnant women. They may have access to hospital emergency rooms and very sophisticated equipment in the event of an emergency for themselves or for their newborn child, but they may not be able to receive less-expensive, ongoing prenatal care. Disparities in health care access often follow racial lines. In the United States the infant mortality rate for non-Hispanic black babies is more than twice as high as for non-Hispanic white babies (CDC 2020).

While many have called for a national health care system in the United States, most reform plans have been aimed at filling gaps in the present

private-pay system. Medicaid, a joint federal and state program, provides care for the poorest people. Some states have added protection for the children of the working poor, who have jobs and may not qualify for Medicaid but often do not have work-related insurance and cannot afford other insurance. Attempts have been made to make insurance "portable" between jobs. Still, most Americans have their health insurance through an employer, and those who change jobs, are unemployed, or have jobs with no benefits are often left out of the system. In early 2010 between 35 and 50 million Americans were in this situation.

The social and economic strain of this situation led to health care reform being one of the Obama administration's first domestic priorities. It proved to be enormously controversial. After rejecting proposals to create a public option for those without private insurance, Congress narrowly passed a reform bill in March 2010—the Affordable Care Act. Among the provisions of the act were: the requirement that all uninsured people buy private insurance; government subsidies to those who purchased insurance under this plan; requirement of insurance companies to insure individuals, even if they had preexisting conditions; and the allowance that parents' insurance cover their children until the age of 25. As of 2019, health insurance is no longer mandated at the federal level, but the plan's other stipulations, including insurers may not refuse to take people with preexisting conditions, have been retained.

Canada

Canada has used a **single-payer health care system** since the early 1970s. In this system, physicians are still in private practice; except for a few specialists who work outside the system, they send their bills to the government in a program shared by the national and provincial governments. All Canadian citizens have a health card issued by the government that is their assurance of access to care. Patients are allowed to choose their doctors and develop relationships with them over time.

This system is considerably less expensive than that in the United States, since emphasis is placed on preventive rather than high-end care. Also, duplication of services between hospitals is limited, and hospitals and doctors' offices only need to bill one source, greatly reducing overhead and administrative costs. The government sets fees for particular services and caps physicians' incomes, although Canadian doctors are still well paid.

The biggest downside of this system can be long waits for certain services, since facilities are run at full capacity and there is no incentive not to seek unnecessary care (except the deterrent of a long wait). Impatient Canadians sometimes seek care outside the government-paid system or in the United States. Yet most Canadians approve of this system, which provides broader coverage for less cost than the system to the south.

Sweden

One of the earliest efforts at **national health care** came in Sweden, which in 1891 instituted health care for all its citizens. Hospitals are government run, and most physicians are government employees. Their salaries are considerably lower than those of U.S. and Canadian doctors. While the care can be more impersonal, the technical level is quite high.

The Swedes have one of the longest life expectancies in the world, and their system costs considerably less than the Canadian system and less than half the U.S. system. The Swedish system has been termed **socialized medicine** (a term sometimes wrongly applied to the Canadian system), since it is largely owned and operated by the national government.

Great Britain

Great Britain has used a hybrid system since shortly after World War II. The National Health Service provides health care to anyone who needs it, but an extensive private system remains in place for those who can afford to pay. The British system thus ensures care for all and preserves choice for some, but it does so at the risk of a two-tier system (not unlike the British school system), with better care for those who are better-off.

Japan

Japan also retains private physicians, but most health care costs are paid by the government, as in the Canadian system. Private insurance makes up the difference. Everyone is covered through large insurance pools. An extensive and well-regarded health care system, coupled with a traditionally healthy diet and exercise, has given the Japanese the longest life expectancy and the longest healthy life expectancy of people anywhere in the world. The Japanese do suffer chronic illnesses related to high levels of smoking and occupational and educational stress. The influence of a higher-fat Western diet and a greater dependence on cars, which reduces the amount of walking, are starting to add to the incidence of chronic illness. An aging population will also be a concern.

Still, a combination of low rates of obesity and low rates of violence, coupled with a highly efficient health care delivery system, gives Japan some of the lowest health care costs in the advanced industrial world. Payment levels are set by the government, often at one-half to one-third of U.S. levels, and targeted toward primary care. In Japan, primary care can be more lucrative than specialties, ensuring that a larger portion of Japanese medical facilities target primary and preventive care (Arnquist 2009).

Russia

The Soviet Union, not surprisingly, had a far-reaching system of socialized medicine. While the technology and expertise were not always at the highest level, the system did reach almost everyone. Like many institutions in post-Soviet Russia, the health care system is in disarray. Physicians are paid very poorly, often earning no more than teachers or factory workers, and they are often paid irregularly. Over two-thirds of Russian doctors are women, reflecting an early opening of opportunities for Russian women as well as the fact that health care is not considered a very lucrative profession. Many physicians' training is comparable to that of a nurse-practitioner in the United States. Better care is offered in large cities and in military hospitals. The Russian system can be very impersonal, or at times, personal to the extreme.

The smoking rate is high in Russia, and the rate of alcoholism is one of the highest in the world. Russian life expectancy of 73.2 years is 97th in the world, behind El Salvador, Bangladesh, and Vietnam (World Health Organization 2020). Russia seems to combine the chronic illnesses of the industrialized world with the infectious diseases and poor care of the developing world. With a very low birth rate and relatively high infant and child mortality rates, Russia has one of the world's fastest-shrinking populations.

China

China is faced with limited resources and a huge budget. It first gained world attention by addressing this problem with a system of "barefoot doctors." Part paramedic, part nurse, and part public health official, these doctors traveled to rural villages to provide basic preventive health care and education. China continues to struggle, however, to provide access to specialists and sophisticated health care in its vast rural areas (Song 2018). The remote western reaches of the country are particularly underserved.

The government has made an effort to make Chinese health care more technologically proficient and equal but is struggling with the latter (Li et al. 2020). The government owns and operates all the hospitals, as in Russia and Sweden, but as in Great Britain, people with cash can secure private care. Ironically, in China the gap between the quality of government care and private care is often much greater than in Great Britain—sometimes, the difference between life and death. Chinese doctors, like British doctors, often "moonlight" in the private sector. In China this can take new forms. Chinese surgeons, as in the United States, often stop by to reassure family members before the surgery of a loved one. One tradition has family members stuffing money into the pockets of the surgeon's white coat as he or she walks by with his or her sanitized hands and arms in the air. Some surgeons don't proceed into the operating room, where the already anesthetized patient is waiting, until their pockets are sufficiently filled!

While the Chinese health care delivery system, that is, its treatment of symptoms and diseases, is looking more and more Western, many traditional Chinese healing practices continue to prevail. A hospital may have a very Western-looking pharmacy, dispensing prescription drugs, and also a large kitchen, where healing herbs are carefully prepared according to ancient traditions. The Chinese contend that they have blended the best of the Eastern and Western healing arts. Indeed, many of these herbs have been found to have healing properties, and interest in ginger, gingko biloba, jasmine, and other traditional herbs and spices has grown in Western countries.

The ideals of balancing the forces of *yin* and *yang* and particularly of channeling the body's vital energy, or *chi*, have no direct parallel in modern Western medicine but continue to guide Chinese medical thought. *Chi* can be channeled through medicine and herbs but also through practices such as massage and exercise. A warm morning in any Chinese park will likely have many people, especially older adults, out practicing the slow and precise movements of Tai Chi Chuan. Tai Chi is related to martial arts, but its main purpose is the improvement of health through the channeling of chi. It has gained wide following in the United States and Europe, as well. Similarly, yoga—an ancient Indian discipline that uses a combination of breathing, balancing, and stretching exercises to promote health, peace of mind, and well-being—has become extremely popular in North America and Europe.

Other Asian Countries

Both China and India have made great gains in lowering infant mortality and raising life expectancy, despite very low average incomes. The southern Indian state of Kerala has combined socialized medicine with extensive village-level care, broad-based public health education, and particular attention to prenatal care and children's health. As a result, it has achieved a level of healthy life expectancy as high as the levels in the most industrialized countries. Sri Lanka, off the coast of India, has also achieved very impressive results with a very limited average income. Singapore has surpassed the United States in lowering infant mortality.

Continuing these successes will require continuing to ensure broad-based health care access while adopting new technologies. It will also be necessary to avoid the risk factors—lack of exercise, obesity, poor-quality environments—that can come with new technology and raise the risks of chronic illness.

Living Well, Staying Well

Many aspects of human physiology (how the body works) and pathology (what goes wrong) are still mysteries, but many others are not. We know the basic elements of individual health and well-being: A balanced, diverse diet that avoids excess fat, sugar, salt, and alcohol; the avoidance of tobacco and dangerous drugs; an active lifestyle with regular exercise; meaningful work without extreme dangers or extreme stress; and healthy relationships are all key factors. We don't always follow all of these guidelines, however, either because we are unwilling or because we are unable.

We also know the basics of good public health—how to build healthy societies and communities. Health care must be available and affordable to all. And while new technologies and discoveries are important, the emphasis needs to be on prevention, particularly in the areas of sanitation and nutrition as well as early diagnosis. Prevention goes beyond health care access to education, both general education and specific public health education. People need to be able to learn about the basic elements of good health, in whatever context they nurture themselves and their families—rural or urban, Eastern or Western, traditional or modern. In this, women's education remains a key, in part because it has been so long neglected in so many places and in part because in most places, women remain the primary caregivers for both the young and the old. An ironic relationship exists between health and population: The sickest populations with the most endangered lives and the least educated women and children also have the highest rates of population growth. As a result, seeing each person as unique, precious, and worthy of great investments of time and money goes hand in hand with slowing population growth.

We know what to do. Yet many societies remain unable or unwilling to make these investments in their people and their future. Developing countries must themselves make health and population control two of their top priorities. Wealthy countries must make access to health care for all—including poor, immigrant, and minority populations—one of their top priorities. Moreover, wealthy nations, foundations, and influential international organizations must recognize that the health of the planet respects national boundaries no more than does the latest epidemic. Whether these become global priorities will determine whether our future is as dismal as the most nightmarish Malthusian projection or a continued transition to a healthy, stable population with hope for themselves and their children.

Key Ideas

- The world's population continues to grow, although the pace of growth is slowing. The current population of almost eight billion will reach nine to 10 billion by the middle of the century before growth levels off in a process known as demographic transition.
- Almost all the population growth is in the world's poorer countries. Advanced industrial nations have stable or even shrinking populations whose average age continues to climb.
- Fertility rates, the average number of children born to a woman in her lifetime, are falling everywhere. They are below replacement level in much of Europe, East Asia, and North America. Fertility rates are higher in rural Latin America and South Asia, and highest of all are in Africa and the Middle East.
- Infectious disease, spread between people, is still a major concern around the world. Vaccines have provided protection against some old killers, but other diseases, such as malaria and TB, are becoming drug resistant, and new difficult-to-treat diseases, most notably AIDS, have emerged.
- Chronic disease can accompany malnutrition and poor living conditions and limit people's ability to work and to learn. Late-in-life chronic disease is also becoming a growing concern in countries with aging populations and sedentary lifestyles.
- Countries around the world struggle with the best way to provide affordable health care. Most countries offer a system of national health care, but in many places this is severely underfunded or unavailable.

For Review and Discussion

1. How many children would you like to have in your lifetime? What are the factors that go into people's decisions about family size as well as their preference for boys or girls?
2. Good health is one of the most basic human needs. Why has it been so difficult to provide the means for a healthy life to many of the world's people?
3. What are the advantages and disadvantages of the differing health care systems used by various countries? Are there some systems that seem preferable in reaching the most people the most effectively and efficiently?

Making Connections

Pandemic

➤ To see the impact of great pandemics over history, see *The Washington Post* graphic "Retropolis" on "History's deadliest pandemics, from ancient Rome to modern America" at https://www.washingtonpost.com/graphics/2020/local/retropolis/coronavirus-deadliest-pandemics/?itid=hp_dontmiss. For tallies on the impact of COVID-19, see Johns Hopkins Data Repository and the "visual desktop" the latest data, charts and maps at https://www.arcgis.com/apps/opsdashboard/index.html#/bda7594740fd40299423467b48e9ecf6.

World Health Organization

➤ This United Nations organization has been at the forefront of the campaign to eradicate disease, vaccinate children, and improve health care and health education around the world. Its site at www.who.int contains information on global health concerns and major campaigns. Special attention is given to HIV/AIDS and to global epidemics, most notably the COVID-19 pandemic. Information can be found by country or by topic. In addition to AIDS and COVID-19, what are the current prime concerns of the WHO?

Healthy Lives and Well-being

➤ UN Sustainable Development Goal 3:"Ensure healthy lives and promote well-being for all at all ages." See more on global health efforts at https://www.un.org/sustainabledevelopment/health/. What goes into "well-being for all ages"? How is this linked to the emphasis on maternal and child health?

Making a Difference

Population Connection

➤ Formerly called Zero Population Growth (ZPG), this group changed its name to reflect a broader concern for population issues, including family planning, health care, and education, though limiting growth is still a major concern. The site at www.populationconnection.org contains a wide array of information, legislative action alerts, and other ways to get involved. What are their current projects and legislative initiatives?

Health Clinics

➤ What is available on your campus or in your community for health education and health care for the uninsured? Begin with your campus health office or campus office. Then visit local clinics and health offices. What are they doing to provide care and education? What are their main emphases and biggest challenges? How can individuals and groups become involved?

AIDS Services

➤ Find out what is available in your community for AIDS services, HIV testing, and AIDS-prevention education. Are these programs offered on campus, in the schools, at community clinics, or through specialized agencies and programs? What types of services are offered, and how do they attempt to reach people in the community?

➤ For further information on AIDS, HIV, tuberculosis, and efforts to combat related infectious diseases around the world, see the AIDS Education Global Information System at https://www.guidestar.org/profile/33-0661931.

11
Technology and Energy

Prometheus's Fire or Pandora's Box?

Global Encounters

Japan

Japan manages to combine the Asian graciousness we have learned to love with the Western sense of efficiency that many have missed. Japan is a country that works hard and works well. Our first great task is to learn the trains: There are three regular lines, a PortLiner, a separate subway, and the Shinkansen bullet train. Every one of them runs precisely to the minute, maybe to the second. The trains won't wait for you, but if you miss one, another will be along in a matter of minutes. Because of this, Kobe is the first major city we have been in that isn't clogged with cars. The handful of cars on the roads tends to be small, efficient, and increasingly hybrids. The result is a crowded city but one without the constant odor of smog and diesel.

The city of Kobe occupies a narrow strip along the coast, and beyond are the forested mountains. Silent gondolas whisk us up into the mountains, where nature occasionally is interrupted for a hot springs spa or a winding herb garden. These are not so much for tourists as for the Japanese themselves to escape the urban bustle. Walking down past a series of waterfalls, we encounter painters at every bridge, sketching in black ink and doing watercolor washes. Not much true wilderness in this crowded place, but a clear love of nature is evident everywhere, along with the means to protect it. Our Latin American ports had similar hills as well, but they were lined top to bottom with the shantytowns of those desperate for a home.

Old and new, things borrowed and things homegrown also blend in Japan as they have for centuries. Intrigued by escalators that only start up when someone approaches them, we are sucked down into the great underground malls and covered arcades. Amid a blend of Christmas carols and raunchy rap lyrics, all in English, young people mill about in the latest fashions (truly latest—what is here now we may see in Chicago next year and in South Bend the year after that). They seem drawn to the lines of stores offering the latest technological gimmickry. Here even the restroom toilets sing to you and the toilet paper rolls are automatic. The most crowded store seems to be the Disney Store, packed with a few parents and many of the under-30 set.

Our students' favorite topic of discussion is a film we saw on Japan's "parasite singles," young people and especially young women who live at home, enjoy spending their income on luxuries, and have little interest in marriage or having children. The older generation worries that these young people have lost the sense of commitment and sacrifice that characterized Japan's rise to prominence. Yet given the prospect of losing one's hard-won career at first pregnancy (mothers are expected to work, at most, part-time at lesser jobs) and raising children to exacting standards in a cramped apartment with a husband who is away at work from early morning until late at night, one can hardly blame these young women for enjoying an unattached life for as long as they can. Their first real experience of family obligation may come in caring for aging parents. Japan's birth rate is one of the lowest in world, and with little in-migration, the population is aging and will be shrinking.

Japan has faced a stagnant economy for over a decade and has been passed by China as the world's second largest economy. Japan is also especially vulnerable to resource shortages, since all the pillars of its industrial economy are imported. The great cranes of the port of Kobe operate day and night loading and unloading huge cargo containers. These cranes may be Japan's real national bird, the country's lifeline to the world. At the same time, the Japanese have a strong sense of their unique identity—Japanese exceptionalism—and their place of leadership in Asia as its only truly First World power.

Japan is exceptional in its rapid rise to economic prominence and its unique blending of cultures. But maybe the Japanese, like Americans, need to get over their sense of being absolutely exceptional. The problems facing Japan are not exceptional; in many ways, they offer a glimpse at what the entire advanced industrial world will face. The Japanese technological response has been superb. If the United States shared Japan's commitment to efficient public transportation, we could be close to self-sufficient in oil and would cut our greenhouse gas emissions by more than half. Yet Japan has foundered on making the social changes these new challenges pose, including making their workplace more flexible and open to new ideas and more friendly to the aspirations of women and the needs of children and families.

Power Surge: The Advance of Technology

The ancient Greeks were fond of new ideas but also afraid of the changes they might bring. They told stories about these hopes and fears. The story of Prometheus tells of how he delivered fire to humanity in defiance of the gods, who feared that humans with control of fire would become godlike themselves. In another story, Pandora opened a box that was not meant to be opened and unleashed suffering and pestilence on humankind, but with an enduring bit of hope. Similarly, the scientists who watched the world's first nuclear blast over the deserts of New Mexico in 1945 wondered whether they were seeing a new Prometheus's fire or opening a Pandora's box. As technological advances continue to occur at an exponential rate, questions about their value versus danger remain.

In one sense, technology has been around as long as humans have. None of us would last very long if we had to depend on our teeth and toenails to bring down game or dig up food. Humans need tools; they always have. For many millennia the way to craft these tools was based on trial and error and that experience was passed down through the generations. There were exceptions to this approach, but they were few.

The Greek mathematician Archimedes (ca. 287–212 BCE)—known for his claim that with the right lever and a place to stand he could move the world—came up with some clever inventions to build and defend Syracuse (on the island of Sicily). The story about him leaping naked from his bath and shouting "Eureka" at having discovered the principle of buoyancy may be true; the one about him burning invading Roman ships with giant mirrors most likely is not. The invading Romans admired Archimedes (although they killed him) and came up with some important engineering advances of their own: concrete, the self-supporting dome, arched aqueducts, paved roads, and so forth. But technical innovation continued to proceed slowly.

New attention to science came with the Italian Renaissance. Leonardo da Vinci (1452–1519) designed everything from helicopters to submarines to tanks, although he never contrived a reasonable way to propel them. His inventions were impractical, but he was on the first wave of a new age, the age of science. Fellow Italian Galileo Galilei (1564–1642) studied the stars as people have done since the first human looked up, but he quickly adapted, refined, and employed a telescope. More important than any single invention, he refined and spread a hugely important idea: the experiment. Plenty of mathematics and a good measure of trial and error were still involved, but careful, systematic observation of a controlled event became one of the foundations of science.

The Fires of Industry

Science made Europe. Once the idea of technology took hold—wedding science, math, and craftsmanship to create new machines—Europe ruled the world. The Royal Academy of Sciences met in London with such greats as Isaac Newton (1643–1727), but tinkerers and craftspersons, if they understood science, also could join the elite club. In short order, the British built everything from tea kettles to huge steam engines. Across the channel, French chemists conducted industrial espionage in China and then went to work fabricating new forms of porcelain, racing to keep ahead of the Dutch. In this atmosphere of rivalry, competition, greed, and inventive excitement, the industrial world was born.

Ancient Egypt and ancient Greece, as well as the early Chinese, Arab, and Maya states, all had great mathematicians. Mostly they studied the stars and helped design monumental buildings. Later mathematicians built machines, and unlike da Vinci, they devised ways to propel them, first using the power of falling water and then the pressure of boiling water. The smelly, sooty, intensely productive age of steam was born.

The Europeans needed resources for their technology and markets for their mass-produced products. Just as with the creations of Archimedes and da Vinci, as well as Galileo's telescopes, great inventions were employed in the service of war. Those who resisted the European expansion faced the brutality of science in bigger, deadlier guns, which were often mounted on bigger, faster ships and eventually driven by steam. Gunboat diplomacy forced the industrial idea on the rest of the world.

By the late 1800s Germany, the United States, and finally Japan had joined the industrial world as major powers. The rest of the world succumbed to the power of what had been small states. The age of the machine had become the age of the machine gun.

But industrial technology was not all about brute force and raw power. Machines must be both powered and controlled. One of the first great inventions of the industrial age was the Jacquard loom, named for its French inventor. Jacquard's 1801 design used punch cards, which looked like the IBM punch cards that guided the first computers, to guide the looms. And so a craft that normally took years to master and painstaking hours to execute could now be mechanically programmed and driven by waterpower. The English stole and perfected the idea, and soon England was producing more textiles than the rest of the world's countries combined. Competing textile mills quickly sprang up along waterways across Europe and North America. Clothing for the average person went from a single garment of homespun cloth to multiple possibilities, ending in the array that today fills our closets.

Technological change has been a steady feature of human society, often in slow increments, but three power surges changed our world. Improvements to the steam engine by James Watt and others in the late 1700s led to a changed world in the 1800s: steam-driven industry plus the steam-driven trains and ships to transport it. A world that had depended on animal power plus a window and some water power now had portable power. By the time the *HMS Great Britain* steamed out of port in Bristol in 1840 en route to New York, the was world was new—centered in Great Britain but spreading quickly. Two lines of inquiry in the late 1800s were similarly transformative. The development of the petroleum propelled internal combustion engine made possible the cars, trucks, tractors, diesel trains, airplanes, and even submarines of the twentieth century. Power was now portable enough to fly. At the same time, advances in the production and transmission of electrical power in the 1800s remade the twentieth century—cities came alive at night with light—soon coming into homes with lighting, refrigeration, and all the electric appliances of a new age. The third great transformation came with work on tiny transistors and personal computers and their connections in the late twentieth century that created the explosion of electronic transformation: the internet, the smartphone, and streaming information of all sorts that continues to remake the twenty-first century year by year.

Booting Up the Electronic Age

Nicolas Lovejoy set off on a trek around the world with only his backpack and his girlfriend, Barbara. It was a wonderful experience, a way for them to enjoy both the planet and the simple life. For one stretch, the two crossed the South Pacific on a sailboat from Tahiti to the Cook Islands. When they get off the boat, they were surprised that their millions of dollars in stock had tripled during the trip.

Nicolas and Barbara are not typical millionaires, if there is such a thing. He began as math teacher and, feeling restless, took a pay cut from his $27,000-a-year salary to go to work for a friend. His friend, Jeff Bezos, was trying to start a business on this thing called the World Wide Web. They decided to call their site "Amazon.com."

With their millions made, Nicolas and Barbara turned to philanthropy and began a multimillion-dollar foundation. Concerned about their community, including low-income families and the environment, they sponsored some community gardens in Seattle (Verhovek 2000). While they were out gardening, their fortune was mostly lost: Amazon's stock plunged in the so-called dot-com crash in the early 2000s. Amazon is back, now one of the fastest growing major companies in the hold. One can hope Nicolas and Barbara kept a bit of their stock.

What does it mean to live and work in an economy in which millions, even billions, can be made and lost before a person reaches the age of 30? Also, how can vast wealth be contained in a business that exists only in cyberspace and went years without ever showing a profit? Have businesses such as Amazon transformed the world of opportunity or created a new boom-and-bust cycle akin to the bank failures and economic panics of the past? Will visionaries like Nicolas and Barbara be able to foster a sense of community and a better life, or have internet businesses and internet society already undermined the face-to-face community?

Modernity is a slippery and elusive term, but in many ways, what became known as the modern world was the industrial world. The world of mass production, mass marketing, mass transportation, and mass consumption of industrial products dominated from the middle of the 1700s to the middle of the 1900s. But mathematicians, engineers, and tinkerers were already creating the beginnings of a new world. The might of Nazi Germany in World War II depended on a multitude of deadly machines—and a secret code to control them all, known as Enigma. Under the might of the Nazis' carefully controlled terror, much of European opposition collapsed. The British and Americans fought back with their own machines. Ultimately, the industrial capacity of the United States was unstoppable, but the key to an early turning of the tides of war was cracking that code. To do that, mathematicians and computing machines were needed. Crude but successful, the machines made their point: Computing power was global power.

Initially computers filled entire buildings, requiring massive staffing and energy supplies, such as the enormous 1946 Electronic Numerical Integrator and Computer (ENIAC) in Philadelphia. In the 1950s and 1960s computers were quickly put to military uses: guiding a global network of submarines and missiles. The transistor allowed the circuitry to become minute and cheap, and soon computers were found in all forms of industries.

The same electronic miniaturization and mass production—ultimately, millions of layers of "chips"—made other electronic items commonplace. The transistor radio brought music and ideas to even the most remote locations. Television went from a curiosity to the central piece of furniture in U.S. homes in the 1950s. Today, from the heights of the Himalayas to the depths of the Amazon basin, the electronic eye of television is everywhere in the world. The same low-cost, miniature electronics could be launched into space and fit into someone's pocket, first as a calculator and then as a cell phone. Whether traveling by beam or by cable, the key to the electronic revolution, along with small size and low cost, is interconnectedness.

The idea of connecting computers in an intercomputer network, or internet, was also born of defense considerations. But soon universities found this a useful way to share information and resources. As late as the 1980s pundits were arguing that only nerdy professors would ever care much about sending mail electronically and that certainly no one would pay for the privilege. But in the 1980s first Apple and then IBM made computers small enough to fit on a desk: personal computers, or PCs. Miniaturization meant that these computers could do far more than the huge ENIAC of 1946. Yet their power was limited if they were used as isolated units. By connecting them in an internet, it was like the synergy of connecting thousands of great minds.

Within a matter of years commercial enterprises such as CompuServe and America Online (AOL) were offering everyone the miracle of instant, worldwide email communication. The development of **HTML,** or **hypertext markup language,** meant that it would become easy to share all types of messages. Any graphic image could be whisked electronically around the world and so the **World Wide Web** was born.

Innovation has always thrived along complex networks. Originally, these were networks of trade, with caravans and caravels plying the deserts and the oceans to connect people, products, and ideas. In places where these networks were most dense, such as the crossroads of the Eastern Mediterranean and the Middle East, civilizations flourished, rich in both products and ideas. In the 1840s the first network of cable, telegraph lines, began its march around the globe. In 1858 transatlantic cable connected the United States and Great Britain. "Glory to God!" wired Queen Victoria. Then the cable proved faulty and the system crashed. But even faulty technology can be powerful, and newer systems are created to replace the old. Telephone networks replaced the telegraph in the 1880s, along with the newly emerging radio.

Networks continue to flourish with newer cables and newer means of beaming messages, such as today's satellite dishes and cell phone towers. Sometimes, these systems crash. But they also intermingle to create new possibilities. Cell phones can receive email messages and search the World Wide Web, take and post digital pictures, and track (and post) one's exact place on the planet with GPS. At the same time, PCs have become laptops, downsized to notebooks and tablets that can be carried anywhere and access a world of information without wires. It is not hard to imagine a multiuse digital companion that merges all these functions into a single tool that will travel with everyone, like the six-shooter of the Wild West or the communicators of *Star Trek*. Some version of a smartphone, tablet like the iPad, electronic reader such as the Kindle, or notebook computer will likely be the only thing many students will bring to class in the near future. The campus bookstore may sell nothing but athletic wear. Books will be ordered online and then beamed or cabled to their recipients, complete with full video and audio, if desired.

Industrial technology built the modern age, and now it seems that postindustrial electronic technology is building a postmodern **information age.** Industrial modernism stressed uniformity, the interchangeable part that allowed U.S. inventor Eli Whitney to mass-produce guns and cotton gins and that allowed Henry Ford to mass-produce automobiles—inexpensive vehicles that all looked alike. There was also a certainty that there was a modern way, seen in the industrial West, which would uniformly transform production, urban environments, and ultimately the people who worked and lived in these places. They would all be modern and somewhat alike.

Postmodernism, based on the incredible diversity that is possible in the information age, stresses a multiplicity of voices, centers, and different approaches. Power lies less in production and more in information. Every year, the United States and the postindustrial economies of Europe and Japan produce less and less that can actually be packaged and held. Instead, they produce designs, programs, patents, and copyrights that allow them to direct and profit from the production of the industrializing world.

The Industrial Revolution of the nineteenth century displaced generations of farm laborers, and many rural dwellers were forced to seek industrial employment, increasingly in urban areas. In the United States farmers and agricultural laborers went from comprising more than 35 percent of the population at the beginning of the 1900s to less than 3 percent by the end of the century. Similarly, postindustrial change has displaced millions of factory laborers, many of whom have had to scramble to try to find places in the service and technology sectors.

Technology has not only changed production and consumption; even social relations have been altered by email, instant messages, texts, and Facebook and TikTok posts. It is now easier to be in contact with others, but less of that contact is face-to-face. Proximity matters less, as people may participate in an international chat room that spans the globe, but they have no idea of the names of their next-door neighbors. On "wired" campuses, roommates fixated on computer screens instant message each other across their dorm rooms, while at home, a teenager calls his or her parents across the house on a cell phone to ask to use the car. Technology can greatly reduce social isolation for those people in remote areas, for the elderly, and for others unable to get out, and it can open a world of global contacts and new relationships. It can also be isolating in its own way, as coffeehouses give way to internet cafes and ultimately to wireless laptops—all communication that is mediated by a keyboard. Virtual communities of virtual relationships are not always the most satisfying, any more than virtual travel to virtual locations to seek virtual romance. The power and limits of electronically mediated connection came to the fore suddenly during the COVID-19 pandemic. Meetings and lectures could move to Zoom and its many competitors, sometimes saving time and commuting. But workers and students also faced Zoom fatigue and depression, and even teen suicide engulfed a generation that was both hyperconnected and profoundly disconnected.

For all its newness, the information age is repeating many of the patterns of the early industrial age. After commerce, one of its primary applications has been in war. In the industrial era, each new advance meant a deadlier weapon. The 1903 *New York Times* article that announced the flight of the Wright brothers noted that the army was interested in their success and that this new machine, just barely off the ground, might be useful for dropping torpedoes. Electronic technology has brought wars that are fought on video screens with weapons guided to their targets by laser beams and satellite signals. The drone has emerged as one of the most feared battlefield weapons. Russia, China, and the United States have all been involved in cyberattacks and counterattacks, as have smaller countries such as North Korea and Iran. The rules of this dangerous game are not at all clear—what constitutes an act of war: cyber espionage, attacking dense systems, crashing a nuclear power plant or a vast electrical grid?

The high tide of the industrial era was also a time of tremendous concentration of wealth and power in the hands of a few. Andrew Carnegie controlled steel, John D. Rockefeller controlled oil, and J. P. Morgan dominated banking. What had been local markets became national markets, and the potential for wealth was enormous. Whether these people were seen as philanthropists, contributing to a better society, or "robber barons," exploiting their monopoly of power, they dominated their era.

So, too, the information era is dominated by a few, now that globally national markets have given way to international markets. Of the richest multibillionaires on the *Forbes* list (2021), almost all are directly related to technology and communications: Jeff Bezos (Amazon), Elon Musk (Tesla and SpaceX), Carlos Slim Helú (Mexico's Telecom), Bill Gates (Microsoft), Larry Ellison (Oracle), Mark Zuckerberg (Facebook), and Larry Page and Sergey Brin (Google). The remainder are retail founders and heirs, capitalizing on a global electronic marketing and distribution boom. Mergers continue to put the largest media companies into fewer hands: AOL–Time Warner (combining what were once separate computer, print, television, and film operations), ABC–Disney (a conglomerate that merged film, newspapers, and books), and then Disney–21st-Century Fox (making Disney an ever greater entertainment giant). The Rupert Murdoch family retained effective control of Fox News and related broadcasting, combining this with control of the sister organization, News Corp, which owns *The Wall Street Journal*, HarperCollins, and other publishing ventures. The postmodern vision is characterized by multiple and diverse perspectives on the world, but increasingly, these are structurally merged in the hands of a few vast multinational corporations.

The musical styles of the times are drawn from the multicultural influences of a "world beat," but once packaged into global "pop," the music is popularized everywhere by MTV and marketed everywhere by a vast music industry. More music is recorded than ever before, but the global market is dominated by a handful of superstars. Similarly, more books are produced than ever, but the massive profits are confined to a few titles that are marketed globally, complete with movie and merchandise rights. Food products and styles are also drawn from all over the planet and then standardized by a few fast-food giants, which control the marketing to offer Taco Bell in Tokyo and KFC in Guadalajara.

The industrial era created great opportunities for urban professionals and tradespersons at the same time that it displaced huge numbers of European peasants and rural people. So, too, the information age has created a **digital divide** between those who have access to the technological tools of the day and are comfortable using them and those for whom this is an alien and alienating world.

Global Cybercafé: The Social Network

In January 2011 Facebook, the social networking site that seems to expand at rates not seen since the big bang, topped 600 million users worldwide, then surged to 2.7 billion by 2021—approaching one-third of the world's population. This is still less than the roughly four billion that use Google. The growth of these giants seems limited only by Chinese restrictions and competition. We live in a world in which information is gathered collectively on Wikipedia (which, whatever teachers may think, has been shown to be as accurate on most topics as the venerable Encyclopedia Britannica). For four years reporters watched Twitter for the latest on U.S. policy from the White House. The most followed account now belongs to another former president, Barack Obama. But he is just ahead of Justin Bieber, Katy Perry, and Rihanna, all with over 100 million followers.

The phenomenal success of Facebook is a reminder that, even as we embrace new technologies, what people often want most is to stay connected to real people. New sites use the power of social networks to allow people to shop together (electronically) and to offer opinions on everything from products to nightlife options. Instagram influencers and Pinterest posters seek ways to rapidly build their network of followers. But one of the most successful Instagram sites during the COVID-19 pandemic was Cottagecore, a Tumblr phenomenon that idealized a country life of homespun fabrics, crafts, baking, and pottery. It has been successful, not with grandmothers, but with young urbanites interacting online.

The global village of Marshall McLuhan is emerging but not in real space so much as in cyberspace. The globe is increasingly hyperlinked in a network of electronically mediated social relationships that, if not quite a village, looks like one vast cybercafé. Particularly significant for sociologists is how this changes our relationship to one other. Physical proximity becomes an afterthought. We may go days without seeing colleagues in the same hallway, or maybe even that reclusive roommate, yet rarely does a day go by that we aren't in contact with colleagues on other continents. We may email back and forth with students several times before realizing they are sitting in the computer lab across the hall. Or the reverse may occur, after the third email, the student may ask to drop by, only to get the reply, "Sorry, no. I'm not working late; I'm emailing you from a cybercafé on the second floor of a department store in Ho Chi Minh City where it is already tomorrow morning." Our social interactions transcend space and even time. I joined Facebook originally as a convenient way to stay in touch with students and colleagues around the globe. In 2005 being on Facebook was pretty hip (or a bit strange) for a college professor. Now it would be unusual for any faculty member not to have a Facebook profile. For most who were born before 1995 this was a new social arena, but the younger set has grown up "meeting" friends on sites like the now defunct Club Penguin to chat and play games with friends: some who may be a thousand miles away and some who may be sitting in the same room. So when Facebook opened to those beyond the campus community, students were ready to join and interact, now with a new presentation of self that no longer includes penguins.

We live in a world being reshaped by electronic globalization, or more properly, electronically mediated social and cultural globalization. The electronically mediated globalization of culture and communication has been one of the most rapid forms of globalization and also one of the least likely to be reversed. It is possible that in the future, high fuel costs, concerns about terrorism, new trade wars, environmental problems, a gradually leveling of wage rates, or just a new fashion of buying local could combine to reduce the huge global exchange of products. Yet the cost of sending messages around the world continues to plummet, and the ease of sending data, greetings, images, and spam, from anywhere to anywhere, continues to increase. In earlier societies, only an intrepid few—explorers, sailors, merchants—traveled far to interact with others. For the first time, we are seeing the creation of a global society in which anyone with access to a computer can daily interact with people and ideas almost anywhere in the world. Language still sets some boundaries on these networks, but even this comes with new incentives in many places to learn international English as the dominant language of the internet.

New technology comes with new concerns that people are losing out on casual contact with one another. Getting together to go to a movie and meeting other friends and neighbors gives way to streaming video from Netflix served at home to one's own laptop. Going out for a night of social bowling is replaced by the same game on one's Wii at home. Sitting in a sidewalk café with friends gives way to watching "reality" TV at home. Yet technology also offers new ways to stay connected in spite of bad weather in Maine and bad roads in the Congo. Technology has the power to both increase isolation and to reduce it. It seems to work best as a way of extending social contact, not replacing it—a balance of Facebook time and face time.

Planet Hollywood: When Reality Is Virtual and Virtual Is Reality

I often miss professional meetings when I am out of the country. But no more! Thanks to video conferencing. My first experience with virtual meetings was few years ago when a conference on teaching and learning was held not in a major conference hotel but on Second Life (SL), a popular electronic web community. To participate one must be sure to have signed up for a free SL account in advance and know the following SL basics:

- How to Force Noon.
- How to walk and sit.
- How to chat and use History window so you do not miss posts.
- How to send (private) instant messages.
- How to keyword search SL for locations.
- How to teleport to University Project.
- How to edit appearance.
- How to edit profile (so people can list their real identity and affiliation if they wish).
- How to get an item out of inventory and wear it.
- How to offer friendship to others and how to offer friends a teleport to your current location.

How wonderfully convenient! We had the option to "edit our appearance" or pull a new outfit from a virtual closet before making a presentation. The possibilities were endless. The reality that struck during the pandemic in 2020 was not nearly as fun—conferencing by Zoom and even by Facebook. Still, colleagues now wonder if it is worth going back to long-distance travel in an age of tight time schedules and tight budgets. But each of us agrees—what we miss is not flying halfway around the world to hear someone read a paper that could have been posted online but rather our informal, spontaneous, in-person conversations that inspire, inform, and build bonds and connections. In some ways the new electronic media are no more than a fancier telephone. In other ways they are transforming our relationship to physical space and to one another.

The line between what is real and what is virtual is becoming ever more blurred. Take virtual currency: The currency is digital, issued and controlled by its developers and unregulated by the government, but is paid for with real U.S. dollars. The digital currency that changes hands within Second Life, to buy, sell, rent, or trade goods or services, is Linden Dollars. In fact some Second Life participants have their primary career in a Second Life occupation, which generates real income, rather than in their day job.

Until the late 1990s, paper money was used for financial transactions. Today little of our income and expenditures are ever in the form of paper money. Every day several trillion dollars move around the world as electronic signals. Even if we are not financiers and hedge-fund managers, we are likely part of this flow of electronic but "real" money. Salaries and financial aid are directly deposited. Payments are made using direct withdrawals or transfers. Credit and debit amounts come out of accounts we only see on a screen. With the right codes, one can draw on these numbers in pesos in Mexico City or Euros in Vienna. Concern over those real currencies has led to the skyrocketing values of cryptocurrencies such as Bitcoin. Backed by no country, it exists only on carefully secured hard drives. Its value is based on how much someone is willing to pay for it—that is, how much others think it is worth.

Stalked by the White Ghost: Electronic Globalization

Electronic technology has also been a powerful force for cultural globalization. No place on the planet is immune from its influence. Some societies are moving directly from the preindustrial to the postindustrial era. In parts of the world the leap, is even greater:

> Deep in the Amazon, the slow tropical twilight beckons villagers to join the fire circle. Here all gather to share the news, to learn of one another's lives, to hear elders tell the old stories, entertain and socialize the young into the right ways of living. Yet there are ever fewer young at this fire circle. The elders explain in hushed tones, "They have fallen to the ghost, the big ghost." For this jungle is haunted.... The big ghost arrives by satellite dish, The Amazon's Kayapo used money from gold and mahogany on the world market to install a small but effective satellite dish.. The chief regrets his decision, "I have been saying that people must buy useful things like knives or fishing hooks. Television does not fill the stomach. It only shows our children and grandchildren white people's things." Bemoans an elder, "The night is the time the old people teach the young people. Television has stolen the night." (Sernau 2000, p. 140; see also Simons 1990)

It is incorrect to view these groups as powerless victims, however. In some cases, they have used technology to their own purposes. Kayapo fighters stalk their enemies silently through the forest. When they have them within range, they carefully site their favorite weapon and release the dreaded whir—not of a blowgun but of a video camera. They have effectively used video to capture the trespasses and violations of foreign oil companies and use this tape to support their complaints before the Organization of American States and other international bodies (Turner 1993). They have grown more sophisticated in their use of electronic media, now recording traditional village dances with cameras mounted on drones and employing sophisticated video editing techniques. Is it still traditional?

In desperately poor rural Bangladesh, the Grameen Bank—a remarkable "microlender" known for its loans to small entrepreneurs, 95 percent of whom are women—has been lending money for cell phones. This sounds like the ultimate in waste and inappropriate technology. But cell phones can be extremely useful in places where regular phones are unavailable or unreliable. Women use the loans to buy phones and then rent them by the minute to villagers. The villagers can contact their relatives in neighboring villages, find out about prices for their commodities in nearby towns and cities, get medical advice, and otherwise access information in minutes that would previously have required a day's walk.

Bhutan is not easy to find. This tiny country is tucked up against the Himalayas north of India and next to Nepal. Like Tibet to the north, Bhutan is a primarily Buddhist country and devotion to this tradition permeates the culture. Bhutan is a very poor and remote state, and until 1999, it had another distinction: It was the last country on earth to get television.

All that changed one day when the "cable guy" showed up. That's how he is known to the villagers, as he goes about connecting homes to the cable service that the government reluctantly agreed to accept. And since cable TV arrived, the country has never been the same. Televisions are now everywhere, humming with foreign programming. One young boy now has a new topic to fight about with his older sister: He likes Cartoon Network and she likes MTV. In the dirt schoolyard, the fights are more energetic, as young boys crash into each other in moves copied from the masked "heroes" of the World Wrestling Federation. An elderly woman, who grew up in a once peaceful land, shakes her head in dismay but also worries that she is neglecting her religious duties to watch soap operas. Cables and satellites now bring not just television but reliable internet. For Bhutanese boys, the traditional discipline of archery must now compete with video games.

Bhutan's mountains withstood millennia of invaders, but they were no match for the cable guy. Within a matter of years, the society has changed forever. Residents wonder what Bhutan has gained and what it has lost. As the earnest young cable guy unrolls yet more spools, is he spreading civilization and culture or destroying it? Bhutan became a democracy, by order of the king, in 2008. The king voluntarily moved from being an absolute ruler to being a constitutional monarch with an elected parliament. Will media access allow democracy to thrive, or will it undermine a sense of common citizenship? Many Bhutanese still wonder.

The Information (and Misinformation) Age

Technology typically has two sides: High-speed computers can give totalitarian dictatorships the means to monitor their populations and track dissidents. At the same time, email and social media messages can zip past censors to coordinate social movements and popular resistance around the world.

Postmodernists such as French social theorist Michel Foucault (1977) note that we are experiencing both more sophisticated means of surveillance and social control and also more diverse and evasive means of resistance. The Chinese government wrestles with Google over the government's right to limit and monitor searches, as when all references to Chinese dissident Liu Xiaobo winning the 2010 Nobel Peace Prize were blocked in China. At the same time, Tunisian rebels in 2011 claimed the first *cyber revolution*, toppling the repressive government in a coordinated campaign of blogs, Tweets, and YouTube videos showing police repression. Even the question of whether increased surveillance is positive depends on whether you see it in the hands of legitimate authority or the repressive hands of a "Big Brother," like the one George Orwell portrayed in his novel *1984*. Likewise, the resistance may be "freedom fighters," dissidents and "free thinkers," or "terrorists," depending on the situation and one's point of view.

We must also face the fact that the *information age* can be the *misinformation age*, in which reality is packaged by corporate media, advertisers, and public relations campaigns. Postmodern theorist Walter Truett Anderson got it right in the title of his 1992 book—*Reality Isn't What It Used to Be*. The public is confronted with media-edited virtual wars that seem to have no casualties, carefully presented celebrity political candidates who have no unpopular policies, and idealized images of products and places that promise paradise in a package.

In such a context the media are as likely to produce international misunderstanding as they are to produce understanding. They also create a climate of intense consumerism, in which people in richer nations are driven to spend and consume beyond their own means and beyond the means of the planet to support their lifestyle. At the same time, new audiences in poorer nations are prompted to emulate the very behavior that is the cause of so many problems for richer, high-consumption countries.

The double-edged sword that is the media can be seen in U.S. political campaigns in which the internet has been used to launch largely unknown candidates and to organize citizens' groups and involve many who could not otherwise meet face-to-face. It has allowed some candidates to raise funds from many small donations and so challenge the power of large donors. It has also allowed for trivialization and misinformation on a colossal scale. Rumors and wild distortions that would bring a libel suit in print can be spread in a matter of days as people email false but enticing information to their friends. New stories that have a momentum of their own even when all the information has been fabricated have been dubbed **urban legends,** and many continue to circulate for years.

The QAnon conspiracy theory posed wild charges—that a cabal of Satan-worshipping pedophiles (in some versions they were cannibals) dominated Hollywood, most of the media, and much of the U.S. Democratic Party and worked out of the basements of pizza parlors (how many pizza parlors actually have basements?). Devoted proponents supposedly had names of politicians and actors, but no supporting evidence. Since most media were suspect, no investigative journalism or published counterevidence would be convincing to QAnon believers. The conspiracy grew on mysterious internet posts and eventually moved beyond U.S. borders to take hold in parts of Europe and beyond. As devotees found one another and held "Save the Children" (also the name of a legitimate charity) rallies, the formation of this conspiracy demonstrates both the power of social media and the power of complete distrust of mainstream media, including their common practice of fact-checking stories. Never has information been so available, and so suspect.

The ability to create "deep fake" images that are pure Photoshop creations, and to spread them to millions instantly, further destabilizes our stream of information. Regulators debate the responsibility of major outlets—Facebook, Twitter, TikTok—to monitor content they did not create. Can the electronic media be harnessed to promote citizenship, rather than mere consumerism, and open dialogue, rather than cycles of repression and terror? The answer to that question will, in large measure, determine whether the information age will be a golden age or a dark age disguised in golden tinsel.

Energy: Fire from Above and Below

The industrial age was built on the idea of using stored energy, the force of falling water, burning wood, or burning coal and oil to replace human and animal power. The electronic age is predicated on the availability of cheap and reliable electrical power.

When a massive power failure shut off the electricity to the northeastern United States and eastern Canada in 2003, economic activity came to a stop. People in tall buildings had no elevators. Urban commuters had no trains. Grocery stores had no refrigeration. Some cities had no water. And most significantly, unless one had batteries or generators, there was no access to the computers that ran everything else. Massive and persistent power failures in Puerto Rico in 2017, following hurricane Maria, and in Texas, following an ice storm in 2021, likewise showed both how dependent we are on networks of electrical transmission and how fragile those networks may be.

Our industrial and electronic economies are all based on the use of large amounts of stored energy. Every year humanity's appetite for energy increases (see figure 11.1). Some economists use energy consumption as a proxy for the level of economic development. Yet there is also a real danger here. Even as the world becomes ever more energy dependent, it has yet to settle on a safe and reliable energy source.

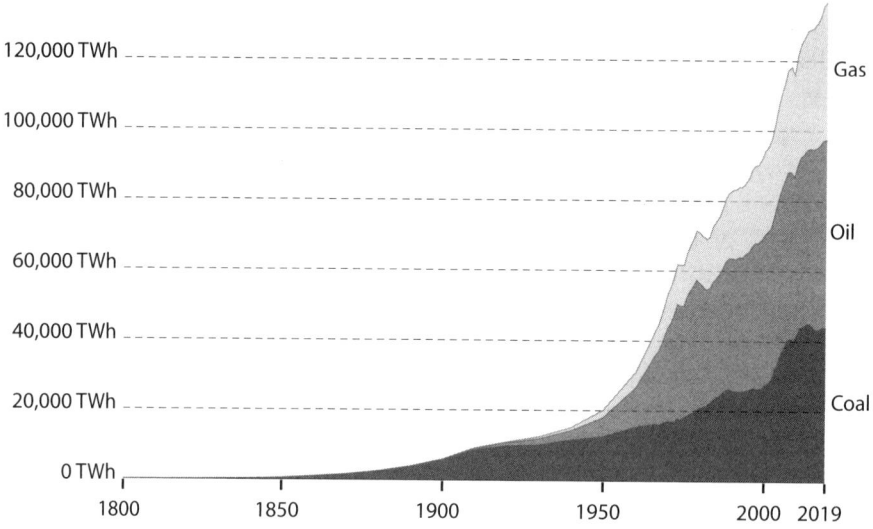

Figure 11.1 Global fossil fuel consumption. (Source: Our World in Data.) For a detailed look at change over time and the energy mix and strategy of individual countries, see https://ourworldindata.org/energy.

Wood

Maybe it was fire that made us what we are. Many ancient peoples have stories about the coming of fire, such as the Greek's tale of Prometheus. Fire allowed people to make food more digestible, to keep warm, and to ward off everything from predators to mosquitoes. Some people may even have used it to change tangled, brush-filled landscapes into the grasslands and open savannas that human hunters prefer.

In many places in the world, wood is still depended on as essential fuel. Herders in dry grasslands have long known that animal dung makes a very usable (if less than elegant) fire. But without enough animals on hand, there is little alternative to what wood can be found. All across the Sahel region of Africa, the dry country just south of the Sahara; on the fringes of the Kalahari Desert in Southern Africa; all across the dry plateau regions of India; and in the rugged highlands of Haiti the land is being stripped of trees by people desperate for fuel. More than two billion people around the world use wood fuel to meet their energy needs (UN Department of Economic and Social Affairs 2017). When larger trees are not available or too difficult to harvest, people walk long distances to collect loads of gnarled sticks to haul back on their gnarled backs. The sticks feed small cooking fires and can be slowly burned in pits to create crude charcoal, which can be sold to urbanites to use as fuel. As wood becomes increasingly scarce, the walks get longer. Many places are being deforested down to the last twig, not by great logging companies or raging forest fires but by the slow, smoky burn of charcoal pits—the only energy and income source for poor and displaced people.

While back-to-nature North Americans and Northern Europeans investigate the idea of heating with high-efficiency woodstoves, many of the world's poor need to find alternatives. One option is **reforestation.** Fast-growing trees, such as the *Melaleuca* being tried in Haiti, can reforest slopes, provide a steady supply of firewood, and also control erosion. For a long time, development workers doubted that poor people would take much interest in planting and protecting trees. Yet once the people have seen that a project will benefit them and their children in years to come and that they won't be denied access to the resource, successful reforestation projects have been undertaken in Haiti, in the Sahel, and in India.

A compatible option is to use the resource more efficiently. Open fires waste wood and can be replaced by high-efficiency stoves and ovens. The same technologies that allow people in cold, wood-rich climates to heat their homes efficiently can help feed people in hot, wood-scarce regions. Some stoves can use grasses for fuel, not unlike the method used by North American prairie pioneers, who found they could use twisted hay, and some can burn dung.

Finally, a hot, dry climate is the perfect place to use direct solar energy. Cookers that use curved mirrors to direct the sun's heat can replace wood altogether.

Coal

Coal fired the industrial age. The age of coal saw huge surges in industrial production and the "dark Satanic mills" that blackened the skies of Britain, Germany, and the northeastern United States. Coal is vastly abundant. Great layers were created as ancient forests sank beneath new layers of sediment, trapping and compressing the carbon in the wood into coal.

The limitations of coal are apparent to anyone who has seen pictures of a coal mine, a coal barge, and a coal furnace. Coal is difficult to extract, difficult to transport, and messy to burn. Large amounts of coal lie under some of the world's most energy-hungry countries, such as the United States and Russia, but it varies greatly in quality and ease of extraction.

The most accessible coal-like substance is peat, the black, dirt-like material that Irish peasants have long harvested from surface peat bogs and burned for fuel. Peat is coal in the making: still loose and crumbly, horribly smoky, but easily accessible and in some places still used. Coal grades improve as this substance moves from crumbly peat through bituminous to hard and cleaner anthracite. Abundant, easy-to-access coal tends to be of the dirtier sort.

Sulfur content is also a problem. The sulfur in coal goes up; as sulfur dioxide mixes with water in the atmosphere, it comes down as sulfuric acid. It is a caustic component of acid rain, which kills trees and fish and eats away the facades of buildings and the finishes on cars.

Coal fires, especially lower-grade coal fires, also put out a lot of particulate matter: soot. The coal soot of early-twentieth-century London provided comic scenes in Mary Poppins. But coal soot so filled the air in parts of Eastern Europe that it blackened the laundry hung out to dry and slowly blackened the lungs of adults and children alike.

Urban air in advanced industrial countries became cleaner as manufacturing went from coal- and steam-driven machinery to electrically driven production. Today the majority of electricity in the United States and elsewhere around the world is produced by coal-fired electrical plants that sit just outside major urban areas. Higher-technology coal-fired plants use "scrubbers" to remove some of the particulate matter from the smoke.

Even the cleanest plant and the cleanest coal, however, mix the carbon of the coal with the oxygen of the air to produce tons of carbon dioxide. Carbon dioxide has not been considered a pollutant, since it is harmless in small quantities, but it is the main "greenhouse gas." Carbon dioxide allows light to pass through but traps the escaping heat of the sun in the same way that the glass of a greenhouse or an automobile on a sunny day captures the heat of sunlight. Climatologists have shown for decades that the carbon dioxide buildup in the atmosphere is causing **global warming** with severe and unpredictable **climate change.**

The other major problem with coal comes before it is burned: in its access and extraction. Cutting peat out of a bog gave way to extracting coal from deep mine shafts. Narrow, dark shafts cut into the black heart of the hills of such places as Scotland, Pennsylvania, and Japan became the daily abode of generations of miners in the 1800s. Young boys were preferred in the mines, since they could crawl into the narrower tunnels. Sometimes boys became the main income earners for their families after their fathers succumbed to "black lung" and other disabling diseases as well as frequent accidents.

Deep-shaft coal mining in the United States shifted southward along the Appalachian Mountains and became the mainstay of rural West Virginia and eastern Kentucky and Tennessee by the 1880s. During the latter part of the twentieth century, coal mining in the United States began a massive shift westward, particularly after the Clean Air Act of 1970. Mines in the Rocky Mountain States contained lower-sulfur coal, and air quality in U.S. cities was becoming a major concern. But just as important, the great reserves in Montana, Arizona, and other western states could be accessed through **strip mines.** Huge excavating machines, some with tires taller than a typical bulldozer, could scour into the mountainsides and extract coal far faster than in the old pick-and-shovel mines. This type of mining was also safer for the workers. New questions emerged, however, about what would be done with the great human-made craters after the coal was gone and what would be done with the tons of rock, called "overburden," which was hauled out to get at the coal.

Meanwhile, mining returned to parts of Appalachia in the 1980s and used western strip-mining methods. **Mountaintop removal mining** literally takes the tops off eastern mountains and ridges to get at the underlying coal, dumping the overburden down the sides to fill streams and valleys with mine tailings. At first the unemployed Appalachian workers rejoiced at the return of their lost industry. Soon, however, residents realized the terrible environmental toll that accompanied this type of mining, which literally tore down the mountains and fouled everything downstream (Vollers 1999; Reece 2006).

Giant excavator mining has become the norm in many huge mines in developing countries such as New Guinea. The production is vast, but the life span of most of these mines is short. Coal remains plentiful but hard to extract, hard to transport, and dirty to burn, with a residue of toxic ash. We are not in danger of running out of coal, but we out running out of atmosphere to contain the carbon dioxide and deadly contaminants.

In West Virginia, USA, massive machinery can devastate a mountain in a matter of days.

India [top] also uses heavy machinery but adds heavy manual labor, where the look of mining, and miners can be quite different. China [bottom] surged past the United States in coal consumption, only to be pushed to a frantic search for alternatives, as coal-burning industry and power plants choked cities with unbreathable air. Coal remains alluring in parts of the world where it is abundant and cheap—if one does not count the environmental and human cost.

Oil

Coal fired the nineteenth century, but oil fueled the twentieth century. In many ways the twentieth century was driven by petroleum and petroleum products: gasoline, kerosene, diesel fuel, jet fuel, and myriad plastics, even pharmaceuticals that are petroleum-based.

The century began with the internal combustion engine, a gasoline burner, becoming the dominant way to power automobiles, rather than steam or electricity. Lighter and more powerful gasoline engines made powered flight a possibility. Diesel fuel was used to power submarines and then gradually replaced coal-fired steam for ships and trains. By midcentury, oil dominated. World War II was fought with oil-burning machines and was often fought over oil fields: in North Africa, in the Soviet sphere, and in the Dutch East Indies, where Japan went to war in part over fears of a U.S.-led oil embargo (Yergin 2008).

The first oil fields were the easiest to tap. The "bubbling crude" came right to the surface. Easy-access fields in Pennsylvania (e.g., the Drake well of 1852) and Texas (e.g., the Lucas well at Spindletop, 1901) made the United States the leader in oil production. These fields were soon insufficient, and the search for new oil went global.

Substantial oil fields have been found in Alaska in North America; in Mexico and Venezuela in Latin America; in Nigeria, Chad, and other parts of West Africa; in the North Sea between Great Britain and Norway; in Indonesia (the former East Indies); in the Caucasus Mountains region of Russia and the new former Soviet Republics; and of course, in the Middle East. The area around the Persian Gulf may contain as much as two-thirds of the world's known accessible oil reserves. Accessibility is a key issue. No doubt much more oil may exist in more remote offshore locations, but it would be very hard to reach and to extract safely and economically.

In advanced industrial economies, oil is power. In the 1970s the Arab oil-exporting countries embargoed their oil exports to the United States and Europe in protest over these regions' support for Israel, which had fought a difficult war with Egypt and Syria in 1973 (Yergin 2008). The embargo was so successful in getting the attention of the Western industrial powers that oil-producing countries continued to work together to exploit this advantage. And so, **OPEC, the Organization of the Petroleum Exporting Countries,** was born. The price of crude (unrefined) oil rose dramatically, and oil became the "black gold" of the world economy, promising an asphalt road to riches for oil producers. That road has proved bumpy for most, however.

Saudi Arabia has the world's largest oil reserves, and its very image is tied to oil and oil wealth. It is true that the Saudi royal family is wealthy with oil money and that Saudi Arabia uses its oil income to buy large quantities of industrial products, consumer goods, and top-shelf weapons. Yet the gross domestic product (GDP) per capita is just topping $20,000, placing Saudi Arabia as a high-middle-income country on par with parts of Latin America and Eastern Europe. Unemployment is very high, inequalities of both gender and class are extreme, and the quality of education and health care is below the standards of most of Asia (Energy Information Administration 2005; UNDP 2020). Oil has brought neither broad-based development nor stability and democratic institutions.

A similar pattern can be seen in Iraq and other oil-rich nations. Iraq's oil financed weapons and disastrous wars, but it has not been able to finance the nation's recovery. Iran's oil wealth first financed the repression of the Shah and then the extremism of the Ayatollah Khomeini, but it still benefits only a few Iranians.

Latin America has fared little better. Mexico's dynamic President Lázaro Cárdenas nationalized the oil industry in the 1930s to secure the profits from primarily U.S.-based companies. But the national monopoly, Pemex, has been rife with corruption and mismanagement. While oil has financed some national programs and oil and petrochemicals are Mexico's leading exports, the entire economy now rises and falls on prevailing oil prices. Venezuela continues to face economic and political turmoil, in spite of large oil reserves.

Africa has had the most troubled times of all in the oil business. In Nigeria oil revenues have risen to hundreds of billions of dollars over the last 25 years, but the country remains desperately poor, often lagging in development behind its neighbors who are not blessed—or cursed—with oil. The only oil many Nigerians along the coast ever see is what leaks from the broken pipes. Some is collected in wheelbarrows and plastic jugs by desperate slum dwellers. In other places, the leaks foul water supplies and fuel deadly fires. Residents of the oil-rich Niger Delta face environmental devastation, which has destroyed traditional fishing and farming, and health risks from heavy metals and other deadly contaminants such that many never see their 40th birthday (DW News 2021). Some see Nigeria's best hope forward lying in greatly reducing its oil export dependence as has happened in Indonesia and the Middle East (Fickling 2021).

Chad, one of the world's poorest countries, worked with ExxonMobil, Chevron, and Petronas (the oil giant of Malaysia) on a huge pipeline to carry its oil though Cameroon to tankers on the Atlantic Ocean. The initial revenues buy weapons and expand the military, while poor residents see few benefits and suffer from the risk of oil spills.

In the worst-case scenario, oil wealth has fueled bitter wars. For years in Angola the government sold oil to arm its soldiers, while rebels sold black-market diamonds to arm themselves. The country was devastated. The potential of oil money to fill the coffers continues to bedazzle world leaders. The tiny islands of São Tomé and Principe, off the equatorial African coast, have huge offshore oil reserves compared to their sizes. These long-overlooked entities are now being courted by the big oil companies. Will they become the next Qatar or Bahrain (both in the Persian Gulf), tiny and rich? Some have described the relaxed life on these small islands where the wealth was once in fresh fruit, as paradise. Will oil enrich them or create a paradise lost?

Oil and repressive government are often paired in what has been termed "petro-tyrannies." American oil companies have poured billions into neighboring Equatorial Guinea since oil was confirmed there in 1995. The man who has ruled the country as president for life after overthrowing his uncle in 1979, Teodoro Obiang Nguema, is now fabulously wealthy, as most of the oil revenue has gone to him and his family members. Most people in the country continue to live on less than a few dollars per day, half have no clean drinking water, and 10 percent of children die before the age of five.

The irony is that while oil producers struggle to find positive ways to use oil income to foster development, nonoil producers struggle under the burden of paying for oil imports in economies that are increasingly dependent on petroleum products for transportation, shipping, industry, and mechanized agriculture.

Oil poses many environmental as well as economic and political problems. Unlike coal, it is liquid, so it can be pumped rather than mined and piped rather than hauled. It can also be spilled. Oil drilling and pumping techniques have improved greatly since the days of flaming gushers, but spills and accidents are still common. As drilling moves to more difficult-to-reach and environmentally sensitive areas, these concerns will only increase, as in the massive gulf oil "spill" (underwater gusher would be more appropriate) of 2010. Despite advanced technology, gulf residents watched in horror as millions of gallons gushed into the Gulf of Mexico with no one certain of how to stop it. The disaster resulted in a temporary moratorium on deep-water drilling and quelled some of the "drill, baby, drill" enthusiasm of the 2008 Republican convention, but many governors of the surrounding gulf states never stopped supporting offshore drilling. Drilling in environmentally sensitive areas such as the Arctic National Wildlife Refuge on the north slope of Alaska remains intensely controversial. Once out of the ground, further danger lies in shipping the oil by tanker. In 1989 the *Exxon Valdez* caused enormous damage in its famous shipwreck off the Alaskan coast. Earlier oil spills had fouled the California coast, and a huge spill contaminated large areas of the Spanish coastline. In each case, both the economy and the environment were devastated. Pipelines carry their own environmental problems and risks for accidents as well as sabotage and terrorism.

Oil poses major threats to the environment as it consumed, as well. Diesel fuel puts a lot of particulates into the air—that black, sooty, smelly smoke that belches from the exhaust of trucks and buses. Gasoline has fewer particulates but contributes a variety of harmful gases, including nitrous oxide. This comes back down as nitric acid and contributes to the acid rain problem. In certain weather conditions, it never escapes the urban atmosphere at all but hovers to create ozone, one of the major and most dangerous components of urban smog.

In this regard, the people in the cities in developing countries don't breathe any easier than those in richer nations and sometimes worse. While developing nations may have somewhat fewer vehicles, those vehicles are often older and in poorer repair. Many of the world's cities exist in a perpetual brown haze that smells like old tobacco. For decades, Beijing and Mexico City topped the list for the world's most polluted urban air, but Athens, London, Los Angeles, and New York also struggled with high levels of automobile-related pollution (World Health Organization 2007). The cities with the worst air quality are now concentrated in South Asia: India, Pakistan, and Bangladesh (IQ*Air* 2020) where the burning of oil in vehicles and coal in industry combines with the burning of crops (BBC News 2019). The burning of oil products is also a major contributor to the greenhouse gases linked to global climate change. Once we worried about running out of oil, now we are just running out of time to find less damaging alternatives.

Natural Gas

Oil often shares its underground cavities with a lighter fossil fuel relative: **natural gas.** Originally natural gas was considered a waste product to be burned off in huge pillars of flame before beginning the serious pumping of oil. Oilmen remembered the dangers of gas buildup in coal mines. Over time, the handling of this fuel has improved, and it is now one of the fastest-growing energy sources.

Natural gas is an important international commodity, just as petroleum has been, and its importance keeps increasing. Canadian gas fields supply much of the natural gas used in the United States. Bolivia exports 84 percent of its natural gas production, mainly to Argentina and Brazil. The gas could be a major source of revenue, but Bolivia's poor, largely indigenous population is not convinced. Bolivian silver traveled the world and made the Spanish Empire rich, but Bolivia remains South America's poorest nation. Can the people expect better from gas exports?

Natural gas can be delivered by pipes across the country and to individual homes. It is primarily methane gas, which burns somewhat cleanly, giving off mostly water vapor and carbon dioxide. This makes it safer and cleaner to use for home heating and allows for the open, unvented flame of a gas stove. Natural gas has also become a popular fuel for electrical generation, again because it is high energy, easy to move, and clean. Some vehicles have been adapted to run on natural gas; they give off less hazardous exhaust, and while they typically have less power than gasoline vehicles, they are often ideal as urban stop-and-go vehicles, such as postal trucks.

Natural gas also has its limitations. It is in short supply, at least at our current rate of consumption, and its harder-to-reach sources carry new dangers and environmental problems. Also, to say that natural gas burns clean, giving off only water and harmless carbon dioxide, is no longer accurate on the global level because carbon dioxide is a major suspect in global warming.

Oil fueled the twentieth century, and the twenty-first is becoming increasingly dependent on oil and natural gas. These fuels fire our machinery, and petrochemicals made from these fuels are the basis for a vast array of synthetic fabrics, medicines, and plastics. The clothes on our backs and the plastic jugs that fill rich countries' landfills and poor countries' streets and hillsides are all based in oil. We wear it, eat and drink from it, put it on as cosmetics, and take it as medicine. Given the importance of oil and natural gas, it is the height of waste and recklessness to continue to burn them up or to spin them into products to be thrown away. Yet few places are developing effective plans for a postpetroleum age.

Nuclear Fission: The Power of Ancient Suns

In one sense, all power is solar power, because our major energy sources are all means of stored solar power. Fossil fuels—oil, coal, and natural gas—release energy that was stored by ancient life that used solar energy to build molecules of carbon, hydrogen, and oxygen. Humanity's favorite fuel over most of its history, wood and charcoal, are products of the same storage processes that occur in living trees. Solar power also drives the wind, the waves, and the currents and evaporates the water that eventually returns as rivers—all sources of alternative energy.

The only exception to this is **nuclear power,** which releases the energy of atomic nuclei from heavy atoms such as uranium, fused in the supernova of primordial suns. And so perhaps it is the ultimate in stored energy. One other experimental energy source, nuclear fusion, imitates the processes of the sun itself in releasing energy as it fuses hydrogen into helium.

Manhattan Project scientists worked feverishly in the 1940s in Los Alamos, New Mexico, to develop a sustainable nuclear fission chain reaction to release the power of uranium and heavy atoms. Their goal was to beat the Nazis in the race to build an atomic bomb. Many of the scientists felt intensely conflicting emotions: The thrill of discovering a new and yet unknown source of vast energy coupled with the fear of what this tremendous energy source might do to the planet and the people who occupy it. Their fears were well grounded. Nuclear weapons hastened the end of World War II only to plunge the world into a cold war in which ever-deadlier "nukes" threatened to destroy whole cities and scorch the planet itself. Nuclear power, an attempt to tame this wild force, is similarly viewed with mixed hopes and fears.

A nuclear fission weapon uses an out-of-control chain reaction, in which each splitting atom produces high-energy neutrons to split other atoms. A nuclear power plant inserts carbon rods into the fuel to absorb the neutrons and slow the reaction. A slow reaction does not explode (one hopes) but produces intense heat. The heat produces steam that drives turbines, and the turbines drive dynamos, or electric generators. The process is as old as Michael Faraday's dynamo and James Watts's steam engine, only the fuel has changed.

Large amounts of water are used to cool the plant to a safe operating temperature. The only waste products are large amounts of steam (the great white plumes billowing from the hourglass-shaped stacks of many nuclear plants); a lot of warm water, which is typically pumped into whatever waterway the plant sits beside; and a small amount of spent fuel. This is the attraction of nuclear power: There is no dependence on great quantities of coal, oil, or natural gas, and there is no carbon- and particulate-laden smoke billowing into the air.

The United States built many nuclear power plants, particularly in the growth-oriented 1960s, and European countries, with less access to oil and coal resources than the United States, became even more nuclear dependent. France embarked on an ambitious nuclear program and now produces a majority of its electrical energy from nuclear power. Other countries have looked to nuclear power as an alternative to oil dependence, and many developing countries are eager to have nuclear plants to meet their growing energy demands.

As the hopes for nuclear power grow, so do the fears. Mining uranium is a difficult and dangerous operation, and it's only economical in certain parts of the world, such as South Africa. Only a certain rare type of uranium, the isotope U-235, is useful for fission, so the fuel must be enriched in a complex and energy-intensive process to increase the amount of fissionable uranium. This enriched form is highly radioactive and must be transported and stored safely without releasing dangerous radiation. A large area in the Caucasus Mountains of Russia shows evidence of severe radiation damage. Once thought to be evidence of a terrible nuclear accident hidden by the Soviet government, it may just be the result of careless practices in the handling, storage, and disposal of radioactive material—the nuclear equivalent of an abandoned open-pit mine.

The process in the plant is highly regulated but not foolproof. The plant can't explode, but a runaway reaction could cause extreme heat and a "meltdown." Other errors could lead to the release of radiation. In the United States, the Three Mile Island plant had a series of mishaps followed by a radiation release that affected nearby areas and threatened to be far worse. The worst known nuclear disaster occurred in 1986 in Chernobyl, near the city of Kiev in Ukraine—at the time, part of the Soviet Union. Radiation was released and sickened and killed hundreds, perhaps thousands in the area. Radioactive particles also rode the winds into Eastern Europe and Scandinavia and ultimately circled the earth in the upper atmosphere.

Part of the fear of radiation is its invisibility, but more important is its durability. Many radioactive substances will emit radiation for thousands, even tens of thousands, of years. (This is often reported as **half-life,** the time it takes for half of the material to break down.) As you read this, you have radioactive strontium and other materials in your bones, emitting minute quantities of radiation, as the result of nuclear accidents, atmospheric tests of nuclear weapons, and other radiation releases. For most people, the amount is too small to pose a health risk. Even so, questions as to how much material, of what kind, and over what period poses a health hazard are still hotly debated.

Time is another problem with nuclear waste. The quantities of material are small, but they are deadly. They must be stored under perfectly sealed conditions and essentially forever. One proposal is to bury nuclear waste in some very stable environment, such as a salt dome far from groundwater, earthquakes, and any other disturbance and preferably in a remote location. Plans to deposit nuclear waste at Yucca Mountain, Nevada, approved by President George W. Bush in 2002, have drawn a storm of controversy not only from the residents of that state but also from others who live along the route that this material would travel by train or truck. Fears of terrorist attacks have only compounded the concern. The current alternative is to store the material onsite, allowing it to build up in the "cellar" of the plant itself. When the plant becomes obsolete after several decades of operation, the fuel will remain stored under its concrete protective dome, a huge monument to be guarded forever.

Nuclear power plant designs, such as the "breeder" reactor, solve part of the mining and enrichment problem by creating fuel as they operate. One process is to turn nonfissionable uranium into a fissionable human-made element: plutonium. Like U-235, plutonium can be used in power plants and in bombs. In fact, the world's newest nuclear powers—that is, holders of nuclear weapons—developed their weapons by diverting technology and materials that were supplied for nuclear power plants. North Korea's nuclear program is about cheap energy but also about the production of nuclear weapons. In 1981 Israeli jets bombed the Iraqi nuclear power plant for fear it would be used to make nuclear weapons materials. Iran has nuclear power, largely of French design, and there is great suspicion about why an oil-rich nation is so eager to develop nuclear power; many suspect it is to become a nuclear power through weapons development.

Nuclear power offers a clean, smoke-free alternative to fossil fuels, one that contributes no greenhouse gases, and so it has stirred new interest. But it also poses the risks of accident, terrorist sabotage or theft of nuclear material, the worldwide proliferation of nuclear weapons, and the prospect of hazardous waste that will outlive us all.

Nuclear Fusion: The Fire of the Cosmos

The sun, like all stars, produces its energy by fusing hydrogen atoms into helium, a process that releases enormous amounts of heat. This is **nuclear** fusion or **thermonuclear reaction.** (The term is a bit misleading, since all nuclear reactions release intense heat.) In the 1950s first the United States and then the Soviet Union built thermonuclear weapons. These weapons used a uranium-type fission bomb to create intense heat and set off a nuclear fission reaction—the hydrogen bomb.

Hydrogen bombs were soon being built that released enormous amounts of energy. The nightmare was that these weapons would be used against major cities in a thermonuclear war; the dream was that this energy could be harnessed for useful power. The small amounts of hydrogen needed (also a special isotope, known as deuterium), could be extracted from water that is an endless source. The radioactive waste produced, mostly another isotope of hydrogen, was far less dangerous and only radioactive for a few years. This seemed to hold promise as an unlimited, clean energy supply.

The problem has been igniting and containing this reaction. Fusion only takes place under conditions of intense heat. In a star, this heat is produced by huge gravitational pressures. In a hydrogen bomb, it comes from a fission bomb. Neither is practical in a power plant. Material this hot is not easy to contain without vaporizing the container it is in. Attempts have been made to bombard material contained by a magnetic field with multiple high-energy laser beams. These and other designs remain experimental. Either they don't work reliably, or they take more energy to operate than they produce.

A brief stir was created over the idea that so-called cold fusion might be possible, but this has also proved unworkable. The tantalizing prospect of nuclear fusion energy remains, but whether it can be turned into safe and affordable energy is still unknown.

Alternative Energy: Sun, Wind, Earth, and Water

The idea of renewable energy and "green power" has moved from being a hobby of environmentalists to being a national priority in many locations (see figure 11.2). Countries as diverse as Sweden and Costa Rica have embraced alternate energy sources and laid plans to be "carbon neutral," adding no net carbon into the atmosphere for their energy needs in upcoming decades. Promoting green energy, and the jobs that this would entail, is a central theme of the of the Build Back Better Plan put forth by President Joe Biden in 2021, who argues that this plan is not just about addressing global climate change but also about maintaining global competiveness in new technology and creating jobs—these are the jobs of the future as surely as coal and oil brought jobs to earlier generations.

One of the most promising options comes up every morning without fail. Why work so hard to create a "miniature sun" when we already have a big one shining down on our backyard every day? This is the idea behind **solar power,** the original energy source. The sun already grows our food and so indirectly

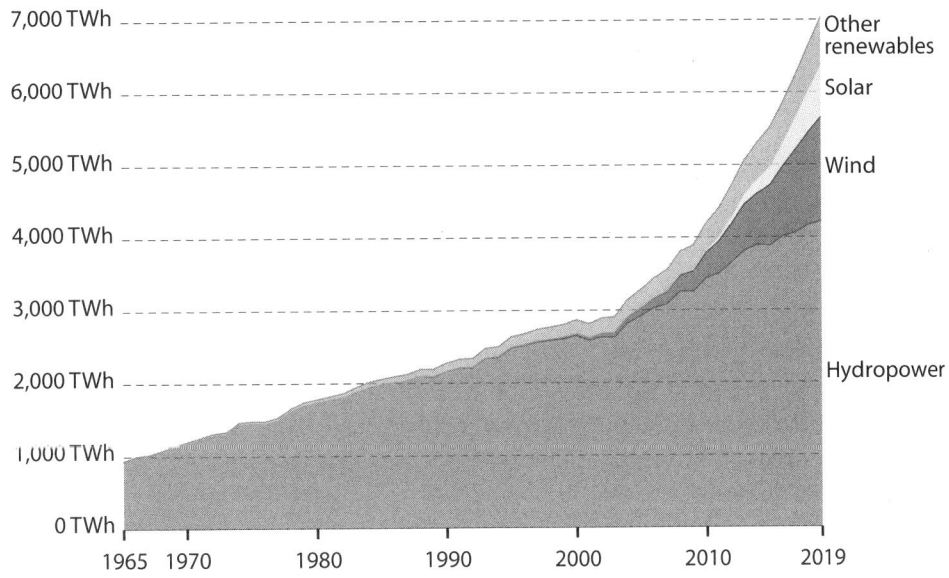

Figure 11.2 Renewable energy generation, world. (Source: Our World in Data.) For a detailed look at change over time and the energy mix and strategy of individual countries, see https://ourworldindata.org/energy.

powers us. It also warms our houses (some days, not enough perhaps, and some days, too much) and propels the weather. The amount of solar energy beaming down on the planet is huge, but the amount on any square meter of space is fairly small. Therein lies the great difficulty: how to harness a power source that is diffused when energy desires are often intense and concentrated.

Like coal and uranium, the sun can be used to generate electricity. Since the intensity in any one place isn't enough to boil water into steam, the usual means is a solar panel, what engineers call a photovoltaic cell. Light striking the substance begins an electric current, the same technique used in a battery-free solar calculator. One vision is to have a vast array of these solar panels in a sunny location to send the electricity to a major metropolitan area—say, from the Mojave Desert to Los Angeles. Cost is a problem with this arrangement but the cost of large solar panels continues to come down, making large-scale solar power look more feasible. China has taken a lead in the mass production of large panels, perhaps hoping to become a global alternative-energy power just as Russia has been a continental power in oil and gas. Currently most solar panels are used on the roofs of single buildings or pieces of equipment. They work well in cloudless space to power satellites but less well in cloudy and smoggy locations. But with each new generation of panels, the cost declines and the efficiency increases. One interesting innovation is solar shingles, where the roofing shingles themselves are high efficiency photovoltaic cells, eliminating the need for large units perched on the roof. A simpler technique for a building is to heat water as it winds through a rooftop solar collector and then use this to heat the building. This works best for places that are sunny yet cold enough to need heat. Still simpler is solar hot water, in which solar-heated water is used for bathing and other hot water needs.

Wind power—essentially an indirect form of solar power, since the sun drives the wind—has much the same promise and limitations. Windmills are ancient, having been used to pump water on the U.S. frontier and to drive mills in flat Holland, where there was little falling water to tap. Modern windmills are less picturesque than the Dutch mills and even the prairie farm mills, but they are far more efficient. Narrow airfoil blades spin on rotors that turn in even the slightest of winds. The turning rotors can spin turbines, which in turn can generate electricity.

Again, this method works well for a single building or piece of equipment. Producing enough electricity to supply an entire metropolitan area requires a large "wind farm." Wind farms have been sprouting on the windy high plains of the United States and on windy ridgelines from the Midwest to Costa Rica. Wind farms can also be established in water to capture offshore winds. For some these are an eyesore, for others they are the look of a cleaner future. Windmills off the shore in New England have been extremely controversial, but one large project in the North Sea off the Danish coast has proven both successful and well accepted.

Other efforts have been made to tap the resources of particular regions. Rising and falling tides can drive turbines, as can strong ocean currents. Both are powerful but diffuse forces. Iceland draws most of its power from **geothermal energy.** Hot water just under the surface of this volcanic land, the stuff of geysers, can also heat homes in the cold Icelandic winter and provide the steam for electrical power plants. This system is clean, efficient, and safe for Iceland, but of course, it only works in areas where there is geothermal activity. Each of the other forms also works best in special locations of high tides, strong currents or strong winds, intense sun, and so forth. While no one means will work everywhere in the world, each can contribute to global energy demands.

Not all uses of the sun, wind, and forces of the earth need to be high technology, however. **Passive solar systems** don't require pumps and photovoltaic cells but work by more efficiently capturing the energy that is already available. Many of these techniques are ancient. The Anasazi Pueblo peoples of the American Southwest have long built their homes with walls of thick adobe mud. The walls insulate from the heat of the day and then slowly release that absorbed heat during the chilly night. People living in hot, dry climates, such as around the Mediterranean, have often built with similarly thick walls and also made use of central courtyards that channel cooling winds. These techniques are still used in Middle Eastern cities, in rural Spain, and in Mexico. Even more efficient were the earth lodges of settled Plains Indian groups such as the Pawnee, a style later seen in sod houses on the frontier plains. Natural insulation, trapping or blocking the sun and capturing or blocking the wind, have long been features of traditional architecture. Only with the advent of central heating and air conditioning, typically powered by nuclear-produced electricity or fossil fuels, have some of these styles begun to disappear.

Passive solar techniques combine old forms with new ideas: south-facing glass to collect sunlight in greenhouse fashion, efficient insulators, heavy materials to absorb and radiate solar heat, and earth-sheltered walls to insulate from the wind and cold or the heat and sun. Carefully placed trees can shelter from the summer sun and in cold climates drop their leaves to allow the desired winter sun to provide heat.

The technology may be as modern as photovoltaic cells, as ancient as a tree-lined courtyard, or more likely a combination of both. Regardless, a planet with an ever-growing energy appetite will have to find better ways of using the energy that is showered on it, rather than burning the "stores" of millions of years in a matter of decades. While we might hope that the urgency of addressing climate change would drive energy change, often economics dominates decisions. Renewable energy sources have new appeal as the costs go down. It is now cheaper to invest in wind power than to try to build a coal fired power plant and much cheaper than a nuclear plant (see figure 11.3).

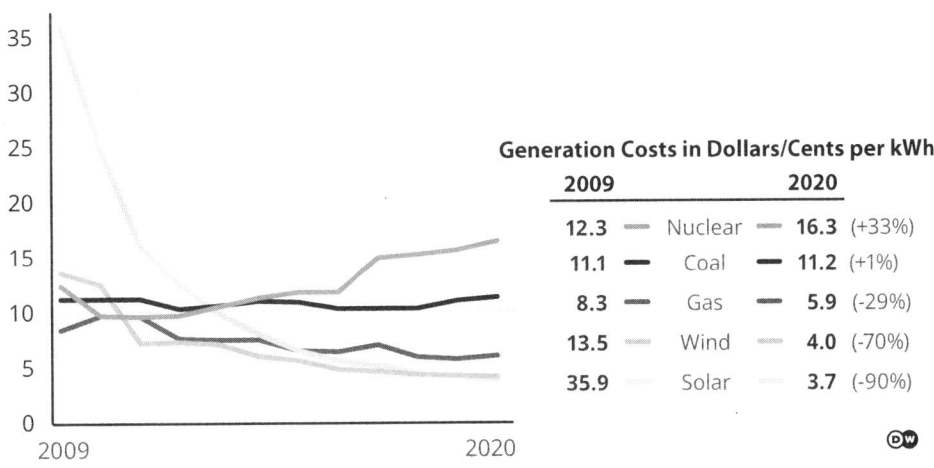

Figure 11.3 World energy prices. © Deutsche Welle.

Chariots of Fire: Automobiles and Transport

Nowhere has our energy appetite grown more quickly than in transportation, particularly our ways of moving ourselves. Until the 1800s all movement was driven by wind or current or powered by muscles—sometimes animal, most often human. With the coal era came the steam train and the steamboat. The internal combustion era, with gasoline and diesel engines, allowed people in the twentieth century to travel by plane and automobile. The first has revolutionized global interactions, and the second has completely reordered our lives.

Automobiles set in motion a cycle of sprawl that turned them from an oddity to a necessity all across North America. Europe shared the fascination with the car but needed a means of travel better suited to smaller spaces and more crowded conditions.

Diesel could also power trains. The first and finest diesel trains were American. The Pioneer Zephyr "Silver Streak" set a new speed record between Denver and Chicago in the 1930s, with a new modern, gleaming silhouette of stainless steel and a quiet, comparatively clean diesel-electric engine that drove the wheels and powered the air conditioning. The great trains were lost in the U.S. building boom of interstate highways and expanding airports.

Train technology shifted to Europe. New designs, new seamless tracks, and new types of electric engines have made high-speed, high-comfort rail travel possible across much of Europe. The trains may no longer have the elegance of the Orient Express, but they provide an affordable and reliable system that has reduced the need for auto and air travel.

When U.S. Commodore Perry visited Japan in 1853, he brought a model steam train, and the Japanese have been fascinated with train travel ever since. Today's Japanese bullet trains are some of the fastest ever built, rivaling air travel between major cities. The Japanese, like the Americans and Europeans, have moved into the automobile business in a major way. Even so, fast intercity trains and efficient urban train transit have limited the need to own and use a car in Japan. South Korea also has entered the auto-manufacturing business but has more closely followed the Japanese pattern regarding domestic use of cars.

Train travel in the United States is most concentrated along the eastern seaboard between Boston and Washington and including New York, Philadelphia, and Baltimore. Yet aging systems and competition from air shuttles and interstate highways have made consistent rail service tenuous.

In Latin America, with a few luxurious exceptions, trains are often old and less than reliable. Partly as a result of this, automobile travel continues to increase dramatically, although buses remain the transport of choice for many. The contrast between Curitiba, Brazil, with its clean, efficient, and low-cost bus system that is used by most urbanites, and São Paulo, with its terrible traffic gridlock, is evidence that Latin America may do best not to imitate its neighbors to the north in automobile dependence.

Americans, who must travel long distances across regions with sometimes sparse populations (and who have a history of seeking independence), have been hard to coax out of their automobiles. They lead the world in oil consumption and will likely continue to do so. Even as gas prices climb, there is still great allure in the car advertisements of sleek vehicles, humming along scenic highways that always seem devoid of any other traffic. The realities of smog, gridlock, and dependence on foreign oil have pushed some to seek alternatives, however. The question is whether the car must go or whether it can clean up its act.

Gasoline-electric hybrids, using a system not unlike those of midcentury trains, get twice the average auto mileage and cut certain emissions by as much as 90 percent. In the early 2000s, when driving my hybrid, I used to get looks as though I had just landed a flying saucer. Increasingly, hybrids have become some of the best-selling and most sought-after vehicles on the road. The energy in most current hybrids still comes completely from gasoline, but plug-in hybrids allow drivers to make short trips entirely on electricity from the electrical grid, only shifting to gasoline for longer trips. This had been offered in Japan in its popular Prius for some time and reached the North American market in 2012.

Hybrids work on newly improved battery systems. A great deal of interest has also gone into **fuel cell cars,** which use a fuel source to create an electric current without combustion or batteries. The fuel may be a petroleum product or hydrogen. Much has been made of hydrogen cars, which have no exhaust but water vapor. The fuel cell combines hydrogen fuel and oxygen from the air to make water, generating electricity in the process. The limitation is how to get the hydrogen. This most abundant element in the universe is not available in pure elemental form. It can be extracted from water, but that takes electrical energy, which must be supplied by some other means. Hydrogen can also be extracted from hydrocarbons, such as petroleum products, but that would merely create just a new form of dependence on fossil fuels.

Affordable fuel cell technology has been elusive, but new battery systems continue to improve with greater range and fewer environmentally damaging components. This has opened a new generation of all-electric cars. Electric cars are not new. Studebaker entered the car market with electrics in 1902. Eventually they gave way to the apparent convenience of gasoline. Now electric is back. The Tesla electric roadster outperforms any sports car on the road (0–60 in under 4 seconds), but with a high purchase price. The Nissan Leaf can take motorists anywhere affordably on electricity—as long as they can find charging stations. New technologies need to be supported by new infrastructure.

Global gridlock has become a common feature of every major metropolitan region as developing economies embrace the automobile (and a few motorbikes) as seen in Bangkok, Thailand [top]. A faster, more efficient and likely much more pleasant alternative is high-speed rail as seen here on a new viaduct in Spain [bottom]. Slower-speed light rail can also be an attractive way to move commuters and claim urban spaces for pedestrians; TriMet in Portland [facing page] was an early integrated system combining light rail with streetcars and buses.

New automobile technologies are promising. But we may need to face the fact that any car, running on any fuel, still takes too many resources to build and operate, too much space to park, and is too hard to recycle to ever be the daily transportation choice of most of the world's people. Some form of public transportation, combined with walking and biking, will likely be needed to have livable communities and sustainable economies.

Turning Down the Heat: Climate Change and Appropriate Technology

The local and regional effects of our desires for transportation and energy have been with us for a long time. England depleted the last of its great forests 200 years ago in an effort to float the world's greatest navy; it needed wood for ships and wood for charcoal to smelt iron. Similarly, we are now seeing the global effects of our choices.

A huge hole in the high atmosphere ozone layer opened up over Antarctica several decades ago as a result of the release of various chemicals, such as the chlorofluorocarbons (CFCs) in aerosol cans. This is not merely a concern to geophysicists or a hazard to penguins. The high-altitude ozone layer protects us against damaging ultraviolet rays from the sun. Australia—a vast, sunny island near this hole—already has the world's highest rate of skin cancer, and ultraviolet exposure is a major concern.

At the other pole, things are also warming up. Adventurous travelers can now trek to the North Pole on Russian icebreakers, their tourist dollars supporting the ailing Russian navy. When they get there in midsummer, they may get to see something no human beings have seen before on or near the pole: open water. The glaciers are retreating in Greenland and Alaska, and now it seems that parts of the polar ice cap may be melting. Santa may need a snorkel to get around his workshop.

Globally, the first decade of the twenty-first century was the warmest on record (Black 2009). Are people to blame? Tons of greenhouse gases, such as carbon dioxide and methane, pour into the atmosphere every day and trap the sun's heat from escaping. How much they contribute to the warming of the planet, and what are the full range of effects, is an enormously complicated projection. The trouble is that no one will know for sure until the process is so far underway that it will take decades to reverse. So far, climate scientists have been dismayed to see effects around the world happening faster than they had originally predicted.

Global warming may not sound so bad if you are reading this in January in Minneapolis or Toronto, but its potential effects are worrisome. Already, residents of low-lying islands such as those of Palau are watching the waves sweep over their homelands. With another meter or so rise in sea level, their homes will be gone.

But this is only the beginning. Most of the world's population is crowded into cities along the seacoasts. If the polar ice were to melt enough to raise the ocean levels several meters, the waves would be in New York, Tokyo, Shanghai, Bombay, and hundreds of other major cities. A rise in ocean level of a few more meters would flood almost the entire country of Bangladesh, home to over 141 million people.

The irony of **global climate change** (a term that some prefer to *global warming*, others have just suggested "global weirding") is that some places might get colder. There is evidence that melting ice water is beginning to submerge the warm waters of the Gulf Stream, the current that flows from the Caribbean across the Atlantic and northward. It warms parts of the extreme eastern United States and Canada and much of Europe. This is the main reason that countries in Northern Europe, such as Great Britain, Norway, and Sweden, are as warm as they are, despite having latitudes as far north as Alaska and Siberia. Without the influence of the warm water, these countries could plunge into a decades-long deep freeze.

Also, while some parts of the world would experience flooding, others would likely experience severe drought as the global winds and weather patterns changed. Agriculture and ecosystems around the world would be disrupted. In 2010 Pakistan experienced record floods just as Russia was experiencing record drought and wildfire—food production in both locations was devastated. Australia appears particularly vulnerable: The dry south of the continent experienced record heat in 2019–2020, sparking lethal bush fires that burned over 12 million acres and affected three billion animals. Sydney was encased in hazardous air for 81 days. In Australia the dry south burns, and the wet north floods: Brisbane, the third largest city in Australia, faced massive flooding in 2011 as unrelenting rains fell on the north. In North America, 2020 saw rampant wildfires in the western United States—the worst year ever for California—and larger and more frequent hurricanes in the southeastern states. Devastation from hurricanes also hit parts of Central America. The Global Humanitarian Forum has dubbed climate change a silent catastrophe, already affecting 300 million people, with possibly 300,000 already dying every year in climate-related disasters and food scarcity—a number that will likely double by 2030 (Whiteman 2009). Climate data show that such worries were not overly alarmist but likely understated the far-reaching impacts (see NASA Global Climate Change at https://climate.nasa.gov/effects/ for more information and continual updates).

Human civilization has grown around a climate that has shown only slight changes in the last 10,000 years. Modern cities have been built along coastlines that have been relatively constant for hundreds of years. A rapidly changing climate could disrupt everything we have learned to take as normal. Moving the homes, farms, and livelihoods of millions, even billions, would be an undertaking of almost unimaginable proportions—post-Katrina New Orleans a thousand times over. All plans for economic development must now consider this danger, what Al Gore famously dubbed "an inconvenient truth" (Gore 2006).

We don't have to wait to know the effects of global warming to take action. The very steps that are needed to slow global climate change would also give us cleaner air to breathe, make us less dependent on limited fossil fuel supplies, and give us less need to damage fragile parts of the planet with drilling and mining. These steps include the following:

1. **Place greater reliance on efficient mass transit, most notably trains.** Reducing our dependence on automobiles and helping the developing world develop alternative, more efficient means of transportation, rather than filling their roads with more cars, would do more than almost anything else to clear the air.

2. **Emphasize energy-efficient homes.** Building homes that effectively use the forces of the sun, wind, and earth to heat and cool them and that rely on materials and designs that make the most of their environment (and thus have the least need for artificial heating and cooling) would greatly reduce the global demand for energy. Again, the wealthy nations may need

The most efficient technology is not always the most complex. Bicycles work well for commuting, relaxing, and improving urban ambience for a family outing in bicycle-filled Amsterdam [top] and for friends enjoying bike sharing in Beijing [bottom].

to relearn the naturally economizing ways and designs of traditional societies, rather than encourage the developing countries to develop a desire for billions of units of central air conditioning.

3. **Explore alternative energy sources in earnest.** There is no magic sorcerer's stone that will provide all our energy needs. Using careful combinations of alternative sources, such as solar and wind, along with creative conservation will be needed.

4. **Reverse the trend toward disposable mass consumption.** We seem to be paving large portions of the planet in concrete and asphalt, and much of the remainder seems to be covered with plastic bottles. Plastic bottles and containers—recent additions to advanced industrial societies and now filling shelves in developing societies everywhere—have come to dominate landscapes around the world. They fill the beaches of Panama and float on the waves. They line the gorges of Mexico and bob under majestic waterfalls. They drift in remote reaches of the Amazon and choke the wildlife. In Africa they have moved from a novelty to a necessity. Most plastic is a petroleum product, spun from oil and molded into shape in processes that require large amounts of energy. Discarded, these products litter the land for centuries and must be replaced by still more fossil fuel inputs. Rich nations must lead the way in recycling and so reduce the energy and waste that goes into this process of turning limited resources into limitless litter. Consumers in both rich and poor countries need alternatives to cheap breakable products in cheap, disposable, and excessive packaging.

Global technology has brought us a worldwide media that assure us that the way to a happy, healthy, rewarding life is through consumption: buying more, accumulating more, and then abandoning it in favor of a new and improved model. In the early 1900s *consumption* referred to the ravages of diseases like tuberculosis that slowly drained a person, leaving him or her withered, gasping, and dying, or suffering from consumption. The planet is now suffering from consumption in its new twenty-first century meaning: withered, gasping, and in places, dying under the demand for energy and products. The truth is more likely that the way to a happy, healthy, rewarding life is by consuming less, making it last longer, and then recycling it into something new. The great challenge for twenty-first century technology will be to make this both a global vision and a global reality.

Key Ideas

> Technological change has driven social change over the centuries. Never has technology advanced so quickly, however, offering both new possibilities and new dangers.

> Electronic media allow people to contact one another easily around the world and build common understanding or united efforts. Popular media can also become a monopoly with tremendous reach in the hands of a few at the expense of local and face-to-face communication.

> The technological era requires enormous inputs of energy. This energy is becoming both scarce and expensive.

> Politics, scarcity, and the difficulty and danger of extraction, along with concern about global climate change, have forced a search for alternatives to fossil fuels. At this time no single energy source is both completely safe and sufficient for all needs. Along with conservation efforts, new attention is going to the search for safer nuclear power and for affordable and practical ways to harness solar and wind power and other renewable resources.

For Review and Discussion

1. How has technology changed the way people interact around the world? How much of your own social interaction is face-to-face and how much is conducted electronically through texts, emails, social networking sites, and similar methods? What are the advantages and costs of each?

2. Does modern media keep people informed or misinformed? Is this a question of government regulation, corporate responsibility, or individuals' responsibility to stay informed?

3. What are the biggest energy users in our world and in our country? What are the biggest energy users in your own life? What will be needed for the world, and for your local community, to curb its energy appetite and practice meaningful conservation?

Making Connections

Urban Legends

> You can see some of the latest urban legends circulating in the area of politics, consumer goods, or anything else at www.snopes.com. Snopes researches the claims made by the most commonly circulated stories on the internet and checks them for accuracy. What are some of the leading

urban legends currently circulating? Why do these spread so far and so fast? What is their appeal?

APC

▶ The Association for Progressive Communications (APC) is a global network dedicated to open access to electronic communication around the world. Its site at www.apc.org explores issues of open, unfettered journalism and broad access to communications in an internet age. Note efforts in various regions of the world: What changes are they seeking to bring about?

Energy Topics and Renewable Sources

▶ The U.S. Energy Information Administration, the statistical agency the U.S. Department of Energy, posts a wide range of data on energy sources and consumption, history and trends at www.eia.gov. A focus on renewable sources can also be found on the site, https://www.eia.gov/renewable/.

Impact of Climate Change

▶ Scholarly but very accessible information on climate change and its impacts can be found at https://climate.nasa.gov/evidence/. What strikes you about the evidence and the impacts?

Making a Difference

Energy Efficiency and Renewable Energy

▶ The U.S. Department of Energy maintains a site with information on energy efficiency and renewable energy at https://www.energy.gov/eere/office-energy-efficiency-renewable-energy. Note its discussion of these topics and the information it provides to groups and individual consumers to increase their energy efficiency and to learn more about alternative energy sources. What can individuals as well as communities do to use less nonrenewable energy?

Transit and Energy

▶ What is being done in your community and on your campus to promote the use of public transportation? Are there ways that individuals and groups can advance these efforts? What are the barriers to greater use of the transit systems available?

▶ What efforts, both private and public, are being made to increase energy efficiency and reduce consumption on your campus and in your community? What resources are offered to help individuals and groups? Does your campus have an energy conservation plan?

Sierra Club Beyond Coal Campaign

➤ The "beyond coal" campaign of the Sierra Club has included sponsorship of the informative looks at economic, social, and environmental consequences of coal dependence in the United States. See https://coal.sierraclub.org/. They include a variety of action steps at https://coal.sierraclub.org/take-action.

350

➤ This international movement was founded on its pledge to reduce global CO_2 levels below 350 parts per million (ppm). Its website, www.350.org, contains information on global climate change and a wealth of photos from climate activists and campaigns around the world.

12
Ecology

How Much Can One Planet Take?

Global Encounters

We live on a planet that is both dazzling and dangerous, both magnificent and much abused. It is also a great biosphere, a circle of life, whose climate and ecology are changing just as we begin to understand its complexity. Consider experiences on two continents. Can we devise ways of living that sustain both human diversity and the natural diversity of our common home?

India

We rumble down this stretch of road and then abruptly pull off onto the monsoon-soaked mud. We find a hidden gate and enter a sudden and unexpected refuge of shade and flowers—the last private farm on this bit of exurban

Chennai. Our host is Arul, the young man who is responsible for this refuge. His extended family once owned a lot of land and enterprise but fell into familial struggles over property and grudges. He and his parents retreated to this bit of land, something no one else wanted just eight years ago. Those 80 acres have now multiplied in value so much that eight years later he is a wealthy man. But he is not sure he can afford to farm. The family had been dairy farmers, supplying milk and yogurt along with fresh produce to the big five-star hotels. But now the hotels want everything packaged and pasteurized, preferably powdered and standardized. He put in the lowest bid for their needs, but they were not interested in his small enterprise. He offered to buy more animals. "Animals?" they wondered. "That is how I get milk, it comes from animals," he explained. That may be, but their suppliers don't acquire animals. They add new processing plants, and the cows are far away in huge operations.

He also grows coconuts but can't sell them in town either. Much produce now comes from Sri Lanka, Thailand, and the Philippines, surplus that is dumped, he claims, in the Indian market, now opened through WTO agreements. He can't compete, so he sells "tender" coconuts on the highway to the hungry throngs that now line the roads. He also grows eucalyptus, no longer for paper, but for poles to make the huts that newcomers throw up along the roads. He gets a good price. He also grows a bit of rice, but rice brings no profit. He can break even if the weather is good, and he employs a lot of people who need work. Rice is labor intensive, which is one reason it is disappearing. He employs an older generation that is dependent on his farm, but their children do not want to work the fields. There is a new government primary school for the village; students go to school through fifth grade, and now they even go to college. These people were outcastes, and then bonded labor, but now, Arul notes, at least in southern India, "No one is any longer untouchable, thank God. Everyone gets a chance."

How will he cope with the rising taxes that come with rising property values, with international and huge agribusiness competition, and changing consumer demand? He wants to keep this, the last farm in the area, in agriculture, but he wonders if he can start a bed and breakfast, maybe a demonstration farm and guest home for the many city people who have never seen a farm. The tourist income would make up for the lack of profit in farming. As I enjoy a snack of water buffalo yogurt, mango chutney, and Coca-Cola under the shade of towering hibiscus, I must admit he would have a wonderful oasis in the midst of the postmodern chaos outside. Far from exotic, his ideas sound incredibly familiar. Are we talking about a farm in India or Indiana? We could be having this conversation with my dairy farming friends back home. Would those Indiana farmers imagine how closely this world parallels theirs? It is not about cheap foreign competition in India, the story is about the changing nature of work, livelihood, and land use worldwide. "The world is changing," Arul notes. "The way of life is changing."

We walk on past groves of trees to a large containment reservoir where families are bathing and washing clothes by slapping them against wet rocks. I'm reminded of Mark Twain's quip that India is the only country where people use clothes to break rocks. The people are newcomers, migrant laborers, but not in agriculture. They are migrant construction laborers, following the road projects. With houses tossed together from palm fronds and eucalyptus poles, they have no other water source. Arul can't keep them off his land, so he has worked out an agreement: They can use the reservoir that is too brackish for irrigation. You can't have water that is used for nothing, he explains.

South Africa

Private game reserves have become a big part of South Africa's postisolationist embrace of tourism. One travels in style in Land Rovers to game overlooks, even accompanied by waiting champagne to toast the first sighting of a lion or rhino. The wild side of Africa? There seems to be a subtle gradation in what is ultimately a zoo. Even in the United States, barred cages have given way to more natural enclosures. And one can now travel to open-air game parks with drive-through tours outside San Diego, in Ontario, or in Disney's Animal Kingdom in Florida. Here the reserves have natural vegetation and climate, but the animals are often purchased at auction and brought in. Is this conservation or just a bigger zoo? Increasingly the two are intertwined as many large species will only survive behind some kind of fence, a barrier against poaching and the endless march of human sprawl. We enjoy watching the ostriches foraging within a few meters of the Atlantic surf at Cape Point, but we get our real close-ups with the animals at an ostrich farm not unlike one that has opened in Indiana, not for tourists but for low-cholesterol steaks. Also at Cape Point, signs not unlike those at Yosemite or Yellowstone warn people to keep their food locked safely in their cars. No bears here, just very bold and very fast baboons— not very intimidating until you get a look at those incisors.

South Africa is in the process of bringing some of its indigenous San peoples back to their ancestral lands, land that is now within large national parks. I wonder if these people can really maintain an ancient culture in a new land. Without this effort, they will only be found in the national history museum we visited. But relocated to the parks, will they simply become part of the bigger zoo? Can they teach us about their heritage, or will they, too, be left watching for cars and waiting for handouts?

One of the most popular private game reserves near here boasts that it is its community's largest employer. The reserve sponsors blanket drives and programs for those who are still unemployed and impoverished. Overnight guests can put down their cocktails and help serve dinner in their soup kitchen program for locals. Our students love the wildlife but feel a bit cheated on seeing "the real Africa." Still, this is the real Africa. Rich and poor, open land and crowded communities, wild and urbane, all stirred together.

Planetary Boundaries

You may have heard the term "carbon footprint." This is not tracking up the carpet after walking through soot or oil drips in the garage. It is the amount of carbon dioxide that our lifestyle releases into the atmosphere. A broader concept is **ecological footprint:** The total amount of demands that we place on the earth's land, air, and water to support our lifestyle. Sometime in the 1980s our combined ecological footprint exceeded one—that is, one earth. We have run out of planet. At this point, we our borrowing—or maybe stealing, since it is without their consent—from our children and grandchildren. Visionaries such as Elon Musk think maybe it is time to look to the vastness of space. But it is inconceivable that a collapsing global civilization could muster the resources to launch billions of people on a space voyage. Space exploration is an inspirational endeavor, but it can only be done by a thriving terrestrial civilization with resources to spare, not one on the brink of collapse. In his book, *Collapse: How Societies Choose to Fail or Succeed* (2011), Jared Diamond uses Easter Island as a metaphor for a too-late realization of impending doom. Having deforested the remote island and depleted its natural resources, the island's inhabitants no longer had enough to survive—and they had no huge trees left with which to build ocean-going canoes. They were stranded in the vastness of the Pacific. Somehow we need to find a way to live within the constraints of our one home. Plus we need to do this in ways that allow its diversity of plants and animals to survive amidst clean air and water, and healthy landscapes—all the elements that make this one human home not only viable, but also beautiful.

Swedish agronomist and environmental researcher Johan Rockström led a project that focused on planetary boundaries. You can see their work summarized in his TED talk at https://www.youtube.com/watch?v=RgqtrlixYR4. He argues that while we may negotiate the global agreements on water, land, and climate, the earth itself does not negotiate. We have to remain within those planetary boundaries. These include not just climate, but nine others including biodiversity, ocean acidity, the ozone layer, and the buildup of phosphorus and nitrogen, largely as part of our industrialized agricultural production.

British economist Kate Raworth (2017) added an inner ring to Johann Rockström's "planetary boundaries." A ring of human need that includes food, water, and health, and broader concepts such as social justice and political voice. Between the outer ring of planetary boundaries and the inner ring of human need, she contends that we need to find a "sweet spot"—a safe and just space for humanity. She calls the result "doughnut economics" (see figure 12.1). What do you think of her approach? And her list of human needs? Is there a "sweet spot" that combines recognition of both human needs and planetary boundaries?

Food: We Are What We Eat

Hunter-gatherers searched for their sustenance from among a diverse supply of natural provisions. When both men and women were crucial to providing food, the two genders tended to have more equal social power. Limited and shifting food supplies meant small, mobile populations. Mobility meant that possessions had to be few and had to be shared, and so members of the band tended to be fairly equal. Although life was dangerous, for many it appears to have been quite satisfying. Food was uncertain but diverse and nutritious.

At some point the growing population, declining resources, and changing climate caused many groups to begin growing food in communal gardens; they became **horticultural societies.** Their impact on their environment increased,

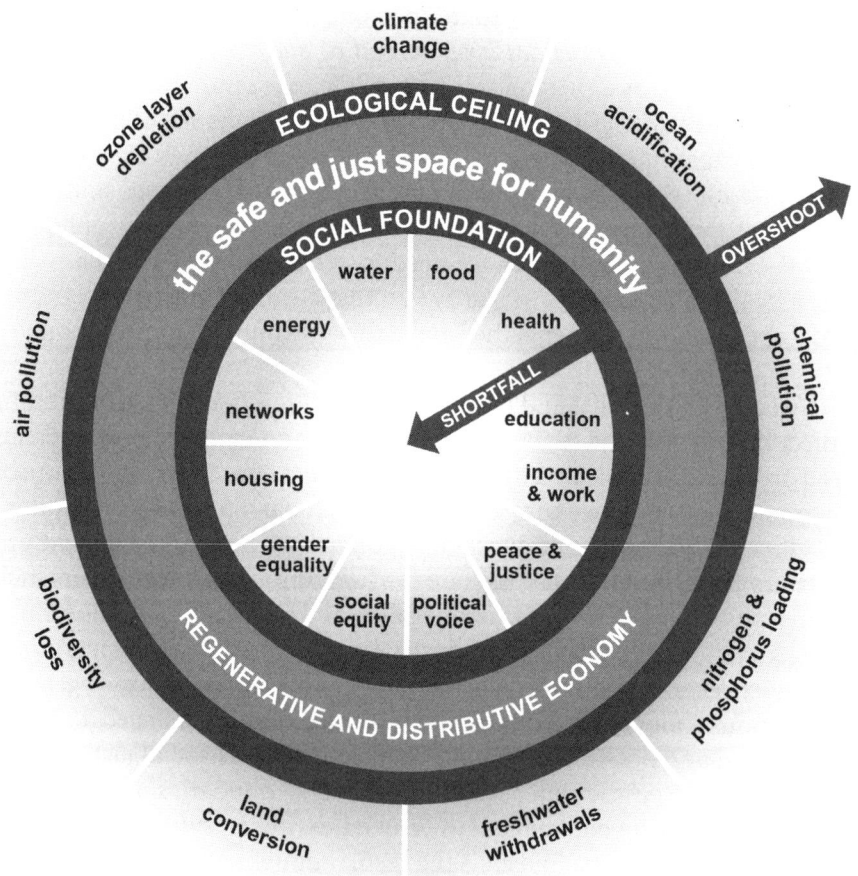

Figure 12.1 Doughnut economic model.

as they now had to clear land for gardens, often by chopping or burning or both. But plots tended to be small and shifting, in part to prevent soil depletion. Both men and women contributed; often, the men cleared and the women tended the land. Working together in common gardens, women were a key to the economy and often held considerable power in the village.

Equal sharing was no longer possible as groups grew larger, and surplus produce had to be redistributed by some central authority, often a man of some influence and prestige. Still, nonperishable possessions were few, and so inequality was not great. The most prized possession was often a respected family name, which would yield influence in community decisions.

In open grasslands and places too dry to garden, one way to survive was to herd grazing animals. As these animals grazed, they turned grass into protein for their herders. People first hunted these animals, including the wild ancestors of the horse and cattle. But as they came to control the movements of the animals, eliminate the competition of predators, and selectively manage the herd size, they shifted from being hunters to herders, forming **pastoral societies.** Smaller, more hardy animals probably were domesticated first: goats (known for eating anything), then sheep, then larger animals such as horses and cattle, and probably last of all, camels (ornery and harder to control) and their South American cousins, llamas.

Herders had to be tough. The animals had to be moved over large areas, especially in arid climates, so as not to exhaust the grass. They also had to be protected from predators and increasingly from other herders. Small animal herding probably involved the whole community, but eventually large herds of large animals were controlled primarily by men, male warriors ready to protect their herds. Eventually horses became more valuable as transportation than as food, and the mounted warrior rode onto the scene.

Large herds can be very hard on the environment, but traditionally herders kept moving. If they mingled with local farmers, they also provided something valuable: organic fertilizer. Herders sometimes used their animals for meat, but that was generally considered too costly, as it reduced the herd. Others learned to extract protein from their animals in the form of blood or, more often, milk, and so were able to keep them alive.

From food sources also came lifestyle and social patterns. Mobile herders had to make do with few possessions. Moving over large areas and among potentially hostile groups, they were often more militant than gardeners and gatherers. If men controlled the herds, they often controlled the society and its women, as well.

Each of these three groups has been discussed in the past tense because so few of them remain. When Europeans set out to explore and conquer the world around 1500, many of these groups still existed. Hunter-gatherers lived in the harsh but bountiful forests of Canada and Alaska and throughout the

North American Rocky Mountains. The highlands and grasslands of South America were also dotted with bands of hunter-gatherers. All of Australia was populated by Aboriginal hunter-gatherers, whereas small but resourceful people of the Pygmy cultural group lived in the rain forest of equatorial Africa. Further south, in the Kalahari Desert, were the San and Khoi peoples, whose simple but effective lifestyle was set in the popular imagination in the movie *The Gods Must Be Crazy* and its sequels. In the far north, Inuit peoples hunted caribou and seals and gathered roots and berries.

Some of these groups remained in remote locations well into the twentieth century, but their lifestyles continued to change due to contact, often forcible, with other societies. The few that remain such as the Baka of Central Africa have a lifestyle that is a blend of older traditions and new impositions. The means of survival that supported humanity for tens of thousands of years is now almost as extinct as the mastodon or, for that matter, the wild horse.

Many of the so-called primitive peoples that European colonizers and conquerors encountered were not true hunter-gatherers, though they often did hunt and fish. Rather, they depended on gardens; they were horticulturalists. Horticulturalists included the native peoples of the eastern woodlands of what is now the United States, as well as the peoples of the Amazon and the Pacific. When the Pilgrims came ashore in New England, they weren't saved by stores of meat or wild nuts but by finding stores of Indian corn in abandoned villages. The eastern woodland tribes survived on staples that had diffused northward from what is now Mexico: corn, squash, and beans. Together, they provide quite complete nutrition; also, corn and beans can be dried and stored for winter use.

Since horticulturalists typically leave large areas of the forest intact, the Europeans thought they were coming to wild lands inhabited by only a few wild people. But the eastern forests were laced with trails that connected villages whose residents hunted and gathered wild foods in the forest yet depended on small garden plots to ensure their survival. Similarly, the Amazon seemed a great wilderness to the explorers, but it was, in fact, home to plant cultivators who domesticated and eventually gave to the world black beans, peanuts, pineapples, and tapioca. In the Pacific, if Tahiti was a tropical paradise, ripe with beckoning fruits, it was only so because Polynesian seafarers had brought their plants with them and carefully cultivated the new islands.

Like hunter-gatherers, horticulturalists are resourceful and they utilize a wide range of both domestic and wild foods to survive harsh times. It was Squanto who saved the Pilgrims from starvation, not the other way around. Yet the number of horticulturalists is typically small in one area. They were ultimately no match for the large number of colonizers who coveted their open spaces. A few simple horticulturalists remain today, often in tropical rain forest environments in South America, Southeast Asia, and pockets of Africa, but they, too, are succumbing to the encroachment of other societies.

By 1500 there were so few hunter-gatherers and horticulturalists in Europe and Asia, as well as North Africa, because most had already succumbed to more powerful neighbors. In the Middle East, by 3000 BCE inventive farmers were learning a new way to put food in their stomachs. Instead of eating or milking the grazing animals, they put them to work pulling a plow. Cereal grains, such as wheat and oats, are grasses that produce seeds edible to humans. It took a lot of land and the soil had to be turned up, but draft animals allowed large areas to come under cultivation. **Agriculture** was born.

The impact on the environment was almost immediate. Large areas came under cultivation, and wild lands and wild animals were limited to remote reaches too hard to farm. Grain could be harvested in mass and stored, feeding larger populations and those not near the farm. Cities also became possible. But urban dwellers could only flourish by bringing more of the hinterland under cultivation and by ensuring, by trade or by force, that the bounty of land came to the central city. The agrarian kingdom and then the agrarian empire were born. **Agrarian societies,** with their larger populations and centralized governments, could field larger, more disciplined armies, and other societies were soon consumed.

The herders held out the longest, especially those who had learned to fight from horseback. Much of European and Asian history in the centuries from 3000 BCE to about 1500 CE reflects the back-and-forth struggle for dominance between settled farmers on the fertile fringes (the Mediterranean and Europe, India, and eastern China) and mounted herders on the great grasslands in-between (Central Asia). Firearms eventually settled the balance in favor of the agrarian states, and independent herding societies gradually dwindled away, coming under the control of more powerful states. A few, such as the Ottoman Turks, settled into their own firearm-equipped empires.

Sowing the Seeds of Civilization

Agrarian states and empires fed their growing populations through the intensive cultivation of a few strains of what had been wild grasses—grasses whose seed grains could be fed directly to humans. A Middle Eastern grass—wheat—was cultivated so successfully that it built the empires of Babylonia and Egypt, fed Rome, and ultimately fed much of Europe and the world. Its cousins—rye, barley, oats, and others—played a supporting role, but over time, wheat conquered the land.

In the wet lowlands of Southeast Asia, the preferred grass was rice. With a warm climate and increasingly sophisticated irrigation, rice could provide two or three crops a year and so came to support the world's most densely populated area. A dividing line still runs across Asia, separating the rice-based cuisine of wet southern Asia from the wheat-based diet of the northern plains. Rice isn't very nutritious, but when combined with vegetables, and especially with protein-rich beans, it has served as the dietary basis of most of Asia's billions. Rice was brought to the tropical Americas by the Spanish and Portuguese, and rice and beans feed millions in Brazil and across the American tropics.

The Mesoamerican Indian states that the Spanish found in place already had their staple grass: maize, or the American corn. Bred from tiny plants into tall stalks, this crop, combined with beans and squash, fed the great empires of ancient Mexico and spread across the southern and eastern parts of North America. American corn now feeds much of the world, either through U.S. exports or through cultivation in China and Africa.

Africa originally built its great states on its own indigenous grains, millet and sorghum, but eventually adopted first wheat and then corn as staples. Ancient American horticulturalists contributed to other key starchy staples: potatoes from the South American highlands and manioc from the tropical lowlands. Potatoes from Peru became the basis of diets from Ireland to Russia, wherever land was scarce and ill-suited to grain production. Manioc, grown as cassava, feeds millions in tropical climates. The grains of these three grasses—wheat, rice, and corn—with some help from the starchy root crops, such as potatoes and cassava, and a few bushy legumes, such as peanuts, black beans, and increasingly, soy beans, now feed almost the entire world.

Wheat, rice, and corn have a 5,000-year history of feeding growing populations, and the root crops and legumes have an even longer history. But how these are grown has changed dramatically. Agrarian states relied on vast fields under cultivation to feed the population, including urban dwellers that grew nothing, and to clothe the population in clothes made from fibers, such as the linen of Egypt and the Middle East. Cotton was apparently domesticated in slightly different varieties independently in Africa, India, and the Americas. Indian cotton produced beautiful gowns and saris, Egyptian cotton clothed Europe's armies and gained fame, but it was the cotton worn by Mesoamerican Indians (now Mexico) and southern North America—which was used for everything, from sun protection to royal robes to warriors' armor—that eventually traveled throughout the world. The pastoralists contributed one other important fiber: wool. All these fabrics were extremely labor intensive to produce. Cotton, in particular, was picked in clumps, cleaned of its seeds, and then spun and woven, all by many hands. Peasant laborers in India and Europe provided these hands; in the Americas, large plantations turned to African slave labor.

As demand grew, so did the desire to speed production. One of the world's first mass-production machines was U.S. inventor Eli Whitney's 1794 cotton gin, which cleaned and processed the cotton fiber. But turning it into clothing was still a slow process. In Europe, a French inventor named Joseph-Marie

Jacquard came up with an ingenious way to operate looms using punched metal cards. The designs were encoded in the cards, rather than in the memory of the master weaver, and the looms could run at high speeds and be operated by workers with simple skills. The great looms were run by water power and sometime later by steam.

France, Germany, and Britain all began to build bigger textile plants. The British, eventually helped by power from English inventor James Watts's more efficient steam engine, took the lead and soon supplied much of the world with textiles. The natural resources were still agrarian products, but production was now fully industrial. The industrial age entered so quickly and completely that it has come to be known as the **Industrial Revolution.** Agrarian states became industrial societies—first in Western Europe, then in the United States and Canada in North America, later in Japan in Asia, and finally in scores of industrializing agrarian states around the world.

Industry did not replace agriculture but rather transformed it. Industrial machinery could dig irrigation canals and then pump water. With the internal combustion engine came the tractor and the harvester, increasingly larger machines that replaced the millions of hands once needed for farm production. In the early 1800s most of U.S. society worked in agriculture. By the early 1900s the number had dropped to one-third, by the beginning of the 2000s it had dropped to below 3 percent of the labor force (U.S. Bureau of the Census 2004), and by 2020 it was 1.3 percent (Statistica 2021). Industrialized agriculture, combined with global marketing of food, or **agribusiness,** feeds an ever-growing portion of the planet's billions (see Kimbrell 2002). It has also changed the face of the planet.

Growing Business: Industrial Agriculture

Flying over the central United States, one can see few natural landforms. Even the water that is visible is usually a dammed reservoir that turns a river into a source of irrigation and a transport route for grain (Brown 2005). What is visible is a great checkerboard of squares—green in the summer, brown the rest of the year, unless mixed with snow.

Most of the squares are filled with corn, which comprises over one-fifth of U.S. cropland. Corn grown in the United States feeds large portions of the world, including places such as Mexico, where corn was probably first cultivated. The hundreds of varieties of so-called Indian corn have been replaced by just a few varieties grown from hybrid seeds provided by large firms, such as Monsanto. Large tractors and harvesters are ideal for working these vast, unbroken fields. Herbicides and pesticides are used to maintain the fields, and most are irrigated, even in wet areas, so that periods of drought do not slow growth.

One allowance for an ancient tradition is made: American Indians grew corn interspersed with beans to provide added nutrition and to replenish the soil with nitrogen, which was drawn out by the corn. These days, this is accomplished by rotating crops of corn with soybeans. Seeing these vast fields, one would suppose that Americans live on nothing but corn and soybeans. In fact, most of the production is either fed to animals or is turned by the food industry into syrups, sweeteners, and oils. Most of the remainder is exported.

American-grown wheat is also exported around the world, although it must compete with that from other industrialized agribusiness centers, such as Canada, Australia, and Argentina. The tremendous U.S. production is supported by large amounts of pesticides and huge amounts of water. In some parts of the western United States, the great squares give way to giant circles, visible only from the air. The circles are not alien creations but merely the result of giant rotating irrigation systems.

When mechanized agriculture covered the American plains with farm fields plowed "fence row to fence row," it helped create the great "dust bowl" of the 1930s. Amid unexpected drought, the turned-up soil simply blew away by the ton. The answer to the dust bowl was primarily **irrigation:** pouring on huge amounts of water from underground aquifers, essentially great underground lakes. These pools of groundwater, built up over thousands of years, are disappearing, however, forcing the need to find ever-deeper wells to tap. Wheat grown in Washington State uses surface water. Huge quantities are pumped from the Columbia River, water that is also sought by the salmon industry (note that even fishing is now an "industry") and rapidly growing communities.

More surprising to many than the country's production of wheat or corn is the fact that the United States is also a major exporter of rice. Half of this production comes from Arkansas, where large areas have been deforested or stripped of natural wetland vegetation to accommodate massive rice production. The wet clay soil retains the moisture that commercial rice needs, but it also breeds many pests, and so using a large quantity of pesticides is part of the process.

If developing countries in the Global South are importing such large quantities of grains from the industrial agribusiness countries, what are they doing with their own land? Increasingly, it is also controlled by agribusiness and used for export crops. Coffee and cacao (the cocoa and chocolate plant) are major industries. Coffee, originally from East Africa but now dominating in the tropical Americas, is second in global trade only to petroleum. Chocolate, originally a Mesoamerican cultivation, now dominates the economy of Ghana and West Africa. In Brazil, black bean production has shifted to massive fields of soy to be turned into oil for export. In West Africa the American peanut is grown to be pressed into vegetable oil for the European market.

Recent growth, however, is not just in crops that need tropical climates but also in crops that need cheap labor. Grains can be planted and harvested by enormous machines that outproduce armies of cheap laborers and so are increasingly concentrated in areas of heavily industrialized agriculture, such as the United States and Canada. This is not so easy with crops such as fruits and vegetables, which must be carefully harvested, often by hand, to avoid damage. The old means of achieving this was to import migrant farm labor. The Imperial Valley of California, acre for acre the most productive land in the United States, combines the sunshine of what should naturally be a desert with vast amounts of irrigation water from the Colorado River (largely draining it dry) and itinerant farm laborers to harvest the crops. This land, along with similar operations in south Texas and Florida, provides most of the U.S. fruit and vegetable production. But an ever-growing portion of that production comes from other countries: Mexico, Brazil, and Chile, in particular.

Agribusiness can transform almost any food product into a large-scale operation. Cotton is more likely to be grown in irrigated portions of California's central valley than in its traditional locations in the Southeast. California also just passed Wisconsin as the leading dairy state. But this is not your grandfather's dairy farm. The little red barns of family farms and children's books have been replaced by lactose mills. At the peak of Wisconsin's claim to be the dairy state, dairy farms in Wisconsin often had only about 80 cows; in California, the number was typically in the thousands, with megaplants holding over 14,000 animals (NPR 2004; Oncken 2021). Most of these animals never see grass. They are housed in block-long open sheds, with apartment-sized blocks of hay. Drainage ditches carry the manure to vast holding lagoons. Old McDonald's farm has been replaced by electric machines and hoses operated by armies of migrant laborers.

These farms are typically located near communities of low-income people of color. The potential for air and water pollution, especially in these communities, is enormous, according to the Center for Race, Poverty, and the Environment. In some places, the air—with its putrid mixture of manure, dust, and the exhaust of both machines and cows—is smoggier than that in Los Angeles (Grossi 2005; KPIX 2016). Yet regulations are rare, for this is farming, after all. The industry notes recent efforts to reduce the emissions and environmental impact, but then came record drought, fire, and new challenges to an intensive industry on a fragile land.

A similar shift in production has occurred with meat. Pork in the Midwest is now a product of huge hog farms, each with over 5,000 animals. Hog waste is washed into great holding lagoons, where it fouls the air and threatens to leech into groundwater. The hogs' carcasses are shipped to huge factory-like slaughterhouses, where again, the workers tend to be low-income men and women of color.

Smithfield Foods is the largest pork processor in the world, with hundreds of corporate-owned farms and contracts with thousands of smaller farms. They are based in Virginia but wholly own by WH Group of China. This massive operation knows how to bring home the bacon, but it also has a dark underbelly. Charlie Le Duff (2000) describes a mix of black, Latino, and American Indian workers looking up at the one white man towering over them, leaning on a balcony railing and looking more like a prison guard or border agent.

> Quota has to be met and the workload doubles. The conveyor belt always overflows with meat around 1 o'clock. So the workers double their pace, hacking pork from shoulder bones with a driven single-mindedness. They stare blankly, like mules in wooden blinders, as the butchered slabs pass by. (p. 1)

As the world's best fishing grounds have been depleted, there is new interest in fish farming in both Asia and North America. The prospect of cultivating a new resource to replace an overtaxed natural resource is appealing. Yet the ecological and social costs can also be high: damaging fragile coastal areas, releasing huge amounts of waste into waterways, and creating breeding ground for disease (NPR 2014; Ballard 2019).

Poultry has become a huge international operation. Chickens are stacked by thousands in high-rise wire compartments, their feet never touching the ground, from egg to market. The slaughterhouse emphasizes mass production. The fast pace, crowded conditions, mental and physical exhaustion, and low wages in meat packing and poultry have raised concern from the days of Upton Sinclair to recent human rights reports calling them places of "blood,

Old McDonald doesn't live here anymore, evidenced by this huge factory operation for broiler chickens.

sweat and fear" (Human Rights Watch 2019). Then came COVID-19. Those same conditions made meatpacking and poultry packing sources of pandemic spread, even as they were labeled "essential" work in an industry that must continue. Workers had new fears as hundreds became sick at the Smithfield plant in South Dakota and across the country.

Tyson chicken has long been battling union organizers, as well as facing Immigration and Naturalization Service (INS) investigations into hiring illegal immigrant workers in its U.S. plants. Tyson claims it is caught in an ever more competitive market. Even though it dominates the domestic market, it is being challenged in the lucrative Asian market by Thai chickens. Thailand is making a major push to develop its agricultural as well as its industrial exports. Chickens can be subcontracted: raised on small farms and then mass-processed for export to Japan, Taiwan, and South Korea. Processed food has become one of Thailand's top manufactured exports, meeting the demands of fast-growing Asian cities and helping Thailand establish itself as Asia's supermarket (McMichael and Weber 2022). Thai chicken exports have soared—until COVID-19 interrupted production and key markets (*Bangkok Post* 2020).

The origin of orange juice, once that symbol of all-American goodness and Florida sunshine, has also become mysterious. The container may say something like: "Made from concentrate from one or more of the following: USA, Brazil, Belize." The label is even more mysterious for a common apple juice: "Concentrate from USA, Hungary, Argentina, and either Poland or Turkey." A package of chicken may soon require similar labeling: "Parts assembled from one or more of the following countries." In the ideal of global capitalism, product has become divorced from place. To be accurate, the label maybe should just say: "Made on Earth, mostly."

"We Are What We Eat"

The way a society gets its food supply is its **food regime.** We now have a global food regime based on industrial agriculture and controlled by corporate agribusiness and massive import and export. In one sense, this system is extraordinarily efficient. Production is massive, enough to feed all 7.9 billion of us and growing. Distribution is global, following prices to wherever there is demand for new items or lower costs. This is the principle of an **economy of scale,** or that more volume under mass production can lower costs.

Yet it is also extremely inefficient. Often more energy is expended in fossil fuels to plant, irrigate, and harvest than is contained in the food. Rather than capture the sun's energy for human use, the entire process is merely an inefficient conversion of hydrocarbons into carbohydrates. The process also involves mining the earth of nutrients and topsoil, as well as groundwater, which are not replaced. The land, at best, is an unending monotony of monocropping; at worst, it is ultimately left barren and unusable.

People, especially rural dwellers in poor countries, are left vulnerable to the vagaries of the marketplace. If their export products thrive, they will earn enough cash to purchase the food they need for themselves. But if their export commodity prices fall or if wages fall, for agricultural workers, they will be left hungry or malnourished. High fuel and food prices, coupled with precarious wages has left South Asian hunger at a 40-year high (BBC News 2009). Mass-produced food products provide consumers in wealthy nations and cities with more food choices, but these foods are often heavily packaged, heavily preserved, and heavily advertised, offering little in nutrition or taste.

One consequence of soaring energy costs has been rising food prices and new food scarcity. When U.S. corn and Brazilian cane can be turned into ethanol, or the soy crop of either location into biodiesel, new competitors are added into global food systems. Intensive grain production in places like the United States, Canada, Australia, and Argentina are also highly energy intensive. Responding to high-energy costs and the dangers of food scarcity, by 2008, 29 countries had sharply limited food exports of basic commodities to protect domestic supplies (Bradsher and Martin 2008). Food is still available for those who can afford to pay, but the world's most vulnerable—the poorest countries as well as those served by aid agencies in conflict-torn or famine-stricken areas—are facing critical food shortages. The world is fed by a system of agricultural intensification that is extremely vulnerable to climate change, changing weather patterns, and shifts in the prices of fuel, fertilizer, and commodity prices. The specter of famine has returned to haunt many of the world's poorest places.

Food was one of the early battlegrounds for competing theories of economic development. Recall from chapter 1 that dependency theory is the perspective that vital resources flow from poor countries to rich countries without sufficient compensation. Modernization theory proposes that societies advance from traditional, low productivity societies to modern, intensely productive ones. Dependency theorists saw export commodity dependence as one of the great legacies of colonialism and one of the great weaknesses of the economies of underdeveloped nations. Modernization theorists saw modern agriculture as finally banishing the age-old curses of hunger and famine. There is some truth in each perspective.

Humanity has been malnourished for the last 5,000 years. Hunter-gatherers had precarious food supplies but also assembled a diet rich in diversity: all those organically grown nuts, fruits, vegetables, and lean meats that dieticians encourage people to eat. Horticulturalists gained more control over their food supply at the price of variety (quite likely, a starch, such as manioc or sweet potato, made up many of their calories), but it was still supplemented by a rich diversity of both wild and garden-based foods. Devastation came with agriculture. Aggressive rulers drove their peasantry to produce more and more food, and crowded populations cleared more and more land. Wetlands were drained, forests cleared, wildlife exterminated, and soil depleted. Crops provided great food security in good times, but they were extremely vulnerable to drought, climate shifts, and the ravages of war. And so, the specter of mass famine was created.

The quality of the food supply also declined for most people. The wealthy and privileged ate better than ever before, but the peasants often subsisted largely on a single starchy crop: rice, wheat, corn, or potatoes. The luckiest of them were able to maintain their own gardens to supplement the bounty of the fields. Colonial empires turned this system into a global food regime, with the finest delicacies, and the spices to keep them fresh, flowing into the colonial capitals, often at the expense of greater vulnerability to famine. The great Indian famines of 1630 and 1770 occurred while the ports were full of grain, tea, and spices (Sen 1999). The Irish potato famine that began in 1845 came from a blight that destroyed the peasants' food supply, yet pricier grains continued to leave Ireland, bound for London and the European capitals, at the height of the famine.

In many ways, our current food regime is merely an intensification of this system. Food flows in great abundance to centers of wealth, while the poor and peripheral areas are left extremely vulnerable. With land, seed, and fertilizer all at a premium, few of the world's people have gardens, or ones that produce enough food to feed them, and so are entirely dependent on the cash economy of the global food regime. The questions for the planet now are: Can we continue to feed our eight billion people, half of whom are urban dwellers, yet also return to a more sustainable and equitable system? Can we find a place for "economies of detail," where small producers feed local markets, taking great care to ensure the long-term viability of the land and the food supply? Can we return to a more diverse landscape that is both healthful and beautiful?

Richer countries have sometimes been able to preserve a landscape of small farms. Japan's rice production is uneconomical in pure market terms, because rice can be grown cheaper elsewhere. But the small rice farmer, along with the carefully tended orchard and other local production, is sustainable as well as traditional and provides a valued part of the Japanese landscape and food supply, one the government is willing to subsidize. Similarly, the French countryside looks quite different than rural American regions with a similar climate, for France is dotted with small farms, vineyards, orchards, and pastures. The French maintain this only by limiting imports and subsidizing local production, but in doing so, they also retain beauty, an environmentally sustainable tradition, and some measure of food independence. Even with the dominance of U.S. corporate agriculture, farmers' markets, food cooperatives, alternative organic markets, roadside farm stands, and other arrangements have preserved some of the local landscape of small farms and varied production, as well as the taste of local produce.

Poor countries that will never be the highest bidders for global commodities need a basis of local production more than other countries, yet they often find it the hardest goal to achieve. In the United States, some people have begun to experiment with eating locally in their own communities as a way to enjoy fresh and seasonal produce, support local farmers, and reduce the huge amount of energy we spend in transporting our food around the world. They have managed this in southern Appalachia (Kingsolver 2007) and even in wintry, mountainous Vermont (McKibben 2007). A major goal of rural development in the twenty-first century will be to feed growing populations with efficient and appropriate technologies, while helping rural communities and "green spaces" around cities maintain and revive diverse, small-scale, and independent local production. The health of the land and its people depend on it.

Pollution

Water: From Open Sewers to Toxic Canals

Our hunting-and-gathering ancestors must have enjoyed largely pristine waters, perhaps only facing the risk of a parasite like *Giardia*, which worries modern backpackers. This changed dramatically as people crowded into cities at the hubs of agrarian states. A few, such as the carefully planned cities of the ancient Indus civilization (modern Pakistan), had sewage systems, but most did not.

In medieval Europe, sewage and household waste were merely dumped into the street, sometimes from the second story, where chamber pots of human waste were emptied out the window. The overhangs of medieval buildings provided some protection, and a true gentleman always walked on the outside, allowing his lady the more protected path closer to the wall! But no one was safe from the stench or the disease. Rats, fleas, and bacteria flourished as bearers of the plague and other killers. Even worse was the water. Wherever a stream or ditch cut through the town, it was likely to be treated as an open sewer. Contaminated drinking water was and remains one of the world's greatest killers.

The greatest gains in life expectancy came not with elaborate medicines but with simple sewers and safe water supplies. Providing covered sewers and piped water systems is the simplest and most cost-effective way to save lives, especially those of children. Yet the industrial age that brought the steel pipe and the concrete drain culvert also brought new killers. Industries poured chemical contaminants into the waterways. For example, the chemicals used in the preparation of fabrics and dyes often contained mercury. The Mad Hatter of *Alice in Wonderland* was quite familiar to those readers who knew of hat makers being driven mad by mercury exposure. As industry expanded, so did the wastes that spilled into the waterways.

Industrial sites were typically on rivers, both for transportation and for waterpower, but these rivers also served as toxic canals. Chemical odors replaced biological ones, as the Thames and the Hudson, the Seine and the Susquehanna, the Danube and the Ruhr all flowed with toxins. In the 1960s and 1970s several rivers, including the Cleveland River, actually caught fire as combustible chemicals covered their surfaces.

Deadlier were the unseen killers. Chemicals dumped into Love Canal from 1920 to 1953 proved silent killers of residents of the area. Chemicals flowing from rivers and canals largely killed Lake Erie and threatened the other Great Lakes throughout the 1960s and 1970s. Warnings went out not to eat Great Lakes fish, which were laced with mercury and other heavy metals, as well as DDT and other human-made toxins. In Japan people who ate fish from Tokyo Bay developed strange and terrible diseases, also from heavy metals dumped into the water.

Then the water got cleaner, at least in some places. Cities in all of the advanced industrial countries strove to clean up their waterways. New sewage plants were more efficient and effective. New industries installed filters to capture wastes. But most important, the industries left. Once-filthy Baltimore harbor is now the bright and gleaming Inner Harbor shopping and entertainment district. The confluence of Pittsburgh's rivers was once a meeting ground of toxins, but now it hosts boats and picnickers along Park Point. The only heavy metal evident on Cleveland's gleaming waterfront is in the Rock and Roll Hall of Fame. London's formerly polluted dockyards are today prime real estate for development. Cities cleaned up old industrial sites and converted the waterways from industrial channels to attractions for recreation and commerce.

Of course, where the industry went, so did the pollution. Export processing zones around the world, often hastily built along waterways, often seethe with pollutants. The Rio Grande on the Texas–Mexico border receives pollutants from the industrial border cities, such as Ciudad Juárez and Reynosa, where U.S. industry has congregated and is now North America's filthiest river. The most dangerous part of a border crossing here may be getting into the contaminated water.

Of course these rivers all carry their burdens to the sea, making the world's oceans a great global (dirty) sink. Hardest hit are the coastal regions, the continental shelf, which also contains most ocean life. Persistent toxins, such as mercury and pesticides, build up in the food chain, contaminating fish and birds. The coast also receives the bulk of human activity and spills: from untreated sewage to devastating oil, which layer the water and cover the beaches. The great spill of the *Exxon Valdez* in Prince William Sound in 1989 captured the world's attention, but continued spills have threatened shorelines from California to Spain. The shallow waters off shorelines and islands are also the prime locations for coral reefs, perhaps the most abundant and diverse habitats on the planet, even surpassing the rain forests. Reefs have been damaged by boats and divers and polluted by spills and fish collectors, stunning their quarry with cyanide.

Trouble on the land also quickly becomes trouble in the water. Erosion from deforested and mined lands spills down the rivers and washes over the coastal reefs in great toxic mud baths. New concern has arisen that global warming may be part of the cause of a bleaching that is diminishing the once brilliant colors of reefs. Around the world virtually every major reef has been damaged, and many are in serious danger of destruction (UNESCO 2017). Coastal waters, not the deep ocean water, are the main habitat for most fish species. Great fisheries have supported entire human societies, both ancient and modern. Many of these fisheries are now collapsing under the weight of overfishing, often with great factory ships, nets that capture and kill indiscriminately, and coastal pollution. Ninety percent of fish stocks "are fully exploited, overexploited or used up (Kituyi and Thomson 2018).

But the perils that have plagued coastal areas are now reaching deep water locations, as spills and toxins travel with the currents. Individual countries have tried to claim stretches of the coasts as their own: originally, the roughly three miles that could be defended with shore cannon is now an agreed-upon 12-mile limit, which some would like to see extended to 200 miles. But no one owns the open ocean. Like the atmosphere that circles the planet, it is the ultimate shared commons. Only international agreement and enforcement can protect the waters that connect and nourish us all.

Solid Waste: A Planet in Plastic Wrap

Archeologists who study ancient societies must often rely on the few enduring remains they find—sometimes only a few bits of pottery or precious metal—to piece together an understanding of how these societies lived. Great communities built of wood and thatch and perishable materials can almost disappear. Future archeologists will have no trouble studying the artifacts of modern industrial society, however. The dumps, landfills, and ditches are filled with every detail of our daily lives, preserved in plastic, glass, and metal.

The coming of industrial society filled the world with products, and increasingly the materials for those products were not agricultural, such as cotton, or wild, such as wood. Rather, they were mined as ores and coal and pumped as petroleum. As these products and their containers have proliferated, few places on the planet remain untouched. Remote waterfalls in South America kick up fertilizer-laden froth, on which bob the brilliant colors of hundreds of plastic bottles, the remnants of beverages and detergents marketed around the world. Remote beaches in Panama, where few tourists ever reach, are lined with great barrier walls of trash, particularly those same bottles, which float out to sea and drift back with the tide. Bottles and containers point the way to Mount Everest in the Himalayas. They fill the sides of gorges in Mexico and tumble across the savanna in East Africa. They freeze into the snowfields around arctic villages and even collect at the South Pole (where a U.S. field station has begun to implement a recycling program).

For millennia, the beverage container of choice was the gourd, grown and hollowed to carry water or sometimes the local beer. A few such containers can still be seen in Latin America and Africa. Once abandoned, it is eaten by animals and then decomposes. More sedentary people could depend on pottery. Once shattered, it returned to the soil. Glass and metal were more enduring, but as long as they were expensive, they had to be reused. Until a decade or so ago, the much-loved *refrescos*, or soft drinks, of Mexico were often consumed right at the store, so that the bottle could be immediately returned. Then came the cheap and disposable plastic bottle, a petroleum product that lasts for centuries. With no incentive to return the bottles and often with erratic trash collection, the bottles have become one of the markers of our age (see figure 12.2).

Great trash dumps have long accompanied cities. When Jesus wanted a vivid metaphor of despair for his followers, he pointed to the trash dump that spilled down the hillside from Jerusalem: Gehenna was crawling with worms

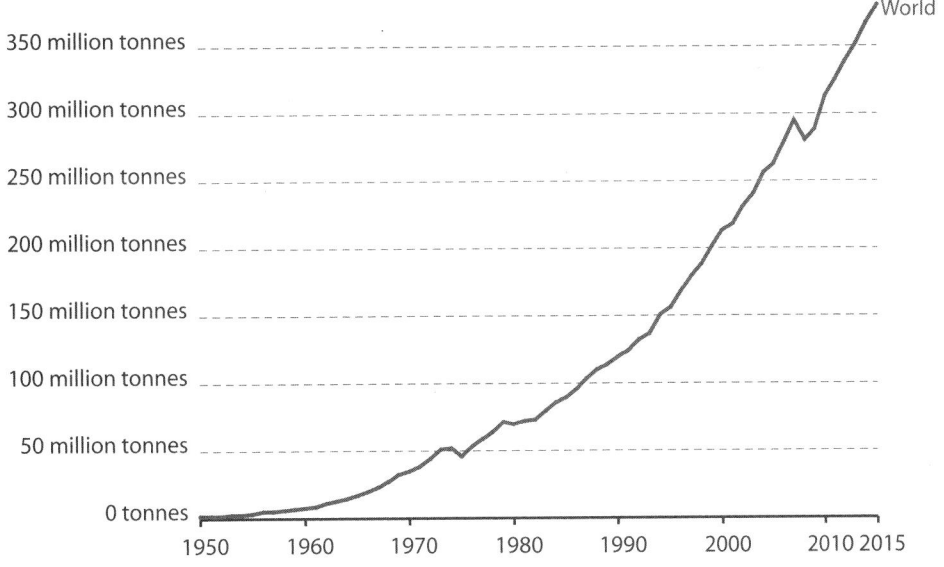

Figure 12.2 Global plastics production, 1950 to 2015. (Source: Our World in Data.) For a closer look at the plastic stream from industry to ocean, see https://ourworldindata.org/plastic-pollution.

and punctuated by smoldering fires that never died out; it is often translated in the New Testament simply as "hell." Smoldering hells still fill the valleys, ravines, and hillsides of many cities: "Smokey Mountain" outside Manila in the Philippines; the great Cairo dump, big enough to fill the pyramids 10 times over; the massive mountainside dump of Rio de Janeiro, Brazil; the huge dumps of San Salvador in Central America and of Mexico City; and the growing Tijuana dump that has already filled its valley and now flows over settlements and cemeteries on the California border.

Like the shopping centers that sell the products and packages that end up here, these dumps have an international sameness to them. Cardboard and rubber smolder and burn. Plastic bags rise up in great white clouds and drift on the wind until snagged by a tree or bed frame, to dangle like crackling ghostly sentries. Great clouds of gulls and vultures circle overhead, swooping down on choice morsels. And people—many who live in, on, or near the dumps—race over the heaps among the rats and the wild dogs, trying to get to resalable materials before someone else does. Children, bandanas pulled up over their grimy faces, are particularly effective at running and digging through the piles to claim prizes. These people are the original recyclers! Without them, the trash piles would be higher. In some cases, they have moved beyond being mere independent trash pickers to form organized unions that contract with industrial recyclers. Yet one can't help but feel that these human-made smoking mountains also represent an incredible waste of both natural resources and human potential.

The postindustrial electronic age has generated solid waste problems of its own. Computers and electronic equipment become obsolete quickly and are thrown away in abundance. Cheaply made appliances have short working lives and are often cheaper to replace than to repair. (New appliances are made with machines in remote, low-wage locations, while repair often requires human hands and must be done close to home.) Electronics and appliances are hard to recycle, since they contain many components, often an intermingling of metal and plastic. They also often contain dangerous materials, such as the heavy metal cadmium and chemicals such as PCBs. Discarded, these materials leech into the ground and water; incinerated, they go into the air.

Recycling is a viable option, if it is done with regard to human safety. Batteries filled with lead and acid, plastics that release toxins, and even radioactive wastes have been flowing to the cities of low-income countries, such as India and Pakistan. The products are recycled to reclaim raw materials, but often the recyclers have no protection against the caustic acids and fumes and the dangerous chemicals. As early as 1993 Greenpeace reported that 23 shiploads of U.S.-made plastic soft drink bottles were shipped to India for this type of recycling. At the same time, this made lower-quality Indian bottles less desirable, and Indian cities were becoming choked with great mountains of plastic trash (Guruswamy 1995).

Ecology CHAPTER 12 437

Trouble in paradise. Tourists seek out Indonesia's beaches, while global consumers desire their electronic and assembled goods, but the trash left behind consumes the landscape [top], and sometimes the lives of young trash pickers [bottom].

The good news is that the same technology that produces new products can be used to find new and more efficient ways to recycle old ones. Small European and Asian countries with nowhere to dump have led the way in recycling ever-larger portions of their waste streams. The ease of printing has meant that the electronic age uses more paper than ever. Yet the hope remains that electronic information can replace the reams of unnecessary paper—information storage that could be recycled with the drag of a mouse. Ultimately, however, reducing the waste stream will require lifestyle and societal choices: producing and consuming fewer products and making those that are, able to last.

Deforestation and Desertification

The Baka have hunted and gathered in the rain forest of western Cameroon in Central Africa for more millennia than anyone knows. They are part of a broad cultural group that has been better known to outsiders simply as "Pygmies." The Baka were one of the last of this resourceful group of people to hold on to their hunter-gatherer lifestyle, which they managed well into the 1990s.

The Baka are now settled near a road that facilitates government aid and government control in a pattern familiar to native peoples in many places around the world. But they have not become completely sedentary. The Baka still walk great distances. They walk on ever-longer treks into the last remaining forest to hunt for game. No longer dependent on bows and blowguns, they have a rifle; one rifle with one bullet is all they can afford. Their chosen marksman, a young man of 17, is a lucky shot, and so for now, their one bullet has brought them a small forest buffalo. All members of the settlement trek into the forest to carve up and carry back the meat.

The Baka also walk into town, a small provincial outpost, to trade and to plead their case before local administrators. They win assurances that their forest will be protected. Yet within a few days, they note the marked trees and hear the deep-throated roar of the chain saw. The whole settlement turns out, but they can only stand and watch in silence, as loggers illegally remove the largest and most valuable trees and haul them down the dirt road.

Resistance is futile. The Baka are a courageous but peaceful people, and besides, they have already used their only bullet. They can again put on their size "small" suits and go in to plead for protection, but with little political clout and no money for bribes, they have little voice ("Voices of the Forest" 2001).

People have been making deserts for a long time (see figure 12.3). The vast Sahara was once a lush forest and grassland, with lakes and vast herds and flocks of wildlife. The desert has been growing ever since, perhaps due in part to natural climate shifts, but people have helped. Egypt once fed ancient Rome; now crops only grow there under intense irrigation. The Sahara continues its southward drift into the region of tenuous grasslands known as the Sahel. Sometimes this drift is dramatic, as entire villages are engulfed in huge dunes of drifting sand. More often, the slow loss of scattered trees and grass allows the last of the soil to drift away, leaving a rocky crust.

Desertification often follows **deforestation.** Helped by the stripping of natural vegetation and the felling of trees, deserts continue to grow in Brazil, India, and Mexico. The desert has only been tamed for a time in the southwestern United States, where massive irrigation projects have drained the rivers dry.

Deforestation is also not new. Plato noted that the rocky treeless forms of many Greek islands had taken over from dense pine forests only with the introduction of people and goats. The brilliant sun of the Aegean islands is undimmed because all of the shade has been cleared. Likewise, Scotland and Ireland should be heavily forested. While we romanticize the heather-clad hills of Scotland and the green pastures of the emerald isle of Ireland, most of both should be covered with rich, moist forests. Most of England was also deforested—first for agriculture and pasture and then finally for wood for ships and charcoal for making steel. To keep the Royal Navy in towering ship masts, the British had to turn to North America.

In turn, most of the eastern United States was also deforested. From pre-colonial times, when a hypothetical squirrel could travel from Massachusetts to the Mississippi without ever touching the ground, to the beginning of the twentieth century, vast forests of old-growth timber came down all across what

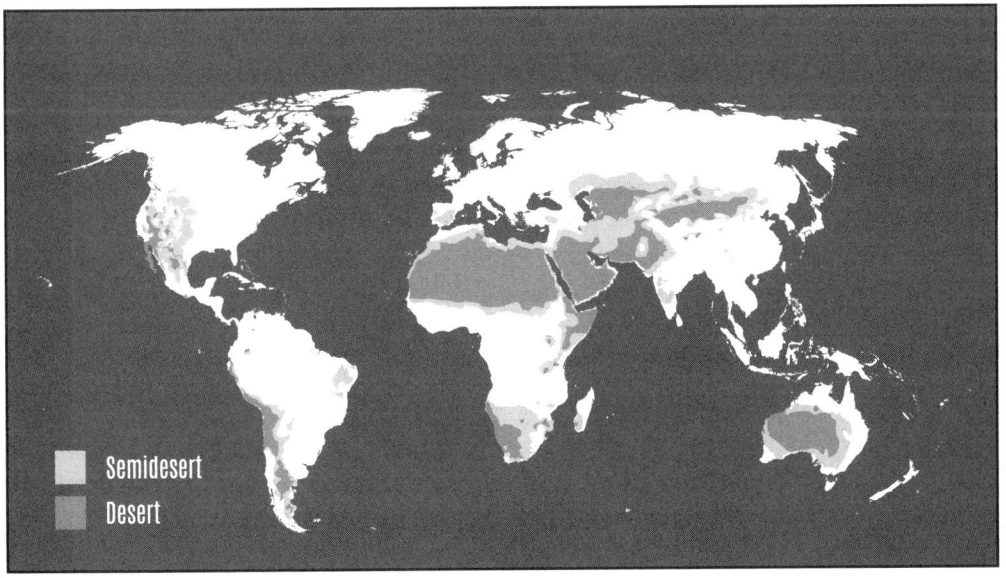

Figure 12.3 Distribution of deserts and arid land worldwide.

is now the eastern United States. Land that is now endless farm fields and subdivisions, with an occasional shade tree or wood lot, was once endless forest, with only an occasional meadow or clearing.

Ironically, as more intense farming has moved westward with irrigation on the plains and in the dry basins of the United States and Canada, some of this land is becoming reforested. In some cases, animal species are being reintroduced, as well. This is **second-growth forest,** often of smaller and faster-growing trees, not the great stands of pine, maple, oak, and beech that once dominated. Likewise, most of the returning wildlife consists of smaller species that are more adapted to living with human neighbors: Whitetail deer do well, but moose, elk, and woodland caribou are much harder to bring back. Coyotes expand onto range once roamed by wolves, and feeder-friendly birds move into the habitat of extinct or disappearing native species.

In recent decades the global concern has focused on the tremendous loss of tropical **rain forests.** Much of the original rain forest has been cleared from Brazil and the Amazon basin, from Central America, from West and Central Africa, and from Indonesia and Southeast Asia. The forest has sometimes been cut for timber. More often it has been cut for farmland and pasture. Small farmers in Latin America, Africa, and Asia, often denied access to more fertile lands that are used for export crops, are driven ever farther into the forest to clear trees and try to farm. Sometimes the export agribusiness industries themselves lead the push. Millions of acres of tropical forestland in Brazil and Central America have been cleared for cattle, to be ground into hamburgers to feed a growing worldwide appetite for U.S.-style fast food. Coffee, tea, rubber, and even citrus can be grown amid tree cover but is often grown in huge plantations cleared of the original large trees.

The fight for forest conservation rages under the canopy of political economy—both national politics and the global economy. For decades, growing demand for palm oil drove deforestation in Indonesia, home to isolated pockets of incredible biodiversity from orangutans to tigers and rhinoceros, all critically endangered. Fires raged across parts of this vast country, scorching Sumatra and Borneo to make room for more palm oil–producing trees. Now intense pressure from the international community, and key corporate buyers, are changing practices (Johnson 2021). Palm oil, like coffee, can be obtained amidst other forest cover. In Brazil the story has been the reverse. Decades of success in stopping the destruction of the Amazon basin was reversed by the Bolsonaro administration in 2019. The reversal has caused fires to return. Soy production has been a culprit, but that, like palm oil, is controlled by large multinationals that may see long-term success tied to sustainable production. Beef cattle production, however, is widely dispersed, with poor ranchers pushing into the forest, then feeding into a decentralized supply chain that leads

The Amazon is burning [top], often illegally, to make way for mining, for soy farms and, most often, for cattle pasture. The result of deforestation is not always scarred, eroded land—it may be quite green, as the in great palm oil plantations of Southeast Asia, but biodiversity is replaced by monocropping with no room for wildlife [bottom].

ultimately to the fast-food drive-through (see figure 12.4). These small producers are unlikely to have access to alternate means to feed their stock.

The loss of the tropical rain forest is of particular concern, as this land is some of the most diverse in the world. The tiny remaining pockets of forest in Costa Rica have as many species of trees and birds as can be found in the entire eastern United States. When the eastern United States was deforested, plants and animals that were distributed over vast areas often survived in Canada and in rugged and less accessible mountain locations. For many endangered species in the tropics, however, there is no place to run. Deforestation will mean extinction.

The thin tropical soil also poses a problem. Stripped of tree cover, it bakes in the tropical sun into brick. Then, what was once the most diverse land habitat on the planet becomes desert. The most remarkable view of deforestation can be seen over Haiti, where land that was once dense forest has been stripped bare of trees and almost all vegetation. There, too, experiments in reforestation have been tried, but they have almost always involved introducing nonnative trees, such as the fast-growing ipilipil, to replace the unique species that have been lost.

Not all tropical forest is rain forest. Often the most fragile lands are **dry forests,** where a delicate balance is maintained among trees, shrubs, and grass. In this environment even subtle human pressures, such as the search for firewood, can tip the balance against the trees. With no trees to hold moisture and soil, dry forests quickly become deserts.

Neither are all rain forests tropical. From northern California along the Pacific Coast into Canada and Alaska is a vast region that once had huge stands of temperate rain forest. It often takes a biohistorian to know which California suburbs now sit on land that was once in the shade of the redwoods. This land has also been intensely logged. Flying over the Canadian and Alaskan Pacific Coast, the deep emerald of dense forest is often broken by vast, pale-brown clearings that cover whole mountainsides and entire valleys. Douglas fir trees become stud walls for the new subdivisions built on these clearings, and the cedar and redwood trees end up as decks and deck furniture in the back. Much of the rest is pulverized into pulp for paper and shipped overseas as wood chips to be pressed into building materials. The largest U.S. national forest, the Tongrass near Juneau and Glacier Bay, continues to be the site of bitter controversy between those who want to preserve the last vast expanse of old growth rain forest in the United States for wildlife and recreation and those who prefer to tabulate how many board feet of lumber are in those trees.

The reforestation of parts of the eastern United States, along with reforestation efforts in the Sahel, the Caribbean, the Himalayas, and elsewhere, show that it is possible to bring back the trees and to hold back the deserts. At the same time, planting rows and woodlots of a fast-growing single species will

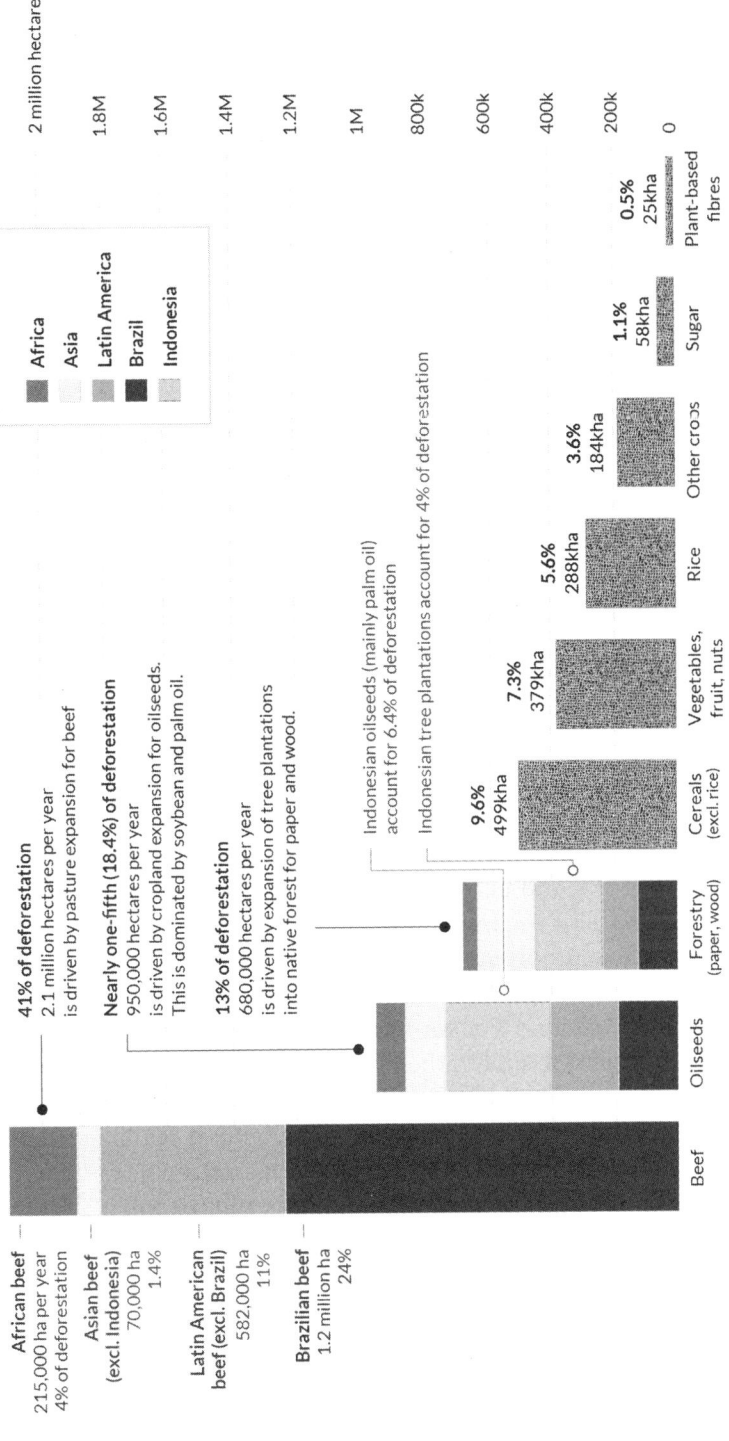

Figure 12.4 Drivers of tropical deforestation, 2005–2013. (Source: "Drivers of Deforestation," by Hannah Ritchie and Max Roser. Our World in Data.) For more detailed data, see https://ourworldindata.org/forests-and-deforestation.

not restore the majesty and diversity of the great old-growth forests once these have been lost. The effort to keep the land green and thriving must be two-pronged. First, land that has already been clear-cut for timber, pasture, and farmland should be restored with careful attention to soil and conservation. Trees, shrubs, and gardens can be reintroduced to create a landscape that is tamed but still lush, productive, and beautiful. Second, but at the same time, the remaining stands of old forest must be preserved for their uniqueness and diversity and awesome presence. We don't have 2,000 years to wait for new giant redwoods to grow. And in the tropics, once gone, it may be impossible to bring back the forests that have dominated the land for millions of years (see figure 12.5).

Recently, rain forest conservation has become fashionable. It is the cause of international conservation organizations, local zoos, and even rock and film stars. Interest in the rain forest has also sparked new interest in **ecotourism.** More and more visitors to tropical locations are not content to sit on the sand or by the pool next to a planted palm tree but instead want to explore the forest interior. Visitors to the ultimate high-rise hotel haven of Cancún, Mexico, increasingly escape hotel row for trips to the interior to see the rain forest and the Maya ruins. Costa Rica, with many beautiful beaches, has staked its claim on the ecotourism market. Visitors can choose between canopy tours on bridges or dangling from ropes and cables, and the numbers of nature parks, both private and public, continue to increase. In the Caribbean, places with few desirable beaches, such as the island of Dominica, promote exploration of the mountains, rivers, and rain forest of "the Nature Island." In Hawaii, the more remote island of Kauai, "the Garden Island," is now a fashionable destination, in part for its lush interior, which includes some of the wettest forest in the world. New resorts and parks in Malaysia and Indonesia likewise feature the natural attractions of the tropical forest and the ancient cultures of its people, largely village-based horticulturalists.

A unique story of ecotourism begins when Moi, a member of the Huaorani people of lowland Ecuador (known to outsiders as "Auca," or savages) went to Washington to talk to the president. He went to plead for help in stopping American-owned oil companies from carving up the last remaining forest home of the Huaorani. Moi brought his eloquent language skills, speaking basic Spanish and English. He also brought his medicine pouch and his eight-foot-long spear. (The Huaorani are not a peaceful people.) The Huaorani are simple horticulturalists, who both hunt and garden, and the way of life that they have guarded from centuries of would-be conquerors is almost ended.

Without seeing the president and receiving only empty assurances from the Ecuadorian ambassador, Moi returned to his South American home. He led a few raids, his young followers armed mostly with video cameras. A terrible oil well fire swept through their homeland, and his supporters thought

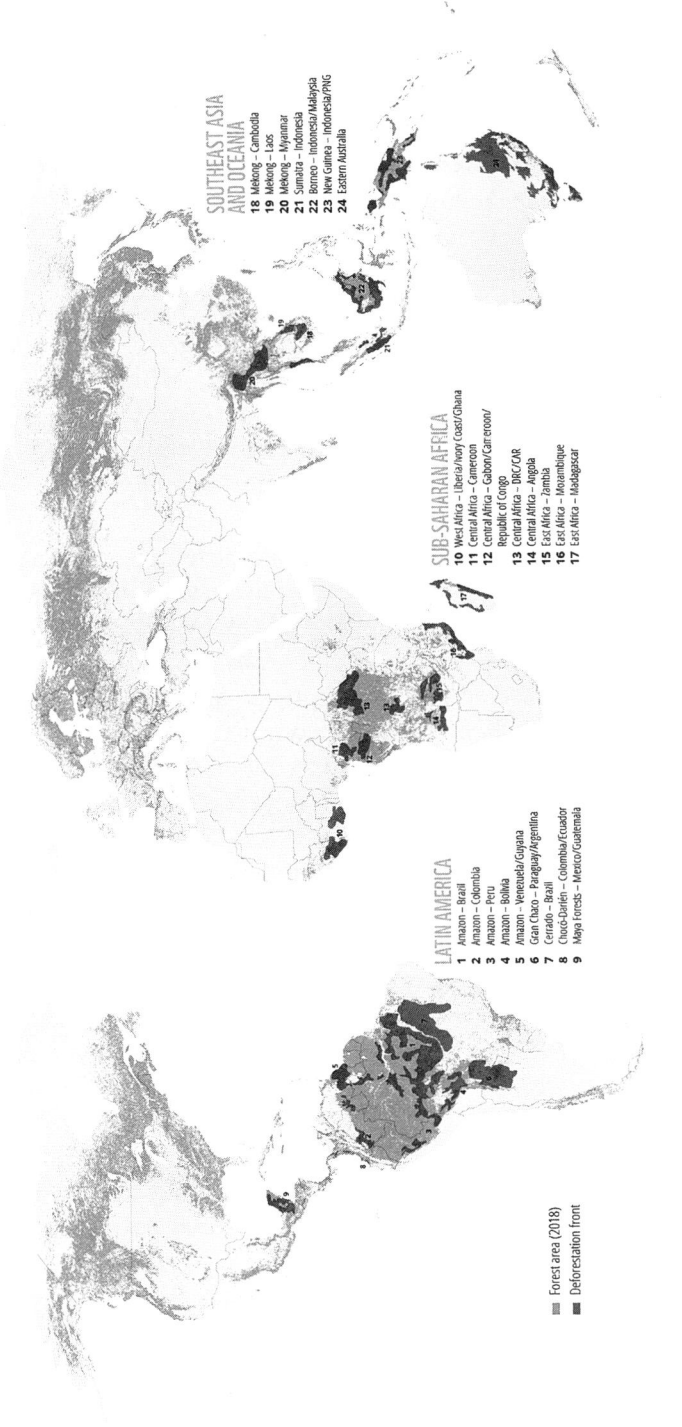

Figure 12.5 Global deforestation map. (Source: P. Pacheco, K. Mo, N. Dudley, A. Shapiro, N. Aguilar-Amuchastegui, P. Y. Ling, C. Anderson, and A. Marx. 2021. Deforestation Fronts: Drivers and Responses in a Changing World. World Wildlife Fund, Gland, Switzerland.)

Moi might have perished (see Kane 1996). But he didn't, and he continued maintaining his website, where visitors could learn about the struggles of the Huaorani and then travel to a once-remote Huaorani village to meet with the elders. The visitors stayed outside the village to preserve its character and participated in ecotourism activities to learn about the rain forest. It was hoped that they will return to North America, Europe, and Asia with a commitment to fight for Huaorani rights.

Ecotourism, however, can be a sham; badly done, it can also be a nightmare. One group being led by a venture through the Amazon became hopelessly lost. The group ended up stripping off their clothes, soaking them in kerosene, and wrapping them around sticks to make torches to alert rescuers. As this poor group of Americans and Europeans huddled nearly naked in the torchlight, they were confronted by native warriors emerging from the grasses. Fortunately, these warriors no longer speared strangers; they worked for Moi and Huaorani ecotourism and came to offer their competitors a bit of help getting back to camp!

Ecotourism has also begun to discover the temperate rain forest. Ecolodges based on exploring the natural world have shown up on Canada's Vancouver Island, Alaska's Kenai Peninsula, and points in between on the harsh but lush northern North American Pacific Coast. The savannah and dry forest of Africa have also received new attention, as safari tourism, based on "bagging" trophy game (much like that once common in western North America), is giving way to ecotourism, dedicated to understanding the land and its people.

At their best, these ventures are new ways for visitors to appreciate the remarkable beauty and diversity of the land and the history and diversity of the people who have shared it. Yet many of the parklands in poor countries are "paper parks," which show up on the map but remain largely unprotected, due to lack of funds and personnel. Poachers, loggers, miners, and others remain in these areas—some out of greed, many out of desperation. The authenticity of the ecotourism experience can also range from meaningful encounters to glitzy tours not much different from the jungle cruise at Disneyland.

Litter from expeditions clutters the tropics and climbs the slopes of the Himalayas. It remains to be seen if new travelers will really tread lightly, leave with all their trash, and insist that governments and operators truly preserve these natural settings. Transportation and lodging also remain big problems. As more of the last wild places are cut by roads and airstrips, few locations are truly remote anymore. Just as urban sprawl consumes wild lands, so does tourist sprawl. The routes in and out of many U.S. national parks are cluttered with commercial sprawl, amusement parks, and so-called attractions that mar the natural setting. Coastal locations around the world are often the most heavily targeted for development. In the tropics of the Global South, natural vegetation, such as the mangrove forest, is stripped away to make room for open stretches of sandy beach, backed by high-rise hotels. The posters promise tropical paradise, but the process is simply a continuation of deforestation followed by desertification—for what is an unbroken beach but a linear desert? Again it remains to be seen whether a new breed of traveler will willingly give up the ocean view that's provided by a wall of windows in a beachside, high-rise hotel for more environmentally friendly lodging that is set back to preserve the coast and is attentive not just to the guests but also to the environment.

Who Invited You? Invasive Species

The travels of humans include a long history of hitchhikers, both intended and unintended. Early sailors took with them intended passengers, such as dogs and pigs, as well as unintended ones, such as rats. Unleashed on tropical island environments, which are particularly vulnerable, all three frequently devastated the local bird and plant life. Polynesian travelers across the Pacific established lovely horticultural and fishing settlements, which the Europeans in the 1700s and 1800s saw as paradise. Yet they exterminated many forms of native wildlife, such as the 12-foot-tall flightless Moa bird, in their wake. With the bigger ships of European colonizers, the destruction increased. Islands, whose native wildlife develops free from outside competition, proved particularly vulnerable to outside invasion.

The brown tree snake, inadvertently brought from Southeast Asia sometime before 1952 thanks to its ability to hide in planes and ships, destroyed most of the native bird life of Guam in a matter of years (Fritts and Leasman-Tanner 2001). Inspectors are trying to keep it out of Hawaii, where it would likely do the same to already endangered Hawaiian native birds, many found nowhere else. Hawaiians are already having enough trouble coping with the cane toad, a large amphibian that is able to make itself at home in abundance in any subdivision or golf course. While amphibians worldwide are in deep trouble, this one seems to be thriving, taking over any habitat it can invade. Like many invaders, this toad was purposefully introduced to control pests and quickly became a pest itself.

The entire island continent of Australia is split by the world's longest fence, intended to keep feral (animals that have gone wild) dogs away from the sheep. The dogs were introduced to the island long ago and the sheep more recently. European colonizers also introduced rabbits in the hope that they would multiply and provide food. The rabbits have multiplied, so much so that they now consume much of the limited vegetation needed by the native wildlife—the distinct marsupials, such as kangaroos, who are the original inhabitants—and the introduced livestock. For a time, societies of European colonists in New

Zealand sought to introduce all the native plants and animals of Europe that they missed from home. However, these introductions quickly began to compete with and sometimes eliminated the unique island wildlife.

North America has also been hard hit by invasive species. Not an island but still largely isolated from the great landmass of Eurasia, North America has been particularly vulnerable to bio imports from across the Atlantic and Pacific. Sometimes the introductions were intentional. For instance, settlers released English sparrows and European starlings, just a few, to give the new world a bit of the feeling of the old. One society, calling itself Shakespearean, sought to introduce every plant and animal mentioned in the bard's plays. While some introductions failed, others succeeded too well. Introduced birds quickly became pests and took over the habitats of native species, which have seen drastic declines.

New plants also arrived with the new settlers. Dandelions, thistles, and tumbleweed quickly adapted to new homes. Sometimes the introductions were intentional. Quick-growing kudzu was used to stabilize eroded banks and provide for a quick landscaping option. Multiplying beyond imagination it has become "the vine that ate the South." Billions of dollars are spent each year fighting invasive plants; once established they are hard to get rid of.

Insect invaders have been the most destructive. The boll weevil, an import from Central America, devastated U.S. cotton production in the early twentieth century. An Asian fungus transported tree to tree by a European beetle almost wiped out the American elm in the Northeast, starting in the 1930s. The gypsy moth, a native of Europe and Asia, introduced into the United States in the 1860s, defoliates vast areas of the northeastern United States each year and continues to spread, hitchhiking on trucks and cars. Seeming never to learn the lesson about intentionally introducing new species, the U.S. Department of Agriculture more recently introduced a new type of ladybug, an Asian lady beetle, to control agricultural pests in the 1970s and 1980s. What seemed like an innovation in biological control has itself become a major nuisance, as the beetles have taken over from their native cousins. Each fall, these flying, foul-smelling, biting bugs enter homes and commercial buildings, trying to escape the onset of winter (Taubman 2002). The emerald ash borer arrived from Asia and is devastating U.S. ash groves as thoroughly as the European beetles did with the elm almost a century earlier. Then in 2020 during the pandemic isolation, as though they had unknowingly signed into some horror film subscription, people heard news of the arrival of giant murder hornets on the West Coast, likely brought over from Japan, where they are eaten. They are very big. "Murder" refers to their ability to kill large numbers of honeybees not to stalk humans, but the danger to beekeeping, and to all crops that need pollinators, is quite real, and it will require extreme vigilance to prevent their spread.

Some Asian invaders are even bigger—much bigger. A female python captured in 2019 was over 17 feet long, weighed 140 pounds, and contained 73 developing eggs. The Burmese python can grow to 23 feet long and is now becoming a top predator in the Everglades. The snakes likely arrived as escaped pets and have found a new wet and warm home, threatening local bird species, local wildlife, and any lost small dog or cat. Florida, a long peninsula with its subtropical climate and wetlands isolated from similar environments elsewhere, is the hotspot of U.S. invasive species. Long hosting sun-seeking "snow birds" from the North, it now hosts myriad sun-seeking reptiles. Green iguanas hang from trees (dropping to the ground during sudden freezes), Nile monitors look for small native owls, the huge Argentine tegu lizard—a favorite pet until it gets just too big—consumes native turtle eggs. The state is now seeking to ban exotic pets (Pittman 2021).

The sea lamprey moved into the Great Lakes through the system of locks and shipping canals in the St. Lawrence Seaway by attaching itself to native fish. It has plagued Great Lakes fishing since the 1950s. More recently, zebra mussels came in, probably released from the holds of cargo ships. They have filled the Great Lakes and continue to move into new waterways, often facilitated by human-built canal systems and the constant movement of pleasure

Invasive species are often small insects and fungi that go unnoticed until they do massive damage. Other invasive species are harder to ignore, such as this fifteen-foot-long Burmese python in the Florida Everglades.

boats. These foreign mussels take over from native species and grow in such abundance that they clog cities' water intake pipes. Their sharp shells make beaches hazardous, and their appetites take nutrients that would go to native aquatic life.

A larger, leaping intruder has been making its way up the Mississippi. The huge Asian silver carp was introduced to keep catfish ponds clear of excessive weed growth. It escaped in the floods of the early 1990s and has been on the move north. It quickly becomes the dominant fish in many waterways and is infamous for flying leaps when disturbed by outboard motors. Boaters and anglers are dismayed to find quiet waters full of leaping fish, and some people have had jaws broken and other injuries from the startled fish. The carp have moved into the Wabash, Illinois, and many tributaries of the Mississippi. Only electric barriers along the Chicago River and shipping canal are keeping them from being the next Great Lakes invader, threatening a huge fishing industry. The Chicago River should not connect to this river network, but in 1887 engineers reversed its flow to keep sewage, and cholera, from the city out of the lake. Better, in their minds, to send it all downstream toward St. Louis and the Gulf of Mexico. They created a path for barge traffic as well, and now a path for carp. Disaster looms if carp are able to find their way into the Great Lakes, and a dangerous nuisance remains in the huge Mississippi watershed. Some are looking to try to turn them into food, but Americans don't relish carp, unless it feeds their cats.

Invasive Asian silver and bighead carp in the Illinois River.

So far, all the new species have actually been the old species of some distant location newly introduced. But now, biotechnology has created the possibility of creating entirely new species, or at least old species with completely new characteristics. The possibilities are enticing: fruit that doesn't freeze, crops that grow faster than ever before, bacteria that are modified to attack other pests, and so forth. Our experience with introducing new species to new locations stands as a warning, however, of what can happen when an introduction is too successful and a plant or organism multiplies beyond the original intent, taking over its own space. Could we create new superbugs or superplants that likewise spread far beyond their intended purpose?

Ecology and Economy: The Search for Sustainable Futures

Sustainability is the power to thrive and to endure. It is taking care of this generation and generations to come. Hunting-and-gathering societies survived for tens of thousands of years. Human hunters may have helped to drive some of the great massive mammals of the ice age over the brink of extinction, but for the most part, they endured by practicing a way of life that was indefinitely sustainable.

Horticultural, pastoral, and agrarian societies also survived for thousands of years. Some agrarian empires may have exhausted their soil with intensive farming and hastened their own collapse, but on the whole, this way of life proved sustainable century after century.

Industrial society is only 250 years old and has dominated the globe for less than a century. Advanced industrial, or postindustrial, information-based society, the electronic age, is less than 50 years old.

As the people of the electronic age, are we already placing more strain on the planet than all other prior societies combined? Can our current way of life be sustained? Can it be globalized and shared by all the world's billions? Lester Brown (2003) estimates that it would take at least six earths to provide all the world's people with the standard of consumption common in the United States. The demands of our ecology and the demands of our economy seem to be seriously at odds.

Ecology and **economy** both come from the same Greek word for "house." Keeping our global house in order will require careful attention to both. The realization that there is a close relationship between ecology and economy has come slowly. For decades, poor countries claimed that it was their turn to pollute—that they needed to exploit resources just as the rich countries had. Wilderness was dismissed as "the rich man's playground." The poor needed jobs, resources, and economic production. Yet the poor also need livable communities. Much of the world's dumping has been inflicted directly by wealthy communities on poor communities (Bullard 1993, 2000).

The environmental justice movement has noted that it is the poor (and often, poor minority communities) that live among the untreated sewage, the piles of industrial and consumer waste, and the stagnant, toxic urban air. The wealthy can at least try to retreat to higher ground and a more secluded environment. They can move from one air-conditioned shell to another, dine on food gleaned from dozens of distant locations, and travel in search of an unspoiled locale. The poor must live, eat, and drink close to their earth and water, in whatever condition they may be.

Rich nations became rich by exploiting the human and natural resources of our world. They could then seek refuge far from the environmental destruction. Once again, the world's poorest nations find themselves last in line. There is no one else, nowhere else, left for them to exploit but their own land and people. Unlike the rich and powerful, they have to sit in their own waste. For this reason, environmental concerns are of prime importance to poor nations and to poor people.

Environmental degradation is often directly related to inequality. The newly rich overconsume as they compete with one another in contests of conspicuous consumption. At the same time, the poorest citizens and refugees are often driven from the best lands to encroach on the last forests and the most fragile environments. Wealthy corporations carry off old-growth timber for greater profits, while poor woodsmen poach the last valuable trees and animals for a few dollars to survive. Wealthy mining companies move whole mountains to get to more profitable deposits, while poor independent miners destroy stream banks and fragile mountainsides in pursuit of a few ounces of salable material.

Environmental degradation is also closely related to violence. In his lectures, Arun Gandhi an Indian American political activist, describes how his grandfather, Mahatma Gandhi, called environmental disregard "violence against the earth." Violence against one another also often claims the natural environment as so-called collateral damage. In ancient times, the Spartans burned and trampled crops to try to drive Athens to surrender, while Roman soldiers poured salt into the ground of Carthage to make it infertile. During the American Indian Wars of the late 1800s, U.S. frontier forces slaughtered bison to starve the Plains tribes.

Modern arsenals are all weapons of mass destruction with regard to the environment. The United States sprayed the defoliant Agent Orange to destroy the rain forest of Southeast Asia during the Vietnam War, with lingering effects for both people and wildlife. Land mines turn former farmland useless. Refugees from war zones are often driven into remote borderlands, where they strip the land of trees and wildlife in an effort to survive. The first Gulf War released streams of oil into the Persian Gulf, and raging fires poured pollutants into the air from burning oil wells. Bombs and mortars destroy indiscriminately and chemicals linger. Nuclear fallout would be the most devastating of all.

We have thus come full circle. The only sustainable world is one in which people have regard for equity and for peace.

Key Ideas

- Human society has been largely shaped by its means of subsistence: the way the people get food and basic needs. Humans have lived as hunter-gatherers, horticulturalists, herders, agrarian farmers, and industrial workers, and in postindustrial service and technology-driven societies.

- Most of the world's people are fed by a system of industrial agriculture and agribusiness in which key grains such as rice, wheat, and maize (corn) are grown in large mechanized operations and transported around the world. Foods such as fruits and vegetables that require labor-intensive harvesting have increasingly become the specialty of countries with low-cost labor.

- Global agribusiness has fed billions, but the system is endangered by poverty, depleted soils and irrigation systems, high fuel costs, and global climate change.

- In advanced industrial countries gains have been made in cleaning the air and water. Industrial pollution remains a huge problem for many around the world, particularly poor urban dwellers. Toxic by-products are increasingly dangerous, and solid waste is accumulating at unprecedented rates.

- Human activity has encouraged the spread of deserts, the depletion of soils, and the destruction of forests, both in temperate and tropical regions. Efforts have begun in earnest to reverse these trends to preserve land for both people and wildlife.

- Global trade and movement has also brought invasive species to new locations and disrupted or even destroyed many ecosystems.

- Preserving healthy natural ecosystems is an important part of maintaining the earth's biodiversity and nurturing a healthy and meaningful life for the earth's inhabitants. From ecotourism to global environmental movements, there is rising alarm and increasing interest in protecting life on the planet.

- Sustainability is the ability of one generation to meet its needs without compromising the ability of future generations to meet theirs. Sustainability has become a key criterion in the quest for economic and social development that respects the natural environment.

For Review and Discussion

1. What factors have affected the ways we eat and our food choices? Do you have friends, family, or acquaintances who are rethinking their food choices for their own health or the health of the planet: choosing organic foods, eating food from local sources, eating a vegetarian diet, or trying to avoid chemical additives? What do you think of such efforts?

2. What has caused the tremendous increase in global trash? How is solid waste handled in your local community? Are there recycling programs? Is there active participation in your community, workplace, or campus?

3. What are the land and resource issues in your local community: loss of farmland, water conservation, forest or open space preservation, wildlife conservation, or others? How do these issues parallel the global challenges?

4. What are the pros and cons of ecotourism/ecotravel? When you travel do you like to experience other cultures and environments or to just relax and escape? Can travel be a force for environmental protection rather than environmental damage?

Making Connections

Agribusiness

➤ Go to the website for Conagra Brands https://www.conagrabrands.com/brands and look at all the product names. Are you surprised at some of the familiar products listed? Why would one company have so many apparently competing brands? You can compare the other U.S. giant, Kraft Heinz, at https://www.kraftheinzcompany.com/brands.html. Look at their range and global reach. How do these huge corporations affect the way we eat, even the way we think about food?

➤ The world's largest and one of the most controversial of the global food giants is Swiss-based Nestlé S.A. They have been boycotted for promoting baby formula over breastfeeding and accused of depriving poor communities of clean water in order to build a bottled water empire. See "Why Nestle is one of the most hated companies in the world": https://www.zmescience.com/science/nestle-company-pollution-children/. Now look at Nestlé's "Net Zero Roadmap": https://www.nestle.com/sites/default/files/2020-12/nestle-net-zero-roadmap-en.pdf. The company says it aims to halve its greenhouse gas (GHG) emissions by 2030 and to achieve net zero by 2050. What are some of their plans for doing that? Do you have a sense the company has changed its focus, or is it just "greenwashing" (pretending to be environmentally and socially aware) its actions?

Making A Difference

Food Alternatives

➤ What are the alternative ways to grow and buy food in your community? Is there a farmers' market or a buying cooperative? Some arrangements link consumers directly to local farmers in "you pick" arrangements or through cooperative arrangements in which everyone buys a share of the farm and then shares in the produce. Many communities are also developing community gardens, where neighbors work together to raise and share produce. Others offer help to those who want to turn some of their chemically maintained lawns into productive garden and wildlife space.

➤ Find out what is available locally, and visit or participate in the operation. How is this group attempting to address concerns about nutrition, food safety, chemical pollution, and so forth?

Recycling

➤ What is being done in your community and on your campus to promote recycling? How can individuals and groups advance these efforts?

Nature Conservancy

➤ The Nature Conservancy operates worldwide, buying environmentally sensitive property and helping landowners preserve portions of their land. Increasingly this group's efforts include ventures in biological "hot spots" and the "last great places" around the world. Go to the conservancy's colorful site at www.nature.org to get a feel for the scope of their mission and reach and look for information on their activities and local chapters. What types of habitats and environments are featured as central to the group's current focus?

Sierra Club

➤ One of the world's oldest conservation organizations, the Sierra Club, has hundreds of local chapters and worldwide activities. These are highlighted at www.sierraclub.org along with information on current environmental issues, upcoming legislation, and other activities including nature trips. What does the Sierra Club see as the urgent environmental issues of the day? What actions does it propose? Are there projects and activities near you?

World Wildlife Fund

➤ For an expansive global conservation organization, see the World Wildlife Fund https://www.worldwildlife.org/. Explore tabs of interest on their page: food, climate, freshwater, wildlife, forests, oceans. Why does a wildlife organization have so much concern about food and agriculture? Why do they offer conservation travel? Other links cover racism, rights of women and girls, and other very human issues for an organization most recognized by its panda logo. How are all these issues intertwined?

Ocean Conservancy

➤ The Ocean Conservancy is an almost half-century old U.S.-based organization with a vision for the world's oceans. See their programs at https://oceanconservancy.org/programs/. What are the current concerns and ongoing projects and efforts?

Environmental Defense Fund (EDF)

➤ Begun in 1967 to combat the use of DDT with its dangers to humans and wildlife, the EDF has expanded to tackle issues of climate, oceans and fisheries and energy. See their site at https://www.edf.org/. What are some of their current initiatives? In what regions of the world are they working?

Conclusion

Making a World of Difference

How wonderful it is that nobody need wait a single moment before starting to improve the world.

—Anne Frank

Never doubt that a small group of thoughtful committed citizens can change the world. Indeed it's the only thing that ever has.

—Margaret Mead

Global Encounters

Coming Home: Honolulu

We have been crossing the Pacific for over a week. It is hard to keep track of the days. It doesn't help that Tuesday, November 29, was followed by a second Tuesday, November 29, as we crossed the international dateline. We have been losing an hour of sleep each night crossing time zones.

We have been crossing some of the clearest, bluest water I have ever seen. But there are also the sudden interruptions of large swirling slicks of trash floating, out from who knows where. Like lost sailors of old, we were cheered to see rugged lush islands come into view. These are part of Hawaii, but not the tourist belt; they are small wildlife sanctuaries accessible only by permit. The first inhabited island we pass is Ni'ihao, wholly privately owned and restricted to a small Native Hawaiian community. Gradually the numbers of soaring seabirds increase and the great volcanoes of the big island of Hawaii emerge from the clouds. I've read that Polynesian seafarers found these specks of land in the vastness of the Pacific by following the birds and the clouds. Closer in, the dark swirls and occasional spouts of the first humpback whales returning to the islands can be seen off the back of the ship. The shadowy whales usher us toward Diamond Head rising on the horizon, followed soon by the great hotels of Waikiki. This is not an easy day to keep students' minds focused on class.

The long Pacific crossing has provided some time for reflection, along with attempts to draw some conclusions from the last 100 days. It is a magnificent world. Maybe that is easier to remember as we edge past palm-fringed beaches to dock at the historic Aloha clock tower. But we have also found that magnificence in less familiar places, from the lush Orinoco Delta of Venezuela to the temple-studded plains of Bagan, Myanmar. It is also a precarious world. Our "near misses" have become a topic of speculation. We just narrowly escaped the fury of Hurricane Katrina as we started south. We rerouted our voyage away from East Africa and later heard of an attempted pirate attack on a small cruise ship off Somalia. The day we left India, the Asian news was filled with reports of flooding in Chennai, with a derailed train in Hyderabad and terrorist bombings in Delhi. A day or two earlier, we had students in each of those locations. We left Myanmar to hear the next day that the junta is moving the capital out of Yangon into the interior and adding new travel restrictions. They claimed to have worries about invasions. Maybe our "invasion" was too much for them, although they should take some comfort in knowing that these invaders could only get in during the month's highest tides. We made it through China before the typhoon, and to Japan after the offshore earthquake, then across the Pacific beneath large winter storms. Still, while I pity parents tracking our voyage and watching the news, the world is really a much safer place than one would glean from CNN. And the scattered "hot spots" are becoming most unpredictable. Outside of the French colonial post office in Ho Chi Minh City, next to Notre Dame Cathedral, we read in the English-language papers of the riots all across France. How fortunate that we were enjoying our glimpse of French architecture in a calm, peaceful country like Vietnam.

Classes for the last several days have focused on that elusive term globalization. Certainly as we have traveled through various ports, and especially our Asian ports, we have seen the tremendous impact of economic, political, and cultural globalization. Having a conversation in English in a distant port, over a Starbucks latte, with citizens of three different countries who are all concerned about the impact of U.S. foreign policy, is now commonplace. At the same time, globalization remains a catch-all term for some very different, and sometimes contradictory, forces. The world is integrating at the same time it is fragmenting. Economic globalization brings new market integration while it divides social classes further from one another and leaves many utterly cut off from productive livelihoods. Global politics keeps nations continually intertwined with one another at the same time that there are new movements for independence and autonomy and more isolated pariah states. Cultural globalization brings us all the same media and the same billboards around the world but also offers new attempts to revive and understand old traditions. The latter is not so much a clash of civilizations as it is a potpourri of cultural identities all mixed together and trying to claim their own space. In great multicultural cities like Honolulu or Hong Kong, or Ho Chi Minh City for that matter, the heritage of many civilizations and traditions may mingle on a single block.

Our final student panel debates the pros and cons of globalization. The truth is, however, that we have found few alternatives to the forces that are both uniting and fragmenting the world. Even the ostensibly communist countries we have visited are pursuing global capitalism with a vengeance (in some cases "vengeance" may be literal). The challenge for us, then, is how to master and harness the forces that seem to be running away with the planet. Can we globalize in ways that are more humane and more respectful of the biosphere that we share? I have become convinced that such a search must be our prime motivation for overseas study and for international travel.

The idea of ecotourism has caught on in many of the ports we visited. Guides offer travel that focuses on learning about the natural world, and doing so in ways that don't damage what we have come to enjoy. Sometimes these ecotrips do just that, but at the other times, ecotourism seems to be nothing more than a Disney-style jungle cruise—but with real insects. We have also had a course on cultural tourism, travel in search of greater cultural awareness and understanding. In this port, that means getting past the Tiki torches and hula skirts to understand a bit of what a cultural blender the Hawaiian

Islands have been for the past couple of hundred years. I am intrigued by this idea of encountering both the natural world and the human cultural world but still balk at the world of "tourism" itself. One of our daily memos began with this quote from Daniel Boorstin on tourism versus travel: "The traveler was active; he went strenuously in search of people, of adventure, of experience. The tourist is passive; he expects interesting things to happen to him. He goes sight-seeing."

Our goal from the beginning has been to be travelers rather than tourists, to complete a voyage, not to take a cruise. Time will tell if we have succeeded. Students around me take study breaks on their computers by cataloging great volumes of amazing digital pictures. Nice collections all, but will they move beyond "snapshots" to form a vision of the big picture? They have been "excited for" many things on our common venture, with that great enthusiasm of 20-year-olds. Now we'll see if they can maintain that enthusiasm as they go on to tend the amazing natural and cultural heritage we have viewed, and to share it more equitably with our global neighbors.

For the moment, the excitement is about coming home. A student has won the opportunity to raise our port flag over the ship. For the first time, the flag is the Stars and Stripes as we enter U.S. waters. He waves it dramatically over his head in the strong Hawaiian breeze. We get a brief 24 hours here as the ship refuels. Exams are in two days but for the moment the surf is up at Waikiki. I share their excitement but also know a secret: We never left home. We need to see the whole planet as our home. And we need to straighten up our room. It is a beautiful place. Aloha.

Making a World of Difference

We have covered a lot of ground in 12 chapters. Perhaps you have the feeling that one sometimes has at the end of a long trip: It's good to be back home. Perhaps you're a bit overwhelmed. Maybe depressed. There is a lot of misery to go around, a lot of reasons to be discouraged about the present and even more pessimistic about the future. There are also many reasons for hope, however.

There is an old Chinese curse that simply says, "May you live in interesting times." We certainly live in interesting times. But with that "curse," there is also endless wonder and growing opportunity. We can predict with certainty that we will continue to live in interesting times, but whether that is a blessing or a curse remains to be seen. The global stage has been set, but the play has not yet been written. And so this is a good time to live, if you love high drama, rapid scene changes, and mounting suspense.

Economic globalization offers new opportunities for both entrepreneurship and innovation, yielding new solutions to old problems. It also offers the prospect of concentrating ever more wealth in the hands of a few and of inflicting reckless schemes and ruthless monopolies.

Political globalization offers the hope that a world of war will be replaced by a world of law, of universal human rights, and of new respect for labor and the environment, built into new transnational agreements. It offers the prospect of petty dictators falling to the contagion of spreading democracy. Political globalization also offers the prospect of rule by global elite, a powerful few who impose their will on the planet through repression, occupation, and the endless reach of bureaucracy.

Cultural globalization promises new opportunities to learn from one another and to respect, appreciate, and delight in our human differences. It also presents the prospect of the destruction of myriad cultural forms and local distinctive styles, to be replaced by bland uniformity or a crass commercial "pop" culture that is created, packaged, and imposed by a profit-driven media elite.

More likely than the utopian vision or the opposite dystopian vision is that forces will continue to pull in both directions. We may have more say in setting the eventual course than we know. Perhaps we should add a fourth force to the global dynamic: social globalization. We have begun to see the globalization of social movements. Women's networks have moved from the extended family to the community, to the nation, and now to international partnerships. Environmental movements now span national borders, seeking protection for global ecosystems. The long struggle for civil rights at the national level has become embedded in a global struggle for human rights. Labor movements cannot remain national while capital goes international, and concern for work and wages now extends to sweatshops, child labor, and working conditions around the globe.

Don't be fooled! The real work is and has always been in our own backyards. It still comes back to how we cultivate our own spaces and lives—how we treat our own neighbors and tend our own neighborhoods. What has changed is that we now live if not in a global village then in some sort of postmodern global cybercafé, where there is no limit to our reach and our contacts. Social networks span the entire earth. Insights and allies may come from different continents. Our challenge is to be open to many currents yet still be true to our core convictions.

Indian political leader and social reformer Mohandas Gandhi, known to his country as the Mahatma, or "great soul," said simply, "I do not want my house to be walled in on sides and my windows to be stuffed. I want the cultures of all the lands to be blown about my house as freely as possible. But I refuse to be blown off my feet by any." Assassinated for calling for the nonviolent accommodation of both Hindus and Muslims, with equal rights for both, he left a simple challenge: "You must be the change you wish to see in the world."

References

AAMC. 2019. "The Majority of U.S. Medical Students Are Women, New Data Show." https://www.aamc.org/news-insights/press-releases/majority-us-medical-students-are-women-new-data-show.

Abrahamson, Mark. 1996. *Urban Enclaves: Identity and Place in America*. New York: St. Martin's Press.

Aizenman, Nurith. 2021. "Gun Violence Deaths: How the U.S. Compares with the Rest of the World." National Public Radio. March 24. https://www.npr.org/sections/goatsandsoda/2021/03/24/980838151/gun-violence-deaths-how-the-u-s-compares-to-the-rest-of-the-world.

Aizenman, Nurith, and Marc Silver. 2019. "How The U.S. Compares With Other Countries In Deaths From Gun Violence." *Goats and Soda*. National Public Radio. August 5.

American Demographics. 2000. "Risk of Violent Crime." *American Demographics Magazine*. December.

Anderson, Walter Truett. 1992. *Reality Isn't What It Used to Be: Theatrical Politics, Ready-to-Wear Religion, Global Myths, Primitive Chic, and Other Wonders of the Postmodern World*. San Francisco: Harper.

Arnquist, Sarah. 2009. "Health Care Abroad: Japan." *New York Times*. August 25.

Baker, Pauline H. 1974. *Urbanization and Political Change: The Politics of Lagos, 1917–1967*. Berkeley: University of California Press.

Ballard, Barclay. 2019. "Fish Farming Is on the Rise, but There's an Environmental Catch." *EuropeanCeo*. October 18. https://www.europeanceo.com/industry-outlook/fish-farming-is-on-the-rise-but-theres-an-environmental-catch/.

Bangkok Post. 2020. "Chicken Exports Expected to Grow by 10% This Year." April 23.

Barber, Benjamin. 1995. *Jihad vs. McWorld*. New York: Times Books.

Barboza, David. 2010. "China Shifts Away from Low-Cost Factories." *New York Times*. September 16.

Barnett, Thomas P. M. 2004. *The Pentagon's New Map*. New York: Putnam.

Barrionuevo, Alexei. 2008. "Strong Economy Propels Brazil to World Stage." *New York Times*. July 31.

Barth, Frederick. 1998. *Ethnic Groups and Boundaries*. Long Grove, IL: Waveland Press. Orig. pub. 1969.

Bashir, Mohsin, and Shoaib Ul-Haq. 2019. "Why Madrassah Education Reforms Don't Work in Pakistan," *Third World Quarterly*, 40:3, 595–611, DOI: 10.1080/01436597.2019.1570820.

BBC News. 2000. "Anger Grows at U.S. Jail Population." February 15. www.news.bbc.co.uk.

BBC News. 2004. "Rwanda: How the Genocide Happened." April 1. www.news.bbc.co.uk/hi/world/africa/1288230.

BBC News. 2009. "South Asian Hunger at 40-year High." June 2. www.news.bbc.co.uk/2/hi/south_asia/8079698.stm.

BBC News. 2010. "Ban Ki-Moon Says UN Millennium Goals 'Can Be Met.'" September 20. www.bbc.co.uk/news/world-11375847.

BBC News. 2019. "Why Is India's Pollution Much Worse than China's?" November 6. https://www.bbc.com/news/world-asia-50298972.

BBC News. 2020. "Myanmar Rohingya: What You Need to Know about the Crisis." January 23. https://www.bbc.com/news/world-asia-41566561.

BBC News. 2021a. "Covid: WHO Scheme Covax Delivers First Vaccines." February 24. https://www.bbc.com/news/world-africa-56180161.

BBC News. 2021b. "Mozambique Insurgency: Children Beheaded, Aid Agency Reports." March 16. https://www.bbc.com/news/world-africa-56411157.

Bearak, Barry. 2009. "Constant Fear and Mob Rule in South Africa Slum." *New York Times*. June 30.

Becker, Gary. 1964. *Human Capital*. New York: National Bureau of Economic Research.

Bellah, Robert. 1957. *Tokugawa Religion: The Values of Pre-Industrial Japan*. Glencoe, IL: Free Press.

Bennhold, Katrin. 2010. "In Sweden, Men Can Have It All." *New York Times*. June 15.

Berger, Peter. 1967. *The Sacred Canopy*. New York: Anchor Books.

Berkey, Jonathan. 2002. *The Formation of Islam: Religion and Society in the Near East, 600–1800*. Cambridge, UK: Cambridge University Press.

Bernal, Díaz del Castillo. 1963. *The Conquest of New Spain*. Translated by J. M. Cohen. Baltimore: Penguin.

Bernard, Jesse. 1981. "The Good Provider Role: Its Rise and Fall." *American Psychologist*, 36 (January): 1–12.

Bernstein, Nina. 2004. "More Teenagers Are Striving for Restraint." *New York Times*. March 7. www.nytimes.com/2004/03/07/nyregion/07TEEN.html.

Biswas, Soutik. 2010. "Conundrum of Kerala's Struggling Economy." BBC News. March 17. www.news.bbc.co.uk/2/hi/south_asia/8546952.stm.

Black, Richard. 2009. "This Decade Warmest on Record." BBC News. December 8. www.news.bbc.co.uk/2/hi/science/nature/8400905.stm.

Bly, Robert. 2004. *Iron John*, 25th anniv. ed. Boston: Da Capo Press.

Bourgeois, Philippe. 2003. *In Search of Respect: Selling Crack in El Barrio*, 2nd ed. Cambridge, UK: Cambridge University Press.

Bradshaw, York, and Michael Wallace. 1996. *Global Inequalities*. Thousand Oaks, CA: Pine Forge.

Bradsher, Keith, and Andrew Martin. 2008. "Hoarding Nations Drive Food Costs Ever Higher." *New York Times*. June 30.

Braudel, Fernand. 1979. *The Perspective of the World*. New York: Harper and Row.

Brodkin, Karen. 1998. *How Jews Became White Folks and What That Says about Race in America*. New Brunswick, NJ: Rutgers University Press.

Brown, Lester. 2003. *Plan B: Rescuing a Planet under Stress and a Civilization in Trouble*. New York: Norton.

Brown, Lester. 2005. *Outgrowing the Earth: The Food Security Challenge in an Age of Falling Water Tables and Rising Temperatures*. New York: Norton.

Brown, Lester. 2011. *World on the Edge: How to Prevent Environmental and Economic Collapse*. New York: Norton.

Bukharin, Nikolai. 1925. *Historical Materialism: A System of Sociology*. New York: International Publishers. Orig. pub. 1917.

Bukharin, Nikolai. 1973. *Imperialism and the World Economy*. New York: Monthly Review Press. Orig. pub. 1917.

Bullard, Robert D. 1993. *Confronting Environmental Racism: Voices from the Grassroots*. Boston: South End Press.

Bullard, Robert D. 2000. *Dumping in Dixie: Race, Class and Environmental Quality*. 3rd ed. New York: Routledge.

Bureau of Justice Statistics. 2005. *Substance Dependence, Abuse, and Treatment of Jail Inmates, 2002*. U.S. Dept. of Justice. July.

Burgess, Eugene W. 1967. "The Growth of the City." In Robert E. Park and Eugene W. Burgess (eds.), *The City*. Chicago: University of Chicago. Orig. pub. 1916.

Campbell, John. 2018. "More Criminal Violence in Nigeria's Middle Belt." Council on Foreign Relations. October 23. https://www.cfr.org/blog/more-communal-violence-nigerias-middle-belt.

Cardoso, Fernando Henrique. 1977. *Latin America: Styles of Development and Their Limits*. Occasional Papers Series, no. 25. New York: New York University.

Cardoso, Fernando Henrique. 1996. "Humanizing Growth—Through Equity." *United Nations, Human Development Report 1996*. New York: Oxford.

Cardoso, Fernando Henrique, and Enzo Falletto. 1979. *Dependency and Development in Latin America*. Berkeley: University of California Press.

CDC. 2021. "Parasites—Malaria." February 17. https://www.cdc.gov/parasites/malaria/index.html.

Children's Defense Fund. 2004. *The State of America's Children 2004*. Washington DC: Children's Defense Fund.

Chivers, C. J. 2010. *The Gun*. New-York: Simon & Schuster.

Chua, Amy. 2003. *World on Fire: How Exporting Free Market Democracy Breeds Ethnic Hatred and Global Instability*. New York: Doubleday.

Chua, Amy. 2007. *Day of Empire: How Hyperpowers Rise to Global Dominance—and Why They Fall*. New York: Doubleday.

Clinton, Hillary Rodham. 1995. *Remarks for United Nations' Fourth World Conference on Women*. New York: United Nations.
Cloward, Richard, and Lloyd Ohlin. 1966. *Delinquency and Opportunity*. New York: Free Press.
Constable, Nicole. 2007. *Maid to Order in Hong Kong: An Ethnography of Filipina Workers*, 2nd ed. Ithaca, NY: Cornell University Press.
Connolly, Katie. 2011. "Why America's Gun Laws Won't Change." BBC News. January 10. www.bbc.co.uk/news/world-us-canada-12158148.
Coontz, Stephanie. 2016. *The Way We Never Were: American Families and the Nostalgia Trap*. Rev. and updated ed. New York: Basic Books.
Council on Foreign Relations. 2021. "Mexico's Long War: Drugs, Crime, and the Cartels." https://www.cfr.org/backgrounder/mexicos-long-war-drugs-crime-and-cartels.
Cox, Harvey. 2013. *The Secular City*. Princeton, NJ: Princeton University Press. Orig. pub. 1965.
Diamond, Jared. 1997. *Guns, Germs, and Steel*. New York: Norton.
Diamond, Jared. 2005. *Collapse: How Societies Choose to Fail or Succeed*. New York: Viking.
Draper, Robert. 2013. "Kinshasa, Urban Pulse of the Congo." *National Geographic*. September.
Duany, Andres, Elizabeth Plater-Zyberk, and Jeff Speck. 2010. *Suburban Nation: The Rise of Sprawl and the Decline of the American Dream*, 10th anniv. ed. New York: North Point Press.
Durkheim, Émile. 1951. *Suicide*. New York: Free Press. Orig. pub. 1897.
Durkheim, Émile. 1964. *The Division of Labor in Society*. New York: Free Press. Orig. pub. 1895.
DW News. 2021. *Oil a Blessing and a Curse for Nigeria's Niger Delta*. April 10. https://www.dw.com/en/oil-a-blessing-and-a-curse-for-nigerias-niger-delta/av-57056185.
Eck, Diana. 2002. *A New Religious America*. San Francisco: HarperSanFrancisco.
Economist. 2018. "Taming the Tiger Mothers: China Sounds Alarm over Its Stressed-out Schoolchildren." August 18. https://www.economist.com/china/2018/08/18/china-sounds-the-alarm-over-its-stressed-out-schoolchildren.
Economist. 2020. "The state of democracy around the world." https://www.eiu.com/n/campaigns/democracy-index-2020/.
Ehrenreich, Barbara, and Arlie Russell Hochschild. 2003. *Global Woman: Nannies, Maids, and Sex Workers in the New Economy*. New York: Metropolitan Books.
Ehrlich, Paul R. 1968. *The Population Bomb*. New York: Ballantine.
Energy Information Administration (EIA). 2005. "Saudi Arabia." *Country Analysis Briefs*. Washington DC: Energy Information Administration.
Ellwood, David. 1988. *Poor Support: Poverty in the American Family*. New York: Basic Books.
Elsner, Alan. 2005. "U.S. Says Drugs War Hampered by Mexican Corruption." Reuters. June 14.
Evans, Peter. 1979. *Dependent Development: The Alliance of Multinational, State and Local Capital in Brazil*. Princeton, NJ: Princeton University Press.
Fanon, Franz. 2004. *The Wretched of the Earth*. Translated by Richard Philcox. New York: Grove Press.
FBI. 2004. *Crime in the United States, 2003*. Washington DC: Dept. of Justice.
Fickling, David. 2021. "Nigeria's Oil Curse Could Become an Opportunity." April 7. *Bloomberg Opinion*. https://www.bloomberg.com/opinion/articles/2021-04-07/nigeria-s-oil-curse-could-become-an-opportunity-for-renewable-power.
Firebaugh, Glenn. 2003. *The New Geography of Global Income Inequality*. Cambridge, MA: Harvard University Press.
Fisher, Helen. 2004. *Why We Love: The Nature and Chemistry of Romantic Love*. New York: Holt.
Fisher, Max. 2021. "Myanmar's Bloodshed Reveals a World That Has Changed, and Hasn't." *New York Times*. April 5.
Fishman, Charles. 2003. "The Wal-Mart You Don't Know." *Fast Company*, Issue 77. December.
Fishman, Ted. 2010. "As Nations Age, a Chance for Younger Nations." *New York Times*, October 17.
Foucault, Michel. 1977. *Discipline and Punish: The Birth of the Prison*. New York: Pantheon Books.
Forbes. 2021. *World's Billionaires List: The Richest in 2021*. https://www.forbes.com/billionaires/.
Forbes Magazine. 2004. "The Forbes 400." October.

Frank, Andre Gundar. 1967. *Capitalism and Development in Latin America*. New York: Monthly Review Press.
Frank, Andre Gunder, and Barry K. Gills. 1993. *The World System: Five Hundred Years or Five Thousand?* London: Routledge.
Freed, Josh. 2004. *Coat of Many Countries*. New York: Filmmakers Library.
Friedman, Thomas L. 1999. *The Lexus and the Olive Tree*. New York: Farrar, Straus and Giroux.
Friedman, Thomas L. 2006. *The World Is Flat: A Brief History of the Twenty-first Century*. New York: Farrar, Straus and Giroux.
Freire, Paulo. 2018. *Pedagogy of the Oppressed*, 50th anniv. ed. Translated by Myra Bergman Ramos. New York: Bloomsbury Academic. Orig. pub. 1968.
Fritts, Thomas H., and Dawn Leasman-Tanner. 2001. *The Brown Tree Snake on Guam*. Fort Collins: U.S. Geological Survey. www.fort.usgs.gov/resources/education/bts/bts_home.asp.
Frontline World. 2008. *Nigeria: God's Country*. www.pbs.org/frontlineworld/flash_point/nigeria/.
Furstenberg, Frank F., Jr. 1988. "Good Dads—Bad Dads: Two Faces of Fatherhood." In Andrew Cherlin (ed.), *The Changing American Family*. Washington, DC: Urban Institute.
Gans, Herbert J. 1982. *The Urban Villagers: Group and Class in the Life of Italian-Americans*. New York: Free Press. Orig. pub. 1962.
Garreau, Joel. 1991. *Edge City: Life on the New Frontier*. New York: Doubleday.
Garrels, Anne. 2002. "Child Labor in Pakistan." *All Things Considered*. National Public Radio. February 13.
Gettleman, Jeffrey. 2020. "Coronavirus Crisis Shatters India's Big Dreams." *New York Times*, September 30.
Giddens, Anthony. 1999. *The Third Way: The Renewal of Social Democracy*. Oxford, England: Blackwell.
Giddens, Anthony. 2000. *Runaway World*. London: Routledge.
Gilmore, David. 1990. "Manhood." *Natural History*. June.
Gimbutas, Marija, and Miriam R. Dexter. 2001. *The Living Goddesses*. Berkeley: University of California Press.
Global Justice Now. 2018, October 17. https://www.globaljustice.org.uk/news/69-richest-100-entities-planet-are-corporations-not-governments-figures-show/.
Goode, William. 1963. *World Revolution and Family Patterns*. New York: Free Press.
Gore, Al. 2006. *An Inconvenient Truth*. Emmaus, PA: Rodale Books.
Gramlich, John. 2020. "Black Imprisonment Rate in the U.S. Has fallen by a Third since 2006." *Fact-Tank*. Pew Research. May 6. https://www.pewresearch.org/fact-tank/2020/05/06/share-of-black-white-hispanic-americans-in-prison-2018-vs-2006/.
Grossi, Mark. 2005. "Cows Emit More Organic Gas Than Cars, Studies Say." *Fresno Bee*. May 7.
Guruswamy, Krishnan. 1995. "World's Waste Is Piling Up in India." *South Bend* (IN) *Tribune*. June 4.
Gutek, Gerald L. 2006. *American Education in a Global Society*, 2nd ed. Long Grove, IL: Waveland Press.
Gutek, Gerald L. 2022. *A History of the Western Educational Experience*, 3rd. ed. Long Grove, IL: Waveland Press.
Gutmann, Mathew. 2006. *The Meanings of Macho*. Berkeley: University of California Press.
Hackbarth, Kurt, and Colin Mooers. 2019. "The Zapatista Revolution Is Not Over." *The Nation*. September 9.
Hannigan, John. 1998. *Fantasy City: Pleasure and Profit in the Post-Modern Metropolis*. London: Routledge.
Hardin, Garrett. 1968. "The Tragedy of the Commons." *Science*, 162: 1241–1252.
Hareven, Tamara. 1982. *Family Time and Industrial Time*. Cambridge: Cambridge University Press.
Hedges, Christopher. 2003. *War Is a Force That Gives Us Meaning*. New York: Anchor Books.
Hedges, Chris. 2007. *American Fascists: The Christian Right and the War on America*. New York: Free Press.
Hedges, Chris. 2008. *I Don't Believe in Atheists*. New York: Free Press.
Hochschild, Arlie. 2001. *The Time Bind: When Work Becomes Home and Home Becomes Work*. New York and London: Picador.
Hochschild, Arlie (with Anne Machung). 2012. *The Second Shift: Working Parents and the Revolution at Home*, Rev. ed. New York: Penguin.

Horowitz, Donald. 2000. *Ethnic Groups in Conflict*. Berkeley: University of California Press.
Human Rights Watch. 2019. "When We're Dead and Buried, Our Bones Will Keep Hurting—Workers' Rights Under Threat in US Meat and Poultry Plants." https://www.hrw.org/report/2019/09/04/when-were-dead-and-buried-our-bones-will-keep-hurting/workers-rights-under-threat.
Huntington, Samuel. 2011. *The Clash of Civilizations and the Remaking of World Order*. New York: Simon & Schuster.
ILO. 2017. *Global Estimates on Child Labour*. Geneva, Switzerland: International Labour Organization.
ILO. 2021. *ILO Monitor: COVID-19 and the World of Work*, 7th ed. January 2021. https://www.ilo.org/wcmsp5/groups/public/@dgreports/@dcomm/documents/briefingnote/wcms_767028.pdf.
IQAir. 2020. "World's Most Polluted Cities 2020 (PM 2.5)." https://www.iqair.com/us/world-most-polluted-cities.
Iyer, Pico. 1997. *Tropical Classical*. New York: Knopf.
Jacobs, Jane. 1970. *The Economy of Cities*. New York: Vintage.
Jacobs, Jane. 1984. *Cities and the Wealth of Nations*. New York: Random House.
Jenkins, Philip. 2011. *The Next Christendom: The Coming of Global Christianity*, 3rd. ed. New York: Oxford.
John, Hassan, Aminu Abubakr, and Jethro Mullen. 2015. "Scores Killed as Church, Mosques Are Targeted in Nigeria." July 6. CNN. https://www.cnn.com/2015/07/06/africa/nigeria-violence.
Johns Hopkins. 2021. Covid-19 Data Repository. https://github.com/CSSEGISandData/COVID-19. Retrieved Feb. 23, 2021; updated daily.
Johnson, Nathanael. 2021. "How to Stop Runaway Deforestation? Look at Indonesia." *Grist*. February 19. https://grist.org/food/how-to-stop-runaway-deforestation-look-at-indonesia.
Kageyama, Yuri. 2004. "'Cool' Hunter Leads Foreign Visitors along Cutting Edge of Japan Fashion." *Japan Times*. February 14.
Kane, Joe. 1996. *Savages*. New York: Vintage.
Karakatsanis, Neovi M., and Jonathan Swarts. 2003. "Migrant Women, Domestic Work, and Sex Trade in Greece." *The Greek Review of Social Research*, 110: 239–270.
Karberg, Jennifer, and Allen J. Beck. 2004. "Trends in U.S. Correctional Populations: Findings from the Bureau of Justice Statistics." Paper presented at the National Committee on Community Corrections, Washington DC, April 16.
Keeney, Bradford. 1994. *Shaking Out the Spirits: A Psychotherapist's Entry into the Mysteries of Global Shamanism*. Barrytown, NY: Station Hill Press.
Keeney, Bradford. 2004. *Bushman Shaman: Awakening the Spirit through Ecstatic Dance*. Rochester, VT: Destiny Books.
Kimbrell, Andrew. 2002. *Fatal Harvest: The Tragedy of Industrial Agriculture*. Washington, DC: Island Press.
Kingsolver, Barbara. 2007. *Animal, Vegetable, Miracle: A Year of Food Life*. New York: HarperPerennial.
Kitroeff, Natalie. 2021. "'We Are Doomed': Devastation from Storms Fuels Migration." *New York Times*. April 6. https://www.nytimes.com/2021/04/06/world/americas/migration-honduras-central-america.html?action=click&module=Top%20Stories&pgtype=Homepage.
Kituyi, Mukhisa, and Peter Thomson. 2018. "90% of Fish Stocks Are Used Up—Fisheries Subsidies Must Stop Emptying the Ocean." World Economic Forum. July 13. https://www.weforum.org/agenda/2018/07/fish-stocks-are-used-up-fisheries-subsidies-must-stop.
Klein, Hilary. 2019. "A Spark of Hope: The Ongoing Lessons of the Zapatista Revolution 25 Years On." *NACLA*. Jan. 18
Konner, Melvin. 1991. *Childhood*. Boston: Little, Brown.
Korten, David C. 2015. *When Corporations Rule the World*, 2nd ed. Oakland, CA: Barrett-Koehler.
Kozol, Jonathan. 1967. *Death at an Early Age: The Destruction of the Hearts and Minds of Negro Children in the Boston Public Schools*. New York: Houghton Mifflin.
Kozol, Jonathan. 1975. *The Night Is Dark and I Am Far from Home*. Boston: Houghton-Mifflin.
Kozol, Jonathan. 1991. *Savage Inequalities*. New York: Crown.
Kozol, Jonathan. 1995. *Amazing Grace*. New York: Crown.
Kozol, Jonathan. 2000. *Ordinary Resurrections*. New York: Crown.

Kozol, Jonathan. 2005. *Shame of the Nation*. New York: Crown.
KPIX. 2016. "California's Dairy Farms Come with Big Environmental Cost." November 13. https://www.youtube.com/watch?v=r2KH2nDZTIY.
Kristof, Nicholas D. 1996. "Who Needs Love? In Japan, Many Couples Don't." *New York Times*. February 11.
Kristof, Nicholas, and Sheryl WuDunn. 2009. *Half the Sky: Turning Oppression into Opportunity for Women Worldwide*. New York: Random House.
Kristof, Nicholas. 2011. "Why Not Regulate Guns as Seriously as Toys?" *New York Times*. January 13.
Lacey, Marc. 2003. "For Ugandan Girls, Delaying Sex Has Economic Cost." *New York Times*. August 18.
Larson, Caleb. 2020. "Israel's Fleet of F-15s and F-16s is Massive—and Highly Specialized." *The National Interest*. https://nationalinterest.org/blog/buzz/israel%E2%80%99s-fleet-f-15s-and-f-16s-massive%E2%80%94and-highly-specialized-141322.
Le Breton, Binka. 2003. *Trapped: Modern-Day Slavery in the Brazilian Amazon*. Bloomfield, CT: Kumarian Press.
Le Duff, Charlie. 2000. "At a Slaughterhouse, Some Things Never Die." *New York Times*. June 16.
Le Duff, Charlie. 2004. "Mexican Americans Struggle for Jobs." *New York Times*. October 13.
Lenin, V. I. 1948. *Imperialism, the Highest Stage of Capitalism*. London: Lawrence and Wishart.
Lewis, Oscar. 1968. "The Culture of Poverty." In Daniel Patrick Moynihan (ed.), *On Understanding Poverty*. New York: Basic Books.
Lewis, Oscar. 2011. *Children of Sanchez*. New York: Random House. Orig. pub. 1961.
Lipton, Eric. 2008. "With White House Push, U.S. Arms Sales Jump." *New York Times*. September 14.
Lipton, Michael. 1977. *Why Poor People Stay Poor: A Study of Urban Bias in World Development*. London: Temple Smith.
MacQuarrie, Kim. 2007. *The Last Days of the Incas*. New York: Simon and Schuster.
Mahtani, Shibani. 2018. "'Nothing But You and the Cows and the Sirens'—Crime Tests Sheriffs Who Police Small Towns." *Wall Street Journal*. May 12.
Malthus, Thomas Robert. 1926. *First Essay on Population 1798*. London: Macmillan. Orig. pub. 1798.
Marshall, Alex. 2001. *How Cities Work: Suburbs, Sprawl and the Roads Not Taken*. Austin: University of Texas Press.
Massey, Douglas, and Nancy Denton. 1993. *American Apartheid*. Cambridge, MA: Harvard University Press.
Matza, Max. 2021. "Jeff Bezos and the Secretive World of Superyachts." May 14. BBC News. https://www.bbc.com/news/world-us-canada-57079327.
McKibben, Bill. 2007. *Deep Economy*. New York: Times Books.
McLellan, David. 1977. *Karl Marx: Selected Writings*. Oxford, England: Oxford University Press.
McLellan, David. 1988. *Marxism: Essential Writings*. Oxford, England: Oxford University Press.
McMichael, Philip, and Heloise Weber. 2022. *Development and Social Change*, 7th ed. Thousand Oaks, CA: Sage.
McNeill, William H. 1991. *The Rise of the West: A History of the Human Community*. Chicago: University of Chicago Press. Orig. pub. 1963.
Merton, Robert. 1938. "Social Structure and Anomie." *American Sociological Review*, 3 (6): 672–682. October.
MEXT (Minister of Education, Culture, Sports, Science, and Technology Japan). n.d. "Report and Statistics: Overview." https://www.mext.go.jp/en/publication/statistics/title01/detail01/1373636.htm. Retrieved May 24, 2021.
Miller, D. T., and Michael Nowak. 1977. *The Fifties: The Way We Really Were*. Garden City, NJ: Doubleday.
Mills, C. Wright. 1956. *The Power Elite*. New York: Oxford.
Mueller, John. 1993. *Retreat from Doomsday*. Boston: Addison-Wesley.
Mukuru Promotion Centre. 2021. Primary School Education. https://www.mercymukuru.co.ke/education/primary-school-education/.

Nanda, Serena. 2019. *Love and Marriage: Cultural Diversity in a Changing World*. Long Grove, IL: Waveland Press.
NCADD. 2016. "From Bar to Bars: Links between Alcohol and Crime." https://www.ncaddesgpv.org/blog/from-bar-to-bars-links-between-alcohol-and-crime.
Nee, Victor, Jimy Sanders, and Scott Sernau. 1994. "Job Transitions in an Immigrant Metropolis: Ethnic Boundaries and Mixed Economy." *American Sociological Review*, 59 (December): 849–872.
Nellis, Ashley. 2016. "The Color of Justice: Radial and Ethnic Disparity in State Prisons." The Sentencing Project. https://www.sentencingproject.org/publications/color-of-justice-racial-and-ethnic-disparity-in-state-prisons/.
Nelson, Susie, Andrew Dunn, and Aria Bendix. 2020. "Moderna's Groundbreaking Coronavirus Vaccine Was Designed in Just 2 Days." December 19. *Insider*. https://www.businessinsider.com/moderna-designed-coronavirus-vaccine-in-2-days-2020-11.
Newman, Katherine S. 1999. *Falling from Grace*. Berkeley: University of California Press.
NIDA. 2020, July 20. "Methamphetamine Research Report: Overview." https://www.drugabuse.gov/publications/research-reports/methamphetamine/overview on 2020. Retrieved November 16, 2020.
Nothdurft, William E. 1989. *SchoolWorks: Reinventing Public Schools to Create the Workforce of the Future*. Washington, DC: German Marshall Fund.
NPR. 2004. "California Becomes America's Biggest Dairyland." *All Things Considered*, November 12.
NPR. 2014. "Can Farmed Fish Feed the World without Destroying the Environment?" June 6. https://www.npr.org/sections/thesalt/2014/06/06/319247280/can-farmed-fish-feed-the-world-without-destroying-the-environment.
O'Donnell, Guillermo. 1979. "Tensions in the Bureaucratic Authoritarian State and the Question of Democracy." In D. Collier (ed.), *The New Authoritarianism in Latin America*. Princeton, NJ: Princeton University Press.
Oncken, John. 2021. "Where's All the Milk Being Produced?" February 24. *Wisconsin State Farmer*. https://www.wisfarmer.com/story/opinion/columnists/2021/02/24/wheres-all-milk-being-produced/6792363002/.
Onishi, Norimitsu. 2000. "In the Oil Rich Nigeria Delta, Deep Poverty and Grim Fires." *New York Times*. August 11.
Orwell, George. 2008. *Burmese Days*. London: Alexandria Press (Archeion). Orig. pub. 1934.
Oxfam. 2021. *The Inequality Virus*. Briefing Paper. January. https://oxfamilibrary.openrepository.com/bitstream/handle/10546/621149/bp-the-inequality-virus-250121-en.pdf.
Palen, J. John. 2018. *The Urban World*, 11th ed. Oxford: Oxford University Press.
Pak, Jennifer. 2021. "Chinese Students, Parents Stressed by Demands of Extracurricular Classes." June 9. *Marketplace*. https://www.marketplace.org/2021/06/09/chinese-students-parents-stressed-by-demands-of-extracurricular-classes/.
Park, Robert. 1914. "Racial Assimilation in Secondary Groups." *American Journal of Sociology* 19 (5): 606–623.
Park, Robert E. 1967. "The City: Suggestions for the Investigation of Human Behavior in the Urban Environment." In Robert E. Park and Eugene W. Burgess (eds.), *The City*. Chicago: University of Chicago. Orig. pub. 1916.
Parsons, Talcott. 1964. *Social Structure and Personality*. New York: Free Press.
Peña, Devon. 1997. *The Terror of the Machine*. Austin: University of Texas.
Pittman, Craig. 2021. "A Reptilian Nightmare: Florida Bans Nonnative Species despite Industry Outcry." *Washington Post*. March 20.Rappeport, Alan. 2021. "Wealthiest Executives Paid Little to Nothing in Federal Income Taxes, Report Says." June 9. https://www.nytimes.com/2021/06/08/us/politics/income-taxes-bezos-musk-buffett.html?action=click&module=Top%20Stories&pgtype=Homepage.
Raworth, Kate. 2017. *Doughnut Economics: Seven Ways to Think Like a 21st-Century Economist*. London: Chelsea Green Publishing.
Reece, Erik. 2006. *Lost Mountain*. New York: Penguin (Riverhead Books).
Ricardo, David. 1996. *Principles of Political Economy and Taxation*. New York: Prometheus. Orig. pub. 1817.

Reynolds, Paul. 2009. "How do you apply pressure on Burma?" BBC News. August 11. www.news.bbc.co.uk/2/hi/asia-pacific/8194868.stm.
Rifkin, Jeremy. 2005. *The European Dream: How Europe's Vision of the Future Is Quietly Eclipsing the American Dream*. New York: Penguin (Tarcher).
Ritzer, George. 2018. *The McDonaldization of Society*, 9th ed. Thousand Oaks, CA: Pine Forge.
Romero, Simon. 2010. "Economies in Latin America Race Ahead." *New York Times*. June 30.
Rosenthal, Elizabeth. 2001. "Without 'Barefoot Doctors,' China's Rural Families Suffer." *New York Times*. March 14.
Royle, David. 1996. *Brazil*. New York: Quality Books.
Rubin, Lillian B. 1976. *Worlds of Pain*. New York: Basic Books.
Rubin, Lillian B. 1994. *Families on the Fault Line*. New York: HarperCollins.
Ruether, Rosemary Radford. 2005. *Goddesses and the Divine Feminine: A Western Religious History*. Berkeley: University of California Press.
Ryan, William. 1976. *Blaming the Victim*, Rev. ed. New York: Vintage Books.
Sachs, Jeffrey. 2006. *The End of Poverty: Economic Possibilities for Our Time*. New York: Penguin.
Sachs, Jeffrey. 2015. *The Age of Sustainable Development*. New York: Columbia University Press.
Sahlins, Marshall. 2018. *Stone Age Economics*. Chicago: Aldine. Orig. pub. 1972.
Sandburg, Carl. 1992. *Chicago Poems*. Champaign: University of Illinois Press. Orig. pub. 1916.
Sanders, Jimy, Victor Nee, and Scott Sernau. 2002. "Asian Immigrants' Reliance on Social Ties." *Social Forces*, 81 (1): 281–314.
Scarr, Sandra, Deborah Phillips, and Kathleen McCartney. 1989. "Working Mothers and Their Families." *American Psychologist*, 44 (11): 1402–1409.
Schell, Jonathan. 2003. *The Unconquerable World: Power, Nonviolence, and the Will of the People*. New York: Holt.
Schlosser, Eric. 2012. *Fast Food Nation*. New York: Houghton Mifflin. Orig. pub. 2001.
Sen, Amartya. 1999. *Development as Freedom*. New York: Anchor.
Sen, Amartya. 2007. *Identity and Terror*. New York: Norton.
Sernau, Scott. 2000. *Bound: Living in the Globalized World*. West Hartford, CT: Kumarian Press.
Sernau, Scott. 2001. *Worlds Apart: Social Inequalities in a New Century*. Thousand Oaks, CA: Pine Forge.
Shabata, Mari. 2019. "Why Japan's 'Shūkatsu' Job-Seeking System Is Changing." BBC. August 21. https://www.bbc.com/worklife/article/20190731-why-japans-shkatsu-is-disappearing-for-japanese-youth.
Shostak, Marjorie. 2000. *Nisa: The Life and Words of a Kung Woman*. Cambridge, MA: Harvard University Press.
Sidel, Ruth. 1998 *Keeping Women and Children Last*, Rev. ed. New York: Penguin.
Simmel, Georg. 1964. "The Metropolis and Mental Life." In K. Wolf (ed.), *The Sociology of Georg Simmel*. New York: Free Press. Orig. pub. 1905.
Simons, Marlise. 1990. "The Amazon's Savvy Indians." *New York Times Magazine*. February 26.
Slater, Philip. 1970. *The Pursuit of Loneliness*. Boston: Beacon Press.
Smith, Adam. 1937. *An Inquiry into the Nature and Causes of the Wealth of Nations*. New York: Modern Library. Orig. pub. 1776.
Smith, Roff. 2008. "Pioneers of the Pacific." *National Geographic*. March.
South, Scott, and Glenna Spitze. 1994. "Housework in Marital and Non-Marital Households." *American Sociological Review*, 59 (June): 327–347.
South Bend Tribune. 2005. "Latinos Divided over Custom of 'Chaperonas' for Daughters." *South Bend Tribune*. June 14.
Southey, Robert. 2004. "Madoc." In Robert Southey: *Poetical Works, 1793–1810*. London: Pickering and Chatto. Orig. pub. 1805.
Spencer, Leighann. 2017. "Vigilantism Is Flourishing in Nigeria—With Official Support." The Conversation. November 9. https://theconversation.com/vigilantism-is-flourishing-in-nigeria-with-official-support-86867.
Stapinski, Helene. 1998. "Let's Talk Dirty." *American Demographics* 20 (11): 50–56.

Statistica. 2020. "Revenue of the Cosmetic and Beauty Industry in the United States from 2002 to 2020." November 24. https://www.statista.com/statistics/243742/revenue-of-the-cosmetic-industry-in-the-us/.

Satistica. 2021. "Distribution of the Workforce across Economic sectors in the United States from 2010 to 2020." March 31. https://www.statista.com/statistics/270072/distribution-of-the-workforce-across-economic-sectors-in-the-united-states/.

Steer, Liesbet. 2014. "Seven Facts about Global Education Financing." Brookings Institution. February 20. https://www.brookings.edu/blog/education-plus-development/2014/02/20/seven-facts-about-global-education-financing/.

Steinberg, Stephan. 2001. *The Ethnic Myth: Race, Ethnicity, and Class in America*, 3rd ed. Boston: Beacon Press.

Stiglitz, Joseph. 2002. *Globalization and its Discontents*. New York: Norton.

Tagliabue, John. 1994. "Vatican Seeks Islamic Allies in U.N. Population Disputes." *New York Times*. August 18. https://www.nytimes.com/1994/08/18/world/vatican-seeks-islamic-allies-in-un-population-dispute.html.

Takaki, Ronald. 2008. *A Different Mirror*, Rev. ed. Boston: Little, Brown.

Taubman, Stephanie. 2002. "Asian Ladybird Beetle." New York: Columbia University Introduced Species Summary Project. http://www.columbia.edu/itc/cerc/danoff-burg/invasion_bio/inv_spp_summ/Harmonia_axyridis.htm.

Thakur, Ramesh. 2021. "India's Growing Democratic Deficit." *Toda Peace Institute*. March 25. https://toda.org/global-outlook/indias-growing-democratic-deficit.html.

Thrush, Glenn. 2021. "U.S. Imposes Additional Sanctions on Myanmar, Targeting Two Companies Linked to the Country's Military." *New York Times*. April 21. https://www.nytimes.com/2021/04/21/us/myanmar-sanctions.html.

Tilly, Charles. 1975. "Reflections on the History of European State-Making." In Charles Tilly (ed.), *The Formation of National States in Western Europe*. Princeton, NJ: Princeton University Press.

Tilly, Charles. 1990. *Coercion, Capital, and European States, AD 990–1990*. Oxford, England: Blackwell.

Timberlake, Michael, and Jeffrey Kentor. 1983. "Economic Dependence, Overurbanization, and Economic Growth: A Study of Less Developed Countries." *The Sociological Quarterly*, 24 (September): 489–907.

Toennies, Ferdinand. 1988. *Community and Society (Gemeinschaft und Gesellschaft)*. New Brunswick, NJ: Transaction Press. Orig. pub. 1887.

Turner, Terrence. 1993. "The Role of Indigenous Peoples in the Environmental Crisis: The Example of the Kayapo of the Brazilian Amazon." In *Perspectives in Biology and Medicine*. Baltimore: Johns Hopkins University Press.

Tutu, Desmond. 2000. *No Future Without Forgiveness*. New York: Doubleday.

UN Department of Economic and Social Affairs. 2017. "More Sustainably Managed Forests Would Help Meet Energy Needs of 1/3 of World Population." March 21. https://www.un.org/esa/forests/news/2017/03/idf2017-un-press-release/index.html.

UN Department of Economic and Social Affairs. n.d. *The World's Women 2020: Trends and Statistics*. https://www.un.org/en/desa/world%E2%80%99s-women-2020. Retrieved May 24, 2021.

UNDP. 2020. *The Next Frontier: Human Development and the Anthropocene*. "Briefing Note for Countries on the 2020 Human Development Report—Saudi Arabia." http://hdr.undp.org/sites/all/themes/hdr_theme/country-notes/SAU.pdf.

UNESCO. 2008. *A View inside Primary Schools*. http://uis.unesco.org/sites/default/files/documents/a-view-inside-primary-schools-world-education-indicators-wei-cross-national-study-en_0.pdf.

UNESCO. 2017. "Assessment: World Heritage Coral Reefs Likely to Disappear by 2100 unless CO2 Emissions Drastically Reduce." June 23. https://whc.unesco.org/en/news/1676.

UNHCR. 2008. "Protecting Refugees and the Role of the UNHCR."

UNHCR. 2020. *Figures at a Glance*. At https://www.unhcr.org/en-us/figures-at-a-glance.html. Updated June 18.

UNICEF. 2005. "Monitoring the Status of Women and Children: Education." January. Available online at www.childinfo.org/areas/education.
UNICEF. n.d. "Pakistan: Education: Giving Every Child the Right to Education." https://www.unicef.org/pakistan/education. Retrieved May 24, 2021.
United Nations, Food and Agriculture Organization (FAO). 2000. *United Nations.* August. Available at www.fao.org.
United Nations. 2003. *Human Development Report 2003.* "Millennium Development Goals: A Compact among Nations to End Human Poverty." http://hdr.undp.org/sites/default/files/reports/264/hdr_2003_en_complete.pdf.
United Nations. 2004. *Human Development Report 2004.* "Cultural Liberty in today's Diverse World." http://hdr.undp.org/sites/default/files/reports/265/hdr_2004_complete.pdf.
United Nations. 2007. *Human Development Report 2007/2008.* "Fighting Climate Change: Human Solidarity in a Divided World." http://hdr.undp.org/sites/default/files/reports/268/hdr_20072008_en_complete.pdf.
United Nations. 2020. *Human Development Report 2020.* "The Next Frontier: Human Development and the Anthropocene." http://hdr.undp.org/sites/default/files/hdr2020.pdf.
UNODC. 2012. *Transnational Organized Crime in Central America and the Caribbean: A Threat Assessment.* https://www.unodc.org/documents/data-and-analysis/Studies/TOC_Central_America_and_the_Caribbean_english.pdf.
UN Sustainable Development Goals. n.d. "Goal 5: Achieve Gender Equality and empower All Women and Girls." https://www.un.org/sustainabledevelopment/gender-equality/. Retrieved May 24, 2021.
U.S. Bureau of the Census. 2004. *Statistical Abstract of the United States.* Washington, DC: U.S. Government Printing Office.
U.S. National Center for Educational Statistics. 1999. *Digest of Educational Statistics.* Washington, DC: Government Printing Office.
Verhovek, Sam Howe. 2000. "After Breaking the Mold in Business, the E-Wealthy Do It Again in Giving." *New York Times.* February 11.
Veterans for Peace. 2003. *Terrorism Is the War of the Poor.* www.veteransforpeace.org.
"Voices of the Forest." 2001. *Africa.* New York: Educational Broadcasting Company and WNET. www.pbs.org/wnet/africa.
Vollers, Maryanne. 1999. "Razing Appalachia." *Mother Jones.* July/August.
Wallerstein, Immanuel. 2011. *The Modern World System.* 4 vols. Berkeley: University of California Press. Orig. pub. 1974.
Wallace-Wells, David. 2020. "We Had the Vaccine the Whole Time." December 7. New York Intelligencer. https://nymag.com/intelligencer/2020/12/moderna-covid-19-vaccine-design.html.
Walljasper, Jay. 1994. "Something Urban in Denmark." *Utne Reader.* September–October.
Washington Post. 2021. "History's deadliest pandemics, from ancient Rome to modern America." Updated Feb. 22. https://www.washingtonpost.com/graphics/2020/local/retropolis/coronavirus-deadliest-pandemics/?itid=hp_dontmiss.
Weatherford, Jack. 1994. *Savages and Civilization.* New York: Ballantine.
Weatherford, Jack. 2012. "Cocaine and the Economic Deterioration of Bolivia." In James Spradley and David W. McCurdy (eds.), *Conformity and Conflict,* 14th ed. Boston: Pearson.
Weaver, James H., Michael T. Rock, and Kenneth Kusterer. 1997. *Achieving Broad-Based Sustainable Development.* West Hartford, CT: Kumarian Press.
Weber, Max. 1997. *The Protestant Ethic and the Spirit of Capitalism.* Los Angeles: Roxbury. Orig. pub. 1905.
Wezeman, Pieter D., Alexandra Kuimova, and Siemon T. Wezeman. 2021. "Trends in International Arms Transfers, 2020." SIPRI Fact Sheet. https://sipri.org/sites/default/files.
Whiteman, Hilary. 2009. "Report: Climate Change Crisis 'Catastrophic.'" CNN. May 29. www.cnn.com/2009/WORLD/europe/05/29/annan.climate.change.human/index.html?eref=rss_world.
Wiener, Myron. 1966. *Modernization: The Dynamics of Growth.* New York: Basic Books.

Wilkinson, Richard, and Kate Pickett. 2010. *The Spirit Level: Why Greater Equality Makes Societies Stronger*. New York: Bloomsbury Press.
Williams, Aaron, and Armand Emamdjomeh. 2018. "America Is More Diverse than Ever—But Still Segregated." *Washington Post*. May 10. https://www.washingtonpost.com/graphics/2018/national/segregation-us-cities/.
Wilson, James Q., and George L. Kelling. 1982. "Broken Windows." *Atlantic Monthly*, March.
Wilson, William Julius. 1996. *When Work Disappears*. New York: Knopf.
World Almanac and Book of Facts. 1991. New York: World Almanac.
World Bank. 2018a. "Nearly Half the World Lives on Less than $5.50 a Day." Press Release. October 17. https://www.worldbank.org/en/news/press-release/2018/10/17/nearly-half-the-world-lives-on-less-than-550-a-day.
World Bank. 2018b. *LEARNING to Realize Education's Promise*. /9781464810961.pdf.
World Bank. 2020a. "Proportion of Seats Held by Women in National Parliaments (%): All Countries and Economies." https://data.worldbank.org/indicator/SG.GEN.PARL.ZS.
World Bank. 2020b. "Literacy Rage, Adult Total (% of People Ages 15 and above)—India." https://data.worldbank.org/indicator/SE.ADT.LITR.ZS?locations=IN.
World Bank. 2020c. "Urban Development: Overview." April 20. https://www.worldbank.org/en/topic/urbandevelopment.
World Bank 2021. *Poverty*. "Overview." 2021. https://www.worldbank.org/en/topic/poverty/overview.
World Economic Forum. 2020. "These Are the Top 10 Manufacturing Countries in the World." https://www.weforum.org/agenda/2020/02/countries-manufacturing-trade-exports-economics/.
World Health Organization (WHO). 2005. "The World Health Organization Warns of the Rising Threat of Heart Disease and Stroke as Overweight and Obesity Rapidly Increase." September 22. https://www.who.int/mediacentre/news/releases/2005/pr44/en/.
World Health Organization (WHO). 2007. *The World Health Report 2007: A Safer Future: Global Public Health Security in the 21st Century*. https://apps.who.int/iris/bitstream/handle/10665/43713/9789241563444_eng.pdf?sequence=1&isAllowed=y.
World Health Organization (WHO). 2021. "Infant Mortality Rate." *The Global Health Observatory*. https://www.who.int/data/gho/data/indicators/indicator-details/GHO/infant-mortality-rate-(probability-of-dying-between-birth-and-age-1-per-1000-live-births).
Yergin, Daniel. 2008. *The Prize: The Epic Quest for Oil, Money and Power*, Updated ed. New York: Simon & Schuster.
Zakaria, Fareed. 2003. *The Future of Freedom: Illiberal Democracy at Home and Abroad*. New York: Norton.
Zwingle, Erla. 2002. "Megacities: The Coming Urban World." *National Geographic*, November.

Index

A

Abortion, 110, 345, 346
Abrahamson, Mark, 309
Absentee fathers, 99
Accommodation and cooperation (and urban neighborhoods), 309
Acid rain, 390, 395
Acquired immune deficiency syndrome. *See* AIDS (acquired immune deficiency syndrome), 109, 353–355, 369
Afghanistan
  arms dealer in, 202
  crime in, 155, 159
  drug trade and, 159, 220
  religion in, 269
  Soviet war in, 202
  Taliban in, 162, 192, 220, 269, 272, 275
  terrorism and, 2, 195, 275
  U.S. military presence in, 275
  war in, 202, 247
Africa
  agriculture in, 71, 95, 423
  AIDS in, 109, 354
  civilization in, 4, 11, 44, 112
  colonization of, 44, 346
  cotton in, 424
  crime in, 156, 170, 171, 172, 176
  economy of, 54, 71, 124, 240, 263, 426
  ecotourism in, 446
  elite education in, 139
  gang activity in, 156, 172, 196
  independence of, 11–12, 125, 266
  poverty in, 11, 44, 109, 348
  regional gap, 140
African Americans
  civil rights of, 244, 270
  drug trade and, 354
  education for, 140, 244
  gender roles among, 339
  nationalism and, 229
  as race, 93, 141
  religion and, 141, 265
  segregation and, 140, 316
  urbanization and, 297
  voting by, 270
Agrarian empires, 183, 259, 322, 423, 451

Agrarian societies, 70, 100, 103, 108, 333, 334, 423, 451
Agribusiness, 416, 425, 426, 427, 429, 440, 453, 454–455. *See also* Industrial agriculture
Agricultural societies, 55, 56
Agriculture
  crops grown in (*See* specific crops)
  energy use and, 429–430
  environmental effects of, 78
  history of, 423
  industrialization of, 322
  irrigation, 423, 425–426
  labor needed for, 56
  origins, 350
  products of (*See* specific products)
  technology and, 13
  urbanization and, 423–425
AIDS (acquired immune deficiency syndrome), 109, 353–355, 369
Air pollution, 299, 343, 427, 432–434. *See also* Pollution
AK-47 (gun), 200–201, 242, 264, 275, 278
Alaska, 3, 9, 166, 393, 395, 408, 422, 442, 446
Alcohol/alcoholism, 96, 113, 159, 160, 167–168, 268, 364, 366
Alexander the Great, 121–122, 225, 233, 263, 295
Alexandria, Egypt, 3, 121, 295, 350
Alice in Wonderland, 343, 432
Alienation (and capitalism), 58, 60, 95, 158
al Qaeda, 196, 273, 274, 275, 318
al Shabab, 274
Alternative energy sources, 397, 400–403. *See also* Energy
Alternative medicine, 365
Amazon, 26, 35, 45, 61–68, 101–102, 411, 422, 440, 446
Amazon.com, 26, 27, 376–377, 380
American Revolution, 186, 235
Amerindians, 6, 133, 141, 252, 257, 301, 358
Amin, Idi, 266
Anderson, Walter Truett, 386
Animist, 229, 258, 259
Anomie, 159, 308

Anthrax, 208
APEC conference. *See* Asian-Pacific Economic Cooperation (APEC) conference
Apprenticeships, 122, 125, 126, 129, 135, 145
Arab nationalism, 229, 230, 263
Archimedes, 374, 375
Argentina, 210, 237, 241, 242, 297, 307, 334, 396, 426, 429, 430, 449
Aristide, Jean-Bertrand, 245
Aristotle, 121, 122, 233, 295
Arms trade, 200–205
Amquist, Sarah, 363
Arranged marriage. *See also* Marriage
Asia
    AIDS in, 109, 355
    cold war in, 191, 194
    colonization of, 346
    drug trade and, 170
    economy in, 71, 136, 192
    education in, 123
    health care in, 364–365
    obesity in, 365
    population of, 330, 346–349
    religion in, 264
    urbanization of, 293
Asian-Pacific Economic Cooperation (APEC) conference, 79
Asoka (emperor), 225, 270
Assimilation (and urban neighborhoods), 309
Athens, Greece, 3, 4, 89, 207, 232, 233, 259, 295, 350, 396, 452
Atomic bombs, 189, 397
Aung San Suu Kyi, 219, 221
Australia, 3, 9, 28, 39, 74, 121, 126, 167, 255, 332, 334, 346, 348, 407, 409, 422, 426, 430, 447
Authoritarianism, 236, 239
Automatic weapons, 154, 173, 175, 196, 264
Automobiles. *See* Cars
Avon (in Amazon), 102
Ayatollah Khomeini, 192, 267, 394
Aztec civilization, 6, 7, 133, 207, 301, 351

B

Baath Party (Iraq), 192
Babylonian Empire, 225, 423
Baha'i, 260
Bahamas (tourism in), 19–20
Baka (hunter-gatherer group), 422, 438
Baker, Pauline H., 304
Bands (of people), 222–228
Bangladesh, 8, 11, 65, 161, 185, 221, 263, 286, 364, 384, 396, 408
Barber, Benjamin, 267, 269
Barnett, Thomas P.M., 213
Barrionuevo, Alexei, 34
Barth, Frederick, 255
Bazooka, 169
Bearak, Barry, 154
Beck, Allen J., 171
Becker, Gary, 136, 268
Beirut, Lebanon, 265, 306
Bellah, Robert, 57
Belt and Road Initiative, 240
Bennhold, Katrin, 98
Berger, Peter, 267
Berlin Wall, 194
Bernal, Diaz del Castillo, 301
Bernard, Jesse, 93
Bernstein, Nina, 109
Bhutan, 166, 385
"Big box" retail, 66–68
Billionaires, 26, 27, 67, 81, 84, 380
Bin Laden, Osama, 263, 267
Biological weapons, 205, 206–208
Biotechnology, 207, 357, 451
BIP. *See* Border Industrialization Program (BIP)
Birthrate, 339. *See also* Fertility rate
    in China, 131, 342
    in Europe, 345
    in Japan, 341
    population growth and, 339
    in Russia, 341
Biswas, Soutik, 87
Black, Richard, 408
Black Death. *See* Bubonic plague
"Black lung" disease, 360, 390
Black Panthers, 279
Blair, Tony, 33, 34
Bly, Robert, 113
Boko Haram, 263, 274
Bolívar, Simón, 229, 240
Bolivia
    cocaine production in, 164
    drug trade in, 165
Bolsheviks, 10, 134, 236
Bolsonaro, Jair, 34, 35, 158, 440
Bombay (Mumbai), India, 25, 54, 86, 296, 303, 408
Border Industrialization Program (BIP), 64
Bourgois, Philippe, 158
Bracero program, 62, 64

Bradshaw, York, 46
Bradsher, Keith, 430
Braudel, Fernand, 167
Brazil
    agriculture in, 71, 95, 158
    crime in, 34–35, 158
    economy of, 34, 158
    education in, 119–120
    government of, 14, 34
    inequality in, 119–120
    military power in, 241
    nuclear programs and, 210
    poverty in, 313
    race/ethnicity in, 251–253, 257
    rain forest in, 440
    social class in, 119–120
    urbanization of, 296, 302, 308, 313, 321
British Empire, 8, 10, 62, 76, 185, 265, 279, 295
Brodkin, Karen, 257
Brown, Lester, 349, 425, 451
Brown v. Board of Education, 140, 143
Bubonic plague, 206, 350, 351, 352
Buddhism, 5, 219, 225, 264, 270, 278, 282
Bukharin, Nikolai, 40
Bullard, Robert D., 452
Burgess, Ernest, 309, 310
Burma (Myanmar), 8, 163, 216–220
Bush, George W.
    diplomatic policies of, 213
    economic policies of, 34, 78–79
    education policies of, 144
    nuclear waste disposal policies of, 399
    population control policies of, 345
    war in Iraq and, 213
"Buy American" philosophy, 67
Byzantine Empire, 205, 234, 260, 263, 295

C

CAFTA. *See* Central American Free Trade Agreement (CAFTA)
Calcutta, India, 41, 86, 88, 292, 303, 306
Cambodia, 11, 181, 191, 192, 219, 264, 271
Cameroon, 394, 438
Canada
    ecotourism in, 446
    health care in, 362
Cannabis, 165–166
Capitalism
    criticism of, 32
    definition of, 12
    division of labor and, 31–32, 57
    globalization of, 81
    history of, 32
    industrialization and, 32
    religion and, 56
Cárdenas, Lázaro, 394
Cardoso, Fernando Henrique, 34, 46
Carnegie, Andrew, 380
Cars, 404–407
    energy consumption and, 343
    population growth and, 342
    technology and, 405
    urbanization and, 407
Carter, Jimmy, 244
Castro, Fidel, 42, 193
Catholicism
    conflict and, 265
    divorce and, 104, 107
    education and, 133
    government and, 226
    history, 260
    nationalism and, 230, 271
    participation in, 261, 262
    political influence of, 234, 271
    regional strongholds of, 252
    work ethic and, 56–57
Central Intelligence Agency (CIA), 191
Central place theory, 306
Chemical weapons, 205–206
Chiefdom, 223–224
Children
    care for, 335, 339
    caregivers of, 108
    chronic diseases and, 358
    education of, 71, 126, 129, 131, 145
    health care of, 361, 362, 366
    as laborers, 68–73, 123
    as labor source, 335
    poverty and, 108
    rights of, 247
    war and, 196
    weapon use by, 196
Chimpanzees, 183
China
    agrarian empires and, 183
    agriculture in, 423–424
    AIDS in, 355
    alternative energy power in, 401
    biological weapon against, 206
    birthrate in, 131
    capitalism in, 46
    children caregiver in, 107
    cholera epidemic in, 353

cities of, 288–291, 294, 299, 303
civilization in, 5
civil rights and, 245, 247
communism in, 35, 189–191
drug trade in, 160, 162
economy, 245
economy of, 12, 26, 28, 43, 60, 80
education in, 121, 130–131
feudalism in, 184
gang activity in, 172
Google and, 386
government of, 232, 240, 386
health care in, 364–365
industrial espionage in, 375
migrant laborers from, 63
nuclear testing by, 210
one-party system in, 239
plague in, 350–351
population of, 328–329, 332, 342, 345
religion in, 264, 265, 278
smoking in, 166–167
Tiananmen Square uprising in, 212–213
Vietnam War and, 190–191
villages in, 299
Chin (or Qin) Empire, 225
Chivers, CJ, 200
Cholera, 120, 313, 353, 450
Christianity, 260–262, 264, 267, 281
Chronic diseases, 357–361
Chua, Amy, 213, 265
Churchill, Winston, 10, 76, 193, 238
CIA. *See* Central Intelligence Agency (CIA)
Cities
    architecture in, 310, 319, 323
    cars and, 317–319
    culture in, 305, 308
    environmental concerns of, 319–320
    globalization and, 296–306
    growth of, 296–299, 317–319
    history of, 3, 293–296, 317–319
    immigration/migration and, 296, 306, 312–313, 315–317
    industrialization and, 296, 299, 304
    lifestyle in, 306–307
    political power of, 307
    poverty in, 312–317
    structure of, 308–310
    sustainable, 321
    transportation and, 317–319
City-state, 25, 225, 232, 304
Civilization (development of), 3–4, 44
Civil rights, 244

Civil War (U.S.), 187, 207
Class (social/economic)
    capitalism and, 31–32
    crime and, 158
    education and, 119–120, 128
    gender and, 92
    theories of, 30–38
Class consciousness, 32
Classical education, 139
Clean Air Act of, 390
Climate change, 286, 390, 408. *See also* Global warming
Clinton, Bill, 34, 135, 138, 170, 192, 244
Clinton, Hillary Rodham, 113, 221
Cloward, Richard, 160
Coal, 70, 360, 389–393
Coca-Cola, 163, 416
Cocaine, 163–165
Coffee (as crop), 73, 426
Cold war, 189–195, 211, 215, 241, 244, 265
College education, 117–119, 126
Colombia, cocaine production in, 164, 165
Communism, 33
    criticism of, 34
    decline of, 34
    definition of, 34
Comparative advantage (and specialization), 73
Competition (and urban neighborhoods), 309
Conflicts, 148
Confucius, 121, 130, 232
Congo, 9, 11, 28, 123, 125, 200, 239, 240, 244, 296, 305, 330, 382
Connolly, Katie, 155
Conservatives (and economic policies), 31, 176, 268
Constable, Nicole, 101
Containment, 190
Contraception, 109, 332, 335, 345, 346
Coontz, Stephanie, 70, 109
Copenhagen, Denmark, 307, 319
Corn, 6, 45, 422, 424, 425–426, 430, 431, 453
Cortés, Hernán, 7, 207, 301, 351
Cosmetics, 101, 257, 397
Costa Rica, 79, 110, 243, 400, 402, 442, 444
Cotton, 59, 70, 78, 424, 427, 434, 438
Cotton gins, 378
Coup d'état, 241
COVID-19, 26, 110, 147, 246, 319, 335, 352, 356, 368, 379, 381, 429
Cox, Harvey, 267
Crack cocaine, 158, 163, 164, 169

Crime, 151–178
   causes of, 156–160
   dislocation and, 158
   incarceration for, 170–171
   and poverty, 156
   prevalence of, 154–156
   prevention of, 176
   and social class, 158
   solutions/responses to, 170–175
   street, 156–158
   trends in, 171–175
   and unemployment, 156
   in urban areas, 155–156
Cuba, 9, 35, 42, 43, 79, 110, 140, 166, 193, 209, 247, 261
Cultural globalization, 1, 3, 382, 384, 461
   challenges, 13
Culture of poverty, 46
Culture shock, 13
Curitiba, Brazil, 313, 321, 404
Cyberrevolution, 386
Czechoslovakia, 193, 226, 227

D

Dairy farms, 416, 427
Dalai Lama, 237, 264, 278, 280, 283
Da Vinci, Leonardo, 295, 374, 375
DDT, 358, 360, 433, 456
Deadbeat dads, 99
Death rate, 333–335. *See also* Life expectancy
Decriminalizing (of marijuana), 165–166
Defoliants (as chemical weapons), 205, 448, 452
Deforestation, 438–447
Deindustrialization, 59, 86, 164
Delhi, India, 86, 88, 303, 304, 458
Demagogue, 227, 233, 280
Democracy
   authoritarianism vs., 236–239
   defined, 230–231
   foundations of, 39
   history of, 230–236
   price of, 242–243
Demographic transition theory, 333–344
Demography, 333
Denmark, 5, 112, 228, 319
Denton, Nancy, 316
Dependency theory, 38–46
Desegregation (of schools), 140, 279
Desertification, 438–447
"Designer" drugs, 169
De Silva, Lula Ignacio, 34

Deterrence, 155, 195, 209
Dewey, John, 123
Diamond, Jared, 6, 207, 350, 419
Digital divide, 381
Dirty war, 240–244
Disease
   agriculture and, 349–353
   chronic form of, 357–360
   in cities, 350, 353, 357
   colonization and, 351–352
   history of, 349–350
   infectious disease, 349–353
   lifestyle and, 360, 366
   nutrition and, 353
   pollution and, 360
Dislocation (economic/cultural/social)
   crime and, 156, 158
   industrialization/deindustrialization and, 38
   urbanization and, 38
Division of labor
   capitalism and, 31–33, 55, 58–61
   definition of, 55
   gender and, 54
   history of, 55–61
   industrialization and, 58–59
   international scope of, 60–61
   productivity and, 55, 58–60
   religion and, 57
   specialization and, 55, 58–61, 73
   theories of, 55–58
   work ethic and, 56–58
Divorce, 94
   marriage and, 102–107
   in United States, 102
Domesticated animals, 350
Domination, dependency theory and, 41
Drug cartel, 164, 169, 174, 175, 275, 348
Drug trade, 160–169
   alcoholism, 167–168
   cannabis, 165–166
   cocaine, 163–165
   crime and, 158
   gang activity and, 158
   opium, 160–163
   poverty and, 158
   violence and, 158–159, 164
Dry forests, 442, 446
Duany, Andres, 320
Dubai, 88, 310, 318
Durkheim, Émile, 56, 159, 308
Dutch East Indies, 11, 41, 62, 229, 393

E

Eastern Europe, 11, 35, 36, 48, 54, 65, 74, 76, 94, 101, 104, 166, 168, 171, 193, 194, 202, 231, 239, 355, 390, 394, 398
Eastern Orthodoxy, 261
Eck, Diana, 264
Economic globalization, 81
    challenges, 13
    definition of, 1
    division of labor and, 60
    inequalities between/among nations, 22–28
Economics (theories of), 38–46. *See also* specific theories
Economy of scale, 429
Ecotourism, 444, 446, 453, 454, 459
Edge cities, 318
Education
    child labor and, 128
    children, 71
    college level of, 117–119, 126
    communication skills and, 144–145
    for democracy, 123
    discrimination and, 140
    foundations of, 121–123
    gender differences in, 92, 123–126
    for girls, 144
    human capital theory and, 136–138
    inequality in, 140–143
    in Islam, 123–124
    nationalism/patriotism and, 135, 145
    race/ethnicity and, 140
    religion and, 123, 133
    rural vs. urban differences in, 123–124
    secondary level of, 125–126
    social class and, 119–120, 140–141
    spending on, 138
    types of, 139
    of women, 92
Egypt, 4, 44, 121, 192, 225, 229, 231, 240, 256, 262, 263, 270, 279, 295, 296, 311, 331, 345, 375, 393, 423, 424, 438
Ehrenreich, Barbara, 101
Ehrlich, Paul R., 333, 343
Eisenhower, Dwight, 211
Electoral democracies, 39, 230–231, 248. *See also* Democracy
Electronics (manufacturer of), 74
Elite education, 139
Ellison, Larry, 27, 380
Ellwood, David, 34
Elsner, Alan, 170
E-mail, 51, 357, 378, 379, 382, 385, 386, 412

Empires (world history of), 8–12, 183
Energy, 387
    alternative, 400–403
    coal, 389–392
    natural gas, 396–397
    nuclear fission, 397–399
    nuclear fusion, 399–400
    oil, 393–396
    wind, 401–403
    wood, 388–389
Environment
    agriculture and, 423, 427, 431
    climate change and, 286, 389, 408
    consumption and, 344
    deforestation/reforestation of, 439–447
    food production and (*See* Food production)
    global warming and (*See* Global warming)
    inequality, 452
    invasive species, 447–451
    oil and, 395–396
    pollution and (*See* Pollution)
    population growth and, 344
    sustainability, 321, 451–453
    urbanization and, 320, 344
Environmental biology, 309
Environmental justice movement, 452
Escobar, Pablo, 164
Ethiopia, 72, 126, 171, 296, 300, 311, 312, 330, 331
Ethnic cleansing, 195
Ethnicity, 255–257. *See also* Race/ethnicity
Ethnocentricism, 256, 280
EU. *See* European Union (EU)
Euro, 228
European colonization, 44
    drug trade in, 161–162, 167
    education and, 123, 139
    empires built by, 9
    lasting impact of, 41
    poverty and, 42
Europeanism, 227
European Parliament, 228
European Union (EU), 79, 210, 228
Evans, Peter, 42
Exploitation, dependency theory and, 41–42
Exploration, 7, 89, 419, 444
Export-processing zones, 54, 59, 60, 96, 433
Extreme poverty, 28, 46–49
Extremists (religious), 271. *See also* Fundamentalism; Religion
Exxon Valdez, 395, 433

F

Falletto, Enzo, 34
Falwell, Jerry, 268
Family/Families, 85–115
    divorce and, 94. *See also* Divorce
    gender roles and, 89–93
    marriage and, 102–107
    patriarchal, 102
    poverty and, 71
    structure of, 107–109
Fanon, Franz, 11
Fascism, 195, 237
Fast-food restaurants, 75
Fatalism, 39, 46
Feminist movement, 112–114
Feminization of poverty, 94, 107
Fertility rate, 339–341
Feudalism, 31, 184
Firebaugh, Glenn, 25
FIRE economy, 156
Fisher, Helen, 102, 103, 221
Fishman, Ted, 342
Food production, 420–432
    agriculture and, 423–432. *See also* Agriculture
    cost of, 429–430
    energy use and, 429–430
    globalization of, 75
    history of, 420–423
    poverty and, 432
Food regime, 429
Foucault, Michel, 385
France
    colonization by, 10, 11, 180, 185, 187
    exploration by, 8
    government of, 234
    maternity leave in, 107–108
    multiple party system in, 239
    nuclear program, 398
    nuclear tests in, 210
    plague in, 350
    population and, 332
    textile plants in, 425
Franco, Francisco, 226, 237, 332
Frank, Andre Gundar, 6, 42
Franklin, Benjamin, 57, 122, 231, 269
Freed, Josh, 74
Free Trade Agreement of the Americas (FTAA), 79
Free trade/Free markets. *See also* Capitalism
    criticism of, 32, 55, 56
    definition of, 78
    regulation of, 33, 55

    specialization and, 73
Free world, 39
Freire, Paulo, 142, 143, 145, 146
French Revolution, 187
Friedman, Thomas L., 61, 213
Fritts, Thomas H., 447
FTAA. *See* Free Trade Agreement of the Americas (FTAA)
Fuel cell cars, 405
Functional illiteracy, 144
Functioning core, 213
Fundamentalism, 267–268
Furstenberg, Frank F., Jr., 100

G

Gadaffi, Muammar, 240
Galilei, Galileo, 374, 375
Gandhi, Arun, 452
Gandhi, Mahatma, 11, 74, 257, 277, 279, 280, 452, 462
Gang activity, 159, 172
Gans, Herbert J., 308, 309
Garreau, Joel, 318
Garrels, Anne, 71
Gasoline-electric hybrids, 405
Gates, Bill, 27, 30, 57, 357, 380
"Gateway" drugs, 163, 166
GATT. *See* General Agreement on Trade and Tariffs (GATT)
Gemeinschaft, 308
Gender
    changing roles, 89–93
    education and, 92, 123–126
    globalization and, 95
    history and, 89–92
    pay gap, 112
    race/ethnicity and, 93–94
    unemployment and, 95
    work and, 89–102
General Agreement on Trade and Tariffs (GATT), 78
Gentrification, 315, 319
George III, King, 59, 235
Geothermal energy, 402
German Empire, 10
Germany
    colonization by, 8
    division of, 189, 193
    education in, 135
    fascism in, 236–237
    industrialization and, 375
    as nation-state, 227

Protestant Reformation in, 261
World War I and, 10, 205, 237
World War II and, 10, 188, 189, 193, 205, 377
Gesellschaft, 308
Giddens, Anthony, 33
Gills, Barry K., 6
Gilmore, David, 99
Global citizenship, 13
Global climate change. *See also* Global warming
Globalization, 1–15
    definition of, 1, 89
    and gender, 95
    history of, 3–13
Global poverty. *See also* Poverty
Global warming, 390, 397, 408, 409, 434
The Gods Must Be Crazy, 422
Goethe, Johann, 248
Golden Triangle, 162–163
Goode, William, 102
Gorbachev, Mikhail, 134, 193, 194, 236
Gore, Al, 409
Government (systems of), 230–240
    authoritarianism/dictatorship, 236–240
    democracy, 230–231
    fascism and, 237
    monarchy, 231
    oligarchy, 232–233
    political parties and, 239
    presidencies vs. parliaments, 238–239
    totalitarianism, 237
Grameen Bank (Bangladesh), 384
Grant, Ulysses S., 187
Great Britain
    colonization and, 184, 185, 230, 303
    colonization by, 8, 11
    democracy in, 234, 237
    drug trade in, 162
    education in, 122, 126–128
    government and, 238, 239
    health care in, 363
    industrialization in, 13, 70
    language in, 256
    as nation-state, 227–228
    nuclear tests and, 210
    regional conflicts and, 195–196
    technology and, 375, 376, 377
    textile plants in, 425
    World War II and, 193
Grossi, Mark, 427
Guantanamo Naval Base, 247–248
Gulf War, 204, 206, 210, 452

Guns, 155–156
    trading in, 171–172
Guruswamy, Krishnan, 436
Gutek, Gerald, 128, 133
Gutmann, Mathew, 95

H

Haiti, 72, 185, 245, 252, 358, 388, 389, 442
Half-life (of nuclear material), 399
Hamilton, Alexander, 236
Hammurabi, 231
Han Chinese, 5, 224
Hannigan, John, 311
Hardin, Garrett, 47
Hareven, Tamara, 339
Hashish, 86, 165, 166
Hawaii, 5, 54, 75, 224, 360, 444, 447, 458, 459, 460
Health care, 349–365
Health insurance, 361–362
Hedges, Chris, 270
Hedges, Christopher, 183
Hemp, 165
Herders/Herding societies. *See also* Pastoral societies
Heroin, 160, 162, 163
Hesse, Hermann, 211
Hindu fundamentalism, 269, 270
Hindus, 264, 265, 273, 462
His Han, 225
Hitler, Adolf, 10, 227, 233, 236, 237, 241, 265, 266
HIV (human immunodeficiency virus), 353–354. *See also* AIDS (acquired immune deficiency syndrome)
Hobbes, Thomas, 235, 238
Ho Chi Minh, 11, 179, 191, 228, 382, 459
Hochschild, Arlie Russell, 94, 96, 98, 100, 101
Hong Kong, 11, 74, 101, 172, 240, 246, 247, 288–290, 304, 317, 319, 343, 459
Horowitz, Donald, 255, 265
Horticultural societies, 55, 103, 108, 421
HTML. *See* Hypertext markup language (HTML)
Human capital theory, 136–138
Human ecology, 309, 319
Human immunodeficiency virus. *See* HIV (human immunodeficiency virus)
Human rights, 244–248
Hunter-gatherers, 3, 6, 43–44, 102, 223, 258, 343, 349, 420, 421–423, 430, 438
Huntington, Samuel, 213

Hussein, Saddam, 192, 206, 230, 240, 265
Hybrid cars, 405. *See also* Cars
Hydrogen bomb, 208, 209, 210, 400
Hypertext markup language (HTML), 378
Hyperurbanization, 306, 307

I

Illegal immigrants, 429
IMF. *See* International Monetary Fund (IMF)
Immigrants, 347
Immigration and Naturalization Service (INS), 429
Immigration/migration
    cities and, 296, 315–317, 334–335
    defined, 346–349
    farm labor, 427
    illegal immigrants and, 429
    population and, 334, 341
    waves of, 347–348
    of women, 100–102
Imperialism, 12, 40, 43, 222
Imperial Japanese Army, 208, 222
Incan Empire, 207, 351
Incarceration, 26, 160, 166, 168, 170–170
Incendiaries, 205
India
    agriculture in, 415–417
    birthrates in, 86
    British rule in, 186, 196
    child labor in, 71
    children caregiver in, 108
    cities, 291–292, 297, 303
    civilization in, 4
    colonization by, 8
    cotton in, 424
    as democratic state, 242, 270
    economy of, 25, 28, 61, 80–81, 86–88
    education in, 117–119, 131, 136
    famines in, 431
    government of, 14, 15
    health care in, 366
    Hindu fundamentalism in, 269
    immigrants from, 317
    independence of, 11, 218, 275
    marriage in, 103
    Mauryan Empire in, 225
    Mogul Empire in, 225, 262
    Muslim population in, 263
    nonviolence and, 276
    nuclear weapons and, 210
    outsourcing to, 61, 86
    and Pakistan, disputes between, 192

    parliamentary system in, 238
    partition of, 277
    peasant laborers in, 424
    population, 330
    poverty in, 306
    race and ethnicity in, 256
    recycling in, 436
    religion in, 258, 262, 264, 269–270
    technology in, 86
    urbanization of, 291–292, 294, 296, 303
    women in, 88
Indian Wars, 9, 452
Indonesia, 5, 7, 11, 41, 62, 65, 71, 141, 155, 185, 220, 229–230, 241, 262, 263, 265, 266, 313, 393, 394, 440, 444
Industrial agriculture, 425–429
Industrialism, 13
Industrialization
    agriculture and, 425–432
    capitalism and, 32
    child labor and, 68–70
    cities and, 296, 300, 304–305
    dislocation and, 38
    division of labor and, 58–59
    effects of, 380, 425
    gender roles and, 90
    history of, 13
    marriage and, 102
    war and, 187–189
    weapons and, 187–189
    women and, 90
Industrial Revolution, 13, 30, 44, 379, 425
Infant mortality, 86, 87, 335, 339, 361, 365
Infectious disease, 334, 347, 349–353
Influenza, 355, 356
Information age, 378, 379, 381, 385–387
Intercomputer network, 377
Intercontinental ballistic missile (ICBM), 209
Internally displaced, 347–348
International Monetary Fund (IMF), 40, 76–77
International terrorism, 172, 195, 271–273
Invasion (and urban neighborhoods), 309
Invasive species, 447–451
Iranian Revolution, 192, 269
Iran-Iraq War, 206
Iraq
    Baath Party in, 192
    Gulf War and, 206
    Nationalism, 230
    nuclear program of, 210
    terrorism and, 273
    U.S. invasion of, 192, 275
    war in, 1, 2, 192, 213, 275

Ireland, 38, 61, 101, 104, 196, 226, 244, 261, 265, 424, 431, 439
Iroquois system of democracy, 231
Irrigation, 417, 423, 425, 426, 427, 438, 439, 440, 453
Islam, 260, 262–264
    education and, 124
Islamic Empire, 262
Islamic fundamentalism, 268, 269
Israeli-Palestinian conflict, 192, 273
Italy, 10, 13, 80, 88, 89, 101, 104, 167, 172, 199, 207, 226, 237, 239, 261, 304, 317, 332, 351, 356
Iyer, Pico, 300

J

Jacobs, Jane, 306, 307
Jacquard, Joseph-Marie, 375, 424–425
Japan
    Battleship Island, 360
    biological weapons and, 206–207
    chemical weapons in, 205
    coal mines in, 70, 360
    divorce rates in, 104
    economy of, 78
    education in, 128–129, 136
    employment in, 128
    fertility rate in, 339
    feudalism in, 184
    Formosa island and, 190
    health care in, 363
    history of, 80
    industrialization in, 128, 375, 425
    life expectancy in, 335
    nationalism in, 228–229
    as nation-state, 222
    Pacific War and, 188–189
    parliamentary system in, 238
    population in, 341
    religion in, 258, 264
    Samurai knights in, 186
    technology and, 371–373
    train travel in, 404
    urbanization in, 296, 299, 304, 341
    women in workforce, 95
    World War II and, 10
Jefferson, Thomas, 9, 30, 39, 59, 123, 235, 236, 244, 248, 269
Jenkins, Philip, 261
Jihad, 266, 267
Jihad vs. McWorld, 267

K

Kane, Joe, 446
Karakatsanis, Neovi M., 101
Karberg, Jennifer, 171
Keeney, Bradford, 258–259
Kelling, George L., 175
Kennedy, John F., 209
Kenya, 80, 143, 240, 307, 308
Kerala, India, 86–88, 131, 365
Khan, Genghis, 9, 186, 195, 224, 265, 271
Khan, Kublai, 195, 296
Khmer Rouge, 180, 181, 191, 192, 200
Khrushchev, Nikita, 209, 236
Kim Jong-un, 190
Kimbrell, Andrew, 425
Kingsolver, Barbara, 432
Konner, Melvin, 169
Korten, David C., 31
Kozol, Jonathan, 141, 142, 143, 313
Kristof, Nicholas D., 104, 114, 125, 155
K'ung Fu-tsu, 121, 130, 232, 259

L

Labor market, 56, 66, 91, 99, 100, 342
Labor migrants, 63, 64, 101, 347
Lacey, Marc, 354
Lagos, 296, 303–304
Laissez-faire capitalism, 30, 31
Language(s), education and, 140–142
Latin America
    AIDS in, 109
    Armies, 242–243
    automobile travel in, 404–405
    conflict in, 192–193
    crime in, 156, 175, 176
    dependency theory and, 42
    dirty wars, 194
    divorce rates in, 107
    drug trade and, 165, 169
    economy of, 36, 37, 78
    education in, 141
    farmers in, 440
    gang activity in, 171
    gender roles in, 93
    government of, 36, 78
    leftist guerilla in, 200
    liberation theology and, 270–271
    military governments in, 237
    nationalism, 231
    obesity in, 361
    oil industry in, 394

INDEX **485**

population in, 342, 347
poverty in, 43, 312–313, 315, 316
presidential system in, 238
race and ethnicity, 255
religion in, 258, 260–261, 270–271
terrorism and, 278
urbanization and, 302, 312–313, 315
US intervention in, 195
women in workforce, 95
League of Nations, 194, 199, 222
Leasman-Tanner, Dawn, 447
Le Breton, Binka, 101
Le Duff, Charlie, 428
Lenin, V. I., 40, 42, 134, 236
Leviathan, 235
Levi Strauss, 67
Lewis, Oscar, 46, 99
Liberals (and economic reform), 31
Libertarians, 31, 47
Libya, 210, 240, 279
Life expectancy, 26, 54, 87, 243, 306, 335–339, 361, 363, 364, 365, 432
Lincoln, Abraham, 134, 230
Lipton, Eric, 202
Lipton, Michael, 307
Liu Xiaobo, 386
Locke, John, 235, 238, 244
Lockheed Martin F-16, 202
LSD, 168, 169
LTTE. *See* Tamil Tigers—Liberation Tigers of Tamil Eelam (LITE)

M

MacArthur, Douglas, 189, 190
MacQuarrie, Kim, 7
Madison, James, 236
Madrassa, 71, 123, 268
Magna Carta, 234
Malaria, 358–360, 367
Malthus, Thomas Robert, 330–332, 345, 366
Mandela, Nelson, 140, 244, 279
Manhattan Project, 206–207, 397
Mao Zedong, 42, 130, 190, 332
Maquiladora, 64, 65, 173
Marijuana, 165
   legalization of, 166
Market conundrums, 47
Marriage, 102–107. *See also* Divorce; Family/Families
Marshall, Alex, 320
Martin, Andrew, 430

Marx, Karl, 31–33, 34, 35, 36, 38, 40, 46, 49, 58, 60, 75, 134, 236, 255, 330–333, 344
Marxism, 130
Massey, Douglas, 316
Matriarchal family, 99
Matrifocal family, 99, 100
Mauritius (economy of), 53–54
Mauryan Empire, 225
Maya culture of Mexico, 183
Mayas, 133
McCartney, Kathleen, 95
McDonald's, 75, 213, 267, 427
McKibben, Bill, 432
McLellan, David, 58
McMichael, Philip, 429
McNeill, William H., 44
MDGs. *See* Millennium Development Goals (MDGs)
Mechanical solidarity, 56
Medellín cartel, 164
Medicaid, 362
Mediterranean, 3, 4, 6, 225, 226, 231, 232, 256, 263, 294, 295, 378, 402, 423
Megacities, 296, 299–304
Men
   as breadwinners, 93–94
   career for, 100
   changing roles of, 89–93
   masculinist movement and, 113
   as parents, 98–100
   pay gap, 110, 112
   unemployment among, 95
Men's movement, 113
Meritocracy, 233
Merton, Robert, 159–160
Mesoamerica, 6, 44, 133, 183, 265, 294, 424, 426
Methamphetamine, 169
Mexican Revolution, 133, 278
Mexico
   border with United States, 64, 172–175
   crime in, 158, 174
   drug wars, 172–175
   economy of, 37
   education in, 133–134, 139
   government of, 37
   immigration from, 64–65
   industry in, 65–66, 96
   revolution in, 133
Mexico City, 22, 133, 207, 294, 296, 301–302, 307, 313, 384, 396, 436
Middle East, 3–4

Migration, 100–101, 297, 346–349
Military expenditures, 211
Millennium Development Goals (MDGs), 48
Miller, D.T., 91
Mills, C. Wright, 211
Mining industry, 70
Moderate poverty, 28
Modernity, 35, 38, 39, 267, 377
Modernization theorists, 58, 102, 430
Modernization theory, 38–40
Moi, Daniel, 240, 444, 446
Monarchy, 39, 231, 233, 235, 238
Mongol Empire, 186, 187, 207, 265
Morgan, J.P., 380
Mothers of the Plaza de Mayo, 241
Mountaintop removal mining, 391
Mueller, John, 211
Mujahedeen, 162, 192, 202
Multinational corporations, 39, 41, 60, 312, 380
Mumbai (Bombay), India, 25, 54, 80, 86, 88, 296, 303
Murphy's Law, 286
Music, 1, 2, 152, 162, 169, 252, 267, 268, 326, 377, 380
Mussolini, Benito, 10, 227, 237, 332
Mustard gas, 206
Myanmar (Burma), 8, 163, 216–220, 221, 222, 264, 348, 458
Mycotoxins, 206

N

NAFTA. *See* North American Free Trade Agreement (NAFTA)
Napoléon, 8, 9, 187, 188, 199, 226, 227, 236, 262, 332
Nasser, Gamal Abdel, 192, 229
Nation, 222
National citizenship, 13
National health care, 361, 363, 367
Nationalism
    defined, 222
    in education, 134, 145
    independence and, 11, 228–230
Nation-state, 184, 185, 196, 221–222
Native Americans, alcoholism among, 168
Natural gas, 396–397
Natural law, 233
Natural resources, 343, 419, 425, 428, 436, 452
Nee, Victor, 316
Neoclassical economics, 31, 38, 49, 76, 78
Neoliberalismo, 36

Neoliberals/Neoliberalism, 31, 34, 36, 39, 48, 49
Neolithic revolution, 44
Neo-Marxists, 36
Neosocial government, 34
Newman, Katherine S., 100
Newton, Isaac, 375
New York City, 299–301
    crime in, 154, 158
Nicotine, 166
Nietzsche, Friedrich, 89–93
Nigeria, 141
    crime in, 158
Nixon, Richard, 193
Nkrumah, Kwame, 229
No Child Left Behind, 143, 144
Nonintegrating gap, 213
Nordic countries, 37, 136
North American Free Trade Agreement (NAFTA), 34, 64, 79, 174
North Atlantic Treaty Alliance (NATO), 193, 194, 203–204, 209, 213, 244
Nothdurft, William E., 135
Nowak, Michael, 91
Nuclear arms race, 209
Nuclear fission, 208, 397–398, 400
Nuclear fusion, 397, 399–400
Nuclear Nonproliferation Treaty, 210
Nuclear power, 380, 397–398, 399, 412
Nuclear weapons, 190, 192, 208–210

O

Obama, Barack, 34, 221, 248, 349, 362, 381
O'Donnell, Guillermo, 242
Offshoring, 60–61
Ohlin, Lloyd, 160
Oil, 393–396
Oligarchy, 232, 233
One-party system, 239
OPEC. *See* Organization of the Petroleum Exporting Countries (OPEC)
Operation Wetback, 64
Opium, 160–163
    global production, 162
Organic solidarity, 56
Organization of the Petroleum Exporting Countries (OPEC), 393
Orwell, George, 218, 386
Ottoman Empire, 7, 10, 192, 199, 230, 262, 266, 271, 423
Outsourcing, 61
Overburden, 391
Ozone, 396, 407, 419

P

Pacific War, 188–189
Pakistan
   child labor in, 71, 124
   education in, 123
Palestinian Arabs, 192
Pandemic, 2, 26, 27, 318–319, 349, 354, 355–357, 368, 379, 381, 383, 429, 448
Parents/Parenting, 107–109
Park, Robert E., 309
Parsons, Talcott, 102
Passive solar systems, 402, 403
Pastoral societies, 112, 421
Patriarchal families, 102
Paul, John, II, 237, 271
Pax Americana, 196
Pax Romana, 195
Peloponnesian War, 207
Personal computers (PCs), 378
Peru, cocaine production in, 165
Peyote, 166, 169
Phillips, Deborah, 95
Philosopher-king, 233, 234
Pizarro, Francisco, 7, 207, 351
Planetary Boundaries, 419
Plebeians, 233
Police action, 155, 175, 190
Political economy, 30, 36, 38, 310, 319, 320, 440
Political globalization, 1
   challenges, 14
Pollution
   solid waste, 434–438
   of water, 432–434
Polynesian, 5, 7, 360, 422, 447, 458
Poor People's Campaign, 270
Population
   control, 344–346
   demographics and, 333–344
   estimates of, 330
   growth of, 330–333
   migration and, 346–349
Postindustrial countries, 60
Poultry, 428, 429
Poverty
   children and, 71
   crime and, 156, 159
   drug trade/use and, 158
   family/families, 71
   history of, 43–46
   single parenting and, 107–108
   women and, 92, 96, 98

Preemptive strikes, 213
Primate city, 307
Private-pay system, 361–362
Privatization, 33, 34, 36, 76
Proletariat, 13, 32, 35, 58, 236
Protestantism
   capitalism and, 57
   work ethic and, 57
Putin, Vladimir, 239

R

Race/ethnicity
   crime and, 160
   definitions of, 255–257
   drug use and, 159
   education and, 140
   gender roles and, 93–94
   in incarceration, 170
   pride in, 255
   religion and, 264–271
   skin color and, 256–257
   social class and, 256
   terrorism and, 278
   and unemployment, 97–98
   war/violence and, 159–160
Rain forests, 4, 102, 220, 422, 434, 438, 440, 442, 444, 446
Reagan, Ronald, 33, 128, 170, 172, 178, 193, 210, 211, 243, 268, 345
Reaganomics, 33
Reality Isn't What It Used to Be, 386
Recycling, 411, 436, 438, 455
Reece, Erik, 391
Reed, Ralph, 268
Reforestation, 389, 442
Refugees, 347
Religion
   capitalism and, 56–57
   divorce and, 104, 107
   and education, 122, 133
   fundamentalism, 267–270
   political involvement by, 267–270
   race/ethnicity and, 264–271
   terrorism and, 277–278
   tribal, 258
   types of, 258–264. *See also* specific types/religions
   work ethic and, 56–57
Religious extremists, 271
Resistance (and urban neighborhoods), 309
Reynolds, Paul, 220
Ricardo, David, 73

Rifkin, Jeremy, 37
Rio de Janeiro (Brazil), 152, 158, 175, 302, 436
Ritzer, George, 75
Robertson, Pat, 268
Rockefeller, John D., 57, 380
Roman Empire, 4, 5, 10, 224, 225, 227, 234, 260, 261, 270, 296, 350, 351
Romero, Simon, 37
Rousseau, Jean Jacques, 235–236, 238
Rousseff, Dilma, 34
Royle, David, 102
Rubin, Lillian B., 109
Ruether, Rosemary Radford, 112
Rural areas
    crime in, 159
    education in, 124, 140
Russia. *See also* Soviet Union
    alcoholism in, 168
    birthrate in, 341
    climate change and, 408–409
    colonization by, 9, 10
    communism in, 35
    drought and wildfire in, 408
    economy of, 35
    education in, 134–135
    food production in, 409
    health care in, 364
    monarchy in, 236
    oil in, 393
    plague in, 350–351
    radioactive material in, 398
    religion in, 261
    revolution in, 134
    smoking in, 168
Russian Empire, 9, 10, 11, 12, 194
Russo-Japanese War, 228
Ryan, William, 46

S

Sachs, Jeffrey, 48, 81
Sahlins, Marshall, 44
Sandburg, Carl, 304
Sanders, Jimy, 309, 316
São Paulo (Brazil), 102, 158, 159, 296, 302, 308, 404–405
SARS virus, 355–356
Scarr, Sandra, 95
Schell, Jonathan, 279, 280
Schlosser, Eric, 75
School-to-work transition, 135, 138–139
Second-growth forest, 440
Second Life (SL), 383

Seljuk Empire, 262
Sen, Amartya, 270, 431
Serfs, 32
Sernau, Scott, 75, 384
Shah of Iran, 192
Shamanism, 258, 259
Shang Empire, 225
Shanghai (China), 62, 74, 164, 303, 305, 321, 328, 329, 408
Shostak, Marjorie, 102
Sidel, Ruth, 94
Sierra Leone, 196, 200, 214, 242, 266
Sikhism, 260
Simmel, Georg, 308
Singapore, 11, 25, 62, 65, 136, 237, 304, 319, 343, 365
Single parents/parenting, and poverty, 107–108
Single-payer health care system, 362
Slater, Philip, 100
Small arms, 172, 196, 200, 201–202
Smallpox, 207, 208, 350, 351, 352, 353, 357, 358
Smith, Adam, 30–31, 33, 34, 36, 38, 39, 47, 49, 55–56, 58, 59, 73
Smith, Roff, 5
Smoking, 163, 166–167
Socialism, application of, 37
Socialized medicine, 363, 364, 365
Social networking, 381, 462
Solar power, 397, 400, 402
Solidarity (and division of labor), 56
Solid waste, 434–438
South, Scott, 94
South Africa
    chronic disease and, 360
    crime in, 154, 170
    education in, 140
    government of, 14
    independence of, 11
    nuclear weapons and, 210
    poverty in, 326–328
    race/ethnicity in, 253–254
    reconciliation policy of, 243–244
    urbanization and, 279
    wild game preserves in, 417–418
South Asia, drug trade and, 160, 165
Southeast Asia, drug trade and, 160
Southey, Robert, 301
Sovereignty, 222, 245, 248
Soviet Union
    and Afghanistan, 192, 202, 206
    as an "evil empire," 194

arms race and, 208–209
biological weapons and, 208
breakup of, 11, 135, 170, 211
chemical weapons and, 206
Cold War and, 189–194
communism and, 193
crime in, 170
dictatorship in, 237
economy of, 40
education in, 134–135
German invasion (World War II) of, 226
modernization theory and, 40
nuclear wagons and, 208, 209
proxy war of, 237
support to India, 192
as weapons supplier, 200–201
World War II and, 189, 227
Spain, 4, 7, 8, 9, 31, 62, 139, 167, 226, 229, 237, 243, 255, 261, 262, 263, 296, 311, 332, 403, 434
Spanish Empire, 396
Specialization (of workforce), 55, 58–61, 73. *See also* Division of labor
Spitze, Glenna, 94
Squatters, 119, 297, 313
Sri Lanka, 196, 244, 264, 272, 273, 348, 365, 416
St. Louis, Missouri, 6, 313, 317, 450
Stalin, Josef, 10, 40, 134, 194, 227, 236
Stapinski, Helene, 94
State
  defined, 222
  terrorism by, 271–277
  violence by, 271–277
State socialist systems, 35
Steinberg, Stephan, 172
Stiglitz, Joseph, 77
Strip mines, 390
Structural adjustments, IMF, 76
Student Nonviolent Coordinating Committee, 279
Sub-Saharan Africa, 4, 5, 11
  incomes in, 25
  poverty in, 44, 48
Suharto, Raden, 230, 241, 266
Suicide bomber, 196, 272, 273
Sukarno, Achmed, 229
Sullivan, Louis, 318
Sustainability (of environment), 451–453
Sustainable Development Goals (SDGs), 48, 50, 51, 83, 110, 115, 147, 177, 249, 323, 368

Sweden, 108, 135, 239, 361, 408
  alternate energy sources in, 400
  health care in, 363
Syria, 200, 229, 239, 271, 273, 279, 348, 393

T

Taiwan, 25, 42, 65, 190, 191, 237, 240, 247, 304, 356, 429
Takaki, Ronald, 257
Taliban, 162, 192, 220, 269, 272, 275
Tamil Tigers—Liberation Tigers of Tamil Eelam (LITE), 272
Tariffs, 2, 64, 77–78
Taubman, Stephanie, 448
Taylor, Charles, 241, 242
TB. *See* Tuberculosis (TB)
Technical education, 139, 142, 146
Technology
  agriculture and, 379, 423
  economy and, 38, 45
  education and, 128–129
  information and, 378–387
  pace of change in, 286
  transportation and, 405, 407
Terrorism
  alternatives to, 277–280
  9/11 attacks, 2, 275
  leadership and, 278–280
  power and weakness of, 273–277
  race/ethnicity and, 278
  religion and, 277–278
  state sponsorship of, 271–273
Textile industry, 54, 61, 64, 68, 74, 90, 360, 375
Thailand, drug trade and, 170, 354
Third Reich, 10
Third-way economics, 33
Thirty Years' War (1618–1648), 186, 261
Three Mile Island plant, 398
The Three Musketeers, 186
Tibet, 5, 237, 247, 264, 278, 283, 385
Tilly, Charles, 183, 184, 225
Tobacco, 166–167
Toennies, Ferdinand, 308
Tokyo, 158, 159, 189, 296, 299, 304, 305, 343
Tolstoy, Leo, 277
Totalitarian, 226, 237, 386
Total war, 186, 187–189
Toys (manufacturer of), 73
Trade (history of), 6–8
Transnational union, 227
Transportation
  forms of, 404–407

technology and, 405
urbanization and, 317–319
Tribal religions, 141, 169, 258–259
Tribal warfare, 183
Trump, Donald, 20, 35, 204, 210, 240, 349
Truth and Reconciliation Commission, 243
Tsunami disaster, 214
Tuberculosis (TB), 357, 369, 411
Turner, Terrence, 384
Tutu, Desmond, 243, 253, 254, 277, 279, 280
Two-party systems, 239
Tyrant, 232, 233

U

UAR. *See* United Arab Republic (UAR)
Ukraine, 11, 172, 212, 342, 398
U.N. Declaration on the Rights of the Child, 247
Unemployment
    crime and, 156
    gender and, 95
    race/ethnicity and, 96
United Arab Emirates, 203, 204, 310
United Arab Republic (UAR), 229
United Nations
    on human rights, 245, 246
    on immigrants, 348
    Korean conflict and, 190
    Millennium Development Goals of, 48
    police action, 190
    on poverty, 28
    war in Iraq and, 2
United States
    agriculture in, 425–427, 430
    alcohol consumption, 168
    biological weapons and, 207
    birthrate in, 334–335
    border with Mexico, 65, 172–175
    chemical weapons and, 206
    Christian fundamentalists in, 269, 270
    chronic diseases in, 360
    cities in, 307, 311, 312–313, 315–317, 320
    civil rights movement in, 270–271
    coal mining in, 389
    Cold War and, 189–194
    colonization by, 9
    crime in, 154, 170, 171, 176
    DDT use in, 358
    decentralized system in, 236
    deforestation in, 439
    as democratic state, 236, 237
    demographics, 342, 343–344
    divorce in, 104
    drug use in, 162, 163
    education in, 123, 124, 126, 133–134, 138–139, 143
    energy consumption in, 387
    fertility rate in, 339, 341
    government system in, 241
    health care in, 361–362
    human rights and, 247
    industrialization and, 188–189, 296, 376, 378, 379
    Israeli-Palestinian conflict and, 192
    Latin American and, 195
    League of Nations and, 194
    life expectancy in, 335, 339
    Manhattan Project, 206–207
    military spending in, 211
    nationalism and, 229, 230
    NATO and, 193
    natural gas and, 396
    nuclear weapons and, 208–209
    oil and, 393
    Pacific War and, 188–189
    population control in, 345
    poverty in, 170, 315
    race and ethnicity in, 256, 257
    rain forest in, 452
    reforestation in, 442
    school-to-work transition, 138–139
    smoking in, 167
    sustainability in, 321
    teenage pregnancy rate in, 108
    terrorism and, 195–196, 267, 275
    terrorism in, 1–2
    terrorist attacks in, 211
    train travel in, 404
    tribal democracy in, 231
    tsunami relief and, 214
    Vietnam War and (*See* Vietnam War)
    and war on drugs, 167
    as weapons supplier, 201–202, 203
    wind farms in, 397–398
Universal Declaration of Human Rights, 245
Urban bias, 307
Urbanization
    cars and, 317–318, 321
    control over, 317–319
    crime and, 155
    culture in, 308
    dislocation and, 38
    education of, 124, 140
    environmental concerns of, 320
    globalization and, 296–306

history of, 294–295, 317–318
immigration/migration and, 297, 306, 312, 315–317
industrialization and, 296, 299–300, 304–305
megacities and, 299–304
poverty and, 312–313
structure of cities, 308–310
theories of, 308–311, 320
transportation and, 317–319, 321
Urban legends, 386, 412–413
Urban sprawl, 317
U.S. Air Force, 202, 203
U.S. Constitution, 238, 239, 244, 269
U.S. Declaration of Independence, 30, 123, 186, 235
U.S. National Guard, 214
U.S. Trident submarine, 209–210
Ustinov, Peter, 196
Utilitarians, 30, 31

V

Venezuela, 36, 155, 240, 348, 393, 394
Verhovek, Sam Howe, 376
Victoria (Queen), 8, 90, 160, 265, 378
Vietnam, 35
Vietnam War, 211, 229, 282, 452
Violence
  drug trade and, 158, 159, 164
  in rural areas, 159–160
Virtual reality, 383–384
Vital statistics, 333
Vocational education, 125, 126, 128, 135

W

Wallace, Michael, 46, 357
Wallerstein, Immanuel, 6, 42
Walljasper, Jay, 319
Walmart, 27, 66–68, 290
Walton, Sam, 67
War
  casualties of, 188–189, 356–357
  children and, 196
  empires and, 8–12
  expenditures for, 211–214
  history of, 183–194
  origins of, 183–185
  regional conflict, 194–200
  types of, 186–194
  weapons of, 200–210
War on drugs, 165, 173
Warsaw Pact, 76, 193, 194, 200

Washington, George, 77, 134, 230, 269, 352
Washington Consensus, 36, 78
Water
  agriculture and, 425, 426
  nuclear power plant and, 209
  pollution of, 432–434
  solar-heated, 401
Weapons, 205–210
  biological, 206–208
  chemical, 205–206
  children and, 196
  nuclear, 208–210
  United States as supplier of, 200, 201–202
Weapons of mass destruction (WMD), 205–210. *See also* Weapons
Weatherford, Jack, 5, 164, 207, 226
Weaver, James H., 46
Weber, Max, 56–57, 255
White Anglo-Saxon Protestant (WASP), 257
Whiteman, Hilary, 409
Whitney, Eli, 378, 424
Wilhelm, Kaiser, 236
Wilkinson, Richard, 26
Wilson, James Q., 175
Wilson, William Julius, 156, 176
Wind power, 402
Women
  careers for, 92
  changing roles of, 89–93
  education of, 92
  in government, 110
  industrialization and, 90–91
  liberation movement of, 89–93, 112–113
  migration of, 100–102
  pay gap, 112
  poverty among, 90, 94, 98
  as property, 103
  as slaves, 100–101
  violence against, 110
  voting by, 113
  in workforce, 89–93, 94–96
Women's movement, 89–93, 112–114
Wood, 388–389
Work
  children and, 68–70
  division of labor in, 55–61. *See also* Division of labor
  exploitation in, 46
  gender and, 55, 89–102
  low-cost labor and, 61–68
  religion and, 56
  trade and, 73–81

Work ethic, 56–57. *See also* Division of labor
World Bank, 28, 39–40, 45–46, 50–51, 77, 82, 136, 194
World systems theory, 42
World Trade Organization (WTO), 33, 78, 79, 194–195
World War I
    casualties of, 188–189, 357
    causes of, 10
    end of, 235, 237, 262
    globalization and, 1
    League of Nations and, 194–195
    weaponry/tactics of, 187–189, 205–206
World War II
    casualties of, 188
    machines used in, 377, 391
    Pearl Harbor, attack of, 213
    superpower rivalries and, 195
    United Nations and, 195
    weaponry/tactics of, 187–189, 205–206
    women's roles in, 90

World Wide Web, 376, 378
WTO. *See* World Trade Organization (WTO)
WuDunn, Sheryl, 114

X

Xi Jinping, 239–240

Y

Yeltsin, Boris, 194
Yergin, Daniel, 393
Yoga, 264, 365
Yugoslavia, 195, 214, 226, 241, 243, 245, 265

Z

Zakaria, Fareed, 237, 242
Zapatista movement, 278
Zionist Jews, 192
Zwingle, Erla, 306